710分
新题型

大学英语 6 级考试

巅峰训练

主　编：王长喜
副主编：赵丙银
　　　　关　淼
编　者：王雅琴
　　　　张　立
　　　　王　洁
　　　　唐　群

学苑出版社

特色栏目 先睹为快

理解特殊句式 听出弦外之音

Lecture 3 第三讲 9 种对话常含句式

四、虚拟句式

　　虚拟语气是英文中一种重要的语法现象，同时也是六级听力考试的重点考查内容之一，它表达的是与事实相反的内容或是一种不可能实现的意愿。

3. wish 后的虚拟语气

【例】 (05-12-7)

[A] He shows great enthusiasm for his studies. [B] He is a very versatile person. [C] He has no talent for tennis. [D] He does not study hard enough.	M: Your son certainly shows a lot of enthusiasm on the tennis court. W: I only wish he'd show as much for his studies. Q: What does the woman imply about her son?

【解析】选 [D]。事实状况题。女士通过虚拟句式 I only wish he'd show... 表达了"希望儿子对学习可以表现出与对网球同样的热情"的愿望，这表明事实上女士的儿子 does not study hard enough（对学习的热情不高）。

学会听前预测 锁定听音重点

Lecture 2 第二讲 10 大听前预测方法

方法四：选项中含有表示评论或感受的词

　　如果选项中含有 think, like, enjoy, agree, reasonable, absurd, disgusting 等一类的词语，听力材料或问题很可能是关于对某人或某事物的评价或感受。

【例】 (710 分样卷 -21)

【预览选项】	【预测信息】
[A] Not clearly specified. [B] Not likely to be met. [C] Reasonable enough. [D] Apparently sexist.	选项均含有表示评论的词语(specified, reasonable 等)，故问题很可能是关于某人对某事物的看法，听音时多留意评论的地方。
【听音验证】	【答案解析】
W: Yes, I think you're asking quite a lot. I mean you're not really prepared to pay all ... ... W: Because personally I think you're asking an awful lot.	21. What does Brenda think of the qualifications Mr. Browning insists on? 【解析】选 [B]。抓住女士(Brenda)话中表达自己观点的标志性词语 I think 和随后的内容即可知，她认为 Mr. Browning 要求的条件 not likely to be met。

敏锐识别线索 快速定位原文

Lecture 3 第三讲 10 大信息定位技巧

技巧三：留意题干中的时间、数量等数字信息处

【例】 (07-12-7)

【原文】	【题目】
According to an International Energy Agency study, if consumers chose those models that would save them the most money over the life of the appliance, they'd cut *global residential power consumption* (and their utility bills) by *43 percent*.	7. *Global residential power consumption* can be cut by *43 percent* if _____. [A] we increase the insulation of walls ad water pipes [B] we choose simpler models of electrical appliances [C] we cut down on the use of refrigerators and other white goods [D] we choose the most efficient models of refrigerators and other white goods

【解析】本题的定位信息是题干中的 43 percent 和 Global residential power consumption，由数字 43 percent 很容易锁定答案出处。

明了设题模式 清晰做题思路

Lecture 1 第一讲 12 种题目原文转换

六、明比较与暗比较之间的转换

　　明比较是指带有明显的比较标志（比较级、最高级）的比较结构，暗比较是指带有含某种比较或变化的词语（如 increase, excess, shorten, while 等）或是暗含某种比较含义的比较结构。

【例】 (710 分样卷 -50)

【原文】	【题目】
While the bottom 10 percent of *American* workers earn just **37 percent** of our average wage, their counterparts in *other industrialized countries* earn upwards of **60 percent**.	50. We learn from the passage that the difference in pay between the lowest paid and the average worker in America is _____ *than* that in other industrialized countries.

【解析】much greater。原文中只给出了两个数字，并没有进行明确的比较，而题目则将其转换成了要求明确比出大小的比较结构。

特色栏目 先睹为快

知道哪易出题 读时适当留意

Lecture 1 第一讲 10 大敏感设题题眼

四、并列、列举、举例处常考

【例】 (04-1-31)

【原文】	【题目】
More recently, this traditional view has begun to be questioned. ***One reason*** for this change was the increasing emphasis given to the historical approach to man. ***Another reason*** for skepticism about the concept of human nature probably lies in the influence of evolutionary thinking.	31. The traditional view of "human nature" was strongly challenged by [A] the emergence of the evolutionary theory [B] the historical approach to man [C] new insight into human behavior [D] the philosophical analysis of slavery

【解析】本段首先提出了最近出现的一种观点: this traditional view has begun to be questioned, 紧接着通过 one reason…, another reason… 列举了支持这种怀疑论观点的两点原因。选项 [B] 与第一点原因内容相符。

熟悉常考错误 炼就火眼金睛

Lecture 1 第一讲 15 种常考错误类型

五、平行结构错误

平行结构要求各部分采用相同的形式, 改错题中经常会出现平行结构的连接词误用或是平行结构中某一部分与其他部分在形式上不统一的错误。

【例1】 (05-12-S7)

Restrict yourself to one or two pages, ***and listing*** any publications or referees on a separate sheet.	S7. _____

【解析】and 连接平行结构, 其前后部分的形式应该保持一致, and 前面的句子 restrict yourself… 是祈使句, and 后面的句子也应该用祈使句, 故应将 listing 改为 list。

【例2】 (04-1-S6)

… feeding 10 billion people will not be easy for ***politics, economic and environmental*** reasons.	S6. _____

【解析】and 连接的并列成分共同修饰 reasons, 形式上应保持一致, economic 和 environmental 均为形容词, 故应将名词 politics 改成形容词 political。

优化句式 让您的句子活起来

Lecture 5 第五讲 6 种灵活句式变换

一、长句和短句的变换

1. 短句变长句

【例】

【原文】	【优化】
Teenagers are pressured by school work. They are also encouraged by their peers. Under such circumstances, they resort to smoking. But sometimes they feel a little guilty. The grading system at our college should be abolished. The students don't like getting grades. The instructors don't enjoy giving grades.	<u>Pressured</u> by school work <u>and</u> <u>encouraged</u> by their peers, teenagers often resort to smoking, <u>though</u> they feel a little guilty sometimes.

【分析】原文中包含四个短句, 语意显得不够连贯。我们将前两个短句改写成用 and 连接的两个并列的分词短语充当句子的状语, 同时将后两个短句合并成一个包含由 though 引导的让步状语从句的主从复合句。

设计亮点 让您的作文眩起来

Lecture 6 第六讲 4 大写作亮点设计

三、开头结尾突破常规

1. 开头的写法

2) 对立法

所谓对立法, 就是引出人们对要讨论问题的不同看法和观点、然后提出自己的看法或者表明自己偏向哪一看法的开头方式。这种开头方式一般用于有争议的主题, 主要适用于对比选择型作文。

【例】

Nowadays there is no agreement among people as to the best measure of a country's success. Some people focus on rich economy while others may think it is the quality of life, which has nothing to do with money.

Those who insists rich economy is the best measure of a country's success believe that economic strength decides everything. Economic prosperity of a country can promote the proserity on all its aspects. …

【分析】第一段文字是关于什么是社会成功的标准的文章开头, 运用了对立法, 自然引出对该问题的两种不同的观点。

前　言

考生的困惑

今年，六级考试结束后，我们对北京、西安、上海、武汉十几所高校的考生做了一次访谈，他们普遍反映，今年试题有点难。

首先，题型不适应。对试卷上几种不同的题型，他们感觉有些茫然，不得要领，每个题型怎么应对、怎么做题，都感觉没有章法。

其次，时间不够用。考前也做了不少的练习题，感觉速度还可以了，可一上场，一下显得捉襟见肘，速度慢了，时间紧张的不行。

考生感觉试题有点难，四、六级考试委员会一项内部阅卷统计也印证了这一点——今年考生成绩平均低于去年，通过率稍有下降。

不同题型，不同考点；不同题型，不同练法，如何在六级考试中有效针对、科学复习，已经成为广大考生迫切思考的问题。

我们的分析

我们分析认为，考生出现对试题不适应、时间紧、得分低这样普遍的现象，主要可能有如下一些原因。

1、题型不熟悉　不同的题型，都有着不同的考查倾向、不同的能力要求、不同的设题方式、不同的做题方法。对各个题型不熟悉、不理解，就不能针对练习、针对提高、形成一套有针对性的做题模式，考场上，也就不能做到不同题型、不同应对、有章有法、胸有成竹。

2、技巧没掌握　不同的考试题型，针对该题型的语料特点、设题方式、问题模式，都有一些行之有效的做题技巧，理解、掌握、运用这些技巧，可以给您的做题能力锦上添花、平添双翼。相反，不熟悉这些技巧，考场上就会影响做题速度、影响做题节奏，时间会变得很紧张。

3、练习不标准　复习备考，练习必不可少，但练习的选择必须标准。很多考生复习中可能也做了不少题目，但能力却没有相应提高，很大的原因就在于所做练习从语料选择、题目设置到难度把握等方面都和真题水平有很大差距，不够标准，结果只能是茫茫做题、苦苦无果。所以，复习中选择练习题目必须严格、标准、有针对性，切忌泛泛，否则练习做得再勤，模拟做得再多，也达不到好的训练效果，甚至造成误导。精挑精练，才会事半功倍。

4、复习没定性　复习备考不是零碎进行、一蹴而就的，它需要一个计划、一个安排。很多考生复习三天打鱼、两天晒网，没有系统、没有计划，导致复习效率低、效果不明显。

为了帮助考生全面熟悉各个题型、清晰形成做题思路、快速提升做题能力，我们在对六级考试各题型潜心研究的基础上，编写了这本书。全书共分五篇，第一至四篇分别对四大题型边讲边练、各个击破，第五篇给出 6 套标准试题，让您在前面每个题型各个击破的基础上，最后整合模拟。

1、45 天计划 一气呵成 全书所有内容——各个题型的讲解、熟悉、演练，以及最后完整的预测模拟，都安排在 45 天里进行，紧凑高效，避免了复习的随意性，确保您复习效率、复习效果。

2、题型特点 清晰透视 第一至四篇每个题型巅峰讲座中，对该题型考查倾向、能力要求、语料特点，一一审视、层层透析，让您清晰理解、深入领会该题型的复习重点、努力方向。

3、设题环节 深度挖掘 第一至四篇每个题型巅峰讲座中，对该题型设题环节、设题方式、设题特点，一一道来、深度解密，让您对每个题设题初衷、对应信息豁然开朗、一目了然。

4、做题思路 个性归纳 第一至四篇每个题型巅峰讲座中，对该题型做题套路、分析方法、答案原则，一一归纳、娓娓讲解，让您对每一种题目类型，都能做到轻松应对、有章有法。

5、实用技巧 独家点拨 第一至四篇每个题型巅峰讲座中，对该题型做题技巧、应急技巧、抢时技巧，一一总结、实用点拨，让您对每一种题目类型，都能做到心有灵犀、一看就通。

6、即讲即练 马上体会 第一至四篇每个题型巅峰讲座中，每一类题型特点、设题环节、做题思路、实用技巧结合实例讲完后，马上给出精选典型练习，让您领会刚刚讲过的内容。

7、巅峰练习 各个击破 第一至四篇每个题型巅峰讲座后，给出一定数量该题型的综合练习，让您在前面讲解、专练后，再对该题型来一个单题型综合训练，全面融会贯通该题型。

8、巅峰预测 整合提升 第一至四篇对各个题型讲练结合、各个击破后，第五篇给出 6 套综合预测试题，让您在前面分题型各个击破基础上，整合模拟、全面升华，培养临考状态。

9、练习充分 设题标准 第一至四篇各题型的即讲即练、巅峰练习和第五篇综合的巅峰预测，合计题量 14 套，练习充分。14 套试题，语料标准、设题标准、难度标准、解析标准。

附：六级试题结构

测试内容		测试题型	数量	比例	
听力理解	听力对话 短对话	多项选择	8个	15%	35%
	听力对话 长对话	多项选择	2段		
	听力短文 短文理解	多项选择	3篇	20%	
	听力短文 短文听写	复合式听写	1篇		
阅读理解	仔细阅读 篇章阅读	多项选择	2篇	25%	35%
	仔细阅读 篇章词汇或短句问答	选词填空或简答题	1篇		
	快速阅读	是非判断＋句子填空或多项选择＋句子填空或其他	1篇	10%	
综合测试	改错或完型填空	错误辨认并改正或多项选择	1篇	10%	10%
写作和翻译	写作	短文写作	1篇	15%	20%
	翻译	汉译英	5句	5%	

目 录

第
1
至
2
天

第
3
天

第4至5天

第6天

第7至8天

第10至11天

第12天

第13天

第二篇　阅读理解

第14至15天

第
14
至
15
天

第
16
天

第
17
至
18
天

第四篇 短文写作

第
33
至
34
天

第
35
天

第
36
天

第
37
天

第五篇　巅峰预测

第一篇

听 力 理 解

第 1 – 13 天

Part 1

第一章 短对话巅峰讲座

六级听力考试中短对话一般为 8 段,每段为一轮对话和一个问题,要求考生能听懂英语国家人士的日常对话,能把握讨论的主题,抓住其中心大意或其中的要点,然后从所给的四个选项中选出最佳答案。每段对话均朗读一遍,每个问题后留有 13 秒的答题时间。

Lecture 1　第一讲　8 类对话常涉场景

短对话涉及的场景十分广泛,但以贴近学生生活、学习的话题或是日常生活和工作的话题为主。常涉及的场景可分为 8 类:校园生活、日常生活、职场工作、医疗健康、旅游交通、饮食娱乐、住房搬家和气候环境,其中以校园生活、日常生活和职场工作居多。

一、校园生活

这类场景主要围绕学生的学习和生活展开,涉及入学、办手续(注册)、选课、听课、作业、论文、借书、买书、学习、考试、课余活动、住宿等一系列话题。

【例 1】 (07-6-12)

[A] He enjoys finding fault with exams.	W: I've never seen you have such confidence before an exam.
[B] He is sure of his success in the exam.	M: It's more than confidence. Right now I feel that if I get less than an A, it'll be the fault of the exam itself.
[C] He doesn't know if he can do well in the exam.	Q: What does the man mean?
[D] He used to get straight A's in the exams he took.	

【解析】本对话的话题是关于考试。男士说如果他这次考试拿不到 A,那一定是 the fault of the exam itself(考试本身的问题),可见他 sure of his success in the exam,故答案为[B]。

二、日常生活

这类场景主要涉及与日常家庭生活相关的话题,包括购物、洗衣、收拾屋子、家庭理财以及其他一些居家琐事等。

【例 2】 (06-6-2)

[A] Set the dinner table.	M: Susan, I am going to change the light bulb above the dining room table. Will you hold the ladder for me?
[B] Change the light bulb.	W: No problem. But be careful while you're up there.
[C] Clean the dining room.	Q: What does the man want the woman to do?
[D] Hold the ladder for him.	

【解析】本对话的话题是关于居家琐事。男士请女士帮忙 hold the ladder(扶梯子),女士回答说 no problem,故答案为[D]。

三、职场工作

这类场景主要涉及学生假期兼职、毕业生找工作、招聘面试、工作选择、工作安排、工作状态、工作往来、职位任免和同事相处等话题。

【例3】 (07-6-15) 🎧

[A] More money.	W: I hear your boss has a real good impression of you and he is think-
[B] Fair treatment.	ing about giving you two more days off each month.
[C] A college education.	M: I hope not. I'd rather get more work hours so I can get enough
[D] Shorter work hours.	bucks to help out my two kids at college.
	Q: What does the man truly want?

【解析】本对话的话题是关于工作目标。男士说他不希望老板给他放假，因为他想 get enough bucks to…(赚更多的钱来供孩子上大学)，故答案为[A]。more money≈enough bucks。

四、医疗健康 ≫

这类场景主要涉及看病就医、健康状况、锻炼身体、健身减肥等话题。

【例4】 (07-6-17) 🎧

[A] Cheer herself up a bit.	W: I'm worried about Anna. She's really been depressed lately. All
[B] Find a more suitable job.	she does is staying in her room all day.
[C] Seek professional advice.	M: That sounds serious. She'd better see a psychiatrist at the conso-
[D] Take a psychology course.	ling center.
	Q: What does the man suggest Anna do?

【解析】本对话的话题是关于心理健康。男士通过典型的建议句式 She'd better…建议 Anna 去 see a psychiatrist at the consoling center(去慰藉中心看精神病医师)，故答案为[C]。

【例5】 (06-6-8) 🎧

[A] At a bookstore.	M: I am afraid there won't be time to do another tooth today. Make sure you
[B] At the dentist's.	don't eat anything like steaks for the next few hours, and we'll fill the
[C] In a restaurant.	other cavity tomorrow.
[D] In the library.	W: All right. Actually, I must hurry to the library to return some books.
	Q: Where does the conversation most probably take place?

【解析】本对话的话题是关于看牙医。由关键词 tooth, cavity 等可推知谈话地点可能为 the dentist's(牙科诊所)，故答案为[B]。

五、旅游交通 ≫

这类场景主要涉及旅行前的准备、旅行选择的交通手段、旅行时的情形、旅行的感受、接人送人、交通状况、交通违章、交通事故等话题。

【例6】 (07-6-16) 🎧

[A] She was exhausted from her trip.	M: I heard you took a trip to Mexico last month. How did you
[B] She missed the comforts of home.	like it?
[C] She was impressed by Mexican food.	W: Oh, I got sick and tired of hotels and hotel food. So now I
[D] She will not go to Mexico again.	understand the saying, "East, west, home's best".
	Q: What does the woman mean?

【解析】本对话的话题是关于旅行感受。男士问女士上个月到 Mexico 的旅行怎么样,女士回答说她 got sick and tired of hotels and hotel food(很厌烦旅馆和旅馆的食物),并说自己现在才明白那句谚语"East, west, home's best"(金窝,银窝,不如自己的草窝)的含义,由此可知她 missed the comforts of home(想念家里的舒适),故答案为[B]。

六、饮食娱乐 ≫

这类场景主要涉及吃饭地点、点菜、对饭菜及用餐环境的评价,以及观看电影、观看演出、购票、评论电影或演出等话题。

【例7】

(新 06-12-18)

[A] The food served in the cafeteria usually lacks variety.
[B] The cafeteria sometimes provides rare food for the students.
[C] The students find the service in the cafeteria satisfactory.
[D] The cafeteria tries hard to cater to the students' needs.

W: The cafeteria provided many kinds of dishes for us today. Did you notice that?
M: Yes, kind of rare, isn't it?
Q: What does the man imply?

【解析】本对话的话题是关于外出就餐。女士提到今天 the cafeteria 的食物种类很多，男士说这种情况 kind of rare（很少有），由此推知通常情况下 the cafeteria 的食物种类很少，故答案为[A]。cater to one's needs 意为"迎合某人的需求"。

七、住家搬房

这类场景主要涉及旅馆住宿、租房买房、居住环境、装饰装修、房屋维修等话题。

【例8】

(新 06-12-12)

[A] The man will rent the apartment when it is available.
[B] The man made a bargain with the landlady over the rent.
[C] The man insists on having a look at the apartment first.
[D] The man is not fully satisfied with the apartment.

W: I'm afraid I can't show you the apartment at the moment, because the tenant is still living in it. It's really a lovely place with a big kitchen and a sunny window for only $200 a month.
M: Sounds good, but we really can't rent an apartment without seeing it first.
Q: What do we learn from the conversation?

【解析】本对话的话题是关于租房。男士通过 but 转折提出要 seeing it first（先看看公寓的情况），然后再决定是否租住，故答案为[C]。

八、气候环境

这类场景主要涉及气候、温度、环境污染以及其对人们生活的影响等方面的话题。

【例9】

(04-6-3)

[A] The temperature is not as high as the man claims.
[B] The room will get cool if the man opens the windows.
[C] She is following instructions not to use the air-conditioning.
[D] She is afraid the new epidemic SARS will spread all over town.

M: Excuse me, Madam. Is the air-conditioning on? This room is getting as hot as a furnace.
W: Sorry, sir. A new epidemic called SARS is threatening us right now. As a preventative measure, we are told to let in fresh air by opening the windows and not to use air conditioners.
Q: What does the woman mean?

【解析】本对话的话题是关于室内空气。女士说为了预防 SARS,他们被告之不要 use air conditioners(使用空调),故答案为[C]。preventative measure 意为"预防措施"。epidemic 意为"流行性的"。

Exercise　即讲即练　边听边记

1. [A] He can't help the woman tonight.
   [B] He broke the calculator the woman lent him.
   [C] He doesn't know how to turn the calculator on.
   [D] He lost the woman's calculator.
2. [A] The woman is now quite satisfied.
   [B] The machine is still out of order.
   [C] The man is fixing the machine now.
   [D] The game the man is watching will end in 3 hours.
3. [A] Vienna.　　[B] Paris.　　[C] Rome.　　[D] Geneva.

4. [A] Husband and wife.　　　　　　　[B] Teacher and student.

 [C] Lawyer and client.　　　　　　　[D] Doctor and patient.

5. [A] Editor.　　　　　　　　　　　　[B] Journalist.

 [C] Teacher.　　　　　　　　　　　[D] Student.

6. [A] It is having financial trouble.

 [B] Its chemistry program is very popular.

 [C] The fees for the chemistry course have been reduced.

 [D] The number of students has doubled.

7. [A] In a drugstore.　　　　　　　　[B] In a hospital.

 [C] In a supermarket.　　　　　　　[D] In the street.

8. [A] She likes cooking only if it takes a short time.　[B] She hates cooking for others.

 [C] She doesn't like the clean-up after the meal.　[D] She dislikes entering the kitchen.

〔边听边记〕

【答案与解析】

1.

[A] He can't help the woman tonight.	W: Could you bring my calculator back? I need it to do
[B] He broke the calcuastor the woman lent him.	my math homework tonight.
[C] He doesn't know how to turn the calculator on.	M: I don't know how to put this, but, er, I dropped it,
[D] He lost the woman's calculator.	and now the on button doesn't light up.
	Q: What is the man's problem?

【解析】本对话的话题是关于借东西。由男士话中的 I drooped it, and now the on button doesn't light up 可知,他把女士借给他的 calculator 摔坏了(broke)。put 意为"表达,说"。

2.

[A] The woman is now quite satisfied.	W: This is going too far. You've been watching the
[B] The machine is still out of order.	game for three hours. You never get the machine
[C] The man is fixing the machine now.	down.
[D] The game the man is watching will end in 3 hours.	M: OK. I'll get it down. But I'll do it when I feel like it.
	Q: What can we learn from the conversation?

【解析】本对话的话题是关于家务活。女士抱怨男士还没有 get the machine down(修好机器),男士说他会修,但前提是他 feel like it(愿意修),言外之意就是他现在不想修机器,所以机器现在还 out of order(没有修好)。

3.

[A] Vienna.	M: Where did you and John go on your vacation?
[B] Paris.	W: We spent four days in Vienna, one week in Paris, and five
[C] Rome.	days in Rome and we had a two-day delay in Geneva before
[D] Geneva.	we went to Italy.
	Q: In which city did the woman and John stay the longest?

【解析】本对话的话题是关于旅行情况。由女士话中的 four days in Vienna, one week in Paris, and five days in Rome...a two day-delay in Geneva 可知,女士和 John 在 Paris 呆的时间最长。

4.

[A] Husband and wife.	M: My throat is sore and I have a fever.
[B] Teacher and student.	W: Let me take a look at your throat. Do you have any chills?
[C] Lawyer and client.	Q: What is the probable relationship between the two speakers?
[D] Doctor and patient.	

【解析】本对话的话题是关于生病就医。男士的嗓子 sore(疼),并且还 have a fever(发烧),女士要求看男士的 throat,并问他是否感到冷,由此可判断二者很可能是 doctor and patient(医生和病人)的关系。

5.

| [A] Editor.
[B] Journalist.
[C] Teacher.
[D] Student. | M: We'll be here in London sitting in a newspaper office or teaching in a classroom full of chalk dust.
W: Well, George, you'd be able to go out in the sunshine sometimes. You are a journalist. I'm the one who has to stay in the classroom. Don't forget.
Q: What is the woman's profession? |

【解析】本对话的话题是关于工作情况。女士话中的 I'm the one who has to stay in the classroom 与男士话中的 teaching in a classroom... 均表明女士是一名 teacher。

6.

| [A] It is having financial trouble.
[B] Its chemistry program is very popular.
[C] The fees for the chemistry course have been reduced.
[D] The number of students has doubled. | M: I was going to take organic chemistry next semester—but now it's been cut.
W: I heard the university's going to double the tuition, too.
Q: What can we infer about the university? |

【解析】本对话的话题是关于选课。男士话中的 it's been cut 表明学校取消了 organic chemistry，女士话中的...going to double the tuition 表明学校要增收学费。学校减少课程、增收学费很可能是因为它面临着 financial trouble(经济困难)。

7.

| [A] In a drugstore.
[B] In a hospital.
[C] In a supermarket.
[D] In the street. | M: Could you tell me where the dental department is?
W: Go down the hall and turn left at the pharmacy. It's just past the nurse's clinic.
Q: Where does the conversation most probably take place? |

【解析】本对话的话题是关于医院诊所。由对话中的关键信息 dental department(牙科)、pharmacy(药房)及 nurse's clinic(临床护理部)可知,对话最有可能发生在 hospital(医院)。

8.

| [A] She likes cooking only if it takes a short time.
[B] She hates cooking for others.
[C] She doesn't like the clean-up after the meal.
[D] She dislikes entering the kitchen. | M: Do you enjoy cooking?
W: Surely not. It takes up too much time and I really hate having to clean up after the meal. I can't stand doing the washing up, drying up, and putting all the dishes and cutlery away.
Q: What can we learn about the woman from the conversation? |

【解析】本对话的话题是关于家务活。女士话中的 I really hate having to clean up after the meal 表明她不喜欢 the clean-up after the meal(饭后的洗刷工作)。doing the washing up, drying up 及 putting all the dishes and cutlery away 都属于 the clean-up after the meal 的范畴。

Lecture 2　第二讲　7种对话常提问题

　　从历年真题来看,六级听力短对话所提问题主要涉及七个方面的内容:事实状况、行为活动、观点态度、地点场景、谈论话题、身份关系和数字信息。对话内容不同,提问的角度和方式也有所不同。

一、事实状况

　　所提问题是关于陈述谈话的一方或双方说了什么、所处状态、做某事的原因何在、结果如何等。
　　常见的提问方式如:
　　What do we learn from this conversation?
　　What does the man mean?

What can be inferred from the conversation?

此类问题解题技巧如下:

1. 根据选项特点判断问题类型。

   这类题的选项一般都是某种事实情况的陈述,选项中句子的时态以一般过去时或一般现在时居多。

2. 正确选项一般不会是原文的细节再现。

   这类题往往需要考生根据对话内容推测出说话人话语中隐含的事实细节,因此正确选项往往不是对话中的原文照搬,而是对话内容的同义转述,或是根据对话内容推断出的事实细节。

3. 注意捕捉选项中的关键词。

   听音前提取选项要点,确定听音时应该捕捉的重点内容。一般某事的原因或结果常为考查重点。

4. 记录关键信息点。

   听音时注意对各选项涉及的关键信息进行标记,然后根据问题对号入座。

【例1】 (新 06-12-17)

[A] They can't fit into the machine. [B] They have not been delivered yet. [C] They were sent to the wrong address. [D] They were found to be of the wrong type.	M: Have the parts we need for the photo copying machine arrived yet? W: I ordered them last week, but something is holding them up. Q: What does the woman say about the parts needed for the photo copying machine?

【解析】事实状况题。女士话中的 something is holding them up 表明她订购的影印机部件还没有寄到,故答案为[B]。hold sth. up 意为"耽误,使不能进行"。

二、行为活动

所提问题是关于谈话的一方或双方做过、正在做、准备去做什么或一方建议另一方去做什么。

常见的提问方式如:

What will the man/woman most probably do?

What are the speakers probably going/trying to do?

What does the woman suggest doing?

此类问题解题技巧如下:

1. 根据选项特点判断题型。

   一般来说这类试题的选项都是动词短语形式,且动词一般为动词原形或动名词形式。

2. 听音时留意对话中的动词,尤其注意与选项中动词相关的信息。

   在留意动词的同时,要记录一些与该动词相关的重要信息,尤其是不只一个选项中的动词在对话中出现的时候,只有留意与动词相关的信息,才能根据问题对号入座。

3. 注意表示请求、建议或提议的短语或句式。

   行为活动类试题的对话中经常会包含提出请求或建议的句式或短语,如:He(She) should, Would you, Why don't you, Let's, You'd better, You don't have to, I have got to, What about, If I were you, I would…, I'd like to, you might as well 等,这些句式后面的内容可能就是建议去做或准备去做的行为活动,很可能与答案直接相关,因此听音时需重点留意。

【例2】 (07-6-11)

[A] Surfing the net. [B] Watching a talk show. [C] Packing a birthday gift. [D] Shopping at a jewelry store.	W: Jim, you are on the net again? When are you going to get off? It's the time for the talk show. M: Just a minute, dear. I'm looking at a new jewelry site. I want to make sure I get the right gift for Mom's birthday. Q: What is the man doing right now?

【解析】行为活动题。由女士话中的 are you on the net again? When are you going to get off?(你又在上网吗?你什么时候出发?)可知,男士正 on the net(在上网);而男士话中的 I'm looking at a new jewelry site(我正在看一个新的珠宝网站)也说明男士正在上网,故答案为[A]。surf the net ≈ on the net。

三、观点态度

所提问题是关于谈话一方对另一方或第三方的行为、品德、观点等的态度或评价。

常见的提问方式如：

What does the woman feel about?

What does the woman/man mean/imply?

How does the woman/man feel about…?

What does the woman/man think of…?

此类问题解题技巧如下：

1. 根据选项特点判断问题类型。

这类试题的选项中一般都含有一些引出观点态度的动词或短语，常见的有：think, believe, find, guess, imagine, consider, as far as I know 等。根据这类线索词判断出试题类型以后，可以更有针对性地去留意对话中说话人对自己观点态度的陈述。

2. 熟悉表示观点态度的常见词语。

表示赞成：approve, agree, share, prefer, wise, reasonable, favorable

表示反对：disapprove, disagree, unwise, ridiculous, foolish, childish

表示赞赏：admire, appreciate, think much of, be proud of

表示批评：critical, criticize

表示喜欢：love, enjoy, wonderful, fascinating, funny

表示讨厌或恨：boring/bored, a shame, hate, hatred, regret

表示积极或消极：positive, negative

表示漠然：indifferent, detached, careless

3. 抓住对话中的一些标识性词语。

听音时应注意抓住一些表明上下文间的因果、转折、比较与对照或举例等逻辑关系的标识性词语(如：but, instead 表转折；if, as long as 表条件；because, due to 表原因；therefore, consequently 表结果)，尤其是转折后的内容，往往表达作者的真实观点或态度，常为考查重点。

【例3】   (07-6-13)

| [A] The man is generous with his good comments on people.
 [B] The woman is unsure if there will be peace in the world.
 [C] The woman is doubtful about newspaper stories.
 [D] The man is quite optimistic about human nature. | W: Just look at this newspaper, nothing but murder, death and war! Do you still believe people are basically good?
 M: Of course I do. But newspapers hardly ever report stories about peace and generosity. They are not news.
 Q: What do we learn from the conversation? |

【解析】观点态度题。女士问男士是否还相信 people are basically good(人是善良的)，男士给予了肯定回答(Of course I do)，由此可推知男士对人的善良天性持 optimistic(乐观的)态度，故答案为[D]。对话中并没有直接表明男士的态度，需要通过双方的对话内容进行推测。

四、地点场景

所提问题是关于对话发生的场合、地点或者涉及到的人或事物所处的位置。

常见的提问方式如：

Where is the conversation most probably taking place?

Where are the two people?

此类问题解题技巧如下：

1. 单个地点题:抓住与特定地点相关的常用词语。

对话中并未提到具体场所,问题要求根据对话内容推测出谈话场所或某人的去向。该类题要求考生能抓住标志信息词,即与特定地点相关的最常用词语。

2. 多个地点题:依赖笔记,抓住提问中的关键词。

对话中提到几个地点,就其中某一个进行提问,解题关键在于区分细节,对与选项中地点相关的信息进行速记,并注意抓住问题中的关键词。

3. 熟悉常考的场景。

主要包括:

诊所或医院 (clinic or hospital)　　　　　餐馆(restaurant)

学校或校园(school or campus)　　　　　书店 (bookstore)

火车站 (railway station)　　　　　机场 (airport)

邮局(post office)　　　　　图书馆 (library)

银行(bank)　　　　　旅馆 (hotel)

【例4】 (06-6-8)

[A] At a bookstore.	M: I am afraid there won't be time to do another tooth today. Make sure you don't eat anything like steaks for the next few hours, and we'll fill the other cavity tomorrow.
[B] At the dentist's.	
[C] In a restaurant.	W: All right. Actually, I must hurry to the library to return some books.
[D] In the library.	Q: Where does the conversation most probably take place?

【解析】地点场景题。只要抓住对话中 "tooth"和 "cavity"这两个线索词就可以推出两人的谈话发生在牙科诊所,故答案为[B]。

五、谈论话题

所提问题是关于对话中所谈论的话题或对象。

常见的提问方式如:

What are they talking about?

What are the speakers talking about?

此类问题解题技巧如下:

1. 根据选项特点判断问题类型。

一般来说,谈论话题题的选项概括性都较强,且常为短语;另外,各选项所陈述的内容往往差别较大。

2. 捕捉与话题相关的关键词。

一般来说,该类题型比较简单,只要能捕捉到对话中与该话题相关的关键词,即可判断出对话谈论的内容。

3. 熟悉常考话题的相关词语。

考生在平时训练中,应留意与某类话题相关的词语并加以记忆,以便在听音时能够更有效地抓取关键词。

4. 注意不要只从对话一方的话语中寻找答案。

由于是考查谈话主题,因此双方的话语中都应含有与主题相关的线索词。

【例5】 (02-6-1)

[A] Registering for courses.	W: The deadline for the sociology and computer courses is the day after tomorrow.
[B] Getting directions.	
[C] Buying a new computer.	M: But I haven't decided which courses to take yet?
[D] Studying sociology.	Q: What are the man and woman talking about?

【解析】谈论话题题。选项均为动词-ing 短语,且内容差别较大,故本题很可能属于考查"谈论话题"类型。由女士话中的关键词 sociology and computer courses 和男士话中的关键词 courses 和 take 可推知对话谈论的主题是 registering for courses(选修课程),故答案为[A]。动词 take 可以表示"选(课)"。

六、身份关系

所提问题是关于对话双方的关系或对话中某个人物的身份职业等。

常见的提问方式如：

What is the probable relationship between the (two) speakers?

What is the most probable relationship between Jim and Bob?

What's the woman's job?

What most probably is Mary?

此类问题解题技巧如下：

1. 捕捉关键词及人物语气。

解答这类试题，不但要熟悉体现某种人物关系或某种职业的相关词汇，而且要注意说话人的语气和态度。比如师生之间、夫妻之间、家长与孩子之间以及老板与员工之间的说话方式和语气均有自己的特点，在听音时应加以留意。

2. 熟悉常考人物关系。

主要包括：

夫妻(husband—wife)	父子(father—son)
母子(mother—son)	师生(teacher—student)
同学(schoolmate)	同事(colleague)
老板与秘书(boss—secretary)	雇主与雇员(employer—employee)
医生与病人(doctor—patient)	服务员与顾客(waiter/waitress—customer)
主人与客人(host/hostess—guest)	警察与司机(policeman—driver)
图书管理员与借阅者(librarian—reader)	房东与租房者(landlord/landlady—tenant)

3. 熟悉常考职业身份。

主要包括：

教授(professor)	秘书(secretary)
医生(doctor)	老板(boss)
服务员(waiter/waitress)	修理工(repairer, plumber, electrician…)
家庭角色(husband, wife, son, daughter, girlfriend…)	

【例6】　　　　　　　　　　　　　　　　　　　　　　　　　(06-6-5)

[A] Tony's secretary. [B] Paul's girlfriend. [C] Paul's colleague. [D] Tony's wife.	M: Hello, Mary. This is Paul at the bank. Is Tony home? W: Not yet. Paul. I don't think you can reach him at the office now, either. He phoned me five minutes ago to say he was stopping for a hair-cut on his way home. Q: Who do you think the woman probably is?

【解析】身份关系题。选项表明本题为考查"身份关系"类型，根据选项中 girlfriend, wife 可知，本题应该是问对话中女士的身份。男士询问女士 Tony 是否在家，由此可初步确定答案为[D]，即女士最可能是 Tony's wife，再根据女士所说的 He phoned me…on his way home 即可进一步确定答案为[D]。听音时一定要注意辨别选项中出现的人名，搞清人物关系。

七、数字信息

所提问题涉及到时间、年龄、数量、速度、价格等信息。

常见的提问方式如：

What time did Suzy leave home?

How much does one ticket cost?

When is the train leaving?

此类问题解题技巧如下：

1. 速记信息。

   这类对话题中一般都不会只出现一个数字,因此一定要速记对话中出现的数字及相关要点信息。
2. 听清问题。

   做这类题目时,必须清楚地抓住问题是针对什么提问,然后才能根据记录的信息将答案对号入座。
3. 不要直接答案。

   这类题的答案一般都不是原文中数字信息的再现,往往都需要经过简单的运算才能得出答案。

【例7】 (97-6-1)

[A] On Thursday.	M: Good morning. I'm here to see Mr. Adison.
[B] On Monday night.	W: Mr. Adison went to Washington last Monday for a conference and
[C] On Friday morning.	he will be back on Thursday night. If you like, you may come again
[D] On Thursday morning.	on Friday morning.
	Q: When will Mr. Adison return?

【解析】数字信息题。对话中一共出现了三个时间:Last Monday, Thursday night, Friday morning,听音时要注意记录三个时间分别对应的事件:Adison went to Washington, Adison back, Man come again,然后根据问题对号入座,故答案为[A]。

Exercise 即讲即练 边听边记

1. [A] Tell the man where the lecture is given.
   [B] Help the man prepare for the lecture.
   [C] Go to the lecture with the man.
   [D] Put on her glasses.
2. [A] Doing nothing but playing.
   [B] Reading the next chapter in the textbook.
   [C] Writing a paragraph about a movie they saw.
   [D] Checking out a book from the library.
3. [A] He is patient. [B] He is reliable.
   [C] He is generous. [D] He is forgetful.
4. [A] In a booking office. [B] In a library.
   [C] In a classroom. [D] In a bookstore.
5. [A] Cleaner. [B] Safeguard.
   [C] Acrobat. [D] Peeper.
6. [A] TV stations. [B] Annoying programs.
   [C] Advertisements. [D] Aids.
7. [A] Buy a more expensive watch. [B] Not buy a pink watch.
   [C] Buy the watch at once. [D] Not buy the watch.
8. [A] Clerk and manager. [B] Traveler and customs officer.
   [C] Reader and author. [D] Customer and shop assistant.

【答案与解析】

1.

[A] Tell the man where the lecture is given.	M: I hear Prof. Miller is going to give a lecture about the
[B] Help the man prepare for the lecture.	development of television, but I don't know when.
[C] Go to the lecture with the man.	W: If you wait until I get my glasses, I'll look at the sc-
[D] Put on her glasses.	hedule for you.
	Q: What will the woman probably do first?

【解析】行为活动题。女士话中的条件状语从句 If you wait until I get my glasses 表明,在告诉男士 Prof. Miller 的讲座时间之前,她要先 put on her glasses(戴上眼镜)。

2.

[A] Doing nothing but playing.	W: Do we have an assignment for Monday? I don't have
[B] Reading the next chapter in the textbook.	anything written down.
[C] Writing a paragraph about a movie they saw.	M: Nothing to read in the book, but we have to see a movie and write a paragraph about it.
[D] Checking out a book from the library.	Q: What is the speakers' assignment for Monday?

【解析】事实状况题。男士话中的转折句 but we have to see a movie… 表明他们的任务就是看一部电影,然后写一篇该电影的 paragraph(短评)。

3.

[A] He is patient.	M: Sam offered to give me a ride to the train station tomorrow.
[B] He is reliable.	I hope he won't forget.
[C] He is generous.	W: Oh. Don't worry. If Sam says he will do something, he does it.
[D] He is forgetful.	Q: What does the woman think of Sam?

【解析】观点态度题。女士话中的 If Sam says he will do something, he does it 表明她认为 Sam 是一个说到做到的人,也就是说 Sam 是一个 reliable(值得信任的)人。

4.

[A] In a booking office.	W: I thought we could check out as many books as we need with a student ID.
[B] In a library.	
[C] In a classroom.	M: No, according to the regulation, ten books for each person.
[D] In a bookstore.	Q: Where does this conversation most probably take place?

【解析】地点场景题。女士话中的 many books 提示动词短语 check out 在此处意为"(向图书馆)借书",由此可知对话最可能发生在 library(图书馆)。

5.

[A] Cleaner.	W: My God, you must get nervous hanging up in the air outside the window like that. Are you sure you are all right?
[B] Safeguard.	
[C] Acrobat.	M: Yes, I'm just doing my job. It's okay.
[D] Peeper.	Q: What is the man's occupation?

【解析】身份关系题。由女士话中的 hanging up in the air outside the window 及男士话中的 I'm just doing my job 很容易联想到悬挂在高楼外面进行擦洗工作的人,由此可推断男士很可能是一名 cleaner。

6.

[A] TV stations.	W: Ads are so annoying. They are often shown in a program.
[B] Annoying programs.	M: Yes, but to some extent it is necessary because the money advertisers pay for them is essential for TV stations' survival and development.
[C] Advertisements.	
[D] Aids.	Q: What are they talking about?

【解析】谈论话题题。女士抱怨说 ads 很烦人,它们经常会在电视节目中间播出,男士说有时确实如此,但是在某种程度上 ads 又是必须的,因为广告商所付的广告费对电视台的生存及发展有很大作用,由此可知二人正在谈论 advertisements(广告)。

7.

[A] Buy a more expensive watch.	W: Look at this pink watch. It looks great, doesn't it? And it's only $20.
[B] Not buy a pink watch.	M: But $20 watch will break in no time, and besides you already have a watch.
[C] Buy the watch at once.	
[D] Not buy the watch.	Q: What does the man suggest the woman do?

【解析】行为活动题。由女士话中的 It looks great 及 it's only＄20 可知，她很想买这块手表，但男士话中的转折句 But＄20… 表明了他的相反意见，即他建议女士 not buy the watch(不应买这块表)。in no time 意为"立刻，马上"。

8.

[A] Clerk and manager.	M: Do you have anything to declare? Was this bottle of whisky bought in the duty free shop?
[B] Traveler and customs officer.	W: Yes, at Paris Airport.
[C] Reader and author.	Q: What's the relationship between the two speakers?
[D] Customer and shop assistant.	

【解析】身份关系题。男士话中的 Was … bought in the duty free shop? 提示 declare 在本对话中意为"申报(纳税的物品)"，由此可知男士是一名 customs officer(海关人员)，而由女士话中的 at Paris Airport 可知，她是一名 traveler(旅客)。

Lecture 3　第三讲　9 种对话常含句式

一、转折句式

转折句式是指一般先说明原本的意图或情势，然后经 but 等词进行转折来说明后来的实际想法或事实结果的句式。设题点往往在转折词之后。

1. but 转折

【例1】 (99-1-2)

[A] She is going to Finland.	M: Why don't you come to our house for dinner some time next week?
[B] She has visitors next week.	W: I'd like to, but we have visitors from Finland, perhaps next week.
[C] She has guests at her home.	Q: Why can't the woman accept the man's invitation?
[D] She has just visited him this week.	

【解析】本题在 but 转折处命题。男士邀请女士去他家吃晚饭，女士通过"先肯定后转折"的句式(I'd like to, but…)表示自己不能接受邀请，but 后陈述了理由(have visitors next week)，故答案为[B]。

2. though, yet, however 等其他转折

【例2】 (01-1-1)

[A] The man thinks travelling by air is quite safe.	W: Have you heard about the plane crash yesterday? It caused a hundred and twenty deaths. I am never at ease when taking a flight.
[B] The woman never travels by plane.	M: Though we often hear about air crashes and serious casual deeds, flying is one of the safest ways to travel.
[C] Both speakers feel nervous when flying.	Q: What do we learn from this conversation?
[D] The speakers feel sad about the serious loss of life.	

【解析】本题在 though 转折处命题。男士的话表明 though(尽管)我们经常会听到有关 air crashes 的报道，但他仍然认为 flying(乘坐飞机)是 safest(最安全的)的旅行方式之一，故答案为[A]。

二、建议句式

谈话的一方向另一方提出建议是六级听力考试中常出现的一类场景，因此掌握一些表达建议的常用句式，将对理解对话和解答问题有很大帮助。

1. had better do sth.（最好…）

【例3】 (05-1-3)

[A] Study in a quiet place.	W: I've been studying all the time, but still can't see any improvement in my grades.
[B] Improve her grades gradually.	M: Maybe instead of studying in your dorm, you'd
[C] Change the conditions of her dorm.	

[D] Avoid distractions while studying in her dorm.	better go some place where there are fewer distractions. Q: What does the man advise the woman to do?

【解析】行为活动题。男士通过句式 You'd better…(你最好…)建议女士找一个 fewer distractions(干扰少的)地方学习,即 study in a quiet place,故答案为[A]。

2. How about/What about doing sth.？（…怎么样？）

【例4】　　　　　　　　　　　　　　　　　　　　　　　　　　　　(03-6-9)

[A] The organization of a conference. [B] The decoration of the conference room. [C] The job of cleaning up the dining room. [D] The cost of renting a conference room.	W: Renting a conference room at the hotel will cost us too much. We are already running in the red. M: How about using our dining room for the meeting? Q: What's worrying the woman?

【解析】事实状况题。女士话中的 Renting a conference room…will cost us too much 表明她正在为租用会议室的费用而发愁,故答案为[D]。男士通过 How about using…提议将餐厅作为会议室来使用。run in the red 意为"出现赤字或亏空"。

3. Why not do sth.？ 或 why don't you/we do sth.？（为什么不…?）

【例5】　　　　　　　　　　　　　　　　　　　　　　　　　　　　(03-6-6)

[A] Not to subscribe to the journal. [B] To buy the latest issue of the magazine. [C] To find a better science journal in the library. [D] Not to miss any chance to collect useful information.	M: Maybe I ought to subscribe to the Engineering Quarterly. It contains a lot of useful information. W: Why not read it in the library and save the money? Q: What is the woman's advice to the man?

【解析】事实状况题。女士通过典型的建议句式 Why not …？ 建议男士 read it in the library,即暗示男士 not to subscribe to the journal(不要订阅期刊),故答案为[A]。

4. should/shouldn't do sth.（应该/不应该…）

【例6】　　　　　　　　　　　　　　　　　　　　　　　　　　　(04-6-10)

[A] It is being forced out of the entertainment industry. [B] It should change its concept of operation. [C] It should revolutionize its technology. [D] It is a very good place to relax.	M: Do you think home video players will replace movie theatres and force them out of the entertainment business? W: We're certainly faced with the grave challenge from the DVD industry. That's why I think we have to revolutionize our concept of movie showing. As I see it, the movie theatre should not just be a place to watch a film, but a place to meet people. Q: What does the woman think of the movie theatre?

【解析】观点态度题。女士话中的 I think we have to revolutionize our concept of movie showing 表明她认为应该对电影的经营概念进行改革,紧接着女士又通过 the movie theatre should not just be…, but…表达了自己对电影院改革的建议,故答案为[C]。revolutionize 意为"革新"。

5. maybe…（或许…）

【例7】　　　　　　　　　　　　　　　　　　　　　　　　　　　(05-6-9)

[A] The man should phone the hotel for directions. [B] The man can ask the department store for help. [C] She doesn't have the hotel's phone number. [D] The hotel is just around the corner.	M: Excuse me, but could you tell me how to get to the Friendship Hotel? I thought it was on this corner, but I seem to have made a mistake. W: I am sorry, but I am a stranger here myself. Maybe you can try calling them. There is a phone over there outside the department store. Q: What does the woman mean?

【解析】观点态度题。男士问女士如何到达 the Friendship Hotel,女士通过 Maybe you can…一句建议男士打电话给酒店,故答案为[A]。

6.反问句表达建议

【例8】 (03-6-8) 🎧

[A] Take courses with a lighter workload. [B] Drop one course and do it next semester. [C] Do the assignments towards the end of the semester. [D] Quit the history course and choose another one instead.	M: Mr. Smith, our history professor, announced that we'll be doing two papers and three exams this semester. I wonder how I'm going to pull through when two other courses have similar requirements. W: Well, can't you drop one course and pick it up next semester? Q: What does the woman suggest the man do?

【解析】行为活动题。女士通过反问句 can't you drop one course and pick it up…? 建议男士 drop one course(放弃一门课程),下个学期再 pick it up(选修它),故答案为[B]。

7.祈使句表达建议

【例9】 (06-6-3) 🎧

[A] He'd like a piece of pie. [B] He'd like some coffee. [C] He'd rather stay in the warm room. [D] He's just had dinner with his friends.	W: It's freezing cold. Let me make some coffee to warm us up. Do you want a piece of pie as well? M: Coffee sounds great. But I'm going to have dinner with some friends in a while so I'd better skip the pie. Q: What does the man mean?

【解析】观点态度题。女士通过祈使句 Let me… 提议 make some coffee,男士话中的 coffee sounds great 表明他觉得女士的提议不错,即 He'd like some coffee,故答案为[B]。

8.虚拟语气表达建议

【例10】 (00-1-1) 🎧

[A] To cancel his trip. [B] To go to bed early. [C] To catch a later flight. [D] To ask for a wake-up call.	M: I hope I won't oversleep. I've simply got to catch the first flight to New York. W: If I were you, I'd request the wake-up call from the hotel reception. Q: What does the woman advise the man to do?

【解析】行为活动题。女士通过虚拟句式 If I were you, I'd… 建议男士向酒店服务台要求 a wake-up call(叫早电话),故答案为[D]。

三、请求句式

1.Will/Would/Can/Could you…?

【例11】 (06-6-1) 🎧

[A] She met with Thomas just a few days ago. [B] She can help with the orientation program. [C] She is not sure she can pass on the message. [D] She will certainly try to contact Thomas.	M: Mary, could you please tell Thomas to contact me? I was hoping he will be able to help me out with the freshmen orientation program next week. W: I would certainly tell him if I saw him, but I haven't seen him around for quite a few days. Q: What does the woman mean?

【解析】观点态度题。男士请求女士给 Thomas 捎个口信(could you please tell…),女士回答中的"先肯定后转折"(I would certainly…, but…)的语气表示自己"没有把握一定能把信传到",故答案为[C]。orientation 意为"入学导向"。

2.I wonder if…

【例12】 (97-6-2) 🎧

[A] Try to help him find rooms in another hotel. [B] Check to see if there are any vacancies in her hotel. [C] Let him move to a room with two single beds.	M: I wonder whether it would be possible to change this double rooms. W: Sorry, sir. All the single rooms are occupied.

| [D] Show him the way to Imperial Hotel. | But if you like, I can check with Imperial Hotel to see if they have any.
Q：What's the woman going to do for the man? |

【解析】行为活动题。男士请求女士 change this double rooms，女士回答说 single rooms 都已经 occupied（被占用了），她可以帮男士看看能不能 find rooms in another hotel，故答案为[A]。

3. Would you mind…?

【例13】 (00-1-3)

| [A] She will save the stamps for the man's sister.
[B] She will no longer get letters from Canada.
[C] She can't give the stamps to the man's sister.
[D] She has given the stamps to the man's roommates. | M：I'm noticed that you get letters from Canada from time to time. Would you mind saving the stamps for me? My sister collects them.
W：My roommates already asked for them.
Q：What does the woman imply? |

【解析】事实状况题。男士通过句式 Would you mind…? 请求女士为他 saving the stamps，女士回答说邮票已经被她的室友要走了，言外之意是说她不能 give the stamps to the man's sister，故答案为[C]。

四、虚拟句式

1. if 虚拟条件句

虚拟语气下的条件句称为虚拟条件句，又称非真实条件句，其所谈论的情况与事实相反或不太可能发生。听音时要注意区分虚拟条件句与真实条件句。

主句和从句的谓语动词基本形式如下：

形式　　时间	if 从句	主句
与现在事实相反	were /did	would /should /might /could ＋do
与过去事实相反	had been /had done	would /should /might /could＋have done
与将来事实相反	should / were to ＋do	would /should /might /could ＋do

【例14】 (06-6-4)

| [A] He has managed to sell a number of cars.
[B] He is contented with his current position.
[C] He might get fired.
[D] He has lost his job. | W：How come Jim lost his job?
M：I didn't say he had lost it. All I said was if he didn't get out and start selling a few cars instead of idling around all day, he might find himself looking for a new job.
Q：What does the man say about Jim? |

【解析】事实状况题。男士通过虚拟语气（might find… a new job）表达了对 Jim 可能失去工作的担忧，故答案为[C]。might find himself looking for a new job≈might get fired（可能被解雇）。这是一个与现在或将来事实相反的虚拟语气，而不是与过去相反，因此选项[D]是错误的。所以，考生除了掌握"反着选"的技巧，还要留心时态问题。

2. 含蓄虚拟条件句

含蓄虚拟条件句是指假设的情况并不以条件从句的形式表示出来，而是通过 without, but for, but that, otherwise, or 等词或短语引出。

【例15】 (03-6-4)

| [A] She suggested a way out of the difficulty for the man.
[B] She took the man to where he wanted to go.
[C] She came a long way to meet the man.
[D] She promised to help the man. | M：Thank you for your helpful assistance. Otherwise, I'd surely have missed it. The place is so out of the way.
W：It was a pleasure meeting you. Goodbye!
Q：Why did the man thank the woman? |

【解析】事实状况题。男士话中的 I'd surely have missed it 明显使用了虚拟语气(谓语为 would have done 的形式),otherwise 在这里相当于虚拟条件句 if there weren't your helpful assistance,实际情况是由于女士的帮助,男士没有错过 it,由后一句可知 it 指代 the place,最后得出答案为[B]。

3. wish 后的虚拟语气

动词 wish 后的宾语从句一般用虚拟语气,表示不太可能或没有把握实现的愿望。其谓语动词有三种形式:表示对现在的愿望,用 were 或动词的过去式;表示对过去的愿望,用 had+动词的过去分词或 would/could have+动词的过去分词;表示对将来的愿望,用 would/should/could/might+动词原形。

【例16】 (05-12-7)

[A] He shows great enthusiasm for his studies.	M: Your son certainly shows a lot of enthusiasm on the tennis court.
[B] He is a very versatile person.	W: I only wish he'd show as much for his studies.
[C] He has no talent for tennis.	Q: What does the woman imply about her son?
[D] He does not study hard enough.	

【解析】事实状况题。女士通过虚拟句式 I only wish he'd show… 表达了"希望儿子对学习可以表现出与对网球同样的热情"的愿望,这表明事实上女士的儿子 does not study hard enough(对学习的热情不高),故答案为[D]。

4. if only 后的虚拟语气

谓语动词用一般过去时表示现在没有实现的愿望,用过去完成时表示过去没有实现的愿望。

【例17】 (四级 06-6-1)

[A] They enjoyed the party better than the other guests.	M: I think the hostess really went out of her way to make the party a success.
[B] They knew none of the other guests at the party.	W: Yes. The food and drinks were great. But if only we had known a few the other guests.
[C] They didn't think much of the food and drinks.	Q: What did the two speakers say about the party?
[D] They went a long way to attend party.	

【解析】事实状况题。女士通过虚拟句式 if only we had known…(要是我们认识几个其他的客人就好了)来表达心愿未遂的遗憾,其中隐含的事实是"他们不认识其他客人",故答案为[B]。

5. should/shouldn't /needn't/…+have done 表虚拟含义

表示"本应该做某事而实际上没有做/本不应该做某事但实际却做了/本不必做某事但实际却做了/…"等含义。

【例18】 (04-1-10)

[A] The woman had been planning for the conference.	M: I thought you were going to call me last night about the plans for the conference on language teaching.
[B] The woman called the man but the line was busy.	
[C] The woman didn't come back until midnight.	W: Sorry, I should have, but Tom and Jane stopped by and stayed until midnight.
[D] The woman had guests all evening.	Q: What do we learn from the conversation?

【解析】事实状况题。女士通过虚拟句式 I should have 表明"她本应该打电话给男士,但实际却没有打",紧接着通过 but 转折说明理由:had guests all evening,故答案为[D]。

6. couldn't have done+形容词或副词比较级表虚拟含义

否定形式表肯定含义,即"再不能更…","非常…"。

【例19】 (00-1-8)

[A] She's never watched a better game.	M: I'm sorry I missed the football game, but I had a terrible cold.
[B] Football is her favorite pastime.	
[C] The game has been canceled.	W: You didn't miss anything. We couldn't have played worse.
[D] Their team played very badly.	Q: What does the woman imply?

【解析】事实状况题。女士通过虚拟句式 We couldn't have played worse 表示他们踢得"不可能再糟糕了",言外之意是他们 played very badly,故答案为[D]。

7. I thought…

表示"原以为…",但事实并非如此。

【例20】　　　　　　　　　　　　　　　　　　　　　　　　　　　　　　(06-6-6)

[A] He was fined for running a red light.	W: Oh! Boy! I don't understand how you got a ticket to-day. I always thought you were slow even driving on the less crowded fast lane.
[B] He was caught speeding on a fast lane.	
[C] He had to run quickly to get the ticket.	M: I'm usually careful. But this time I thought I could get through the intersection before the light turned.
[D] He made a wrong turn at the intersection.	Q: What do we learn about the man?

【解析】事实状况题。男士通过虚拟句式 I thought I could… 表示他本来以为自己可以在 the light turned 之前穿过那个路口的(但实际上没有),再根据女士话中的 got a ticket(得到罚单)可知男士是因为 running a red light(闯红灯)而被 fined(罚款),故答案为[A]。

五、反问句式

反问是用疑问的形式表达确定的意思,反问句无需回答,答案已包含在话语中。反问常用来加强语气,表达强烈的情感。

1. 表示异议

如:Should they be doing that with all the other expenses they have to pay?

　　Why book a hotel? My brother has 2 spare rooms in his apartment.

【例21】　　　　　　　　　　　　　　　　　　　　　　　　　　　　　　(04-1-9)

[A] Jimmy is going to set out tonight.	M: Jimmy is going on a journey tomorrow. Shall we have a farewell dinner tonight?
[B] Jimmy has not decided on his journey.	
[C] There is no need to have a farewell dinner.	W: Do you think it's necessary? You know he'll be away just for a few days.
[D] They may have a dinner when Jimmy's back.	Q: What does the woman mean?

【解析】观点态度题。女士通过反问句 Do you think it's necessary? 表示不同意男士的提议,即没有必要 have a farewell dinner,故答案为[C]。

2. 表示责怪或批评

如:Shouldn't he be working on his term paper?

　　But why do you always wait until the last minute?

【例22】　　　　　　　　　　　　　　　　　　　　　　　　　　　　　　(03-1-2)

[A] The woman is strict with her employees.	W: Morning, Jack! Late again? What's the excuse this time?
[B] The man always has excuses for being late.	M: I'm awfully sorry. I must have turned the alarm off and gone back to sleep again.
[C] The woman is a kind-hearted boss.	
[D] The man's alarm clock didn't work that morning.	Q: What do we learn from the conversation?

【解析】事实状况题。女士话中的反问句 Late again? 中明显带有批评的语气,再根据后面的 What's the excuse this time? 不难推断出男士 always has excuses for being late,故答案为[B]。

3. 表示建议

如:Is that really a good reason to drop the class, Tony?

　　Should they be doing that with all the other expenses they have to pay?

【例23】　　　　　　　　　　　　　　　　　　　　　　　　　　　　　　(00-9-2)

[A] They have different opinions as to what to do next.	W: Next, shouldn't we get a telephone installed in the hall?
[B] They have to pay for the house by installments.	
[C] They will fix a telephone in the bathroom.	M: Fixing the shower pipe is far more important.
[D] The man's attitude is more sensible than the woman's.	Q: What do we learn from the conversation?

【解析】事实状况题。女士通过反问句式 shouldn't we…? 建议在大厅里 get a telephone installed(安装一部电话),男士则说 Fixing the shower pipe(安装沐浴喷水管)更重要,可见二者意见不一,故答案为[A]。

4. 表示惊讶

如：Wouldn't you get bored with the same routine year after year teaching the same things to children?

Are you kidding?

【例24】 (05-12-5)

[A] She admires Jean's straightforwardness. [B] She thinks Dr. Brown deserves the praise. [C] She will talk to Jean about what happened. [D] She believes Jean was rude to Dr. Brown.	M: Jean really lost her temper in Dr. Brown's class this morning. W: Oh, did she? But I think her frankness is really something to be appreciated. Q: What does the woman mean?

【解析】观点态度题。女士通过反问句 did she? 对 Jean 在 Dr. Brown 的课堂上 lost her temper(发脾气)感到惊讶,接着在 but 转折后又对 Jean 的 frankness(直率)表示 appreciate(欣赏),故答案为[A]。straightforwardness 相当于 frankness,admire 相当于 appreciate。

5. 表示委婉拒绝

如：Don't you think that cinema is a little out of the way?

Do you think I could ever win anything if I took part in it?

【例25】 (03-9-7)

[A] Everyone enjoyed himself at John's parties. [B] The woman didn't enjoy John's parties at all. [C] It will be the first time for the man to attend John's party. [D] The woman is glad to be invited to John's house-warming party.	M: Shall we go to John's house-warming party this weekend? Everyone is invited. W: Well, you know what John's parties are like. Do you think I will go again? Q: What can be inferred from the conversation?

【解析】观点态度题。女士用反问句 do you think I will go again? 表明自己不喜欢 John 举办的派对,故答案为[B]。

六、否定句式

1. 含有否定标志的表达

说话人的话语中含有明显的否定标志是考生最熟悉的一种否定表达,也比较容易理解,关键是掌握一些比较常见的否定词或含有否定词的短语。

常见的否定词和短语有：

no, not, none, nobody, nothing, never, neither, nor, hardly, rarely, little, few, without, opposite, not … at all(根本不),not … until(直到…才), no sooner … than(刚一…就), nothing but(仅仅), no more/no longer(不再)等。

【例26】 (05-12-1)

[A] The dean should have consulted her on the appointment. [B] Dr. Holden should have taken over the position earlier. [C] She doesn't think Dr. Holden has made a wise choice. [D] Dr. Holden is the best person for the chairmanship.	M: The dean just announced that Dr. Holden's going to take over as chairman of the history department. W: I knew it all along! He's the obvious choice. All the other candidates are no match for him! Q: What does the woman mean?

【解析】观点态度题。女士话中的否定结构 All the other…no match for him 表明她认为没有一个候选人能够比得上他(Dr. Holden),即 Dr. Holden is the best person for the chairmanship,故答案为[D]。

2. 不含有否定标志的表达

有时说话人的话语中没有明显的否定标志,但在含义上却是否定的,即暗含否定。

常见暗含否定意义的词和短语有：

deny，fail，refuse，ignore，dislike，overlook，miss，doubt，lack，against，beyond，unless，instead of(代替)，far from，short of(短缺)，other than(除了)，rather than(而不是)，too … to(太…而不能…)，anything but(一点也不，根本不)，the last thing ＋定语从句(最不愿意或最不可能做的事)等。

【例27】　　　　　　　　　　　　　　　　　　　　　　　　　　　　　　　　　(02-1-3) 🎧

[A] He believes dancing is enjoyable.	W: Lots of people enjoy dancing, do you?
[B] He definitely does not like dancing.	M: Believe it or not, that is the last thing I'd ever
[C] He admires those who dance.	want to do.
[D] He won't dance until he has done his work.	Q: What does the man mean?

【解析】观点态度题。男士话中的 that is the last thing… 表达否定含义，意思是"那是他最不愿意做的事"，即他 does not like dancing，故答案为[B]。

3. 否定转移

在含有表示"相信"或"臆测"等含义动词的主从复合句中，否定词在形式上是否定主句的谓语，而在意义上其实是否定从句的谓语。

常见的这类动词有：believe，think，imagine，feel，expect，suppose 等。

【例28】　　　　　　　　　　　　　　　　　　　　　　　　　　　　　　　　　(01-1-10) 🎧

[A] Tom has arranged a surprise party for Lucy.	W: I don't think we should have told Tom about the
[B] Tom will keep the surprise party a secret.	surprising party for Lucy.
[C] Tom and Lucy have no secrets from each other.	M: It's all right. He promised not to tell, and he do-
[D] Tom didn't make any promise to Lucy.	es not make promises likely.
	Q: What does the man mean?

【解析】观点态度题。由男士话中的 He promised not to tell 可知 Tom 答应过不说出去的，即 Tom 会 keep the surprise party a secret，故答案为[B]。女士话中的 I don't think we should have told… 包含否定转移结构，意思是"我觉得我们不该告诉 Tom…"，其中 should not have told 表示"本不该告诉但实际却告诉了"的含义。

4. 双重否定

同一个句子里出现两个否定词，即否定之否定，这种结构叫做双重否定结构。

如：**Unless** you have visited the southern United States, you probably **never** heard of Kudzu.

Without them the animals will **not** remain healthy and productive.

【例29】　　　　　　　　　　　　　　　　　　　　　　　　　　　　　　　　　(05-6-4) 🎧

[A] The son.	W: I don't know how you can eat so much yet never put on any weight, son.
[B] The father.	Your father's got the same luck. I can't take a bite without calculating how
[C] The mother.	many calories I am taking.
[D] Aunt Louise.	M: But remember Aunt Louise, Mom? She ate a lot and never gained a pound.
	Q: Who is worried about gaining weight?

【解析】事实细节题。女士话中的 I can't…without… 包含双重否定结构(not…without…)，表达出女士(the moth-er)在控制饮食上谨小慎微，由此可知她十分 worried about gaining weight(担心体重增加)，故答案为[C]。

七、比较句式

形容词、副词的比较级和最高级，以及 as…as，compared with 等引出的比较结构经常是六级听力理解题的设题重点之一，出现比较结构的句子往往提供重要的信息或就是答案的出处。

1. 同级比较

as…as 表示"和…一样"；not so/as…as… 表示"不像…一样"。

【例30】　　　　　　　　　　　　　　　　　　　　　　　　　　　　　　　　　(02-1-2) 🎧

[A] Its results were just as expected.	M: How many students passed the final physics exam in your
[B] It wasn't very well designed.	class?
[C] It fully reflected the students' ability.	W: Forty, but still as many as 20 percent of the class failed,
[D] Its results fell short of her expectations.	quite disappointing, isn't it?
	Q: What does the woman think of the exam?

【解析】观点态度题。女士话中的反意疑问句 quite disappointing, isn't it? 表明她认为考试的结果是 disappointing(令人失望的),即这个考试结果 fell short of her expectations,故答案为[D]。同级比较结构 as many as 20 percent 表示"多达 20％"的含义。

2. 形容词、副词的比较级

单纯表示两者之间的比较,常与 than 连用,前面经常会有 much, even, still, further 等副词修饰,用来加强语气。

【例31】 (06-6-7)

[A] He has learned a lot from his own mistakes.	W: Your dog certainly seems to know you are his master. Did you have to punish him very often when you trained him?
[B] He is quite experienced in taming wild dogs.	
[C] He finds reward more effective than punishment.	M: I found it's much better to praise him when he obeys and not to be so fussy when he makes mistakes.
[D] He thinks it important to master basic training skills.	Q: What does the man say about training dogs?

【解析】观点态度题。男士话中的比较结构 it's much better to praise him… and not to be so fussy… 表明他认为 reward more effective than punishment(奖励比惩罚更有效),故答案为[C]。

3. 形容词、副词的最高级

单纯表示三者或三者以上之最,常是 most＋形容词或副词的原级。

【例32】 (04-6-1)

[A] Dick's trousers don't match his jacket.	W: Oh, Dick. You're wearing a black jacket but yellow trousers. It's the strangest combination I've ever seen.
[B] Dick looks funny in that yellow jacket.	
[C] The color of Dick's jacket is too dark.	M: I know. I got up late and dressed in a hurry. I didn't realize my mistake until I entered the office.
[D] Dick has bad taste in clothes.	Q: What does the woman think of the way Dick dressed?

【解析】观点态度题。女士话中的最高级结构 the strangest combination I've ever seen(我所见过的最奇怪的搭配)表明她认为男士(Dick)的裤子 don't match(不配)他的夹克,故答案为[A]。

4. more…than(与其…不如…)

【例33】 (05-12-9)

[A] Its rapid growth is beneficial to the world.	M: Professor Stevenson, as an economist, how do you look upon the surging Chinese economy? Does it constitute a threat to the rest of the world?
[B] It can be seen as a model by the rest of the world.	
[C] Its success can't be explained by elementary economics.	W: I believe China's economic success should be seen more as an opportunity than a threat. Those who looked upon it as a threat overlooked the benefits of China's growth to the world's economy. They also lack understanding of elementary economics.
[D] It will continue to surge forward.	Q: What does Professor Stevenson think of China's economy?

【解析】观点态度题。女士话中的 more as an opportunity than a threat 意为"与其说是威胁不如说是机遇",由此可知她认为中国的经济增长 beneficial to the world(有利于世界经济),故答案为[A]。

5. more and more…(越来越…)与 the more…, the more…(越…,就越…)

【例34】 (04-1-2)

[A] The air pollution is caused by the development of industry.	W: I can't bear the air pollution in this city any more. It's getting worse and worse.
[B] The city was poor because there wasn't much industry then.	
[C] The woman's exaggerating the seriousness of the pollution.	M: You said it! We've never had so many factories before.
[D] He might move to another city very soon.	Q: What does the man mean?

【解析】观点态度题。女士话中的 worse and worse 表明她认为(城市空气污染)越来越严重了。男士话中的 so many factories before 表明他认为污染是由工厂即 the development of industry(工业发展)造成的,故答案为[A]。You said it!(你说得太对了!)是表示赞同对方看法的常用句式。

八、强调句式

1. 强调句型

强调句型的基本结构是"It＋系动词 be＋被强调成分＋关系代词 who/that＋句子的其他成分"。

如：Mary bought a mobile phone last month.

It was **Mary who** bought a mobile phone last month.（强调主语）

It was **a mobile phone that** Mary bought last month.（强调宾语）

It was **last month that** Mary bought a mobile phone.（强调时间状语）

需要注意的是,有三类句子成分不可以用这个强调句型进行强调,即表语、谓语动词和 though, although, whereas 等引导的让步状语从句或比较状语从句。

2. 谓语动词的强调

强调谓语动词时,通常在该谓语动词前面加助动词 do 或 does(过去时用 did)来加强语气,一般译为"务必,一定,确实"等。

如：If it **does rain**, the whole thing will have to be cancelled.

He **did come** here last night.

【例35】　　　　　　　　　　　　　　　　　　　　　　　(02-6-5)

[A] A prediction of the future of mankind.	M: I must point out that trials of new medicine are expensive and you can never guarantee success.
[B] A new drug that may benefit mankind.	W: But there is a very good chance in this case. I do hope you'll go ahead in view of the potential benefit to mankind.
[C] An opportunity for a good job.	
[D] An unsuccessful experiment.	Q: What are the two speakers talking about?

【解析】谈论话题题。由女士话中的强调句 I do hope… the potential benefit to mankind 可确定二者正在谈论一种可以 benefit mankind 的 new drug,故答案为[B]。

九、推测句式

1. must do, must have done(一定…)

前者表示对现在或将来事实的肯定推测,后者表示对过去事实的肯定推测。

如：The light is on in his room →He **must be** home now. 现在他一定在家。

【例36】　　　　　　　　　　　　　　　　　　　　　　　(02-6-7)

[A] Neither of their watches keeps good time.	W: It's awfully dark for 4 o'clock. Do you think it's going to rain?
[B] The woman's watch stopped 3 hours ago.	M: You'd better do something about that watch of yours. It must have stopped hours ago. Mine says 7.
[C] The man's watch goes too fast.	
[D] It's too dark for the woman to read her watch.	Q: What conclusion can we draw from this conversation?

【解析】事实状况题。男士话中的 It must have stooped hours ago 表示对过去事实的一种肯定推测,由此可知女士的表很可能几小时前就停了,故答案为[B]。

2. may/might do, may/might have done(可能,可以…)

前者表示对现在或将来事实的不肯定推测,后者表示对过去事实的不肯定推测。

如：I suppose he **might have missed** the train. 我猜他可能没赶上火车。

【例37】　　　　　　　　　　　　　　　　　　　　　　　(98-6-1)

[A] He thinks that there won't be enough seats for everybody.	W: Friday's speaker is supposed to be wonderful. Are you going to attend the seminar on that day?
[B] He thinks that the speaker won't show up.	
[C] He thinks the seminar won't be open to the public.	M: Yes. But I haven't been able to get the ticket

[D] He thinks that there might not be any more tickets available.

yet. Since the lecture is open to the public, I imagine that the tickets may have already been sold out.

Q:Why is the man afraid he won't be able to attend the seminar?

【解析】观点态度题。男士话中的 the tickets may have already been sold out 表示对过去事实的一种可能性推测，由此可知他认为票可能已经卖光了，故答案为[D]。

3. can't do,can't have done(不可能…)

前者表示对现在或将来事实的否定推测,后者表示对过去事实的否定推测。

如：There was no light in his room last night→He **can't have been** home last night. 昨晚他一定不在家。

Exercise 即讲即练   🎧 边听边记

1. [A] Take a picture for his mother.　　　　[B] Hang the picture for his mother.
   [C] Buy a frame for his mother.　　　　　[D] Buy a bunch of flowers for his mother.

2. [A] She didn't have a look at her mailbox.　　[B] She is too hurried to check her mailbox.
   [C] The man's note was not in her mailbox.　　[D] She has found the man's note in her mailbox.

3. [A] Go to the volleyball match.　　　　　[B] Try to postpone the match.
   [C] Go to work.　　　　　　　　　　　　[D] Write her chemistry report.

4. [A] The hat is of the right size.
   [B] The color of the hat is just right for the woman.
   [C] The hat is not fit for the woman.
   [D] The woman should bring an umbrella with her.

5. [A] She has hoped for a better conclusion.　　[B] Her committee hasn't been very busy lately.
   [C] This committee is better than the other one.　[D] She is pleased with the results.

6. [A] The man may have to work harder for more money.
   [B] The man will be richer than her.
   [C] The man had worked for too long hours.
   [D] The man took a wrong job.

7. [A] Nick should go home now.
   [B] Nick should leave home right now.
   [C] Nick shouldn't stay in this country for another year.
   [D] Nick should stay in this country for another year.

8. [A] Stay at home.　　　　　　　　　　　[B] Spend more time with his family.
   [C] Devote his time to a trip around the world.　[D] Keep on doing his work at home.

【答案与解析】

1.

[A] Take a picture for his mother.	M: Could you help me to decide what I should buy for my mother's birthday?
[B] Hang the picture for his mother.	
[C] Buy a frame for his mother.	W: I remember that you have taken a picture of her last week. Why not buy her a frame so that she can fix the picture in it?
[D] Buy a bunch of flowers for his mother.	
	Q: What does the woman suggest the man do?

【解析】行为活动题。女士通过典型的建议句式 Why not buy her a frame…? 建议男士买一个 frame(相框)作为生日礼物送给他的母亲。

2.

[A] She didn't have a look at her mailbox.	M: Oh, dear, you needn't have waited for so long a time. Haven't you seen my note?
[B] She is too hurried to check her mailbox.	W: If I had checked the mailbox, I would have found your note.
[C] The man's note was not in her mailbox.	Q: What does the woman mean?
[D] She has found the man's note in her mailbox.	

【解析】事实状况题。女士话中的虚拟语气 If I had checked the mailbox, I would have found your note 表明她没有看到男士的便条是因为她没有 checked the mailbox(查看邮箱)。have a look at≈checked。

3.

[A] Go to the volleyball match.	M: Some of my friends are getting together to go to the volleyball match on Sunday afternoon. Do you want to come?
[B] Try to postpone the match.	W: Oh, I'd love to, but I have to work on my chemistry report.
[C] Go to work.	Q: What will the woman probably do on Sunday?
[D] Write her chemistry report.	

【解析】行为活动题。男士邀请女士去看 volleyball match(排球比赛)，女士通过"先肯定后转折"的句式(I'd love to, but…)表明周日她不能去看排球比赛，but 后陈述了理由(have to work on my chemistry report)。

4.

[A] The hat is of the right size.	W: What do you think of my new hat?
[B] The color of the hat is just right for the woman.	M: I'm sure you'll never need to bring an umbrella with you wearing it. And besides, do you think the color is right for your age?
[C] The hat is not fit for the woman.	Q: What does the man mean?
[D] The woman should bring an umbrella with her.	

【解析】观点态度题。男士话中的 you'll never need to bring an umbrella…表明他认为女士的帽子太大；而反问句 do you think the color is right for your age? 表明帽子的颜色不适合女士。

5.

[A] She has hoped for a better conclusion.	M: I have not seen you like this for weeks.
[B] Her committee hasn't been very busy lately.	W: The committee finally reached the decision and I couldn't have hoped for a better outcome.
[C] This committee is better than the other one.	Q: What do we know about the woman from the conversation?
[D] She is pleased with the results.	

【解析】事实状况题。女士话中的 I couldn't have hoped for a better outcome 表明她对委员会作出的决定非常pleased(满意)。"否定词(not, no, never 等)+比较级"表示肯定意义。

6.

[A] The man may have to work harder for more money.	M: One good thing about it is the higher salary. It's perfect for me.
[B] The man will be richer than her.	W: I'm sure you'll be better off. But I guess you might have to work for longer hours.
[C] The man had worked for too long hours.	Q: What does the woman mean?
[D] The man took a wrong job.	

【解析】观点态度题。女士话中的 you might have to work for longer hours 是对现在或将来事实的不肯定推测。男士要得到 the higher salary 可能需要 work for longer hours(工作更长时间)，也就是说男士不得不要 work harder。

7.

[A] Nick should go home now.	W: Nick would be much wiser to stay in this country for another year and finish his Master's degree than to rush home and take over his uncle's business now. Don't you think so?
[B] Nick should leave home right now.	M: Yes, I can't agree with you more.
[C] Nick shouldn't stay in this country for another year.	Q: What is the man's opinion of Nick?
[D] Nick should stay in this country for another year.	

第一篇 听力理解 ⑥
【解析】观点态度题。由女士话中的比较结构 Nick would be much wiser … than … 可知,她认为 Nick 应该 stay in this country another year,而男士话中的 I can't agree with you more 表明他非常赞同女士的话。

8.

[A] Stay at home.	M: I hear your father will retire next week. I guess he must be willing to spend more time with the family.
[B] Spend more time with his family.	W: I hope so, but he once said that he would like to travel around the world rather than just stay at home doing nothing.
[C] Devote his time to a trip around the world.	Q: What does the woman's father prefer to do after retirement?
[D] Keep on doing his work at home.	

【解析】行为活动题。女士话中的 he would like to … rather than … 表明她的父亲退休后不会只待在家里,他会 travel around the world,即她的父亲更喜欢 devote his time to a trip around the world。

短对话巅峰练习

Exercise 1

边听边记

11. [A] It is not difficult to reach.
    [B] It will not be achieved in a walk.
    [C] It can be gotten with strong determination.
    [D] It does not exist at all.

12. [A] The problem caused by the increase of retirement age.
    [B] The problem caused by the increase of the need of the young and the elderly.
    [C] The problem caused by the aging population.
    [D] The problem caused by the decrease of welfare.

13. [A] The man has bought some jewels for his mother.
    [B] The man was thinking about to buy what for his mother.
    [C] The man has bought a shirt for his sister.
    [D] The man has bought presents for each of his family.

14. [A] He received an e-mail message from his old African friend.
    [B] He was reading some economic news on the web.
    [C] He read the latest news on current affairs.
    [D] He sent an e-mail message to his old friend.

15. [A] 1:00.   [B] 1:30.
    [C] 2:00.   [D] 3:00.

16. [A] China.   [B] Japan.
    [C] America.   [D] Canada.

17. [A] It was boring.   [B] It was very nice.
    [C] It saved time.   [D] It was less comfortable.

18. [A] His car was out of gas.   [B] He couldn't fix his car.
    [C] He had a car accident.   [D] He had to go back for clean clothes.

Exercise 2

11. [A] The woman would understand if she did Betty's job.
    [B] The woman should do the writing for Betty.
    [C] The woman should work as hard as Betty.
    [D] The woman isn't an efficient writer.

12. [A] George was late for school on the first day.
    [B] George was the first friend of the woman.
    [C] The man and George were in the same class.
    [D] George likes to make a face in class.

13. [A] See a movie.   [B] Read the paper.
    [C] Have dinner in town.   [D] Go bungee jumping.

14. [A] Because the man sometimes turns his radio too loud.
    [B] Because the man sometimes makes too much noise.
    [C] Because the man sometimes gets angry.

[D] Because the man sometimes make a mess of the room.

15. [A] $120.   [B] $108.

    [C] $90.   [D] $40.

16. [A] The disadvantage of a restaurant.   [B] The disadvantage of a hotel.

    [C] The disadvantage of a hospital.   [D] The disadvantage of an airport.

17. [A] To visit more places in the city.   [B] To take a lot of pictures of the beautiful city.

    [C] To take some pictures of his friends.   [D] To spare some time to meet his friends.

18. [A] At a newsstand.   [B] At a car dealer's.

    [C] At a publishing house.   [D] At a newspaper office.

答案与解析

Exercise 1

11.

[A] It is not difficult to reach. [B] It will not be achieved in a walk. [C] It can be gotten with strong determination. [D] It does not exist at all.	W: Parents usually give their children more freedom in my country. Sometimes they give them too much freedom. M: It's almost impossible to get the right balance. If you are too strict, kids might ignore you. If you are too lenient, they might go wild. Q: How does the man think of the balance between strictness and lenience?

【解析】观点态度题。由男士话中的两个并列的条件复合句可知，the right balance 指的是 strictness 和 lenience 之间的 right balance(平衡)，又由男士话中的 It's almost impossible to… 可知，男士认为 strictness 和 lenience 之间的平衡 will not be achieved in a walk(是很难达到的)。in a walk 意为"轻而易举地"。

12.

[A] The problem caused by the increase of retirement age. [B] The problem caused by the increase of the need of the young and the elderly. [C] The problem caused by the aging population. [D] The problem caused by the decrease of welfare.	W: Nowadays the problem of an aging population is so great that it will soon affect most of the world. M: You can say that again. I heard that the government might need to increase the retirement age, because otherwise there will not be enough workers to support the young and the elderly. Q: What are the speakers talking about?

【解析】谈论话题题。女士话中的 the problem of an aging population… 提示本对话与 aging population 引起的问题有关，而男士话中的 …there will not be enough workers… 也是 aging population 引起的问题，由此可知二人谈论的是 the problem caused by the aging population。

13.

[A] The man has bought some jewels for his mother. [B] The man was thinking about to buy what for his mother. [C] The man has bought a shirt for his sister. [D] The man has bought presents for each of his family.	W: I suppose you've bought some gifts for your family. M: Well, I have bought a shirt for my father, and two books for my sister. But I haven't decided what to buy for my mother. Probably some jewels. Q: What can be inferred from the conversation?

【解析】事实状况题。由男士话中的 I haven't decided to buy what for my mother 可知，男士还没有想好给他妈妈买什么礼物。

14.

[A] He received an e-mail message from his old African friend.	W: I was busy reading the latest news on the web just now.
[B] He was reading some economic news on the web.	M: Me too! I also sent an e-mail message to my old friend in the United States.
[C] He read the novels on the web.	
[D] He sent an e-mail message to his old friend.	Q: What did the man do just now?

【解析】行为活动题。男士话中的 I also sent an e-mail message…表明，他刚才除了看网上的最新新闻，还 sent an e-mail message to his old friend(给美国的老朋友发了一封电子邮件)。

15.

[A] 1：00.	W: What time do you usually have lunch?
[B] 1：30.	M: Around 1:00, but this week I have been occupied with my work, so I've been eating my lunch at 1:30, or 2:00, even as late as 3:00.
[C] 2：00.	
[D] 3：00.	Q: What time does the man usually have his lunch?

【解析】数字信息题。女士问男士通常什么时间吃午饭，男士话中的 Around 1：00 表明他通常会在 1：00 左右吃午饭，后面出现的三个时间 1：30、2：00 与 3：00 是男士这个星期的吃午饭时间。

16.

[A] China.	M: Miranda is Canadian, but now she's lived in the Far East for most of her life.
[B] Japan.	
[C] America.	W: Yes. She speaks Japanese and Chinese as well as English.
[D] Canada.	Q: Which country is Miranda from?

【解析】地点场景题。由男士话中的 Miranda is Canadian 可知，Miranda 来自加拿大(Canada)。

17.

[A] It was boring.	M: Did you mind coming back by bus instead of by air?
[B] It was very nice.	W: No. I didn't mind at all. It took a lot longer, but it was very comfortable and it was much cheaper.
[C] It saved time.	
[D] It was less comfortable.	Q: How did the woman feel about coming back by bus?

【解析】观点态度题。男士问女士是否介意 coming back by bus，女士话中的 I didn't mind at all 表明她并不介意坐车回去，因为坐车非常 comfortable，并且还 much cheaper，由此可知女士认为还是坐车回去好。

18.

[A] His car was out of gas.	W: Do you know that you are an hour late?
[B] He couldn't fix his car.	M: I'm terribly sorry, Cathy. My car broke down on the way and my clothes got so dirty while I was trying to fix it. I had to go home to change.
[C] He had a car accident.	
[D] He had to go back for clean clothes.	Q: Why was the man late?

【解析】事实状况题。男士话中的 My car broke down…my clothes got so dirty…表明，他迟到一个小时是因为车在路上坏掉了，而他在修车时又把衣服弄脏了，所以不得不 go back for clean clothes(回家换干净的衣服)。

Exercise 2

11.

[A] The woman would understand if she did Betty's job.	W: Betty is always complaining about her job.
[B] The woman should do the writing for Betty.	M: Maybe if you tried writing letters every day, you'd see what it's like.
[C] The woman should work as hard as Betty.	
[D] The woman isn't an efficient writer.	Q: What does the man mean?

【解析】观点态度题。男士话中的条件句 if you tried writing letters … you'd see… 表明他认为女士如果像 Betty 一样每天都 writing letters,她就会 understand(明白)Betty 为什么经常抱怨自己的工作。

12.

[A] George was late for school on the first day.	M: Do you know George? He's in your class.
[B] George was the first friend of the woman.	W: Certainly. In fact, he was the first person I got to know in my class. I still remember the look on his face when he showed up late on the first day of school.
[C] The man and George were in the same class.	
[D] George likes to make a face in class.	Q: What can we learn from the conversation?

【解析】事实状况题。女士话中的…when he showed up late on the first day of school 表明 George 上学第一天就迟到了。

13.

[A] See a movie.	W: It's a shame to spend Saturday evening at home. Let's go bungee jumping tomorrow.
[B] Read the paper.	M: That's exactly what I've been thinking about. Let me get the paper and see what's on tonight.
[C] Have dinner in town.	
[D] Go bungee jumping.	Q: What are the two speakers going to do tomorrow?

【解析】行为活动题。男士话中的 That's exactly what I've been thinking about 表明他也打算明天 go bungee jumping(去蹦极)。bungee jumping 意为"蹦极跳"。

14.

[A] Because the man sometimes turns his radio too loud.	W: Do you like living in the dormitory?
[B] Because the man sometimes makes too much noise.	M: It's not too bad. Sometimes Tom turns his radio too loud and makes too much noise. Then I get angry. Sometimes, I leave my books and clothes lying around and he gets angry. But usually we get along.
[C] Because the man sometimes gets angry.	
[D] Because the man sometimes make a mess of the room.	Q: Why does Tom sometimes get angry?

【解析】事实状况题。男士话中的 I leave my books and clothes lying around and he gets angry 表明,Tom 生气是因为男士总是 leave books and clothes lying around(把书和衣服乱放),即 make a mess of the room(把房间弄得乱乱的)。

15.

[A] $120.	M: I'll take these shoes. Please tell me how much I owe you.
[B] $108.	W: They are $40 a pair, so 3 pairs make a total of $120. But today we're offering a 10% discount.
[C] $90.	
[D] $40.	Q: How much does the man have to pay?

【解析】数字信息题。女士话中的 we're offering a 10% discount 表明鞋子现在打九折,即鞋子的现价是原价的90%,男士要买 3 pairs 鞋,因此他应付款 $120×90%= $108。

16.

[A] The disadvantage of a restaurant.	M: They may be proud of their new facility, but, frankly speaking, I'm disappointed. The nurses are friendly, but everything seems to be running behind schedule.
[B] The disadvantage of a hotel.	
[C] The disadvantage of a hospital.	W: Not to mention the fact that it's noisy because no one observes visiting hours.
[D] The disadvantage of an airport.	Q: What are the people discussing?

【解析】谈论话题题。由男士话中的 nurses 及女士话中的 visiting hours(探病时间)可知,二人所谈论的话题与 hospital 有关,再由男士话中的 everything seems to be running behind schedule 及女士话中的 it's noisy…可以判断,二人正在谈论 the disadvantage of a hospital(医院的不足之处)。

17.

[A] To visit more places in the city. [B] To take a lot of pictures of the beautiful city. [C] To take some pictures of his friends. [D] To spare some time to meet his friends.	W: Oh, this is a beautiful city. I'm really glad I brought my camera. M: Yes, there are lots of things to take pictures of here. But I hope you will not plan to spend all your time taking pictures. I have some friends who would like to meet you. Q.: What does the man want the woman to do?

【解析】行为活动题。男士话中的转折句 But I hope…表明,他希望女士不要把所有时间都用来拍照,因为他的朋友想见见她,由此可知男士希望女士 spare some time to meet his friends(空出一些时间去见见他的朋友)。

18.

[A] At a newsstand. [B] At a car dealer's. [C] At a publishing house. [D] At a newspaper office.	M: Excuse me. I'd like to place an advertisement for a used car in the Sunday edition of your paper. W: OK, but you have to run your advertisement all week. We can't carry it for just Sunday. Q: Where is the conversation most probably taking place?

【解析】地点场景题。由男士话中的 I'd like to place an advertisement…in the Sunday edition of your paper 可知,他很可能是在一家 newspaper office(报社)。

长对话巅峰讲座

第三章

长对话不同于短对话的一问一答,原材料是以多组对话的形式给出,由一男一女两人的对话组成,考查方式类似于短文理解。长对话涉及的内容更深入,人物态度、语气、情感变化更复杂,一般不能简单根据某个关键词句来判断整篇对话的含义。

Lecture 1　第一讲　7大敏感设题题眼

长对话一共两组,平均每组长对话的长度在260词左右,每组长对话后设3—4题,共7题。题目的顺序一般是按照对话的顺序分布。常见的设题题眼包括:

一、对话的开头处

对话的开头部分一般都会引出谈话的主题,比较容易设主旨题,主要考查对谈话主题或所涉及场景的把握。

【例1】　　　　　　　　　　　　　　　　　　　　　　　　　　　　(710分样卷-19)

[A] To interview a few job applicants.

[B] To fill a vacancy in the company.

[C] To advertise for a junior sales manager.

[D] To apply for a job in a major newspaper.

M: Morning, Brenda.

W: Good morning, Mr. Browning.

M: Er, did you, did you put that ad in yesterday?

W: Yes, yesterday afternoon.

M: The ad for a junior sales manager, I mean.

...

19. What did Mr. Browning ask Brenda to do?

【解析】本题的设题题眼在开头处。根据男士话中的 did you put that ad in yesterday? 和 The ad for a junior sales manager 可知,Mr. Browning 是要求 Brenda 在报纸上刊登一则招聘广告。本题只需抓住 ad 一词(advertisement 的缩写)即可确定答案为[C]。

二、对话的结尾处

对话结尾往往会涉及对话双方的态度、建议或决定等总结性的内容,而且经常能够进一步体现对话的主题及场景,也是出题者设题时考虑的重点。

【例2】　　　　　　　　　　　　　　　　　　　　　　　　　　　　(710分样卷-21)

[A] Not clearly specified.

[B] Not likely to be met.

[C] Reasonable enough.

[D] Apparently sexist.

...

W: Well sir, I wish you the best of luck and hope ...

M: Well, yes?

W: ...I think you're asking an awful lot.

21. What does Brenda think of the qualifications Mr. Browning insists on?

【解析】本题的设题题眼在结尾处。根据女士在结尾处所说的 you're asking an awful lot 可推知,她认为 Mr. Browning 对应聘人员的要求太多,不太可能会得到满足,故答案为[B]。

三、对话中问答处

长对话由于仍然是以对话形式出现,双方会就对话主题进行讨论,故其中经常会包含一些对话双方的一问一答,这些地方往往是长对话设题的重点。

【例3】　　　　　　　　　　　　　　　　　　　　　　　　　　　　　　(710 分样卷-20)

| [A] A hard working ambitious young man.
[B] A young man good at managing his time.
[C] A college graduate with practical working experience.
[D] A young man with his own idea of what is important. | W: What kind of person have you got in mind for this job?
M: Oh, well, somebody fairly young, you know, twenty something, like 21, or 25. A man, I think.
...
W: Erm, what sort of a young man have you...?
M: ..., someone with plenty of ambition, plenty of drive. ... .
20. What kind of person will meet the job requirements? |

【解析】本题的设题题眼在问答处。根据男士话中的 fairly young, plenty of ambition, plenty of drive 等关键词可知,招聘者想要寻找的是一个工作努力、有抱负的年轻小伙子,故答案为[A]。

四、对话中逻辑关系处

长对话中经常会涉及到表示转折、因果等逻辑关系的短语或句式,这些地方也很受出题人的青睐。

【例4】　　　　　　　　　　　　　　　　　　　　　　　　　　　　　　(新 06-12-23)

| [A] Bad weather.
[B] Human error.
[C] Breakdown of the engines.
[D] Failure of the communications system. | W: What were the circumstances? Were there bad weather, a fire, or engine failure?
M: Apparently, there were some low clouds in the area, but mostly it was just miscommunication between the pilots and the air traffic controllers.
23. What was the cause of the tragedy? |

【解析】本题的设题题眼在问答处和转折处。女士问男士事故发生时情形如何,男士通过 but 转折引出悲剧发生的主要原因:miscommunication between the pilots and the air traffic controllers(飞行员和控制人员之间的沟通失误),这明显属于 human error(人为失误),故答案为[B]。

五、对话中列举或举例处

对话中出现列举或举例的地方往往也是出题的重点,因此,当听到 such as, for example, for instance, the first, the second 等一类词语时,应加以留意。

【例5】　　　　　　　　　　　　　　　　　　　　　　　　　　　　　　(07-6-21)

| [A] Took balanced meals with champagne.
[B] Ate vegetables and fruit only.
[C] Refrained from fish or meat.
[D] Avoided eating rich food. | W: Well, I didn't drink any alcohol or coffee and I didn't eat any meat or rich food. I drink a lot of water and fruit juice and I eat the meals on the well-being menu. They are lighter. They have fish, vegetables and noodles, for example. And I did some of the exercises in the program.
21. What did the woman do to follow the well-being menu? |

【解析】本题的设题题眼在列举或举列处。女士说她不吃 meat or rich food(肉或高脂肪的食物),但是会喝 a lot of water and fruit juice(很多水和果汁),并且会吃 the meals on the well-being menu(健康菜单上的食物),包括 fish, vegetables 和 noodles,故答案为[D]。本题答案虽并未直接来自于所举例子,但该例子内容可作为排除干扰项的主要依据。

六、对话中比较或对比处

含有形容词或副词的比较级和最高级、as...as 以及 compared with, in contrast, while, whereas 等引出比较或对比结构的句子往往提供重要信息或就是答案的出处,这些地方也是长对话设题的重点之一。

【例6】　　　　　　　　　　　　　　　　　　　　　　　　　　　　　　(新 06-12-20)

[A] Trim the apple trees in her yard. [B] Pick up the apples that fell in her yard. [C] Take the garbage to the curb for her. [D] Remove the branches from her yard.	W: Well, I don't think you're quite finished yet—some of the larger branches fell over into my yard, and I think you should come and get them. 20. What did the woman ask the man to do?

【解析】本题的设题题眼在比较处。女士说 some of the larger branches 掉进了她的院子里,要求男士 come and get them,由此可知她是想让男士把掉到她院子里的苹果枝清走,故答案为[D]。

七、对话中数字信息处

对话中出现年代、价格、时间等相关信息的地方,也经常被作为长对话设题的一个重点,但要注意,除了单纯地考查数字或时间以外,还经常会考查与数字或时间相关的其他细节信息。

【例7】　　　　　　　　　　　　　　　　　　　　　　　　　　　　　　(新 06-12-24)

[A] Two thousand feet. [B] Twelve thousand feet. [C] Twenty thousand feet. [D] Twenty-two thousand feet.	M: The pilots were told to descend to "two-two thousand" feet. … Unfortunately, the terrain of the mountains in Norweija extends up 20,000 feet. 24. How high are the mountains in Norweija?

【解析】本题的设题题眼在数字信息处。抓住男士话中的 the terrain of the mountains in Norweija extends up 20,000 feet,即可确定 Norweija 地区的山有两万英尺高,故答案为[C]。terrain 意为"地带,地势"。

Exercise 　　　　即讲即练 　　　　🎧 边听边记

Conversation One

1. [A] People's parents.
   [B] The environment people live in.
   [C] The TV and movies.
   [D] People's partners.
2. [A] The bad influence of TV and movies.
   [B] Parents' improper way of educating their child.
   [C] The degenerative ethos.
   [D] The loss of morality of teenagers themselves.
3. [A] He is quiet and introverted. 　　　　　　[B] He is hardworking and outgoing.
   [C] He is strong-willed. 　　　　　　　　　　[D] He is considerate and lenient.

Conversation Two

4. [A] Seven days. 　　　[B] Eight days. 　　　[C] Ten days. 　　　[D] Two weeks.
5. [A] It will be held after April 28th.
   [B] It is held for the third time.
   [C] It will be held at Sydney Opera House.
   [D] It aims at films only for high school students.
6. [A] The organizer of the Hawaii International Film Festival.
   [B] The lighting engineer of Hawaii International Film Festival.
   [C] The producer of the Hawaii International Film Festival.
   [D] The presider of the Hawaii International Film Festival.
7. [A] To select excellent producers and directors from the whole world.
   [B] To demonstrate outstanding films before people.
   [C] To promote the understanding and cultural exchange among different areas.
   [D] To encourage the development of fashion.

【答案与解析】

Conversation One

【听力原文】	【答案解析】

【听力原文】

W: How do you think people get their personalities?

M: I think [1] it's mainly from the environment a person lives in.

W: Don't you think people get their personalities from their parents?

M: No, but parents control a lot of the environment that kids grow up in, so they certainly influence their kid's personalities a lot.

W: So why do you think many kids have personalities that are so different to their parents.

M: Maybe when they become teenagers, they want to be completely different to their parents.

W: You might be right. I guess most parents want their kids to be like them, but kids today grow up in a different environment. You know, they know much more about the world from the internet, newspapers, and TV.

M: Do you think that teenagers get a lot of their bad behavior from TV and movies?

W: Maybe some of it. [2] I think a lot of people blame TV and movies when the real problem is that the parents aren't bringing their child up correctly.

M: Parents have a difficult job. They have to bring up their children and usually have to work too.

W: Yes, that's fine. Your son is doing well at school, isn't he?

M: Yes, he is. [3①] He's very hardworking when he's at school. Then he comes home from school and does homework before dinner. After dinner, he goes out with his friends.

W: So, he's not a bookworm? It's good that [3②] he has an outgoing personality. Some kids are very quiet and introverted. You wonder they'll survive in the real world without their parents to support them.

【答案解析】

1. Where do people's personalities come from, according to the man?

【解析】选[B]。设题点在对话的开头处。对话一开始女士就问男士人的 personalities(性格)是如何形成的,男士回答说他认为性格的形成主要源于 the environment a person lives in(人们所生存的环境)。

2. What does the woman think that teenagers' bad behavior should be ascribed to?

【解析】选[B]。设题点在对话中比较处。在说到青少年的坏习惯时,女士说很多人都把青少年的坏习惯归咎于 TV 和 movies,但其真正的原因应是 parents aren't bringing their child up correctly(家长们没有正确地教导孩子)选项[B]是原文的同义转述。

when 在此句中作用同 although,含有对比意义。

3. What personality does the man's son possess?

【解析】选[B]。设题点在对话的结尾处。对话结尾处,由男士话中的 He's very hardworking 和女士的话中的 he has an outgoing personality(他有着开朗的性格)可知,男士的儿子既勤奋,又性格开朗。

Conversation Two

【听力原文】

W: Mr. Anderson, would you tell us when the festival will be held?

M: Well, this is the 5th Annual Hawaii International Spring Film Festival. [4] It will be running from April 19th—28th with [5] the third Annual Student Film Festival running April 26th—28th at the Grand Theatres. The Student Film Festival is one part of the Hawaii International Spring Film Festival. It aims at films for kids and teenagers.

W: Can you name some famous stars who will be present at the festival?

M: Sure, we never disappoint the fans. In the Opening Night Ceremony, we have Peter Bogdanovich and South Korean director Jeong Jaeeun who has attracted critical praise worldwide.

W: Oh, that sounds interesting.

M: Yes, other guests include last year's Audience Award Winner at

【答案解析】

4. How long will the 5th Annual Hawaii International Spring Film Festival last?

【解析】选[C]。设题点在对话中数字信息处。对话开头处,男士提到 It will be running from April 19th—28th, it 指代 the 5th Annual Hawaii International Spring Film Festival,由此可知 the 5th Annual Hawaii International Spring Film Festival 将举办 10 天时间。

5. What can we learn about the Student Film Festival?

【解析】选[B]。设题点在对话中逻辑关系处。男士话中的 the third Annual Student Film Festiva…表明学生电影节是第三

the Sundance Film Festival, and the director, Stacy Peralta, of the humorous "Z-Boys". Many of the original Z-Boys and producer Agi Orsi will be in attendance at the screening.

W: That's great. Then let's go on. Mr. Anderson, [6] as a successful organizer of the Hawaii International Film Festival, would you comment on it?

M: Sure, from 1981, [7] when we held it for the first time, the Hawaii International Film Festival has been dedicated to advancing the understanding and cultural exchange among the people of Asia, the Pacific and North America through the medium of film. Besides showcasing a full slate of feature films, documentaries and short subjects, the festival will conduct seminars, workshops, special award presentations and receptions with top Asian, Pacific and North American filmmakers participating. We hope for a brighter future for the film industry and for a peaceful world for all human beings.

W: Thanks, you will impress the public.

M: Thank you, too. See you then.

次举办。

6. Who is Mr. Anderson?

【解析】选[A]。设题点在对话中逻辑关系处。女士在介绍 Mr. Anderson 提到 as a successful organizer of the Hawaii International Film Festival，由此可知 Mr. Anderson 是 the organizer of the Hawaii International Film Festival。

7. What was the purpose of the first Hawaii International Film Festival?

【解析】选[C]。设题点在对话的结尾处。对话结尾处，男士明确提到 when we held it for the first time, Hawaii International Film Festival has been dedicated to advancing the understanding and cultural exchange among…，由此可知第一届 Hawaii International Film Festival 的目的是为了促进不同地区人们之间的了解和文化交流。

Lecture 2 第二讲 10 大听前预测方法

　　听力题中很多选项都有比较明显的特点，或者使用某种专门的表达形式，如均为动词原形或均为人物角色等；或者含有一些标志性的词语，通过这些选项特点我们便可以推测问题可能考查的核心内容。另外，我们经常可以通过对选项的分析，排除一些比较明显的干扰项，缩小听音范围，从而在听音时更有针对性。

方法一：各题主题揭示对话主题

　　将各题所考查的主题内容结合在一起，往往可得出整篇对话的主题。如果某一题目是考查对话主题，其中的一个选项明显能够概括其他各题选项的内容，那么该选项很可能为答案。

【例1】　　　　　　　　　　　　　　　　　　　　　　　　(710 分样卷-Conversation One)

【预览选项】	【预测信息】
19. [A] To interview a few job applicants. 　[B] To fill a vacancy in the company. 　[C] To advertise for a junior sales manager. 　[D] To apply for a job in a major newspaper. 20. [A] A hard-working ambitious young man. 　[B] A young man good at managing his time. 　[C] A college graduate with practical working experience. 　[D] A young man with his own idea of what is important. 21. [A] Not clearly specified.　　[B] Not likely to be met. 　[C] Reasonable enough.　　[D] Apparently sexist.	预览三道题各选项，由 19 题中的 interview, applicants, vacancy, advertise for a manager, apply for a job 等词语可以推测对话与刊登招聘广告或应聘工作有关。而 20 题中的 hard-working, ambitious, good at managing his time, with practical working experience, with his own idea 等词语则表明对话中还涉及到对所招聘人员的要求。

方法二：选项均以动词的某种形式开头

　　含有这类选项的问题为考查"行为活动"类型。根据动词的不同形式，问题考查的重点也可能不同。
　　选项均以动词原形开头，问题大多是关于建议某人做某事，有时也表示为了某种目的要做某事。
　　选项均为动名词，问题大多是关于正在进行的动作或计划打算。
　　选项均为不定式，问题很可能是关于做某事的目的，或是计划、承诺或要求做某事。

【例2】

【预览选项】	【预测信息】
[A] File a lawsuit against the man. [B] Ask the man for compensation. [C] Have the man's apple tree cut down. [D] Throw garbage into the man's yard.	选项均为动词原形,故本题应该是考查某人的行为活动。四个选项均是针对男士的行为,故本题很可能是关于某人与男士发生争吵或冲突时所采取的应对措施。

【听音验证】

W: Get the branches off my property or I'll have to sue you.

M: Yeah? For what?! You're taking those law classes too seriously! I've gotta go, I have to pick up my son.

W: You'll be hearing from me.

M: Yeah, yeah. See you in court, Jane.

21. What did the woman threaten to do?

【例3】

【预览选项】	【预测信息】
[A] To interview a few job applicants. [B] To fill a vacancy in the company. [C] To advertise for a junior sales manager. [D] To apply for a job in a major newspaper.	选项均为不定式短语,故本题应该是考查某人将要采取的行动。[A]、[C] 是关于招聘工作(interview, advertise),[B]、[D] 则是关于申请工作(fill, apply for),故听音时应留意该行为是关于招聘还是应聘。

【听音验证】

M: Morning, Brenda.

W: Good morning, Mr. Browning.

M: Er, did you, did you put that ad in yesterday?

W: Yes, yesterday afternoon.

M: The ad for a junior sales manager, I mean.

19. What did Mr. Browning ask Brenda to do?

方法三:选项中含有表示意愿或建议的词

　　如果选项中含有 should, had better, would like 等一类的词语,问题很可能是考查"观点或建议"。

【例4】

【预览选项】	【预测信息】
[A] Accurate communication is of utmost importance. [B] Pilots should be able to speak several foreign languages. [C] Air controllers should keep a close watch on the weather. [D] Cooperation between pilots and air controllers is essential.	由选项中的 should 可推知,本题应该是考查某人的观点或建议。选项内容表明问题应该与确保安全飞行的因素有关。

【听音验证】

W: So the pilots did descend to the wrong altitude then, thinking they were following the air controllers' instructions.

M: Sadly enough, yes they did. It was a really bad mistake. Many people died as a result of the simple misunderstanding.

W: Wow, that's a powerful lesson on how important it can be to accurately communicate to each other.

25. What lesson could be drawn from the accident?

方法四:选项中含有表示评论或感受的词

　　如果选项中含有 think, like, dislike, enjoy, agree, disagree, mind 等一类的词语,听力材料或问题很可能与某人或某事物的评价或感受有关。

　　四个选项中如均含有表示评论或感受的词,则表示问题是关于对人或事物的评价或感受;如其中只有个别选项含有表示评论或感受的词,则表示听力材料中很可能涉及到对人或事物的评价或感受,问题则不一定会涉及。

【例5】　　　　　　　　　　　　　　　　　　　　　　　　　　　　　　(710 分样卷-21)

【预览选项】	【预测信息】
[A] Not clearly specified.　　[B] Not likely to be met. [C] Reasonable enough.　　[D] Apparently sexist.	四个选项中均含有表示评论的词语(specified, reasonable 等),故问题很可能是关于某人对某事物的看法。

【听音验证】

W: Yes, erm, what sort of education are you actually looking for?

M: Well, you know, a couple of A levels. Must have English, of course.

W: Yes, I think you're asking quite a lot. I mean you're not really prepared to pay all…

M: No, I'm not prepared to give him a big salary to start with. Nevertheless, I want someone with plenty of ambition, plenty of drive. You know, not looking at the clock all the time.

W: Well sir, I wish you the best of luck and hope you have some very successful interviews.

M: Well, yes?

W: Because personally I think you're asking an awful lot.

21. What does Brenda think of the qualifications Mr. Browning insists on?

方法五：选项中含有比较结构

　　如果选项中含有形容词或副词的比较级或最高级,或是其他表示比较的词语,则听力材料或问题很可能涉及人或事物之间的异同点或优劣的比较。

　　四个选项中如均含有比较级或表示比较的词,则表示问题是关于人或事物之间的比较;如其中只有个别选项中含有比较级,则表示听力材料中很可能涉及到人或事物之间的比较,问题则不一定会涉及。

【例6】　　　　　　　　　　　　　　　　　　　　　　　　　　　　　　(四级 710 分样卷-22)

【预览选项】	【预测信息】
[A] Their competitors have long been advertising on TV. [B] TV commercials are less expensive. [C] Advertising in newspapers alone is not sufficient. [D] TV commercials attract more investments.	由选项中的 advertising on TV, advertising in newspapers 以及比较级 less expensive, attact more 可知本题很可能涉及到电视广告和报纸广告之间优劣的比较。故听音时应留意比较级或其他陈述二者优劣特点的词句。

【听音验证】

W: Marketing has some interesting ideas for television commercials.

M: TV? Isn't that a bit too expensive for us? What's wrong with advertising in the papers, as usual?

W: Quite frankly, it's just not enough anymore. We need to be more aggressive in order to keep ahead of our competitors.

M: Will we be able to afford all this?

W: I'll look into it, but I think higher costs will be justified. These investments will result in higher profits for our company.

22. Why does the woman suggest advertising on TV?

方法六：选项均为名词短语

　　如选项均为概括性较强的名词或是名词短语,且各项内容差异较大,问题则可能是关于对话所谈论的主题或对话中出现的某一事件或问题的主题。

【例7】　　　　　　　　　　　　　　　　　　　　　　　　　　　　　　(710 分样卷-22)

【预览选项】	【预测信息】
[A] The latest developments of an armed rebellion in Karnak. [B] The fall of Karnak's capital city into the hands of the rebel forces. [C] The epidemic that has just broken out in the country of Karnak.	选项均为名词短语,且概括性均较强,故本题很可能考查对话的主旨。由 armed rebellion, the rebel forces, peace talks between the rebels and the government 等词以及多次出现的 Kar-

[D] The peace talks between the rebels and the government in Karnak.	nak 可推知本对话很可能与 Karnak 国反政府武装叛乱有关。

【听音验证】

W: We now interrupt our regular scheduled news program to bring you live up-to-date coverage on the civil unrest in the newly formed country of Karnak, where our man Stan Fielding is stationed. Stan…

M: This is Stan Fielding reporting live from the suburbs of the capital city. Just 20 minutes ago, rebel forces launched the biggest offensive against the ruling government in the 18-month conflict here in this country.

W: Now Stan, is this a sign that the peace process has been totally abandoned?

M: Well, so far, peace negotiations have failed, and any resolution to end the civil war appears bleak at this moment. As you can see… Whoa.

22. What is the news coverage mainly about?

方法七：与对话主题或其余选项内容不同的选项往往不是答案

如果某一选项明显与对话主题不相关,那么该选项往往不是答案。

如果某一选项明显与其他三个选项内容不同,即与该题主题明显不相关,那么该选项往往不是答案。

【例8】　　　　　　　　　　　　　　　　　　　　　　　　　　　　　　　　　　(新 06-12-19)

【预览选项】	【预测信息】
19. [A] He picked up some apples in his yard. 　　[B] He cut some branches off the apple tree. 　　[C] He quarreled with his neighbor over the fence. 　　[D] He cleaned up all the garbage in the woman's yard. 20. [A] Trim the apple trees in her yard. 　　[B] Pick up the apples that fell in her yard. 　　[C] Take the garbage to the curb for her. 　　[D] Remove the branches from her yard. 21. [A] File a lawsuit against the man. 　　[B] Ask the man for compensation. 　　[C] Have the man's apple tree cut down. 　　[D] Throw garbage into the man's yard. 22. [A] He was ready to make a concession. 　　[B] He was not prepared to go to court. 　　[C] He was not intimidated. 　　[D] He was a bit concerned.	由各选项中的 apple, tree, yard, branches, trim(修剪)等词可推知对话主题应该与苹果树枝条和院子有关,再根据选项中出现的 quarreled, lawsuit(诉讼), compensation(赔偿), concession(让步), court(法庭)等词可推知对话还可能涉及到对话双方的争吵。 　　19 题各选项中谓语动词的过去式形式表明本题应该是考查男士过去的活动。[A]、[B]、[C] 均与苹果树和院子有关,只有[C] 是关于 fence(栅栏),与其他三项内容差别较大,且与其他各题选项内容均不相关,故[C] 为答案的可能性较小。
【听音验证】	【答案解析】
W: Hello, Patrick, is that you? M: Yeah, Jane, what can I do for you? W: I was calling about the apple tree that you were trimming yesterday. M: That was hard work!	19. What did the man do yesterday? 【解析】选[B]。由女士话中的 the apple tree that you were trimming yesterday 可知男士昨天给苹果树剪枝了。trim 意为"修剪,修整"。

方法八：包含其他选项内容的选项往往不是答案

有的选项明显包含其他选项的含义,如果该选项成立,那么其包含的选项也将成立,故包含其他选项内容的选项往往不是答案。

【例9】　　　　　　　　　　　　　　　　　　　　　　　　　　　　　　　　　　　　(托福)

【预览选项】	【预测信息】
[A] She was impressed by it. [B] It was a waste of money.	由选项中的 impressed, a waste of money, amazed, like 等可推知本题是针对某事物的看法设题的。选项

[C] She was <u>amazed</u> it had opened so soon. [D] She didn't <u>like</u> it as much as the other wings.	[A]说"it"给她留下了深刻印象,选项[C]说她对"it"这么快就开张(或开放)感到吃惊,其含义包含[A]的含义在内,故[C]很可能不是答案。
【听音验证】 M: Hey, how was your trip? W: Wonderful. I spent most of my time at the art museum. <u>I especially liked the new wing. I was amazed</u> to hear the guide explain all the problems they had building it.	【答案解析】 34. What did the woman think of the new wing of the museum? 【解析】选[A]。细节题。由对话中出现的 amazed, unusual, impressive 等可知女士对美术馆新侧厅的修建费用以及修建过程中的种种问题大感吃惊,并且对里面的设计印象非常深刻,故答案为[A]。

方法九：明显不符常理的选项往往不是答案

有的选项明显不符合该对话情景下的常识或常理,那么该选项往往不是答案。

【例10】 (新06-12-25)

【预览选项】	【预测信息】
[A] Accurate communication is of utmost importance. [B] Pilots <u>should</u> be able to speak several foreign languages. [C] Air controllers <u>should</u> keep a close watch on the weather. [D] Cooperation between pilots and air controllers is essential.	由选项中的 should 可推知,本题应该是考查某人的观点或建议。选项内容表明问题应该与确保安全飞行的因素有关。[B]是说飞行员应该会说几门外语,这不大合乎常理,因为飞国内行线的飞行员并不一定要会好几门外语,故[B]为答案的可能性较小。
【听音验证】 M: Sadly enough, yes they did. It was a really bad mistake. Many people died as a result of the simple misunderstanding. W: Wow, that's a powerful lesson on <u>how important it can be to accurately communicate to each other</u>.	【答案解析】 25. What lesson could be drawn from the accident? 【解析】选[A]。对话的最后女士总结了这次事故的教训:how important it can be to accurately communicate to each other,答案是对此的同义转述。utmost 意为"极大的"。

方法十：意思相近的选项往往都不是答案

如果有两个选项意思明显相近,那么这两个选项往往都不是答案。

【例11】 (新06-12-22)

【预览选项】	【预测信息】
[A] He was ready to make a <u>concession</u>. [B] He was not prepared to <u>go to court</u>. [C] He was not <u>intimidated</u>. [D] He was a bit <u>concerned</u>.	由选项中的 concession(让步),go to court,intimidate(威胁),concerned(担心)等词可推测问题应该与男士对某事的反应有关。[A]是说他准备让步,[B]是说他不准备上法庭,二者都表示男士要"妥协退让"的含义,故很可能都不是答案。
【听音验证】 M: Get the branches off my property or I'll have to sue you. M: Yeah? For what?! ... W: You'll be hearing from me. M: <u>Yeah, yeah. See you in court</u>, Jane.	【答案解析】 22. What was the man's reaction to the woman's threat? 【解析】选[C]。女士说让男士等着收法庭的传票(hear from me),男士的回答"Yeah, yeah. See you in court(法庭见)"表明他根本 not intimidated(不怕威胁)。

Exercise　　　　　　即讲即练　　　　　　　🎧 边听边记

Conversation One

1. [A] The necessity of fashion.
   [C] The development of fashion.
   [B] The waste of resources.
   [D] The popularity of fashion.
2. [A] Positive.
   [C] Neutral.
   [B] Critical.
   [D] Indifferent.
3. [A] Whether they are expensive.
   [C] Whether they are comfortable.
   [B] Whether they are suitable for him.
   [D] Whether they are of his favorite.

Conversation Two

4. [A] The celebration day of American Labor Day is later than that of Chinese Labor Day.
   [B] There are more workers celebrating Labor Day in America than in China.
   [C] American Labor Day is much more formal than Chinese Labor Day.
   [D] The influence of American Labor Day is not as great as that of Chinese Labor Day.
5. [A] Having a parade.
   [C] Raising workers' salary.
   [B] Giving workers a day off.
   [D] Presenting gifts to workers.
6. [A] It is welcomed by all the American workers.
   [B] It is accompanied by satisfaction and suffering.
   [C] It is beneficial for workers.
   [D] It disappeared immediately since the establishment of Labor Day.
7. [A] Survival and poor harvest.
   [C] Death and harvest.
   [B] Death and Hope.
   [D] Evil and Hope.

【答案与解析】

Conversation One

【预览选项】	【预测信息】
1. [A] The necessity of fashion. [B] The waste of resources. [C] The development of fashion. [D] The popularity of fashion. 2. [A] Positive.　　[B] Critical. [C] Neutral.　　[D] Indifferent. 3. [A] Whether they are expensive. [B] Whether they are suitable for him. [C] Whether they are comfortable. [D] Whether they are of his favorite.	预览三道题各选项,由第 1 题选项中多次出现的 fashion(时尚)可知,对话应该与时尚有关,再结合第 2 题选项中表达人物态度的词语可推测,对话主题很可能是关于对话双方对时尚的不同看法。 1. 选项均为名词短语,且均具有较强的概括性,故本题很可能是考查对话所谈论的主题。听音时重点判断对话主要谈论的是时尚的哪一方面(necessity, development 还是 popularity)。 2. 选项均为形容词且都是表达感受的词,由此可推断本题很可能与某人对某一事物的态度有关。 3. 由选项中的 expensive、suitable、comfortable 及 of his favorite 可知,本题很可能与某物的性质或男士对某物的态度有关。而再根据选项中均含有 whether 可知,本题很可能与男士在选择某一事物时考虑的因素有关。
【听音验证】	【答案解析】
M: In my opinion, [1①] fashion is a complete waste of time, money and resources. W: [1②] [2] I disagree entirely. The world would be a very boring place without change. M: Fashion doesn't only involve change. It's a very dishonest form of marketing based on artificial images	1. What are the speakers talking about? 【解析】选[A]。主旨题。对话一开始,男士就提出自己的观点 fashion is a complete waste of time, money and resources,女士接着就说她 disagree entirely,在接下来的对话中男士和女士分别对自己的观点进行了论证,但论证的目的都是为了证明 fashion 是否有必

which never translate into reality.

W: But everyone understands that the images are there to capture attention. People think they're fun. Haven't you ever looked through a fashion magazine?

M: Only at the dentist's.

W: What about the glossy magazines you get when you buy a Sunday newspaper? They're full of fashionable advertisements.

M: That's true, but don't you think they're a terrible waste of paper? How many people throw them straight into the dustbin?

W: A lot of people must read them and they don't add to the cost of the newspaper.

M: There is the point here. The advertiser may pay, but the costs are passed on to the consumer.

W: That isn't strictly true. If a company can sell in bulk, prices can be brought down. You can't expect to sell unless the consumer knows the product exists.

M: I wouldn't mind publicity if it told you something about the product, but by getting fashion models to market clothes and even cars, you are hiding the truth. [3] When I buy clothing, I want to know if it's comfortable and how long it's going to last.

W: That may be your reason, but some people buy clothes because they want to look nice. People have always liked dressing up.

M: That may be so. What worries me is today's throw-away society where some people waste the world's precious resources while other people go out.

W: Well, I don't see why you should blame the fashion industry for social injustice.

要存在。

2. What is the woman's attitude toward fashion in life?

【解析】选[A]。推断题。对话开头处，女士提到她 disagree entirely 男士对 fashion 的观点，由此可推断女士对 fashion 持有的态度是 positive(积极的)。

3. What does the man concern when he buys some clothes?

【解析】选[C]。细节题。对话结尾处，男士提到 When I buy clothing, I want to know if it's comfortable …，由此可知男士买衣服所考虑的主要因素就是衣服是否 comfortable 和 how long it's going to last(衣服能穿多久)，衣服是否 comfortable 是其中一个方面。

Conversation Two

【预览选项】

4. [A] The celebration day of American Labor Day is later than that of Chinese Labor Day.

[B] There are more workers celebrating Labor Day in America than in China.

[C] American Labor Day is much more formal than Chinese Labor Day.

[D] The influence of American Labor Day is not as great as that of Chinese Labor Day.

5. [A] Having a parade.

[B] Giving workers a day off.

[C] Raising workers' salary.

[D] Presenting gifts to workers.

6. [A] It is welcomed by all the American workers.

[B] It is accompanied by satisfaction and suffering.

[C] It is beneficial for workers.

[D] It disappeared immediately since the establishment of Labor Day.

7. [A] Survival and poor harvest.　　[B] Death and Hope.

[C] Death and harvest.　　[D] Evil and Hope.

【预测信息】

预览四道题各选项，由选项中的 American / Chinese Labor Day 以及多次出现的 workers 可推测，对话应该与美国劳动节和中国劳动节的不同习俗有关。

4. 选项中均含有比较级结构，且都是在 American Labor Day 和 Chinese Labor Day 之间进行比较，由此可推断本题很可能与 American Labor Day 和 Chinese Labor Day 之间的不同点有关。

5. 选项均为动名词且多次出现 workers，由此可推断本题很可能与某人在 labor Day 那天对 workers 所作出的行为活动有关。

6. 选项均以 it is 开头，由此可推断本题很可能与某物的性质或某物对工人的作用有关。选项[A]说某物受到所有美国工人的欢迎，很明显该选项太过绝对，可初步排除;选项[D]说某物自劳动节形成就立即就消失了，很明显该选项不太符合常理，故也可初步排除。

7. 选项均为名词短语，且均表示某种抽象意义，故很可能与某种主题或象征意义有关。

【听音验证】

W: As you have given us detailed information about Christmas and Easter in America just now, could you name some other

【答案解析】

4. What is the difference between American Labor Day and our Chinese Labor Day?

important holidays and special days?

M: Well, Labor Day, Halloween, New Year's Day, Valentine's Day, Mother's Day and Father's Day.

W: Oh, is American Labor Day the same as our Chinese Labor Day?

M: No, [4] it is celebrated on the first Monday in September. [5] People parade to honor workers. Labor Day began in the 19th century with the dream of a carpenter named Peter J. McGuire, who eventually grew up to become the president of a national union of carpenters. Since [6] he was fully aware of both the satisfaction and the suffering that accompany hard work, he wanted to establish a holiday "to honor the industrial spirit, the great vital force of the nation." At his suggestion, the first Labor Day parade was held in New York City in 1882. In 1894, Labor Day became a federal holiday in the United States.

W: What do people do on this special day?

M: Since the holiday also marks the end of the summer vacation period for many people, it is often the time for an outing to the beach, a picnic in the park, or a barbecue in the backyard.

W: That's great. Then, how about Halloween?

M: Well, Halloween is a short way of saying All Halloween's Eve, which means the night before the Roman Catholic holy day of All Saint's Day. It comes from two different sources: an ancient Celtic festival in honor of the lord of death and a Roman festival in honor of the goddess of gardens and orchards. [7] The Halloween colors, black and orange, suggest death and harvest.

W: That's why we often have pumpkin lanterns with candlelight.

【解析】选[A]。推断题。女士问 American Labor Day 是否和中国的 Labor Day 一样时,男士给出否定回答,并说美国庆祝 Labor Day 是在 the first Monday in September,而中国庆祝 Labor Day 是在 1st, May,由此可知 American Labor Day 和 Chinese Labor Day 的不同之处在于二者庆祝的时间不同,美国比中国的庆祝时间要晚。

5. How do Americans do to honor workers on Labor Day?

【解析】选[A]。细节题。男士向女士介绍美国的 Labor Day 时说到 People parade to honor workers,由此可知在劳动节这一天美国人会以 parade(游行)的形式表达对工人们的尊重。

6. What can we learn about "hard work" from the conversation?

【解析】选[B]。细节题。男士提到 Peter J. McGuire 提议设立劳动节,正是因为他清楚地明白 the satisfaction and the suffering that accompany hard work(伴随着辛苦劳作的满足感与辛酸),由此可知 hard work 是要伴随 satisfaction 和 suffering 的。

7. What do the two traditional Halloween colors symbolize?

【解析】选[C]。细节题。对话结尾处男士说 Halloween colors, black and orange, suggest death and harvest,由此可知 black 和 orange 分别代表 death 和 harvest。

Lecture 3　　第三讲　6大边听边记技能

长对话的篇幅较长,想要听过之后就能将主要的内容都清楚地记在脑子里,几乎是不可能的。考生只有听一遍的机会,只能边听、边记、边答。

边听边记是听力中一项非常重要的技能,但是作笔记并不是要把听到的每一个单词都记下来,笔记无非是帮助记忆的手段,只要能把重要的信息用可识别的符号记录下来,就算达到了目的。因此为了提高听与记的效率,应注意把握一定的技巧和原则。

技能一:抓住首尾句

主题句常常是在对话的开头,它对整个对话的内容起一个概括和提示的作用,实际上是说话人所谈论的中心话题。长对话中的第一题很可能是针对对话的开头提问,考查考生对整个对话的主题或所谈话题的把握。

结尾处往往涉及到某种建议、决定或下一步要做的事情,它对整个对话起到一个总结的作用。长对话的最后一题经常是针对对话的结尾设题,故留意结尾处的关键动词对解题至关重要。

【例1】　　　　　　　　　　　　　　　　　　　　　　　　　　(07-6-19)

【预览选项】	【边听边记】
[A] To go sightseeing.	M: Hi, Ann, welcome back. How's your trip to the states?
[B] To have meetings.	
[C] To promote a new champagne.	W: Very busy, I had a lot of meetings. ……

| [D] To join in a training program. | 19. Why did the woman go to New York? |

【答案解析】

选[B]。细节题。对话一开始,男士就问女士去美国的旅行怎么样,女士回答说很忙,她 had a lot of meetings(要参加很多会议),由此可知女士去纽约是去参加会议。

技能二：留意对话中的一问一答

　　长对话中,对话双方往往出现多个一问一答,而这一恰恰是长对话的一个出题重点,对话后面的问题往往就是对话原文中问题的照搬或是同义转述,因此其答案就是对话中紧接问题之后的答语,而且一般不会有同音或近音词的干扰,因此对于这类题目答案的基本原则就是"听到什么选什么"。

【例2】 (07-6-25)

【预览选项】	【边听边记】
[A] Data collection.	W: What's your line of business, Mr. Johnson?
[B] Training consultancy.	M: We are a training consultancy.
[C] Corporate management.	25. What is the man's line of business?
[D] Information processing.	

【答案解析】

选[B]。细节题。女士的提问即为本题的提问,答案就在男士接下来的回答中。女士问男士 What's your line of business(做哪一行),男士回答说他们是 a training consultancy(一家培训咨询公司),由此可知答案为[B]。

技能三：留意重复率较高的词或短语

　　对话的主要内容理所当然会得到说话人的强调,而一个非常重要、也是非常明显的强调方式就是重复,而且重复的词语往往能够揭示对话的主题。因此,对那些对话双方多次提到的词语或内容应进行重点记忆。

【例3】 (710 分样卷-22)

【预览选项】	【边听边记】
[A] The latest developments of an armed rebellion in Karnak.	W: …bring you live up-to-date coverage on the civil unrest in the newly formed country of Karnak, …
[B] The fall of Karnak's capital city into the hands of the rebel forces.	M: …, rebel forces launched the biggest offensive against the ruling government in the 18-month conflict here in this country.
[C] The epidemic that has just broken out in the country of Karnak.	…
[D] The peace talks between the rebels and the government in Karnak.	M: …, rebel forces are also using heavy artillery to pound the positions of government forces around the city center. Rebel forces are closing in, …
	…
	M: …this war-torn country…, but that is always a concern if this war lingers on.
	22. What is the news coverage mainly about?

【答案解析】

选[A]。主旨题。主旨题的答案往往在开头或结尾,而本题的答案就出自开头的第一句。选项中的 latest(最新的)对应该句中的 live up-to-date(最新直播),armed rebellion(武装叛乱)对应 unrest(动乱)。另外,对话的主题往往会得到多次重复,因此根据后面多次出现的 rebel forces, conflict, war 等与"叛乱"相关的词语,也可判断本题答案为[A]。

技能四：留意选项中的要点内容

　　正确选项往往与原文相似,或是原文的同义表达,而错误选项也往往是根据原文而设,因此应注意提取选项中的关键点,在听音时留意其是否在文中出现并对其相关信息加以记录。

【例4】　　　　　　　　　　　　　　　　　　　　　　　　　　　　　(710分样卷-25)

【预览选项】	【边听边记】
[A] Inadequate medical care. [B] Continuing social unrest. [C] Lack of food, water and shelter. [D] Rapid spreading of the epidemic.	W: …what other pressing concerns are there for the citizens of the city? M: Well, since the beginning of the conflict, starvation, and lack of clean water and adequate shelter have been the biggest daily obstacles facing the citizens of this war-torn country. 25. What is the pressing concern of the citizens of Karnak?

【答案解析】
选[C]。细节题。四个选项中只有[C]项内容在对话中出现，其他三项均未涉及到，故只要抓住对话中 starvation, and lack of clean water and adequate shelter 或其部分内容，即可判断答案为[C]。starvation 意为"饥饿"。

技能五：留意数字、人名、地名、时间、年代等相关信息

　　遇到数字、人名、地名、时间、年代时要对相关信息作简要记录，尤其是选项中出现相互类似的概念时，在听音时更应重点留意。

【例5】　　　　　　　　　　　　　　　　　　　　　　　　　　　　　(710分样卷-24)

【预览选项】	【边听边记】
[A] Late in the morning. [B] Early in the afternoon. [C] Sometime before dawn. [D] Shortly after sunrise.	M: …Rebel forces are closing in, and it's feared that they will be able to take the capital building before daybreak where, it is believed, many government officials are holding out. 24. At what time of day do you think this news report is being made?

【答案解析】
选[C]。细节题。根据原文中 …it's feared that they will … before daybreak 可知，当时报道的时间应该是在 before daybreak(黎明破晓前)。dawn 相当于 daybreak。

技能六：学会使用缩略语

　　作笔记一定要迅速，要想在有限的时间内尽可能比较全面地记录重点信息，使用一定的缩略语和熟悉的符号是十分必要的。

　　1. 利用数学符号。

　　如 equal 写成"="；"≠"表示"unequal"；"↑"表示 increase/up；"←"表示 result from/because/since/for/as；"→"表示 lead to/result in/has become/turn into；"↓"表示 decrease/drop/dip/fall；"≈"表示 about/almost；">"表示 more than；"<"表示 less than；"＋"表示 include/cover；"－"则表示 exclude 等。

　　2. 利用数字和其他固定符号。

　　能用阿拉伯数字或其他固定符号代表的词全部用符号代替，这样既能节约时间，又能避免拼写错误，如：twenty 记作 20；nineteen eighty four 记作 1984；dollar 记作 $；pound 记作 £；11 in the morning 记作 11 a. m.；11 in the evening 记作 11 p. m. 等。

　　3. 创造自己的速写符号。

　　在平时的训练中也可以使用和创造一些符合自己习惯的缩略语和符号，如 u 可代表 understand(ing)；m 可代表 minute；s 可代表 second；h 可代表 hour；imp. 可代表 important/importance；nec. 可代表 necessary 等。

Exercise　　　　　　　　　　　即讲即练　　　　　　　　　　　🎧 边听边记

Conversation One

1. [A] They should think carefully about the advice from older people.
　[B] They should not ask their friends of their age for advice.
　[C] They should not care too much about things except study.
　[D] They should learn to respect the older people.

2. [A] Because older people can't understand the problem the young face.

[B] Because older people don't want to understand the young.

[C] Because older people always think they are right at any time.

[D] Because the young want to be different from older people.

3. [A] Happy.   [B] Satisfied.

[C] Frightened.   [D] Depressed.

Conversation Two

4. [A] How to deal with hardships.

[B] Whether it is right for students to live off campus.

[C] How to create nice surroundings for study.

[D] The importance of a good study environment.

5. [A] They can have a quieter environment for study and rest.

[B] They have more freedom without supervision of the students.

[C] They have more chances to learn to be independent.

[D] They can save some money.

6. [A] Many universities have common problems.

[B] Most college students can't afford better conditions.

[C] The conditions can't be improved in short time.

[D] The conditions can be improved soon.

【答案与解析】

Conversation One

【听力原文】	【答案解析】
M: I was young once myself, you know. I know what it's like to be young. W: But you don't know what it's like to grow up in our world, Mr. Perkins. You had a brave new world to fight for, didn't you? But what have we got to look forward to? Pollution and the population explosion …, if we're not destroyed first by the H bomb! M: We'll survive, Susan. The young will realize the world one day. They'll learn and grow up. W: You think we should grow up to be like you, don't you? You sometimes laugh at us when we talk about universal love and understanding between people! When people demonstrate about what is happening in other countries, you say, "What right do they have to interfere? It's none of their business!" But it is our business, Mr. Perkins. M: But international demonstrations only make misunderstandings worse. A lot of you are so sure you've got the answer to everything. [1] You won't accept guidance at all from older people. W: Mr. Perkins, [2] it's very difficult for older people to give proper guidance these days. They didn't have the same kind of problems. That's what the generation gap is all about. M: Well, I don't think the generation gap in this country is as great as you make it out to be. In fact, I suspect you go to your mother for advice just as often as you go to friends of your own age!	1. What does Mr. Perkins suggest the young do? 【解析】选[A]。推断题。本对话主要是关于 generation gap，女士抱怨大人们不了解她所成长的世界，无法给她们合理的建议，男士则说年轻人太过相信自己，并且 won't accept guidance at all from older people(不接受大人的教导)，由此可推断男士(Mr. Perkins)建议年轻人应该 accept guidance from older people。 2. Why can't older people give proper guidance nowadays, according to the woman? 【解析】选[A]。推断题。女士说现在 older people 要想给年轻人合理的指导及建议是很难的，因为他们 didn't have the same kind of problems(没有遇到年轻人所遇到的困难)，言外之意就是 older people 不能切实地了解年轻人所遇到的困难(can't understand the problem the young face)，所以女士认为 older people 不能给出合理的指导。 3. What is Susan's opinion of getting older? 【解析】选[C]。细节题。对话结尾处，女士说自己 frightened of getting older，由此可知女士对 getting older 是很 frightened(害怕的)。

W: Perhaps you are right. But, Mr. Perkins, [3] I'm almost frightened of getting older! Will I be talking like this to my children one day?

Conversation Two

【听力原文】

M: As far as I know, [4①] many students who choose to live off campus have good reasons. For example, they think the school doesn't offer satisfactory accommodation.

W: Yes, I agree with you to some extent. Conditions in university accommodation need to be improved. [4②] But students come to the university for the purpose of gaining knowledge and preparing themselves for future career. So living conditions should be their second consideration.

M: [4③] I don't think you are right here. Nice surroundings will stimulate our learning. [5] Students who rent a house off campus can have a nicer and quieter environment in which to study and rest.

W: But don't you see that we can still work better at our lessons with poor dormitory rooms? At any rate, if we want to study, we can go to the library or the classrooms.

M: [4④] I truly can't agree with you. School dormitories are usually noisy and crowded. Some rooms are very damp. These kinds of living conditions will seriously affect the quality of our rest. Without good rest, how can we study with enough energy?

W: To certain degrees, what you said is true. However, crowdedness and noises are something that can't be avoided in our daily life. So we should learn to be tolerant of hardships. If we can't be adaptive and flexible at the university, how can we expect ourselves to survive in the society? Not to mention making a success of our life.

M: Hardships can teach us many things, but it will also make us pay for it. I don't think living on campus to experience the hardships is a good choice when other options are available. Anyway, if the university can offer satisfactory accommodation, maybe no one will live off campus.

W: I'm afraid you are off the point. [6] The conditions can't be improved within one day, so let's face the reality.

【答案解析】

4. What are the two speakers talking about?

【解析】选[B]。主旨题。对话一开头,男士就表明了自己的观点:学生在校外住 have good reasons(是有理由的),女士话中的 but 转折句表明她认为学生的主要任务是学习,住宿条件应该放在次要位置。接着由下文男士话中频繁出现的 I don't think you are right here 及 I truly can't agree with you 和女士话中的 But…,However,… 等可知对话双方在讨论学生是否应住在校外(whether it is right for students to live off campus)。

5. According to the man, what is the possible reason for students to rent a house off campus?

【解析】选[A]。细节题。男士在说明居住环境对学生学习的影响时说到在校外租房的学生能够有 a nicer and quieter environment in which to study and rest(一个更好更安静的学习环境和休息环境),而这正是学生出去租房住的原因。

6. What does the woman think of the accommodation conditions in university?

【解析】选[C]。细节题。对话结尾处,女士提到 the conditions can't be improved within one day(住宿情况不可能在短期内有所改善)。in short time ≈ within one day。

Chapter 4

长对话巅峰练习

Exercise 1

 边听边记

Conversation One

19. [A] How to improve spoken English.
    [B] How to speak fluently.
    [C] How to speak correctly.
    [D] How to study English successfully.

20. [A] The person's spoken English will be improved greatly.
    [B] The person will feel nervous or embarrassed about speaking English publicly.
    [C] The person will be motivated to learn more about how to improve spoken English.
    [D] The person will speak English more fluently.

21. [A] To make recording of her monologue.
    [B] To ask her friends' opinion about her progress.
    [C] To make monologue often.
    [D] To be more confident and natural when speaking English.

Conversation Two

22. [A] Because the son spends little time on his schoolwork.
    [B] Because the son doesn't want to have dinner.
    [C] Because the son doesn't know how many hours he has played.
    [D] Because the son takes the computer to the playground.

23. [A] She doesn't believe her son has known so much about computer.
    [B] She doesn't know much about Internet.
    [C] She thinks her son should not study on the Internet.
    [D] She thinks her son should not make friends through Internet.

24. [A] By learning from his French friends known on Internet.
    [B] By learning from his French teachers.
    [C] By learning from some websites which teach French.
    [D] By teaching himself.

25. [A] Opposed.   [C] Interested.
    [B] Doubtful.   [D] Critical.

Exercise 2

Conversation One

19. [A] It is a term for the process of explaining the causes of behavior.
    [B] It is a term created by some physicians.
    [C] It is a term used to judge who should be blamed to some negative behaviors.
    [D] It is a term for explaining all the human behaviors.

20. [A] They usually blame others' carelessness.
    [B] They usually automatically attribute others' behavior to an internal factor.

　　[C] They usually ask the reason of others' negative behavior.

　　[D] They usually use the theory to explain others' negative behavior.

21. [A] Legal factor.　　　　　　　　　　[C] External factor.

　　[B] Internal factor.　　　　　　　　　[D] Subconsciousness.

Conversation Two

22. [A] The things a new secretary needs to pay attention to.

　　[B] How to write an apologizing letter.

　　[C] What the secretary's daily work is.

　　[D] When is the proper time to write an apologizing letter.

23. [A] In the office.

　　[B] At the company's data bank.

　　[C] At the man's home.

　　[D] On line.

24. [A] Because the time to deliver goods is delayed.

　　[B] Because her company can't cooperate with it this time.

　　[C] Because the goods MN company asked are damaged.

　　[D] Because her company can't pay the losses of the delay of goods.

25. [A] She doesn't know how to write business letter at all.

　　[B] She is not confident of dealing well with the apologizing letter.

　　[C] She came to the company earlier than the man.

　　[D] She asks the man to write an apologizing letter for her to MN company.

答案与解析

Exercise 1

Conversation One

【听力原文】	【答案解析】
W: John, [19①] I have some difficulties in my spoken English. M: What's your problem? W: [19②] I find that if I try to speak fast, I make more mistakes. If I slow down, there may be fewer errors but it sounds unnatural. M: Oh, I know your problem. That is why we must balance accuracy and fluency in spoken English. [20]If you tend to focus on accuracy, you may worry too much about making mistakes. This can make you nervous or embarrassed about speaking English in public. W: So that's why my spoken English hasn't improved. Can you tell me how I can develop that? M: [19③] First, you should find what kind person you are—one who focuses on accuracy or one who focuses on fluency. Think about situations where you've used English and how you feel about making mistakes. Do you always try new words even though they might not be correct? Or do you feel embarrassed by mistakes? W: I'm always in a dilemma. M: [19④] The solution is to focus on one problem at a time. When you speak English, find the mistakes you make most often. The next time you use English, try to work on those problems you have identified. W: That's a good idea. How do I know if I've made progress in my spoken English?	19. What are the speakers discussing? 【解析】选[A]。主旨题。对话一开头,女士就说自己在 spoken English 上遇到了一些困难:如果英语说得太快那她就会出很多错,但说得太慢就显得不自然,男士说自己理解女士的问题,并先后就女士如何弄清自己是什么样的人及如何弄清楚自己怎样才能知道自己的进步给出了相关建议,由此可知二人正在谈论 how to improve spoken English(如何提高口语)。 20. What is the result of one's focusing on accuracy in spoken English? 【解析】选[B]。细节题。男士提到如果你过于注重 accuracy(正确度),那么你就会过分地担心出错,而这造成的结果就是你会 nervous or embarrassed about speaking English in public,[B] 中的 publicly 是 in public 的同义转述。 21. What does the man suggest the woman to do to know her progress in spoken English?

M: [19⑤] [21] Try recording yourself. Take a tape recorder and record a monologue you should speak naturally! A two-or three-mi-
   nute recording is enough. The more you record yourself, the more
   confident and natural sounding you will become.

W: Thank you for your advice.

M: My pleasure. Good luck to you.

【解析】选[A]。细节题。女士问男士她怎样才能知道自己口语的进步,男士建议她 try recording yourself(给自己录音),而录音的具体内容就是把自己的 monologue(独白)录下来。

Conversation Two

【听力原文】	【答案解析】

【听力原文】

W: Jim, dinner is ready.

M: Wait a minute, mom.

W: Jim, these days I am really worry about you. Ever since we
   bought the computer for you, you have turned it into an electronic
   playground. You know how much time you are spending on your
   computer every day?

M: A couple of hours, I guess.

W: You call this a couple of hours? [23] You shouldn't spend so
   much time playing all these games; you've totally neglected your
   schoolwork.

M: Mom, you just don't understand. The computer is really fascinating! It can be a great help. Actually, the computer helps a lot in
   my academic study.

W: I don't see how the computer contributes to your study.

M: Well, the biggest use of the computer is that it connects me with
   the Internet. I am now able to get online. You know WWW and
   Internet?

W: [24] I have heard of people talking about it, but have no idea
   what you can actually do on the Internet.

M: Oh, there are countless things you can do there. For instance, I
   use e-mail to send messages to my friends every day. It's faster
   and safer. Sometimes I chat online and meet different people from
   different parts of the world.

W: [25①] That sounds interesting.

M: It does. Also there are many educational websites. [24①] I know
   some websites that help people learn French. I visit the sites almost every day.

W: Then I hope you can speak French more fluently.

M: [24②] I think I've made much progress. This is only a small portion of what the Internet can do for people. At the moment, more
   and more companies do business through the Internet and people
   can stay at home and shop online.

W: Oh, really? [25②] I want to learn it someday.

【答案解析】

22. At the beginning of the conversation, why is the mother worried about her son?

【解析】选[A]。细节题。对话一开头,女士就说自己非常担心 Jim,因为自从有了电脑,Jim 花在电脑上的时间太多了,几乎 neglected(忽略了)他的 schoolwork(作业),[A] 中的 spends little time on his schoolwork 是 neglected…schoolwork 的同义转述。

23. What can we learn about the mother according to the conversation?

【解析】选[B]。推断题。Jim 问他的妈妈是否知道 WWW and Internet,女士回答说她听过别人谈论 WWW and Internet,但她 have no idea what you can actually do on the Internet(不知道可以利用因特网干些什么事情),由此可推断女士对 Internet 知识了解得并不多。

24. How does Jim make so much progress in French?

【解析】选[C]。细节题。Jim 说他法语已经 made much progress(取得了很大的进步),并说这只是 a small portion of what the Internet can do for people(Internet 可以为人们做的事情中的一小部分),具体地说就是 Internet 上提供的 websites that help people learn French(帮助人们学习法语的网站)帮助 Jim 在法语上取得了进步。

25. What's the mother's attitude towards computers finally?

【解析】选[C]。推断题。由女士话中的 That sounds interesting 及 I want to learn it someday 可推断女士开始对电脑 interested(感兴趣了)。

Exercise 2

Conversation One

【听力原文】	【答案解析】

M: One of the most common questions we ask about people's behavior is why. Why did she say this? Why did he do that? Sometimes the reason is obvious. For example, when someone is driving down the street, the light turns red. They stop, why?

W: Because they have to, legally I mean.

M: Exactly! In this sense the reason is obvious, so we usually don't question it. But when the reason is not so obvious and especially when the behavior could have negative consequences, we'll be more likely to feel a need to explain the causes of the behavior. [19] Social psychologists have a term for this, for the process of explaining the causes of behavior, which is called causal attribution.

W: That sounds reasonable. But could you give me an example?

M: One theory suggests there's a pattern in the way we go about attributing causes to people's behavior. According to the theory, there are two categories of reasons: internal factors and external factors. Again, Lucy, say you're driving down the road and all of a sudden a guy turns into the lane right in front of you, and you have to slam on your brake to avoid an accident. How do you react?

W: I'll probably get very angry.

M: Because…

W: Well, he's not paying attention, he's a bad driver.

M: [20] So you automatically attribute the driver's behavior to an internal factor. He himself is to blame because he is careless.

W: So if I said it was because of heavy traffic or something, I'd be attributing his behavior to an external factor, something beyond his control.

M: Good. [21①] Now how do you usually explain our own negative behavior?

W: [21②] We blame external factors.

M: That's right.

19. What can be learned about causal attribution?
【解析】选[A]。细节题。男士提到 social psychologists(社会心理学家)使用 causal attribution 这一术语来说明 the process of explaining the causes of behavior(解释行为原因的过程),[A] 是原文的细节再现。

20. How do people usually do to others' negative behavior?
【解析】选[B]。推断题。男士问女士当别人突然从右侧将车开到她的车前面时,为避免发生事故,她不得不紧急踩刹车,这时她生气的理由是什么,当女士将原因归咎到那个司机 not paying attention 上时,男士说女士是 automatically attribute the driver's behavior to an internal factor,由此可推断,当人们遇到别人的 negative behaviors 时,人们通常会把原因归咎到别人的 internal factor 上。

21. What do people usually attribute their own negative behavior to?
【解析】选[C]。细节题。对话结尾处,男士问女士如何解释人们自己的 negative behavior 产生的原因,女士回答说人们通常会把它归于 external factors(外部因素),言外之意就是当人们要解释导致自己 negative behavior 产生的原因时,他们通常会把原因归咎于 external factor。

Conversation Two

【听力原文】	【答案解析】

W: [23] Excuse me, I'm the newcomer secretary. Could you please give me some advice?

M: OK. Can I be of any help?

W: You see, [24] the general manager asked me to draft out a business letter to MN company, to apologize for the delay of goods several days ago. [22①] However, as a newcomer, I'm not very skilled in it and need some advice from you.

M: No problem. [25①] I suppose you've already got some information about it, but are not very confident.

W: [25②] That's true. What I know is that apologizing letters should be written in a cordial way. It should first express our gratitude for the letter they wrote us, then tell them that we

22. What is the conversation mainly about?
【解析】选[B]。主旨题。对话开头处,女士说自己不太会写道歉信,希望男士给点建议。接下来的对话主要是围绕男士为女士解答疑问而展开,如 It's the usual way of writing apologizing letters, But need I say anything else? 等,由此可推断本对话主要在谈论 how to write an apologizing letter。

23. Where does the conversation most likely take place?
【解析】选[A]。推断题。由对话开头处女士的自我介绍以及接下来的对话都是围绕如何

are earnestly regretful for the delay of the goods.

M: That's right. [22②] It's the usual way of writing apologizing letters. Then what follows?

W: [22③] After that, we should explain the reasons for the delay, for example it's because of the weather, or other unexpected reasons.

M: That is. You are right on the way.

W: [22④] But need I say anything else? I'm not sure about that.

M: You can express the hope to cooperate with the company, adding what we have done or what measures we will take to reduce the losses. Moreover, do not forget to express our apologies for the loss they suffered.

W: Can that be followed by the signature?

M: Yes, that's usually the case. But you may deal flexibly according to the circumstances. I'm sure you can do properly.

W: Thank you so much. You've been really very helpful.

写道歉信这一工作内容展开可知，本对话很可能发生在公司的 office(办公室)里。

24. Why should the woman's company apologize to MN company?

【解析】选[A]。细节题。对话开头处，女士说到总经理让她写一封商业信给 MN 公司，to apologize for the delay of goods several days ago(为几天前货物的延期而道歉)，由此可知女士所在的公司要向 MN 公司道歉的原因是他们公司发货延期了。

25. What can we know about the woman from the conversation?

【解析】选[B]。推断题。男士认为女士已经掌握了一些写道歉信的知识，只是她 not very confident(不是很有自信)，女士给予了肯定回答，由此可推断女士没有自信能写好道歉信。

第五章 短文理解巅峰讲座

短文理解是六级听力考试的常规题型,其内容和题材比较丰富,从历年真题来看,常涉及的题材有以下六类:人物故事类、科学技术类、社会习俗类、社会问题类、文化教育类和工作生活类。

Lecture 1　第一讲　9大敏感设题题眼

每篇短文的长度一般在240－260词之间,共三篇,10道题目,其题目顺序基本按照文章的顺序分布。常见的设题题眼包括:

一、短文首尾处

短文的开头与结尾,尤其是开头,是设题的重点,一般是考查对短文主旨或所讨论话题的把握。短文的主题句一般都出现在开头,而且往往是第一道题的答案出处。而短文的结尾也往往对整篇文章的内容起一个概括和提示的作用,因此同样不可忽视。

【例1】　　　　　　　　　　　　　　　　　　　　　　(05-12-14)

[A] By making laws.	Laws have been written to govern the use of the American National Flag and to ensure proper respect for the flag. …
[B] By enforcing discipline.	
[C] By educating the public.	14. How do Americans ensure proper respect for the National Flag?
[D] By holding ceremonies.	

【解析】主旨题。本题的设题题眼在短文的开头。

【例2】　　　　　　　　　　　　　　　　　　　　　　(05-1-17)

[A] Getting rich quickly.	… A major difference between American culture and most East Asian cultures is that in East Asia, the community is more important than the individual. Most Americans are considered a success when they make a name for themselves.
[B] Distinguishing oneself.	
[C] Respecting individual rights.	
[D] Doing credit to one's community.	17. What is encouraged in American culture according to the passage?

【解析】细节题。本题的设题题眼在短文的结尾。

二、短文中列举或举例处

短文中为说明一个问题,常常会使用列举或进行举例,这些地方往往是考查的重点。因此当听到 such as, for example, for instance, the first, the second 等一类的词语时,应加以留意。

【例3】　　　　　　　　　　　　　　　　　　　　　　(03-9-11)

[A] Rally support for their movement.	…Women's liberation groups in Britain, for example, have used graffiti to show their anger at the sex discrimination of many advertisements where women's bodies are used to sell goods. …
[B] Liberate women from tedious housework.	
[C] Claim their rights to equal job opportunities.	
[D] Express their anger against sex discrimination.	11. What do women's liberation groups in Britain do with graffiti?

【解析】细节题。本题的设题题眼在列举处。

三、短文中逻辑关系处

转折处,尤其是 but 之后,不仅是对话的考查重点,在短文理解中也常常备受关注。另外表示并列、因果、条件等其他逻辑关系的地方也往往是短文理解的出题重点。因此,当短文中出现 as well as, not only…but also, but, however, because, since, so, if, even if/even though 等表示逻辑关系的连接词的时候,需重点关注。

【例4】   (04-6-17)

[A] It will be consumed by more and more young people.	…But until our attitudes to food change fundamentally, it seems that insect-eaters will remain a select few.
[B] It will become the first course at dinner parties.	
[C] It will have to be changed to suit local tastes.	
[D] It is unlikely to be enjoyed by most people.	17. What does the speaker say about the future of this type of unusual food?

【解析】细节题。本题的设题题眼在 but 转折处。

四、短文中强调处

强调的地方肯定是短文的重点所在,因此短文理解中的强调句型也是考查的重点之一。

【例5】   (02-6-19)

[A] One of Etna's recent eruptions made many people move away.	…Let's take Mount Etna for example. It does erupt frequently, but those eruptions are usually minor. …
[B] Etna's frequent eruptions have ruined most of the local farmland.	
[C] Etna's eruptions are frequent but usually mild.	
[D] There are signs that Etna will erupt again in the near future.	19. What will people living near Mount Etna do in the face of its eruptions?

【解析】细节题。本题的设题题眼在强调处。

五、短文中比较或对比处

短文中的形容词或副词的比较级和最高级、as…as 同级比较,以及 while, whereas, in contrast, compared with 等引出的对比结构也经常是短文理解的设题题眼之一。

【例6】   (02-12-14)

[A] There were fewer fish in the river.	… However, my studies indicate that they took fewer fish because there were fewer fish to catch, not because they were trying to preserve fishes…
[B] Over-fishing was prohibited.	
[C] The local Chamber of Commerce tried to preserve fishes.	
[D] The local fishing cooperative decided to reduce its catch.	14. Why was the annual catch of fish in the Biramichi River reduced according to the speaker?

【解析】细节题。本题的设题题眼在比较处。

六、短文中数字信息处

短文中经常会涉及到时间、价格、数量等与数字相关的信息,这些数字以及与这些数字相关的重点信息,常常是短文理解的重要设题题眼之一。

【例7】   (06-6-17)

[A] She won the 1945 Nobel Prize in Literature.	…In 1945, she gained worldwide recognition by winning the Nobel Prize in literature, the first South American to win the prize.
[B] She was the first woman to win a Nobel Prize.	
[C] She translated her books into many languages.	
[D] She advised many statesmen on international affairs.	17. How did Gabriela Mistral become famous all over the world?

【解析】细节题。本题的设题题眼在年代处。

七、短文中目的处

短文中涉及到目的、目标的地方也经常会受到出题人的青睐,这类题目的选项多为动词原形或不定式短语。

【例8】　　　　　　　　　　　　　　　　　　　　　　　　　　　　　　(03-9-11)

| [A] Rally support for their movement.
[B] Liberate women from tedious housework.
[C] Claim their rights to equal job opportunities.
[D] Express their anger against sex discrimination. | Writing on walls is a way to comment on the world we live in. Women's liberation groups in Britain, for example, have used graffiti to show their anger at the sex discrimination of many advertisements where women's bodies are used to sell goods.
11. What do women's liberation groups in Britain do with graffiti? |

【解析】细节题。本题的设题题眼在目的处。

八、短文中定语从句处

短文中的定语从句,尤其是非限制性定语从句经常是短文理解的设题题眼之一,定语从句的内容往往就是答案所在或为解题提供重要的信息提示。

【例9】　　　　　　　　　　　　　　　　　　　　　　　　　　　　　　(新 06-12-35)

| [A] In areas with few weeds and unwanted plants.
[B] In areas with a severe shortage of water.
[C] In areas lacking in chemical fertilizer.
[D] In areas dependent on imported food. | Scientists say Low Till Farming is becoming popular in South Asia, which is facing a severe water shortage.
35. Where is Low Till Farming becoming popular? |

【解析】细节题。本题的设题题眼在定语从句处。

九、短文中 it 充当形式主语或宾语处

it 常用来代替不定式、动名词短语或从句,充当形式主语或形式宾语,这也是短文理解的重要设题题眼之一,题目的答案往往出自 it 所代替的真正主语。

【例10】　　　　　　　　　　　　　　　　　　　　　　　　　　　　　(新 06-12-29)

| [A] He grieved to death over the loss of his wife.
[B] He committed suicide for unknown reasons.
[C] He was shot dead at the age of 40.
[D] He died of heavy drinking. | It is said that he was found dead after days of heavy drinking.
29. How did Edgar Allen Poe's life come to an end? |

【解析】细节题。本题的设题题眼在形式主语处。

Exercise　　　　　　　即讲即练　　　　　　　边听边记

Passage One

1. [A] American.　　　[B] Japanese.　　　[C] British.　　　[D] Canadian.
2. [A] 113 years.　　　　　　　　　　　　[B] Nearly 114 years.
   [C] About 116 years.　　　　　　　　　[D] About 118 years.
3. [A] Less work pressure and more outdoor exercises.
   [B] Fresh air, fresh food and a simple way of life.
   [C] Healthy diet and clean environment.
   [D] A simple way of life and developed medical care.

Passage Two

4. [A] To demonstrate the use of new measurement device.
   [B] To provide background for the next assignment.

[C] To review what students know about volcanic activity.

[D] To explain the answer to an examination question.

5. [A] P waves can pass through liquids, but S waves can't.

[B] S waves can pass through solids, but P waves can't.

[C] P waves are longer than S waves.

[D] S waves can travel deeper than P waves.

6. [A] Volcanoes.   [B] Molten lava.

[C] Quartzite.   [D] Limestone.

🎧 边听边记

【答案与解析】

Passage One

【听力原文】

Thousands of people in the world are a hundred years old or more. There are about two thousand centenarians in Britain alone, and certain parts of the world are famous for the long lives of their inhabitants: Georgia in the Soviet Union, the Vilacamba Valley in Ecuador, and the home of the Hunzas in the Himalayas. [1] But the oldest person in the world is Japanese. In 1983 Mr. Shigechiyo Izumi, aged 118, held first place in *The Guinness Book of Records*. He was born on June 29th, 1865 and beat the previous record on his 114th birthday. [2] Before Mr. Izumi broke the record, the longest life was that of an American woman, Mrs. Eveline Filkins. She lived for 113 years, 214 days, from 1815 to 1928. During her lifetime she saw the invention of the first camera, the first telephone, the first car, the first airplane and the first television. There are official papers to prove the date of birth of Mr. Izumi and Mrs. Filkins, but many other people claim to be as old or older.

Why do so many people live to the healthy old age? What is the secret of their long lives? [3] Three things seem to be very important: fresh air, fresh food and a simple way of life. People work near their homes in the clean, mountain air instead of traveling long distances to work by bus, car or train. They do not sit all day in busy offices or factories, but work hard outdoors in the fields. They take more exercise and eat less food than people in the big cities.

【答案解析】

1. What nationality is the oldest person, according to the passage?

【解析】选[B]。设题点在短文中逻辑关系处。短文一开始就指出世界上有成千上万位年龄超过百岁的人,在介绍各个国家的情况时提到 the oldest person in the word is Japanese。

2. How many years did the American woman, Mrs. Filkins live?

【解析】选[B]。设题点在短文中数字信息处。短文中指出,在日本人 Mr. Izumi 打破年龄记录以前,活得最久的是一位名叫 Mrs. Eveline Filkins 的美国妇女,她生存的时间总共是 113 年 214 天,也就是说她活了将近 114 年。

3. What are the important factors for people's long healthy lives?

【解析】选[B]。设题点在短文的结尾处。短文结尾处首先提出两个问题 Why do so many people live to the healthy old age? What is the secret of their long lives? 接着给出答案 Three things seem to be very important…,由此可知人们长寿的最重要因素是 fresh air, fresh food 和 a simple way of life。

Passage Two

【听力原文】

I'm glad you've brought up the question of our investigations into the makeup of the earth's interior. In fact [4] since this is the topic in your reading assignment for next time, let me spend these last few minutes of class talking about it. There were several important discoveries in the early part of this century that helped geologists develop a more accurate picture of the earth's interior. The first key discovery had to do with seismic waves. Remember they are the vibrations caused by earthquakes. Well, scientists found that they travel thousands of miles through the earth's interior. This finding enabled geologists to study the inner parts of the earth.

【答案解析】

4. What is the purpose of this passage?

【解析】选[B]。设题点在短文中逻辑关系处。短文开头部分,作者说 since this is the topic in your reading assignment for next time(因为这是学生下一次的阅读作业),所以他会花几分钟的时间讲解一下学生提出的问题,而这几分钟的讲解会 provide background for the next assignment(为学生下一个阅读任务提供背景知识)。

5. What is the difference between P waves and S waves?

【解析】选[A]。设题点在短文中比较处。短文中

You see, the studies revealed that these vibrations were of two types: compression or P waves and shear or S waves. And researchers found that [5] P waves travel through both liquids and solids while S waves travel only through solid matter. In 1906, a British geologist discovered that P waves slowed down at certain depths but kept traveling deeper. On the other hand, S waves either disappeared or were reflected back. So he concluded that the depth marked the boundary between a solid mantle and a liquid core. Three years later, another boundary was discovered that between the mantle and the earth's crust, there is still a lot to be learned about the earth. [6] For instance, geologists know that the core is hot. Evidence of this is the molten lava that flows out of the volcanoes. But we are still not sure what the source of heat is.

提到 P waves travel through both liquids and solids while S waves travel only through solid matter（P waves 既可以通过 liquids 也可以通过 solids，而 S waves 只能通过 solid matters），由此可知 P waves 和 S waves 的不同之处就在于 P waves 可以通过 liquids，但 S waves 不可以通过 liquids。

6. **What can prove that the earth's core is hot?**

【解析】选[B]。设题点在短文中举例处。短文结尾处，作者为证明关于地球还有很多东西要学习时举例说地质学家知道地心是热的，紧接着又说证据就是 the molten lava that flows out of the volcanoes（从火山流下来的火山岩）。

Lecture 2　第二讲　3招巧做主旨题

主旨题主要考查考生对全文的主旨大意或所谈论话题的理解。

常见的提问方式有：

What is the topic of the passage?

What is the speaker's purpose in giving this talk?

What is the passage mainly about?

主旨题在一套考题中所占的比例很小，一般只有一道，甚至没有，但这并不意味着理解主旨大意不重要。事实上，在听一篇短文时，如果没有对文章大意的理解，把握其事实细节是很难的。常用的解题招术如下：

第一招：根据各题选项推测主题

听力理解的每道题都是围绕听力材料的主要内容而设，故根据各选项中反复出现的相同或相关的词语，往往可大致推测出其所要陈述的主题。

第二招：留意首尾处

主题句常常出现在短文的开头，它对整篇短文的内容起一个概括和提示的作用，实际上是说话人所谈论的中心话题。另外，结尾处也往往含有总结性的语言，故也应加以留意。

在听音时应尽快抓住能概括材料中心思想的主题句和关键词，这样就能比较容易地听懂其内容，更有助于主旨题的解答。

1. 主题句在开头

主题句为首句时，听清开场白，对于了解文章的主题、听懂大意、了解全文的中心思想非常重要。

2. 主题句在结尾

主题句出现在段落结尾时，是先摆出一些事实或情节，然后归纳总结本段或本文的主题。

第三招：留意重复频率较高的词或短语

短文的主要内容理所当然会得到说话人的强调，而一个非常重要、也是非常明显的强调方式就是重复。因此，对那些短文中多次提到的词语或内容应进行重点记忆。

【例】　　　　　　　　　　　　　　　　　　　　　　　　　　　　　(06-6-Passage Three)

【预览选项】	【预测信息】
18. [A] How <u>animals</u> survive harsh conditions in the wild. [B] How <u>animals</u> <u>alter colors</u> to match their surroundings. [C] How <u>animals</u> <u>protect</u> themselves against <u>predators</u>.	预览三道题各选项，可知本文涉及到 animals 与 predators（食肉动物），再由 protect，alter colors，disguise（伪装），offensive（难闻的）smell 等线索词可推测本文主题很可能与动物保护自己免受食肉

[D] How <u>animals</u> learn to <u>disguise</u> themselves effective-ly.

19. [A] Its enormous size.

　　[B] Its <u>plant-like appearance</u>.

　　[C] Its instantaneous response.

　　[D] Its <u>offensive smell</u>.

20. [A] It helps improve their <u>safety</u>.

　　[B] It allows them to swim faster.

　　[C] It helps them <u>fight</u> their <u>predators</u>.

　　[D] It allows them to avoid twists and turns.

动物侵食的方法有关。

18. 选项的概括性都很强,故本题很可能是考查短文的主题。根据前面对主题的分析,本题答案为[C]的可能性较大。

19. 选项及对主题的推测表明本题是关于某种动物保护自己的方法。文中可能会出现不只一种动物保护自己的方法,因此听音时需注意搞清与选项中涉及的方法相对应的动物,然后根据问题对号入座。

20. 选项中的 help, improve, allow 等词表明本题很可能是问"it(很可能是某种保护方法)"起到什么样的作用。

【听音验证】

　　[18①] Over time animals have developed many ways to <u>stay away from predators</u>. A [18②] <u>predator</u> is an animal that hunts and eats other animals. Hiding is one of the best ways to stay alive. Some animals hide by looking like the places where they live. To see how this works, let's look at the sea dragon. It's a master of disguise. The sea dragon is covered with skin that looks like leaves. [19] <u>The skin helps the dragon look like a piece of seaweed</u>. A hungry meat eat-er would stay away from anything that looks like seaweed. Other animals stay safe by showing their colors. They want other animals to see them. Scientists call these bright colors warning colors. You have probably seen animals that have warning colors. Some grasshoppers show off their own bright colors. Those colors don't just look attractive; they tell their enemies to stay away. Of course, hungry [18③] <u>predators</u> sometimes ignore the warning. They still go off the grasshopper. If that happens, the grasshopper has a backup of defense. It makes lots of foams. The foams taste so bad that the [18④] <u>predator</u> won't do it again. Color doesn't offer enough protection for some other animals. They have different defenses that help them survive in the wild. Many fish live in groups or schools. [20] <u>That's be-cause of the safety in numbers</u>. At the first sign of trouble, schooling fish swim as close together as they can get. Then the school of fish makes lots of twists and turns. All that movement makes it hard for [18⑤] <u>predators</u> to see individ-uals in a large group.

【答案解析】

18. What is the speaker mainly talking about?

【解析】选[C]。主旨题。主旨题的答案往往在短文的开头或结尾,而本题的答案出处就是短文开头的第一句。由该句可知本文主要是讨论 many ways to stay away from predators,即 how animals protect themselves against predators(动物如何保护自己免受食肉动物的侵食),由此可知答案为[C]。另外,短文中多次出现了 predator 一词,抓住该词也有助于本题答案的选择。

19. What protects the sea dragon from the meat eater's attack?

【解析】选[B]。推断题。本题的答案不是对话中某个细节的再现,而是在细节基础上的推断。由文中 The skin helps the dragon look like a piece of seaweed 一句可推知是 plant-like appearances(像海草的外表)保护了 sea dragon 免遭食肉动物的攻击,由此可知答案为[B]。

20. According to the passage, why do many fishes stay in group?

【解析】选[A]。细节题。本题的答案是对话中的细节再现。由文中 That's because of the safety in numbers 一句可知,许多鱼 stay in group 是为了 safety(安全)。只要抓住 safety 一词即可确定答案为[A]。

Exercise 即讲即练 🎧 边听边记

Passage One

1. [A] The advantages of telephone.

　[B] The history of telephone.

　[C] The influence of telephone on people's life.

　[D] The convenience of telephone.

2. [A] To avoid being disturbed.　　　　[B] To keep their private life secret.

　[C] To be different from common people.　[D] To attract the public's attention.

3. [A] Critical.　　　　[B] Positive.　　　　[C] Indifferent.　　　　[D] Neutral.　　　🎧 边听边记

Passage Two

4. [A] Americans should follow the example of more relaxed cultures.
   [B] It is impolite to arrive more than an hour late to a party in the U.S.
   [C] Americans hurry more at night than in the daytime.
   [D] Time plays a very important role in American culture.

5. [A] Half an hour or an hour.　　　　　　　[B] Twenty minutes.
   [C] One and a half hour.　　　　　　　　　[D] Forty minutes.

6. [A] They think it is all right.　　　　　　　[B] They think it is unpardonable.
   [C] They think it is unbelievable.　　　　　[D] They think it is unreasonable.

【答案与解析】

Passage One

【听力原文】

When it comes to the telephone, people always think of a great American inventor, Alexander Graham Bell. It was Bell who introduced a fast means of communication to people all over the world. [1①] No one can deny the fact that it has brought about a lot of profits and convenience to our daily life. A successful bargain may be struck by no more than dialing the right number and making a negotiation without bothering to meet the partner. Over phone one can also hear the familiar, sweet voice of his daughter when he travels overseas. Another case in point is that we can phone to order goods. It's no exaggeration to say that telephone has become an indispensable part of modern life.

[1②] However, the telephone also has its disadvantages. How many times have you been woken up from a sound sleep by a wrong call at midnight? How often are you troubled with the unwanted calls while you're being pressed with your work? What is more, [2] some people just use it for fun to disturb the famous singers, football stars who, as a result, have to change their telephone numbers frequently. Besides, some children are fascinated with hot lines, especially with international calls, which inevitably lead to a fast drop in their studies.

[3] By and large, the advantages of telephone outweigh its disadvantages. If Bell could see how enormously we depend on his invention today, surely he would feel somewhat proud.

【答案解析】

1. What is the passage mainly discussing?
【解析】选[C]。主旨题。由各选项中的 telephone 可初步推测本对话很可能与 telephone 有关。短文第一段指出…it has brought about a lot of profits and convenience to our daily life(电话给人们的日常生活带来了好处及方便),这是在说电话对人们生活的积极影响,但短文第二段又指出 the telephone also has its disadvantages,根据下文可知本处的 disadvantages 指的是电话对人们生活的消极影响,综合来讲本文主要是讲电话对人们生活的 influence。

2. Why are those famous stars always changing their phone numbers?
【解析】选[A]。细节题。短文在证明 the telephone also has its disadvantages 时所举的例子中有明星经常受到电话骚扰一例。文中指出 some people just use it for fun to disturb the famous singers…,所以明星们不得不经常换电话号码,由此可知明星经常换电话号码是为了 avoid being disturbed。

3. What is the speaker's attitude toward telephone?
【解析】选[B]。推断题。短文结尾处,作者提到大体上来说,the advantages of telephone outweigh its disadvantage(电话的好处多余坏处),由此可推断 the speaker 对 telephone 抱有的态度是 positive(乐观的)。

Passage Two

【听力原文】

[4①] For most Americans, clocks and watches are very important. They are always aware of them. In the morning some people have to get up when it is still dark. Others sleep through several hours of sunlight. But both groups wake up when they hear their alarm

【答案解析】

4. What is the main idea of the passage?
【解析】选[D]。主旨题。本文开头部分的 For most Americans, clocks and watches are important 和结尾处的 time is so

clock ring. While they get dressed and eat breakfast, they listen to the radio, and the radio tells them again and again exactly what time it is.

On the way to work or school, people look at their watches. If they think they are going to be late, they hurry. At work, Americans think it is important to arrive at meetings on time. [5] Their lunch breaks are short, lasting only half an hour or an hour. Late in the afternoon, they check their watches often to see how soon they can go home.

In the evenings, however, Americans are more relaxed. They try to arrive on time, but they don't worry if they are a few minutes late to meet friends in a restaurant. Also, people who arrive a few minutes late to a movie are usually in time to see the main feature film. [6] If a party at a friend's house starts at 8, some people come an hour later, but nobody minds.

Americans are used to living by clocks and watches. It is hard for them to understand that people in many parts of the world don't think that [4②] time is so important.

important 均提示本文很可能与时间有关,而且文中多次出现的 watches、time 可以确定本文的主旨是时间对美国人的重要作用。

5. How much time do Americans have to have lunch?

【解析】选[A]。细节题。短文明确提到美国人的午饭时间特别短,只有 half an hour or an hour。

6. What do people think of the one who is late for his friend's party?

【解析】选[A]。细节题。文中提到,在晚上美国人就不像白天那样紧张,如果他们的朋友晚上 8 点钟举办一个晚会,但是一些人却迟到了一个小时,这时 nobody minds(没有人会介意),即他们认为 it is all right。

Lecture 3　第三讲　4 招巧做推断题

主要考查考生对重要细节引申含义的理解及考生的推理判断能力。

常见的提问方式有:

What can be inferred from…?

What do we learn about sth. from…?

推断题是相对较难的一种题型,它要求考生对听力材料的主旨或某些细节有深层次的理解,即在理解原文所直接陈述的观点或事实的基础上,进行合乎逻辑地推断,领悟作者的言外之意。常用的解题招术如下:

第一招:根据选项确定应关注的重点细节

根据选项特点及选项内容,推测问题可能考查的核心内容,确定在听音时应重点关注哪些细节,以便更好地进行推断。

第二招:注意与主题密切相关的选项

听力材料都是围绕一定的主题展开,问题考查的内容也一般都与主题相关,因此,听音时应重点留意那些与主题密切相关的选项,那些与主题明显无关的选项往往可以初步排除。

第三招:注意关联词,把握短文发展的脉络

短文常使用一些连接手段,如表示并列、转折或因果等关系的连接词,它们表明上下文的逻辑关系,使文章成为一个有机的整体。熟悉这些关联词,有助于抓住重点信息,从而提高推理和判断的准确性。

第四招:听到的往往不是解

推断题难度相对较大,正确选项一般不会是对话中某个细节的再现,而是需要根据某个细节来进行推断。推断最重要的是要合乎逻辑,不能根据只言片语胡乱猜测。

【例】　　　　　　　　　　　　　　　　　　　　(06-6-Passage One)

【预览选项】	【预测信息】
11. [A] Social work. 　　[B] Medical care. 　　[C] Applied physics.	预览三道题各选项,由 medical care(医疗护理), hospitals,以及 therapists(治疗专家)可推测本文可能与医疗工作有关;由 special education(特殊教育),

　　[D] Special education.

12. [A] The timely advice from her friends and relatives.

　　[B] The two-year professional training she received.

　　[C] Her determination to fulfill her dream.

　　[D] Her parents' consistent moral support.

13. [A] To get the funding for the hospitals.

　　[B] To help the disabled children there.

　　[C] To train therapists for the children there.

　　[D] To set up an institution for the handicapped.

disabled(残疾的)和 handicapped(残疾的)可推测本文很可能与残疾人特殊教育有关,但 12、13 题各选项并没有涉及到任何有关教育的问题。因此综合来看,本文的主题很可能是关于残疾人的医疗工作。

11. 四个选项均是某一学科领域,由前面对主题的分析可推断本题答案为[B] Medical care 的可能性较大,听音时再确认具体是哪个领域。

12. 选项特点表明本题很可能是关于影响"她"做某种决定的因素(friends and relatives, parents, training, determination)。听音时主要判断是来自"谁"的因素。

13. 选项均为不定式形式,表明本题很可能是考查某人做某事的目的或原因。[A]是有关资金问题,偏离主题,不太可能为答案。听音时需留意以下要点:help disabled children; train therapists; set institution for handicapped。

【听音验证】

Born and raised in central Ohio, I'm a country girl through and through. [11] I'm currently studying to become a physical therapist, a career path that marks a greater achievement for me. At Ohio State University, admission into the physical therapy program is intensely competitive. I made it pass the first cuts the first year I applied, but was turned down for admission. I was crushed, because for years I have been determined to become a physical therapist. I received advice from friends and relatives about changing my major and finding another course for my life. I just couldn't do it. I knew I could not be as happy in another profession. [12] So I stilled myself, began to work seriously for another year and reapplied. Happily I received notice of my admission. Later, I found out that less than 15% of the applicant had been offered positions that year. Now in the first two years of professional training, I couldn't be happier with my decision not to give up on my dream. My father told me that if I wanted it badly enough, I would get in. Well, Daddy, I wanted it. So there.

After graduation, I would like to travel to another country, possibly a Latin American country and [13] work in a children's hospital for a year or two. So many of the children there are physically handicapped but most hospitals don't have the funding to hire trained staff to care for them properly. I would like to change that somehow.

【答案解析】

11. What is the speaker's field of study?

【解析】选[B]。推断题。本题是问说话者研究的领域是什么。由文中的 studying to become a physical therapist 可知说话人目前在学习成为一名理疗师,而 physical therapist 明显属于 medical care 的范畴,由此可推知说话人的学习领域属于 medical care(医疗)范畴,故答案为[B]。解答此题时切忌将 physical therapist(理疗师)中的 physical 与 physics(物理学)联系起来而误选[C]。

12. According to the speaker, what contributed to her admission to Ohio State University?

【解析】选[C]。推断题。本题是问说话者被俄亥俄州立大学录取的原因是什么。根据文中 So I stilled myself, began to work seriously for another year and reapplied 一句可知说话人坚持了自己的梦想,并努力为实现梦想而奋斗,由此可推知她最终被录取是因为她 determination to fulfill her dream(实现梦想的决心),故答案为[C]。解答本题要注意不能根据只言片语妄下结论,如听到 received advice from friends and relatives 就误选[A]。

13. Why does the speaker want to go to a Latin American country?

【解析】选[B]。细节题。本题是问说话者想去拉美国家的原因是什么。根据文中 work in a children's hospital for a year or two. So many of the children there are physically handicapped but most hospitals don't have … 可知说话人想去拉美国家是为了 help the disabled children there(帮助那里的残疾儿童),故答案为[B]。

Exercise　　　　　　　即讲即练　　　　　　🎧 边听边记

Passage One

1. [A] Building is more useful for common people than architecture.
   [B] Building can not be without architecture.
   [C] Building and architecture developed at the same time.
   [D] Building and architecture are the achievement of individuals.
2. [A] They are not rotten.　　　　　　　[B] They are endurable and not burnable.
   [C] They are huge enough.　　　　　　[D] They are resistible to pressure.
3. [A] The use of stone and lime.
   [B] The use of marble and glass.
   [C] The expanses of glass and the use of reinforced concrete.
   [D] The use of brick and tile.

Passage Two

4. [A] What influenza is.　　　　　　　　[B] What the sub-group of type A virus is.
   [C] How to find type A virus.　　　　　[D] Whether WHO could find type A virus is.
5. [A] About 15%—20% of its population.　[B] About 5%—12% of its population.
   [C] About 35%—40% of its population.　[D] About 50%—75% of its population.
6. [A] Its sub-groups have not been recognized.　[B] There are no effective drugs to defeat it.
   [C] It can kill the one who was infected.　[D] It spreads at low speed.

【答案与解析】

Passage One

【听力原文】

[1] Architecture is to building as literature is to printed word. The best buildings are often so well constructed that they outlast their original use. They then survive not only as beautiful objects, but as documents of the history of cultures. These achievements are never wholly the work of individuals. Architecture is a social art.

The renaissance brought about an entirely new age, not only in philosophy and literature but in the visual arts as well. In architecture, the principles and styles of ancient Greece and Rome were brought back to life and reinterpreted. They remain dominant until the 20th century.

Many kinds of stone are used as building materials. [2] Stone and marble were chosen for important monuments because they are not burnable and can be expected to endure. Stone architecture was often blended with stone sculpture. The use of stone has declined, however, because a number of other materials are more adaptable to industrial use.

The complexity of modern life calls for a variety of buildings. More people live in mass housing and go to work in large office buildings; they spend their income in large shopping centers, send their children to many different kinds of schools, and when they are sick they go to specialized hospitals and clinics. All these different types of buildings accumulated experiences needed by their designers.

By the middle of the 20th century, modern architecture, which was influenced by new technology and mass production, was dealing

【答案解析】

1. What is the relationship between architecture and building, according to the passage?
【解析】选[B]。推断题。短文一开始就说 Architecture is to building as literature is to printed word(建筑学对建筑物就像文学对书面语言一样),printed word 离不开 literature,也就是说没有了 literature,printed word 也就没有了它存在的基础,可见 architecture 和 building 的关系也是如此,所以说 building can not be without architecture.

2. What are the special characteristics of stone and marble?
【解析】选[B]。细节题。文中提到许多种 stone 可以用作建筑材料,但 stone 和 marble 经常被用来建造纪念碑,因为它们 not burnable 并且能 endure,也就是说正是 stone 和 marble 具有 not burnable(不可燃性)和 endurable(持久性)的特点,它们才会被作为建造纪念碑的材料。

3. What are the most important features of modern architectural works?
【解析】选[C]。细节题。短文结尾处提

with increasingly complex social needs. [3] Important characteristics of modern architectural works are expanses of glass and the use of reinforced concrete. Advances in elevator technology, air conditioning, and electric lighting have all had important effects.

到在 20 世纪中期 modern architecture 受到了 new technology 和 mass production 的影响，modern architectural works 最重要的特点就是 glass 的大量运用和 reinforced concrete（钢筋混凝土）的使用。

Passage Two

【听力原文】

In 1957 a doctor in Singapore noticed that hospitals were treating an unusual number of influenza like cases. Influenza is sometimes called "flu" or a "bad cold". He took specimens from the throats of patients in his hospital and was able to find the virus of this influenza. There are three main types of influenza virus. The most important of these are types A and B, each of them having several sub-groups. With the instruments at the hospital, [4] the doctor recognized that the outbreak was due to a virus group A, but he did not know the sub-group. He reported the outbreak to the World Health Organization in Geneva. WHO published the important news alongside reports of [5] a similar outbreak in Hong Kong, where about 15%—20% of the population had become ill.

As soon as the London doctors received the package of throat samples, they began the standard tests. They found that by reproducing itself at a very high speed, [6①] the virus had multiplied more than a million times within two days. Continuing their careful tests, the doctors checked the effect of drugs used against all the known sub-groups of type A virus on this virus. None of them gave any protection. [6②] This then, was something new, a new influenza virus against which the people of the world had no ready help whatsoever.

Having isolated the virus they were working with, the two doctors now conducted tests on some specially selected animals, which contract influenza in the same way as human beings do. In a short time the usual signs of the disease appeared. These experiments revealed that the new virus spread easily, but that [6③] it was not a killer. Scientists, like the general public, called it simply "Asian flu".

【答案解析】

4. What puzzles the doctor in Singapore?
【解析】选[B]。细节题。文中提到 the doctor in Singapore 知道了流感病毒的爆发是由 a virus group A 引起的，但他不知道 type A virus 的 sub-group，由此可知 the doctor in Singapore 感到困惑的是 what the sub-group of type A virus is。

5. How many people were infected by virus of influenza in Hong Kong mentioned in the passage?
【解析】选[A]。细节题。由文中的 a similar outbreak in Hong Kong … about 15%—20% of its population become ill 可知，香港有大约 15%—20% 的人口感染上了流感病毒。

6. What can we learn about type A virus, according to the passage?
【解析】选[B]。推断题。文中提到 type A virus 是 a new influenza virus（新的流感病毒），这种病毒传播速度很快，但它不会置人于死亡，the people of the world had no ready help，由此可推断还没有研制出有效的药物（effective drugs）可以消灭 type A virus。

Lecture 4　　第四讲　6 招巧做细节题

细节题主要考查考生对短文中细节内容的确切含义的理解，经常针对听力材料中的某个细节（如人名、地名、时间、原因、数据、目的、年代等）进行提问。

常见提问方式如：

Why are…?

How is…?

Where is…?

细节题是六级听力考试中出现频率最高的一种题型，10 道题中通常都占 5 道以上，有时多至 8、9 道。常用的解题招术如下：

第一招：根据选项确定应关注的重点细节

根据选项特点及选项内容,推测问题可能考查的核心内容,确定在听音时应重点关注哪些细节。另外,听音时应重点留意那些与主题密切相关的选项。

第二招：捕捉转折、因果、条件等逻辑关系处

转折处,尤其是 but 之后,不仅是对话的考查重点,在短文理解中也常常备受关注。另外表示并列、因果、条件等其他逻辑关系的地方也往往是短文理解的出题重点。因此,当短文中出现 as well as, not only … but also…, but, however, because, since, so, if, even if /even though 等表示逻辑关系的连接词的时候,需重点关注。另外,一些表示上下文逻辑关系的词或短语也应加以留意。

听力中常出现的关联词有:

表并列:and, also, besides, furthermore, in addition, what's more, as well as, apart from

表转折:although, but, however, in spite of, otherwise, instead

表因果:because, therefore, since, for, why, as

表顺序:first, last, before, after, next, then

表举例或解释:such as, namely, that is, for example, for instance

表对比与比较:compared with, while, whereas

第三招：捕捉列举或举例处

为说明一个问题,常常会使用列举或进行举例,这些地方往往是考查的重点。因此,当听到 such as, for example, for instance, the first, the second 等一类的词语时,应加以留意。

第四招：捕捉强调处

短文中强调的地方往往都是短文的重点内容,所以也是出题的重点所在。

第五招：捕捉比较或对比处

短文中的形容词、副词的比较级和最高级、as…as 同级比较以及 compared with, in contrast 等引出的对比结构也经常是短文理解的设题点之一。

第六招：捕捉含有年代、数量、价格等数字的句子

需要注意的是,直接考查数字的情况往往较少,而多数是考查与数字相关的信息,因此当听到录音中出现数字时,应关注与其相联系的重点信息。

【例】 (04-1-Passage Two)

【预览选项】	【预测信息】
14. [A] Coca Cola. [B] Sausage. [C] Milk. [D] Fried chicken. 15. [A] He has had thirteen decayed teeth. [B] He doesn't have a single decayed tooth. [C] He has fewer decayed teeth than other people of his age. [D] He never had a single tooth pulled out before he was fifty. 16. [A] Brush your teeth right before you go to bed in the evening. [B] Have as few of your teeth pulled out as possible. [C] Have your teeth X-rayed at regular intervals. [D] Clean your teeth shortly after eating.	由15、16题各选项内容可推测本文的主题应该是关于牙齿保健的。 14.选项都是食物或饮料,结合对文章主题的分析,本题很可能是问哪种东西对牙齿有害。根据常识,四种食物或饮料中 Coca Cola 最容易伤害牙齿,因为其含糖量较高,故[A] 为答案的可能性较大。 15.选项表明本题考查的是某人的牙齿状况(是否有蛀牙)。[A]、[B]、[C] 都是关于蛀牙的问题,[D]则是关于拔牙的问题,故可初步排除。 16.选项表明本题考查的是保护牙齿的正确方法。根据对前两题的分析可推知,本题很可能是关于预防蛀牙的方法,并且很可能与饮食有关。因此[B]、[C] 为答案的可能性较小;而[A]、[D] 为答案的可能性较大。

【听音验证】

How many teeth have you had filled in the past 2 years? If you follow the advice of Dr. Forstic, you may be able to reduce the number of your visit to a dentist. Dr. Forstic conducted a two-year survey to find out how to prevent or reduce dental decay. 946 students took part in the experiment. 523 students cleaned their teeth within 10 minutes of eating. When possible, they used toothbrush. When this was impossible, they washed their mouth thoroughly with water. The remaining 423 students merely cleaned their teeth when they went to bed and when they got up in the morning. All the students had their teeth X-rayed at the end of the first and second years. At the end of the first year, the night-and-morning group had three times as many decayed teeth as the clean-after-each-meal group. At the end of the second year, the latter group had 53% fewer decayed teeth than the former group. [15] Dr. Forstic has cleaned his teeth after every meal for 13 years, and has not had a single decayed tooth. [14] He pointed out that sugar is a major agent in dental decay, particularly the sugar in sweets, cakes and soft drinks. Ideally, [16] you should keep a toothbrush in your pocket and use it immediately after you have finished eating. When this is impractical, you can at least make sure that you have a drink of water and let the water through your teeth, to force out any particles of food. Seven out of ten people lose at least half their teeth by the time they are fifty. Many have a complete set of false teeth by that time. In any case, neither toothache nor a visit to a dentist is very pleasant. So, it is worthwhile making an effort to keep your own teeth as long as possible. The main preventive agent is simply water.

【答案解析】

14. According to the passage, what type of food or drink is most likely to cause dental decay?

【解析】选[A]。细节题。根据文中 sugar is a major agent in dental decay, particularly the sugar in sweets, cakes and soft drinks. 可知 sugar, 尤其是 sweets(甜点)、cake 和 soft drinks(软饮料)中含有的 sugar, 是引起蛀牙的一个 main agent(主要原因), 而 Coca Cola 就属于 soft drinks 的一种, 故答案为[A]。注意表示强调的副词 particularly。

15. What does the passage tell us about the condition of Doctor Forstic's teeth?

【解析】选[B]。细节题。根据文中的 Dr. Forstic has cleaned his teeth after every meal for 13 years, and has not had a single decayed tooth 可知 Dr. Forstic 13 年来每次饭后都会 clean his teeth, 因此 not had a single decayed tooth(没有一颗蛀牙), 故答案为[B]。注意本题是在并列关系处命题。

16. What does Doctor Forstic suggest to prevent dental decay?

【解析】选[D]。细节题。根据文中的 you should keep a toothbrush in your pocket and use it immediately after you have finished eating 可知 Doctor Forstic 认为 clean your teeth shortly after eating(饭后保持牙齿的清洁)是防止蛀牙的有效方法, 故答案为[D]。注意本题也是在并列关系处命题。

Exercise

即讲即练

🎧 边听边记

Passage One

1. [A] Adults.　[B] Juveniles.
   [C] Ill people.　[D] Crazy people.
2. [A] They are not given proper treatment.　[B] They refused to see any strangers.
   [C] They are dangerous to society.　[D] They are protected perfectly.
3. [A] Other's consideration.　[B] Careful listening.
   [C] Other's well-wishing.　[D] Proper treatment.

Passage Two

4. [A] Radio.　[B] Newspaper.
   [C] TV.　[D] Magazine.
5. [A] By Internet.　[B] By tape-recorders.
   [C] By teleprinters.　[D] By electric wave.
6. [A] To be natural.　[B] To be interesting.
   [C] To be vivid.　[D] To be abstract.

【答案与解析】

Passage One

【听力原文】

Dr. Linda A. Teplin, professor of psychiatry and behavioral sciences, presented research about young people with mental disorders in the juvenile justice system. Dr. Teplin has spent two decades studying adults with mental illnesses. [1] She turned her research attention to juveniles because it is a natural extension of her previous work, but more importantly, because she is worried that mentally ill youths—like their adult counterparts—are receiving prison terms without benefit of treatment.

Using research as the sword, [2] Dr. Teplin spoke of striking a blow against public policies that imprison, rather than treat, young people with mental disorders. The Northwestern Juvenile Project, headed by Dr. Teplin, is the first large study of the mental health of delinquent youths. The project is following the paths of 1,830 juveniles in the Cook County Detention Center. [3] Many of the participants in the study are eager to be involved, saying "You don't have to pay me for the interview. It's just enough that you listen to me." Teplin's staff sends them birthday cards and receives thank-you notes in return. One juvenile wrote, "Thank you for remembering my birthday. You were the only person who did."

The data from the study thus paint a gloomy picture: two-thirds of the detainees have tested positive for one drug or more; twenty-five of the participants have died, all violently; and mood disorders run rampant. Twenty-two percent of the female participants suffer from major depression—an extremely high rate. Two-thirds of the participants with an affective disorder also abuse alcohol or drugs. Clearly, many of these young people have very serious problems and have been failed by the treatment system.

【答案解析】

1. Who is the new study object of Dr. Teplin's research?

【解析】选[B]。细节题。文中明确提到 Dr. Teplin 把她的研究重心从 adults with mental illness 上转到了 juveniles 上，由此可知 Dr. Teplin 的新研究对象是 juvenilves(青少年)。

2. What can we learn about juveniles with mental disorders?

【解析】选[A]。细节题。文中提到 Dr. Teplin 抨击了 public policies，因为这些政策只是把 young people with mental disorders(精神上有问题的年轻人)关起来，却没有对他们进行治疗(treat)，也就是说他们没有得到 proper treatment。

3. What do the participants in Dr. Teplin's study of the mental health of delinquent youths really need?

【解析】选[B]。细节题。由文中参与者话中的 You don't have to pay me for the interview. It's just enough that you listen to me 可知，这些参与者最渴求的是别人能够听他们说话，即别人对他们的 listening(倾听)。

Passage Two

【听力原文】

Reading newspapers, listening to the radio or watching television are the three methods of communication that bring daily news to millions of people everywhere. They are known as the mass media.

The main job of a newspaper is to inform us what is going on in the world. [4] Newspapers are probably the least entertaining of the media, but the most informative. The news is gathered by reporters. The editor of a newspaper decides which items of news to be published and which page they will appear on. It is the editor's job to make sure that the piece is not too long, the story is interesting and people will be able to understand it.

TV and radio stations also have reporters. They interview people and their interviews are filmed. The news editor decides to use which pieces of film in the television news. Radio interviews are tape-recorded. An important source of world news for the broadcasting media is news agencies. There are several

【答案解析】

4. What is the least entertaining yet the most informative among the mass media according to the passage?

【解析】选[B]。细节题。短文开头介绍了三种获得信息的方法：reading newspapers, listening to the radio 和 watching television。在介绍第一种大众传播媒介 newspapers 时，文中明确提到报纸是 the least entertaining of the media, but the most informative。

5. How do the news agencies' headquarters send their reports overseas according to the passage?

【解析】选[C]。细节题。短文在介绍 news agencies(新闻社)如何收集及传播信息时说到，所有记者收集到的新闻都集中在 news agencies' head-quartersl(新闻社总部)，然后由总部 by teleprinters(经由电传打字机)将新闻传送到世界各国。

worldwide news agencies which employ correspondents in different places all over the world to make reports. [5] These reports are gathered at the agencies' headquarters and then sent overseas by teleprinters. [6] One of the most important jobs of the news editors at the radio and TV stations is re-writing these reports so that they sound natural when the news reader reads them over the air.

6. What do the editors at the radio and TV station want the reports to be by rewriting them?

【解析】选[A]。细节题。短文结尾处提到电台编辑的一项最重要的工作就是 rewriting 新闻，以使这些新闻听起来 natural(自然)，由此可知使新闻听起来 natural 正是编辑们重新写新闻的目的。

Chapter 6

短文理解巅峰练习

Exercise 1

边听边记

Passage One

26. [A] Because it is their tradition.
    [B] Because it contains certain chemicals.
    [C] Because a lot of important business is conducted in teahouses.
    [D] Because it can dispel the heat and bring on an instant coolness.

27. [A] They can't live without tea for a single day.
    [B] They almost don't drink tea.
    [C] They drink tea every three days.
    [D] They drink tea only a time in one day.

28. [A] Drink other refreshments instead of tea.
    [B] Don't drink tea constantly.
    [C] Don't drink over-strong tea.
    [D] Realize the negative effects of over-strong tea.

Passage Two

29. [A] The custom of wedding in Britain.
    [B] The arrangement of wedding in Britain.
    [C] The announcement of wedding in Britain.
    [D] The entertainment of wedding in Britain.

30. [A] Long white dresses.   [B] White suits.
    [C] Long dresses in attractive colors.   [D] Formal suits.

31. [A] In a restaurant.   [B] In a local hall.
    [C] In church.   [D] In the bride's home.

Passage Three

32. [A] It is usually moderate in length.
    [B] It is a style of immediate impact and rapid persuasion.
    [C] It is easily accepted by the audience.
    [D] It is what the advertisers and audience care about.

33. [A] The sender of information.
    [B] The collector of money.
    [C] The beneficiary of advertising.
    [D] The producer of information.

34. [A] It should be abstract, reasonable and short in length.
    [B] It should be accurate, definite, recognizable and moderate in length.
    [C] It should be easy, emotional and moving.
    [D] It should be equivocal, motivated and ambitious.

35. [A] Exhibition.   [B] Movie.
    [C] Neon lights.   [D] Broadcasts.

Exercise 2

Passage One

26. [A] He killed them.
    [B] He chased them away from his territory.
    [C] He made them become his servants.
    [D] He intimidated them.

27. [A] Because she loves him for a long time.
    [B] Because she wants to protect her people.
    [C] Because she is afraid of him.
    [D] Because she was forced by her parents.

28. [A] Her stone necklace.
    [B] Her ring.
    [C] Her earring.
    [D] Her hairpin.

Passage Two

29. [A] An hour a week.
    [B] An hour a day.
    [C] Eight hours a week.
    [D] Eight hours a day.

30. [A] Online questionnaires and offline interviews.
    [B] Online chatting and in-person interview.
    [C] Communication and interview.
    [D] Examination and questionnaires.

31. [A] Online chatting.
    [B] Online gaming.
    [C] E-mail.
    [D] Online education.

Passage Three

32. [A] How to keep healthy.
    [B] How to keep clean.
    [C] How to exercise.
    [D] How to be wealthy.

33. [A] It can increase the flow of the bloodstream and circulation.
    [B] It can improve the nourishment of the body cells.
    [C] It can make people feel energetic.
    [D] It can keep people slim.

34. [A] They are not as good as regular meals for health.
    [B] They contain more nutrients.
    [C] They are not suggested by the doctors.
    [D] They are beneficial to people.

35. [A] Relaxation and periods of rest.
    [B] Intense exercise.
    [C] Special care and training.
    [D] Opportunity to connect with others.

答案与解析

Exercise 1

Passage One

【听力原文】

Tea has been one of the daily necessities in China since time immemorial. Countless numbers of people like to have their after-meal cup of tea.

[26] In the summer or in warm climates, tea seems to dispel the heat and bring on an instant coolness together with a feeling of relaxation. For this reason, teahouses abound in towns and market villages in Southern China provide elderly retirees with a place to meet and chat over a cup of tea.

Medically, tea may help to break down meat and fat and thus promote digestion. It is, therefore, of special importance to people who live mainly on meat, like many of the ethnic minorities in China. A popular proverb among them says, [27] "Rather go without salt for three days than without tea for a single day."

Tea is also rich in various vitamins and, for smokers, it helps to discharge nicotine from the system. After drinking alcohol, strong tea may prove to be a sobering pick-me-up. The above, however, does not go to say that the stronger the tea, the more advantages it will yield. Too much tannic acid will affect the secretion of the gastric juice, irritate the membrane of the stomach and cause indigestion. Constant drinking of over-strong tea may induce heart and blood-pressure disorders in some people, reduce the milk of a breast-feeding mother, and put a brown color on the teeth of young people. [28] It is not difficult to get rid of these undesirable effects. Just don't make your tea too strong.

【答案解析】

26. Why do people in warm areas like to drink tea?

【解析】选[D]。细节题。文中提到,在夏天或在温暖的天气里,茶可以 dispel the heat and bring on an instant coolness together with a feeling of relaxation(起到驱热、清凉的作用并且可以使人放松),而这也正是生活在 warm areas 的人们喜欢喝茶的原因。

27. What does tea mean to people of some ethnic minorities in China?

【解析】选[A]。推断题。文中提到,中国一些少数民族有这样一个谚语 Rather go without salt for three days than without tea for a single day,该谚语的意思是人们可以三天不吃盐,但是却一天也离不开茶,即 people can't live without tea for a single day。

28. What is the speaker's advice to avoid the negative effect of over-strong tea?

【解析】选[C]。细节题。文中结尾处提到要想 get rid of these undesirable effects(消除浓茶带来的负面影响)很简单,只要你 don't make your tea too strong(不把茶泡得太浓)就可以了,言外之意就是 don't drink over-strong tea(不要喝太浓的茶)。

Passage Two

【听力原文】

[29①]In Britain, the arrangements for inviting and entertaining guests at a wedding are usually the responsibility of the bride's family. In most cases, it is mainly friends and relatives of both families who are invited. It is, however, the bride's mother who has the job of sending out the formal printed invitation cards.

[29②] In the case of a church wedding, the vicar of each parish in which the bride and bridegroom live is normally informed about a month in advance of the ceremony so that an announcement of the coming wedding can be made in church on each of three Sundays before it takes place. Anyone who may know of an existing marriage of either partner is ordered to give information about it, though this means of avoiding bigamy. Often up to a hundred or more people attend the religious service and [30] the bride usually wears a traditional long white dress and veil, while her bridesmaids, wear long dresses in attractive colors.

[29③] The reception which follows may be held in a restau-

【答案解析】

29. What is the passage mainly about?

【解析】选[A]。主旨题。文中依次介绍了英国的 the arrangements for inviting and entertaining guests at a wedding(邀请朋友参加婚礼或在婚礼上招待客人的安排)、举办婚礼的场所、新婚人穿的服装及在婚礼招待宴席上,如何招待客人等,用一句话概括就是 the custom of wedding in Britain(英国的婚礼习俗)。

30. What do the bride's bridesmaids usually wear at a wedding?

【解析】选[C]。细节题。文中明确提到,在婚礼上,新娘通常会 wears a traditional long white dress and veil(穿传统的白色长裙,带着面纱),而她的 bridesmaids(女傧相)通常会 wear long dresses in attractive colors(穿颜色鲜艳的长裙)。

rant, a local hall or, [31] when there are few guests, in the bride's own home. Refreshments are provided, and a special iced wedding-cake is cut, usually to the accompaniment of speeches and distributed to the guests. At some point in the celebration, the bride goes off to change into everyday clothes and then leaves the party with her husband to go on their honeymoon.

31. Where is the reception probably held if there are few guests?

【解析】选[D]。细节题。短文结尾处明确提到婚礼招待宴席可能会在 restaurant 和 local hall 举行，但如果客人较少，招待宴席可能会在 the bride's own home 举行。

Passage Three

【听力原文】

The American Marketing Association defines advertising as "the non-personal communication of information usually paid for and usually persuasive in nature about products, services or ideas by identified sponsors through the various media." However, whatever the marketing strategies advertising takes, language is the main carrier of the message. [32] The advertising language is a style of immediate impact and rapid persuasion.

According to the definition of advertising, most of the advertisements should have the following components.

Firstly, [33] the advertiser is the sender of information, and all the advertising activities should be consistent with the purpose and willingness of the advertiser. Therefore, the advertiser is the main body of advertising. There are two features of an advertiser: firstly, it's easy for the target audience to recognize the company and the products, which will promote the sale of its products; secondly, it will establish a high reputation for the group, the enterprise, or the individual so that the consumer will trust the brand.

Secondly, the advertising fees are paid by the advertiser whether it's operated by itself or other agencies. Because advertising is a kind of marketing action, an advertiser has to pay for its advertisement.

Thirdly, advertising information is the principal content an advertisement wants to disseminate. Advertising is a series of planned actions, so the information in advertisements should be aimed at certain target markets and consumers and should avoid aimlessness. [34] The dissemination of information should be accurate, definite, recognizable and moderate in length.

Lastly, different medias including newspapers, magazines, broadcasts, TV programs, billboards and mail are all the means of dissemination of advertising. [35] The newspapers, magazines, broadcasts and TV are called the four main medias of advertising. Different kinds of media have different features, disseminating areas, target audiences and speeds.

【答案解析】

32. What is the advertising language like?

【解析】选[B]。细节题。文中提到语言是广告信息的载体，advertising language（广告用语）是 a style of immediate impact and rapid persuasion（一种产生即时影响和快速劝服效果的语言形式。

33. What role does the advertiser play in advertising?

【解析】选[A]。细节题。文中提到advertisements 有四个组成部分，其中在介绍第一个组成部分时提到 the advertiser（广告商）是 the sender of information（信息的发送者）。

34. What are the characteristics of the standard dissemination of information?

【解析】选[B]。细节题。文中在介绍advertisements 的第三个组成部分时明确提到 the dissemination of information（信息的传播）的特点应该是 accurate, definite, recognizable and moderate in length。

35. Which of the following medias is one of the four main medias of advertising?

【解析】选[D]。细节题。文中在介绍advertisements 的组成部分时提到newspapers, magazines, broadcasts 和 TV 是广告的四大主要传播媒介，broadcasts 属于其中一种。

Exercise 2

Passage One

【听力原文】

When the earth was long and flat, and the moon was cold and plain, there lived a spirit named Obweji. Obweji was very powerful because he was the Spirit of the Sky. He owned the universe and the

26. How did Obweji treat those people who are against his will?

【解析】选[A]。细节题。文中提到当 Obweji

great flat earth. He had many servants on Earth, and they were all a-fraid of him and did his bidding.

On Earth there was a beautiful maiden named Pateka. Her hair was the color of a raven's wing, and her eyes sparkled like fire. She was kind and respectful to her people, and she loved the sun.

One day, Obweji came down to Pateka's village to choose a bride. [26] All of the people were obligated to give forth their daughters, and the families who didn't were killed. When Obweji saw Pateka, he chose her right away because of her great beauty. [27] Pateka cried and cried but went with him for the sake of her people.

She cried for many nights, and the only thing that pleased her was staring into the sun for many hours. Obweji was sorry, but very mad at Pateka for being disrespectful to him.

One night, Pateka told Obweji, "I am leaving you because you are cruel to my people!" The words shocked Obweji, and he became furious at her. He grabbed her stone necklace from her neck. But Pateka was too quick and darted away from him. [28] He held the broken necklace as she ran away, never to be seen again.

Where is Pateka? She ran to the spirit of the sun and married him. They were very happy and had many children. They named them—Venus, Mercury, Mars, Jupiter, Saturn, Uranus, Pluto and Neptune. They lived happily ever after.

去 Pateka 所住的村庄挑选新娘的时候，所有的人都要把自己的女儿送出来供他挑选，如果有的家庭 who didn't (不愿意把女儿送出来)，他们就会被 killed，也就是说如果有人违背了 Obweji 的意愿，Obweji 就会 killed them。

27. Why did Pateka finally agree to marry Obweji?

【解析】选[B]。推断题。文中提到 Pateka 被 Obweji 选为新娘时十分伤心，但最后 for the sake of her people (为了她的人民)，她还是跟着他走了，由此可推断 Pateka 最终同意嫁给 Obweji 是为了 protect her people (保护她的人民)。

28. What was left when Pateka run away from Obweji?

【解析】选[A]。细节题。文中提到，当 Pateka 告诉 Obweji 她要离开他时，Obweji 非常气愤，他抓住了 Pateka 的 stone necklace 试图制服 Pateka，但是 Pateka 还是巧妙地逃脱了，只是她的 stone necklace 却被 Obweji 抓住了。

Passage Two

【听力原文】

According to a report released yesterday by the China Internet Network Information Center, the number of Internet users in China at the end of June rose 28 percent from a year ago to hit 87 million. The Internet users now account for 6.7 percent of the total population of the world. It is, however, still below the world's average rate of 12.2 percent and is even lower compared to the rate in developed countries, which ranges from 63 percent in Canada to 77 percent in Sweden.

[29] The report defines a Chinese citizen who uses the Internet for at least an hour a week as an Internet user. The figure didn't include users in Macau, Hong Kong and Taiwan. [30] The survey, which is conducted through online questionnaires and offline interviews, said the error margin of the online population is 5 percent.

According to the report of the nation's Ministry of Information Industry, [31] the percentage using e-mail slipped from 88.4 percent to 84.3 percent, but it still remained at the top of the frequently used services provided on the Internet. Meanwhile, the report, which is published every six months, also found that more people placed online chatting, online gaming and online education into their often-used services.

The report also said the environment of China's e-commerce is improving as over half of the respondents plan to do online shopping within the next year. The percentage of those who use online banking for payment also continued to grow and is now 13 percent more than those paying cash on delivery for the goods they bought online, the report said.

【答案解析】

29. How long a Chinese person uses Internet can be defined as an Internet user, according to the report?

【解析】选[A]。细节题。文中提到 the report 对 Internet user 的定义是 a Chinese citizen who uses the Internet for at least an hour a week (每周至少能用一个小时网络的中国公民)，也就是说只要能使用网络至少 an hour a week 就可以被称为 Internet user。

30. How is the survey on Internet users conducted?

【解析】选[A]。细节题。文中明确提到对上网人数的调查是通过 online questionnaires 和 offline interview 进行的。

31. What service on Internet is most frequently used?

【解析】选[C]。细节题。文中提到根据报告显示使用 e-mail 的人数由 88.4% 下降到 84.3%，但仍然还是 at the top of the frequently used services provided on the Internet (使用频率最高的网上服务)。

Passage Three

【听力原文】	【答案解析】
[32①] Health is the most precious possession a man can have. You may be very rich, have plenty of friends, have a good education, and be very powerful—but if you are not healthy, you cannot enjoy what you have. This is the reason for the saying "Health is wealth."	32. What is the topic of the passage? 【解析】选[A]。主旨题。短文一开头就提出一种观点 Health is the most precious possession a man can have(健康是人类最宝贵的财富),而下文中的 The first rule for stay healthy …, Another health rule is …, A balanced diet is necessary to good health 及 The last health requirement 都是在讲如何保持健康,由此可判断本文的主题是 How to keep healthy。
[32②] The first rule for staying healthy is to observe cleanliness. A daily bath or wash will help keep your body clean and pleasant smelling. With cleanliness goes clean clothes. Food must be served on clean plates and eaten in clean surroundings. Fresh air and adequate sunshine help keep our body healthy. We often hear the saying, "open wide the windows and let the air and sunshine come in."	33. What can exercise do to our body, according to the passage? 【解析】选[A]。细节题。文中在提到第二个保持健康的方法时说到 Exercise increases the flow of the bloodstream and … circulation(锻炼身体能增强血液循环),而 improve the nourishment of the body cells 是 the flow of the bloodstream 和 circulation 增强后带来的影响。
[32③] Another health rule is to exercise systematically. [33] Exercise increases the flow of the bloodstream and, therefore, of circulation. This in turn improves the nourishment of the body cells, increases the elimination of waste products, strengthens the heart, and stimulates the liver, kidneys, and spleen.	34. How does the speaker think of snacks? 【解析】选[A]。细节题。文中在提到第三个保持健康的方法时说到 Regardless of the good nutrients they contain, regular meals are better for health than snacks eaten frequently,言外之意就是说对健康而言 snacks 不如 regular meals 好。
[32④] A balanced diet is necessary to good health. A person should know that fresh fruits and vegetables, as well as meat, fish, eggs, and milk, help keep the body strong. Plenty of liquids are important too. Doctors tell us that we should drink around eight glasses of water a day. [34] Regardless of the good nutrients they contain, regular meals are better for health than snacks eaten frequently. Rest and sleep restore the body energy. [35] Relaxation and periods of rest—perhaps a nap in addition to eight hours of sleep are especially needed by a growing boy or girl.	35. What does a growing child need besides nutrition? 【解析】选[A]。细节题。文中在提到第三个保持健康的方法时说到 Relaxation and periods of rest … are especially needed by a growing boy or girl,即成长中的孩子特别需要 relaxation 和 periods of rest。
[32⑤] The last health requirement is a sound mind. Negative emotions like fear, anger, worry, or hate, especially in large doses, cause ill health.	

Chapter 7

短文听写巅峰讲座

第 七 章

短文听写是大学英语六级听力考试中唯一的主观题型,包括对听力材料的理解能力(即"听")和一定的书面表达能力(即"写")两方面的测试。六级短文听写的长度一般在 240—260 词之间,包括 8 个单词填空和 3 个句子填空。

短文一共朗读三遍。第一遍朗读时,中间没有停顿,供考生听懂全文内容;第二遍朗读时,单词填空处没有停顿,句子填空处大约有 50—60 秒的停顿时间,要求考生把听到的内容填入空内;第三遍朗读与第一遍朗读一样,中间没有停顿,供考生核对所填内容。

Lecture 1　第一讲　10 大单词填空考查点

单词填空主要集中在名词、动词和形容词三种词性的考查上,偶尔也会涉及到副词。

一、动词的考查重点

动词主要考查其单复数形式、时态和语态以及某些特殊形式的过去式和过去分词,以及情态动词、虚拟语气中动词的正确形式。

【例1】　　　　　　　　　　　　　　　　　　　　　　　　　　　　　　　　(07-6-36)

> As nurses, we **are** (36) <u>licensed</u> **to** provide nursing care only.（系动词 are 和不定式 to 提示所填词应为动词的过去分词形式）

【例2】　　　　　　　　　　　　　　　　　　　　　　　　　　　　　　　　(05-6-S6)

> If the parents **can** (S6) <u>afford</u> **it**, each child will have his or her own bedroom.（情态动词 can 和代词 it 提示所填同应为动词原形）

二、名词的考查重点

名词主要考查单复数问题、表示数量的名词、一些单复数同形的名词,以及一些常见的名词后缀。

要注意根据空格前面的修饰词和后面的谓语动词等线索来判断名词的单复数形式。像 percent, percentage, million, billion 等表示数字的名词与具体数量连用时,一般不用复数形式。

【例3】　　　　　　　　　　　　　　　　　　　　　　　　　　　　　　　　(07-6-42)

> …we have a legal (42) <u>responsibility</u> to question that order or refuse to carry it out.（注意名词后缀-lity）

【例4】　　　　　　　　　　　　　　　　　　　　　　　　　　　　　　　　(99-6-S3)

> Mr. Clinton will ask Congress this coming week for nearly **three** (S3) billion **dollars** to fund a five-year program called "America Reads".（数词 three 和表示金钱的名词 dollars 提示所填词应为表示数量的名词）

三、形容词的考查重点

形容词主要考查近音易混形容词、分词演化来的形容词、与介词搭配使用的形容词以及带有前缀后缀的形容词。

【例5】　　　　　　　　　　　　　　　　　　　　　　　　　　　　　　　　(07-6-41)

> …we feel that a physician's order is (41) <u>inappropriate</u> or unsafe, …（注意否定前缀-in）

【例 6】 (710 分样卷-40)

The second charge stemmed from his association with numerous young men who came to Athens from all over the (40) civilized world to study under him. (注意由 civilize 分词演化来的形容词 civilized 意为"文明的")

四、副词的考查重点

副词主要考查用于说明动词发生时的情形或状态的情状副词,以-ly 结尾的副词居多。

【例 7】 (01-1-S2)

You are (S2) constantly *harnessing* and consuming energy through the intricate (S3) mechanism of your body in order to remain in energy balance. (副词 constantly 修饰动词 harnessing)

五、对易混词的考查

英语中存在很多近音异义词或近形异义词,这些词会对听力理解形成很大的障碍,尤其在听写时,更会对考生造成比较大的干扰,影响考生的判断。

【例 8】 (07-6-38)

We provide health teaching, (38) assess physical as well as emotional problems, … (assess 很容易误写成 access)

【例 9】 (99-6-S6)

…it would also give (S6) grants to help parents help children read by the third grade, or about age eight. (grants 很容易误写成 grounds)

六、对较难单词拼写的考查

六级短文听写经常会涉及一些拼写较复杂的单词,像拼写中含有前缀后缀,或含有重复字母的词汇等,并且这类难词多为名词或形容词。

【例 10】 (07-6-41)

…we feel that a physician's order is (41) inappropriate or unsafe, … (注意前缀-in)

【例 11】 (99-6-S4,S5)

The program would fund the (S4) coordination efforts of 20 thousand reading (S5) specialists and it would… (注意前缀 co-、后缀-tion 和 -ist)

七、对习惯搭配的考查

习惯搭配也是六级短文听写的一个考查点,常见的有形容词与介词、动词与介词、名词与介词、名词与名词的搭配等。

【例 12】 (07-6-40)

If, *in any* (40) circumstance, we feel that a physician's order is (41) inappropriate or unsafe. (in any circumstance 是固定短语,意为"在任何情况下")

【例 13】 (710 分样卷-39)

The second charge stemmed from his (39) association *with* numerous young men who came to Athens from all over the civilized world to study under him. (association 后面常接介词 with)

八、对并列、排比或列举处的考查

常见的并列连接词有 and, as well as, or, together with, along with, coupled with, with 等。

【例 14】 (07-6-38, 39)

We *provide* health teaching, (38) assess physical as well as emotional problems, (39) coordinate patient-related services, *and make* all of our nursing decisions based upon what is best or suitable for the patient. (所填词与 provide, make 是并列的谓语动词)

【例15】

> If, in any (40) circumstance, we feel that a physician's order is (41) inappropriate ***or unsafe***, we have a legal responsibility to question that order or refuse to carry it out. （所填词与 unsafe 并列充当表语）

九、对转折等其他逻辑关系的考查

常见的转折连接词有 but, however, whereas, while, instead 等。

【例16】

> Anyone may go there and read anything in the collection. ***But*** no one is (S5) permitted to take books out of the building. （but 前说"anyone 都可以…"，后面应该说"anyone 都不可以…"）

十、对上下文照应或复现的考查

所填词前后句中经常会有与其相照应的词或短语，或是该词的近义或反义复现，这也是短文听写重点考查的内容之一。

【例17】

> Closely (S2) associated with the value they ***place on*** individualism is the importance Americans (S3) assign to privacy. Americans assume that people "need some time to themselves" or "some time alone" to think about things or … （assign to 是该句前面 place on 的近义复现）

【例18】

> The program would ***fund*** the coordination efforts of 20 thousand reading specialists and it would also give (S6) grants to help parents help children read by the third grade, or about age eight. （give grants to 是前面句中 fund 一词的近义复现）

Exercise　　　　　　　　　　即讲即练　　　　　　🎧 边听边记

If you want to spark a heated debate at a dinner party, bring up the (S1)_____ of genetically modified foods. For many people, the concept of genetically altered, high-tech crop production raises all kinds of environmental, health, safety and (S2)_____ questions. Particularly in countries with long agrarian traditions the idea seems against nature.

In fact, genetically modified foods are already very much a part of our lives. At present, a third of the corn and more than half the (S3)_____ and cotton grown in the U. S. are the product of biotechnology, according to the Department of Agriculture. More than 65 million acres of genetically modified crops are being planted in the U. S.

Yet there are clearly some very real issues that need to be resolved. Like any new product entering the food chain, genetically modified foods must be subjected to strict testing. In wealthy countries, the debate about biotech is (S4)_____ by the fact that we have a full range of foods to choose from and a supply that far (S5)_____ our needs. In developing countries desperate to feed fast-growing and (S6)_____ populations, the issue is simpler and much more urgent: Do the benefits of biotech outweigh the risks?

The (S7)_____ on population growth and hunger are disturbing. The U. N. estimates that nearly 800 million people around the world have (S8)_____. The effects are shocking. About 400 million women of (S9)_____ age are lacking in iron, which means their babies are (S10)_____ to various birth defects. As many as 100 million children suffer from lack of vitamin A, a leading cause of blindness.

【答案与解析】

【听力原文】	【答案解析】

【听力原文】

　　If you want to spark a heated debate at a dinner party, bring up the (S1) topic of genetically modified foods. For many people, the concept of genetically altered, high-tech crop production raises all kinds of environmental, health, safety and (S2) ethical questions. Particularly in countries with long agrarian traditions the idea seems against nature.

　　In fact, genetically modified foods are already very much a part of our lives. At present, a third of the corn and more than half the (S3) soybeans and cotton grown in the U. S. are the product of biotechnology, according to the Department of Agriculture. More than 65 million acres of genetically modified crops are being planted in the U. S.

　　Yet there are clearly some very real issues that need to be resolved. Like any new product entering the food chain, genetically modified foods must be subjected to strict testing. In wealthy countries, the debate about biotech is (S4) tempered by the fact that we have a full range of foods to choose from and a supply that far (S5) exceeds our needs. In developing countries desperate to feed fast-growing and (S6) underfed populations, the issue is simpler and much more urgent: Do the benefits of biotech outweigh the risks?

　　The (S7) statistics on population growth and hunger are disturbing. The U.N. estimates that nearly 800 million people around the world have (S8) malnutrition. The effects are shocking. About 400 million women of (S9) childbearing age are lacking in iron, which means their babies are (S10) exposed to various birth defects. As many as 100 million children suffer from lack of vitamin A, a leading cause of blindness.

【答案解析】

S1. 空前的定冠词 the 和空后的介词 of 提示所填词应为名词。本句条件状语中的 debate(辩论)提示所填词应该表示"话题,主题"的含义。topic 意为"话题,主题"。

S2. 空前的连词 and 和空后的名词 questions 提示所填词应与 environmental, health, safety 在词性及语义上构成并列关系,共同修饰 questions, 故所填词应为形容词或名词。ethical 意为"民族的"。

S3. 空前的定冠词 the 和空后的连词 and 提示所填词应为名词,与 cotton 构成并列关系,故所填词很可能是某种农作物。soybeans 意为"大豆"。

S4. 空前的系动词 is 和空后的介词 by 提示所填词应为动词的过去分词。tempered 意为"缓解"。

S5. 分析句子结构及主句时态可知,所填词应为动词的第三人称单数形式。由 we have a full range of food to choose from 以及连词 and 可知本句主要讲发达国家的优势,所以就常理而言,在发达国家供应大于需求,故所填词很可能表示"超过,大于,多于"的含义。exceeds 意为"超过,多于"。

S6. 空前的连词 and 提示所填词应与 fast-growing 构成并列关系,故所填词应为形容词。由后面的 hunger, lacking in iron 及 lack of vitamin A 可知,在发展中国家人们面临着饥饿以及营养不良等问题,故所填词应表示"营养不良,吃的不饱"的含义。underfed 意为"营养不良的,吃的不饱的"。

S7. 分析句子结构可知所填词应为名词,在句中作主语。下文中的数字 800 million 及 400 million 均表明所填词的含义应与"数字"有所联系。statistics 意为"统计数字"。

S8. 根据上下文可推测空前的 have 为实义动词,故所填词应为名词。本段中的 hunger, lacking in iron 及 lack of vitamin A 均说明世界上有 800 million 人吃不饱或者营养不良,故所填词可能表达"营养不良"的含义。malnutrition 意为"营养不良"。

S9. 空前的介词 of 和空后的名词 age 提示所填词应为名词或形容词。定语从句中的 their babies 提示所填词应与"怀孕"有关。childbearing 意为"分娩"。

S10. 空前的系动词 are 提示所填词应为形容词或动词的分词形式,且能与介词 to 搭配。exposed 意为"面临"。

Lecture 2　第二讲　7 大句子填空设题处

　　句子填空要求考生写出所空句子的原文或其要点。分析历年真题得知,六级短文听写考查的句子结构一般都比较复杂,通常为并列句或主从复合句,其长度在 12—30 个单词之间,平均长度约为 18 个单词。句子填空常见的设题处有:

一、与主题密切相关的细节内容

　　段落的主题一般已给出,要求同学们补全支撑细节。

【例1】 (05-6-S10)

Americans' attitudes about privacy can be hard for foreigners to understand. (S10) American's houses, yards, and even their offices can seem open and inviting. Yet, in the minds of Americans, there are boundaries that other people are simply not supposed to cross. (空格前面一句是该段的主题句,紧接着的一句显然应该用来说明这一主题)

二、段落主题句或结论句

全文中概括性的结论或主题句一般情况下出现在文章开头或末尾,而段落的概括性的结论或主题句多出现在段首或段尾。

【例2】 (05-6-S9)

Americans assume that (S9) people will have their private thoughts that might never be shared with anyone. Doctors, lawyers, psychologists, and others have rules governing "confidentiality" … (所填句为该段的主题句,后面的部分是对该句的进一步说明)

三、并列、转折结构处

这类句子中往往含有 and, as well as, but, yet 等标志性的词语。

【例3】 (01-1-S8)

The term body image refers to the mental image we have of our own physical appearance, and (S8) it can be influenced by a variety of factors, including how much we weigh, or how that weight is distributed. (and 提示所填内容的主题与前面一致,应该都是有关"body image"的情况)

四、比较或对比处

句子由 whereas, while 等表示对比含义的连词连接,或是句中含有 as…as, than 等引出的比较结构,或是句中含有形容词或副词的比较级或最高级。

【例4】 (710分样卷-45)

Socrates (45) had the right to ask for a **less severe** penalty, and he probably could have persuaded the jury to change the verdict. (该句中包含比较级 less severe)

五、含有从句的句子

短文听写的句子很少有简单句,因此含有状语从句、同位语从句或定语从句的复合句往往是其命题重点。

【例5】 (05-6-S8)

Having one's own bedroom, even as an infant, fixes in a person *the notion that* (S8) she is entitled to a place of her own where she can be by herself, and keep her possessions. (该句为同位语从句)

六、含有非谓语动词短语或独立结构的句子

含有不定式、动名词、分词短语或是分词的独立结构的句子往往也是短文听写重点考查的句式。

【例6】 (01-1-S8)

The term body image refers to the mental image we have of our own physical appearance, and (S8) it can be influenced by a variety of factors, **including** how much you weigh or how that weight is distributed. (现在分词短语 including…在句中充当定语)

七、含有年代等数字的句子

含有数字(年代、增长或降低的数据、百分比、比分等)的句子也是短文听写中的一个考点,听的过程中注意做好笔记。

【例7】 (99-6-S10)

The president says many of the Philadelphia summit's corporate sponsors will recruit tutors. (S10) **Dozens of** colleges and universities are prepared to send **thousands of** their students in support of the program. (dozens of 和 thousands of 均为表示数字的短语)

Exercise　　　　　即讲即练　　　　　　　　🎧 边听边记

Nature has supplied every animal except man with some covering for his body such as fur, feathers, hair, or a thick hide. But man has nothing but (S1) _____ — though the earliest men may perhaps have been hairier than modern man.

It is only when we begin to think about it a little that we realize that clothes are worn (S2) _____. For instance, we wear clothes to some extent in order to decorate our-selves—to make ourselves, if possible, look more graceful than we are. Even (S3) _____ that they form a kind of decoration, and the material itself is of a kind and color that (S4) _____—though ideas about what looks nice change very much from time to time.

Besides decorating us, our clothes have to link us up with the people amongst whom we live. We feel uncomfortable if they do not "look right"—(S5) _____. Some-times, even in civilized countries, people wear some jewel of charm. These are (S6) _____, or because it is connected with their religious beliefs.

【答案与解析】

【听力原文】

Nature has supplied every animal except man with some covering for his body such as fur, feathers, hair, or a thick hide. But man has nothing but (S1) <u>a thin skin and for thousands of years human beings must have wandered about the world with no other covering</u>—though the earliest men may perhaps have been hairier than modern man.

It is only when we begin to think about it a little that we realize that clothes are worn (S2) <u>for a great many reasons that have nothing to do with the climate or with our need for warmth</u>. For in-stance, we wear clothes to some extent in order to decorate ourselves—to make ourselves, if possi-ble, look more graceful than we are. Even (S3) <u>the plainest clothes worn by civilized people have their buttons, collars and so forth arranged in such a way</u> that they form a kind of decoration, and the material itself is of a kind and color that (S4) <u>we think suits us, and is cut or arranged in a way that we think looks nice</u>—though ideas about what looks nice change very much from time to time.

Besides decorating us, our clothes have to link us up with the people amongst whom we live. We feel uncomfortable if they do not "look right"—(S5) <u>if they are not similar to those which other people of our age, sex, country and period are wearing</u>. Sometimes, even in civilized countries, people wear some jewel of charm. These are (S6) <u>because they believe that it will bring them luck or protect them from evil or illness</u>, or because it is connected with their religious beliefs.

【答案解析】

S1. 浏览整篇文章可知,本文主要讲的是服饰对人类的作用。文章第一句指出:除了人类自然赋予了各种动物遮盖物,本句空前的转折连词 but 提示所填句子应表示人类拥有动物身上所没有的东西。

【Main Points】a thin skin and for thousands of years **human** must have wandered **around** the world **without** other covering

S2. 下句中的 For instance 提示下句是对本句所说内容的举例说明,通过浏览文章可知,下句主要是讲人类穿衣服的目的或原因,由此可推断本句应该是概括说明人类穿衣服的目的或原因。

【Main Points】for **many** reasons **which** have nothing to do with the climate or **the** need for warmth

S3. 空前表递进关系的副词 Even 提示所填句子是对上句内容的进一步解释,也应是与 clothes 有关。

【Main Points】the **most common** clothes worn by civilized people have their buttons, collars **and so on** arranged in such a way

S4. 分析句子结构可知,所填句子的主语为 the material it-self,根据主语可以推断所填内容主要是与衣服的材料有关。

【Main Points】we think **fits** us and is cut or arranged in a way that we think **is** nice

S5. 空前破折号提示所填句子是对破折号前的内容进一步解释说明。破折号前的内容是讲如果人们的衣服看起来不合适,人们就会感到不自在,那么破折号后的内容就应该与穿衣不合适有关。

【Main Points】if they are not similar to those **clothes that** oth-er people **who are** of our age, sex, **period** and **country** are wearing

S6. 空后的连词 or 提示所填句子也应是由 because 引导的原因状语从句,说明人们 wear some jewel of charm 的原因。

【Main Points】because they **think** that it will bring **luck to them** or protect them from evil or illness

Lecture 3　第三讲　5招扫清填词障碍

第一招：利用句子的语法结构

　　根据句子的主谓搭配、动宾搭配、修饰关系以及虚拟、倒装等语法结构关系,判断所填词在句中的成分,从而推测出所填词的词性及形式(名词单复数或动词的时态、语态等)。

【例1】　　　　　　　　　　　　　　　　　　　　　　　　(05-6-S7)

If the parents can afford it, each child will have his or her own bedroom. Having one's own bedroom, even as **an** (S7)_____ , fixes in a person the notion that…

【解析】空前的不定冠词 an 提示所填词应为一个以元音音素开头的单数可数名词。本空答案为 infant。

第二招：利用语义连贯

　　根据上下文中的关键词与空格前后词语在语义上的连贯,判断出所填词可能的含义。

【例2】　　　　　　　　　　　　　　　　　　　　　　　　(05-6-S6)

If the parents can (S6)_____ it, each child **will have his or her own bedroom**.

【解析】空前的情态动词 can 和空后的代词 it 提示所填词应为动词原形。if 引导的条件状语从句应是后一句的前提,而要做到每个孩子都有自己的卧室,前提必须是父母能够承担得起费用。本空答案为 afford。

第三招：从逻辑衔接中寻找线索

　　根据上下文及句际间的逻辑关系,如并列、转折、因果等推测所填词可能的含义(主要通过连接词、介词短语和副词来判断)。

【例3】　　　　　　　　　　　　　　　　　　　　　　　　(01-1-S7)

However, sometimes the overall energy balance is upset, and your normal body weight will **either fall or** (S7)_____ .

【解析】either…or…连接两个语法结构相同的并列成分,用于表示在两个可能性中选择一个。either 后面为动词原形 fall, or 后面也应为动词原形且意思应与 fall 相对。本空答案为 increase。

第四招：注意上下文的照应

　　根据同一语境中所填词的近义词、反义词、上、下义词推测所填词可能的形式和含义。近义词和反义词出现时常伴有表示并列或转折关系的信号词;上、下义词是指词的总括或分解关系,上义词是总称词,下义词是其包含的个体或种类。

【例4】　　　　　　　　　　　　　　　　　　　　　　　　(99-6-S6)

The program would **fund** the (S4) coordination efforts of 20 thousand reading (S5) specialists and it would also give (S6)_____ to help parents help children read by the third grade, or about age eight.

【解析】and…also 提示所填词所表达的含义应与前面的 fund(资助)形成照应,故所填词也应表示"资助"或"补助"等相关含义。本空答案为 grants(补助)。

第五招：注意是否构成固定搭配

　　根据所填词与其前后词语可能构成的固定搭配或习惯表达来推测所填词的形式和含义。如动词＋介词、形容词＋介词或其他习惯性表达方式等。

【例5】　　　　　　　　　　　　　　　　　　　　　　　　(05-6-S5)

Americans **have great** (S5)_____ **understanding** foreigners who always want to be with another person, who dislike being alone.

【解析】由空前的 have great 以及空后的动名词 understanding 可以比较容易联想到固定搭配 have difficulty (in) doing sth。本题答案为 difficulty。

Exercise   即讲即练   🎧 边听边记

The history of man's exploration of the earth extends over 5,000 years. The earliest (S1)_____ _____ explored in a very (S2)_____ way: they had to go out to gather plants and hunt animals to feed themselves. Also, in order to feel more secure in their homes, they had to (S3)_____ their surroundings quite thoroughly. But the wider world remained a (S4)_____ to them. It was only later, once the necessities of life had been obtained, that people began to (S5)_____ what lay on the other side of the hill. Whether the forest around them ever came to an end, or where the sun went after it had fallen into the sea. This curiosity caused them to discover previously unknown lands and seas.

The explorers of today are the astronauts and their (S6)_____ is space, but this does not mean there is nothing left to explore on earth. It is true that with the (S7)_____ this century of jet aircraft and spaceships, every part of the world has been (S8)_____ and maps made of it. But there is still much left to find out. Enormous parts of other continents remain practically unknown. And yet all these places are nowadays (S9)_____ easy to reach. There is little difference in attitude between the men sent into space in our time and the explorers of an earlier age. The universe is as mysterious and (S10)_____ for them as our planet seemed to the people in the past. Man's natural curiosity drives him on to explore the unknown and to travel where no one has traveled before, even at the risk of his life.

【答案与解析】

【听力原文】

The history of man's exploration of the earth extends over 5,000 years. The earliest (S1)cavemen explored in a very (S2)limited way: they had to go out to gather plants and hunt animals to feed themselves. Also, in order to feel more secure in their homes, they had to (S3)investigate their surroundings quite thoroughly. But the wider world remained a (S4)mystery to them. It was only later, once the necessities of life had been obtained, that people began to (S5)wonder what lay on the other side of the hill. Whether the forest around them ever came to an end, or where the sun went after it had fallen into the sea. This curiosity caused them to discover previously unknown lands and seas.

The explorers of today are the astronauts and their (S6)territory is space, but this does not mean there is nothing left to explore on earth. It is true that with the (S7)invention this century of jet aircraft and spaceships, every part of the world has been (S8)photographed and maps made of it. But there is still much left to find out. E-normous parts of other continents remain practi-

【答案解析】

S1. 分析句子结构可知所填词应在句子中作主语,故所填词为名词。由冒号后的复数代词 they 可知,所填词应为复数名词。cavemen 意为"穴居人,野人"。

S2. 空前的副词 very 和空后的名词 way 提示所填词应为形容词。冒号后的句子是对冒号前的句子的解释说明,冒号后的句子提到人们只是为了基本生活而探索周围世界,而段末提到后来人们渐渐开始去探索先前并不知道的陆地和海洋,由此可知早期人们对地球的探索是有限的,故所填词应表示"有限的"含义。limited 意为"有限的"。

S3. 空前的不定式 to 和空后的名词 surroundings 提示所填词应为及物动词。investigate 意为"调查"。

S4. 空前的不定冠词 a 和空后的介词 to 提示所填词应为名词。本句句首的转折连词 but 提示本句内容应与上句内容构成对比关系,通过分析不难发现本句想表达早期的人们对 the wider world 还不太了解。mystery 意为"神秘"。

S5. 空前的不定式 to 和空后的名词性从句提示所填词应为及物动词。由下句中的 whether 及 where 引导的状语从句可知,所填词应能表达早期人类对 what lay on the other side of the hill(山外事物)的好奇。wonder 意为"想知道,好奇"。

S6. 分析句子结构可知,所填词在分句中作主语,故所填词应为名词。空前形容词性物主代词 their 指代的是 the astro-nauts,根据 and 前的分句可推测本句要表达 the astronauts 的探索范围是太空,故所填词应表示"范围,地域"的含义。territory

cally unknown. And yet all these places are nowadays (S9) <u>comparatively</u> easy to reach. There is little difference in attitude between the men sent into space in our time and the explorers of an earlier age. The universe is as mysterious and (S10) <u>exciting</u> for them as our planet seemed to the people in the past. Man's natural curiosity drives him on to explore the unknown and to travel where no one has traveled before, even at the risk of his life.

意为"领土,地域"。

S7. 空前的定冠词 the 和空后的介词 of 提示所填词应为名词。由 jet aircraft 和 spaceships 推测所填词应含有"发明"的含义。invention 意为"发明"。

S8. 分析句子结构可知,所填词应在句中作谓语,空前的 been 提示所填词应为动词的过去分词形式。photographed 意为"拍照片"。

S9. 空前的系动词 are 和空后的形容词 easy 提示所填词应为副词。comparatively 意为"相对地"。

S10. 空前的并列连词 and 提示所填词应为形容词与 mysterious 并列。exciting 意为"令人兴奋的"。

Lecture 4 第四讲 6 招攻克填句难关

短文听写的句子结构一般都比较复杂,如果在不了解其内容的情况下直接听写,很难抓住全部信息。因此,我们应该在听音前根据空格前后逻辑关系、上下文内容及短文整体脉络和内容对句子可能陈述的主题进行推测,从而在听音时可以更有效地抓取更多的信息。

第一招:抓住文章和段落的主题句

文章的开头或段首往往会出现主题句,之后的内容进一步展开,说明或论证该主题。抓住这些主题句,把握文章和段落的组织结构,可以更好地理解文章或段落意义,更容易把握所缺单词或句子的含义。

【例1】 (05-6-S8)

Certain phrases one commonly hears among Americans capture their devotion to individualism: "Do your own thing." "I did it my way." "You'll have to decide that for yourself." "You made your bed, now lie in it." "If you don't look out for yourself, no one else will." "Look out for number one." …

If the parents can (S6) <u>afford</u> it, each child will have his or her own bedroom. Having one's own bedroom, even as an (S7) <u>infant</u>, fixes in a person the notion that (S8) _____. She will have her clothes, her toys, her books, and so on. These things will be hers and no one else's.

【解析】文章的第一句就点出了主题"individualism",接下来的内容是对这一主题的展开,从各个方面讲述美国人对待隐私的态度。空前的 the notion that 提示所填句应该是 the notion(观念)的同位语,根据本文的主题,该观念很可能与美国人对待隐私的态度有关。本空答案为 she is entitled to a place of her own where she can be by herself, and keep her possessions。

第二招:根据段落主题推测段落首尾处空格内容

段落的开头或结尾往往起到承上启下的作用,常为主题或总结性的内容,因此应注意根据上下文的细节内容进行总结,推测段首或段尾的句子填空处可能表达的内容。

【例2】 (05-6-S9)

Americans assume that (S9) _____. Doctors, lawyers, psychologists, and others have rules governing "confidentiality" that are intended to prevent information about their clients' personal situations from becoming known to others.

【解析】本空考查的是段首句。空后句子谈到医生、律师、精神病专家等职业人士都有要为客户保密个人信息的规定,应该是对段首句子的展开,因此所填句很可能是讲美国人认为人们应该有对自己的想法或信息进行保密而不让他人知道的权利。本空答案为 people will have their private thoughts that might never be shared with anyone。

第三招：理清句子间的逻辑关系

作者在组织篇章和段落时，经常会使用一些表达逻辑关系的词或短语，如顺承关系、因果关系、对比关系、转折关系等。通过分析句子结构，把握这些关键词，理清句子间的逻辑关系，可以推测所填句子所表达的大致含义，从而在听音时可以更准确地抓取有效信息。

【例3】　　　　　　　　　　　　　　　　　　　　　　　　　　(710 分样卷-46)

But Socrates, as a firm believer in law, reasoned that it was proper to submit to the death sentence. (46) ＿＿＿＿＿＿ ＿＿＿＿＿＿.

【解析】空格前面的句子说苏格拉底是法律的坚定信奉者，他认为服从死刑是应当的，so 表示前后句子是因果关系，因此当听到 so 后便可推测后面很可能是表达他接受了判决的含义。本空答案为 So he calmly accepted his fate and drank a cup of poison in the presence of his grief-stricken friends and students。

第四招：根据前后句意推测空格处内容

句与句之间在语义上要保持连贯，因此要利用空格前后句意，对所填句子可能表达的含义进行推测。

【例4】　　　　　　　　　　　　　　　　　　　　　　　　　　　(01-1-S9)

Research has revealed that about 40 percent of adult men and 55 percent of adult women are dissatisfied with their current body weight. (S9) ＿＿＿＿＿＿＿＿＿＿＿＿. At the college level, a study found that 85% of both male and female first-year students desired to change their body weight.

【解析】空前描述了对自己体重不满的成年人的比例，空后描述了对自己体重不满的大学新生的比例，由此可推测所填句子很可能是关于某个年龄阶层的人对体重的不满情况。本空答案为 Similar findings have also been reported at the high school level mainly with female students。

第五招：明确代词的指代关系

空格后面句子中的代词往往为空格所在句中出现过的词，因此要学会利用后面句子的内容明确代词的指代内容，从而推测所填句要陈述的内容。

【例5】　　　　　　　　　　　　　　　　　　　　　　　　　　　(01-1-S8)

The term body image refers to the mental image we have of our own physical appearance, and (S8) ＿＿＿＿＿＿＿ ＿＿＿＿＿＿.

【解析】根据上文可知，所填句子的主语 it 指代的是 body image（体形），由此可推知所填句子的陈述对象是"体形"。本空答案为 it can be influenced by a variety of factors including how much we weigh and how that weight is distributed。

第六招：学会记录关键词

由于短文听写的句子结构比较复杂，而且考试时间有限，考生想要在听音时将句子完整地写下来不太现实，因此考生应学会记录关键词，然后调动自己的语法知识、词汇知识、语篇分析能力、语感和思维判断能力，将所记录的关键词整理成完整、准确的句子。可见，足够信息量的笔记是写好要点的重要条件。

首先，要学会使用缩略语。缩略语不一定要求规范，甚至可用些符号，所记内容不一定要求完整，只要能起到提示的作用就行了。这里的基本要求是快速、省时，并能表达含义。

其次，要有选择地作笔记。由于短文听写的句子结构都比较复杂，即使使用缩略语也很难记下全句，因此考生应有选择地作笔记。英语中实词具有表意功能，而虚词多具语法功能，所以所记词应以实词为主。

再次，重点记录句子主干。因为短文听写的句子填空只要求写出内容要点，所以考生应重点记录句子的主干中心词，在记下主干的前提下尽可能记全信息。

总之，弄清句子的前后关系并进行适当地分析和推理是准确填写出所填内容的关键。但是，技巧只是提纲挈领的，能帮助提高准确度，但只注重技巧而忽视实践，不多练习也不会取得很好的成绩，因此必须把两者有机地结合起来，才会取得事半功倍的效果。

Exercise

即讲即练

🎧 边听边记

Many insurance companies share in appreciation of the importance of the driver education program in reducing the soaring accident rate. Most large insurance companies charge more money for automobile insurance coverage when a car is to be driven by a man under twenty-five. However, (S1) _____. In a number of states, a person under eighteen who wishes to obtain a motor-vehicle operator's license must successfully complete a state-approved driver education program. The courses in driver education (S2) _____. The age at which a driver may apply for a license varies in different places.

(S3) _____. These figures represent the minimum number of hours and many programs exceed them. The students use cars that are equipped with two controls. The instructor has (S4) _____, if necessary. In the practice-driving sessions, the pupil learns to operate the car. In class, he is taught (S5) _____. In addition to helping students realize the importance of developing proper attitudes and skills, driver education (S6) _____.

【答案与解析】

【听力原文】

Many insurance companies share in appreciation of the importance of the driver education program in reducing the soaring accident rate. Most large insurance companies charge more money for automobile insurance coverage when a car is to be driven by a man under twenty-five. However, (S1) if the driver has successfully completed a state-approved driver education course, a reduction in the rates is possible. In a number of states, a person under eighteen who wishes to obtain a motor-vehicle operator's license must successfully complete a state-approved driver education program. The courses in driver education (S2) are given to pupils who have already reached, or are about to reach the legal driving age. The age at which a driver may apply for a license varies in different places.

(S3) Typical programs consist of thirty hours of classroom instruction and six hours of behind-the-wheel instruction. These figures represent the minimum number of hours and many programs exceed them. The students use cars that are equipped with two controls. The instructor has (S4) an extra brake on his side of the car that enables him to bring the car to a halt, if necessary. In the practice-driving sessions, the pupil learns to operate the car. In class, he is taught (S5) the theory of driving and the rules he must know in order to take his place behind the wheel. In addition to helping students realize the importance of developing proper attitudes and skills, driver education (S6) stresses the relationship between alcohol and the responsibility of driving and the dangers in the combination.

【答案解析】

S1. 本句句首的转折连词 however 提示本句表达的含义与上句内容相反。上句主要讲大多数大的保险公司会对小于 25 岁的驾驶者收取更多的保险费,所以本句就应该讲保险公司在什么样的情况下收取较少的保险费。

【Main Points】if the driver has successfully **finished** a **driver education course approved by state**, a reduction in the rates is possible

S2. 根据上下文语义联系可知,本句中的 the course 就是上句中的 driver education course,而下句句首的 the age 肯定是承接本句而来,那么本句肯定与驾驶者教育课程的授课对象的年龄有关。

【Main Points】are given to **students** who have reached or **will soon** reach the legal driving age

S3. 由下句中的 These figures, hours 和并列连词 and 后面的 programs 以及该句的整体含义可推断本句应与某些 programs 所需时间有关。

【Main Points】Typical programs **include** thirty hours of classroom instruction and six hours of **driving** instruction

S4. 上句是讲学习驾驶者使用带有两个刹车装置的车,根据上下文语义联系可推测,本句主要是与 the instructor(教练)如何操作刹车装置有关。

【Main Points】**another** brake on his side of the car that enables him to **let the car stop**

S5. 本句的主语 he 指代的是上句中的主语 the pupil,即学习驾驶者。根据本句所给出的提示 In class, he is taught 可推测所填句子应该与学习驾驶者在课堂上所学的课程内容有关。

【Main Points】the theory of driving and the rules he must know **to** take his place **when he is driving**

S6. 本句句首的状语 In addition to helping... 是在讲 driver education 的作用,所以根据 in addition to 的用法可知所填内容应该是讲 driver education 的其他作用。

【Main Points】stresses the relationship between **drinking** and the **duty** of driving and the dangers in the combination

短文听写巅峰练习

Exercise 1

边听边记

As regards social conventions, we must say a word about the well-known English class system. This is an (36)_____subject for English people, and one they tend to be ashamed of, though during the present century class-consciousness has grown less and less, and the class system has become less rigid. But it still (37)_____below the surface. Broadly speaking, it means there are classes, the "middle-class" and the "working-class". We shall (38)_____for a moment the old "upper-class", including the hereditary aristocracy, since it is extremely small in numbers; but some of its members have the right to sit in the House of Lords, and some newspapers take a (39)_____ interest in their private life. The middle class (40)_____chiefly of well-to-do businessmen and (41)_____people of all kinds. The working class includes manual and (42)_____ workers chiefly.

The most(43)_____difference between them is in their accent. Middle-class people use slightly varying kinds of "received pronunciation" which is the kind of English Spoken by BBC announcers and taught to overseas pupils. Typical working-class people(44)_____ ____.

One of the biggest barriers of social equality in England is the two-class education system. (45) _____. The middle classes tend to live a more formal life than working-class people, and are usually more cultured. Their midday meal is "lunch" and they have a rather formal evening meal called "dinner", whereas (46)_____.

Exercise 2

British postmen have a reputation for being cheerful. Of course, there are some (36)_____ postmen, who make you think that every letter contains (37)_____news, but the majority is (38)_____and good-humored. This is quite surprising, because delivering the (39)_____ each morning is a job which is not very well paid and there are a great many problems.

Normally, the city postman has to go on foot, not only along streets but also up and down stairs, as many (40)_____of flats still have no (41)_____and no down-stairs letter box. If he has a (42)_____letter to deliver, he has to wait for someone to come to the door to sign for it. That person may (43)_____him in a most unfriendly way if he has just been woken from a deep sleep very early in the morning.

In the country, (44)_____, nevertheless he has his problems too. (45) _____when this makes the journey half an hour longer. In winter, the postmen often have to carry on in the rain or the snow. Sometimes it is on foot, like his city colleague. Most country people keep a dog. He is forced to go in whether the dog is dangerous or not. So every day the country postman knows that, (46)_____.

答案与解析

Exercise 1

【听力原文】

As regards social conventions, we must say a word about the well-known English class system. This is an（36）<u>embarrassing</u> subject for English people, and one they tend to be ashamed of, though during the present century class-consciousness has grown less and less, and the class system has become less rigid. But it still（37）<u>exists</u> below the surface. Broadly speaking, it means there are classes, the "middle-class" and the "working-class". We shall（38）<u>ignore</u> for a moment the old "upper-class", including the hereditary aristocracy, since it is extremely small in numbers; but some of its members have the right to sit in the House of Lords, and some newspapers take a（39）<u>surprising</u> interest in their private life. The middle class（40）<u>consists</u> chiefly of well-to-do businessmen and（41）<u>professional</u> people of all kinds. The working class includes manual and（42）<u>unskilled</u> workers chiefly.

The most（43）<u>obvious</u> difference between them is in their accent. Middle-class people use slightly varying kinds of "received pronunciation" which is the kind of English spoken by BBC announcers and taught to overseas pupils. Typical working-class people（44）<u>speak with many different local accents which are generally felt to be rather ugly and uneducated</u>.

One of the biggest barriers of social equality in England is the two-class education system.（45）<u>To have been to a so-called "public school" immediately marks you out as one of the middle class</u>. The middle classes tend to live a more formal life than working-class people, and are usually more cultured. Their midday meal is "lunch" and they have a rather formal evening meal called "dinner", whereas（46）<u>the working man's dinner, if his working hours permit, is at midday, and his smaller, late-evening meal is called supper</u>.

【答案解析】

36. 空前的不定冠词 an 和空后的名词 subject 提示所填词应为一个以元音音素开头的形容词。本句中的代词 this 及 one 指代的都是 the well-known English class system，所以所填词应与 ashamed of 构成语义并列关系。embarrassing 意为"令人为难的，麻烦的"。

37. 分析句子结构及上下文句子时态可知，所填词应为动词的第三人称单数形式。转折连词 but 提示本句话的含义应与上句含义相反，上句说英国的社会等级观念已经慢慢淡化了，那么本句就应该讲在英国社会里等级观念依然存在，故所填词应表示"存在"的含义。exists 意为"存在"。

38. 空前的情态动词 shall 提示所填词应为动词原形。句中的 since 引导原因状语从句，由此可知 the old "upper-class" 数量极其少造成的后果可能是人们会将其遗忘，故所填词应含有"遗忘或忽略"的含义。ignore 意为"忽略"。

39. 空前的不定冠词 a 和空后的名词 interest 提示所填词应为形容词。surprising 意为"令人震惊的"。

40. 分析句子结构可知所填词应为动词，在句中充当谓语，再根据上下文时态及句子主语可知所填词应为动词的第三人称单数形式，且能与 of 搭配。本句主语 the middle class 与下句主语 the working class 的关系为语义场复现，所以所填动词也应与下句谓语 includes 构成语义复现关系，故所填词应表示"包括，由…组成"的含义。consists 意为"包括，由…组成"。

41. 空前的并列连词 and 和空后的名词 people 提示所填词应为形容词。professional 意为"专业的"。

42. 空前的并列连词 and 和空后的名词 workers 提示所填词应为形容词，且与 manual 并列，共同修饰 workers。unskilled 意为"无技能的"。

43. 空前的形容词最高级 the most 和空后的名词 difference 提示所填词应为形容词。obvious 意为"明显的"。

44.【Main Points】speak with many different local accents **that** generally felt to be **quite** ugly and uneducated

45.【Main Points】**Having** been to a so-called "public school" marks you out as one of the middle class **at once**

46.【Main Points】the working man's dinner, if his working **time allows**, is at **noon**, and his smaller, late-evening meal is called supper

Exercise 2

【听力原文】

British postmen have a reputation for being cheerful. Of course, there are some（36）<u>gloomy</u> postmen, who make you think that every letter contains（37）<u>tragic</u> news, but the majority is

【答案解析】

36. 空前的形容词 some 和空后的名词 postmen 提示所填词应为形容词。根据上下文内容可推测所填词与上句中的 cheerful 含义相反，即所填词可能表示"不高兴的"的含义。gloomy 意为"郁闷的，悲伤的"。

(38)jolly and good-humored. This is quite surprising, because delivering the (39)mail each morning is a job which is not very well paid and there are a great many problems.

Normally, the city postman has to go on foot, not only along streets but also up and down stairs, as many (40)blocks of flats still have no (41)lifts and no down-stairs letter box. If he has a (42)registered letter to deliver, he has to wait for someone to come to the door to sign for it. That person may (43)greet him in a most unfriendly way if he has just been woken from a deep sleep very early in the morning.

In the country, (44)a postman may have a bicycle or a small van, so he does not have to walk so far, nevertheless he has his problems too. (45)It is very annoying to be compelled to go all the way to an isolated house simply to deliver a postcard when this makes the journey half an hour longer. In winter, the postmen often have to carry on in the rain or the snow. Sometimes it is on foot, like his city colleague. Most country people keep a dog. He is forced to go in whether the dog is dangerous or not. So every day the country postman knows that, (46)if the dog is not safely tied up, it may bite him on the leg or tear his trousers.

37. 空前的动词 contatins 和空后的名词 news 提示所填词应为形容词。由从句的主语 every letter 和宾语 news 可推测，所填词应是表达 news(消息)的好坏。tragic 意为"不幸的"。

38. 空前的系动词 is 和空后的并列连词 and 提示所填词应与 good-humored 并列，为形容词。上文提到有些邮递员心情不好，那么 but 后面的句子应表达大多数邮递员都很高兴的含义，故所填词应表达"高兴的"的含义。jolly 意为"快乐的，高兴的"。

39. 分析句子结构可知所填词应作 delivering 的宾语，故所填词应为名词。delivering the _____ 是 postmen 的工作，所以可推测所填词应与信件有关。mail 意为"邮件"。

40. 空前的形容词 many 和空后的介词 of 提示所填词应为复数名词。blocks 意为"街区"。

41. 空前的形容词 no 和空后的并列连词 and 提示所填词应为名词。lifts 意为"电梯"。

42. 空前的不定冠词 a 和空后的名词 letter 提示所填词应为形容词。registered 意为"记名的"，registered letter 意为"挂号信"。

43. 空前的情态动词 may 提示所填词应为动词原形。根据常识可知人们早上起床后遇到外人时通常会先问候他，故所填词应表示"问候"的含义。greet 意为"问候"。

44. 【Main Points】a postman may have a **bike** or a small van, so he **needn't** walk so far

45. 【Main Points】It is very annoying to be **forced** to go all the way to a isolated house **only to send** a postcard

46. 【Main Points】if the dog is not **well** tied up, it may bite **his leg** or tear his trousers

Chapter 9

听力理解巅峰练习

Test 1

Section A

🎧 边听边记

11. [A] Drive him to the restaurant. [B] Show him the way to the restaurant.
    [C] Go to eat with him. [D] Take him home.

12. [A] Three days. [B] One week.
    [C] Five days. [D] Half a week.

13. [A] A new shirt. [B] A shirt and a tie.
    [C] An old shirt. [D] Something informal.

14. [A] His new apartment is quite dirty. [B] The traffic is too noisy.
    [C] His neighbor always makes some noise. [D] His neighbors don't like him.

15. [A] Ask Dr. Smith to alter his decision. [B] Ask Dr. Smith to call the library.
    [C] Get the book directly from Dr. Smith. [D] Get Dr. Smith's written permission.

16. [A] Relatives. [B] Roommates.
    [C] Colleagues. [D] Neighbors.

17. [A] She teaches a foreign language. [B] She wants to go golfing.
    [C] She is busy with her work. [D] She has an appointment with someone.

18. [A] They should wish the professor good luck.
    [B] They should ask for three weeks to do the work.
    [C] They shouldn't push the project buttons.
    [D] They shouldn't make too many requests.

Questions 19 to 21 are based on the conversation you have just heard.

19. [A] To watch a basketball match. [B] To have a birthday party.
    [C] To celebrate Christmas. [D] To appreciate an ancient porcelain vase.

20. [A] It is five hundred years old. [B] It broke the computer.
    [C] It was knocked over. [D] It is a gift from Henry's grandmother.

21. [A] To ask for forgiveness. [B] To show his love.
    [C] For the funeral. [D] For their wedding anniversary.

Questions 22 to 25 are based on the conversation you have just heard.

22. [A] Winter. [B] Early spring.
    [C] Late autumn. [D] Late spring.

23. [A] Changeable. [B] Stable.
    [C] Always sunny and warm. [D] Very cold at night.

24. [A] The highest spring temperature is 13℃.
    [B] It seldom rains.
    [C] The average spring temperature is 21℃ to 24℃.
    [D] The weather begins to get warmer since the middle of March.

25. [A] 24℃. [B] 40℃.
    [C] 14℃. [D] 41℃.

Section B

Passage One

Questions 26 to 28 are based on the passage you have just heard.

26. [A] The increasing homicide.
    [C] The increasing burglary and theft.
    [B] The increasing suicide.
    [D] The increasing misprision.
27. [A] The law enforcement officials.
    [C] The strict laws.
    [B] The stimulated citizenry.
    [D] The various organizations.
28. [A] The local enforcement police.
    [C] Local residents.
    [B] The local police chief.
    [D] The head of the neighborhood organization.

Passage Two

Questions 29 to 31 are based on the passage you have just heard.

29. [A] It was once the center of government.
    [B] It is different from other buildings.
    [C] There are no decorations in it.
    [D] It has no record of its designers.
30. [A] The City Hall can't provide them enough room.
    [B] The City Hall is too old to accommodate them.
    [C] The City Hall is put on the list of reserve.
    [D] The City Hall is under construction.
31. [A] The trueness of the government.
    [B] The cleanliness of the government.
    [C] The steeliness of the government.
    [D] The righteousness of the government.

Passage Three

Questions 32 to 35 are based on the passage you have just heard.

32. [A] Nonverbal behavior can reveal one's subconscious.
    [B] Nonverbal behavior can have more expressions than verbal expressions.
    [C] Nonverbal behavior is more reasonable than verbal expressions.
    [D] Nonverbal behavior can protect the person's real mind from being recognized.
33. [A] By their verbal expressions.
    [B] By their angry facial expressions.
    [C] By their different gestures from the leader's.
    [D] By their unwilling decisions.
34. [A] He keeps his left hand over the right one with the palms down.
    [B] He keeps his right hand cover the left one.
    [C] He sits with crossed legs and arms.
    [D] He touches the nose gently with his index finger.
35. [A] The listener encourages the speaker to go on speaking.
    [B] The listener wants the speaker to finish quickly.
    [C] The listener wants to interrupt the speaker.
    [D] The listener wants to have the opportunity to ask questions.

Section C

　　A few years ago it was fashionable to speak of a generation gap, a division between young people and their elders. Parents complained that children did not show them (36)_____ respect and (37)_____ while children complained that their parents did not understand them at all. What had gone wrong? Why had the generation gap suddenly (38)_____? Actually the generation gap has been around for a long time. Many (39)_____ argue that it is built into the (40)_____ of our society.

One important cause of the generation gap is the (41) _____ that young people have to choose their own lifestyles. In more traditional societies, when children grow up, they are expected to live in the same area as their parents, to marry people that their parents know and (42) _____ __of, and often to continue the family occupation. In our society, young people often travel great (43) _____for their education, move out of the family home at an early age, marry or live with people whom their parents have never met, and choose occupations different from those of their parents.

(44) _____: to find better jobs, to make more money and to do all the things that they were unable to do. Often, however, (45) _____; often they discover that they have very little in common with each other.

Finally, the speed at which changes take place in our society is another cause of the gap between the generations. (46) _____.

边听边记

答案与解析

Section A

11.

[A] Drive him to the restaurant.	M: Excuse me. Where is the closest place to eat?
[B] Show him the way to the restaurant.	W: Down the street about four blocks. I can take you there if you'd like.
[C] Go to eat with him.	
[D] Take him home.	Q: What is the woman offering the man to do?

【解析】行为活动题。男士问女士最近的餐馆在哪里,女士回答说她可以 take you there if you'd like, 即 drive him to the restaurant(开车送他去餐馆)。"take sb. 十地点名词"通常指开车送某人到某个地方。

12.

[A] Three days.	W: I heard that you've been abroad. Can you tell me where you went?
[B] One week.	M: I spent four days in Italy, three days in Scotland, one week in Spain and half a week in Switzerland.
[C] Five days.	
[D] Half a week.	Q: How long did the man stay in Scotland?

【解析】数字信息题。由男士话中的 I spent…three days in Scotland…可知,他在 Scotland 呆了三天。

13.

[A] A new shirt.	W: I thought you'd wear a shirt and a tie.
[B] A shirt and a tie.	M: But it's formal. A T-shirt is more comfortable in this hot weather.
[C] An old shirt.	
[D] Something informal.	Q: What is the man wearing?

【解析】事实状况题。男士话中的 it's formal 表明他认为穿衬衫打领带太 formal(正式)了,言外之意就是他会穿 something informal(不太正式的衣服)。A T-shirt is more comfortable…进一步证明了男士会穿不太正式的衣服。

14.

[A] His new apartment is quite dirty.	W: Oh, what's the matter? You look so annoyed.
[B] The traffic is too noisy.	M: My new apartment is quite nice, but my neighbor is too noisy. He sings, dances… Well, I simply can't concentrate on anything.
[C] His neighbor always makes some noise.	
[D] His neighbors don's like him.	Q: What is the man complaining about?

【解析】事实状况题。男士话中的 my neighbor is too noisy…表明他的邻居制造的噪音太大,使他无法专心地做任何事情,由此可知他是在抱怨邻居制造的 noise。

15.

[A] Ask Dr. Smith to alter his decision. [B] Ask Dr. Smith to call the library. [C] Get the book directly from Dr. Smith. [D] Get Dr. Smith's written permission.	M: May I take this book out? I need it to work on a paper for Dr. Smith's history class. W: I'm afraid not. The book has been put on the shelf by Dr. Smith. Unless you have his written permission, I won't lend it out. Q: What should the man do to borrow the book?

【解析】行为活动题。女士话中的条件状语从句 Unless you have his written mission 表明如果没有 Dr. Smith 的 written permission,男士是不可以把书借走的,由此可知女士要想借书,必须拿到 Dr. Smith 的 written permission(书面允许)。

16.

[A] Relatives. [B] Roommates. [C] Colleagues. [D] Neighbors.	M: I've just brought your ladder back. Thanks for lending it to me. Where should I leave it? W: Just lean it against the wall there. Use the ladder again at any time. Q: What's the probable relationship between the two speakers?

【解析】身份关系题。由男士话中的 brought your ladder back 及女士话中的 use the ladder again at any time 可知,本对话主要围绕借梯子和还梯子展开的,而像借还东西这种日常生活琐事经常会发生在 neighbors(邻居)之间,故两人可能是邻居关系。

17.

[A] She teaches a foreign language. [B] She wants to go golfing. [C] She is busy with her work. [D] She has an appointment with someone.	W: Tom, would you mind watching the children this afternoon while I go golfing? M: I'm sorry. I have a foreign student that I'm helping with English this afternoon. Q: Why does the woman ask the man to help watch the children?

【解析】行为活动题。女士话中的…I go golfing 表明她请男士帮忙照看孩子的原因是她下午要去 go golfing(打高尔夫)。

18.

[A] They should wish the professor good luck. [B] They should ask for three weeks to do the work. [C] They shouldn't push the project buttons. [D] They shouldn't make too many requests.	W: If Professor Thomson is willing to give us a three-day extension to finish the project, maybe she'll give us a few more days. M: Let's not push our luck, Mary! OK? Q: What does the man mean?

【解析】观点态度题。男士话中的 Let's not push our luck 表明他认为 Professor Thomson 多给了三天时间已经很不错了,女士不应该有让 Professor Thomson 再给 a few more days 的想法,也就是说男士认为女士不应该 make too many requests。push one's luck 意为"得寸进尺"。

Conversation One

【听力原文】	【答案解析】
W: Hey, Henry, how's everything going, and [21①]what's with the flowers? M: They're for my wife. W: Oh, a wedding anniversary or something? M: [21②]To tell the truth, it couldn't be worse. You see. I have to pick my wife up from the airport this evening, but while she was gone, there were a few minor mishaps. W: Oh, really? What happened?	19. Why did Henry's friends come over to his house on Friday night? 【解析】选[A]。细节题。男士提到周五晚上他邀请朋友去他家watch a basketball game on TV(看篮球比赛),[A]为原文的同义转述。

M: Well, [19] I had some of the guys over Friday night to watch a basketball game on TV, but one of them got all excited, and started horsing around, waving his arms, and [21③] he accidentally knocked over my wife's 250-year-old Chinese porcelain vase given to her by her grandmother, and broke it beyond repair.

W: Man, have you tried…?

M: Super glue? Yeah, but she would be able to tell in a second. I was trying to pull something over her eyes.

W: Oh, wow. You're in hot water now.

M: If it had only been that.

W: Oh, there's more?

M: Yeah, you see, the water from the vase spilled all over the manuscript of a book my wife had been writing for the past two years. It blurred the ink over many of the pages. And so [21④] one of the guys had the bright idea of drying the pages by the fire while we watched, uh, the rest of the game, but a spark from the fire must have blown out and burned the manuscript to a crisp.

W: What about an electronic file copy? She had one, didn't she?

M: Well, actually, her computer crashed the day before while I was playing some computer games and I hadn't been able to get it to work since.

W: Man, you are in trouble now. You're going to have a hard time digging yourself out of this one.

20. What has been mentioned about the vase?

【解析】选[C]。细节题。男士提到，他的一个朋友由于看球太过兴奋，开始手舞足蹈起来，不小心knock over(打翻)了他妻子的祖母送给她的那只有着250年历史的瓷花瓶，[C]是原文的细节再现。

21. Why does the man send flowers to his wife?

【解析】选[A]。推断题。对话一开始女士就问男士买花是不是为了他的结婚周年纪念，男士回答说it couldn't be worse(再糟糕不过了)，接着告诉女士他的一个朋友先是把他妻子的那只有着250年历史的花瓶打破了，然后又把他妻子两年来的手稿给弄脏并烧毁了，由此可判断男士买花给妻子是想 ask for forgiveness(请求原谅)。

Conversation Two

【听力原文】

M: What lovely weather we're having today!

W: Yes, [22] it's wonderful after the cold winter.

M: What season do you like best?

W: Spring, I think.

M: Why so?

W: Because nature awakens from her long winter sleep. Everything becomes green little by little, and the air rings with the sweet songs of birds. The sun is usually bright and the weather gets warmer gradually.

M: That's true. By the way, do you often have fine weather in spring in your hometown?

W: I'm afraid not. And [23] the weather usually varies, sometimes beyond one's expectations.

M: Is that so?

W: Yes. In late spring, it rains from time to time. For example, the sun may be shining brightly in the morning. After a while it may be hidden, and the sky may begin to cloud over.

M: It seems if you go out without an umbrella in the morning, you'll probably get us through in the afternoon. Right?

W: You're clever. Indeed we have lots of rain in spring. Sometimes it drizzles, sometimes it pours, and sometimes there are showers and storms. Once spring sets in, there seems to be no end to the rain.

M: I dare say, people have a dislike for such long spells of rain.

W: Perfectly right. What about spring for the U.S., then?

M: [24] Spring begins in the middle of March and continues to the middle of June.

【答案解析】

22. What season is it when the dialogue takes place?

【解析】选[B]。细节题。对话一开头，女士就说 it's wonderful after the cold winter(寒冷的冬天过去后有这么一个好天真是太妙了)，由此可知对话可能发生在早春。

23. What's the weather like in spring in the woman's hometown?

【解析】选[A]。细节题。女士提到在她的家乡里，春天的 the weather usually varies, sometimes beyond one's expectations(天气经常变化，有时会出人意料)，即在她的家乡里春天的天气是 changeable(多变的)。

24. What's spring like in the U.S.?

【解析】选[D]。推断题。男士说到美国春天一般是

In spring the weather gets somewhat warmer. The average spring temperature is around 13°C. It also rains often during this period.

W: And summer?

M: Summer temperatures vary widely according to the different regions of the country, but we may say that the average summer temperature, as a whole, is 21°C to 24°C.

W: It's warm, but not very hot.

M: Now, tell me something about your summer.

W: It's very hot there. [25] During the hottest days, the temperature in the sun rises as high as 40°C. It is usually very stuffy indoors, and outside there's seldom any breeze either. We can hardly stand the heat.

M: That's terrible. Anyhow, autumn is a good season for both Chinese and Americans. I presume.

W: I think so. There is a saying among us: spring is flowery, and autumn is fruitful.

从 the middle of March 开始,一直持续到 the middle of June,由此可推测在美国 3 月中旬就开始变得暖和了。

25. What degree will the temperature reach in the hottest days in the woman's hometown?

【解析】选[B]。细节题。对话结尾处,女士说在她的家乡里,夏天最热的时候气温高达 40°C。

Section B

Passage One

【听力原文】

[26] There is increasing concern throughout the States about the growing incidence of burglary and theft in rural areas. Rural residents are taking steps to assist law enforcement officials in dealing with this growing problem. These efforts have come to be known as neighborhood crime prevention or neighborhood crime watches.

One of the most effective crime prevention measures is the establishment of a neighborhood organization to maintain surveillance of local properties, roads and highways. The existence of such a group serves as a prevention of theft and burglary.

Other measures a neighborhood organization can take are immediately reporting suspicious people and acts and the location of questionable vehicles with license plate numbers to law enforcement officials.

Experience has shown that the three steps of prevention organization, reporting and marking valuable property can sharply reduce the amount of criminal activity in rural areas.

[27] It has often been said that nothing is as potent as a stimulated citizenry. [28] Even in cities and towns, law enforcement officials cannot be everywhere all the time. So it is "Mr. and Mrs. Average Citizen" who become the additional eyes and ears needed to maintain law and order.

Organization is the key to effective action. The local residents must band together and take responsibilities not previously fulfilled.

Beyond the organizational activities, individual households must be given attention to minimize the chances of becoming the targets of thieves. Such things as night lights, locks and the care of equipment and livestock must all be taken into account.

【答案解析】

26. What has been disturbing the rural people, according to the passage?

【解析】选[C]。细节题。短文开头处提到乡村地区 the growing incidence of burglary and theft(入室行窃及偷窃事件连续不断的发生)越来越受到整个国家的关注,由此可推断乡村地区的人们会经常受到 burglary 和 theft 的困扰。

27. Who are the most potent to defeat criminal activities in rural area?

【解析】选[B]。细节题。文中提到在打击犯罪活动时 nothing is as potent as a stimulated citizenry(没有比被激发起来的公民更加有力的了),言外之意就是 the stimulated citizenry 是最有力的。

28. Who are "Mr. or Mrs. Average Citizen"?

【解析】选[C]。推断题。文中提到即使是在城镇里,law enforcement officials(执法人员)也不能照顾到各个方面,这时"Mr. and Mrs. Average Citizen"就能起到维护法律秩序的作用。根据整篇短文都在讲乡村居民在打击入室行窃及偷窃等违法犯纪中的重要作用可推断 Mr. or Mrs. Average Citizen 指的就是 local residents(当地居民)。

Passage Two

【听力原文】

If you walk along Padang you will not miss the magnificent City Hall building which stands facing the Esplanade. City Hall is a historical building. [29] It was the seat of the British Government of Singapore and, in earlier times, was the center of government. Even in recent times, it was an important building. At one time, it housed the Prime Minister's office and the offices of several ministers. [30] It was only after the ministries grew in importance and size that many of them moved out to occupy larger complexes. City Hall is the site of many milestone events in Singapore. It is where the Japanese surrendered to the British in 1946. Also, most of the important announcements with regard to the country, were made from the building.

The building is made of solid granite in many parts and, like most old buildings, is able to withstand bombardment. If you look closely, you will see that each pillar seems to have been placed lovingly with a view that the building should stand forever. The building is filled with carvings and statues from Greek mythology. [31] It is painted white to symbolize the cleanliness of the government. Indeed, the City Hall building is a masterpiece and a beautiful building to represent the solid foundation upon which our nation is founded. It stands today as a monument of the high standards set by our forefathers. We know that it is more than a building: it is a part of our history to remind us that we struggled to establish this beautiful country.

【答案解析】

29. What can we learn about the City Hall?

【解析】选[A]。细节题。短文开头处指出 the City Hall 是 the seat of the British Government of Singapore(新加坡英国政府的所在地),并且在早期也曾经是 the center of government(政府的中心所在地)。

30. Why did many of ministries move out of the City Hall?

【解析】选[A]。推断题。文中提到因为政府部门的重要性及政府部门的增加,许多部门 moved out to occupy larger complexes(搬往更大的建筑中去了),言外之意就是 the City Hall can't provide them enough room(无法满足政府部门的空间需求)。

31. What does the white color of the City Hall building stand for?

【解析】选[B]。细节题。文中在描述 the City Hall building 时提到,它被粉刷成白色以表明 the cleanliness of the government(政府的廉洁)。

Passage Three

【听力原文】

The knowledge of nonverbal communication helps a manager understand the behavior of others and thus manage his workforce effectively. It is also a useful and powerful tool for handling serious and sensitive situations tactfully. [32] Nonverbal behavior is more reliable than verbal expressions since it is the language of the subconscious and is therefore difficult to manipulate.

Experienced managers are alert to notice harmony or dissent in gestures. A group of workers once came to ask me for a facility which I knew was going to be misused. All of them were unanimous in pressing for it. When I observed them closely, however, [33] I found that their leader had been sharing his gestures only with a handful of people; the rest were displaying a different set of gestures a clear indication that the leader was forcing his decision on an unwilling majority.

[34] During a meeting or presentation, you know that you are being listened to intently if the listener is keeping his left hand over the right one, with his palms down. However, if the right hand covers the left one, the person is probably disagreeing with what is being said and is wait-

【答案解析】

32. Why is nonverbal behavior more reliable than verbal expressions?

【解析】选[A]。推断题。文中提到 Nonverbal behavior is more reliable than verbal expressions since it is the language of the subconscious(非语言行为比语言表达更为可靠,因为它是潜意识的表达方式),言外之意就是非语言行为能够 reveal one's subconscious(反映出人们的潜意识行为)。

33. How does the speaker know that most workers didn't share the idea with their leader?

【解析】选[C]。细节题。文中提到曾有工人要求 the speaker 把 a facility(一套设备)给他们,当他仔细观察这些工人的时候,发现有几个工人的手势与那个工人领导相同,the rest were displaying a different set of gestures…(其他工人的手势都与工人领导不同),the speaker 由此判断那个工人领导 forcing his decision on an unwilling majority(把自己的意志强加到大多数工人身上),由此可知 the speaker 是通过大多数工人的 different gestures from the leader's 判断出他们与领导的意见不一致。

34. What gesture can show the listener is listening

ing for an opportunity to interrupt. During my training programs, I often ask questions from uninterested participants to keep them alert and attentive. They tend to sit with crossed legs and arms showing their mental withdrawal or resistance to what is being said. Rubbing behind the ear or touching the nose gently with the index finger shows dislike, doubt, uncertainty or the inability to avoid or answer a question. By nodding his head, the listener conveys that he is listening and encourages the speaker to go on. [35] Rapid nods of the head, or a gentle, rhythmic tapping of the head or stomach may mean that the listener wants the speaker to finish quickly.

to you carefully?

【解析】选[A]。细节题。文中提到在会议或演讲中，如果听众 keeping his left hand over the right one, with his palms down(把左手放在右手上，且手掌朝下)，那么该听众就是在仔细听你讲话。

35. What does the gesture of rapid nods of the head mean?

【解析】选[B]。细节题。短文结尾处提到 rapid nods of the head 表明听者 wants the speaker to finish quickly(希望讲话者快点结束讲话)。

Section C

　　　　　　　　　　【听力原文】

A few years ago it was fashionable to speak of a generation gap, a division between young people and their elders. Parents complained that children did not show them (36)<u>proper</u> respect and (37)<u>obedience</u> while children complained that their prents did not understand them at all. What had gone wrong? Why had the generation gap suddenly (38)<u>appeared</u>? Actually the generation gap has been around for a long time. Many (39)<u>critics</u> argue that it is built into the (40)<u>fabric</u> of our society.

One important cause of the generation gap is the (41)<u>opportunity</u> that young people have to choose their own lifestyles. In more traditional societies, when children grow up, they are expected to live in the same area as their parents, to marry people that their parents know and (42)<u>approve</u> of, and often to continue the family occupation. In our society, young people often travel great (43)<u>distances</u> for their education, move out of the family home at an early age, marry or live with people whom their parents have never met, and choose occupations different from those of their parents.

(44)<u>In our upwardly mobile society, parents often expect their children to do better than they did</u>: to find better jobs, to make more money and to do all the things that they were unable to do. Often, however, (45)<u>the ambitions that parents have for their children are another cause of the division between them</u>; often they discover that they have very little in common with each other.

Finally, the speed at which changes take place in our society is another cause of the gap between the generations. (46)<u>In a traditional culture, elderly people are valued for their wisdom, but in our society the knowledge of a lifetime may become obsolete overnight.</u>

　　　　　　　　　　【答案解析】

36. 空前的动词 show 和代词 them 与空后的名词 respect 提示所填词应为形容词。proper 意为"适当的"。

37. 空前的并列连词 and 提示所填词应为名词，与 respect 并列，共同作动词 show 的直接宾语。obedience 意为"服从，顺从"。

38. 分析句子结构可知，句子缺少谓语动词，根据空前的助动词 had 可推测出，所填词应为动词的过去分词形式。appeared 意为"出现"。

39. 分析句子结构可知，所填词在句中作主语，根据空前的形容词 many 可以推断出所填词应为复数名词。critics 意为"评论家，批评家"。

40. 空前的定冠词 the 和空后的介词 of 提示所填词应为名词。fabric 意为"构造"。

41. 空前的定冠词 the 和空后的同位语从句提示所填词应为名词。opportunity 意为"机会"。

42. 空前的并列连词 and 提示所填词应与 know 并列，共同作定语从句的谓语，故所填词应为动词原形，并能与介词 of 搭配。approve 意为"同意，允许"。

43. 空前的形容词 great 和空后的介词 for 提示所填词应为名词。根据上下文内容可知所填词所在的句子是想表明现代社会与传统社会不同，以前父母希望子女和他们住一起，但是现在子女们因学业等原因会远离家庭，会自己选择婚姻及事业。由此可以推测所填词应能使句子表达出年轻人会因学业离家很远的含义。distances 意为"距离"。

44. 【Main Points】In our **advancing** society, parents often **hope** their children **can** do better than they did

45. 【Main Points】the ambitions parents have for their children **can also cause** the division between them

46. 【Main Points】In a traditional culture, **old** people are **respected because of** their wisdom, but in our society the knowledge of a lifetime may **be outdated** overnight

Test 2

Section A .... 🎧 边听边记

11. [A] At a bookstore.　　　　　　　　[B] In a workshop.
    [C] At an art gallery.　　　　　　　[D] In a department store.
12. [A] Fifteen days later.　　　　　　　[B] On the first day of the exhibition.
    [C] Every day during the exhibition.　[D] On the second day of the exhibition.
13. [A] Black.　　　　　　　　　　　　[B] Dark brown.
    [C] Light blue.　　　　　　　　　　[D] Dark blue.
14. [A] Go camping.　　　　　　　　　[B] Attend a conference.
    [C] Join the man.　　　　　　　　　[D] Cancel the meeting.
15. [A] Their parents cut back the loan.
    [B] The woman doesn't want the man to take another English course.
    [C] They can't pay the rent this month.
    [D] The woman's boss refused to give her a raise.
16. [A] Take a course given by another professor.
    [B] Concentrate on the textbook only, not the lectures.
    [C] Borrow his notes to study for the exams.
    [D] Write down and remember what Professor Smith said in class.
17. [A] He has studied for a whole night.
    [B] He has paid for private lessons.
    [C] He has given Spanish tests to students.
    [D] He has studied continually for two weeks.
18. [A] Joe and Carl both graduated from art schools.
    [B] Joe and Carl are equally competent for the job.
    [C] Joe and Carl majored in different areas of art.
    [D] Joe and Carl are both willing to draw the posters.

Questions 19 to 21 are based on the conversation you have just heard.

19. [A] The illness of the people.　　　　[B] The solution of environmental pollution.
    [C] The solution of water pollution.　[D] The problem with the soil.
20. [A] Carbon dioxide.　　　　　　　　[B] Oxide.
    [C] Carbon monoxide.　　　　　　　[D] Hydrogen and oxygen.
21. [A] They worried about them.　　　　[B] They thought them useful.
    [C] They hated them.　　　　　　　[D] They thought them ugly.

Questions 22 to 25 are based on the conversation you have just heard.

22. [A] At the airport.　　　　　　　　[B] At the bank.
    [C] On the street.　　　　　　　　[D] In the police station.
23. [A] 0.1%.　　　　　　　　　　　　[B] 0.2%.
    [C] 0.21%.　　　　　　　　　　　[D] 0.25%.
24. [A] When the monthly balance is less than $250.
    [B] When the monthly balance is less than $50.
    [C] When there is no balance on the account.
    [D] When the monthly balance is less than $100.
25. [A] Deposit account and savings account.
    [B] Current account and traveling account.
    [C] Checking account and savings account.
    [D] Savings account and transaction account.

Section B

Passage One

Questions 26 to 28 are based on the passage you have just heard.

26. [A] How to keep away from cold weather.   [B] Some expressions related to "cold".
    [C] How cold weather formed.   [D] The effect of cold weather on people's minds.
27. [A] The temperature of one's shoulder.
    [B] The physical act of turning back toward others.
    [C] The legend about shoulder.
    [D] The mental activity toward someone's remark.
28. [A] To get cold feet.   [B] Cold shoulder.
    [C] Cold fish.   [D] Out in the cold.

Passage Two

Questions 29 to 31 are based on the passage you have just heard.

29. [A] The newspaper subsidized by the colonial.
    [B] The development history of newspaper.
    [C] The first successful newspaper.
    [D] The low cost of newspaper.
30. [A] 43.   [B] 53.
    [C] 33.   [D] 23.
31. [A] It didn't bring too many benefits to newspapers.
    [B] It made newspapers available for common people.
    [C] It made newspapers the province of the wealthy.
    [D] It made newspapers full of advertisement.

Passage Three

Questions 32 to 35 are based on the passage you have just heard.

32. [A] Stealing and violence.   [B] Suicide and murder.
    [C] Arson and kidnapping.   [D] Blackmail and rape.
33. [A] Because they are given more freedom to go where they want.
    [B] Because they are more in need of money.
    [C] Because they are more willing to show they are different.
    [D] Because they are more easily to get away from the police.
34. [A] The strict punishment.   [B] The familiarity among people.
    [C] The contribution of local people.   [D] The good order of society.
35. [A] The society.   [B] The education.
    [C] The teachers.   [D] The parents.

Section C

Many new plays are presented first on Broadway, the theatre district of New York City. If they are successful, they later go "on the road" to (36)_____ of cities throughout the country. More than 50 (37)_____ are presented each season on Broadway. To many Americans, seeing a Broadway show is a high point in their visit to the nation's largest city. However, a movement known as "(38)_____ theatre" has developed across the United States, and playhouses are (39)_____ eagerly in cities throughout the nation.

In recent years another side of the New York Theatre has developed, known as "off Broadway". These plays are (40)_____ staged in small playhouses, but some (41)_____ with the best Broadway performances in (42)_____ skill, and many enjoy long runs.

After the regular theatre season has closed, more than 300 summer theatres go into action in rural areas, in suburbs and seashore and mountain (43)_____. Well-known actors often appear in these plays. At the same time, (44)_____.

Motion pictures remain a favorite form of entertainment despite the popularity of television. (45)_____. Many movies are now made by independent producers with fresh i-deas and approaches. They select their stories and treat the subjects in ways that reflect their creative ideas. Modern methods of movie making, (46)_____.

🎧 边听边记

答案与解析

Section A

11.

[A] At a bookstore.	M: Cathy, what is the title of this oil painting?
[B] In a workshop.	W: Sorry, I don't know for sure. But I guess it's an early 18th century work. Let me look it up in the catalog.
[C] At an art gallery.	
[D] In a department store.	Q: Where does the conversation most probably take place?

【解析】地点场景题。由对话中的关键信息 oil painting 及 an early 18th century work 可推断,对话最可能发生在 an art gallery(艺廊)。

12.

[A] Fifteen days later.	M: I was interested to hear about your exhibition. How long will it stay open?
[B] On the first day of the exhibition.	W: Ten days. I do hope you'll come to the opening.
[C] Every day during the exhibition.	
[D] On the second day of the exhibition.	Q: When will the man go to the exhibition if he accepts the invitation?

【解析】数字信息题。女士话中的 I do hope you'll come to the opening 表明,她希望男士 the opening(开幕式)那天能来,即希望男士在 the first day of the exhibition 能来。

13.

[A] Black.	M: I think blue suits you best, Madam.
[B] Dark brown.	W: Yes… well, I think I'll take the light blue. No, perhaps the dark blue will go better with my black shoes.
[C] Light blue.	
[D] Dark blue.	Q: What color will the woman most probably take?

【解析】事实状况题。女士开始说她会 take the light blue(买浅蓝色的),但接着用 No 对前面的话进行了否定,并说 the dark blue 会和她的黑鞋子更搭配,由此可知女士所买物品的颜色是 dark blue。

14.

[A] Go camping.	M: Let's go camping this weekend.
[B] Attend a conference.	W: I wish I could join you, but I have to attend a meeting in LA. If only the meeting could be cancelled!
[C] Join the man.	
[D] Cancel the meeting.	Q: What is the woman going to do this weekend?

【解析】行为活动题。女士话中的转折句式 but I have to attend a meeting in LA 表明这周她要去参加一个会议,不能和男士一起去野营。conference ≈ meeting。I wish…, but…是委婉地拒绝别人邀请或请求的一种常用句式。if only…用来表示虚拟语气,表明对一件无法实现的事情的一种渴望。

15.

[A] Their parents cut back the loan.	W: Frank, we've got a problem. We don't have enough money to pay the rent this month. I think we'd better ask Mom and Dad for a loan, or ask my boss for a raise.
[B] The woman doesn't want the man to take another English course.	M: Well, I don't know. But maybe I'd better not take another English course this semester.
[C] They can't pay the rent this month.	
[D] The woman's boss refused to give her a raise.	Q: What's the problem the two speakers face?

【解析】事实状况题。女士首先说他们 got a problem,接着就解释说他们这个月 don't have enough money to pay the rent(没有钱付房租),由此可知他们面临的问题就是 can't pay the rent this month 女士话中的 ask Mom and Dad for a loan,ask my boss for a raise 及男士话中的 I'd better not… 都是为解决没有钱交房租这一问题而要采取的措施。

16.

[A] Take a course given by another professor.	W: I'm taking Professor Smith's course next semester. Anything I need to know about it?
[B] Concentrate on the textbook only, not the lectures.	M: If I were you, I'd take careful notes. His exams are based on his lectures.
[C] Borrow his notes to study for the exams.	Q: What advice does the man give to the woman?
[D] Write down and remember what Professor Smith said in class.	

【解析】事实状况题。男士话中的虚拟语气 If I were you, I'd take careful notes 实际上是在建议女士上 Professor Smith 的课时要仔细作笔记,因为 Professor Smith 的考试是以他的上课内容为基础的。[D] 是 take careful notes 的同义转述。

17.

[A] He has studied for a whole night.	W: You seem well prepared for this Spanish midterm test. I'm impressed.
[B] He has paid for private lessons.	M: I'd better be prepared. I've spent the last fortnight cramming for it.
[C] He has given Spanish tests to students.	Q: What can we learn about the man from the conversation?
[D] He has studied continually for two weeks.	

【解析】行为活动题。男士话中的 I've spent the last fortnight cramming for it 表明,他为迎接 Spanish midterm test 已经准备了 fortnight(两周)时间。two weeks ≈ fortnight。

18.

[A] Joe and Carl both graduated from art schools.	M: I don't know whether to ask Joe or Carl to draw the posters.
[B] Joe and Carl are equally competent for the job.	W: What difference does it make? They are both excellent artists.
[C] Joe and Carl majored in different areas of art.	Q: What can be inferred from the conversation?
[D] Joe and Carl are both willing to draw the posters.	

【解析】事实状况题。女士话中的反问句 What difference does it make 表明她认为不管是让 Joe 还是让 Carl 画海报都是一样的,因为他们都是 excellent artists,即 Joe 和 Carl 都能 competent(胜任)for the job。

Conversation One

【听力原文】	【答案解析】
M: The more I learn about the world around me, the more aware I become of the problems facing us.	19. What problem are the speakers talking about?
W: Do you mean the problems here in China?	【解析】选[B]。主旨题。对话开头部分就指出目前全世界面临的严重问题:environmental pollution。紧接着男士提到他通过读文章知道了现在有一种通过 bacteria 帮助控制环境污染的方法,后面的对话都围绕着 bacteria 的实用性而展开,由此可推断本对话主要是与 environmental pollution 的解决方法有关。
M: Yes, here and over the world.	
W: Well, there's one problem I'm certainly aware of and [19①] that is the environmental pollution all around us.	
M: That is one of the great problems, but in many parts of the world, as people become more aware and apply new technology to solving the pollution problem, there is hope for the future.	
W: What technology will help with pollution control?	
M: Well, for example, [19②] I've recently read an article about using certain types of bacteria to help control some pollution problems.	20. What can bacteria produce after they absorb petroleum in controlling environmental pollution?
W: How could that be? I thought bacteria just caused illness.	
M: That's not true. Bacteriologists have identified certain strains of bac-	

teria that "eat" petroleum products, such as oil and gasoline.

W: That sounds very strange. How does it work?

M: [20] They absorb the petroleum and give out hydrogen and oxygen, leaving a clean environment behind them.

W: Could they use those little bugs to clean up big oil spills?

M: Yes, as a matter of fact, they are being proven to be the most successful method of cleaning land-based oil spills and are also useful for marine spills.

W: Wow! Are there other types of pollution those microbes like to eat?

M: Sure, bacteria have been used to remove arsenic from the sludge produced by gold mining operations. There are even experiments being done now to reduce nuclear waste to a harmless residue.

W: [21] Maybe those bacteria that we used to worry about will eventually save the world!

【解析】选[D]。细节题。男士在向女士解释 bacteria 如何起作用时说到，bacteria 能够吸收 petroleum (石油)，并释放出 hydrogen and oxygen。

21. What do the people think of the bacteria before, according to the woman?

【解析】选[A]。细节题。对话结尾处，女士话中的 Maybe those bacteria that we used to worry about will eventually save the world 中的定语从句 that we used to worry about 表明，过去人们会 worry about bacteria (担心细菌)。

Conversation Two

【听力原文】

W: Next… can I help you?

M: Yes. [22①] I'd like to open an account.

W: Certainly. Do you have any identification with you?

M. Yes. I have my passport and a driver's license.

W: That'll be sufficient. What type of account are you interested in?

M: I don't know, really. Could you explain the options to me?

W: Of course. There are several accounts suited to your specific needs. What will you be using it for?

M: I'm going to have my salary deposited into it. I want to be able to pay my bills, and I also want to use it to save some money.

W: Will you be [22②] making regular deposits?

M. I usually put away two hundred dollars each pay check.

W: I see. Well, I'd recommend that you open two separate accounts, [22③] one savings account and one transaction account.

M: Why not just one account?

W: The advantage of the savings account is that it gives you better interest.

M: Oh, what's the difference in the interest rates?

W: Well, let's see. I'll just check. [23] The interest rate on the savings account is currently zero point two percent. Interest is paid monthly.

M: Hmm. I see. What's the interest on the transaction account?

W: [24] It's only zero point one percent, and there are no fees unless your monthly balance falls below two hundred and fifty dollars.

M: And can I have a cheque book with that account?

W: Yes, of course. And you can have the two accounts linked to one card.

M: Oh, that's convenient.

W: Yes, you can also have a portion of your salary automatically transferred into your savings account when you get paid.

M: Oh, great. That sounds good. [25] I think I'll open both accounts.

W: All right. I'll get the application forms.

【答案解析】

22. Where does the conversation most probably take place?

【解析】选[B]。细节题。由对话中多次出现的 account (账户) 及 making regular deposits, one savings account and one transaction account 可推测对话可能发生在 bank。

23. How much interest rate will the man get if he opens savings account?

【解析】选[B]。细节题。女士告诉男士 savings account 的利率为 zero point two percent，也就是说如果男士开立储蓄存款账户，他会得到 0.2% 的利率。

24. When will not the owner of transaction account get interest, according to the woman?

【解析】选[A]。细节题。女士提到交易账户的利率是 0.1%，并且如果该账户月余额 falls below two hundred and fifty dollars (低于 250 美元)，那么交易账户的持有者就不会得到 fees (利息)。

25. What kind of account does the man choose to open at last?

【解析】选[D]。细节题。对话结尾处，男士说他会 open both accounts (开立这两种账户)，由上面的对话可知，这两种账户指的是 savings account 和 transaction account。

Section B

Passage One

【听力原文】	【答案解析】
Cold weather has a great effect on how our minds and bodies work. Maybe that is [26①] why there are so many expressions that use the word cold. For centuries, the body's blood has been linked closely with emotions. People who show no human emotions or feelings are said to be "cold-blooded". Cold can affect other parts of the body, too, the feet, for example. Heavy socks can warm your feet, if your feet are really cold. Yet there is an expression, [26②] "to get cold feet", that has nothing to do with cold or with your feet. The expression means being afraid to do something you had decided to do. Cold can also affect your shoulder. You give someone the [26③] "cold shoulder" when you refuse to speak to them. You treat them in a distant, cold way. [27] The expression probably comes from the physical act of turning your back toward someone instead of speaking to him face to face. A [26④] "cold fish" is not a fish. [28] It is a person. But it is a person who is unfriendly, unemotional and shows no love or warmth. A cold fish does not offer much of himself to anyone. [26⑤] "Out in the cold" is an expression often heard. It means not getting something that everybody else got. A person might say that everybody but him got a pay raise, and that he was left out in the cold. It is not a pleasant place to be.	26. What does the passage mainly talk about? 【解析】选[B]。主旨题。短文开头处就指出也许是 cold weather 对我们的思想和身体的影响太大,所以才会有那么多 expressions that use the word cold,下文紧接着对习语"to get cold feet"、"cold shoulder"、"cold fish"、"out in the cold"分别作出解释,由此可推断本文主要讲 some expressions related to "cold"(与 cold 有关的一些表达方式)。 27. What does the expression "cold shoulder" probably come from? 【解析】选[B]。细节题。文中在解释说明 cold shoulder 时明确提到,cold shoulder 很可能是来自于 the physical act of turning your back toward someone …(一个背对他人的动作)。 28. Which expression can be used to express someone who is unfriendly and unemotional? 【解析】选[C]。细节题。文中明确提到 a "cold fish"并不是指鱼,而是指 a person who is unfriendly, unemotional and shows no love or warmth(那种不友好、没有感情、没有爱和热情的人)。

Passage Two

【听力原文】	【答案解析】
[29①] In America the first successful newspaper was the *Boston News Letter*, begun by postmaster John Campbell in 1704. Although it was heavily subsidized by the colonial government, the experiment was a near-failure, with very limited circulation. [29②] Two more papers made their appearance in the 1720's, in Philadelphia and New York. By the eve of the Revolutionary War, some two dozen papers were issued in all of the colonies, although Massachusetts, New York, and Pennsylvania would remain the centers of American printing for many years. Articles in colonial papers, brilliantly conceived by revolutionary propagandists, were a major force that influenced public opinion in America from reconciliation with England to full political independence. [29③] [30] At the war's end in 1783, there were forty-three newspapers in print. The press played a vital role in the affairs of the new nation; many more newspapers were started, representing all shades of political opinion. [29④] The ratification of the Bill of Rights in 1791 at last guaranteed the freedom of the press, and America's newspapers began to take on a central role in national affairs. [29⑤] In the 1830s, advances in printing and papermaking technology led to an explosion of newspaper growth; the emergence of the Penny Press made it possible to produce a	29. What is the passage mainly talking about? 【解析】选[B]。主旨题。短文一开始就提到 1704 年 *Boston News Letters* 是美国第一份成功的报纸,下文以时间为序,分别说明了各个阶段报纸的发展情况,由此可推断本文主要讲的是 the development history of newspaper(报纸的发展史)。 30. How many newspapers in print were there in 1783? 【解析】选[A]。细节题。文中明确提到 1783 年战争结束时,美国有 forty-three newspapers in print(43 种发行的报纸)。 31. What change did Penny Press bring to newspapers? 【解析】选[B]。推断题。文中提到 Penny Press 的出现使得报纸的成本

newspaper that could be sold for just a cent a copy. [31①] Previously, newspapers were the province of the wealthy, literate minority. The price of a year's subscription, usually over a full week's pay for a laborer, had to be paid in full and "invariably in advance". [31②] This sudden availability of cheap, interesting reading material was a significant stimulus to the achievement of the nearly universal literacy now taken for granted in America.

降低,从而使 newspapers were the province of the wealthy(报纸是有钱人的领域)的局面被打破了,言外之意就是 Penny Press 使报纸 available for common people。

Passage Three

【听力原文】

One sort of crime which particularly worries people is juvenile delinquency—that is, crimes committed by young people. [32] There are two main types of juvenile crimes: stealing and violence. Most people do not understand why young people commit these crimes. They tend to put all the blame on the children. In fact, there are a large number of different reasons.

These crimes are not usually committed by people who are poor or in need. Young people often dislike and hate the adult world. They will do things to show that they are rebels. [33] Also in Britain today it is easier for young people to commit crimes because they have more freedom to go where they want and have more money to do what they want.

There are two other possible causes which are worth mentioning. More and more people in Britain live in large towns. In a large town, no one knows who anyone else is or where they live. They may have been next-door neighbors for years, but have never spoken to one another. When a stranger appears in the neighborhood, nobody takes any notice. [34] But in the village, crimes are rare because everybody knows everyone else.

Although it is difficult to explain, the last cause is very important. Perhaps there is something in society which encourages violence and crime. It is a fact that children are exposed to films and reports about crime and violence all the time. Many people do not agree that this influences the young people, [35] but young people are very much influenced by the society they grow up in. The fault may be as much with the whole society as with these young people.

【答案解析】

32. What kind of crime do young people usually commit, according to the passage?
【解析】选[A]。细节题。短文一开头就明确提到 juvenile crimes(青少年犯罪)的两大主要类型是 stealing and violence,[A] 是原文的细节再现。

33. Why is it easier for juvenile to commit crimes in Britain?
【解析】选[A]。细节题。文中明确提到,在 Britain 年轻人更容易犯罪,因为他们 have more freedom to get where they want(有更多的自由去他们想去的地方),[A] 是原文的细节再现。

34. What contribute to the less crimes in village, according to the passage?
【解析】选[B]。推断题。文中提到,乡村不经常发生犯罪事件,是因为 everybody knows everyone else(人们之间互相认识),言外之意就是人们之间的 familiarity(熟识性)使犯罪事件很少。

35. What should be blamed for juvenile crimes as mentioned in the passage?
【解析】选[A]。细节题。短文结尾处明确提到,引起青少年犯罪的一个重要原因就是一些关于犯罪和暴力的电影和报道影响到了青少年的成长,尽管有些父母并不承认这一事实,但孩子们成长的 society 确实对他们有影响,由此可知 society 是引起青少年犯罪的主要原因。

Section C

【听力原文】

Many new plays are presented first on Broadway, the theatre district of New York City. If they are successful, they later go "on the road" to (36) scores of cities throughout the country. More than 50 (37) productions are presented each season on Broadway. To many Americans, seeing a Broadway show is a high point in their visit to the nation's largest city. However, a movement known as "(38) regional theatre" has developed

【答案解析】

36. 空前的动词短语 go to 和空后的介词 of 提示所填词应为名词,再结合介词 of 后面的名词 cities 可知所填词应为复数名词。本句中的 they 指代的是上句中的 many new plays,由此可推测本句大致是讲如果这些新剧在 Broadway(百老汇)演出成功,它们就会 throughout the country(在全国)尽心演出,故所填词很可能表示"很多不同的"城市。scores of 意为"很多的"。

37. 空前的数词 50 和空后的系动词 are 提示所填词应为复数名词。本文首句指出 Broadway 是上演戏剧的地方,由此

across the United States, and playhouses are (39)attended eagerly in cities throughout the nation.

In recent years another side of the New York Theatre has developed, known as "off Broadway". These plays are (40)modestly staged in small playhouses, but some (41)rank with the best Broadway performances in (42)professional skill, and many enjoy long runs.

After the regular theatre season has closed, more than 300 summer theatres go into action in rural areas, in suburbs and seashore and mountain (43)resorts. Well-known actors often appear in these plays. At the same time, (44)ambitious young students of the theatre have an opportunity to work under experienced actors and directors.

Motion pictures remain a favorite form of entertainment despite the popularity of television. (45)Not as many feature films are being made today as 20 years ago, but the quality of the films has improved. Many movies are now made by independent producers with fresh ideas and approaches. They select their stories and treat the subjects in ways that reflect their creative ideas. Modern methods of movie making, (46)such as the wide screen, color film and improved sound, have enhanced realism and audience enjoyment.

可知此处应表达"50多部戏剧作品"的含义。productions 意为"产品"。

38. 空后的名词 theatre 提示所填词应为形容词。regional 意为"地区的"。

39. 空前的系动词 are 提示所填词应为形容词或动词的过去分词形式。根据副词 eagerly 在句中的位置可进一步判断所填词应为动词的过去分词形式。attended 意为"出席，参加"。

40. 空前的系动词 are 和空后的过去分词 staged 提示所填词应为副词。modestly 意为"适当地"。

41. 分析句子结构可知，所填词应在句中作谓语，故所填词应为动词，并与 with 构成搭配。空前的形容词 some 指的是在 small playhouse(小剧院)上演的 some plays(一些戏剧)，又由转折连词 but 可知，句子想要表达的是尽管有些戏剧是在小剧院上演的，但有些却可以和 the best Broadway…"媲美"的含义。rank with 意为"与…并列"。

42. 空前的介词 in 和空后的名词 skill 提示所填词应为形容词。professional 意为"专业的"。

43. 空前的并列连词 and 和名词 mountain 提示所填词应为名词，与 seashore 构成并列关系。resorts 意为"胜地"。

44. 【Main Points】ambitious young **learners** of the theatre **could** work under experienced actors and directors

45. 【Main Points】Not as many feature films are being **produced** today as 20 years ago, but **the films' quality** has improved

46. 【Main Points】**for example**, the wide screen, color film and improved sound, have **increased** realism and audience enjoyment

第二篇

阅读理解

第14-26天

Part 2

快速阅读巅峰讲座

　　快速阅读要求考生在 15 分钟内读完一篇 1200 字左右的文章并解答后面的 10 道题。大纲规定,其题目类型为"是非判断+句子填空+其他",目前考过的题目类型包括是非判断题、句子填空题和多项选择题,题目数量分配一般为"4 道是非判断题+6 道句子填空题"或"7 道多项选择题+3 道句子填空题"。尽管快速阅读的题目类型有些多样化,但每类题目所测试的重点都是一样的,即考生在有限的时间内利用略读和寻读两种技能掌握文章主旨大意、快速查找特定信息的能力。

Lecture 1　　第一讲　11 大是非题判断原则

　　是非判断题要求考生判断题目内容是 Y(for YES),N(for NO)还是 NG(NOT GIVEN),而大多数考生对于 Y,N 和 NG 三类答案的判断标准并不十分明确,尤其是容易混淆 N 和 NG。因此,我们在此将三类答案所代表的具体内涵及判断原则给大家总结如下:

一、题目是原文的同义表达—Y

　　如果题目是用同义词或同义结构对原文内容的转述,即题目就是原文的同义表达,那么该题的答案即为 Y(for Yes)。

【例 1】

(710 分样卷-2)

【原文】	【题目】
They receive nearly the same amount of sunlight, and therefore heat, all year. Consequently, the weather in these regions **remains fairly constant**.	2. There is **not much change** in the weather in the tropical rainforests all the year round.

【解析】[Y]。题目中的 not much change 对应原文中的 remains fairly constant;主谓结构转换成了存在句。

二、题目是对原文的归纳或推断—Y

　　如果题目是根据原文中的某两处或两处以上的细节内容作出的归纳或简单推断,那么该题的答案为 Y(for Yes)。

【例 2】

(07-6-2)

【原文】	【题目】
Mary Lyn Miller, **veteran career consultant** and founder of the Life and Career Clinic, … she has **helped thousands of dissatisfied workers reassess life and work**.	2. Mary Lyn Miller's job is to **advise people on their life and career**.

【解析】[Y]。Mary Lyn Miller 后面的同位语 veteran career consultant 表明她的职业是职场顾问,而由该段最后一句可知,她通过各种方式帮助人们解决在生活和工作中遇到的问题,题干正是对此的归纳概括,故答案为[Y]。

三、题目与原文直接相反—N

　　如果题目是用反义词、not 加同义词或反义结构等来直接表达与原文相反的意思,那么该题答案为 N(for No)。这类题目相对简单,因此在六级快速阅读中并不常见。

【例3】

【原文】	【题目】
Frozen and tinned fruit and vegetables can be just **as nutritious as** fresh varieties.	1. Compared with fresh fruit and vegetables, frozen and tinned varieties are **lack of nutrients**.

【解析】[N]。原文指出冷冻、罐装水果和蔬菜所含营养同新鲜水果和蔬菜所含营养是一样的(…as nutritious as fresh varieties),而题目中的 are lack of nutrients 与原文表达意思恰好相反。

四、题目与原文某项事实相矛盾—N

题目将原文中已经确定的原因、结果或是其他明确的事实说成是另外的情况,那么该题答案为 N(for No)。

【例4】 (新 06-12-1)

【原文】	【题目】
Lance Bass of N Sync was supposed to be the third to make the $20 million trip, but he did not join the three-man crew as they blasted off on October 30, 2002, **due to lack of payment**.	1. Lance Bass wasn't able to go on a tour of space **because of health problems**.

【解析】[N]。原文说 Lance Bass 原定是第三个到太空旅行的人,但最终没能成行的原因是 lack of payment(费用不够),题目中则将原因说成是 health problems(健康问题),与原文事实相矛盾。

五、题目将原文信息张冠李戴—N

如果题目将原文中相邻信息的主语、宾语、定语、条件状语等成分换位,造成原有信息的张冠李戴,那么该题答案为 N(for No)。

【例5】

【原文】	【题目】
The United States ranks somewhere in the middle of the major countries (United Kingdom, Canada, Germany, France and Japan) in landfill disposal. **The United Kingdom ranks highest**, burying about 90 percent of its solid waste in landfills…	2. Compared with other major industrialized countries, **America buries a much higher percentage** of its solid waste in landfills.

【解析】[NG]。原文是说 the United Kingdom 在 landfills 填埋 solid waste 的比例最高(ranks highest),而题目中则将 the United Kingdom 换成了 America,明显属于张冠李戴。

六、题目使用了与原文不同范畴、频率或可能性的词语—N

如果题目中增加、减少或删除了原文中的范畴、频率或可能性,或是题目将原文中的绝对概念变成了相对概念或是将相对概念变成了绝对概念,那么该题答案为 N(for No)。比如原文中是 many(很多)、sometimes(有时)以及 unlikely(不太可能)等词语,题目中却换成了 all(全部)、usually(通常)、always(总是)以及 impossible(完全不可能)等词语;或是原文中是 both…and, and, or 以及 also 等词语,题目中则是 must 或 only 等词。

【例6】 (710分样卷-1)

【原文】	【题目】
Today, tropical rainforests cover only 6 percent of the Earth's ground surface, but they are home to **over half** of the planet's plant and animal species.	1. Virtually **all** plant and animal species on Earth can be found in tropical rainforests.

【解析】[N]。原文中是说热带雨林是地球上一半以上(over half)的动植物物种的家园,而题目则将其转述成地球上所有(all)动植物物种在热带雨林均能够找得到,故题目与原文不符。

七、题目将原文中表示比较概念的词语误用或混淆—N

如果题目将原文中的比较级转述成最高级,或将最高级转述成比较级,或是将原文中的比较对象相混淆,那么该题答案为 N(for No)。

(710 分样卷-4)

【例7】

【原文】	【题目】
Their top branches spread wide in order to capture maximum sunlight. This creates a thick *canopy*(树冠) level at the top of the forest, with **thinner greenery** levels **underneath**.	4. **Below** the canopy level of a tropical rainforest grows an **overabundance of plants**.

【解析】[N]。原文中是说顶部的树枝为了最大限度地吸收阳光而向外扩展,从而形成了厚厚的树冠(canopy),而下面的植物相对则较稀疏(thinner greenery),而题目则是说在树冠以下(below)植物生长非常茂盛(overabundance of plants),显然与原文不符。

八、题目在原文中找不到对应信息或依据—NG

如果题目中的某些信息在原文中根本没有提及或在文中找不到依据,即我们根据原文内容无法判断其正确与否,那么该题答案为 NG(for Not Given)。

【例8】 (07-6-3)

【原文】	【题目】
Mary Lyn Miller, veteran career consultant and founder of the Life and Career Clinic, says that when most people are unhappy about their work, their first thought is to get a different job.	3. Mary Lyn Miller herself was once quite dissatisfied with her own work.

【解析】[NG]。原文中介绍了 Mary Lyn Miller 的职业,并提到了某些人在对工作感到不满(unhappy)时的一些想法,但并没有提到 Miller 自己是否曾经对工作不满(dissatisfied)。

九、题目将原文具体化—NG

如果原文涉及一个较大的概念,而题目涉及的内容比原文更具体,那么该题答案为 NG(for Not Given)。

【例9】 (710 分样卷-3)

【原文】	【题目】
Since **rainforests** are at the middle of the globe, located **near the equator**, they are not especially affected by this change.	3. The **largest number of rainforests** in the world are located on the **African continent**.

【解析】[NG]。原文只提到热带雨林是位于地球中部地区的赤道附近(near the equator),而并没有具体提到世界上最大数量的热带雨林是位于非洲大陆(African continent)。

十、题目是无根据比较—NG

如果原文中提及某些事物,但并未对其作出任何比较,而题目却将其放在一起比较,那么该题答案为 NG(for Not Given)。

【例10】

【原文】	【题目】
2. **Take advantage of site features**. CareerBuilder. com, for example, offers three levels of privacy from which job seekers can choose. The first is standard posting… The second is… The third is…	1. Of the three options offered by Career-Builder. com in Suggestion 2, the third one is apparently most strongly recommended.

【解析】[NG]。原文中说 CareerBuilder. com 提供了三个层次的隐私保护,然后分别对它们进行了列举说明,但并未对三者作出比较,更没有强烈推荐其中任何一个,因此题目中的 most strongly recommended 属无根据比较。

十一、题目将原文的抽象概念说成事实—NG

如果题目将原文中的目标、目的、想法、愿望、保证、发誓等说成是事实情况,那么该题答案为 NG(for Not Given)。这类题目原文中常使用 aim(目标)、purpose(目的)、promise(保证)、swear(发誓)以及 vow(发誓)等词,题目中则一般使用实义动词。

【例 11】

【原文】	【题目】
David promised he would never come back.	1. David never came back.

【解析】[NG]。原文中 promised 表示 never come back 是他的承诺,但事实上他到底有没有遵守承诺无从考证,而题目则将这种承诺说成了事实,故本题答案应为[NG]。

Exercise 　　　　　　　　即讲即练

Very Small Business

Technologist Eric Drexler foresaw a future in which machines far smaller than dust motes would construct everything from chairs to rocket engines, atom by atom, in which microscopic robots would heal human ills, cell by cell. Sixteen years after the publication of Drexler's book *Engines of Creation*, the technologies most immediately available to consumers are somewhat less fantastic: stain-resistant cloth and more durable tennis balls.

Much of the trend is gone from nanotechnology, the term Drexler popularized for his world of very small wonders. But something more interesting has crept in: sales. The cloth and tennis balls are bringing in money, as are dozens of other new products made and enhanced through nanotechnology. To be sure, most nanotech companies are still investing more in R. and D. (research and development) than they are collecting in revenue. But many commercial applications are in advanced stages of development or already on sale. Says Richard Smalley, a Rice University professor and Nobel Prize-winning chemist: "We are only beginning to see the things nanotechnology can do."

Nanotechnology takes its name from a nanometer (nm), a billionth of a meter, or about one-hundred-thousandth the diameter of a human hair. In common usage, it refers to an array of new machines and materials whose key parts are smaller than 100 nanometers and to the new tools, such as Veeco Instruments' atomic-force microscopes and Nanometrics' inspection tools for semiconductor makers, which allow the tiny parts and particles to be observed and manipulated. It is a mysterious realm in which the laws of classical physics yield to those of quantum mechanics, in which the powerful bonds between atoms overtake the effects of gravity that rule the big world. Yet scientists have moved beyond the basic exploration of nanotech to its exploitation. The National Science Foundation in the US foresees a $1 trillion market by 2015 for nano products, and businesses and governments around the world are rushing to cash in.

The US government has proposed that $710 million be spent on nanotech research next year — a 17% increase over the 2002 budget — on the development of everything from water-filtration equipment to military uniforms made from "smart" materials that can guard against germ warfare. Governments in Asia and Europe are investing $2 billion in similar R. and D., according to CMP-Cientifica, a research firm in Madrid. "Nanotech is a three-legged race right now," says Mark Modzelewski, executive director of the NanoBusiness Alliance, based in New York City.

Even enthusiasts like Modzelewski caution that no one should expect an overnight nanotech revolution. The technology will evolve — "radically", he says — as its benefits seep into virtually every crevice of human industry, from toys to tanks. And even professional investors are cautious. "True venture capitalists are not investing. They are watching," says Glenn Fishbine, author of The Investor's Guide to Nanotechnology and Micromachines. Only a handful of "pure play" nanotech stocks exist, including Nanophase Technologies, in Romeoville, Illinois, which makes nanoscale powders. Still, investors in big companies such as Intel, Samsung and Dupont have been indirectly funding nanotech development for years.

Some sectors surveyed here — consumer goods, computer chips and cars — deserve particular attention for the progress they have made toward bringing profitable products to market.

Cloth and Tennis Balls

InMat, physicist Harris Goldberg's seven-employee company in Hillsborough, New Jersey, regularly ships to Wilson Sporting Goods 55-gallon drums filled with am environmentally safe liquid containing l-nm-thick sheets of clay. When the material covers the inside of a tennis ball, it traps air far more effectively than standard rubber alone and doubles the life of the ball. Wilson's Double Core, which was launched more than a year ago, sells at a high price in US tennis shops and this year became the official ball of the Davis Cup competition.

InMat will take in just $250,000 this year, but Goldberg expects to double that figure in each of the next few years.

A chemical process that adds "nano-whiskers" to cotton fabrics and renders them wrinkle and stain resistant explains new products from Eddie Bauer and Lee Jeans. The fabrics were developed by Nano-Tex, a Greensboro, North Carolina, company that is 51% owned by Burlington Industries, a textile firm that is struggling to emerge from bankruptcy. Nano-Tex has also developed active-wear fabrics that disperse and dry sweat. Later this year, it will launch a line, destined for socks, underwear and T shirts, that will channel body odors through the structure of the fibers.

Computer Chips

If the company of Greg Schmergel, a serial entrepreneur, is successful, it will eventually add about five minutes to everyone's day. The company, Nantero, wants to build an "instant-on" computer that doesn't need to boot up.

In a year, Nantero expects to produce a chip which won't forget how to run all its programs when the power is switched off. The technology uses arrays of 2-nm strands of carbon atoms, called carbon nanotubes. Pairs of tubes store data by locking together when a current runs through them and stay together even when the computer power is switched off and back on. The tubes remain linked until separated by a countercurrent, so their memory is retained. And these chips have other advantages. Schmergel says that within three years, Nantero can bring to market chips that can store 10 times as much data as a silicon chip the same size while operating faster and with less heat. "They're not saying much publicly about their approach," says Steven Glapa, president of the nano-consulting firm In Realis, "but what they're promising sounds pretty breathtaking."

Nanotubes could be the first commodity in the nanotech economy. Nano-lab, in Brighton, Massachusetts, is one of the few nanotech companies turning a profit. It sold $200,000 worth of made-to-order nanotubes in 2001 and is on track to more than double that amount this year.

Plastic Cars

Every big carmaker promises that any year now, it will have a fuel-cell car on the road a vehicle that will travel silently, spit drinkable water from its tail pipe and provide power to your house when you plug it into the garage. In the meantime, auto manufacturers are putting nanotechnology to work in other ways. Toyota was the first to experiment with strong, light-weight nanocomposite materials in the late 1980s, and US automakers are starting to move nanocomposites out of the lab and into vehicles. General Motors is using advanced plastics to make step assists for 2002 GMC Safari and Chevrolet Astro vans. The new materials are stiffer, lighter and less brittle in cold temperatures than other plastics. Improvements in strength and reductions in weight lead to fuel savings. The next step is for GM to use nanocomposites in car interiors and bumpers and eventually into load-bearing structural parts, such as vehicle frames.

As nanotechnology produces more products and processes, will the technology ever catch up with Eric Drexler's theories? Says Steve Bent, a Washington patent lawyer for nanotech firms, "That will be the research agenda for the rest of the century."

1. What Drexler predicted 16 years ago has come true.
2. According to the passage, most nanotech companies haven't made much profit from the nanotechnology.
3. Scientists haven't employed the nanotechnology in producing nano products because of insufficient financial support.
4. The success in the future germ warfare will largely depend on the usage of nanotechnology.
5. Spain is also planning to launch enough money into the nanotech research and development.
6. There are not many "pure play" nanotech stocks existing because the true venture capitalists are not investing in nanotech.
7. Whether the tennis ball is durable lies on whether the air inside is easy to leak from it.
8. The person who wears the active-wear fabrics will not sweat.
9. Once the chip which can store more data is brought into market, it will make more money for the company than the silicon chip.
10. Every big carmaker has a fuel-cell car being put in to practice any year now.

【答案与解析】
1.【定位】根据题目中的关键信息 16 years 可将搜索范围定位在第一段最后一句。

【解析】[N]。题目中 what 引导的主语从句与该段第一句中的定语从句相对应,但该段第二句指出在 Drexler 的著作"Engines of Creation"发表后 16 年,与消费者们联系最紧密的却是那些不太新奇的科技,如 stain-resistant cloth 和 more durable tennis balls,而不是 Drexler 所说的 machines far smaller than dust motes…和 microscopic robots would heal human ills…,由此可见 16 年前 Drexler 的预想并没有变为现实,题目与原文直接相反,故答案为[N]。

2.【定位】根据题目中的关键信息 most nanotech companies 可将搜索范围定位在第二段第四句。

【解析】[Y]。由该句中的比较级 more…than…不难看出,对大多数 nanotech companies 来说,它们仍然是 investing (投资)多于 collecting in revenue(收益),也就是说,most nanotech companies 还没有从 nanotechnology 中获得很大利润,题目是原文的同义表达,故答案为[Y]。

3.【定位】根据题目中的关键信息 scientists, nano products 可将搜索范围定位在第三段倒数一、二句。

【解析】[N]。该段倒数第二句中的 scientists have moved beyond the basic exploration of nanotech to its exploitation 表明现在科学家们已不再局限于对纳米技术的 exploration(钻研),而是开始转向对纳米技术的 exploitation(利用),而最后一句则指出世界上很多企业以及政府部门都投入了大量的资金以支持 nano products。题目与原文事实相反,故答案为[N]。

4.【定位】根据题目中的关键信息 germ warfare 可将搜索范围定位在第四段第一句。

【解析】[NG]。该句指出美国政府计划明年投资 7 亿 1 千万美元用于 nanotech research,来发展从 water-filtration equipment 到 military uniforms 的所有东西。该句中 that 引导的定语从句 that can guard against germ warfare 只是说明"smart" materials 能够用以抵御细菌战,但是并没有说明将来能够在细菌战中取得胜利将很大程度上依赖于纳米技术的使用,题目在原文中找不到依据,故答案为[NG]。

5.【定位】根据题目中的关键信息 Spain 和 research and development 可将搜索范围定位在第四段第二句。

【解析】[NG]。Madrid 是 Spain 的首都,但该句只是说明 CMP-Cientifica 是位于 Madrid 的一家研究公司,它指出 Asia 和 Europe 的各国政府也投入 20 亿资金以用以纳米技术的研究和开发。Spain 虽然是 Europe 国家,但原文并没有指出它也投入资金用以纳米技术的研究和开发,题目将原文信息具体化了,故答案为[NG]。

6.【定位】根据题目中的关键信息 pure play, nanotech stocks 和 true venture capitalists 可将搜索范围定位在第五段第三、四句。

【解析】[N]。该段第三句指出 true venture capitalists 并不投资于 nanotech,而是在 watching(观望)形势。第四句指出目前 only a handful of "pure play" nanotech stocks exist(只存在很少一部分专门用以研究纳米技术的股票),这两句只是指出了一些事实,两句之间并不存在因果关系,题目是将原文中的信息张冠李戴,故答案为[N]。

7.【定位】根据题目中的关键信息 tennis ball, air 可将搜索范围定位在小标题 Cloth and Tennis Balls 下第一段。

【解析】[Y]。该段第二句指出当把 1-nm-thick sheets of clay 用在 tennis ball 的内壁时,它就会 traps air far more effectively than standard rubber alone and doubles the life of the ball,由此可推断 tennis ball 不耐用是因为它里面的空气很容易漏走,也就是说如果 tennis ball 里面的空气不易漏走,那么它就会很耐用。题目是对原文的正确推断,故答案为[Y]。

8.【定位】根据题目中的关键信息 active-wear fabrics 可将搜索范围定位在小标题 Cloth and Tennis Balls 下第三段。

【解析】[N]。该段倒数第二句中的定语从句表明了 active-wear fabrics 的作用,即 disperse and dry sweat。是说在人体出汗后,active-wear fabrics 可以使汗变干,但并不是说穿了 active-wear fabrics 就不会出汗,题目表达与原文的表达范畴不同,故答案为[N]。

9.【定位】根据题目中的关键信息 chip, store more data, silicon chip 可将搜索范围定位在小标题 Computer Chips 下第二段。

【解析】[NG]。该段指出了新芯片的一些优点,如:在电源关闭后仍能储存资料,容量大,运行更快,产生的热量更少等。该段倒数第二句只是说在未来三年内,Nantero 可能会出售 chips than can store 10 times as much data as a silicon chip the same size,但是并没有说明哪个会更赚钱,题目是无根据比较,故答案为[NG]。

10.【定位】根据题目中的关键信息 every big carmaker, fuel-cell car 可将搜索范围定位在小标题 Plastic Cars 下第一段。

【解析】[NG]。由该段第一句中的 promises 可知 any year now, it will have…是 every big carmaker 的承诺,但该承诺究竟会不会变成现实还无从考证,而题目将这种承诺说成了现实,故答案为[NG]。

Lecture 2　　第二讲　8种选择题设题题眼

快速阅读中多项选择题的出题形式与传统的篇章阅读一样,要求考生根据文章内容从四个选项中选出最佳答案,其题目主要有以下设题题眼:

一、数字信息处

时间、比例、人数、价格等数字信息处是快速阅读多项选择题最常见的设题题眼之一,答案一般都是原文中数字的再现或需要进行简单运算得出,其干扰项多为文中出现的数字。解题的关键在于利用题干中的关键信息迅速定位,找到与其相对应的数字,有时选项中的数字也可以作为定位信息。

另外,有些题目虽然不是直接考查数字,但题干中包含数字,这时数字则可以作为很好的解题定位信息。

【例1】　　　　　　　　　　　　　　　　　　　　　　　　　　　　　　　(07-12-4)

【原文】	【题目】
Forty percent of that powers old-fashioned incandescent light bulbs— a 19th-Century technology that wastes most of the power it consumes on unwanted heat.	4. How much of the power consumed by incandescent bulbs is converted into light? 　[A] A small of portion.　　[B] Some 40 percent. 　[C] Almost half.　　[D] 75 to 80 percent.

【解析】[A]。本题是问 incandescent bulbs(白炽灯泡)消耗的电力中有多少被转化成光能。文中说 incandescent light bulbs 所使用的技术将大部分电力都浪费在产生无用的热能上,由此可推知它所消耗的电力中只有 a small of portion 转化成光能。

二、段落主题处

针对段落主题所设的题目有时题干中会指定段落,有时则需要考生根据题干中关键词定位段落。其答案一般需要结合段落其他内容归纳得出,有时也可从段落主题句直接摄取。

【例2】　　　　　　　　　　　　　　　　　　　　　　　　　　　　　　　(07-12-1)

【原文】	【题目】
Forget the old idea that conserving energy is a form of self-denial-riding bicycles, dimming the lights, and taking fewer showers. These days conservation is all about efficiency: getting the same — or better — results from just a fraction of the energy.	1. What is said to be the best way to conserve energy nowadays? 　[A] Raising efficiency. 　[B] Cutting unnecessary costs. 　[C] Finding alternative resources. 　[D] Sacrificing some personal comforts.

【解析】[A]。本题是问目前保护能源最好的方式是什么。本段第二句为主题句:现在保护能源都与效率有关,结合冒号后面对其的解释可知,目前保护能源最好的方式是 raising efficiency(提高效率)。

三、方式方法处

这类题目题干中一般会含有 by,the way 等表示方式方法的标志性词语,但原文中经常没有明显的标志性词语,因此解题时不能将 by, the way 等类词语作为主要的定位线索词,而应该利用题干中其他关键信息词进行定位,找出原文中隐含的方式方法。

【例3】　　　　　　　　　　　　　　　　　　　　　　　　　　　　　　　(07-12-5)

【原文】	【题目】
Several countries have used subsidies to jump-start the market, including Japan, where almost 1 million heat pumps have been installed in the past two years to heat water for showers and hot tubs.	5. Some countries have tried to jump-start the market of heat pumps by _____. 　[A] upgrading the equipment 　[B] encouraging investments 　[C] implementing high-tech 　[D] providing subsidies

【解析】[D]。本题是问一些国家想要通过什么方式尽快起动热泵市场。原文中的谓语 used subsidies 转换成题目中的方式状语 by _____，故答案为[D](提供津贴)。

四、举例或列举处

作者经常会使用举例或列举的方法来论证观点或说明事实，针对举例或列举所设的题目有时是题干为事例，答案为相关观点或事实；有时是题干为观点或事实，答案为相关事例。定位原文时，要留意原文中出现 as, such as, for example, for instance, take … as an example, First(ly) …, Second(ly) …, Third(ly) …, Finally …, On the one hand …, on the other hand … 等表示举例或列举的标志性词语的地方。需要注意的是，有时原文中并不含有这类标志性词语，这时就需要考生利用题干提供的线索在原文中定位。

【例4】 (四级 07-12-5)

【原文】	【题目】
Globalization is also reshaping the way research is done. One new trend involves sourcing portions of a research program to another country. Yale professor and Howard Hughes Medical Institute investigator Tian Xu directs a research center focused on the genetics of human disease at Shanghai's Fudan University, in collaboration with faculty colleagues from both schools.	5. An example illustrating the general trend of universities' globalization is _____. [A] Yale's collaboration with Fudan University on genetic research [B] Yale's helping Chinese universities to launch research projects [C] Yale's student exchange program with European institutions [D] Yale's establishing branch campuses throughout the world

【解析】[A]。本题是问能够阐释大学全球化这一总趋势的例子是哪一个。该段首先说全球化也在重塑研究方式，之后以耶鲁大学和复旦大学在基因研究方面的合作为例来说明大学全球化的这一总的趋势。

五、解释说明或补充说明处

文章中经常会对某人或某事物进行解释或补充说明，有时是通过破折号、冒号等特殊标点引出，有时是通过定语从句或同位语从句引出，因此在定位原文时要重点留意这些地方，答案往往就在特殊标点之后，或在定位从句或同位语从句中。

【例5】 (07-12-4)

【原文】	【题目】
Forty percent of that powers old-fashioned incandescent light bulbs — a 19th-Century technology that wastes most of the power it consumes on unwanted heat.	4. How much of the power consumed by incandescent bulbs is converted into light? [A] A small of portion. [B] Some 40 percent. [C] Almost half. [D] 75 to 80 percent.

【解析】[A]。本题是问 incandescent bulbs(白炽灯泡)消耗的电力中有多少被转化成光能。破折号后面是对 old-fashioned incandescent light bulbs 的补充说明，由该句可知这种白炽灯泡将大部分电力都浪费在产生无用的热能上，由此可推知它所消耗的电力中只有 a small of portion 转化成光能。

六、组织机构观点或行为处

这类题目往往会针对文中涉及的某项组织或机构的观点、态度、措施或行为进行设题，解题时要注意利用题干或选项中给出的该组织或机构的名称进行定位。

【例6】 (07-12-2)

【原文】	【题目】
On Jan. 10, the European Union unveiled a plan to cut energy use across the continent by 20 percent by 2020.	2. What does the European Union plan to do? [A] Diversify energy supply. [B] Cut energy consumption. [C] Reduce carbon emissions. [D] Raise production efficiency.

【解析】[B]。本题是问欧盟计划做什么。通过题干中的 the European Union 我们很容易就能够找到答案出处。

七、并列、递进、转折处

这类题目的题干中一般都不含有表示并列、递进或转折关系的标志性词语,因此无法识别题目的设题题眼,但由于这些地方是设题的高发点,因此考生在利用题干中关键词语定位原文的同时,应重点留意出现 and, or, but, however, even, not only…but also, not …but, on the other hand 等表示并列、递进或转折关系的标志性词语的地方。

【例 7】　　　　　　　　　　　　　　　　　　　　　　　　（四级 07-12-7）

【原文】	【题目】
Most politicians recognize the link between investment in science and national economic strength, but support for research funding has been unsteady.	7. What is said about the U. S. federal funding for research? [A] It has increased by 3 percent. [B] It has been unsteady for years. [C] It has been more than sufficient. [D] It doubled between 1998 and 2003.

【解析】[B]。本题是问关于美国联邦政府在研究方面的拨款文中说了什么。由 but 转折后内容可知,该项拨款一直不太稳定。

八、条件、因果等逻辑关系处

这类题目的题干或选项中经常会含有体现该逻辑关系的连接词或短语,定位原文时,要留意 if, because, so, so that, in order that 等表示逻辑关系的连接词。但需要注意的是,题干或选项可能会对原文中逻辑关系进行转换,因此定位时要多方面考虑。

【例 8】　　　　　　　　　　　　　　　　　　　　　　　　（07-12-3）

【原文】	【题目】
The most advanced insulation follows the law of increasing returns: if you add enough, you can scale down or even eliminate heating and air-conditioning equipment, lowering costs even before you start saving on utility bills.	3. If you add enough insulation to your house, you may be able to _____. [A] improve your work environment [B] cut your utility bills by half [C] get rid of air-conditioners [D] enjoy much better health

【解析】[B]。本题是问如果给房子加上足够的保暖材料,可以带来什么样的好处。利用 if 及关键词 insulation(隔热,保暖)可快速在原文中定位,由分词短语 lowering costs…可知,这样做可能会将购置取暖设备的费用减少一半。

Exercise 即讲即练

Animal Tests — More Than a Cosmetic Change

Every time you reach for an eye-drop or reapply a lip salve, you do be so confident that the chemicals they contain are safe to use. But the *toxicology* (毒物学) tests on which regulators rely to gather this information are largely based on wasteful and often poorly predictive animal experiments. Efforts in Europe are about to change this, and the man charged with bringing toxicology into the 21st century is a plain-talking German: Thomas Hartung. Although Hartung acknowledges the immense challenges ahead, he sees this as an opportunity for toxicology "to turn itself at last into a respectable science".

Three years ago, Hartung became director of the European Centre for the Validation of Alternative Methods (ECVAM) in Ispra, Italy. ECVAM was set up in 1993 to support European Union policy aimed at reducing the number of animals used in regulatory testing.

The centre, which sits on the sleepy shores of Lake Maggiore in the Italian Alps, originally had ten members of staff and faced an uphill struggle to cut back the millions of animal tests carried out in Europe every year. Then in 2003, two major policy changes were announced from above, increasing the pressure on the center's labs. ECVAM found itself facing an unexpectedly short deadline for delivering a slew of animal-free methods for testing chemical toxicity.

Rule Change

The first change was to the European Union's Cosmetics Directive, which phases out over ten years the use of animals in cosmetics testing. A short while later, the European Commission proposed its controversial REACH legislation (Registration, Evaluation and Authorization of Chemicals). Europe produces some 30,000 chemicals for which toxicity data have never been registered. REACH aims to make registration mandatory for both future and existing chemicals — even those that have been on the market for decades.

If, as expected, the REACH directive is approved next year, it will come into effect in 2007. Animal-welfare groups fear that this will mean millions more animals will be used in tests to meet the regulatory requirements. And industry claims that the testing process could cost billions of euros. Almost overnight, industry's interest in cheaper, animal-free testing skyrocketed.

Last month ECVAM was put in charge of developing, with industry and regulatory agencies, the testing strategies for REACH. Now commanding 50 staff, Hartung is rising to the challenge. "The toxicity tests that have been used for decades are simply bad science", he explains. "We now have an opportunity to start with a clean slate and develop evidence-based tests that have true predictive value."

Many of the animal tests used today were developed under crisis conditions. The notorious Draize test, which assesses the irritation or damage caused by chemicals simply by putting them into the eyes of rabbits, is a prime example. It was developed by the US Food and Drug Administration in 1944 after reports in the 1930s that some cosmetics were causing permanent eye injuries. One 38-year-old woman had gone blind after dyeing her lashes with Lash-Lure, a product that contained a derivative of coal tar.

Then came the calamity of *thalidomide*(镇静剂), which was given to a pregnant woman in the late 1950s to control morning sickness, but which caused horrific birth defects. By this time, governments were highly sensitive to public concerns and called on their authorities to develop animal-based tests that would predict all conceivable toxic effects of drugs and chemicals. The principles behind most of those tests remain more or less unchanged today.

Safety Catch

Each chemical that goes through the multiple tests required for registration can use up to 5,000 animals — or 12,000 if the chemical is a pesticide. The cost of doing this for the 30,000 unregistered chemicals so that they comply with REACH has been estimated at between 5 billion (US$6 billion) and 10 billion.

In the decade since ECVAM was established, the number of animals used in toxicology testing has fallen slightly, although it still hovers at about one million per year. This reduction is a result of the refinement of existing tests, and the introduction of some alternative methods that rely on in *vitro* (试管) tests using cell cultures.

ECVAM believes that it can halve the total number of animals used for regulatory testing within a decade. It has just completed its first large-scale validation study of an *in vitro cytotoxicity* test, which monitors death of cultured cells following short-term exposure to a chemical. Chemicals shown to be harmful in this test would be excluded from any animal tests. At least 70% of the chemicals registered in the past two decades fall into this category, says Hartung. And this is just the beginning.

Poor Prediction

Most animal tests over-or under-estimate toxicity, or simply don't mirror toxicity in humans very well. The relevant industries also acknowledge the poor quality of those tests.

Take the embryo-toxicity test in which chemicals are fed to pregnant animals and the fates of their embryos, and the progeny of two subsequent generations, are studied. "Animal embryo-toxicity tests are not reliably predictive for humans," says Horst Spielmann, a toxicologist at the Federal Institute for Risk Assessment in Berlin. "When we find that cortisone is embryotoxic in all species tested except human, what are we supposed to make of them?"

The same goes for cancer. To test a single chemical for its potential to cause cancer takes 5 years and involves 400 rats, each of which is treated with the maximum tolerated dose. It is dramatically over-predictive: more than 50% of the results are positive, of which 90% are false positive, yet the number of compounds proved to be carcinogenic to humans is very low — the International Agency for Research on Cancer in Lyons, France, has identified just 95 proven and 66 probable human *carcinogens*(致癌物质).

Life or Death

Scientists also cannot assume that *in vitro* alternatives are automatically better, says Spielmann. In 1971, a comparison of animal Draize tests in different labs revealed the test to be hopelessly non-reproducible. But Spiehnann's 1995 study of animal-free alternatives to the Draize test showed that they were equally unreliable. Since then the *in vitro* tests have been standardized, and they are intrinsically more reproducible. "Although reproducibility and relevance are not the same thing," Spielmann cautions.

Relevance requires a good match between the test results and human data. At an ECVAM workshop in February, 30 industrial scientists met to develop the most effective strategy for using the alternative Draize tests, so that the false negatives and false positives of each test compensate for each other. This strategy is now going through the crucial validation procedure, in which human data, often from occupational health data-bases, will be used as points of reference. ECVAM has so far seen 17 alternative tests through validation — 11 use in vitro methods, another six involve refining in vitro tests to reduce the number of animals used.

Most of the new tests assess acute toxicity, but animal use is highest when testing for the toxic effects of prolonged exposure to chemicals for long-term consequences such as cancer and reproductive toxicity.

1. What are largely used for toxicology tests, according to the first paragraph?
   [A] Vitro.　　　[B] Animals' embryos.　　　[C] Animals' cells.　　　[D] Animals.
2. The original number of staff in ECVAM was _____.
   [A] 50　　　[B] 10　　　[C] 30　　　[D] 17
3. According to the REACH legislation proposed by European Commission, both future and existing chemicals must _____.
   [A] cut down the use of animals　　　[B] be within the law
   [C] register　　　[D] be without toxicity
4. The Draize test was developed _____.
   [A] in the 1930s　　　[B] under crisis condition
   [C] to reduce the calamity of thalidomide　　　[D] in the late 1950s
5. What result did the thalidomide bring to the pregnant woman who used it in the late 1950s?
   [A] Her morning sickness was controlled.　　　[B] Her child had horrific defects.
   [C] She died from using it.　　　[D] Her eyes were blind.
6. How many animals will be used to reach the requirement for registration if the chemical is a pesticide?
   [A] 5,000.　　　[B] 12,000.　　　[C] 30,000.　　　[D] 3,000.
7. The amounts of animals used in toxicology testing _____, since the establishment of ECVAM.
   [A] has fallen slightly　　　[B] has fallen greatly
   [C] has risen slightly　　　[D] has risen greatly
8. In vitro cytotoxicity test is the one that monitors death of _____.
   [A] cultured cells　　　[B] animals　　　[C] embryos　　　[D] organs
9. Human data, used in validation procedure, usually come from _____.
   [A] ECVAM　　　[B] occupational health data-bases
   [C] European Union　　　[D] European Commission
10. In testing chemicals' effects for cancer, _____ seems to be most frequently used.
    [A] embryos　　　[B] cultured cells　　　[C] in vitro　　　[D] animals

【答案与解析】

1. 【定位】根据题目中的关键信息 toxicology tests, first paragraph 可将搜索范围定位在第一段。
   【解析】选[D]。段落主题处设题。该段第二句指出 toxicology tests 很大程度上依赖于 animal experiments,接下来的内容都是围绕为解决 toxicology tests 大量依赖 animal experiments 作出的努力,由此可知大量用于 toxicology tests 的是 animals。
2. 【定位】根据题目中的关键信息 ECVAM 可将搜索范围定位在第二段。
   【解析】选[B]。数字信息处设题。该段尽管涉及到 ECVAM,但是并没有涉及到 ECVAM 的人数,故应将搜索范围扩展到第三段,该段第一句中的 originally had ten numbers of staff 表明 ECVAM 最初有 10 名工作人员。
3. 【定位】根据题目中的关键信息 REACH legislation, European Commission 可将搜索范围定位在小标题 Rule

Change 下第一段。

【解析】选[C]。组织机构观点处。该段最后一句 REACH legislation 的目标,即 make registration mandatory for...(强制那些将来及目前已经存在的化学药品注册),由此可知根据 REACH legislation,both future and existing chemicals 都必须 register。

4. 【定位】根据题目中的关键信息 Draize test 可将搜索范围定位在小标题 Rule Change 下第四段。

【解析】选[B]。举例处设题。该段第一句即本段的主旨,它指出现在许多的 animal tests 都是在 crisis conditions 的情况下发展起来的,接着举出了 Draize test 的例子。很明显 Draize test 是在 crisis condition 的情况下发展起来的。

5. 【定位】根据题目中的关键信息 thalidomide,1950s 可将搜索范围定位在小标题 Rule Change 下第五段。

【解析】选[B]。因果处及转折处设题。结合该段第一句中的转折连词 but 及其中隐含的因果关系可知,thalidomide 引起的最终结果是 caused horrific birth defects。[B]是该句中 horrific birth defects 的同义转述。

6. 【定位】根据题目中的关键信息 pesticide 可将搜索范围定位在小标题 Safety Catch 下第一段。

【解析】选[B]。数字信息处及条件处设题。该段第一句中破折号后的内容表明如果杀虫剂要达到注册要求,那么用于实验的动物数量将会达到 12,000。

7. 【定位】根据题目中的关键信息 amounts of animals,establishment 可将搜索范围定位在小标题 Safety Catch 下第二段。

【解析】选[A]。转折处设题。由该段第一句可知,自 ECVAM 建立后,用于实验的动物总量 has fallen slightly。

8. 【定位】根据题目中的关键信息 in vitro cytotoxicity 可将搜索范围定位在小标题 Safety Catch 下第三段。

【解析】选[A]。解释说明处设题。通过该段的定语从句可知,in vitro cytotoxicity test 是 monitors death of cultured cells... 的实验。

9. 【定位】根据题目中的关键信息 human data,validation procedure 可将搜索范围定位在小标题 Life or Death 下第二段。

【解析】选[B]。补充说明处设题。该段倒数第二句中的 often from occupational health data-bases 是对 human data 的补充说明,表明了 human data 的来源。

10. 【定位】根据题目中的关键信息 effects,cancer 可将搜索范围定位在小标题 Life or Death 下最后一段。

【解析】选[D]。举例处设题。该段指出大多数的 new tests(如 in vitro tests)只是用来评估 acute toxicity 的,而最常用来测验化学药品的毒性所产生的长期性后果的是 animal use,句中的 such as 提示 cancer 和 reproductive toxicity 是对毒性所产生的长期性后果的举例。句中的 highest 提示在测验化学药品的毒性所产生的长期性后果中,animals 是最经常被使用的。

Lecture 3　第三讲　2种填空题出题方式

句子填空题的答案基本都是原文中的原词,个别时候需要根据句子结构的变换进行词性上的转换或简单的句式转换,答案一般由 1—5 个单词构成。

一、题目句子结构与原文没有明显区别

这类题目的句子结构与原文的句子结构没有明显的区别,即在句式上没有变换,只是个别词语进行了转换。这类题目的答案一般为原文中的原词或需要进行简单的词性转换。

【例1】 (710 分样卷-5)

【原文】	【题目】
New tree seedlings rarely survive to make it to the top unless **some older trees die**, creating a "hole" in the canopy.	5. New tree seedlings will not survive to reach the canopy level unless _____ .
【解析】some older trees die。题目句子与原文句子结构没有明显的区别,只是进行了个别词语的转换,其中 not 对应 rarely,reach the canopy level 对应 make it to the top。	

二、题目句子是原文的同义转述或细节归纳

这类题目的句子是原文中句子的同义转述,或是两处或两处以上细节内容的归纳,在用词或句式上均有变化,如主被动的转换、简单句变复杂句、"形+名"结构转换成"动+副"结构等。这类题目的答案可能为原文中原词或需要进行词性上的转换,有时也可能需要进行结构上的转换。

【例2】 (710 分样卷-7)

【原文】	【题目】
Some epiphytes eventually develop into stranglers. … Eventually, the strangler may block so much light from above, and absorb such a high percentage of nutrients from the ground below, that **the host tree dies**.	7. Stranglers are so called because they _____ by blocking the sunlight and competing for the nutrients.

【解析】kill the host tree。原文中的谓语部分(block…)转换成题目中的介宾短语(by blocking…)充当方式状语，而原文中的结果状语从句(that the host tree dies)则应相应的转换成题目句子的谓语部分，即 kill the host tree。

Lecture 4　　　第四讲　10 大信息定位技巧

　　快速阅读，顾名思义，就是要求考生能够在规定时间内迅速地阅读完文章并正确解答文章后的题目，而能否做到这一点在很大程度上取决于考生能否快速而准确的将题目信息在原文中定位，这就需要考生掌握一些实用有效的信息定位技巧。

技巧一：题目顺序基本与行文顺序一致

　　一般情况下，快速阅读的题目顺序与原文的行文顺序是基本保持一致的(偶尔会有个别题目顺序颠倒)，把握这一规律，将有助于我们节省寻读时间，提高定位信息的速度和准确度。

【例1】　　　　　　　　　　　　　　　　　　　　　　　　　　　　　　　　　　(07-6)

【原文】	【题目】
Many people today find themselves in unfulfilling work situations. [1] In fact, one in four workers is dissatisfied with their current job, according to the recent "Plans for 2004" survey. Their career path may be financially rewarding, but it doesn't meet their emotional, social or creative needs. They're stuck, unhappy, and have no idea what to do about it, expect move to another job.　　[2] Mary Lyn Miller, veteran career consultant and founder of the Life and Career Clinic, says that when [3] most people are unhappy about their work, their first thought is to get a different job. Instead, Miller suggests looking at the possibility of a different life. …　　…　　**Step 1: Willingness to do something different**　　Breaking the cycle of doing what you have always done is one of the most difficult tasks for job seekers. [4] Many find it difficult to steer away from a career path or make a change, even if it doesn't feel right.　　**Step 2: Commitment to being who you are, not who or what someone wants you to be**　　[5] Look at the gifts and talents you have and make a commitment to pursue those things that you love most.	1. According to the recent "Plans for 2004" survey, most people are unhappy with their current jobs.　2. Mary Lyn Miller' job is to advise people on their life and career.　3. Mary Lyn Miller herself was once quite dissatisfied with her own work.　4. Many people find it difficult to make up their minds whether to change their career path.　5. According to Mary Lyn Miller, people considering changing their careers should commit themselves to the pursuit of _____.　…

【解析】[N]。本篇快速阅读10道题目的设题题眼的顺序与行文顺序完全保持一致。

技巧二：留意小标题和首尾段

　　定位信息时，首先要留意各个小标题及该标题下的首尾段，这样往往可以迅速缩小搜索范围，更加快速准确地寻找到题目信息的出处。

【例2】　　　　　　　　　　　　　　　　　　　　　　　　　　　　　　　　　　(07-6-4)

【原文】	【题目】
Step 1: Willingness to do *something different*.　　Breaking the cycle of doing what you have always	4. Many people find it difficult to make up their minds whether to *change* their *career path*.

done is one of the most difficult tasks for job seekers. Many find it difficult to steer away from a ***career path*** or make a ***change***, even if it doesn't feel right.

【解析】[Y]。本题的定位信息是 change career path，浏览小标题发现 Step 1 中的 something different 正好与 change 相匹配，故很快将本题出处定位在该小标题下，进一步寻读发现第二句即是本题答案的出处。

技巧三：留意时间、数量等数字信息

如果题目中包含数字，可以成为很好的题眼，因为数字在文章中一般是以阿拉伯数字的形式出现，比较容易寻找，方便快速定位。

【例3】   (07-12-7)

【原文】	【题目】
According to an International Energy Agency study, if consumers chose those models that would save them the most money over the life of the appliance, they'd cut global residential power consumption (and their utility bills) by 43 percent.	7. Global residential power consumption can be cut by 43 percent if _____ . [A] we increase the insulation of walls ad water pipes [B] we choose simpler models of electrical appliances [C] we cut down on the use of refrigerators and other white goods [D] we choose the most efficient models of refrigerators and other white goods

【解析】[D]。本题的定位信息是题干中的 43 percent 和 Global residential power consumption，由数字 43 percent 很容易锁定答案出处。

技巧四：留意人名、地名、机构名称等专有名词

专有名词都是以大写字母开头，与数字信息一样，它们在文章中显得比较突出，比较容易寻找，方便快速定位。但需要注意的是，有时候，该专有名词可能就是文章所讨论的主题，在文章中反复出现，那么就不适合用来充当定位信息。

【例4】   (新 06-12-1)

【原文】	【题目】
Lance Bass of N Sync was supposed to be the third to make the ＄20 million trip, but he did not join the three-man crew as they blasted off on October 30, 2002, **due to lack of payment**.	1. ***Lance Bass*** wasn't able to go on a tour of space **because of health problems**.

【解析】[N]。本题的定位信息是人名 Lance Bass，通过寻读很快将题目出处锁定在第二段，该段第一句话就揭示了答案。

技巧五：留意比较或对比关系

形容词、副词的比较级或最高级，或是表示比较的词语或结构，经常会被作为快速阅读的设题题眼，查读时需重点留意，尤其是题目中含有表示比较关系的词语时。

【例5】   (新 06-12-8)

【原文】	【题目】
The Most Expensive Vacation … Each **spacecraft** requires millions of pounds of **fuel** to take off into space, which makes them ***expensive*** to launch. One pound of payload（有效载重）costs about ＄10,000 to put into Earth's orbit.	8. What makes going to space ***the most expensive vacation*** is the enormous cost involved in _____ .

【解析】the fuel of spacecraft。本题的定位信息是最高级 the most expensive vacation，通过它很容易将题目出处锁定在小标题 The most Expensive Vacation 下，进一步寻读发现答案出自该标题下第一段结尾处。

技巧六：留意破折号、冒号、括号、引号等特殊标点

快速阅读经常会针对破折号、冒号或括号等特殊标点的地方设题，因此，即使题目中不含有这些标点，当寻读到文章中这些特殊标点处时也应给予重点关注。

【例6】　　　　　　　　　　　　　　　　　　　　　　　　　　　　　(07-6-8)

【原文】	【题目】
Step 5: Vision Miller suggests that job seekers develop a vision that embraces the answer to "**What do I really want to do?**"	8. **Mary Lyn Miller** suggests that a job seeker develop a **vision** that answers the question"_____"

【解析】What do I really want to do? 本题的定位信息是 vision(构想)以及双引号。由 vision 一词很容易将题目出处定位到小标题 Step 5 下,通过引号则可以迅速找到答案所在。

技巧七：留意表示因果、并列、转折等逻辑关系的词

　　逻辑关系处是快速阅读的重要设题点之一,因此题目中的 because,since,so,therefore,but,while 等逻辑关系词语往往可以成为重要的信息定位点之一。但需要注意的是,题目可能会对原文中的逻辑关系词语进行替换,查找时要注意。另外,我们还可以利用逻辑关系判断哪些信息是相对重要的信息,哪些信息是相对不重要的信息,从而简化阅读。

【例7】　　　　　　　　　　　　　　　　　　　　　　　　　　　　(新 06-12-6)

【原文】	【题目】
Even Hilton Hotels has shown interest in the space tourism industry and the possibility of building or co-funding a **space hotel**. **However**, the company did say that it believes such a **space hotel** is 15 to 20 years away.	6. **Hilton Hotels** believes it won't be long before it is possible to build a _____.

【解析】space hotel。本题的定位信息是 Hilton Hotels,另外如果能够在寻读时注意到表示递进的副词 even 和表示转折的副词 however,也将有助于更加快速地定位信息点。

技巧八：留意表示程度、范围或频率的词语

　　题目中描述事物的程度、范围或频率的词语往往可以作为信息定位的关键词语。

【例8】　　　　　　　　　　　　　　　　　　　　　　　　　　　　(新 06-12-10)

【原文】	【题目】
Within the next 20 years, space planes could be taking off for the Moon at the same frequency as airplanes flying between New York and Los Angeles.	10. **Within the next two decades,** _____ could be as common as intercity air travel.

【解析】space travel。本题的定位信息是表示时间范围的短语 within the next two decades,通过它很快可以将题目出处定位在文章的结尾处。

技巧九：留意列举或举例处

　　表示举例或列举的标志性词语,如 like,such as,for example,for instance,include,consist of 等,也常可以作为信息定位的关键词语。

【例9】

【原文】	【题目】
Healthy snacks include: fresh fruit, vegetable sticks (carrots, peppers), dried fruit, toast, small sandwiches, and yogurt.	1. Chicken is also a kind of **healthy snacks** better for children in the first years.

【解析】[NG]。本题的定位信息是 healthy snacks。文中列举了一些健康快餐,但列举的项中没有提到 chicken。

技巧十：留意题目中的新信息

　　选择定位信息时注意不要选文章中多次出现过的词语,这样的词语即使在题目中处于比较中心的位置,也很难成为有效的定位信息。一般来说,每道题中都会有一些明显不同于其他词的新信息,那么该信息往往可以成为定位的关键词语,这类词语多为名词。

【例 10】

【原文】	【题目】
Step 2: *Commitment* to being who you are, not who or what someone wants you to be Look at the gifts and talents you have and make a ***commitment*** to ***pursue*** those things that you love most.	5. According to Mary Lyn Miller, people considering changing their careers should ***commit*** themselves to the ***pursuit*** of _____.

【解析】those things that they love most。尽管本题是陈述 Mary Lyn Miller 的观点,但文章很大的篇幅都是在陈述他的观点,因此不宜将其作为定位信息。本题适合作定位信息的是 commit themselves to the pursuit。

Exercise　　即讲即练

Missing in Action

　　Amelia Earhart was flying into the sun. It was shortly after dawn on July 2, 1937, and the aluminium wings of her Lockheed Electra were ablaze with light. Earhart nosed the twin-engine aircraft down through the clouds and, at 300m above the water, she began searching for her microscopic destination: a 3-km-long coral island with an airstrip in the middle of the Pacific Ocean. She had nearly completed her record-smashing journey around the globe. After a 20-hour flight, she had 35 minutes of fuel remaining, leaving her only the tiniest margin for error.

　　Earhart apparently never located that dot of an island. She made no final distress call. The world's most famous aviatrix kept her nerve until the end. In her last radio message, there was only a slight fraying on the edge of her normally cool voice as she tried to eyeball Howland Island: "We are on the line of position 157 — 337. We are running north to south." The bodies of Earhart and her navigator Fred Noonan were never found, and neither was the Lockheed Electra's wreckage, giving rise to one of early aviation's greatest mysteries — and to outlandish speculation and conspiracy theories about their disappearance. Persistent rumours suggested she was a secret US government agent or, alternatively, a Japanese prisoner of war.

　　The fact is, no one wanted to believe this heroic icon was dead. After a solo crossing of the Atlantic in 1932, Earhart became the most admired woman in America. She was a proto-feminist who, as a girl, scissored out newspaper stories of women who had broken into male-dominated professions. In addition to courage, Earhart was endowed with puckish glamour and an ethereal, up-in-the-clouds smile, as though she didn't need metal wings to fly. There were as many "sightings" of Amelia as of Elvis after his death years later.

　　Two rival groups of Earhart enthusiasts are convinced that they can at long last solve the riddle of her crash. Their hypotheses are wildly different — and yet both are plausible. One group, led by Ric Gillespie from Delaware-based TIGHAR, the International Group for Historic Aircraft Recovery, believes that Earhart and Noonan wandered far off course. After running out of fuel, they crash-landed on Nikumaroro, a tiny crust of an atoll far south of their intended destination. The searchers believe that Earhart and Noonan, injured after ditching the plane, survived for at least several days before perishing on the deserted atoll. Since Aug. 27, a 12-member expedition has been scouring Nikumaroro for any signs of the aircraft's wreckage and human remains. The team members speak of searing heat, voracious bugs and possible gravestones that, so far, have turned out to be chunks of coral. But their four previous expeditions on the island between 1989 and 1997 unearthed several tantalizing, though far from substantiating, clues: aircraft debris and a leather sole "consistent with shoes worn by Earhart," says Gillespie.

　　Even more promising evidence was discovered not on Nikumaroro but in the national archives in Tarawa, capital of the Kiribati archipelago. There, TIGHAR researchers found letters from a British colonial officer who visited Nikumaroro in 1940 and found human remains, a bottle of Benedictine brandy and evidence of a campfire. The brandy could conceivably have been in the plane's emergency rations. The bones were examined in Fiji, and a doctor concluded that they probably belonged to a "muscular middle-aged male of European descent", according to TIGHAR's report. That might fit Noonan's description, but there is no way of knowing: the bones disappeared during World War II. On another front, the researchers tracked down former settlers on Nikumaroro who claimed that on their arrival in 1938, they found two corpses — of a man and a woman in Western clothes. The settlers also reportedly discovered pieces of aircraft wreckage strewn about the jungle-covered atoll.

　　The finds are intriguing, but skeptics say TIGHAR explorers are overlooking some crucial details: a US navy ship that was part of the search effort passed by the island six days after the crash and saw no wreckage and no casta-ways on the beach waving for help. Elgen Long, an aviation expert and co-author with his wife, Marie, of the 1999 book Amelia Earhart: The Mystery Solved thinks that the pilot, who was flying against strong 42-km/h headwinds, simply did not have enough fuel to reach Nikumaroro and ditched in the ocean.

Another problem with TIGHAR's hypothesis: there is no convincing explanation of why Noonan, one of the best navigators of his day, would have been so wide of the mark. The weather was calm and the visibility good. From the cockpit, Noonan had a compass and an octant, a device that uses the sun to plot positioning, and these instru-ments should have kept him from straying so far south. Moreover, says Long: "We know from the strength of her radio beam that Earhart was within 160 km of Howland Island before she started running out of fuel."

Meanwhile, David Jourdan, founder of Nauticos, the Maryland-based outfit that plumbed many of the secrets of the sunken Titanic, is heading in another direction. In January, Jourdan and crew will utilize the latest sonar technol-ogy and fibre-optic cables to explore a roughly 52,000 sq. km area of the ocean floor northwest of Howland Island. The sensors will dangle below Nauticos' ship, picking up sounds bounced off any odd shapes on the flat ocean floor. The Nauticos team selected the search area based on new, high-tech analysis of the radio-beam strength of Earhart's last messages, wind speed and just how far her 42,000 litres of fuel would have taken her.

Long thinks the Nauticos' effort is more sensible. He believes the crashed plane drifted to the bottom of the deep plains, some 5,000 m below the surface. Because there is little oxygen, gelid temperatures, no currents and no plant life at those depths, the wreckage may be in perfect condition. The bodies would have disintegrated long ago, but Jourdan's experience with the Titanic leads him to believe that Earhart's notebook, the postcards from her stops a-round the world, her jewellery and her aviator glasses may still be preserved. "That would be kind of haunting," he says. But only then would the enigma of Earhart's disappearance finally be put to rest.

1. The fuel in Amelia Earhart's plane only allowed it to fly for twenty hours and thirty five minutes.
2. Earhart didn't lose her nerve even though she was faced with death, because of her professional training.
3. Early in 1932, Amelia Earhart had flied across the Atlantic with the accompany of Fred Noonan.
4. The passage doesn't imply that the Earhart enthusiasts will unveil the mystery of Earhart's crash at last.
5. According to the hypotheses of TIGHAR, the place, Nikumaroro where Amelia Earhart and Fred Noonan landed lied on _____.
6. The clues that Gillespie's group had found, including aircraft debris and a leather sole, haven't _____.
7. There is no way proving that the bones left on Nikumaroro belong to Fred Noonan, because _____.
8. Different from TIGHAR researchers' opinion in the aspect of the place where Earhart landed, Elgen Long believes that Earhart even didn't _____.
9. _____ will be used by Jourdan to search for the pieces of aircraft wreckage or something belonged to Ear-hart on the ocean floor.
10. If there is a need to make a choice among who will disclose the truth of Earhart's disappearance at last, Long will choose _____ rather than TIGHAR.

【答案与解析】
1.【定位】根据题目中的时间 twenty hours and thirty five minutes 可将搜索范围定位在第一段最后一句。
　【解析】[Y]。该句指出在 20 小时的航行之后,Amelia Earhart 驾驶的飞机上所剩的燃料只够维持 35 分钟的航行时间,由此可知 Amelia Earhart 飞机上的燃料只能支撑 20 小时 35 分钟,题目是原文的同义表达。
2.【定位】根据题目中的关键信息 Earhart, nerve 可将搜索范围定位在第二段第三句。
　【解析】[NG]。该句指出 Earhart 直到最后也 kept her nerve(没有慌张),题目中的 didn't lose her nerve 与它相对应。但是文中并没有说明为什么 Earhart 到最后也没有慌张,题目中表述的原因在文中找不到对应信息。
3.【定位】根据题目中的关键信息 1932, Atlantic 可将搜索范围定位在第三段第二句。
　【解析】[N]。该句指出在 solo crossing of the Atlantic in 1932 之后,Earhart 成为美国最受崇拜的女性。题目中的 flied across the Atlantic with the accompany of Fred Noonan 与原文的信息不符,故答案为[N]。
4.【定位】根据题目中的关键信息 the passage 可将搜索范围定位在全文。
　【解析】[Y]。文章第四段第一句指出两组 Earhart 的狂热者们 are convinced that they can at long last solve the riddle of her crash(相信到最后他们会揭开 Earhart 飞机失事的谜团),但这只是他们的一种想法,究竟会不会变成现实还有待考证。并且下文分别介绍了两组 Earthart 的狂热者们在揭开 Earhart 飞机失事谜团的过程中所采取的措施,仍然没有明确表明他们会最终揭开谜团,题目表述与原文一致,故答案为[Y]。

5.【定位】根据题目中的关键信息 hypotheses of TIGHAR,Nikumaroro 可将搜索范围定位在第四段第四句。

【解析】far south of their intended destination。该句指出在燃料烧完之后,Amelia Earhart 和 Fred Noonan 坠落在 Nikumaroro,句中的同位语 a tiny crust of an atoll far south of their intended destination 表明了他们的降落地点的位置在 far south of their intended destination(预定目的地的南部较远地区)。

6.【定位】根据题目中的关键信息 aircraft debris,a leather sole 可将搜索范围定位在第四段最后一句。

【解析】been substantiated。该句指出在 Gillespie 领导的小组的前四次考察中,他们找出了一些线索,如:aircraft debris 和 a leather sole。由该句中的 though far from substantiating 可知,Gillespie 小组找出的线索并没有经过证实,由此可知 far from substantiating 即为本题出处,the clues 与"证实"之间存在被动关系。

7.【定位】根据题目中的关键信息 bones,Fred Noonan 可将搜索范围定位在第五段。

【解析】they disappeared during World War II。该段指出一名医生认为 Nikumaroro 上遗骨的主人生前拥有强健的体魄且为欧洲血统的中年男子(muscular middle-aged male of European descent),并推测认为这些描述符合 Noonan 的特征,但 but 后陈述了事实:there is no way of knowing,其后的冒号表明 the bones disappeared during World War II 是 there is no way of knowing 的原因,故此处为本题答案的出处。因题目中 that 引导的宾语从句中的主语为 the bones,所以为了避免重复,答案中的 the bones 应用代词 they 代替。

8.【定位】根据题目中的关键信息 Elgen Long,the place where Earhart landed 可将搜索范围定位在第六段。

【解析】have enough fuel to reach Nikumaroro。在作本题之前,应首先弄清 TIGHAR 的研究者们对 Earhart 降落地点的观点。由前两段可知,他们认为 Earhart 降落在 Nikumaroro,由此就可以进一步缩小本题的搜索范围,即在第六段中寻找 Elgen Long 对 Earhart 的降落地点的观点。通过阅读第六段可发现,该段最后一句中的 simply did not have enough fuel to reach Nikumaroro 即为本题的答案出处。

9.【定位】根据题目中的关键信息 used,Jourdan,ocean floor 可将搜索范围定位在倒数第二段。

【解析】The latest sonar technology and fibre-optic cables。由题目中的谓语动词 will be used 可以推测本题很可能是要问 Jourdan 搜寻飞机残骸和 Earhart 的遗留物的方法。题目中的 used 与该段第二句中的 utilize 相对应,由此可知 utilize 的宾语即为本题的答案出处。

10.【定位】根据题目中的关键信息 Earhart's disappearance 以及题目的出题顺序可将搜索范围定位在最后一段。

【解析】Nauticos。分析题目大意可知,本题问的是一种假设情况,即 Long 对谁会揭开 Earhart 失踪之迷持有的信心更大。最后一段首句 Long thinks the Nauticos' effort is more sensible 表明了 Long 的态度,即:Nauticos 所做的努力更有意义,由此可推断 Long 认为 Nauticos 最有可能解开 Earhart 失踪之谜。

快速阅读巅峰练习

Exercise 1

Turning History into Tourism

Renate Horst wanted to visit Africa, but she was not only interested in running around the bush looking for zebras and hippos. "I told my travel agent I didn't just want to be a tourist. I wanted to go where ordinary people don't get to go," says Horst, a resident of Munich. Today, this middle-aged woman is getting her wish. As her car pulls into Cape Town's crime-plagued Langa township, guide Ntobeko Peni, 27, starts reciting a capsule history of the apartheid struggle, starting with bloody 1960 protests against the country's passed law for blacks. He takes his visitor by police stations where marchers rallied, through a squatter-camp beer hall, then finally pulls up to the street in Khayelitsha township where a mob stoned and stabbed to death American exchange student Amy Biehl in 1993. Four people served time in prison for the murder, the result of a party's efforts to block scheduled elections by creating unrest; they were later released. Peni adds casually: "One of them is now involved in tourism, and he is driving for you." Horst doesn't appear to be bothered, and after the tour is complete declares: "That was a good thing."

A growing number of her fellow visitors to South Africa seem to agree. World outrage over apartheid sparked international sanctions that squeezed South Africa's economy until the system fell in 1994. But the memory of apartheid lives on — thanks in part to thriving tourism businesses. In the last year interest in attractions that highlight the nearly 50 years of segregation has been growing rapidly. Last week Robben Island, where Nelson Mandela and other political prisoners suffered for decades in jail, announced that 300,000 people visited its prison turned museum over the last 12 months, a record. Private tours of Soweto, the huge black township outside Johannesburg, are booming. Four museums devoted to the apartheid era have opened in the last year, one adjacent to a casino. In Cape Town, Peni caught on to the possibilities while working as a business strategist for the Amy Biehl Foundation Trust, having been publicly forgiven by the victim's parents. He led his first tour for the charity in June. "I saw an opportunity," he explains.

Although apartheid was unique to South Africa, the idea of teaching people a little history and making some money out of the lesson is not. "It's well known that tourists all over the world are more and more interested in culture," says Mohammed Valli Moosa, South Africa's minister of Environmental Affairs and Tourism. "People don't just want to lie on the beach any more they want to see things they are not able to see anywhere else in the world." So his department promotes South Africa's multi-cultural, multi-religious society, an ethnic stew in which there isn't a single majority language. And Moosa's department hasn't shied away from exploiting the country's segregationist history or, as he prefers to describe it, "the heroic struggle against racism". A Johannesburg native, he admits to being surprised by the depth of cultural and historical interest in South Africa internationally. "I never would have thought in all my dreams that people would find this place so interesting," he said.

The biggest attraction among apartheid-related sites is undoubtedly the Robben Island Museum, a half-hour ferry ride from the Cape Town waterfront. A national inonument since 1997, the museum logged its millionth visitor last December. Much of its appeal derives from its 30 tour guides: all are former activists who were arrested by the state and imprisoned on the island.

The popularity of Robben Island has inspired other projects, some of them unusual. Last year casino developers built the Apartheid Museum in Johannesburg to fulfill a public-service requirement imposed by the municipality. It has been built on a former prison. Visitors are separated by race at the entrance, and enter through separate doors. Inside, a ceiling hung with ropes symbolizes the political prisoners hanged during apartheid. Most people walk hesitantly beneath them. "I'll remember this for a long time," says Hillary Davidson, 61, a retired British librarian. Yet as visitors exit the dim museum, they also hear the screams of people on the roller coaster at the casino across the parking lot, interrupted by a recording of elephants trumpeting.

　　Another new venture will reconstruct Liliesleaf Farm in Rivonia, a suburb of Johannesburg, where police raided and captured rebel leaders from the African National Congress. The co-owner, lawyer Harold Wolpe, bribed his way out of jail and fled to London. His son Nicolas, a business consultant, now plans to add a conference centre to the site, which is currently a hotel.

　　In the end, and not surprisingly, it may be Mandela himself who beats everyone at this game. Two weeks ago a series of lithographs based on his drawings of Robben Island scenes went on sale at the trendy Belgravia Gallery in London. Nearly 200 of them already have sold at £ 1500 each, says the gallery's Anna Hunter, adding, "We've been inundated with calls from throughout the world." Mandela's publisher plans more exhibitions soon in the United States. Mandela also plans to go on the road next year for a series of seminars with top-level US executives — just as Margaret Thatcher and Bill Clinton have done before him. The organizer is calling it the "Mandela Legacy Tour". Income from both the tour and the lithographs goes to the Mandela Trust, which supports several children's charities.

　　Not everyone is pleased with the new tourist attractions. In July several of the black tour guides at the Robben museum accused the management of corruption; the director resigned, protesting his innocence. Nearly every Soweto tour includes a visit to the small "matchbox" house in the Orlando East neighbourhood where Mandela lived briefly with his second wife, Winnie, while working as a lawyer in Johannesburg. Income from visits is said to go to some charitable trust. But this year a parliamentary ethics committee blamed Winnie Mandikizela-Mandela, now divorced from the former president, partly for failing to disclose a financial interest in the Mandela Family Museum. Police had charged her with stocking liquor on the premises — in effect, running an illegal pub. However, Mandikizela-Mandela denies the charges. Most South Africans would agree, though, that the benefits of educating locals and foreigners about the country's painful past far outweigh such stumbles.

1. Ordinary people don't travel in places like Langa township because of the bad order there.
2. The murder of Amy Biehl was a premeditated one, which a party hoped to make use of to stop scheduled elections.
3. We learn from Peni that one of the four people who had murdered Amy Biehl now becomes a guide in Khayelitsha township.
4. Because of the thriving tourism business in South Africa, the memory of apartheid hasn't faded away.
5. There were no more than _____ who came to visit its prison in 12 months before Robben Island's announcement.
6. The idea that a country can earn money from its historical lesson is _____ .
7. In order to appeal to tourists' new interest in culture, Moosa's department devotes its effort to the development of South Africa's _____ .
8. The Robben Island museum's tour guides also attract tourists much because they were once _____ as activists.
9. The money gotten from Mandela Legacy Tour and the lithographs based on Mandela's drawings of Robben Island scenes will be used to _____ .
10. Income from the visits to the house of Mandela is handed to some _____ , according to the passage.

Exercise 2

UN: Women Gain in Political Clout, Lag in Schooling

　　A new report by the United Nations indicates that women are gaining political power around the world, while they continue to suffer unequal access to education and employment. "There's some good news, but we've still got a long way to go," says Diane Elson, professor of Sociology and Human Rights at Essex University, in northern England, and principal author of Progress of the World's Women 2002: Vol. 2. "After compiling data from all over the world, I can say this isn't simply a case of poor countries lagging behind rich countries. There isn't a country anywhere that meets our requirements for full gender parity and female empowerment."

　　Progress of the World's Women 2002 tracks improvements made toward women's empowerment within the context of a set of eight goals created at the U. N. Millennium Summit in September 2000. By creating a framework for all to follow, the international community hopes to be able to end poverty, hunger, and inequality by 2015. Number three on the list is "Promote gender equality and empower women," with a target date of 2005 for achieving full parity between the sexes in access to education. This report assesses the world's progress during the past two years.

Only 7 countries met Elson's criteria for "high levels" of gender equality and they're all in Northern Europe: Sweden, Denmark, Finland, Norway, Iceland, Netherlands and Germany. Although none of these nations has achieved a perfect ratio, they do have nearly even numbers of girls and boys enrolled in primary, secondary and tertiary schools. The illiteracy rates among women aged 15 to 24 is comparable to men in that same age group and wages are generally equal between the sexes. And — perhaps most importantly — women hold at least 30 percent of parliamentary seats in each country, which Elson says is crucial for affecting real change.

30 Percent Is Tipping Point

"We've found that it's not enough to get one or two or even ten women into political positions, although those are important first steps. But to really make a difference, women need to reach the 'tipping point' of 30 percent in a political body." The "tipping point" theory might help explain why the progress made in these 7 northern European countries is not reflected in the rest of the developed world. Three of the world's richest countries ranked surprisingly low in political parity when compared to many countries in the developing world. In the United States, France and Japan, women's share of political positions is below 12 percent. Meanwhile, 13 developing nations in sub-Saharan Africa, which is experiencing the greatest regional poverty in the world, have much higher percentages of female participation in government, as do 38 developing countries in Asia and Latin America.

In terms of overall improvement in access to education, employment and political empowerment for women and girls in the past two years, Elson determined that Argentina, Costa Rica and South Africa far outstripped all other nations, leading her to believe that political will, not national wealth, is the real reason women progress. That is certainly the case in France, which grudgingly agreed to set quotas (名额) in 2000 and has since done little to enforce them, allowing political parties to pay a small fine rather than put women on the ballot.

Nations Committed to Change Saw Rapid Improvement

"In countries that committed to change and set quotas," she says, "we saw real and rapid improvement." Progress 2002 discovered that countries that willingly implement quotas rapidly achieve the 30 percent mark which, in turn, leads to policy changes that improve women's lives. However, in countries that do not establish quotas (such as the United States and Japan), or only do so reluctantly (like France), women are occasionally elected — sometimes to very prominent positions — but they largely work in isolation, unable to build momentum among other like-minded politicians. "It makes life harder for all women," says Elson, "because they don't have adequate representation in the government and therefore their issues and needs aren't being discussed."

In many developing nations, women are frequently the heads of households, and it's predominantly women who perform the agricultural labor that keeps economies going. Nudged by the international community, governments in that part of the world are growing in their understanding of the maxim: What's good for women is very often good for the country as a whole. More are now taking steps to make sure women have a real political presence. As evidenced by the findings in Elson's report, the majority of developed nations have yet to fully grasp that concept.

Although poorer nations have outperformed the developing world in the political arena, they continue to lag behind in almost every other aspect of gender parity. National poverty is still a major factor in determining what type of life a girl will have, particularly regarding her access to education.

In sub-Saharan Africa and South Asia, where a scarcity of resources and strong cultural preferences for males are ever-present factors, young girls often have never seen the inside of a primary level classroom. Women and girls in these regions and in many parts of Latin America often take agricultural jobs or work in factories — both of which are low-paying and vastly undercounted in employment statistics. There are now an estimated 140 million illiterate young people in the world, 60 percent of whom (86 million) are young women. "If we want to halve the number of people living on less than a dollar a day," Noeleen Heyzer, executive director of UNIFEM writes in Progress 2002, "then it's critical that the feminization of poverty receive systematic attention — especially in this era of globalization."

In years leading up to the 21st century, world leaders did seem to be paying attention to women's issues. There were numerous forums on advancing gender equality, such as the International Conference on Population and Development (1994), the Fourth World Conference on Women (1995), and the World Summit on Social Development (1995). Yet many say little was achieved in terms of actual change.

"It's sometimes known as the 'Decade of Promises' among activists," says Caren Grown, director of the Poverty Reduction and Economic Growth project at the International Center for Research on Women. "What we have to do now is move into the 'Decade of Implementation and Accountability'." Grown's group is part of a task force assigned by the United Nations Secretary General to research ways in which the Millennium Development Goals can be a-chieved.

A Personal Suggestion

Grown and her team have several unorthodox suggestions on how to wipe out cultural practices that discriminate against girls. Grown endorses setting up regional programs that will pay families for allowing their daughters to get an education, providing the economic incentive she believes could change the usual fate of girls: Female children in sub-Saharan Africa and parts of Asia are often sold into slavery for quick profit by desperate parents; also in Africa, with its high number of female-headed households, girls are often kept at home to be "mom" while the mother works outside.

A special approach is needed to help girls living in conflict-ridden areas, where there's almost no chance they'll ever get to crack the books. Not only is there usually a disintegration of social services — such as public education — but parents often are reluctant to permit girls to leave their homes for fear they will be attacked or kidnapped.

"Without a doubt, violence against women is the largest obstacle to full parity and empowerment," says Grown. "A recent study by the World Health Organization found that 1 in 3 women suffers from some kind of physical assault in her lifetime — that's a public health issue, like an epidemic."

Elson's research turned up such startling information that Grown and other activists are preparing to lobby U. N. Secretary General Kofi Annan to head a worldwide campaign to end violence against women.

UNIFEM is also looking at ways to improve women's lives right now. Progress 2002 will be used to educate wealthy donor nations about the importance of honoring long-standing commitments to gender equality and empower-ment. "Lip-service is no longer going to cut it," says Elson, "when we have hard data like this. It's time for world leaders to start making real policy changes if they truly want to achieve the Millennium Development Goals."

1. The goal "Promote gender equality and empower women" ranks _____ in the eight goals created at the U. N. Millennium Summit.
   [A] the third　　　　　　[B] the first　　　　　　[C] the second　　　　　　[D] the fourth
2. Those that met Elson's criteria for "high levels" of gender equality are _____ .
   [A] Northern American countries　　　　　[B] Southern African countries
   [C] Northern European countries　　　　　[D] Southern Asian countries
3. In each of the 7 countries which met Elson's criteria for "high levels" of gender equality, _____ of parliamenta-ry seats are held by women.
   [A] 12%.　　　　　　[B] 60%.　　　　　　[C] 13%.　　　　　　[D] 30%.
4. Which of the following developed countries ranked surprisingly low in political parity?
   [A] France, Japan and Korea.　　　　　[B] Norway, Iceland and Germany.
   [C] Sweden, Denmark and Finland.　　　　[D] The U. S., France and Japan.
5. The factor that contributes to women progress is _____ , according to Elson.
   [A] political will　　　　　　[B] national wealth
   [C] enforcement of political parity　　　　[D] equal treatment
6. What can we know about France establishing quotas?
   [A] It rejects doing it.　　[B] It reluctantly does it.　[C] It willingly does it.　　[D] It never does it.
7. How many young women are illiterate in the world?
   [A] 86 million.　　　　[B] 140 million.　　　　[C] 30% of young people.　　[D] 60% of young people.
8. The numerous forums held in years leading up to the 21st century were mainly to advance _____ .
9. In conflict-ridden areas, many girls are deprived of the education right both for safety reasons and _____ .
10. Since the goal of improving women's lives can't be realized by words any more, Elson suggests world leaders _____
    _____ to achieve it.

答案与解析

Exercise 1

1. 【定位】根据题目中的关键信息 ordinary people, Langa township 可将搜索范围定位在第一段第二、四句。

【解析】[NG]。该段第四句指出 Renate Horst 到 Cape Town's crime-plagued Langa township 旅游,结合第二句中的 I wanted to go where ordinary people don't get to go 可知,ordinary people 一般不会去像 Langa township 这样犯罪活动猖獗的城镇旅游,但是文中并没有具体说明 ordinary people 不去像 Langa township 这样的地方旅游的原因,题目在原文中找不到依据,故答案为[NG]。

2.【定位】根据题目中的关键信息 Amy Biehl, a party, scheduled elections 可将搜索范围定位在第一段倒数第三、四句。

　【解析】[Y]。该段倒数第三句中 murder 的同位语 the result of a party's efforts to block scheduled elections by creating unrest 表明了谋杀 Amy Biehl 的目的是为了阻止预定的选举,由此可推断,谋杀 Amy Biehl 是有预谋的,题目是对原文正确的推断,故答案为[Y]。

3.【定位】根据题目中的关键信息 one of the four people 可将搜索范围定位在第一段倒数第二句。

　【解析】[N]。该句中的 them 指代上句提到的被疑谋杀 Amy Biehl 的四个人。由 Peni 介绍中的 he is driving for you 可知,其中一人现在是一名旅游司机,而不是题目中所说的 guide,题目与原文事实相矛盾,故答案为[N]。

4.【定位】根据题目中的关键信息 thriving tourism business, the memory of apartheid 可将搜索范围定位在第二段第三句。

　【解析】[N]。该句指出人们对种族隔离制度记忆犹新,thanks in part to thriving tourism business(部分原因是由于兴盛的旅游业),该句强调兴盛的旅游业是人们对种族隔离制度记忆犹新的部分(in part)原因,而题目中却将原因完全归结于兴盛的旅游业,题目与原文表示原因的范围不一致,故答案为[N]。

5.【定位】根据题目中的关键信息 visit its prison, Robben Island, announcement 可将搜索范围定位在第二段第五句。

　【解析】300,000 people。该句中 announced 后的宾语从句指出在过去 12 个月中,有 300,000 people 参观了 Robben Island 的监狱,turned museum…a record(破了博物馆参观人数的记录),由此可知在 Robben Island 公布该数字之前的 12 个月内,参观人数不足 300,000 人,题目是对原文的同义转述。

6.【定位】根据题目中的关键信息 idea, lesson 可将搜索范围定位在第三段第一句。

　【解析】not unique。该句指出 apartheid 对南非来说是独一无二的,但 the idea of teaching people a little history and making some money out of the lesson is not(通过传授人们历史知识,并通过历史教训赚钱的办法却不是),本句的主句省略了之前出现过的表语 unique,由此可知答案为 not unique。

7.【定位】根据题目中的关键信息 culture, Moosa's department 可将搜索范围定位在第三段。

　【解析】multi-cultural, multi-religious society。该段第四句句首的 So 提示 Moosa 的部门 promotes South Africa's multi-cultural, multi-religious society 的原因应从上几句中寻找。上句中的 they want to see things they are not…是其直接原因,但该原因所反映的情况就是:tourists all over the world are more and more interested in culture。Moosa 的部门促进南非 multi-cultural, multi-religious society 的发展,是为了迎合旅游者们对文化的兴趣。题目中的 devotes its effort to the development of South Africa's…是原文中 promotes South Africa's…的同义转述.

8.【定位】根据题目中的关键信息 Robben Island museum, tour guides, activists 可将搜索范围定位在第四段在最后一句。

　【解析】arrested by the state and imprisoned on the island。句中的冒号解释说明了 Robben Island museum 的多数吸引力来自于它的 tour guides 的原因,即他们都是激进主义分子,曾经被 arrested by the state and imprisoned on the island,此处即为本题答案的出处。

9.【定位】根据题目中的关键信息 Mandela Legacy Tour, the lithographs, drawings of Robben Island scenes 可将搜索范围定位在倒数第二段。

　【解析】support several children's charities。根据题目的主干 The money…will be used to…可知,本题问的是由 Mandela Legacy Tour 和 the lithographs…得来的钱的用途。通读该段可知,该段最后一句与得来的钱的用途有关。由该句中的定语从句可知,钱被用来 support several children's charities。

10.【定位】根据题目中的关键信息 income, visits, the house of Mandela 可将搜索范围定位在最后一段第四句。

　【解析】charitable trust。该句中的 visits 指的就是到 Mandela 曾经住过的房子参观。通过该句可知,来自参观的收入都 go to some charitable trust,题目中的 is handed to 与原文中的 go to 属同义表达,由此可知答案为 charitable trust。

Exercise 2

1.【定位】根据题目中的关键信息 Promote gender equality and empower women 可将搜索范围定位在第二段。

【解析】选[A]。该段倒数第二句中的 Number three on the list 指的就是 Promote gender equality and empower women 在 U. N. Millennium Summit 所提出的 eight goals 位居第三。

2. 【定位】根据题目中的关键信息 Elson's criteria, high levels 可将搜索范围定位在第三段。

【解析】选[C]。该段首句指出符合 Elson's criteria for "high levels" of gender equality 的有 7 个国家，它们都位于 Northern Europe，也就是说它们都是北欧国家。

3. 【定位】根据题目中的关键信息 parliamentary seats 可将搜索范围定位在第三段。

【解析】选[D]。该段最后一句指出在这 7 个北欧国家，每个国家中女性都至少占有 30％ 的 parliamentary seats。

4. 【定位】根据题目中的关键信息 ranked surprisingly low 可将搜索范围定位在小标题 30 Percent Is Tipping Point 下第一段。

【解析】选[D]。该段第四句指出和许多发展中国家相比，世界三大最富有国家在 political parity 方面排名却非常差，第五句指出这三大最富有国家是：the United States，France 和 Japan。

5. 【定位】根据题目中的关键信息 women progress 可将搜索范围定位在小标题 30 Percent Is Tipping Point 下第二段。

【解析】选[A]。由该段第一句中的 Elson determined that . . . leading her to believe that political will, not national wealth, is the real reason women progress 可知，Elson 认为引起 women progress 的是国家的 political will。

6. 【定位】根据题目中的关键信息 France, establishing quotas 可将搜索范围定位在小标题 Nations Committed to Change Saw Rapid Improvement 下第一段。

【解析】选[B]。由该段第三句中的 only do so reluctantly（like France）可知，France 是 reluctantly（不情愿地）establish quotas。

7. 【定位】根据题目中的关键信息 young women, illiterate 可将搜索范围定位在小标题 Nations Committed to Change Saw Rapid Improvement 下第四段。

【解析】选[A]。该段第三句指出目前据估计全世界共有 140 million illiterate young people，其中 60％ 是 young women，根据括号中的数字可知，全世界的 illiterate young women 共有 86 million。

8. 【定位】根据题目中的关键信息 numerous forums, 21st century 可将搜索范围定位在小标题 Nations Committed to Change Saw Rapid Improvement 下第五段。

【解析】gender equality。该段第二句指出了 numerous forums 举行的目的，即 advancing gender equality，题目为该段第一二句的综合概括，故答案为 gender equality。

9. 【定位】根据题目中的关键信息 conflict-ridden areas 可将搜索范围定位在小标题 A Personal Suggestion 下第二段第一句。

【解析】a disintegration of social services。题目中的 both 与该句中的并列结构 Not only. . . but. . . 相对应，safety reasons 与该句中 but 后所陈述的原因对应，故所填内容就应该与 Not only 后所陈述的原因对应，由此可知答案为 a disintegration of social services。

10. 【定位】根据题目中的关键信息 improving women's lives, world leaders 以及出题顺序可将搜索范围定位在小标题 A Personal Suggestion 下最后一段。

【解析】start making real policy changes。结合上文可知，Elson 所说的 Lip-service is no longer going to cut it 是指要想改善女性的生存状况，只靠说是不行的，如果世界领导者们真想达到 Millennium Development Goals，那他们就需要 start making real policy changes，而这正是 Elson 的个人建议。题目中的 can't be realized by words. . . 是 Lip-service is no longer. . . it 的同义表达。

第三章 短句问答巅峰讲座

短句问答与篇章词汇是作为二选一题型出现的,其分值为 10%。文章长度一般在 400－450 词之间,共包含 5 个问题或补全句子题,要求考生用简洁的语言(不超过 10 个词)回答问题或完成句子。

Lecture 1　第一讲　12 种题目原文转换

短句问答题的题目一般不会是原文内容的照搬,它往往会对原文信息进行一定程度的改变,用另外的语言或结构将其表现出来,旨在考查考生对原文信息的识别、理解能力以及利用语法和相关知识对原文信息所表达的含义进行重组、概括及推理的能力。

六级短句问答的题目和原文之间的转换形式主要有以下 12 种:

一、词汇与词汇之间的转换

这类转换是指将原文中某个单词转换成另外的词性或是其近义词,比如将 success 转换成 successful,将 use 转换成 handle。

【例 1】   (新 06-12-47)

【原文】	【题目】
Losing *everything you own* under such circumstances can be distressing, but the people I've heard from all saw their loss, *ultimately*, as a blessing.	47. Many people *whose possessions* were destroyed in natural disasters *eventually considered* their loss _____.

【解析】as a blessing。原文中的 everything you own 转换成了题目中的 whose possessions,saw 转换成了 considered,ultimately 转换成了 eventually。

二、词汇、短语和句子之间的转换

这类转换是指将词汇转换成短语或句子,或是将短语转换成词汇或句子,或是将句子转换成词汇或短语。

【例 2】   (98-6-S3)

【原文】	【题目】
There are various factors that can cause you to *expose yourself to the media selectively*, avoiding much of the material with which you disagree.	S3. *For one reason or another*, *people's exposure to the media is* often _____.

【解析】selective and influenced by different factors。原文中的句子 There are various factors that… 转换成了题目中的短语 for one reason or another,原文中的短语 expose yourself to the media selectively 转换成题目中的句子 people's exposure to the media is often…。

三、陈述主题的转换

一般来说,文章中除了重点陈述的主题外,还包含一些非重点主题,有些题目就是将这些非重点陈述的主题用新的句式表达出来,这要求考生在充分理解原文的基础上将该主题陈述完整。

【例3】 (98-1-S2)

【原文】	【题目】
But…, … to keep *the boat* from *tumbling over*. … After …, people … have become a team, working together to cope with the unpredictable twists and turns of the river.	S2. Why was it easy for *boats to tumble over* in the Colorado?

【解析】Because the river is full of twists and turns. 原文中此处主要是想说明他们在面对有翻船(boats to tumble over)危险时所表现出来的"团队精神",题目中则将"boats to tumble over"作为陈述主题,考生需要充分理解上下文才能正确解答此题。

四、代词的转换

这类转换是指将原文中代替上文中的词汇、短语或是句子的代词转换成其所代替的具体内容,即将代词明确化。

【例4】 (710 分样卷-51)

【原文】	【题目】
Almost 40 years ago, when Lyndon Johnson declared war on poverty, *a family with a car and a house in the suburbs* felt prosperous. Today *that same family* may well feel poor, overwhelmed by credit card debt, a second mortgage and the cost of the stuff that has become the backbone of American life.	51. According to the author, how would *an American family with a car and a house in the suburbs* probably feel about themselves today?

【解析】Poor. 代词 that same family 代指的即是前面提到的 a family with a car and a house in the suburbs。

五、明否定与暗否定之间的转换

明否定是指带有明显否定词(如 not, never, nothing 等)的否定结构,暗否定是指带有暗含否定意义的词语(如 lack, ill, beyond 等)或含否定意义的前缀或后缀(如 un-, dis-, non-, -less 等)的词语的否定结构。

【例5】 (新 06-12-51)

【原文】	【题目】
Make another list *of things you wouldn't acquire* again no matter what, and in fact would be happy to be rid of. When you're ready to start unloading some of your stuff, that list will be a good place to start.	51. What does the author suggest people do with *unnecessary things*?

【解析】Make a list of them before unloading them. 原文中的明否定结构 things you wouldn't acquire 转换成了题目中的暗否定结构 unnecessary things。

六、明比较与暗比较之间的转换

明比较是指带有比较级、最高级(如 more, less, better, best, worse, worst, -er, -est 等)这样明显比较标志的比较结构,暗比较是指带有暗含某种比较或变化的词语(如 increase, decrease, excess, shorten, enlarge, while 等)的比较结构或是句子中暗含的某种比较的含义。

【例6】 (710 分样卷-50)

【原文】	【题目】
While the bottom 10 percent of *American* workers earn just 37 **percent** of our average wage, their counterparts in *other industrialized countries* earn upwards of *60 percent*.	50. We learn from the passage that the difference in pay between the lowest paid and the average worker in *America* is _____ *than* that in *other industrialized countries*.

【解析】much greater. 原文中只给出了两个数字,并没有进行明确的比较,而题目则转换成了要求明确比出大小的比较结构。

七、逻辑关系之间的转换

逻辑关系的转换包括两种：一种是不同逻辑关系之间的转换(如原因转换成条件)；另一种是明逻辑与暗逻辑之间的转换。明逻辑是指通过表示原因、结果、条件、转折等逻辑关系的连词、副词或短语(如 because, so, if, but, consequently, due to 等)明确表达出来的逻辑关系，暗逻辑是指不含有这些逻辑关系词但句中或句子之间却隐含着某种逻辑关系。

【例7】(07-6-50)

【原文】	【题目】
Perhaps their biggest stroke of luck came early on when they tried to sell their technology to other search engines, but no one *met their price, and they built it up on their own*.	50. Brin and Page decided to set up their own *business because* no one would _____.

【解析】meet their price。原文中 and 表示承接，前后行为之间隐含着因果关系，即由于 no one met their price，所以 they built it up on their own。题目用 because 引导的原因状语从句将这种隐含的逻辑关系明确表达了出来。

【例8】(新06-12-48)

【原文】	【题目】
And *once* all those things were no longer there, she and her husband saw how they had weighed them down and complicated their lives.	48. *Now that* all their possessions were lost in the fire, the woman and her husband felt that their lives had been _____.

【解析】simplified。原文中的 once 引导的时间状语从句转换成了题目中 now that 引导的原因状语从句。

八、主动与被动之间的转换

主动和被动的转换除了单纯的主动句和被动句之间的转换以外，经常还会出现表示主动的非谓语动词短语与表示被动的非谓语动词短语之间的转换，或是表示主动的非谓语动词短语与被动句之间或表示被动的非谓语动词短语与主动句之间的转换。这类转换往往涉及到主语或逻辑主语的变换。

【例9】(710分样卷-48)

【原文】	【题目】
American Dream for the well to do *grows from* the bowed backs of the working poor, who too often have to choose between groceries and rent.	48. What is the American Dream of the well to do *built upon*?

【解析】The bowed backs of the working poor。原文中的主动结构 grows from 转换成了题目中的被动结构 is…built upon。

九、主语与宾语之间的转换

在没有主动和被动转换的时候，短句问答题也常会涉及到(逻辑)主语和(逻辑)宾语之间的转换，以此来考查考生对句子的理解程度。

【例10】(07-6-48)

【原文】	【题目】
It was Page who, at Stanford in 1996, initiated the academic project that eventually became *Google's search engine*.	48. *Google's search engine* originated from _____ started by L. Page.

【解析】the academic project。原文中 became 的宾语 Google's search engine 转换成了题目中的主语，became 的逻辑主语 the academic project 就相应转变成的题目中的宾语。

十、强调句与一般句之间的转换

强调句的基本结构是：It is(was)＋强调部分＋that(who)＋句子其他成分。在理解强调句时，可以先把强调句还原成一般句，然后再与题目进行对应分析。

【例11】　　　　　　　　　　　　　　　　　　　　　　　　　　　　　　(07-6-47)

【原文】	【题目】
Google owns much of its success to the brilliance of S. Brin and L. Page, but also to a series of fortunate events.	47. Apart from a series of fortunate events, *what is it that has made Google so successful?*

【解析】the brilliance of S. Brin and L. Page。原文中的一般陈述句转换成了题目中的强调句。

十一、there be 句型与一般句之间的转换

这类转换是指将原文中用 there be 句型陈述的主题用一般句来转述，或是将原文中的一般句用 there be 句型来转述。考生要注意理清 there be 句型中各成分之间的内在关系。

【例12】　　　　　　　　　　　　　　　　　　　　　　　　　　　　　(新 06-12-50)

【原文】	【题目】
Obviously, there's a tremendous **difference** between *getting rid of possessions and losing them through a natural disaster* without having a say in the matter.	50. According to the author, *getting rid of possessions and losing them through* a natural disaster are vastly _____.

【解析】different。原文中的 there be 句型转换成了题目中的一般陈述句，there be 句型中的表语转换成了题目句中的主语，there be 句型中的主语转换成了题目句中的表语。

十二、祈使、感叹或疑问语气与一般语气之间的转换

短句问答题的题目设置一般不会使用祈使句、感叹句或一般疑问句，因此原文中表达祈使、感叹或疑问语气的地方经常会被转换成一般陈述语气。

【例13】　　　　　　　　　　　　　　　　　　　　　　　　　　　　　(新 06-12-51)

【原文】	【题目】
Make another list of *things you wouldn't acquire* again no matter what, and in fact would be happy to be rid of. When you're ready to start unloading some of your stuff, that list will be a good place to start.	51. What does the author suggest people do with *unnecessary things*?

【解析】Make a list of them before unloading them。原文中的祈使句 Make another list of… 转换成题目中的陈述语序 the author suggest people…。注意祈使句常用来表达建议。

Exercise　　　　　　　即讲即练

The period of adolescence, i. e., the period between childhood and adulthood, may be long or short, depending on social expectations and on society's definition as to what constitutes maturity and adulthood. In primitive societies adolescence is frequently a relatively short period of time, while in industrial societies with patterns of prolonged education coupled with laws against child labor, the period of adolescence is much longer and may include most of the second decade of one's life. Furthermore, the length of the adolescent period and the definition of adulthood status may change in a given society as social and economic conditions change. Examples of this type of change are the disappearance of the frontier in the latter part of the nineteenth century in the United States, and more universally, the industrialization of an agricultural society.

In modern society, ceremonies for adolescence have lost their formal recognition and symbolic significance and there no longer is agreement as to constituting initiation ceremonies. Social ones have been replaced by a sequence of steps that lead to increased recognition and social status. For example, grade school graduation, high school graduation and college graduation constitute such a sequence, and while each step implies certain behavioral changes and social recognition, the significance of each depends on the socio-economic status and the educational ambition of the individual. Ceremonies for adolescence have also been replaced by legal definitions of status roles, rights, privileges and responsibilities. It is during the nine years from the twelfth birthday to the twenty-first that the protective and restrictive aspects of childhood and minor status are removed and adult privileges and responsibilities are granted. The twelve-year-old is no longer considered a child and has to pay full fare for train, airplane, theater and movie tickets.

Basically, the individual at this age loses childhood privileges without gaining significant adult rights. At the age of sixteen the adolescent is granted certain adult rights which increase his social status by providing him with more freedom and choices. He now can obtain a driver's license; he can leave public schools; and he can work without the restrictions of child labor laws. At the age of eighteen the law provides adult responsibilities as well as rights; the young man can now be a soldier, but he also can marry without parental permission. At the age of twenty-one the individual obtains his full legal rights as an adult. He now can vote, he can buy liquor, he can enter into financial contracts, and he is entitled to run for public office. No additional basic rights are acquired as a function of age after majority status has been attained. None of these legal provisions determine at what point adulthood has been reached but they do point to the prolonged period of adolescence.

1. The period of adolescence is much longer in industrial societies because more education is provided and _____ are made.

_____

2. According to the passage, it is true that in the late 19th century in the United States the dividing line between _____ no longer existed.

_____

3. _____ that used to mark adolescence have given place to graduations from schools and colleges.

_____

4. Generally speaking, a twelve-year-old individual no more enjoys privileges as a child and is not entitled to _____ .

_____

5. According to the passage, starting from 22, one won't get _____ than when he was 21.

_____

【答案与解析】 ....

【文章大意】
青春期的长短根据社会各方面条件的不同而有所变化。过去的青春期仪式在当今社会已被系列教育以及法律规定的各种权利和义务所代替。

1. 【定位】根据题干中的关键信息 the period of adolescence, industrial societies, education 可将搜索范围定位在第一段第二句。
【解析】laws against child labor。在 while 引导的状语从句中,介词短语 with patterns of... 在句中充当伴随状语,该伴随状语与状语从句中的主句 the period of adolescence is much longer... 之间隐含着因果关系,即因为工业社会中 patterns of prolonged education 和 laws against child labor 使得青春期的时间更长,题目用 because 引导的原因状语从句将这种隐含的逻辑关系明确的表达了出来。

2. 【定位】根据题干中的关键信息 19th century, United States 可将搜索范围定位在第一段最后一句。
【解析】adolescence and adulthood。该句中的 this type of change 指的即是 the length of the adolescent period(青春期的长度)和 the definition of adulthood status(成年人的社会地位的定义)的变化。the length of the adolescent period 可以变长,也可以变短,这些都是随社会和经济情况的变化而变化的。the disappearance of the frontier 指的是 adolescent period 和 adulthood 之间分界线的消失,原文中的名词 frontier 转换成了题目中的短语 the dividing line(分界线),故答案为 adolescent period and adulthood。

3. 【定位】根据题干中的关键信息 adolescence, give place to, graduations, schools 及 colleges 可将搜索范围定位在第二段第一至三句。
【解析】Former social ceremonies/ Social ceremonies。联系上下文可知,第二句中的代词 ones 指代的即是第一句中的 ceremonies for adolescence,原文中的介词短语 for adolescence 转换成了题目中的定语从句 that used to mark adolescence;原文中的被动语态 have been replaced 转换成了题目中的主动语态 have given place to;原文中的并列短语 grade school graduation, high school graduation and college graduation 转换成了题目中的 graduations from schools and colleges。

4. 【定位】根据题干中的关键信息 twelve-year-old individual 及 privileges 可将搜索范围定位在第二段第七句。
【解析】significant adult rights。原文中的 this age 指的即是 twelve-year old;原文中的暗否定 loses childhood privileges 转换成了题目中的明否定 no more enjoys privileges as a child;原文中的介宾短语 without gaining

significant adult rights 转换成了题目中的句子 is not entitled to…,故原文中的 significant adult rights 即是本题答案。

5. 【定位】根据题干中的关键信息 21 可将搜索范围定位在第二段倒数第一至四句。

   【解析】more basic rights。该段倒数第四句指出到了 21 岁,一个人就可以得到作为成年人所有的合法权利;倒数第三句对这些合法权利作了简要说明;倒数第二句对合法权利作了一个补充说明:在到了成年的法定年龄之后 No additional basic rights are acquired as a function of age(基本权利不会再随年龄的增长而增加),原文此处主要是说明到了 21 岁,人的基本权利就不会再增加,题目中则将"从 22 岁开始"作为陈述主题;原文此处的暗比较也转换成了明比较…than…,所以应将原文中的 additional 改写为形容词比较级 more。

Lecture 2　第二讲　4 类题型解题思路

一、事实细节题

此类题型要求考生在阅读和理解文章的基础上根据问题的需要,寻找文中所提供的事实细节,对某一具体事实做出准确回答。此类题型所占比重较大,常见的问题表现形式如:

What is it that …?

The … is generated from _____?

How serious did the author predict …?

此类题目一般就文章中所涉及到的事件发生的时间、地点、人物、原因、结果等来设问,也可能就文章中出现的统计材料、例证材料等来提问,答案一般为原文中的原词或将其稍做词性或时态等方面的改动。由于题目涉及到的都是文章中的一些局部信息,所以一般采取查读的方法去搜索答案。通常的解题思路为:

1. 略读全文,了解文章结构、大意及各段中心。

2. 阅读题目,确定题目中关键信息点。

3. 根据关键信息点,在文章中迅速定位问题出处。

4. 仔细对照题目与原文,根据题目需要给出答案。

【例 1】 (07-6-49)

【原文】	【题目】
…*Google's search engine*. … They were both Ph. D. candidates when they devised the **search engine** which was better than the rest and, without any marketing, **spread** by word of mouth from early adopters to, eventually, your grandmother.	49. How did *Google's search engine spread* over the world?

【解析】By word of mouth。根据题目中的关键词语 search engine 可将搜索范围定位在文章第二段,再由 spread 一词将答案锁定在该段最后一句。Spread 后面的 by word of mouth(通过口头的方式)即为 Google 搜索引擎的传播方式。

二、语义理解题

此类题型要求考生能利用学过的语言知识及上下文提供的信息、线索推测出所选单词、短语或句子的含义。常见的问题表现形式如:

By saying "…(Line?, Para?)", the author suggests that _____.

What does the word … probably mean according to the context of the passage?

What do we know about the author's … from the sentence "… (Line?, Para?)"

此类题型一般不能在原文中直接找到答案,需要考生在理解原文意思的基础上,运用综合逻辑推理能力对文章中的信息进行分析,并用准确精炼的语言将其表达出来。通常的解题思路为:

1. 略读全文,了解文章结构、大意及各段中心。

2. 根据题目提示,定位问题出处。

3. 阅读所考查单词、短语或句子所在段落,重点阅读其前后句子,找出上下文的关联。

4. 结合上下文语境理解所考查单词、短语或句子在句中的语义,然后根据题目需要,用准确精练的语言给出答案。

【例2】

【原文】	【题目】
Though we've never had a catastrophic loss such as that, ***Gibbs and I did have a close call*** shortly before we decided to **simplify**. At that time we lived in a fire zone. One night a firestorm raged through and destroyed over six hundred homes in our community. That tragedy gave us the opportunity to look objectively at the goods we'd accumulated.	49. What do we know about the author's house from the sentence "***Gibbs and I did have a close call …***"(*Lines 1—2, Para. 4*)?

【解析】Their house needs to be simplified。根据括号中的句子出处迅速将答案定位在文章第四段。由"Gibbs and I …"一句可知,作者夫妇在决定精简(家里的东西)之前差点发生一件危险的事(have a close call),根据后面一句的解释可知,此处是说他们在社区的一场大火中幸免于难,而这场悲剧让他们有机会客观地审视他们 accumulated(积攒下来)的东西,由此可推知,作者夫妇的家需要简化。第二、三段内容对答案的提炼起提示作用。

三、归纳概括题

此类题型要求考生寻找或提炼文章大意或主题,或是对文中两处以上的细节内容进行归纳概括。常见的问题表现形式如:

What is the passage mainly about?

The previous paragraph most probably discusses _____.

What are the two ways …?

此类题要求考生在了解整个篇章或段落的结构和内容的基础上,根据文中的细节内容进行综合性的概括,答案一般不会是原文的原词。通常的解题思路为:

1. 略读全文,了解文章结构、大意及各段中心。

2. 确定题目所考查的范围是整篇文章还是具体段落。

3. 若是篇章层次的考查,重点阅读首尾段及各段首尾,寻找主题句,概括文章大意。

4. 若是段落层次的考查,首先根据题目定位到具体段落,然后寻找题目与原文的对应点,找出上下文之间的关联,然后根据题目需要,用精炼的语言归纳概括出答案。

【例3】

【原文】	【题目】
I once knew a dog named Newton who had ***a unique sense of humor***. Whenever I tossed out a *Frisbee* (飞碟) for him to chase, he'd take off in hot pursuit but then seem to lose track of it. Moving back and forth only a yard or two from the toy, Newton would look all around, even up into the trees. He seemed genuinely puzzled. Finally, I'd give up and head into the field to help him out. But no sooner would I get within 10 ft. of him than he would run in—variable straight over to the Frisbee, grab it and start running like mad, looking over his shoulder with what looked suspiciously like a grin. …	S2. Why does the author say Newton had ***a unique sense of humor***?

【解析】Because Newton intended to deceive him。由题目中的 a unique sense of humor 可将搜索范围定位在文章首段。本题的答案需要从该段内容中归纳概括得出。该段中说 Newton 起初好像不知道该去哪找飞碟,但当作者要帮他时,他却直接跑向飞碟抓起它,开始发疯似地跑,好像还在咧着嘴角笑,由此可以看出 Newton 是在挑逗、欺骗作者,因此作者认为 Newton 具有 a unique sense of humor。

四、推理判断题

此类题型要求考生在充分理解原文的基础上,根据文中所陈述的细节内容对其隐含的意思进行推理判断。此类题型一般都是针对文中某一细节的推理,因此从提问方式上与事实细节题差别不是很大,常见的问题表现形式如:

What happened to… in…?

How serious did the author think…?

此类题型是相对较难的一种题型,一般不能在原文中找到答案,需要考生充分理解原文,并能够挖掘出原文中

隐含的事实细节,虽并不常见,但也不容忽视。通常的解题思路为:

1. 略读全文,了解文章结构、大意及各段中心。
2. 根据题目中的中心词,在文中定位问题出处。
3. 仔细阅读上下文,注意把握上下文的逻辑关系。
4. 结合题目,推测文中隐含的事实细节,根据题目需要,用精炼的语言给出答案。

【例4】 (新 06-12-48)

【原文】	【题目】
" *The fire* saved us the agony of deciding what to keep and what to get rid of," one woman wrote. And once all those things were no longer there, *she and her husband* saw how they had weighed them down and complicated their lives.	48. Now that all their possessions were lost in *the fire, the woman and her husband* felt that their lives had been _____.

【解析】simplified。根据题目中的关键信息 the fire 和 the woman and her husband 可将搜索范围定位在文章第二段。由该段最后一句可知,火灾后女士和丈夫才明白,他们家中的东西曾经令他们的生活是多么复杂和繁琐,由此可推断,失去这些东西,他们应该是感到生活被简化了。

Exercise 即讲即练

Sporting activities are essentially modified forms of hunting behavior. Viewed biologically, the modern footballer is revealed as a member of a disguised hunting pack. His killing weapon has changed into a harmless football and his prey into a goalmouth. If his aim is accurate and he scores a goal, he enjoys the hunter's triumph of killing his prey.

To understand how this transformation has taken place we must briefly look back at our ancient ancestors. They spent over a million years evolving as co-operative hunters. Their very survival depended on success in the hunting field. Under this pressure their whole way of life, even their bodies, became radically changed. They co-operated as skillful male group attackers. Then, about ten thousand years ago, after this immensely long formative period of hunting their food, they became farmers. Their improved intelligence, so vital to their old hunting life, was put to new use — that of penning, controlling and domesticating their prey. The hunt became suddenly out of date. The food was there on the farms, waiting for their needs. The risks and uncertainties of the hunt were no longer essential for survival.

The hunting skills and the hunting urges remained, however, and demanded new outlets. Hunting for sport replaced hunting for necessity. This new activity involved all the original hunting sequences, but the aim of the operation was no longer to avoid starvation. Instead, the sportsmen set off to test their skill against prey that were no longer essential to their well-being. To be sure, the kill may have been eaten, but there were other much simpler ways of obtaining a meaty meal. The chase became exposed as an end in itself. The logical extension of this trend was the big game hunter who never ate his kill, but merely hung its stuffed head on his wall, and the foxhunter who has to breed foxes in order to release them to hunt them down.

An alternative solution was to transform the activities of pack into other patterns of behavior. The key to the transformation lies in the fact that there was no longer any need to eat the prey. This being so, then why bother to kill any animals? A symbolic killing is all that is needed, provided the thrill of the chase can be retained. The Greek solution was athletics field sports involving chasing, jumping, and throwing. The athletes experienced the vigorous physical activities so typical of the hunting scene, and the patterns they performed were all elements of the ancient hunting sequence, but their triumph was now transformed from the actual kill to a symbolic one of "winning".

1. According to the passage, aiming is also _____ of hunting behavior.

_____

2. Hunting for sport replaced hunting for necessity because our ancient ancestors learned to _____.

_____

3. According to the passage, a hunter breeds foxes maybe just because he wants to _____.

_____

4. Hunting for food transformed into modern competitive sports because of a key fact that _____ didn't exist any more.

_____

5. The difference between athletics and the ancient hunting lies in the fact that athletes today never _____ in their games.

_____ _____ _____ _____ _____ _____ _____ _____

【答案与解析】

【文章大意】

体育活动基本上是一种变相的狩猎活动。本文中作者向我们讲述了以满足生存所需为目的而进行的狩猎活动被以运动为目的的狩猎活动所代替的演变过程，同时作者也阐述了运动与狩猎活动的区别。

1.【定位】根据题干中的关键信息 aiming，hunting behavior 可将搜索范围定位在第一段最后一句。

【解析】a modified form。该段第一句即指出 Sporting activities are essentially modified forms of hunting behavior，紧接着举出 modern footballer 的例子进行解释说明。modern footballer 踢球被认为是 modified forms of hunting behavior，由此可推知，踢球过程中的 aiming 也应是一种 modified form of hunting behavior。

2.【定位】根据题干中的关键信息 Hunting for sport replaced hunting for necessity 可将搜索范围定位在第三段。

【解析】pen, control and domesticate their prey / raise domestic animals。第三段只是指出了 hunting for sport replaced hunting for necessity 这一结果，具体导致这一结果产生的原因可以从第二段中寻找。该段前半部分主要是讲人们进行狩猎主要是为了满足生存需求；后半部则主要是讲 the hunt became suddenly out of date 的原因：人们开始耕种土地，他们学会了 penning, controlling and domesticating their prey（对捕获的猎物进行圈养、控制以及驯化），这样人们就没有必要再去为满足生存需要而狩猎。

3.【定位】根据题干中的关键信息 breed foxes 可将搜索范围定位在第三段最后一句。

【解析】release them to hunt them down。题目中的 a hunter breeds foxes 对应该句中的 the foxhunter who has to breed foxes，题目中的 because 对应该句中的 in order to，故答案为 release them to hunt them down。

4.【定位】根据题干中的关键信息 transformed，key fact 可将搜索范围定位在第四段第二句。

【解析】the need to eat the prey。题目中的 hunting for food transformed into modern competitive sports 对应第四段第一句中的 transform the activities of pack into other patterns of behavior，第二句指出这种变化的决定性因素即是：there was no longer any need to eat the prey。原文中的 there be 句型转换成了题目中的一般句式，故答案为 the need to eat the prey。

5.【定位】根据题干中的关键信息 athletics 可将搜索范围定位在最后一段。

【解析】make the actual kill / hurt each other。该段最后一句中的 their triumph was now transformed from the actual kill to a symbolic one of "winning"表明体育运动与古代人狩猎之间的区别就是，古代人狩猎是将动物杀死，而体育运动则只是追求胜利的标志，并不是 make the actual kill 或 hurt each other（以杀死或伤害对方为目的），这就是体育运动区别于古代人狩猎的不同之处。

Lecture 3 第三讲 5 大做题避错要诀

要诀一：不要过早下笔

先通读全文，了解文章的主题，把握全文的结构，领会作者的意图，然后浏览要求解答的问题，找出问题的关键信息，再带着问题到文章的相关部分寻找答案依据。

要诀二：注意提问方式

解答问答题时，要注意根据引导问题的特殊疑问词确定答案的性质。回答 what 的提问，一般要用名词、名词性短语或名词性从句，但如果谓语动词是 do，则要用动词短语或表示动作、行为的句子来回答；回答 who 的提问，一般要用表示人或机构的名词或名词性短语；回答 why 的提问，一般要用 because(of)，due to 之类表示原因的词引导的短语或句子；回答 how(表示方式)的提问，常用 by 之类的表示方式的短语。

解答句子补充题时，要注意根据句子的其他成分推测所缺部分的性质和内容。如系动词后很可能是分词或形容词，及物动词后可能是名词、名词性短语或名词性从句。

【例1】 (新 06-12-51)

【原文】	【题目】
Make another list of things you wouldn't acquire again no matter what, and in fact would be happy to be rid of. When you're ready to start unloading some of your stuff, that list will be a good place to start.	51. What does the author suggest people do with unnecessary things?

【解析】Make a list of them before unloading them。本题是问作者建议人们如何处理不需要的东西，suggest 表示建议时，后面从句的谓语动词要求用(should)do 的形式，因此本题答案应以动词原形开头。

要诀三：用简短的语言回答

短句问答题要求答案不超过 10 个单词，考生要遵循简短的原则，回答尽量求简，具体来讲就是，能用单词、短语回答的就不用句子，能用一个单词回答的就不要用两个单词。

【例2】 (新 06-12-48)

【原文】	【题目】
"The fire saved us the agony of deciding what to keep and what to get rid of," one woman wrote. And once all those things were no longer there, *she and her husband* saw how they had weighed them down and complicated their lives.	48. Now that all their possessions were lost in *the fire*, the woman and her husband felt that their lives had been _____ .

【解析】simplified。针对本题有些同学可能会给出这样的答案：made complicated no longer 或是 made more simple，但其实就是想表达 simplified(简化)的含义。

要诀四：谨慎照抄原文

短句问答题中有的答案可以直接用原文中的原词回答，但有很多时候，由于问题是对原文的转述，而且提出的方式或角度可能与原文的叙述不同，所以很难直接套用原文中的语句，需要考生根据问题对原文进行适当的加工，或是根据原文内容，用自己的语言组织出答案。

【例3】 (07-6-50)

【原文】	【题目】
Perhaps their biggest stroke of luck came early on when they tried to sell their technology to other search engines, but no one **met their price**, and they *built it up on their own*.	50. Brin and Page decided to *set up their own business because* no one would _____ .

【解析】meet their price。原文用的 meet 的过去式 met，而题目(would)则要求填动词原形，答题时稍一疏忽就有可能直接照抄原文。

要诀五：仔细检查句法和用词

做完题目以后，要认真细致地核查一遍问题和答案，以避免出现语法和语言形式的错误。常见的语法错误包括：主谓不一致、时态混乱、搭配不当、句子结构不完整、用词不当等。常见的语言形式错误包括：拼写错误，大小写和标点符号错误等。如果是问答题，那么答案的第一个单词的首字母要大写；如果是句子补充题，那么答案的第一个单词的首字母不要大写(专有名词或位于句首时除外)。

短句问答巅峰练习

Exercise 1

We have emphasized so far the significance of scarcity — the limited means to satisfy human wants. Because of scarcity, choices are necessary. An easy example of the problem of choice is a person's decision about how to allocate his or her time. As the old saying goes, "There are only 24 hours in a day." If we take off 8 hours for a reasonable night sleep, this leaves 16 hours to be allocated among all other possible things — working at one or more jobs, watching TV, studying, playing tennis, etc. — one can do with the limited available waking hours. Clearly, each person must make choices about how much of their limited available time will be spent on each possible activity.

When choices are made among alternatives such as those just described, it becomes plain that choosing one alternative often involves giving up another. For example, suppose you go to classes 4 hours a day and get 8 hours of sleep. You will have an additional 12 waking hours to allocate per day. Suppose now that the only other activities you view as worth pursuing are watching TV and studying. If you choose to watch TV for 12 hours a day, no time will be left for studying, assuming you continue to sleep for 8 hours in each 24 hour period and do not cut classes. If you choose each day to devote 6 hours to studying, only 6 of the 12 waking hours will be available for watching TV. You must give up the opportunity of watching more hours of TV in the process of choosing to study. We can therefore say that the decision to study costs you 6 hours of TV watching.

Economists use the term "opportunity cost" to mean the cost of a specific choice measured in terms of the next best alternative choice. In other words, it is what the decision maker must forego in order to make the choice that is finally made. Thus, in our example, the opportunity cost of studying for 6 hours was 6 hours of watching TV. We can see many other examples of opportunity costs around us. For example, governments are faced with limited budgets and therefore with limited resources that can be used to provide goods and services to citizens. If a government chooses to improve its military forces, it may well do so by allocating fewer resources for libraries or schools. The opportunity cost of a strong defense may be a reduction in the size of library holdings or educational services.

47. According to the passage, choices must be made because we have _____.

_____ _____ _____ _____ _____ _____ _____ _____ _____

48. We often need to _____ when we choose one among alternatives.

_____ _____ _____ _____ _____ _____ _____ _____ _____

49. In the example cited in the passage, the opportunity cost of studying for 4 hours per day was _____.

_____ _____ _____ _____ _____ _____ _____ _____ _____

50. According to the economists, the opportunity cost of a specific choice is giving up _____.

_____ _____ _____ _____ _____ _____ _____ _____ _____

51. According to the passage, if a government chooses to allocate more of its resources to its military forces, it is possible for it to reduce resources _____.

_____ _____ _____ _____ _____ _____ _____ _____ _____

Exercise 2

A report consistently brought back by visitors to the US is how friendly, courteous and helpful most Americans were to them. To be fair, this observation is also frequently made of Canada and Canadians, and should best be considered North American. There are, of course, exceptions. Small-minded officials, rude waiters, and ill-mannered taxi drivers are hardly unknown in the US. Yet it is an observation made so frequently that it deserves comment.

For a long period of time and in many parts of the country, a traveler was a welcome break in an otherwise dull existence. Dullness and loneliness were common problems of the families who generally lived distant from one another. Strangers and travelers were welcome sources of diversion, and brought news of the outside world. The harsh realities of the frontier also shaped this tradition of hospitality. Someone traveling alone, if hungry, injured, or ill, often had nowhere to turn except to the nearest cabin or settlement. It was not a matter of choice for the traveler or merely a charitable impulse on the part of the settlers. It reflected the harshness of daily life: if you didn't take in the stranger and take care of him, there was no one else who would. And someday, remember, you might be in the same situation.

Today there are many charitable organizations which specialize in helping the weary traveler. Yet, the old tradition of hospitality to strangers is still very strong in the US, especially in the smaller cities and towns away from the busy tourist trails. "I was just traveling through, got talking with this American, and pretty soon he invited me home for dinner-amazing." Such observations reported by visitors to the US are not uncommon, but are not always understood properly. The casual friendliness of many Americans should be interpreted neither as superficial nor as artificial, but as the result of a historically developed cultural tradition. As is true of any developed society, in America a complex set of cultural signals, assumptions, and conventions underlies all social interrelationships. And, of course, speaking a language does not necessarily mean that someone understands social and cultural patterns. Visitors who fail to "translate" cultural meanings properly often draw wrong conclusions. For example, when an American uses the word "friend", the cultural implications of the word may be quite different from those it has in the visitor's language and culture. It takes more than a brief encounter on a bus to distinguish between courteous convention and individual interest. Yet, being friendly is a virtue that many Americans value highly and expect from both neighbors and strangers.

47. According to the report from visitors, _____ are believed most friendly to them.

_____ _____ _____ _____ _____ _____ _____ _____ _____ _____

48. In the past, many Americans liked the coming of strangers because they felt dull and _____.

_____ _____ _____ _____ _____ _____ _____ _____ _____ _____

49. In the past, where would a weary traveler most probably go for help on the frontier?

_____ _____ _____ _____ _____ _____ _____ _____ _____ _____

50. The behavior of an American's providing a hungry traveler food showed that on the frontier _____.

_____ _____ _____ _____ _____ _____ _____ _____ _____ _____

51. According to the passage, what is it that makes many Americans show hospitality to strangers casually?

_____ _____ _____ _____ _____ _____ _____ _____ _____ _____

答案与解析

Exercise 1

【文章大意】

时间、物资等等一切资源都是有限的。一天 24 小时里,我们要学习、工作、娱乐,如何合理的分配和利用时间,我们面临种种选择。对于政府也是如此。如果政府选择加强军事力量,那么它很可能就会减少对学校和图书馆的资源分配。为此,经济学家提出了"机会成本"这个概念。

47.【定位】根据题干中的关键信息 choices 及短句问答出题顺序原则可将搜索范围定位在第一段。

　　【解析】limited means to satisfy our wants。该段第一句中的破折号表明 the limited means to satisfy human wants 是对 scarcity 的解释说明。该段第二句指出正是因为 scarcity,所以选择才是必须的。题目中的 choices must be made 对应原文中的 choices are necessary,题目中的原因状语从句应该对应 Because of scarcity,但如果将 scarcity 作为答案,we have scarcity 明显不符合词语的常用搭配以及句意。所以应将 scarcity 的解释 limited means to satisfy human wants 作为 have 的宾语,但因为主语是 we,所以应将 human 相应的改为 our。

48.【定位】根据题干中的关键信息 choose one among alternatives 可将搜索范围定位在第二段第一句。

　　【解析】give up other alternatives。该句指出当要进行选择时,choosing one alternative often involves giving up another(选择了一个就意味着放弃另一个)是最平常不过的了。题目中的 when we choose one among alternatives 对应原文中的 choosing one alternative。题目中的 to 为不定式,故其后应用动词原形。

49.【定位】根据题干中的关键信息 the opportunity cost 可将搜索范围定位在第三段。

【解析】4 hours of watching TV。题干中的 example 指的就是文中举出的花 6 小时学习就意味着要少看 6 小时电视这一例子,由该段第三句中的 the opportunity cost of studying for 6 hours was 6 hours of watching TV 可推断,如果花 4 小时学习就意味着它的机会成本是 4 hours of watching TV。

50.【定位】由题干中的 economists, opportunity cost 可将搜索范围定位在第三段。

【解析】the next best alternative choice。该段第一句指出经济学家使用 opportunity cost(机会成本)这一术语来表示通过 the next best alternative choice 来衡量 a specific choice 所花费的成本,也就是说作出 a specific choice 是以放弃后面的 the next best alternative choice(次佳选择)为代价的。

51.【定位】根据题干中的关键信息 government,military forces 可将搜索范围定位在最后一段。

【解析】allocated for libraries or schools /education。该段举出 government 对资源分配的例子是为了证明我们身边有很多关于 opportunity cost 的例子。如果 government 分配大量的资源给 military forces,那么分配给 libraries or schools 的资源就会减少,题目表达的正是此意,由此可知所填内容应该表示分配给学校图书馆或学校的资源。

Exercise 2

> **【文章大意】**
>
> 美国人素有好客之名,本文对美国人好客的原因进行了分析。文章第一段指出一种事实:北美洲的人,尤其是美国人和加拿大人都十分好客;第二段分析了过去人们好客的原因:人们自身的无聊感以及孤独感使然,加之边疆地区日常生活的残酷事实;第三段分析了现在美国人们仍然好客的原因:历史遗留下来的文化传统。

47.【定位】根据题干中的关键信息 report,visitors,most friendly 可将搜索范围定位在第一段第二句。

【解析】North Americans。根据该段第一句话可知,本句中的 this observation 指的是游客对他们所游览的国家中的人们对游客态度的观察。句中的 also 表明除了美国人,Canadians 对游客也是非常友好的,而后一分句中的最高级 best be considered North American 则表明在根据游客反映所作出的报告中 North American 对游人最为友好。题干中的谓语为复数,故 North American 应变成复数名词形式,答案为 North Americans。

48.【定位】根据题干中的关键信息 In the past,dull 可将搜索范围定位在第二段第二句。

【解析】lonely。结合该段第二、三句可知,以前人们欢迎陌生人和游客是因为游客可以带来外部世界的消息,而根本原因则是当时人们相互之间离得很远,在这些人当中普遍存在着 dullness 和 loneliness 的问题,即这些人普遍感到 dull 和 lonely。故答案为 lonely。

49.【定位】根据题干中的关键信息 weary,traveler,frontier 可将搜索范围定位在第二段第四、五句。

【解析】The nearest cabin or settlement。该段第五句中的介词 except 表明,除了 the nearest cabin or settlement,在边疆地区旅游的游客 had nowhere to turn(没有地方可去),即 the nearest cabin or settlement 是疲惫不堪的游客唯一的选择。

50.【定位】根据题干中的关键信息 on the frontier,showed 可将搜索范围定位在第二段。

【解析】daily life was harsh。该段倒数第三句指出独自到边疆地区出游的人在饥饿、受伤或生病的情况下只能去 the nearest cabin or settlement 求助,这并不只是游客选择求助地或是居住者仁慈的问题,而是反映了边疆地区的 the harshness of daily life 的问题。题干中的 showed 是原文中 reflected 的同义词,故 reflected 的宾语即为本题答案,但 showed 后的 that 提示所填内容应该是一个句子,所以应对 the harshness of daily life 进行改写。

51.【定位】根据题干中的关键信息 casually 可将搜索范围定位在最后一段第五句。

【解析】A historically developed cultural tradition。该句中的 neither…nor…,but…结构表明 the casual friendliness of many Americans 应归因于 but 后所指出的实际情况,即 a historically developed cultural tradition。题干中的 many Americans show hospitality to strangers casually 是 the casual friendliness of many Americans 的同义转述,故答案为 A historically developed cultural tradition。注意题干使用的是强调句式。

Chapter 5

篇章词汇巅峰讲座

篇章词汇理解文章长度一般在 250—300 词之间,主要测试考生对篇章语境中的词汇的理解和运用能力,要求考生阅读一篇删去若干个(一般为 10 个)词汇的短文,然后在所给的选项(一般为 15 个)中选择适当的词汇填充,使短文复原。

篇章词汇理解是六级考试改革后新增的一种阅读题型,至今六级考试中尚未出现过,但六级考试大纲中明确规定,篇章词汇理解与短句问答是作为二选一题型出现,因此考生对其也要有充分的准备。

Lecture 1　第一讲　4种重点考查词性

篇章词汇理解主要测试的是考生在实际语境中对单词的理解和把握,因此重点考查的词性是名词、动词、形容词和副词等主要实词,而一般不会涉及介词、冠词等不具有实际意义的虚词。

一、名词

名词通常作主语或宾语,如果空白处位于主语或宾语的位置,那所填词的选择范围就应该定位在选项中的名词上。名词前常有冠词和形容词充当的定语成分,这也可作为判断所填词为名词的依据。

确定所填词应为名词后,要根据修饰该名词的冠词以及主谓一致的原则等线索判断所填名词的单复数形式。

【例 1】

【原文】	【选项】
When Roberto Feliz came to the USA from the Dominican Republic, he knew only a few words of English. Education soon became a ___47___.	[A] wonder　　[E] nightmare　　[F] native [G] acceptance　　[N] breakthrough

【解析】选[E]。分析空格所在句子结构可知,所填词在句中充当 became 的宾语,而空前的 a 提示,所填词应为可数名词单数形式,[G] 为不可数名词,且不能跟在 a 后面,故将其排除,由此可将答案锁定在[A]、[E]、[F]、[N] 四个选项中。

二、动词

动词通常作谓语或以非谓语动词的形式出现充当主语、宾语、定语、状语、补语等各种成分。动词前后最常见是名词、代词、介词和副词。名词或代词充当动词的(逻辑)宾语或(逻辑)主语,介词与动词构成习惯搭配,副词修饰动词,不定式符号 to 后面跟动词原形,这些均可作为判断所填词为动词的依据。

确定所填词应为动词后,要根据上下文含义及语法结构来判断所填动词是及物动词还是不及物动词,其形式是原形、第三人称单数、过去式、过去分词、现在分词还是动名词。

【例 2】

【原文】	【选项】
"I couldn't understand anything," he said. He ___48___ from his teachers, came home in tears, and thought about dropping out.	[B] acquired　　[D] regained [I] hid　　　　[M] recalled

【解析】选[I]。分析句子结构可知,此处缺少一个谓语动词,故所填词应为动词,而后半句中与其并列的 came 和 thought 表明,所填动词应该为一般过去式,而空后的 from 提示,所填动词应该为不及物动词,[B]、[D] 均为及物动词,故排除,由此可将答案锁定在 [I]、[M] 两个选项中。

三、形容词

　　形容词通常作定语或表语。形容词前后最常见的是名词、副词、系动词或半系动词、表示比较级或最高级的more，less，most，least等词，这些均可作为判断所填词为形容词的依据。

　　确定所填词应为形容词后，要根据上下文含义及语法结构来判断所填形容词是原形、比较级还是最高级。

【例3】

【原文】	【选项】
Then Mrs. Malave, a bilingual educator, began to work with him while teaching him math and science in his ___49___ Spanish.	[F] native　　[H] effective　　[J] prominent [K] decent　　[L] countless

【解析】选[F]。分析句子结构可知，所填词在句中充当Spanish的定语，因此最有可能是一个形容词，由此将答案初步锁定在[F]、[H]、[J]、[K]、[L]五个选项中。

四、副词

　　副词通常作状语。副词修饰形容词、动词或整个句子。如果句子的主干成分齐全，而空白处又不适合填形容词，那么所填词极有可能为副词。

　　篇章词汇考查的副词一般都是具有实际意义的情状副词，而且多半是以-ly结尾的副词。

【例4】

【原文】	【选项】
In Arizona and Texas, bilingual students ___55___ outperform their peers in monolingual programs.	[C] consistently　　[O] automatically

【解析】选[C]。分析句子结构可知，空格所在句主谓宾齐全，而空白处明显不能填形容词，故所填词应该是一个副词，修饰动词outperform，由此可将答案锁定在[C]、[O]之间。

Exercise　　　即讲即练

　　No one should be forced to wear a uniform under any circumstance. Uniforms are demeaning to the human spirit and totally __1__ in a democratic society. Uniforms tell the world that the person who wears one has no value as an individual but only lives to function as a part of the whole. The individual in a uniform loses all self-worth. There are those who say that wearing a uniform gives a person a sense of __2__ with a large, more important concept. What could be more important than the individual oneself? If an organization is so __3__ that it must rely on cloth and buttons to inspire its members, that organization has no right to continue its existence. Others say that the practice of making persons wear uniforms, say in school, eliminates all envy and __4__ in a matter of dress, such that a poor person who cannot afford good-quality clothing. Why would anyone strive to be better? It is only a short step from forcing everyone to wear the same clothing to forcing everyone to drive the same car, have the same type of house, eat the same type of food. When this happens, all __5__ to improve one's life is removed. Why would parents __6__ to work hard so that their children could have a better life than they had when they know that their children are going to be forced to have __7__ the same life that they had? Uniforms also __8__ the economy. Right now, billions of dollars are spent on the fashion industry yearly. Thousands of persons are __9__ in designing, creating, and marketing different types of clothing. If everyone were forced to wear uniforms, artistic __10__ and salespersons would be superfluous.

[A] competition	[B] employees	[C] weak	[D] function	[E] illogical
[F] bother	[G] incentive	[H] personnel	[I] unnecessary	[J] identification
[K] exactly	[L] hurt	[M] employed	[N] absolutely	[O] useless

【答案与解析】

> **【词性分析】**
>
> 名　词:competition(竞争,竞赛);employees(雇员,职工);function(作用,职责);incentive(动机,激励);personnel(人员,职员);identification(证明,视为同一);hurt(伤痛,伤害)
>
> 动　词:function(运行,行使职责);bother(烦扰,麻烦);hurt(伤害);employed(雇佣)
>
> 形容词:weak(弱的,无力的);illogical(不合逻辑的,不合理的);incentive(激励的);unnecessary(不必要的,多余的);useless(无用的,无价值的)
>
> 副　词:exactly(正确地,严密地);absolutely(绝对地,完全地)

1. 选[I]。and 连接两个并列分句,后一分句省略了系动词 are,故所填词可能为动词的现在分词、动词的过去分词或形容词。备选项中没有动词的现在分词形式,所以所填词最有可能为形容词或动词的过去分词。本句的主语为 uniforms,结合本分句的其他成分可知,本处用动词的过去分词形式明显不符合逻辑,所以所填词只能为形容词。本文第一句作者便阐明了自己的观点:No one should be forced to wear a uniform under any circumstance,那么在 democratic society(民主社会)中,制服当然也就没有其存在的必要了,备选形容词中只有[I] unnecessary(不必要的)符合句意。

2. 选[J]。空前介词 of 及空后介词 with 提示所填词应为名词。由第三句可知,制服强调的是整体性、同一性。那些认为有必要穿制服的人会觉得穿制服能够使人作为整体的一部分而受到肯定,备选项中的名词在意义上符合本句语境的只有[J] identification(证明,视为同一)。

3. 选[C]。空前系动词 is 及句型 so…that 提示所填词应为形容词。该句指出如果一个组织到了需要统一的着装来激励员工的话,那么它就没有存在的必要了,[C] weak(弱的,无力的)用在句中能表达该组织的无能。

4. 选[A]。空前连词 and 提示所填词应与 envy 构成并列关系,故所填词应为名词。结合句意可知,envy 和所填词都应表示在学生中会出现的情况,所以所填词和 envy 应是语义场共现的关系,故答案为[A] competition(竞争)。

5. 选[G]。分析句子结构可知,所填词在句中作主语,故应为名词。本句时间状语中的 this 指代的是上一句中所说的各种情况,即:每个人都被强迫开同样的车、住同样的房子、吃同样的食物。这些都是作者预想中的事情,但是它反映了一个问题:过分的强调同一性会磨灭一个人作为个体的价值,每个人都被强迫去做同样的事情,那么他们就会丧失提高自我生活的 incentive,故答案为[G] incentive(动机)。

6. 选[F]。分析句子结构可知,所填词在句中作谓语,空前的助动词 would 提示所填词应为动词原形。空后不定式符号 to 提示所填词应能与 to 搭配使用,备选项中是动词原形且能与 to 搭配使用的只有[F] bother(烦恼)。

7. 选[K]。分析句子结构可知,所填词应在句中作状语,故所填词应为副词。备选项中的两个副词的不同之处在于:exactly 为焦点副词,对其后所修饰的词起加强语气作用;而 absolutely 为程度副词,强调某一事物的程度。本句是作者对统一性的质疑,统一性已经表明两个或者更多事物之间是相同的,所以不必再用 absolutely 来强调,而 exactly 则适合用于此处,用以唤起人们对 the same life 的注意,故答案为[K] exactly(完全地)。

8. 选[L]。分析句子结构可知,所填词在句中作谓语,故应为动词。主语 uniforms 为复数且本文通篇使用的都是一般现在时态,故所填词应为动词原形。本文开头部分就指出了 uniforms 的一个缺点,本句中的副词 also 表明本句要讲 uniforms 的另一个缺点。备选项中的动词既是动词原形又能表达 uniforms 的缺点的只有[L] hurt(伤害)。

9. 选[M]。空前系动词提示所填词可能为动词过去分词、动词现在分词或形容词。备选项中没有动词的现在分词形式,故所填词只有可能为形容词或动词过去分词。将备选项中的形容词带入原文,都不符合句意,而动词的过去分词 employed 则符合句意,故答案为[M] employed(雇佣)。

10. 选[H]。空前形容词及连词 and 后的名词提示所填词应为名词。本句假设了一种情况,即:如果每个人都被强迫穿制服。结合上句可知,如果该假设变成现实,那么被雇佣 designing, creating, and marketing different types of clothing 的人就会显得 superfluous(多余)。该句中的 salespersons 对应上句中的 marketing different types of clothing 的人,所以 artistic _____ 则应该对应 designing, creating different types of clothing 的人,故所填词应为[H] personnel(人员),以与 salespersons 对应。

Lecture 2 ## 第二讲　5 大经常涉及考点

　　篇章词汇理解比较注重词汇在文章中的实际运用,它侧重考查考生对连贯性、一致性、逻辑关系等语篇、语段整体特征的理解以及在实际语境中对单词含义的把握,它要求考生在理解全文的基础上弄清文章的宏观结构并把握每个单词的微观含义。具体来讲,该部分的主要考点包括:

一、对句子语法结构的分析

篇章词汇理解备选选项的词性和形式各不相同,这就要求考生根据空格所在句子的语法结构来判断所填词的词性和形式,从而缩小选择范围。

【例1】

【原文】	【选项】
Afro-American arts and crafts started ___47___ on the west coast of Africa where they were important in all aspects of communal life.	[G] originally　　[N] mostly

【解析】选[G]。分析句子结构可知,空格所在句的主干成分是 arts and crafts started,由主语 arts and crafts 可知 started 在此应是不及物动词,故后面不需要再接宾语,排除所填词是名词的可能性。空后充当句子状语的介词短语 on the west… 以及该短语中包含的定语从句也是完整的结构,不缺少任何成分,由此可知,所填词只能是一个副词,用来修饰谓语动词 started,故可将答案锁定在[G]与[N]之间。

二、对前后语义衔接的理解

篇章词汇理解题中,对每一个词的考查都不是孤立地限定于某一个单独的句子,所填词仅能使单个的句子通顺是不行的,还需要确保上下文语义的合理衔接。

【例2】

【原文】	【选项】
"I couldn't understand anything," he said. He hid from his teachers, came home in tears, and thought about dropping out. Then Mrs. Malave, … "She helped me stay smart while teaching me English," he said. Given the chance to demonstrate his ability, he ___50___ confidence and began to succeed in school.	[B] acquired　　[D] regained [I] hid　　　　[M] recalled

【解析】选[D]。分析句子结构可知,所填词应该是一个及物动词,并能与 confidence 构成合理的搭配。单从空格所在句来看,[B] acquired(获得)和[D] regained(重获)均可以使句子通顺,但由上段内容可知"他"根本听不懂老师讲的内容,变得非常灰心,而现在有机会 demonstrate his ability(展现自己的能力),他应该是恢复了信心,符合此语义要求的是[D] regained。

三、对近义词细微差别的了解

篇章词汇注重考查对词汇的精确理解,选项中往往会出现一组或多组近义词,要求考生分清楚它们在实际运用中的细微差别。

【例3】

【原文】	【选项】
Decades ago, there were only a limited number of drugs available, and many of them caused ___56___ side effects in older people, including dizziness and fatigue.	[C] significant　　[H] magnificent

【解析】选[C]。分析句子结构可知,所填词应为形容词,修饰 side effects(副作用)。表面上看,[C] significant 和[H] magnificent 都含有"大"的意思,但[H] magnificent 主要是用来表示事物的"宏伟"、"壮观"和"伟大",而[C] significant 则可以表示事物是"重大的"、"影响深远的",能与 side effects 构成合理的修饰关系。

四、对上下文逻辑关系的把握

解答篇章词汇理解题,不能只考虑句子意思上的通顺,还要充分把握上下文的因果、条件、转折、并列等逻辑关系,然后根据这些逻辑关系选择适合的选项。

【例4】

【原文】	【选项】
It is not hard to see how women who have been through all this might be just a little bit angry. And this is a society where the twisting of feminism's goals and career dreams has ___56___ to the increasing number of divorces.	[A] converted　　　[C] stimulated [I] satisfied　　　[J] privileged [K] resulted　　　[L] depressed [O] contributed

【解析】选[O]。分析句子结构可知,所填词应该充当谓语动词,由空前的 has 可推测所填词应该为动词的过去分词。由空格所在句意可知,the twisting of feminism's goals and careers dreams 是造成 the increasing number of divorces 的原因,由此可将答案范围缩小到[K] resulted 和[O] contributed 两项之间,而 resulted 表示"导致"时通常与 in 搭配,contributed 能与 to 构成合理搭配,故为答案。

五、对词语习惯搭配的掌握

篇章词汇理解虽很少在短语层面上考查词汇,但有时除了考查词汇在语篇、段落层次上的实际运用以外,也会涉及到对词语习惯搭配的测试。

【例5】

【原文】	【选项】	
That's why a growing number of hospitals now depend upon physicians who ___51___ in pain medicine.	[D] range [O] specialize	[M] respect

【解析】选[O]。分析句子结构可知,所填词在句中充当从句的谓语动词,其逻辑主语是 physicians,结合时间状语 now 和句子的一般现在时态可知,所填词应为动词原形,由此可将答案锁定在[D]、[M]、[O] 三项中。空后的介词 in 提示,所填词还必须能与其构成合理搭配,由此可确定答案为[O] specialize。specialize in 意为"专攻,专门研究",符合此处语境。

Exercise 即讲即练

Today, there are many avenues open to those who wish to continue their education. However, nearly all require some break in one's career in order to attend school full time. Part-time education, that is, attending school at night or for one weekend a month, tends to drag the process out over time and puts the ___1___ of a degree program out of reach of many people. Additionally, such programs require a ___2___ time commitment which can also impact negatively on one's career and family time. Of the many approaches to teaching and learning, however, perhaps the most flexible and accommodating is that called distance learning. Distance learning is an educational method, which ___3___ the students the flexibility to study at his or her own pace to achieve the academic goals, which are so ___4___ in today's world. The time required to study may be set aside at the student's ___5___ with due regard to all life's other requirements. Additionally, the student may enroll in distance learning courses from ___6___ any place in the world, while continuing to pursue their chosen career. Good distance learning programs are characterized by the inclusion of a subject evaluation tool with every subject. This ___7___ the requirement for a student to travel away from home to take a test. Another characteristic of a good distance-learning program is the ___8___ of the distance-learning course with the same subject materials as those students taking the course on the home campus. The resultant diploma or degree should also be the same whether distance learning or on-campus study is ___9___. The ___10___ of the professor/student relationship is another characteristic of a good distance-learning program. In the final analysis, a good distance learning program has a place not only for the individual students but also the corporation or business that wants to work in partnership with their employees for the educational benefit, professional development, and business growth of the organization.

[A] completion	[B] virtually	[C] fixed	[D] allows	[E] irregular
[F] employed	[G] unfamiliarity	[H] convenience	[I] individuality	[J] efficient
[K] amazingly	[L] excludes	[M] necessary	[N] precludes	[O] equivalence

【答案与解析】

【词性分析】

名　词:completion(完成);unfamiliarity(不熟悉,陌生);convenience(方便,有益);individuality(个性,独特性);necessary(必需品);equivalence(同等)

动　词:fixed(确定,固定);allows(允许,承认);employed(使用,雇佣);excludes(拒绝接纳,排斥);precludes(排除)

> 形容词：fixed(确定的,固定的)；irregular(不规则的,无规律的)；efficient(有效率的,能干的)；necessary(必要的,必需的)
>
> 副　词：virtually(几乎是,近乎)；amazingly(可惊地,令人惊讶地)

1. 选[A]。空前定冠词及空后介词提示所填词应为名词。本句主要指出 part-time education 的缺点：drag the process out over time 和 puts the _____ of a degree program out of reach…。part-time education 是指在晚上或周末上课,所以如果学习 a degree program(学位课程)的话,就会消耗大量时间,换句话说就是,part-time education 使完成一门课程变得艰难,所以所填词应该含有"完成"之意,故答案为[A] completion(完成)。

2. 选[C]。空前不定冠词及空后名词提示所填词应为形容词。本义第一至四句主要是说明许多全日制或非全日制教学的缺点。第五句则指出了另一种教学模式：distance learning,这种教学模式是 the most flexible and accommodating(最灵活、最方便的),根据上下文可知,distance learning 的优点则说明了 part-time education 的缺点就是：不灵活、不方便。这种不灵活就体现在上课时间固定、不能根据学习者自己的时间而设定上课时间,所以所填词应该有"固定"的含义,故答案为[C] fixed(固定的)。

3. 选[D]。分析句子结构可知所填词在句中作谓语,故所填词应为动词。which 引导非限制性定语从句,其先行词为单数名词,故所填词应为动词的一般现在式,故可将答案限定在[D] allows、[L] excludes 和[N] precludes 中。但句中的不定式短语 to study…提示所填词还应该能与 to 构成搭配,形成动词短语… to do sth. ,[L] excludes、[N] precludes 都没有此用法,故可排除,答案为[D] allows(允许)。

4. 选[M]。空前系动词及程度副词提示所填词应为形容词。备选项中的形容词单从意义上可以首先将[C] fixed 和[E] irregular 排除。空前 which 引导的非限制性定语从句修饰前面一整句话,将[J] efficient 带入该非限制性定语从句中,该从句句意明显不符合逻辑,故也可排除,答案为[M] necessary。

5. 选[H]。空前形容词及空后介词提示所填词应为名词。第五句已经指出远程教育是 the most flexible and accommodating,本句是讲远程教育的时间安排,所以所填词应和 flexible,accommodating 属于同一语义场,备选项中的名词只有[H] convenience(便利,方便)符合要求,故为答案。

6. 选[B]。分析句子结构可知,所填词应为副词,故可将答案限定在[B] virtually 和[K] amazingly 中,如果单从副词意义上来看,二者都适合本句,但在用法上却有所差别：amazingly 通常作为评注性副词,表示某种情感,而 virtually 则为程度副词,本句明显不带有感情色彩,故可排除[K] amazingly(令人惊讶地),答案为[B] virtually(几乎是,几乎)。

7. 选[N]。分析句子结构可知,所填词在句中作谓语,故所填词应为动词。本句主语为 this,再根据上下文时态可知,所填词应为动词的一般现在时。根据第 3 小题的分析可首先将[D] allows 排除,答案限定在[L] excludes 和[N] precludes 中,二者是近形、近义词,但在用法上稍有区别：exclude 作"排斥,拒绝接纳"讲时,是指故意将某物或某事排除在外,含有主观臆动性,而 preclude 则不含有主观臆动性。本句明显不含有主观因素,故可将[L] excludes 排除,答案为[N] precludes(排除)。

8. 选[O]。空前定冠词及空后介词提示所填词应为名词。分析句子结构可知,所填词应能与 with 搭配使用,故答案可限定在[G] unfamiliarity 和[O] equivalence 中。本句是讲远程教育的优点,所以可将含有否定意义的[G] unfamiliarity 排除,且该词含义也与句意不符,故答案为[O] equivalence(同等)。

9. 选[F]。空前系动词提示所填词可能为形容词、动词过去分词或动词现在分词,但备选项中没有动词的现在分词形式,故可初步确定所填词可能为形容词或动词过去分词。distance-learning 和 on-campus study 是两种不同的教育方式,本句想表达的意思是：不论是采用哪种教育方式,最后的证书或文凭都应是一样的,故所填词应含有"使用,采用"之意,答案为[F] employed(使用)。

10. 选[I]。空前定冠词及空后名词提示所填词应为名词。本题的选择可以采用排除法,将备选项中的各个名词分别带入原文,从句意的逻辑性上判断最佳选项。答案为[I] individuality(独特性,个性)。the individuality of the professor/student…意为"好的远程教育的另一个特点就是师生关系的独特性"。

Lecture 3　第三讲　8 招识别常见干扰

第一招：留意一词多性

　　在对备选项进行词性归类时要注意一词多性,有些单词既是名词又是动词,有些单词既是形容词又是名词,而有些分词也可以充当形容词,备选项中的这种一词多性的现象无形中扩大了考生的选择范围,经常会干扰考生的正确选择。

【例1】

【原文】	【选项】
Decades ago, there were only a ___55___ number of drugs available, and many of them caused significant side effects in older people, including dizziness and fatigue.	[C] significant [H] magnificent [J] limited

【解析】选[C]。分析句子结构可知,所填词应为形容词,修饰 number。如果不了解 limited 的形容词用法而将其归到动词的过去分词一类的话,将很难做对本题。

第二招:留意一词多义

篇章词汇题的备选项中有很多单词都是一词多义,而且经常是考查单词的某个不太常用的词义,因此考生在根据词义排除选项时不可过于匆忙,要对该选项的含义进行全面考虑。

【例2】

【原文】	【选项】
Given the chance to demonstrate his ability, he regained confidence and began to succeed in school. Today, he is a ___51___ doctor, runs his own clinic, and works with several hospitals.	[F] native [H] effective [J] prominent [K] decent [L] countless

【解析】选[J]。分析句子结构可知,所填词应为形容词修饰名词 doctor。从上下文来看,此处应该填一个表示积极意义的词,描述"他"现在的成功。[J] prominent 是一个多义词,主要含义有"突起的,凸出的"、"显著的,显眼的"以及"杰出的,著名的",如果只了解其前两个含义,则很容易误选[K] decent 项。[K] decent 也是一个多义词,它可以表示"(行为、衣着等)得体的,合乎礼节的"、"(薪水、饭菜等)相当不错的"以及"(某人)和善的,亲切的",但其均不符合此处的语境。

第三招:寻找近义词

篇章词汇理解的一个考查重点是考生对词汇的精确理解,要求考生清楚把握词汇间的细微区别。所以,如果备选项中出现一组近义词时,往往有一个是干扰选项。

【例3】

【原文】	【选项】
"I couldn't understand anything," he said. He hid from his teachers, came home in tears, and thought about dropping out. Then Mrs. Malave, … "She helped me stay smart while teaching me English," he said. Given the chance to demonstrate his ability, he ___50___ confidence and began to succeed in school.	[B] acquired [D] regained [I] hid [M] recalled

【解析】选[D]。分析句子结构可知,所填词应该是一个及物动词,并能与 confidence 构成合理的搭配。[D] regained 和[M] recalled 是一组近义词,故很可能有一个是干扰项,recall 的意思是"召回,收回"或"记起,想起",它可以表示"重新获得对某事或某人的记忆",而不能表示"重获"信心,故本题答案应为[D]。

第四招:寻找反义词

篇章词汇理解的又一考查重点是考生对于上下文语义的准确理解和整篇文章语境色彩的把握。所以,如果选项中出现一组反义词时,往往有一个是干扰选项。

【例4】

【原文】	【选项】
As a solution to this problem, slaves were employed in every conceivable fashion. The ___53___ of occupations held by slave artisans is a clear example of why skilled slaves became very important agents in the rise of manufacturing.	[F] scarcity [K] plenty [M] diversity [O] implements

【解析】选[M]。空前的定冠词 the 和空后介词 of 提示所填词应为名词,而后面的谓语动词 is 提示所填名词应为单数形式,故将答案限定在[F] scarcity,[K] plenty 和[M] diversity 三个选项之中。[F] scarcity(不足,缺乏)与[K] plenty(充足,大量)和[M] diversity(多样性)在某种程度上构成反义关系,故此处可以通过判断空格处是表示"多"还是"少"来进一步缩小答案范围。前一句是说奴隶们被雇佣进入各种可能的行业,故此处应该是表示奴隶从事工作的"多样化",故排除[F]。而[K] plenty 是强调同一事物的数量充足,不符合此处语境,而且该词一般不会用在定冠词后。

第五招：小心局部通顺的陷阱

有些选项带入空格中,可能会使空格所在句本身看起来很通顺,但却不符合上下文的语境,无法构成上下文的合理衔接。因此,考生在做题时,一定要小心这种局部通顺的陷阱,每填一个空格,都要确保其所在句与前后文形成合理的衔接。

【例5】

【原文】	【选项】
Unlike the Europeans, who tended to perceive art objects only as "curios(古玩)", Africans viewed the art as functional and art objects were created for specific use in ceremonies as well as in numerous ___48___ activities. Many Africans were master artisans, demonstrating various skills and great proficiency in the fashioning of wood, bone, and ivory, in weaving, in pottery-making, and in the making of clothes, tools, and other…	[B] attractive　[D] aesthetic [E] economic　[L] domestic

【解析】选[L]。分析句子结构可知,所填词最可能是形容词,修饰名词 activities。单从空格本身来看,似乎备选项中的四个形容词都可以修饰 activities,但这只是一种局部的通顺,我们必须将其放到上下文的语境中来进一步判断。…as well as…表明空格处所表示的活动与前面的 ceremonies(典礼,仪式)相对应,而且是空格后面一句中所描述的织布、制作工具等活动的概括,符合此语境要求的只有[L] domestic(家庭的)。

第六招：小心汉语的误导

英语中有些单词在使用语境和词语色彩上有很大差别,但对应的汉语却可能是同一个词。还有一些单词,其对应的汉语意思放在句中似乎合适,但其实际表达的英文含义却不符合该句的语境。因此,考生在选择答案时,不能只考虑选项的汉语意思,而忽略了其英文的用法和含义。

【例6】

【原文】	【选项】
Not long ago, many car dealers insulted women shoppers by ignoring them or suggesting that they come back with their husbands. Now car companies have realized that women are ___54___ customers.	[F] affordable　[K] voluntary [L] excessive　[D] extreme [I] potential

【解析】选[I]。分析句子结构可知,所填词应为形容词,修饰名词 customers,将备选项中的形容词带入空格,从意思上来看,似乎[F] affordable(买得起的)和[I] potential(潜在的,有可能的)都符合上下文语境,但需要注意的是,affordable 虽然从表面的汉语意思上来看符合语境,但它实际表达的英文含义是 that can be afforded,只能用来表示"某物是人们可以买得起的",而不能用来表示"人具有潜在的购买能力",因此并不符合此处的语境。

第七招：利用词语的语义色彩

根据整个语篇色彩及空格前后文语境,往往可以判定所填词是应该表达积极意义还是消极意义,比如描述的是优点或好处,所填词就应该表达积极意义;描述的是缺点或坏处,所填词就应该表达消极意义。这样就可以排除那些不符合语义色彩要求的词,缩小选择范围。

【例7】

【原文】	【选项】
When Roberto Feliz came to the USA from the Dominican Republic, he knew only a few words of English. Education soon became a ___47___.	[A] wonder　[E] nightmare [F] native　[G] acceptance [N] breakthrough

【解析】选[E]。分析空格所在句子结构可知,所填词在句中充当 became 的宾语,而空前的 a 提示,所填词应为可数名词单数形式,[G] 为不可数名词,且不能跟在 a 后面,故将其排除,由此可将答案锁定在[A]、[E]、[F]、[N]四个选项中。空格前一句是说 Roberto Feliz 刚到美国时只认识很少的英文单词,由此可判断所填词应表达消极意义,备选名词中表达消极意义的只有[E] nightmare(恶梦)。

第八招：寻找复现和共现关系

复现包括近义复现、反义复现、上义词复现、下义词复现以及同根词复现,共现则主要是指语义场共现,即属于描述同一个语义场景的词汇的共现。

篇章词汇理解中,每一个空格都不是孤立地存在于一个句子当中,它往往与上下文形成某种复现或共现关系,通过这一线索往往可以排除明显不符合该复现或共现关系的选项。

【例8】

【原文】	【选项】
Calexico, Calif., implemented bilingual education, and now has dropout rates that are less than half the state average and college ___56___ rates of more than 90%.	[A] wonder　[E] nightmare [F] native　[G] acceptance [N] breakthrough

【解析】选[G]。分析句子结构可知,所填词很可能是名词,与 rates 搭配,表示某种比率。考生只需稍加留意就不难发现,上文中出现了 dropout rates(辍学率),而句中又包含比较关系,由此可知　56　 rates 应该与 dropout rates 相对,故所填词很可能与 dropout 构成反义复现,由此不难联想到 acceptance rates(入学率)。

Exercise　　　即讲即练

British scientists are breeding a new generation of rice plants that will be able to grow in soil containing salt water. Their work may enable abandoned farms to become productive once more.

Tim Flowers and Tony Yeo, from Sussex University's School of Biological Sciences, have spent several years researching how crops, such as rice, could be made to grow in water that has become salty. The pair have recently begun a three-year programme, funded by the Biotechnology and Biological Sciences Research Council, to ___1___ which genes enable some plants to survive salty conditions. The aim is to breed this ___2___ into crops, starting with rice.

It is estimated that each year more than 10m hectares of agricultural land are ___3___ because salt gets into the soil and stunts plants. The problem is caused by several factors. In the tropics, *mangroves*(红树林) that ___4___ swamps and traditionally formed ___5___ to sea water have been cut down. In the Mediterranean, a series of ___6___ have caused the water table to drop, allowing sea water to seep in. In Latin America, irrigation often causes problems when water is ___7___ by the heat, leaving salt deposits behind. Excess salt then enters the plants and prevents them functioning ___8___. Heavy concentrations of minerals in the plants stop them drawing up the water they need to survive. To overcome these problems, Flowers and Yeo decided to breed rice plants that take in very little salt and store what they do absorb in cells that do not affect the plants' growth. They have started to breed these characteristics into a new rice crop, but it will take about eight harvests before the resulting seeds are ready to be considered for ___9___ use. Once the characteristics for surviving salty soil are known, Flowers and Yeo will try to breed the ___10___ genes into all manners of crops and plants. Land that has been abandoned to nature will then be able to bloom again, providing much needed food in the poorer countries of the world.

[A] evaporated	[B] barriers	[C] normally	[D] economic	[E] excluded
[F] lost	[G] droughts	[H] perfectly	[I] create	[J] capability
[K] establish	[L] ensure	[M] capacity	[N] commercial	[O] appropriate

【答案与解析】

【词性分析】

名　词：barriers(障碍,屏障)；droughts(干旱,缺乏)；capability(能力)；capacity(容量,生产量)

动　词：evaporated(蒸发)；excluded(拒绝接纳,排斥)；lost(丢失,失去)；create(产生,引起)；establish(确定,建立)；ensure(确保,保证)

形容词：economic(经济的,产供销的)；lost(迷失的,失去的)；commercial(商业的)；appropriate(适当的)；evaporated(蒸发的,脱水的)

副　词：normally(正常地,通常地)；perfectly(完全,完美地)

1. 选[K]。空前不定式符号 to 及空后从句提示所填词应为及物动词原形,故可将答案限定在[I] create、[K] establish 和[L] ensure 中。疑问连接词 which 提示 Tim Flowers 和 Tony Yeo 进行一项为期三年的研究,目的就是为了明确哪种基因决定植物能生存在含有盐分的土壤中。establish 是个多义词,主要含义有"建立"、"安置"及"确定",该词的前两个含义为其常用含义,如果忽略了最后一个含义,会很容易误选[L] ensure,但 ensure 后接宾语通常为肯定句,而不是疑问句,故答案为[K] establish(确定)。

2. 选[J]。分析句子结构可知所填词在句中作 breed 的宾语,故所填词应为名词。分析备选项中的名词[J] capability 和[M] capacity 在某种程度上为近形、近义词,故二者中很可能有一个是干扰项。本句句首的 the aim 指的即是上句所说的"establish which genes enable some plants to survive salty condition"的目的,该句中的 enable 提示所填词应该是表示"能力"的名词,故答案为[J] capability(能力)。

3. 选[F]。空前系动词提示所填词可能为动词的过去分词、动词的现在分词或形容词,但选项中并没有动词的现在分词,故所填词只可能为动词的过去分词或形容词。备选项中动词的过去分词都不能与 agricultural land 构成被动关系,故所填词只能为形容词。如果不了解 lost 的形容词用法而将其归结为过去分词,则很难答对本题。

4. 选[I]。分析句子结构可知,所填词在句中作谓语,故所填词应为动词,that 引导的定语从句修饰的先行词为复数名词,故所填词应为动词原形,因此可将答案限定在[I] create 和[K] establish 和[L] ensure 中,结合第 1 小题的分析,可将答案进一步限定在[I] create 和[L] ensure 中。从意义上可判断[I] create(产生)更符合语境。

5. 选[B]。分析句子结构可知,所填词在句中作 formed 的宾语,故所填词应为名词,且该名词应能与 to 搭配使用,故可将答案定位在[B] barriers、[M] capacity 中。第二句提示本句是举例说明每年会有 10 万公顷的农业用地变为盐碱地的原因。本句的定语从句主要讲的是 mangroves 的作用,由此可知,mangroves 能阻挡海水侵入热带雨林的土壤中,故答案为[B] barriers(障碍,屏障)。

6. 选[G]。空前介词及空后助动词提示所填词应为名词,由短语 a series of 可知,所填词应为复数名词,故可将答案限定在[B] barriers 和[G] droughts 中。the water table to drop(地下水位下降)是由干旱引起的,故答案为[G] droughts(干旱)。

7. 选[A]。空前系动词提示所填词可能为形容词、动词过去分词或动词现在分词,因备选项中没有动词现在分词,故可初步判断所填词应为形容词或动词过去分词。由主语 water 和介词 by 的宾语 heat 不难判断,高温会导致水蒸发,故所填词应该含有"蒸发"之意,答案为[A] evaporated(蒸发)。

8. 选[C]。分析句子结构可知,所填词应为副词,故可将答案限定在[C] normally 和[H] perfectly 中,如果单从句意上来看,二者都符合本句句意,但二者在用法上稍有差别：normally 为方式副词,强调某事发生或做某事的方式；perfectly 为程度副词,强调某事的程度。结合本句可知,本句主要强调的是植物 functioning(发挥作用)的方式,故答案为[C] normally(正常地)。

9. 选[N]。空前介词及空后名词提示所填词应为形容词。备选项中的形容词[D] economic 和[N] commercial 之间为语义场共现的关系,故二者中有一个应为干扰项。[D]economic 强调的是利益,而本句主要是强调新水稻品种的 use(用途),故可将其排除。[N]commercial 通常能与 use 构成搭配,commercial use 意为"商业用途",符合句意。

10. 选[O]。空前定冠词和空后名词提示所填词为形容词。将备选项中的形容词分别带入本句中可知,[O] appropriate(适当的)符合句意以及逻辑。

篇章词汇巅峰练习

第六章

Exercise 1

Individuals differ greatly in the degree in which culture shock affects them. Although not common, there are individuals who cannot live in foreign countries. However, those who have seen people go through shock and on to a satisfactory adjustment can __47__ steps in the process. During the first stage most individuals are __48__ by the new. They stay in hotels and associate with nationals who speak their language and are polite and gracious to foreigners. This honeymoon stage may last from a few days or weeks to six months, depending on circumstances. If one is very important, he or she will be shown the places, will be pampered and petted, and in a press interview will speak __49__ about goodwill and international friendship.

But this __50__ does not normally last if the foreign visitor remains abroad and has seriously to cope with real conditions of life. It is then that the second stage begins, __51__ by a hostile and aggressive attitude toward the host country. This hostility evidently grows out of the __52__ difficulty which the visitor experiences in the process of adjustment. There are house troubles, __53__ troubles, shopping troubles, and the fact that people in the host country are largely indifferent to all these troubles. They help, but they don't understand your great concern over these difficulties. Therefore, they must be __54__ and unsympathetic to you and your worries. The result, I just don't like them. You become aggressive, and you band together with others from your country and criticize the host country, its way, and its people. But this criticism is not a(n) __55__ appraisal. Instead of trying to account for the conditions and the historical circumstances which have created them, you talk as if the difficulties you experience are more or less created by the people of host country for your special __56__ .

[A] fascinated	[B] discern	[C] glowingly	[D] objective	[E] mentality
[F] impressed	[G] adaptation	[H] insensitive	[I] discomfort	[J] publicly
[K] characterized	[L] unreasonable	[M] disadvantage	[N] genuine	[O] transportation

Exercise 2

An unidentified wit once said, "Laugh, and the world laughs with you. Snore, and you sleep alone." Yet snoring is far from a laughing matter, as those unfortunates with good hearing, who are rightly __47__ to the sounds of the snoring disorder, will testify.

It has been estimated that one of eight Americans snores; this means that there are approximately 21 million people — women as well as men — who render an __48__ sound when they are asleep. And assuming that each snorer disturbs the sleep of at least one other person, it __49__ follows that there are 21 million unhappy listeners. While a sleeping person breathes, either in or out, several structures in his nose and throat __50__ the snoring. The sounds, coming from the soft *palate* (腭) and other soft structures of the throat, are caused by vibratory responses to inflowing and inflowing air. When the soft tissues of the mouth and throat come close to the lining of the throat, the vibrations that occur are caused by the position of the tongue. In short, the noise made by snoring can be __51__ to the noise when breezes flutter a flag on a pole. The __52__ of the vibrations depends on the size, __53__ and elasticity of the affected tissues and on the __54__ of the air flow. Although it is usually the process of inhaling or exhaling through the mouth that cause snoring, short snores come from the nose of an open-mouthed sleeper. In all fairness to snorers, however, it should be emphasized that snoring is an __55__ act which stops as the offender is __56__ .

[A] involuntary	[B] density	[C] necessarily	[D] unpleasant	[E] force
[F] unexpected	[G] subjected	[H] awakened	[I] incur	[J] compared
[K] sequence	[L] frequency	[M] speed	[N] generally	[O] generate

答案与解析

Exercise 1

【文章大意】

　　本文的主要内容是关于人们在异乡生活的文化冲击问题。本文主要说明了个人在国外生活时会经历的几个心理阶段，并分析了各个阶段的具体心理状况和成因。

【词性分析】

名　词：mentality(心态,思想方法)；adaptation(适应,改编)；discomfort(不便之处,不适)；disadvantage(不利条件,弱点)；transportation(交通,运输)；objective(目标,目的)

动　词：discern(看出,识别)；fascinated(强烈的吸引,迷住)；impressed(给…以深刻的印象)；characterized(成为…的特征,描绘…的特性)

形容词：objective(客观的,依据事实的)；insensitive(无感情的,麻木的)；unreasonable(不讲道理的,不合理的,过度的)；genuine(真正的,真心的)

副　词：glowingly(热情洋溢地,热烈赞扬地)；publicly(当众地,公开地)

47. 选[B]。空前情态动词 can 提示所填词为动词原形。空后的 steps in the process 指的是人们经历文化冲击的各个阶段。本句的主语为 those who…(经历过文化冲击,并最终适应了外国文化的人)，很明显这些人是能够清楚地认识及了解 steps in the process 的，故答案为[B] discern(认识,领悟)。

48. 选[A]。空前系动词 are 和空后介词 by 提示所填词很可能为动词的过去分词，符合此要求的选项有[A] fascinated、[F] impressed、[K] characterized。下文中的 this honeymoon stage 指的是本句中的 the first stage，honeymoon 提示所填词为积极词，所以可将中性词[K] characterized 排除。[F] impressed 强调影响既深刻又持久，但通读整篇文章可知，大多数人对 the new 的态度在第二阶段(the second stage)有所改变，这与 impressed 强调的深刻性及持久性相背离，故[F] impressed 也可排除，答案为[A] fascinated(迷住,强烈的吸引)。

49. 选[C]。分析语法结构可知，所填词应为副词，符合此要求的只有[C] glowingly(热情洋溢地)和[J] publicly(公开地)。press interview 本身就意味着接受采访的人所说的话是公开的，所以没有必要再用 publicly 进行强调，故答案为[C] glowingly(热情洋溢地)。

50. 选[E]。空前指示代词 this 提示所填词应为名词。转折连词 but 提示"this _____"是对上段内容的总结概括。第一段主要讲人们刚受到文化冲击时，对外国文化所持有的态度，这种态度主要是心理方面的，备选项中表示心理状态的名词只有[E] mentality(心态)。

51. 选[K]。分析句子成分可知"_____ by…"在句中作后置定语，修饰 the second stage，由此可判断，所填词应为动词的过去分词形式。结合第48题的分析，可确定本题答案应为[K] characterized(描述…特点)。此处是在描述第二阶段的特点。

52. 选[N]。空前定冠词 the 和空后名词提示所填词应为形容词。将备选项中的形容词依次带入原句中，根据该词语义是否符合语境的原则来寻找答案，最终可确定答案为[N] genuine(真正的,真心的)。

53. 选[O]。分析句子结构可知，_____ troubles 与 house troubles 及 shopping troubles 并列，所以所填词可能为名词或形容词。备选项中只有[O] transportation 能与 house 及 shopping 构成语义场共现关系，故答案为[O] transportation(交通)。

54. 选[H]。连词 and 提示所填词应与 unsympathetic 并列，故所填词应为形容词，且该词也应含有否定意义。备选项中含有否定意义的形容词有[H] insensitive 和[L] unreasonable，本句句首的 Therefore 表明上句是本句的原因，而东道主国家的人不了解外来者的困难造成的后果就是，他们对外来者及外来者所担心的事物不关心、不同情，故答案为[H] insensitive(无感情的,麻木的)。

55. 选[D]。空前不定冠词及空后名词提示所填词应为形容词。本段末句的 Instead of…表明人们通常会把困难归咎于东道主国家的人而不是东道主国家的社会条件及历史情况，而本句中的 not 提示人们的这种想法是错误的，由此可知，人们对东道主国家的 criticism 并不是依据事实作出的，故答案为[D] objective(客观的)。

56. 选[I]。空前形容词提示所填词应为名词。通读整句话可知，本句主句的大意为"东道主国家的人所造成的困难给你带来了_____。"根据常理不难推测，difficulties 当然会引起人们的不便，故答案为[I] discomfort(不适,不便)。

Exercise 2

【文章大意】

本文的主要内容是关于打鼾。文章开始就说在美国打鼾人群的数量和受影响人群的数量都是惊人的,接着从生理结构方面解释了打鼾的原因,最后指出打鼾是一种完全无意识的行为,只有打鼾者醒来,鼾声才会停止。

【词性分析】

名　词:density(密集,密度);force(武力,力量,影响力);sequence(连续,次序);frequency(次数,频率,频繁);
　　　　speed(速度,迅速)

动　词:force(强迫,用力推开);subjected(受…支配,易受…);awakened(醒来,唤醒);incur(招致,遭受);com-
　　　　pared(比较,相比,比得上);speed(加速,急行);generate(产生,发生)

形容词:involuntary(无意识的);unpleasant(使人不愉快的);unexpected(想不到的,意外的)

副　词:necessarily(必要地,必定地);generally(一般地,普遍地)

---

47. 选[G]。空前系动词 are 及空后介词 to 提示所填词可能为动词的过去分词或形容词,且能与 to 搭配使用。本句末的 testify(证明)的内容是 snoring is far from a laughing matter(打鼾是一件令人不快的事)。所填词所在的句子是修饰 unfortunates 的定语从句,结合分析可知,本句主要讲那些听力好的人在什么样的情况下会证明 snoring is far from a laughing matter,很明显该情况就是他们遭受鼾声打扰的时候。故答案为[G] subjected(受…支配)。be subjected to… 意为"使受到…,使遭到…"。

48. 选[D]。空前不定冠词 an 及空后名词提示所填词应为形容词。分析本句结构可知,an _____ sound 指的就是 snores。由上句中的 snoring is far from a laughing matter 可知,snores 会让人产生不快,故答案为[D] unpleasant(使人不愉快的)。

49. 选[C]。分析句子结构可知,所填词应为副词。上句指出美国至少有 21 million 的人打鼾,而本句提出一种假设情况:若 1 人打鼾会打扰 1 个人的睡眠,那么根据该假设情况,美国有 21 million 的人受到鼾声的影响则是一种必然性,故答案为[C] necessarily(必要地,必定地)。

50. 选[O]。分析句子结构可知所填词应为动词,在句中作谓语。本句主要讲 snoring 是如何产生的,故所填词应选[O] generate(产生,发生)。

51. 选[J]。分析句子结构可知,所填词可能为动词的过去分词或形容词,且能与 to 搭配使用。the noise made by snoring 与 the noise when… 二者本身并没有必然联系,但因其在同一句子中,所以所填词就应该具有将二者联系起来的功能,备选项中只有[J] compared(比较,相比,比得上)符合要求,本句是将鼾声比喻成微风吹着旗帜发出的声音。

52. 选[L]。空前定冠词 the 及空后介词 of 提示所填词应为名词。vibrations 意为"振动",备选项中的名词通常与 vibrations 搭配使用的是[L] frequency(次数,频率,频繁),the frequency of the vibrations 意为"振动频率"。

53. 选[B]。连词 and 提示所填词应与 size 及 elasticity 并列,所以所填词词性应为名词,而同样根据并列关系可知,备选名词中只有[B] density 能与 size 及 elasticity 构成语义场共现,故答案为[B] density(密集,密度)。

54. 选[E]。空前定冠词 the 及空后介词 of 提示所填词应为名词。本处句意为:振动的频率也取决于空气流的_____。备选名词中[E] force 意为"武力,力量,影响力",而[M] speed 意为"速度,迅速",相比较而言,"空气流的力量"要比"空气流的速度"更适合此处的语境,故答案为[E] force(力量)。

55. 选[A]。空前不定冠词 an 及空后名词提示所填词应为形容词。第二段第三句话"While a sleeping person breathes, …"讲鼾声是如何产生的,由该句话可知鼾声产生的前提是人要睡着,因此可推断人在睡眠中打鼾是他本人意识不到的,所以鼾声是一种无意识的行为,故答案为[A] involuntary(无意识的,不知不觉的)。

56. 选[H]。空前系动词提示所填词可能为形容词或动词的过去分词。结合第 55 小题的分析可知,鼾声是在人无意识的情况下发出的,由此可推断鼾声停止时自然是人醒着的时候,故答案为[H] awakened(醒来)。

篇章阅读巅峰讲座

六级考试中篇章阅读一共两篇,长度一般在 400—450 词之间。篇章阅读主要测试考生在不同层面上的阅读理解能力,包括理解主旨大意和重要细节的能力、综合分析能力、推理判断能力以及根据上下文推测词义的能力等。

Lecture 1 第一讲 10 大敏感设题题眼

一、篇首、篇尾、段首、段尾处常考

文章的主题句经常出现在首段,段落的主题句经常出现在段首。另外,首段的末句或第二段的首句也是文章主题句的高发区。文章的尾段或段落的结尾一般会是概括或总结性的陈述,经常会得出某种结论或提出某项建议。

因此,文章的篇首、篇尾、段首、段尾处经常被作为篇章阅读题设题的重要题眼,而且大多是考查对文章或段落主旨的理解。

【例 1】   (03-9-25)

【原文】	【题目】
In 1985 when a Japan Air Lines (JAL) jet crashed, its president, Yasumoto Takagi, called each victim's family to apologize, and then promptly resigned. And in 1987, when a subsidiary of Toshiba sold sensitive military technology to the former Soviet Union, the chairman of Toshiba gave up his post. These executive actions, which Toshiba calls "the highest form of apology", may seem bizzare to US managers. No one at Boeing resigned after the JAL crash, which may have been caused by a faulty Boeing repair. The difference between the two business cultures centers around different definitions of delegation. ...	25. The passage is mainly about _____. [A] resignation as an effective way of dealing with business crises [B] the importance of delegating responsibility to employees [C] ways of evading responsibility in times of crises [D] the difference between two business cultures

【解析】 作者在文章第一段以两个例子(例一:日航总裁和东芝总裁分别因飞机事故和由于下属所造成的事故而引咎辞职;例二:尽管日航公司的飞机事故可能是由于美国波音公司飞机修理失误所造成的,但波音公司的上层领导却无一辞职)开篇作为引子,然后在第二段段首引出了他要论述的主题:the difference between the two business cultures(两种不同的商业文化)。

二、转折处常考

作者常常会借用转折连词或副词来引出某项重要的事实或观点,转折词之后的内容往往表达的是作者真实的写作目的、观点或态度,因此出题人经常会围绕转折词前后内容来设题。

篇章阅读中常见的表示转折关系的连词或副词有 however, but, yet, nevertheless, while , though, although, at the same time 等。另外, indeed, in fact, virtually, practically 也常常用来表示前后语义的转折。

【例 2】   (05-12-25)

【原文】	【题目】
When I think about all the problems of our overpopulated world and look at our boy grabbing at the lamp by the sofa, I wish I could have turned to Planned Grandparenthood when my parents were putting the grandchild squeeze on me.	25. What does the author really think of the idea of having children? [A] It does more harm than good. [B] It contributes to overpopulation.

If I could have, I might not be in this parenthood *predicament*（窘境）. But here's the crazy irony, I don't want my child-free life back. Dylan's too much fun.	[C] It is troublesome but rewarding. [D] It is a psychological catastrophe.

【解析】文章结尾作者先是用虚拟语气表示,如果她当时能够求助于 Planned Grandparenthood 的话,可能她现在就不会处在这种为人父母的窘境中了,不过紧接着作者又使用转折语气表达了自己的真正想法:具有讽刺意味的是,她再也不想回到没有孩子的日子了。由此可知,作者对待养育孩子的真正看法是:虽然 troublesome(很麻烦)但是 rewarding(很值得)。

三、对比、比较处常考

　　阅读文章中的对比常常表现为新老观点的对比、错误与正确观念的对比、新事物与旧事物的对比等,而比较则常常表现为两种或多种事物的优点、缺点、用途、功能、原理等特点的比较。这些对比或比较关系经常会受到出题人的青睐。

　　篇章阅读中常见的表示对比或比较关系的词或短语有 while, whereas, than, compared with, in contrast to 等。解题时要留意这些词或短语,并注意出现比较级、最高级的地方,另外要注意搞清对比或比较对象。

【例3】　　　　　　　　　　　　　　　　　　　　　　　　　　　　　　　　　　　　(02-6-38)

【原文】	【题目】
In conducting research on culture and ethnic minority issues, investigators distinguish between the emic approach and the etic approach. *In the emic approach*, the goal is to describe behavior in one culture or ethnic group in terms that are meaningful and important to the people in that culture or ethnic group, without regard to other cultures or ethnic groups. *In the etic approach*, the goal is to describe behavior so that generalizations can be made across cultures. …	38. Compared with *the etic approach, the emic approach* is apparently more _____. [A] culturally interactive [B] culture-oriented [C] culturally biased [D] culture-specific

【解析】本段开头指出,在文化和少数民族问题的研究中有两种不同的方法:the emic approach(音位学法)和 the etic approach(非音位学法),接着对两种方法进行了比较:the emic approach 旨在描述单一文化或少数民族中有意义的行为,即注重文化个体;而 the etic approach 则旨在描述所有文化中共同适用的行为,即注重文化整体。

四、并列、列举、举例处常考

　　并列、列举处是指用 First(ly)…, Second(ly)…, Third(ly)…, Finally …; Not only… but also; In addition; Furthermore; Moreover; Above all; On the one hand …, on the other hand … 等表示顺承或并列关系的词语列举出的一系列并列的事实情况。并列处和列举处是事实细节题的主要设题题眼。

　　为了使自己的观点更有说服力、更加明确,作者还经常会使用举例的方法来进行论证,常由 as, such as, for example, for instance, take … as an example 等引出,这些例子经常会成为出题人设问的焦点。

【例4】　　　　　　　　　　　　　　　　　　　　　　　　　　　　　　　　　　　　(04-1-31)

【原文】	【题目】
More recently, this traditional view has begun to be questioned. One reason for this change was the increasing emphasis given to the historical approach to man. … Another reason for skepticism about the concept of human nature probably lies in the influence of evolutionary thinking. …	31. The traditional view of "human nature" was strongly challenged by _____. [A] the emergence of the evolutionary theory [B] the historical approach to man [C] new insight into human behavior [D] the philosophical analysis of slavery

【解析】文章开头首先提出了最近出现的一种观点:this traditional view has begun to be questioned(关于人性的传统观点遭到质疑),紧接着通过 one reason…, another reason… 列举了支持这种怀疑论观点的两点原因。选项[B]与第一点原因内容相符。

五、指示代词处常考

为了简洁明了地表达事物及其逻辑关系,写作时常利用各种代词来代替前面提到过的人或事物,当代词前后的句子结构比较复杂、代词与其代替的人或事物相隔较远或代词周围出现多个事物时,这种指代关系往往不易区分清楚,因而常常受到出题人的青睐。

【例5】　　　　　　　　　　　　　　　　　　　　　　　　　　　　　　　　　　　(05-12-35)

【原文】	【题目】
… Even if the professor holds no consultancy with any firm, some people may still distrust him because of his association with those who do, or at least wonder about the source of some of his research funding. 　　This attitude can have ***damaging effects***. It questions the integrity of individuals working in a profession that prizes intellectual honesty as the supreme virtue, and plays into the hands of those who would like to discredit scientists by representing them as *venal* (可以收买的). This makes it easier to dismiss all scientific pronouncements, but especially those made by the scientists who present themselves as 'experts'….	35. Why does the author say that public distrust of scientists can have ***damaging effects***? 　[A] It makes things difficult for scientists seeking research funds. 　[B] People would not believe scientists even when they tell the truth. 　[C] It may dampen the enthusiasm of scientists for independent research. 　[D] Scientists themselves may doubt the value of their research findings.

【解析】此处提到,公众认为科学家的论断可能会受到为他们提供科研经费的单位的影响,因而对其持怀疑态度,紧接着指出,this attitude 会带来 damaging effects(危害),因为 this 很容易使公众不接受所有的 scientific pronouncements(科学声明),也就是说即使这些 pronouncements 是真的,公众也不相信。

六、观点态度处常考

文章中表达作者对于某人或某事物的观点或态度或涉及到的其他人或组织机构的观点或态度的地方也常受到出题人青睐。解题时要留意文章中出现 doubt, appreciate, hate, against 等表达观点态度的词语,以及一些带有感情色彩的特殊句式(祈使句、感叹句、反问句等)。

【例6】　　　　　　　　　　　　　　　　　　　　　　　　　　　　　　　　　　　(07-6-59)

【原文】	【题目】
They are using fewer of the very deferential "women's" forms, and even using the few strong forms that are known as "men's." This, of course attracts considerable attention and has led to an outcry in the Japanese media against ***the defeminization of women's language***. Indeed, we didn't hear about "men's language" until people began to respond to girls' appropriation of forms normally reserved for boys and men. There is considerable sentiment about the ***"corruption" of women's language*** — which of course is viewed as part of the loss of feminine ideals and morality — and this sentiment is crystallized by nationwide opinion polls that are regularly carried out by the media.	59. How do some people react to ***women's appropriation of men's language forms*** as reported in the Japanese media? 　[A] They call for a campaign to stop the defeminization. 　[B] They see it as an expression of women's sentiment. 　[C] They accept it as a modern trend. 　[D] They express strong disapproval.

【解析】本段提到,女性们越来越少地使用"具有女性特征"的敬语,而是越来越多地使用被公认为属于男性的强硬语言,而 this 当然引起了广泛关注,并在 Japanese media 上掀起了反对 defeminization of women's language(女性语言中女性特征弱化)的呼声,由此可知人们对女性语言中女性特征的弱化,即女性使用男性语言是持反对意见的。另外,该段最后一句中说,在媒体组织的全国民意测验中许多民众都对女性语言的"堕落"表现出极大的伤感,这也说明人们反对女性使用男性语言。

七、因果关系处常考

两个事件内在的因果关系常常成为出题人的设题点,一般来说,这种题有两种形式:给原因推结果或是给结果找原因。

【例7】　　　　　　　　　　　　　　　　　　　　　(03-9-26)

【原文】	【题目】
As machines go, *the car* is not terribly noisy, nor terribly polluting, nor terribly dangerous; and on all those dimensions it has become better as the century has grown older. *The main problem* is its prevalence, and the social costs that ensue from the use by everyone of something that would be fairly harmless if, say, only the rich were to use it. It is a price we pay for equality.	26. As is given in the first paragraph, the reason why *the car has become a problem* is that _____. [A] poor people can't afford it [B] it is too expensive to maintain [C] too many people are using it [D] it causes too many road accidents

【解析】 本段提到，汽车带来的噪音、污染、车祸并不是主要问题，主要问题是 its prevalence(车的普遍流行)，也就是说汽车成为主要问题是因为有太多的人使用汽车。

八、特殊句式常考

篇章阅读题经常考查的特殊句式包括强调句、倒装句、虚拟语气句，以及包含 not…but…，prefer doing to doing 等特殊结构的句子，这些句式中经常暗含作者想要表达的某种观点态度或想要陈述的事实细节。

【例8】　　　　　　　　　　　　　　　　　　　　　(04-6-31)

【原文】	【题目】
When we worry about who might be spying on our private lives, *we usually think* about the Federal agents. *But* the private sector outdoes the government every time. It's Linda Tripp, not the FBI, who is facing charges under Maryland's laws against secret telephone taping. It's our banks, not the Internal Revenue Service (IRS), that pass our private financial data to telemarketing firms.	31. *Contrary to popular belief*, the author finds that spying on people's privacy _____. [A] is mainly carried out by means of secret taping [B] has been intensified with the help of the IRS [C] is practiced exclusively by the FBI [D] is more prevalent in business circles

【解析】 本段提到，通常人们都认为侵犯个人隐私主要是政府部门的行为，但实际上 the private sector 在侵犯隐私方面要远胜于政府部门，紧接着通过两个强调句型(It's Linda Tripp, not the FBI, who…和 It's our banks, not the Internal Revenue Service (IRS), that…)举出两项实例来说明侵犯隐私的行为在商业领域要比政府部门 more prevalent(更普遍)。

九、特殊标点处常考

特殊标点符号主要包括：破折号(主要表解释或补充说明)；括号(主要表解释)；冒号(主要表解释或列举)；引号(主要表引用或引号里的内容有特殊含义)；分号(主要表并列或进一步解释说明)等等。出题人经常会针对这些特殊标点的前后设题，考查考生对特殊标点含义及其前后内容的准确理解。

【例9】　　　　　　　　　　　　　　　　　　　　　(新06-12-52)

【原文】	【题目】
In a purely biological sense, fear begins with the body's system for reacting to things that can harm us — the *so-called fight-or-flight response*. "An animal that can't detect danger can't stay alive," says Joseph LeDoux. Like animals, humans evolved with an elaborate mechanism for processing information about potential threats. At its core is a cluster of *neurons*(神经元) deep in the brain known as the *amygdala*(扁桃核).	52. The " *so-called fight-or-flight response* " refers to " _____ ". [A] the biological process in which human being's sense of self-defense evolves [B] the instinctive fear human beings feel when faced with potential danger [C] the act of evaluating a dangerous situation and making a quick decision [D] the elaborate mechanism in the human brain for retrieving information

【解析】 破折号前面的内容是对 so-called fight-or-flight response 的解释，该句指出，当我们面对可能伤害到我们的事情时，我们的身体就会产生纯粹生理上的害怕，这就是所谓的 fight-or-flight response。选项[B]是破折号前面内容的同义转述。

十、引言处常考

作者为论证自己的观点，常会引用其他人或组织机构的论断或发现等，出题人常会在此处设计题眼。

【例 10】 (新 06-12-55)

【原文】	【题目】
Hallowell insists, though, that there's *a right way to worry*. "Never do it alone, get the facts and then make a plan," he says. Most of us have survived a recession, so we're familiar with the belt-tightening strategies needed to survive a slump.	55. Which of the following is *the best way to deal with your worries* according to *Hallowell*? [A] Ask for help from the people around you. [B] Use the belt-tightening strategies for survival. [C] Seek professional advice and take action. [D] Understand the situation and be fully prepared.

【解析】由本段引用的 Hallowell 的话可知，他认为应对恐惧的最好的办法就是 get the facts and then make a plan（了解形势然后制定计划），[D] 是其同义转述，其中 understand the situation 对应 get the facts，be fully prepared 对应 make a plan。

Exercise 即讲即练

Computer science and technology is developing so fast that no one can predict exactly what new technology might be developed in the near future, and the development of computer law can hardly keep up with the developing computer technology. The wide spread application of computers in business has created new situations that no existing laws are adequate to cope with. In the following cases, computer generated information was used as evidence but was not all accepted by the court.

A man received some treatment at a hospital but refused to pay the hospital bill because he claimed the figures were not correct. The hospital sued the man. As proof of the amount owed to it, the hospital offered in evidence a computer printout of the services rendered to the defendant and the amounts owed for them. Hospital employees testified that information as to amounts owed by patients in the hospital were stored in a computer as part of a regular business routine. The man objected to the admission of the computer printout as evidence on the ground that there was not a proper comparison checking of original slips showing services rendered against the computer printout.

The court decided that the computer printout was admissible as evidence when it was shown that the entries were made with proper equipment in a regular course of business. The objection that there was not a sufficient checking of the printout did not make the printout inadmissible. It was up to the jury to decide how much weight or importance should be attached to computer printout.

In order to make it possible to admit evidence produced by computer, the law of evidence of the United States has changed greatly. According to the new rule, computer printouts of business records stored on electronic computing equipment are admissible in evidence if relevant to the material, without the necessity of identifying, locating, and producing as witnesses the individuals who made the entries in the regular course of business, if it is shown that the electronic computing equipment is recognized as standard equipment, the entries are made in the regular course of business at or reasonably near the time of the happening of the event recorded, and the foundation testimony satisfies the court that the sources of information, method and time of preparation were such as to indicate its trustworthiness and justify its admission.

1. The man refused to pay the hospital bill because _____.
   [A] the amount of money charged by the hospital was higher than what he should pay
   [B] he couldn't afford the money asked by the hospital
   [C] the computer printout offered by the hospital was not consistent with original slips
   [D] the hospital couldn't show any proof for the amount of money he should pay

2. The court's final decision is _____.
   [A] the man must pay the bill　　　　　　　　　　[B] the computer printout was not admissible
   [C] the hospital failed for lack of evidences　　　　[D] not mentioned in the passage

3. According to the passage, which of the following is true?

[A] The computer printout was not in keeping with the service rendered.

[B] The computer printout was in keeping with the service rendered.

[C] The computer printout was checked to compare it with the service rendered.

[D] The computer printout was not checked to compare it with the service rendered.

4. In order to make the computer evidence admissible, the United States _____.

[A] has completely changed the law of evidence　　　　[B] has begun to draw up the law of evidence

[C] has abolished the law of evidence　　　　[D] has revised the law of evidence

5. The best title for this passage is _____.

[A] The Computer Evidence　　　　[B] The Law of Evidence

[C] The Computer and the Law of Evidence　　　　[D] A Case on Computer

【答案与解析】

【文章大意】

　　计算机科学与技术飞速发展,没人能够准确地预测其将来,然而涉及计算机的法规已明显滞后。作者在第二、三段举例讲述了一人在一家医院接受治疗后因认为费用数据有误而拒付医疗费。随后,医院为此而上诉,并拿出计算机打印账单作为证据,但在计算机打印账单是否符合医院实际提供的服务上,双方发生了争论。最后作者指出美国已经就有关法律做了重大修改以适应新的科技发展形势的需要。

1. 选[A]。举例处常考。根据第二段首句 A man received some treatment at a hospital but refused to pay the hospital bill because he claimed the figures were not correct 可知,这个人拒付医药费是因为他觉得医院的收费金额有问题,故答案为[A]。[B]"他无力承担医药费"文中没有提及;[C]"医院提供的打印账单和原始账单不符"和[D]"医院不能提供证据证明病人应该支付的金钱数额"与原文第二段第三句 As proof of the amount owed to it, … owed for them 意思不符。

2. 选[D]。段尾处常考。本文指出法庭裁决计算机打印单据如果能符合一定的条件可以作为证据,其重要性应由陪审团来决定,但没有明确说明哪一方胜诉,故答案为[D]。

3. 选[D]。对比处常考。原文第二段末句 The man objected to the admission of the computer printout as the evidence on the ground that there was not a proper comparison checking of original slips showing services rendered against the computer printout 表明此人认为医院提供的电脑打印单据未与实际提供的服务核对过,故答案为[D]。

4. 选[D]。段首处常考。第四段第一句 In order to make it possible to admit evidence produced by computer, the law of evidence of the United States has changed greatly 明确指出为了使电脑记录的证据尽可能的被认可,美国对证据法做了重大改动,[D] 中的 revised 是 changed greatly 的同义转述,故为答案。

5. 选[C]。观点态度处常考。文章第一段谈到由于计算机技术的发展,涉及计算机的法规已明显滞后,接着作者在第二、三段举例进一步说明这一问题。最后一段作者指出美国已经就有关法律做了重大修改以适应新的科技发展形势需要,[C] 是对全文的概括总结,故为答案。

Lecture 2　第二讲　5招巧做主旨大意题

　　主旨大意题主要测试考生对文章主题的理解和把握能力以及对文章大意的归纳概括能力。这类题目常就文章的主题、大意、标题或写作目的进行设问,因此主旨大意题还可细分为主题型主旨大意题、标题型主旨大意题和目的型主旨大意题。

　　常见的题干表现形式如下:

The passage is mainly about _____.

The passage mainly discusses _____.

The passage centers on _____.

The main idea (central idea) of the passage is _____.

The best title for the passage would be _____.

Which of the following titles best summarizes the main idea of the passage?

What's the author's purpose in writing this article?

The author's main purpose in writing the passage is to _____.

常用的解题招术如下：

第一招：优先考虑概括性较强的选项

能够表现文章的主旨大意的选项一般都具有较强的概括性，经常含有像 way，approach，concept，chance，opportunity，general，necessity，importance 等抽象名词和概括性词语，因此在选择时应优先考虑这类选项。

第二招：切忌选择内容片面的选项

针对主旨大意题的干扰选项经常是文章中部分内容的节选，其本身内容与原文相符，但只是文章所陈述主题的一部分，而不能概括整篇文章的主旨，因此在解答主旨大意题时，要从文章的整体考虑，切忌根据文章某一段落而误选内容片面、单一的选项。

第三招：重点阅读首尾段和各段首尾

文章的首尾段往往揭示文章的主题，各段的首尾也往往是各段主题句的出处，因此，一般来说，阅读完首尾段及各段首尾就可以准确概括出文章的主旨大意。

第四招：寻找文章或段落的主题句

一般而言，主题句在句法结构上有以下特点：所表达的意思具有概括性；句子结构简单明了；文章或段落中的其他句子都是对其的进一步解释、说明、论证或扩展。全文的主题句一般是在首段开头或第二段开头；段落的主题句一般是在段落的开头。如果全文没有主题句，文章的主旨也往往可以根据各段的主题句归纳概括出来。

第五招：注意出现频率较高的词语

文章中重复频率较高的词语很可能就是蕴含文章中心思想的关键词，这类关键词可能是同一个词语多次出现，也可能是同一类词语贯穿全文。

【例】　　　　　　　　　　　　　　　　　　　　　　　　　(03-6-Passage Four)

【原文】	【题目】
[36①] Take the case of public education alone. The principal difficulty faced by the schools has been the tremendous *increase in the number of pupils*. This has been *caused by* [37] the advance of the legal age for going into industry and the impossibility of finding a job even when the legal age has been reached. In view of the technological improvements in the last few years, business will require in the future proportionately fewer workers than ever before. The result will be still further raising of the legal age for going into employment, and still further difficulty in finding employment when that age has been attained. [36②] If we cannot put our children to work, we must put them in school. We may also be quite confident that the present trend toward a shorter day and a shorter week will be maintained. [36③] [38] We have developed and shall continue to have a new leisure class. Already the public agencies for adult education are swamped by the tide that has swept over them since the depression began. They *will be little better off* when it is over. [36④] Their support must come from the taxpayer. It is surely too much to hope that [36⑤] these increases in the cost of public education can be borne	36. What is the passage mainly about? [A] How to improve the public education system. [B] How to solve the rising unemployment problem. [C] How to persuade local communities to provide more funds. [D] How to cope with the shortage of funds for public education. 37. What is *the reason for the increase in the number of students*? [A] The trend toward a shorter workday. [B] Raising of the legal age for going to work. [C] The requirement of educated workers by business. [D] People's concern for the future of the next generation. 38. The public agencies for adult education *will be little better off* because _____. [A] the unemployed are too poor to continue their education [B] they are still suffering from the depression [C] an increase in taxes could be a problem [D] a new leisure class has developed 39. According to the author, the *answer to the problem of public education* is that the Federal government _____.

by the local communities. They cannot care for the present restricted and inadequate system. The local communities have failed in their efforts to cope with unemployment. They cannot expect to cope with public education on the scale on which we must attempt it. [39①] [40] The answer to the problem of unemployment has been Federal relief. *The answer to the problem of public education* may have to be much the same, and properly so. If there is one thing in which the citizens of all parts of the country have an interest, it is in the decent education of the citizens of all parts of the country. Our income tax now goes in part to keep our neighbors alive. It may have to go in part as well to make our neighbors intelligent We are now attempting to preserve the present generation through Federal relief of the *destitute*(贫民). [39②] Only a people determined to ruin the next generation will refuse such Federal funds as public education may require.

[A] should demand that local communities provide support

[B] should raise taxes to meet the needs of public education

[C] should allocate Federal funds for public education

[D] should first of all solve the problem of unemployment

40. Why does the author say "Only a people determined to ruin the next generation will refuse such Federal funds as public education may require"(Para. 3)?

[A] Educated people are determined to use part of the Federal funds to help the poor.

[B] People all over the country should make contributions to education in the interest of the next generation.

[C] Citizens of all parts of the country agree that the best way to support education is to use Federal funds.

[D] Only by appropriating adequate Federal funds for education can the next generation have a bright future.

36. 【解析】主旨大意题。解答本题需从全文考虑，前两段提出问题：学生人数不断增加，公共教育面临巨大经济压力；第三段讨论解决措施。

37. 【解析】事实细节题。第一段第三句便是学生人数增加的原因。选项中的 Raising of the legal age 对应文中的 the advance of the legal age；going to work 对应文中的 going into industry。

38. 【解析】事实细节题。文章第二段提到，经济好转后由于工作时间的缩短和工作日的减少，就形成了一个 leisure class(休闲阶层)，这些人就会利用空闲时间寻求培训提高自身水平，因此成人教育机构的压力局面丝毫不会 better off(有所好转)。

39. 【解析】推理判断题。综合第三段五、六句可知公共教育资金问题的解决要依靠 Federal relief(政府救济)，也就是说要用 Federal funds 来缓解目前的压力。

40. 【解析】语义理解题。结合上题分析和本句内容可知，作者之所以说"只有决心毁掉下一代的人才会拒绝给公共教育提供联邦基金"是因为他认为，只有联邦政府为公共教育适度拨款，下一代才能拥有光明的未来。

Exercise 即讲即练

At least two million children have died in the past decade as a result of wars launched by adults, many targeted as non-combatants or killed in action as soldiers. Three times that number were disabled or seriously injured, with many more suffering from disease, malnutrition, sexual violence, and the hardships of forced flight. And countless children struggle with the agony of losing their homes, their possessions and those closest to them. Virtually every aspect of a child's development is damaged in such circumstances, and the psychological *toll* (代价) of armed conflict is incalculable.

The criminal exploitation and targeting of children in conflict is an assault not only on their rights, but also on the very cause of international peace and security. When children are denied the opportunity to grow up in an atmosphere of trust, tolerance and justice, the prospects for stemming war over succeeding generations are dim indeed. It is clear, for example, that the kind of warfare we have seen in the Middle East is hardening many children in the belief that violence is an acceptable way of resolving disputes.

Yet it is also true that we have seen significant progress in efforts to protect children in conflict situations, as well as steps to ensure that their interests are central to peacemaking, peacekeeping and peace-building activities. The pending establishment of an International Criminal Court means that the world will have an institution dedicated to challenging the *impunity* (免受惩罚) of war crimes against children and other civilians. At the same time, the role of business in intensifying or prolonging conflict and instability has come under scrutiny as a result of investigations into the links between armed conflict and the illegal trading of diamonds.

A global ban is now in force on the production and use of anti-personal *landmines*（地雷）, which indiscriminately kill or disable children and other civilians for decades after the end of fighting, while posing a comparably long-term threat to reconstruction and development. The shameless *proliferation*（扩散）of small arms and light weapons, which are easily handled by child soldiers, is now being addressed. And the increasing attention paid to war-affected children by the UN Security Council and a number of regional organizations has helped move children closer to the center of the international peace and security agenda.

1. In discussing the impact of wars on children, the author focuses on _____.
   [A] the intensity and causes of the impact
   [B] the scope and result of the wars
   [C] the intensity and scope of the impact
   [D] the causes and brutality of the wars
2. "The criminal exploitation" of children (Line 1, Para. 2) refers to "_____".
   [A] recruiting child soldiers
   [B] killing children as combatants
   [C] targeting children as civilians
   [D] sexual violence on children
3. Children will see violence and war as an acceptable way of resolving violence if _____.
   [A] they find there is little hope to stem wars
   [B] they think their rights are infringed upon
   [C] they are constantly exposed to warfare
   [D] their fathers and forefathers told them so
4. What do we know about the International Criminal Court from this passage?
   [A] It is regarded as an effort in progress to protect children in conflict situations.
   [B] It examines the role of business in intensifying and prolonging conflicts.
   [C] Whether this institution should be established is still undecided.
   [D] The institution has put an end to impunity of war crimes against children.
5. This passage is mainly about _____.
   [A] the impact of wars on children
   [B] how to protect war-affected children
   [C] criminal exploitation of children
   [D] children and world peace

【答案与解析】

【文章大意】
　　世界上几乎每天都在发生战争,战争给人类带来的伤害是勿庸置疑的。本文则着重阐述了战争对少年儿童的影响,在过去的十年里,至少有200万儿童死于战争。同时作者也讲述了针对处于战乱状态下的少年儿童而做的工作已经取得了重大的进步。

1. 选[C]。推理判断题。文中第一段开头指出在过去的十几年中,至少有200万的少年儿童在战争中死去,这足以表明战争的影响范围之大。接着作者又将战争带给孩子们的其他各项灾难一一列举出来,如:disability, disease, malnutrition, sexual violence, homelessness 等等,其中最为严重的影响是给孩子们心灵上带来的伤害,并指出 the psychological toll of armed conflict is incalculable(战争冲突带给孩子们心理上的伤害无法衡量),仅通过第一段即可发现战争对孩子影响的范围之广,深度之大。

2. 选[A]。推理判断题。第一段谈及战争对孩子影响的范围之广,深度之大;第二段首句进一步谈到了战争对孩子们的严重影响:征集童军以及将儿童作为攻击的对象不仅侵害到儿童的权利,而且对国际安全和平事业也构成威胁。由文章首段第一句即主题句"…many targeted as non-combatants or killed in action as soldiers"可推测"the criminal exploitation"是指招募儿童当兵。criminal exploitation 意为"非法利用"。

3. 选[C]。事实细节题。第二段的最后一句话中作者以中东频繁战事为例说明对战争习以为常的孩子们理所当然地认为战争是解决争端的合理方式。作者在此处使用了进行时态说明孩子们的想法在频繁不断的战争影响下逐渐根深蒂固的这一情况。选项[C]即是该句话的同义转述。

4. 选[A]。事实细节题。第三段首句即为该段的主题句:保护处于战乱境遇中的儿童的努力已经有了极大的进展,接着提到国际刑事法庭的设立,由此可以推测国际刑事法庭是为保护处于战乱境遇中的儿童所做出的努力之一,而本段第二句中的 challenging the impunity of war crimes against children and other civilians 也证明了这一点。

5. 选[D]。主旨大意题。文章第一二段主要谈到了战争对儿童的影响,第三四段主要谈到了为保护处于战乱境遇的儿童所做出的努力,如将他们的利益作为 peacemaking,peacekeeping 和 peace-building 活动的中心等,[D]是对原文内容的总体概括,故为答案。[A]、[B]两项都不够全面,[C]项只谈到了文章中的一个小的细节。

Lecture 3 **第三讲　6招巧做事实细节题**

事实细节题主要测试考生对文章中某项事实内容的辨认和理解,如时间、地点、人物、事件、原因、结果等。

事实细节题可大致分为三类:一类是细节辨认类,答案几乎是原文中某处细节内容的再现,在句式和用词上变化不大;另一类是同义转述类,答案是对原文中某处内容的转述,在句式和用词上都有较大变化;还有一类是细节归纳类,答案是根据原文中某两处或以上的细节内容归纳总结得出。从六级考试历年真题来看,篇章阅读题主要考查的是后两类事实细节题。

常见题干表现形式如下:

According to the passage, it is _____ that ...

According to the passage, the best solution to ... is _____.

According to the passage, the problem of ... partly arises from _____.

The author describes ... as ... because _____.

常用的解题招术如下:

第一招:根据题干中关键词语在原文中定位

解答事实细节题,往往可以根据题干中的人物、地点、时间、陈述对象等关键词语在原文中定位,然后再根据原文内容进行选择。

第二招:只读题目出处内容

根据题干中的关键词语在原文中定位以后,只需仔细阅读题目出处的细节内容,而对文中其他内容一带而过,不需要深入理解。

第三招:注意题目与原文的转换

在定位题目出处和选择答案时,要注意识别和理解题干和选项对原文内容的转述表达,这样才能快速而准确地定位信息点并选出答案。

第四招:识别细微之处的干扰

事实细节题是针对文中的细节内容而设置,因此干扰选项经常被设计成只在非常细微的地方与原文不同,因此在解答这类题目时,要将四个选项与原文一一进行仔细地对照,识别细微差别,排除干扰项。

第五招:过于绝对的选项为答案的可能性较小

一般来说,含有模糊性概括词语,如 some,sometimes, certain, someone,more ... than, (not)as ... as ..., less, probably, possible 等的选项为答案的可能性较大;而含有绝对含义较强的词,如 only,everything, all, none, must, never, always, alone, everyone, entirely, absolute , any, no, completely 等的选项为答案的可能性较小。

第六招:符合一般规律的选项为答案的可能性较大

篇章阅读题中,尤其是议论文体中,符合一般规律、意义深刻、富有哲理的选项为答案的可能性较大;而那种明显不符合大众思维、违背常理的选项为答案的可能性较小。

【例】　　　　　　　　　　　　　　　　　　　　　　　　　　　　　　(05-1-Passage Three)

【原文】	【题目】
Throughout the nation's more than 15,000 school districts, [31①] widely differing approaches to *teaching science and math* have emerged. Though there can be strength in diversity, a new international analysis suggests that this [31②] variability has instead contributed to *lackluster* (平淡的) achievement scores by U. S. children relative to their peers in other developed countries. Indeed, concludes William H. Schmidt of Michigan State	31. According to the passage, the *teaching of science and math* in America is _____. [A] focused on tapping students' potential [B] characterized by its diversity [C] losing its vitality gradually [D] going downhill in recent years 32. The *fundamental flaw of American school education* is that _____.

University, who led the new analysis, [31③] "no single intellectually coherent vision dominates U. S. educational practice in math or science. " The reason, he said, "is because the *system is deeply and fundamentally flawed.*"

The new analysis, released this week by the National Science Foundation in Arlington, Va. , is based on data collected from about 50 nations as part of the Third International Mathematics and Science Study.

Not only do approaches to teaching science and math vary among individual U. S. communities, the report finds, but [32] there appears to be little strategic focus within a school district's curricula, its textbooks, or its teachers' activities. This contrasts sharply with the coordinated national programs of most other countries.

On average, [33] U. S. students study more topics within science and math than their international counterparts do. This creates an educational environment that "*is a mile wide and an inch deep*," Schmidt notes.

For instance, eighth graders in the United States cover about 33 topics in math versus just 19 in Japan. Among science courses, the international gap is even wider. U. S. curricula for this age level resemble those of a small group of countries including Australia, Thailand, Iceland, and Bulgaria. Schmidt asks whether the United States wants to be classed with these nations, whose educational systems "share our pattern of *splintered* (支离破碎的) visions" but which are not economic leaders.

The new report "couldn't come at a better time", says Gerald Wheeler, executive director of the National Science Teachers Association in Arlington. "*The new National Science Education Standards* [34] provide that focused vision," including the call "to do less, but in greater depth".

Implementing the new science standards and their math counterparts will be the challenge, he and Schmidt agree, *because* [35] the decentralized responsibility for education in the United States requires that any reforms be tailored and instituted one community at a time.

In fact, Schmidt argues, reforms such as these proposed national standards "face an almost impossible task, because even though they are intellectually coherent, each becomes only one more voice in the *babble* (嘈杂声)."

[A] it lacks a coordinated national program

[B] it sets a very low academic standard for students

[C] it relies heavily on the initiative of individual teachers

[D] it attaches too much importance to intensive study of school subjects

33. By saying that the U. S. educational environment is "*a mile wide and an inch deep*" (Para. 5), the author means U. S. educational practice _____.

[A] lays stress on quality at the expense of quantity

[B] offers an environment for comprehensive education

[C] encourages learning both in depth and in scope

[D] scratches the surface of a wide range of topics

34. The *new National Science Education Standards* are good news in that they will _____.

[A] provide depth to school science education

[B] solve most of the problems in school teaching

[C] be able to meet the demands of the community

[D] quickly dominate U. S. educational practice

35. *Putting the new science and math standards into practice will prove difficult because* _____.

[A] there is always controversy in educational circles

[B] not enough educators have realized the necessity for doing so

[C] school districts are responsible for making their own decisions

[D] many schoolteachers challenge the acceptability of these standards

31.【解析】事实细节题。首段中的 widely differing approaches,diversity 和 variability 都明确体现了美国的数学或科学教育中教学方法的 diversity(多样性)。另外,第二段中的 no single intellectually coherent vision dominates… 也从侧面说明了这个问题。be characterized by …"以…为特色"。

32.【解析】推理判断题。第二段提到美国的数学和科学教育缺乏一种主导性的理念,第四段又指出美国的教学方法多样化与一些国家的 coordinated national programs 形成鲜明对比,这都说明美国缺乏系统有序的全国性教学计划。

33.【解析】语义理解题。第六段的例子对上段中的"a mile wide and an inch deep"(即题干)起到了解释说明的作用。结合美国孩子所学的课题数(比日本同年级的孩子多出 14 个)及其产生的教育结果(第一段中提到的"与其他发达国家同龄孩子相比显得成绩平平")可知,尽管美国学校中开设的课题很多,但每个课题深入的力度却不够,[D] 项"只触及了许多课题的表面"与此意思相近,为答案。

34.【解析】事实细节题。第七段末句指出国家科学教育标准要求"to do less, but in greater depth",but 后的内容为其强调的中心。选项对应文中的 in greater depth,意指要求学校的科学教育要达到一定的深度。

35.【解析】事实细节题。题干中的 putting…into practice 对应文中的 implementing(贯彻,实行);will prove difficult 对应文中的 will be the challenge,because 后面的内容即为本题的答案出处。该句意为"美国的教育权限相对分散,任何一项改革只能一次一个校区地进行调整和实施",也就是说各学区对于自己是否推行新的国家教育标准有决定权,即每个学区对自己负责。

Exercise 　　　　　即讲即练

The popular dietary supplement ginseng is said to improve one's mood and all-around vigor, but a new study published in the Journal of the American Dietetic Association suggests that ginseng has little of any effect on psychological health. The study, conducted by researchers at Oregon State University and Wayne State University, is one of the most extensive peer-reviewed studies of ginseng ever conducted.

"Ginseng is being marketed to relatively healthy young people as a way to feel even better — a kind of *yuppie* (雅皮士) supplement," said Bradley J. Cardinal, an associate professor in the College of Health and Human Performance at Oregon State, "We found it had no real effect on mood at all. It certainly did not live to some of its over-enthusiastic marketing claims." Among the claims, the authors say, were that ginseng enhances mood, leads to positive well-being, and generally makes you feel better. Marketing *ploys* (策略) used to push ginseng promoted its use by astronauts and professional athletes, and claimed it did everything from easing childbirth to working as an *aphrodisiac* (壮阳剂).

The study by Cardinal and Hermann J. Engels of Wayne State University focused only on the alleged psychological properties of ginseng. The researchers gave a regular, 200-mg daily dose of ginseng to one group of volunteers for eight weeks. A second group received a doubled dose of 400-mg daily; the third group received a sugar pill. None of the individuals knew what they were taking. At the end of the eight-week period, the researchers measured the effects of the supplements on the volunteers' "total mood disturbance" using a 65-question "Profile of Mood States" inventory. To eliminate bias, the researchers evaluated the tests without initially knowing which subjects were taking ginseng and which were taking placebos. They compared the results with a baseline survey of the volunteers taken just prior to the study. They found no significant difference among the three groups.

"What these findings on psychological effect do is to extend earlier research from our lab that examined physiological outcomes of ginseng," said Wayne State University's Engels. "Our previous research found, using a controlled physical exercise stress test, that ginseng had no effects when given to normal, healthy adults."

1. What is the main idea of the passage?

    [A] Ginseng is the most popular dietary supplement.

    [B] New study questions role of ginseng as mood enhancer.

    [C] The study of ginseng is one of the most extensive peer-reviewed studies.

    [D] The study focused on the alleged psychological properties of ginseng.

2. It can be concluded that Cardinal's attitude toward marketing claims about ginseng is _____.

    [A] questioning 　　　　[B] neutral 　　　　[C] positive 　　　　[D] negative

3. The study conducted by Cardinal and Wayne aims to _____.

    [A] analyze the reason for the popularity of ginseng

    [B] demonstrate the unwanted side effects of ginseng

    [C] evaluate the alleged effect of ginseng on psychological health

    [D] eliminate bias by both the volunteers and the researchers themselves

4. Placebos (Line 7, Para. 3) refer to _____ in the passage.

    [A] poor-qualified ginseng 　　　　　　[B] high-qualified perfume

    [C] small tablet 　　　　　　　　　　　[D] sugar pill

5. We learn from the last paragraph that _____.

[A] all groups experienced increase in positive feeling during the eight weeks

[B] ginseng didn't seem to enhance the psychological well-being of normal, healthy adults

[C] the popular dietary supplements ginseng had no effects at all

[D] it was impossible that ginseng had an effect on certain individuals

【答案与解析】

【文章大意】

营养价值高的人参被作为一种高级补品已普遍被人们接受。人们普遍认为人参能够调节情绪，使人精力充沛，但目前这一观点受到了置疑。发表在美国饮食协会杂志上的一篇研究报道指出在改善人们的心理健康这方面，人参所起的作用并不大。

1. 选[B]。主旨大意题。文章第一段首句首先指出人参作为膳食补充可以改善人的情绪，增强全身的活力，但是转折连词 but 后的内容却说明了实际情况：ginseng has little of any effect on psychological health。以下内容都是围绕该实际情况而展开的，[B] 表述内容与文章主旨一致，故为答案。

2. 选[D]。观点态度题。由文章第二段第一句中 Cardinal 话中的"We found it had no real effect on mood at all. It certainly did not…"可知，Cardinal 对宣传所说的 ginseng 的效用持有 negative(否定)观点，故答案为[D]。

3. 选[C]。事实细节题。文章第三段首句指出 The study by… focused only on the alleged psychological properties of ginseng，题干中的 aims to 对应原文中的 focused on，所以原文中介词 on 的宾语就是本题的主体内容，[C] 项是原文中 on 的宾语的同义转述，故为答案。

4. 选[D]。语义理解题。文章第三段第七句中的 subjects 指的就是参加实验的三组志愿者，由上文可知，这三组志愿者前两组分别服用了剂量不等的人参，而第三组只服用了 sugar pill，由此可判断 taking placebos 指的就是服用 sugar pill 的人，故答案为[D]。

5. 选[B]。事实细节题。文章最后一段最后一句指出 ginseng had no effects when given to normal, healthy adults，而通过上一句可以发现 the effects 主要指的是心理方面的作用，[B] 为该句话的同义转述，故为答案。

Lecture 4　第四讲　5 招巧做推理判断题

推理判断题主要测试考生根据文章中的细节或局部内容，利用上下文的逻辑关系和内容上的关联，推断出隐含在事实或细节中的深层次含义，理解文字所表达的言外之意。这类题目不但要求考生充分理解文章所表达的字面含义，还要掌握一定的逻辑思维和推理判断能力。

此类题的题干中一般都含有 imply，infer，deduce，conclude 等表示推理和判断的词语。

常见的题干表现形式如下：

It can be inferred from the passage that _____.

What do we learn from the last paragraph?

It can be concluded from the passage that _____.

常用的解题招术如下：

第一招：根据题干中的关键词在原文中定位

推理判断题一般是针对文中的某个事实或细节而设置，因此也可以根据题干中的人物、地点、时间、陈述对象等关键词语在原文中定位，然后再根据原文内容进行正确的推理和判断。

第二招：不要试图在原文中直接寻找答案

推理判断题的答案是根据文中的细节或局部内容推理得出的，是文中细节内容中隐含的深层次含义，因此不可能在原文中直接找到对应的陈述。

第三招：注意原文中事实细节的干扰

推理判断题的干扰选项往往根据文中其他的事实细节而设，这些题干本身看来与原文相符，但实际却与题干要求并不相符，因此，在解答推理判断题时，一定要注意结合题干要求，不要受到其他细节的干扰。

第四招：理清上下文的逻辑关系

解答推理判断题时，除了仔细分析题干出处的细节内容的含义以外，还要理清上下文的逻辑关系，根据这些逻辑关系线索，从上下文的陈述中推出答案。

第五招：不要只在只言片语中寻找答案

推理判断题虽然大多是针对文中的某项细节而设，但往往并不能直接从该细节中得出答案，而是需要结合细节前后的内容甚至细节所在的段落内容综合推断得出，因此，在解答这类题时，不要只是根据只言片语硬推答案，而是要充分结合上下文。

【例】
(06-12-Passage One)

【原文】

  It used to be that people were proud to [26①] work for the same company for the whole of their working lives. They'd get a gold watch at the end of their productive years and dinner featuring speeches by their bosses praising [26②] their loyalty. But today's rich capitalists have *regressed* (倒退) to the "survival of the fittest" ideas and [27①] their loyalty extends not to their workers or even to their stockholders but only to themselves. Instead of giving out gold watches worth a hundred or so dollars for forty or so years of work, [27②] they grab tens and even hundreds of millions of dollars as they sell for their own profit the company they may have been with for only a few years.

  The new rich selfish act on their own to unfairly grab the wealth that the country as a whole has produced. The top 1 percent of the population now has wealth equal to the whole bottom 95 percent and they want more. [28] *Their selfishness* is most shamelessly expressed in downsizing and *outsourcing* (将产品包给外公司做) because these business maneuvers don't act to create new jobs as the founders of new industries used to do, but only to cut our jobs while keeping the money value of what those jobs produced for themselves.

  To keep the money machine working smoothly the rich have bought all the politicians from the top down. The president himself is constantly leaving Washington and the business of the nation because he is summoned to "fundraising dinners" where *fat cats* pay a thousand or so dollars a plate to worm their way into government [29] not through service but through donations of vast amounts of money. Once on the inside they have both political parties busily tearing up all the regulations that protect the rest of us from the greed of the rich.

  The middle class used to be loyal to the free enterprise system. In the past, the people of the middle class mostly thought they'd be rich themselves someday or have a good shot at becoming rich. But nowadays income is being distributed more and more unevenly and corporate loyalty is a thing of the past. [30①] The middle class may also wake up to forget its loyalty to the so-called free enterprise system altogether and the government which governs only the rest of us while letting the corporations do what they please with our

【题目】

26. It can be inferred from the first paragraph that *people used to place a high value on* _____.
  [A] job security
  [B] bosses' praise
  [C] corporate loyalty
  [D] retirement benefits

27. The author is strongly critical of *today's rich capitalists* for _____.
  [A] not giving necessary assistance to laid-off workers
  [B] maximizing their profits at the expense of workers
  [C] not setting up long-term goals for their companies
  [D] rewarding only those who are considered the fittest

28. The immediate consequence of *the new capitalists' practice* is _____.
  [A] loss of corporate reputation
  [B] lower pay for the employees
  [C] a higher rate of unemployment
  [D] a decline in business transactions

29. *The rich* try to sway the policy of the government by _____.
  [A] occupying important positions in both political parties
  [B] making monetary contributions to decision-makers
  [C] pleasing the public with generous donations
  [D] constantly hosting fundraising dinners

30. What is the author's purpose in writing this passage?
  [A] To call on the middle class to remain loyal to the free enterprise system.
  [B] To warn the government of the shrinking of the American middle class.
  [C] To persuade the government to change

jobs. As things stand, [30②] if somebody doesn't wake up, the middle class is on a path to being downsized all the way to the bottom of society.

its current economic policies.

[D] To urge the middle class to wake up and protect their own interests.

26.【解析】推理判断题。题干中的 place a high value on 对应文中的 were proud to。were proud to 后面的 work for the same company for the whole of their working lives 体现的就是对公司的 loyalty(忠诚),另外,后面句中的 loyalty 对解答本题也是一个重要提示。

27.【解析】推理判断题。由 their loyalty extends not to…, but to… 和 they grab…millions of dollars as they sell … 两句话可推知,现在的 rich capitalists(富有的资本家)只对自己忠诚,他们为了使自己的利益最大化,不惜牺牲员工的利益。

28.【解析】推理判断题。文中说,资本家的这种自私行为的最无耻的表现就是 downsizing(裁员)和 outsourcing(产品外包),因为这样的行为不但不会创造就业机会,反而只会 cut out jobs(减少就业机会),由此可推知新兴资本家的行为的直接后果就是失业率的上升。

29.【解析】事实细节题。题干中的 the rich 对应文中的 fat cats(大亨),由 where 引导的定语从句可知,这些富人们能够跻身政府不是通过他们的服务,而是通过 donations of vast amounts of money(大量的捐款),而由接下来的一句可知,他们进入政府的目的是想要撕毁那些不利于他们的规章制度,也就是题干中所说的要 sway the policy of the government(左右政府的政策)。

30.【解析】主旨大意题。作者通篇都在强调资本家对中产阶级的剥削,并在末段强烈呼吁中产阶级尽早 wake up(觉醒)来 protect their own interests(保护自己的利益)。

Exercise　　　即讲即练

On March 25, 1911, one of the five hundred employees of the Triangle Shirtwaist factory in New York noticed that a rag bin near her eighth-floor workstation was on fire. Workers immediately tried to extinguish the flames. Their efforts proved futile, as piles of fabric ignited all over the eighth floor. The manager of the factory ordered his employees to unroll the fire extinguisher *hose* (水管), but they found it rotted and useless.

The shirt factory occupied the top three floors of the ten-story Asch Building. The seventy employees who worked on the tenth floor escaped the fire by way of the staircases or climbed onto the roof, where students from New York University, located across the street, stretched ladders over to the Asch Building.

The 260 workers on the ninth floor had the worst luck of all. Although the eighth floor workers tried to warn them by telephone, the call did not reach them, and by the time they learned about the fire, their routes of escape were mostly blocked. Some managed to climb down the cables of the freight elevator. Others crammed into the narrow stairway. Still others climbed onto the single, inadequately constructed fire escape. But that spindly structure could not support the weight of hundreds of people, and it separated from the wall, falling to the ground and carrying many people with it.

To combat the disaster, the New York Fire Department sent thirty-five pieces of equipment, including a hook and ladder. The young women trapped on the ninth-floor window ledge watched in honor as the ladder, fully raised, stopped far below them, reaching only as far as the sixth floor. Within minutes, the factory — a fire trap typical of the period's working conditions — was consumed by flame, killing 146 workers, mostly immigrant women. City officials set up a temporary *morgue* (太平间) on 26th Street, and over the next few days streams of survivors filed through the building to identify the dead.

The Triangle Shirtwaist fire brought a public outcry for laws to regulate the safety of working conditions. The New York Factory Investigating Commission was formed to examine the working conditions in factories throughout the state. Their report introduced many new regulations. The fire had occurred during an era of progressive reform that was beginning to sweep the nation, as people decided that government had a responsibility to ensure that private industry protected the welfare of working people.

1. What does the passage mainly discuss?
   [A] The causes of a fire in a shirt factory.
   [B] Working conditions in New York City.
   [C] Escaping from a fire in a shirt factory.
   [D] The events surrounding a tragic fire.

2. The word "ignited" (Line 3, Para. 1) could best be replaced by _____.

[A] became wet   [B] caught fire

[C] exploded   [D] spread

3. How did many workers on the top floor manage to escape?

[A] They were saved by the fire escape.   [B] They escaped by taking an elevator.

[C] They escaped by way of ladders.   [D] They escaped by ropes.

4. It can be inferred from Para. 4 that _____.

[A] New York had a well-equipped fire department

[B] fire fighters were able to rescue the women on the ninth floor

[C] the women on the window ledge probably died

[D] the women probably took the stairs down to the sixth floor

5. Which one of the following statements is true?

[A] The Triangle Shirtwaist fire had no influence on public opinion.

[B] The Triangle Shirtwaist factory was rebuilt.

[C] After the fire, working conditions in factories remained the same as before.

[D] Disasters can lead to a demand for reform.

【答案与解析】

> **【文章大意】**
>
> 　　本文是一篇事件报道。文章讲述了 1911 年 3 月 25 日发生在纽约的三角女衣厂的一起火灾。作者描述了起火原因、火灾过程以及火灾所造成的影响。火灾的严重性引起了公众的强烈反应,他们呼吁相关部门制定有关确保工人工作环境安全的法律。

1. 选[D]。主旨大意题。文章第一段讲述了起火原因,第二至四段主要讲述了火灾过程,最后一段主要讲述了火灾所带来的影响,[D] 是对文章总体内容的概括,故为答案。[A]、[B]、[C] 陈述的都是文章的细节,均不能概括全文,应排除。

2. 选[B]。语义理解题。由文章首段第一二句中的 a rag bin near her eighth-floor workstation was on fire 及 …extinguish the flames 可以推断首段倒数第二句中的 ignited 应与"着火"有关,故答案应为[B],caught fire 意为"着火"。

3. 选[C]。事实细节题。文章第二段在讲述顶层的 70 名工作人员的逃生方法时提到他们有的 escaped the fire by way of the staircases(通过楼梯逃生),有的爬上楼顶,那里有街对面纽约大学的学生伸过来的梯子,由此可推断有一部分人可能是通过梯子逃生的。[C] 是其中的一种逃生方法,故为本题答案。

4. 选[C]。推理判断题。第四段第二句提到由于梯子不够高只能够到六楼,The young women trapped on the ninth-floor window ledge watched in honor(被困在 9 楼阳台上的年轻妇女们只能看着远在脚下的梯子),由此可推知这些妇女们很有可能被火烧死,故答案为[C]。

5. 选[D]。推理判断题。本文讲述在三角女衣厂的一场大火之后,人们开始关注和呼吁制定法律以改善工作条件,确保工作人员的安全,由此可推测在发生一次严重的灾难之后,通常会有相应的改革以弥补过去的不足之处,故答案为[D]。

Lecture 5　第五讲　7 招巧做语义理解题

　　语义理解题主要测试考生对阅读文章中出现的关键词、短语或句子含义的理解能力。此类题目的考查方式通常为两种,一种是对单词和短语的考查;一种是对句子含义的考查。而对于文中单词的考查又无外乎三种情况:第一种是在特定语境中判断多义常用词的具体含义;第二种是根据上下文推测出生僻词汇的含义;第三种根据上下文推测出代词所指代的具体内容。

　　常见的题干表现形式如:

　　The word "…" mostly probably means _____.

　　By saying "…", the author means _____.

　　The word "…" mostly probably refers to _____.

Which of the following is the closest in meaning to the word "..."?

The statement "..." probably means _____.

The word "they" in the sentence" ... "refers to _____.

常用的解题招术如下：

第一招：不可仅根据孤立的句子进行判断

解答这类题目时不能孤立地根据某个句子或短语做出判断，应把它放到上下文中去理解。

第二招：通过连接词判断词义

一般来说，由 and 连接的两项内容在含义上是接近或递进的，而以 or 连接的两项内容在含义上往往相反，但有时 or 后面的内容也是对前面内容的进一步解释和说明。另外，其他表递进、转折、因果等关系的信号词均可用来帮助判断词或短语的含义。

第三招：利用所举例子进行判断

作者经常会在生词、难词、短语或句子的后面列举实例来进一步解释或重申上文的内容。通过这些例子往往可以推断出所考词汇、短语或句子的含义。

第四招：从标志性词语或特殊标点符号中寻找线索

一般来说，如果所考词汇是超出六级词汇大纲的生词，那么在该词的前后往往会有该词的定义或对其的解释说明，这类定义或解释说明经常可以通过像 namely，that is，in other words 等标志性词语或是破折号、冒号或括号等特殊的标点符号来识别。另外，有时候这种定义或解释说明也会通过定语从句表达出来。

第五招：不要仅从单词的字面意思来理解

对于所考词汇或短语，尤其是属于六级词汇大纲的词汇，注意不要单从其字面意思来理解，因为这类词往往是多义词，干扰选项经常是根据我们所熟知的含义设置，如果仅根据平时对单词词义的记忆而匆忙选择，则很容易掉进出题人的陷阱。考生在解答这类题时，一定要结合上下文，确保自己所理解的词或短语的含义能够使语义通顺。

第六招：结合文章和段落主旨进行判断

这一点主要针对对句子的语义理解。句子所表达的意思一定是和文章或段落的主旨相关的，因此在判断句子的含义时，要结合文章或段落的主题，在不违背文章或段落主题的前提下，利用上下文判断句子所表达的含义和所起的作用。

第七招：将各选项放到原文中检验

如果直接判断词或短语的含义比较困难，也可以将各选项代入原文，代替所考查词汇或短语在原文中的位置，看其是否能使上下文语义通顺，利用排除法进行选择。

【例】　　　　　　　　　　　　　　　　　　　　　　　　　　(03-9-Passage Three)

【原文】	【题目】
Crying is hardly an activity encouraged by society. [31] Tears, be they of sorrow, anger, or joy, typically make Americans feel uncomfortable and embarrassed. [32①] The shedder of tears is likely to apologize, even when a *devastating*（毁灭性的）tragedy was the provocation. [32②] The observer of tears is likely to do everything possible to put an end to the emotional outpouring. But judging from recent studies of crying behavior, [33①] links between illness and crying and the chemical composition of tears, *both those responses to tears* are often [33②] inappropriate and may even be *counterproductive.*	31. It is known from the first paragraph that _____. [A] shedding tears gives unpleasant feelings to Americans [B] crying may often irritate people or even result in tragedy [C] crying usually wins sympathy from other people [D] one who sheds tears in public will be blamed 32. What does "*both those responses to tears*"

Humans are the only animals definitely known to shed e-motional tears. Since evolution has given rise to few, if any, purposeless physiological responses, it is logical to assume that [34] *crying has one or more functions that enhance survival.*

Although some observers have suggested that crying is a way to elicit assistance from others (as a crying baby might from its mother), the shedding of tears is hardly necessary to get help. Vocal cries would have been quite enough, more likely than tears to gain attention. So, it appears, there must be something special about tears themselves.

Indeed, *the new studies* suggest that [35] emotional tears may play a direct role in alleviating stress. University of Minnesota researchers who are studying the chemical composition of tears have recently isolated two important chemicals from emotional tears. Both chemicals are found only in tears that are shed in response to emotion. Tears shed because of exposure to a cut onion would contain no such substance.

Researchers at several other institutions are investigating the usefulness of tears as a means of diagnosing human ills and monitoring drugs.

At Tulane University's Tear Analysis Laboratory Dr. Peter Kastl and his colleagues report that they can use tears to detect drug abuse and exposure to *medication* (药物), to determine whether a contact lens fits properly or why it may be uncomfortable, to study the causes of "dry eye" syndrome and the effects of eye surgery, and perhaps even to measure exposure to environmental pollutants.

At Columbia University Dr. Linsy Faris and colleagues are studying tears for clues to the diagnosis of diseases away from the eyes. Tears can be obtained painlessly without invading the body and only tiny amounts are needed to perform highly refined analyses.

(Para. 1) refer to?

[A] Crying out of sorrow and shedding tears for happiness.

[B] The embarrassment and unpleasant sensation of the observers.

[C] The tear shedder's apology and the observer's effort to stop the crying.

[D] Linking illness with crying and finding the chemical composition of tears.

33. "*Counterproductive*" (Para. 1) very probably means "_____".

[A] having no effect at all

[B] leading to tension

[C] producing disastrous impact

[D] harmful to health

34. What does the author say about crying?

[A] It is a pointless physiological response to the environment.

[B] It must have a role to play in man's survival.

[C] It is meant to get attention and assistance.

[D] It usually produces the desired effect.

35. What can be inferred from *the new studies* of tears?

[A] Emotional tears have the function of reducing stress.

[B] Exposure to excessive medication may increase emotional tears.

[C] Emotional tears can give rise to "dry eye" syndrome in some cases.

[D] Environmental pollutants can induce the shedding of emotional tears.

31.【解析】事实细节题。由文章首段第二句可知,无论是什么样的眼泪都会让美国人感到 uncomfortable and embarrassed(不适和尴尬),答案是对该内容的同义转述,其中 unpleasant feelings 对应原文中的 feel uncomfortable and embarrassed。

32.【解析】语义理解题。those 为指示代词,所以其修饰限定的 responses to tears 一定在前面提到过。经过寻读发现,这两种对眼泪的反应分别对应首段第三句中的 The shedder of tears is likely to apologize …以及第四句中的 The observer of tears is likely to do …。答案中的 effort to stop the crying 对应文中的 do everything possible to put an end to the emotional outpouring。

33.【解析】语义理解题。"counterproductive"是在描述研究结果时提到的词,由前面提到的该项研究所涉及到的 links between illness and crying 可推知,"counterproductive"一词应和疾病有关。再基于与形容词 inappropriate(不恰当的)的并列及递进关系,不难推知"counterproductive"应意为"对健康有害的"。counterproductive 本意为"起反作用的"。

34.【解析】事实细节题。由第二段末句可知,作者认为"哭泣一定对人类的生存起某种作用",答案是对该内容的同义转述,其中 have a role to play 对应文中的 has one or more functions。

35.【解析】事实细节题。由第四段开头可知,新的研究表明,emotional tears 可能会对 alleviating stress(缓解压力)起到直接的作用,答案是对该内容的同义转述,其中 have the function 对应文中的 play a direct role;reducing stress 对应文中的 alleviating stress。

Exercise　　　　　即讲即练

Global reserves of fresh water add up to more than 37 million cubic kilometers, enough to fill the Mediterranean 10 times over. More than three fourths of this water is bound up in glaciers and polar ice, however, where it is largely beyond the reach of present technology. Almost all the rest consists of water in underground *aquifers* (蓄水层), which are not yet exploited intensively. The main sources of supply — the waters of lakes and rivers and the water vapor in the atmosphere — make up less than 1 percent of the total.

The ultimate source of fresh water is the continuous distillation of the oceans by solar radiation. The annual evaporation of water (including transpiration by plants) is roughly 500,000 cubic kilometers, of which 430,000 comes from the oceans and the remaining 70,000 from waters on the continents. Because the amount of water vapor in the atmosphere is essentially constant, the same amount of water must fall back to the surface as rain and snow. It is of vital importance to *terrestrial* (陆地的) life that a disproportionate share of this precipitation fall on land. Whereas the continents lose 70,000 cubic kilometers of water to evaporation, they receive 110,000 from precipitation, so that the effect of the hydrologic cycle is to transfer some 40,000 cubic kilometers of fresh water each year from the oceans to the continents.

Although the net continental *influx* (流入) is 40,000 cubic kilometers per year, not all of it is available for man's use. Much is lost through floods or is held in the soil or in swamps. The maximum that might reasonably be applied to human purposes is about 14,000 cubic kilometers per year, which is the base flow, or stable runoff excluding flood waters, of all the world's rivers and streams and of those isolated underground aquifers that discharge directly through evaporation. Of this volume about 5,000 cubic kilometers flow in regions that are uninhabited and are likely to remain so because they are climatically unsuited to human settlement. Hence the effective world water resource, from which all needs will have to be met for some years to come, is about 9,000 cubic kilometers per year.

1. Of all the reserves of fresh water in the world, more than three fourths _____.
   [A] is mostly out of the reach of present technology　　　　[B] is in solid form and is very expensive to melt
   [C] is covered by glaciers and polar ice　　　　　　　　　[D] is converted into sea water annually

2. Fresh water, as the passage states, originates mainly from _____.
   [A] the water vapor in the atmosphere　　　　　　　　　　[B] ocean water through distillation by solar radiation
   [C] lakes and rivers　　　　　　　　　　　　　　　　　　[D] underground aquifers

3. The word "precipitation" (Line 6, Para. 2) in the passage most probably means "_____".
   [A] the evaporation of water from the land　　　　　　　　[B] the water reserves on land
   [C] water falling in the form of rain and snow　　　　　　[D] the unevenly distributed rain and snow falls

4. Every year the continents get back _____.
   [A] more water than that it evaporates
   [B] less water than that it evaporates
   [C] the same amount of water as is lost to evaporation
   [D] different amounts of water based on weather conditions

5. It is implied in the last paragraph that the fresh water finally available for mankind to utilize each year is _____.
   [A] enough to meet all human needs
   [B] a little more than enough for all human needs
   [C] not adequate for all human needs
   [D] adequate now but will not be enough for some years later

【答案与解析】..

【文章大意】

　　全球淡水储量多达 3700 万立方千米,但冰川和极地冰中所含淡水储量就占据了其中的四分之三,其余大部分都储存在蓄水层中,还未被充分开发。淡水的最终来源还是海水通过日照被蒸发后以不同形式到达陆地所形成的淡水。最后作者还列举了淡水流失,不为人类所用的种种原因。

1. 选[A]。事实细节题。文章首段第一句话中 where 引导的定语从句表明超过四分之三的淡水资源中 largely be-

yond the reach of present technology(大部分是现代科技也望尘莫及的),[A]是该定语从句的同义转述。

2. 选[B]。事实细节题。文章第二段首句指出最主要的淡水资源来自于 the continuous distillation of the oceans by solar radiation(太阳辐射产生的海水连续蒸馏),题干中的 originates mainly from 对应该句中的 the ultimate source of fresh water,由此可知,该句的表语即为本题的答案,[B]是原文的细节再现,故为答案。下文中的 … of which 430,000 comes from the oceans 也可以证明这一点。

3. 选[C]。语义理解题。precipitation 前的指示代词 this 提示前面会有关于 precipitation 的解释,根据上下文的逻辑连接关系可推断 precipitation 应指降雨和降雪,另外第五句中的两个并列分句中,lose … water to evaporation 和 receive … from precipitation 是对应关系,由此也可看出,precipitation 应指降雨和降雪。

4. 选[A]。推理判断题。第二段最后一句指出如果陆地表面蒸发了7万立方千米的水分,那么它们会得到11万立方千米的降水量,由此可推知陆地所接收到的降水量比它蒸发掉的水量要多,故答案为[A]。选[C]的同学受了第二段第三句中 same amount of water must fall back to the surface 的影响,但没有注意到这里是说降落在 surface 上(包括海洋和陆地表面),即蒸发总量和降水总量相等,而陆地蒸发量和陆地降水量就不一定相等了。

5. 选[D]。推理判断题。文章最后一段主要列举了淡水流失的种种渠道,或不能为人类所用的原因,到最后只剩下9000立方千米的淡水可被人类所用,而且最后一句中 all needs will have to be met 和"9000"这个数字形成鲜明的对比,故可推断出作者想要强调的是淡水资源很有限,另外句中的时间状语 for some years to come 说明作者指的是未来,故选[D]。

Lecture 6　　第六讲　6招巧做观点态度题

观点态度题主要测试考生根据文章内容发现或推断出作者对某人或某事物的观点或态度、作者的行文基调、文中某人(机构)对其他人或事物的观点或态度的能力。

常见的题干表现形式有:

It's the author's view that _____.

What is the author's attitude toward …?

The author's attitude toward … could be described as _____.

Which of the following best describes the author's tone in this passage?

… believes that _____.

According to … , … _____.

常用的解题招术如下:

第一招:辨别清楚文章的文体

议论文中,文章的中心句一般暗示作者的态度;而说明文因为其体裁的客观性,作者的态度也往往近乎中立。在描述性文章中,因为其文章观点往往不直接提出,而且作者写作时也常带有某种倾向性,所以,考生在阅读这种文体时要细心捕捉表达或暗示情感态度的词或短语,捕捉那些烘托气氛、渲染情感的词句。

第二招:利用人名或组织机构名称进行定位

如果考查的是文中人物或组织机构的观点或态度,那么往往可以根据题干中的人名或组织机构名称在原文中进行定位,然后再根据上下文判断其所持的态度或观点。

第三招:结合所举例子进行判断

作者常会通过举例来论证观点,因此结合例子内容往往可以推断出作者所持的态度或观点。

第四招:结合文章主题综合推断

对于考查作者的行文基调和作者的态度或观点的题,需要分析文章走向,理解文章中心思想,从语篇的层次来判断。切忌根据文章局部内容所体现出来的感情色彩,对作者的态度妄下判断。

第五招：注意文中表示假设、想象之类的词语

当文章中出现 claimed as, suppose, perceive as, ranked as 等表示假设或声称之类的词语时，其后所体现的观点往往与作者的观点相反。

第六招：熟悉具有感情色彩的词语

文章中经常会出现能够直接体现人物态度或观点的带有感情色彩的词语，根据这些词语往往可以推断出作者的观点或态度。一般来讲，如果文中出现的褒义词比较多，那作者的观点就应该是正面（赞成）的；如果文中出现贬义词较多，那作者的观点就是负面（反对）的；如果文章中没有出现多少表示褒贬的词语，而通篇使用的都是中性词语，那作者的观点往往就是客观中立的。

另外，观点态度题的选项中也经常会出现这类具有感情色彩的词语，所以要解答观点态度题，熟悉和掌握常见的具有感情色彩的词语是必须的。

常见的这类词语有：

positive(赞成的); supporting(支持的); praising(赞扬的); optimistic(乐观的); admiring(羡慕的); interesting(有趣的); humorous(幽默的); serious(严肃的); enthusiastic(热情的); pleasant(愉快的); polite(礼貌的); concerned(关切的); sober(冷静的); disgusted(感到恶心的，厌恶的); critical(批评的); negative(否定的，反对的); suspicious(怀疑的); tolerant(容忍的，忍让的); worried(担忧的); pessimistic(悲观的); depressed(沮丧的); disappointed(失望的); ironic(讽刺的); sarcastic(挖苦的); bitter(痛苦的); cynical(玩世不恭的); sentimental(感伤的); emotional(激动的); angry(气愤的); indifferent(冷淡的，不关心的); impassive(冷淡的，不动感情的); uninterested(无兴趣的，不感兴趣的); ambivalent(情绪矛盾的); neutral(中立的); impersonal(不带个人感情的); subjective(主观的); objective(客观的); informative(提供信息的); impartial(不偏袒的); apathetic(漠不关心的)。

【例】

(05-6-Passage Three)

【原文】	【题目】
Supporters of the biotech industry have accused an American scientist of misconduct after she testified to the New Zealand government that [21①] a genetically modified (GM) bacterium could cause serious damage if released.	21. The passage centers on the controversy _____.
	[A] between American and New Zealand biologists over genetic modification
The New Zealand Life Sciences Network, an association of pro-GM scientists and organizations, says the view expressed by Elaine Ingham, a soil biologist at Oregon State University in Corvallis, was exaggerated and irresponsible. It has asked her university to discipline her.	[B] as to whether the study of genetic modification should be continued
	[C] over the possible adverse effect of a GM bacterium on plants
But Ingham stands by her comments and says the complaints are an attempt to silence her. "They're trying to cause trouble with my university and get me fired," Ingham told New Scientist.	[D] about whether Elaine Ingham should be fired by her university
The controversy began on 1 February, when *Ingham testified before New Zealand's Royal Commission* on Genetic Modification, which will determine how to regulate GM organisms. Ingham claimed that a GM version of a common soil bacterium could spread and destroy plants if released into the wild. Other researchers had previously modified the bacterium to produce alcohol from organic waste. But [22] Ingham says that when she put it in soil with wheat plants, all of the plants died within a week.	22. Ingham insists that her testimony is based on _____.
	[A] evidence provided by the EPA of the United States
	[B] the results of an experiment she conducted herself
	[C] evidence from her collaborative research with German biologists
	[D] the results of extensive field tests in Corvallis, Oregon
"We would lose *terrestrial*(陆生的)plants … this is an organism that is potentially deadly to the continued survival of human beings," she told the commission. She added that the U. S. Environmental Protection Agency (EPA) canceled its approval for field tests using the organism once she had told them about her research in 1999.	23. According to *Janet Anderson*, the EPA _____.
	[A] has cancelled its approval for field tests of the GM organism
	[B] hasn't reviewed the findings of Ingham's research

But last week [21②]the New Zealand Life Sciences Network accused Ingham of "presenting inaccurate, careless and exaggerated information" and "generating speculative *doomsday scenarios*(世界末日的局面)that are not scientifically supportable". They say that her study doesn't even show that the bacteria would survive in the wild, much less kill massive numbers of plants. What's more, the network says that contrary to Ingham's claims, the EPA was never asked to consider the organism for field trials.

[25①] The EPA has not commented on the dispute. But an e-mail to the network from **Janet Anderson**, director of the EPA's *bio-pesticides*(生物杀虫剂)division, says [23][25②] "there is no record of a review and/or clearance to field test" the organism.

Ingham says EPA officials had told her that the organism was approved for field tests, but says she has few details. It's also not clear whether the organism, first engineered by a German institute for biotechnology, is still in use.

Whether Ingham is right or wrong, her supporters say opponents are trying unfairly to silence her.

[24] "I think her concerns should be taken seriously. She shouldn't be harassed in this way," says **Ann Clarke**, a plant biologist at the University of Guelph in Canada who also testified before the commission. "It's an attempt to silence the opposition."

[C] has approved field tests using the GM organism

[D] hasn't given permission to field test the GM organism

24. According to **Ann Clarke**, the New Zealand Life Sciences Network _____.
[A] should gather evidence to discredit Ingham's claims
[B] should require that the research by their biologists be regulated
[C] shouldn't demand that Ingham be disciplined for voicing her views
[D] shouldn't appease the opposition in such a quiet way

25. Which of the following statements about Ingham is TRUE?
[A] Her testimony hasn't been supported by the EPA.
[B] Her credibility as a scientist hasn't been undermined.
[C] She is firmly supported by her university.
[D] She has made great contributions to the study of GM bacteria.

21.【解析】主旨大意题。文章开头就指出,生物技术产业的支持者们在美国科学家 Elaine Ingham 提出转基因细菌如果被释放会对植物造成严重破坏的论断后对其提起了诉讼,接着分别阐述了争议双方就转基因细菌究竟是否会对植物造成严重破坏这一问题的观点,由此可知,本文论述的主题就是有关转基因细菌到底会不会对植物有负作用这一问题的展开的争议。

22.【解析】推理判断题。第四、五段详细讲述了 Ingham 向新西兰转基因皇家委员会论证(testified)其观点的经过,由第四段最后一句可知,Ingham 坚持她的证词是建立在她的实验结果基础上的。答案中 experiment she conducted 指的是文中的 she put it in soil with wheat plants, results 指的是 all of the plants died within a week。

23.【解析】观点态度题。第七段中,Janet Anderson 的声明(EPA 不存在任何审批或取消对这种转基因有机物的现场试验的记录)其实是针对 Ingham 提到的 EPA canceled its approval for field tests using the organism once she had told them about her research in 1999 这种说法,她其实是想说明 EPA 从来就没允许过对转基因有机物的现场试验,更谈不上得知 Ingham 的研究结果后最终取消决定这件事。

24.【解析】观点态度题。由最后一段中 Ann Clarke 所说的话可知,Ann Clarke 认为新西兰转基因皇家委员不应该禁止 Ingham 发表她的言论,也就是说她认为 Ingham 不应该 be disciplined for voicing her views(因为发表自己的言论而受到谴责)。

25.【解析】推理判断题。根据第七段内容并结合第 23 题分析很容易得知,Ingham 的证词并没有得到 EPA 的支持。

Exercise   即讲即练

Some consumer researchers distinguish between so-called rational motives and emotional (or irrational) motives. In a marketing context, the term rationality implies that the consumer selects goals based on totally objective criteria, such as size, weight, price, or miles per gallon. Emotional motives imply the selection of goals according to personal or subjective criteria (the desire for individuality, pride, fear, affection and status).

The assumption underlying this distinction is that subjective or emotional criteria do not maximize utility or satisfaction. However, it is reasonable to assume that consumers always attempt to select alternatives that, in their view, serve to maximize satisfaction. Obviously, the assessment of satisfaction is a very personal process, based upon the individual's own need structure as well as on past behavioral, social, and learning experiences. What may appear as irrational to an outside observer may be perfectly rational within the context of the consumer's own psychological field. For example, a product purchased to enhance one's self-image (such as a fragrance) is a perfectly rational form of consumer behavior. If behavior did not appear rational to the person who undertakes it at the time that it is undertaken, obviously he or she would not do it. Therefore the distinction between rational and emotional motives does not appear to be warranted.

Indeed, some researchers go so far as to suggest that emphasis on "needs" obscures the rational, or conscious nature of most consumer motivation. They claim that consumers act consciously to maximize their gains and minimize their losses; that they act not from *subconscious* (下意识的) drives but from rational preferences, or what they perceive to be in their own best interests.

Marketers who agree with this view are reluctant to spend either time or money to uncover subconscious buyer motives. Instead, they try to identify problems that consumers experience with products then on the market. For example, instead of trying to identify any special needs that consumers may have for dog food, the marketer will try to discover any problems that consumers are experiencing with existing brands of dog food. If the marketer discovers that many dog foods leave an unpleasant odor in the refrigerator, he or she can develop a new product that solves this consumer problem and then run advertisements that announce to dog owners that the new product does not impart unpleasant odors. Thus, rather than address consumers' expressed needs, such marketers attempt to discover and solve consumers' problems and thereby achieve market success.

1. According to the consumer researcher, which of the following consumer behaviors would be most probably based on rationality?

　[A] Buying a product which was made in one's own country.

　[B] Buying a hat simply because his idol is wearing it.

　[C] Buying a car which saves gas.

　[D] Buying a high-end computer to play computer game.

2. According to the author, why is the purchase of a fragrance a rational form of consumer behavior?

　[A] It is based on an objective criteria.

　[B] The consumer believes that it is useful.

　[C] Fragrance is only used by rational people.

　[D] The consumer can afford it.

3. The phrase "this view" (Line 1, Para. 4) refers to the fact that _____.

　[A] there is not enough emphasis on consumer needs

　[B] consumers make purchases which are not based on their subconscious needs

　[C] consumers often fail to make rational purchases

　[D] consumers act unconsciously to maximize their gains and minimize their losses

4. Marketers mentioned in the last paragraph would be most interested in developing _____.

　[A] an equipment that consumers need to clean indoor air

　[B] a medicine that satisfies consumers' need to remove hair on the clothes

　[C] a pill that cures cancers successfully

　[D] a computer monitor that will emit no harmful radiation

5. In the author's opinion, _____.

　[A] emotional criteria do not maximize satisfaction

　[B] consumers cannot distinguish between rational and irrational purchases

　[C] there is no absolute distinction between rational and irrational purchases

　[D] few customers make purchases according to subjective criteria

【答案与解析】

【文章大意】

　　作者论述了对消费者理性和非理性购买动机的定义,理性与不理性在某些情况下很难区分。其实只要能够满足消费者心理需求的消费就是理智的消费。

1. 选[C]。推理判断题。文章首段第二句解释了 rationality 所涉及到的内容。该句指出 rationality 意指消费者是基于客观标准来选择目标产品,例如 size,weight,price 及 miles per gallon。省油属于客观标准,由此可知买省油的汽车是一种理智的消费方式,故答案为[C]。

2. 选[B]。推理判断题。第二段第四句指出旁观者眼中的非理性行为,从消费者本人的心理看来,也许就是理性的,下文以购买香水为例支持这一观点,因此对香水购买者来说,正因为他相信香水能够提升自身形象所以才会有购买这一行为,从这一点来看,其行为属于理性行为,而第五句更是支持了这一观点,故答案为[B]。

3. 选[B]。事实细节题。指示代词 this 提示答案应从前文刚刚谈及的内容中寻找。第三段最后一句指出消费者是有意识地将他们的所得最大化而将损失最小化;他们的行为不是来自于潜意识而是出自理性的优先选择,或是他们认为的最高利益。而依据第四段中 marketers who agree with this view 会及时发现并解决消费者遇到的问题而不是满足消费者的特殊需要可以判断出,this view 指的就是消费者的行为不是来自于潜意识而是出自理性的优先选择,或是他们认为的最高利益,故答案为[B]。

4. 选[D]。推理判断题。第四段最后一句指出商人不是通过满足消费者的需求,而是通过试图发现及解决消费者遇到的问题来取得市场上的成功,[A]、[B]、[C]都是消费者的需求,所以不太可能是商人感兴趣的,只有[D]是现在市场上已有的,但是消费者对它还有不满意之处,而这也是文中商人有兴趣生产的东西。

5. 选[C]。观点态度题。通读文章可知,作者的观点是理性和非理性消费是相对于消费者而言的,只要能够满足消费者的心理需要,那便是理智消费,也就是第二段最后一句 the distinction between rational and emotional motives does not appear to be warranted(区分理性动机和感性动机的标志并不是固定不变的),选项[C]是其同义转述。

篇章阅读巅峰练习

Exercise 1

Passage One

Money-laundering has been one of the world's fastest growing industries over the past decade despite increasing efforts by the world's financial authorities to stamp it out. Following is a simple guide to the world of money-laundering.

Money-laundering is the process by which money obtained by illegal means is given the appearance of legitimate income and returned into circulation. The word and the practice are widely believed to have been invented by the US *Mafia* (黑手党). As a means of mixing the dirty cash obtained from prostitution, gambling, gun-running, blackmail and its other wicked activities, so that both came out more or less clean, the Mafia bought up and operated large numbers of Laundromats. As good cash businesses they were a good means of providing the appearance of honest cash flow.

Various techniques can be employed as the means of money-laundering, but they essentially boil down to three stages. Step One: moving the money from the scene of the crime (A) to a remote location (B), ideally in another country, preferably a bank account, if possible one that is anonymous. Step Two: disguising the trail leading from A to B. Step Three: making the cash available to the criminals, along with a plausible explanation of how it came legally into their possession.

Apart from harming the economies that it feeds off, the money-laundering industry is essential to organized crime. As the head of the UN's crime fighting wing Pino Arlacchi remarked, organized crime "brutalizes society and diminishes respect for the values like honesty and cooperation upon which successful societies are based". Or as a senior US official said in 1999, "money-laundering may look like a polite form of white-collar crime, but it is the companion of brutality, deceit and corruption."

The liberalization of markets around the world and deregulation of exchange controls are regarded as the chief causes of the rapid expansion of money-laundering over the past decade. Together they have opened up many more channels for laundering dirty money and provided more opportunities to hide its origins. UN officials believe the most important single measure in eliminating money laundering is the ending of bank secrecy.

52. We know from the passage that money-laundering _____.
    [A] has almost been stamped out by the world's financial authorities
    [B] has greatly promoted the development of the world's industries
    [C] only has a ten-year history but has grown rapidly
    [D] has expanded rapidly over the past decade

53. Which of the following is closest in meaning to the phrase "stamp it out" in the first paragraph?
    [A] To put an end to it completely.　　　　[B] To mark a sign by pressing on it.
    [C] To announce it illegal.　　　　　　　 [D] To do harm to it.

54. The reason why the Mafia bought up and ran substantial Laundromats is that _____.
    [A] the Mafia can carry out large numbers of illegal transactions in them
    [B] the Mafia has many wicked activities like prostitution and gambling in them
    [C] the Laundromats can give the dirty cash the appearance of legitimate income
    [D] the Laundromat is such a profit-making industry that has attracted the Mafia

55. In money-laundering, money would be moved from the scene of the crime to _____.
    [A] the financial authorities　　　　　　 [B] the circulation fields
    [C] Laundromats operated by the Mafia　　[D] anonymous bank account in another country

56. With the worldwide liberalization of markets, money-laundering has expanded rapidly by _____.

   [A] deregulating the exchange controls

   [B] buying and operating more Laundromats

   [C] having more channels to launder dirty money

   [D] tightening the bank secrecy rules

Passage Two

Ronald Coase, winner of the 1991 Nobel Prize for economics, was not exactly waiting by the telephone. Neither the Nobel committee nor the University of Chicago, where Mr. Coase is *emeritus* (退休的) professor, knew where he was on October 15, 1991, when the award was announced. A Reuters correspondent tracked him down in Tunisia the next day, and told him the honor and the $1 million that goes with it.

Mr. Coase is a typical prizewinner in one way: his best work published decades ago. He is old-fashioned in other ways, too. He published sparingly, never for its own sake, always scoring hits; he wrote in plain English; he does not have a Ph. D. . Yet he is also thoroughly modern: his best papers have had more influence in the past ten years than ever before.

Mr. Coase published *The Nature of the Firm* in 1937. It asked, why do entrepreneurs, managers and workers choose to tie themselves together in that way, rather than buying and selling each other's services in a spot market? The answer is that transactions are costly. Contractual relationships evolve to reduce these costs. So think of the firm not as a collection of people and machines but as a web of mutually advantageous contracts. More than 50 years later, modern theorists do justify that.

The Problem of Social Cost, published in 1960, asked, how can conflicts over the use of resources be solved? Mr. Coase considered the case of a locomotive whose sparks might set fire to a farmer's field. Common sense and e-conomists before Mr. Coase, believed that in such cases the allocation of resources would be decided by the law — i. e. by the distribution of property rights. If the train-operator is obliged not to set fire to the field, he will spend money to reduce the emission of sparks; otherwise, not.

Mr. Coase said this need not to be so. As long as the property rights can be bought and sold, resources will be used in exactly the same way regardless of how they are initially distributed. For instance, suppose farmers had the right to stop spark-emitting trains crossing their land: train-operators would simply pay them for permission to pass through.

In practice, as Mr. Coase realized, the scope for such arrangements is limited by transaction costs. But the basic insight — that markets in property rights reduce the scope for government intervention to improve, or even after, the allocation of resources — inspired a literature that, in turn, fueled the worldwide drive to deregulation during 1980s.

57. What can be inferred about Ronald Coase from the passage?

   [A] He is a person who is enthusiastic about traveling.

   [B] He is not wild about getting Nobel Prize.

   [C] He likes to simplify the complicated problems.

   [D] He has ideas different from all the other economists.

58. What does "a typical prizewinner" (Line 1, Para. 2) want to convey?

   [A] The one who gets the Nobel Prize usually has ideas different from others.

   [B] The one who gets the Nobel Prize usually is a knowledgeable person.

   [C] The one who gets the Nobel Prize finally usually needs to wait many years.

   [D] The one who gets the Nobel Prize usually doesn't pay too much attention to it.

59. As explained in *The Nature of the Firm*, Mr. Coase recommended _____ as a way of tying each other.

   [A] contract   [B] transaction

   [C] agreement   [D] recognizance

60. What will happen when the train-operators paid for permission to pass through the farmers' land, according to the passage?

   [A] The farmers will not have the right to use the land.

   [B] The train-operators have the right to set fire to the land.

   [C] The farmers lost the right to stop the train pass through their land.

[D] The farmers cannot promise others to pass through their land.

61. Which of the following may be the best title for the passage?

[A] The Foreknowledge of Ronald Coase

[B] 1991 Economics Nobel Winner

[C] A Typical Noble Prize Winner

[D] Theories Proposed by Ronald Coase

Exercise 2

Passage One

Western tattooists work with a special electrical instrument, something like a dentist's drill. It holds a number of very fine needles which, for the purpose of reproducing the approved drawing, are dipped in black ink. When the current is switched on, and the instrument passed rapidly over the outline, the action of the needles drives the ink into the skin. The tattooist is constantly wiping away excess ink as he works. This is where skill is so important, for the speed of the instrument means that he must work rapidly over lines which are almost permanently covered over.

The basic drawing then has to be colored in, using the same method but with non-poisonous paint now replacing the ink. The average tattoo contains four or five colors, each injected with a separate instrument. How many needles are used each time will depend on the area to be covered, but it is possible to use as many as ten or twelve, giving up to 300 injections a minute. Filling in is a lengthier process than outlining, and since most people find half an hour under the needles quite enough, a major tattoo can take a number of visits to complete. Every visit will leave the skin sore and stinging, and to prevent infection on the area is finally treated with an *antiseptic*(消毒的，抗菌的) cream and covered with a dressing. After a few days it finally heals over, leaving the new tattoo clearly visible under the skin.

And there it stays, for, as those who get tattooed and think better of it soon discover that getting rid of the tattoo is a far more difficult business than getting it. The tattooist is powerless to undo what he has done and can only refer unhappy customers to their doctors who, no matter how sympathetic, are able to offer little encouragement. Removing a tattoo, if it can be done at all, has to be by one of two methods, neither of them pleasant or even completely satisfactory. The first is by surgery and skin replacement, an operation which leaves permanent marks. The other possibility is to re-tattoo over the offending design with a special acid-based substance which absorbs the colors as it goes. This is a painful and lengthy process which, though less expensive than private surgery, is still quite costly.

It is such a common event that responsible tattooists refuse to work on areas which cannot normally be covered up. "The trouble is that most people don't think about it until it's too late," says one tattooist who had his own hands tattooed some years ago, and freely admits to regretting it. "I realize now that it looks in bad taste."

52. What is the effect of using fine needles in the process of tattoo?

[A] It can drive the ink into the skin.

[B] It can draw paints.

[C] It can cure disease.

[D] It can reproduce the approved drawing.

53. Before a large scale tattoo is finished, the customer may _____.

[A] have to go to the tattooist several times

[B] pay for the work in several times

[C] be injected with four or five instruments

[D] be operated for several times

54. It's known from the passage that a dressing is used to _____.

[A] make colors more distinct

[B] cover the outline of tattoo

[C] prevent the skin from infection

[D] keep warm for the customers

55. Why don't doctors offer encouragement to the customers who want to get rid of the tattoo?

[A] Because doctors are not sympathetic.

[B] Because customers will suffer a lot.

[C] Because no methods are entirely successful.

[D] Because doctors are not willing to have operations on them.

56. What is the author's attitude toward tattoo?

[A] Critical.

[B] Indifferent.

[C] Positive.

[D] Neutral.

Passage Two

These are the words written around the Olympic flame, burning in the latest ultra-modern stadium, the latest *venue*（比赛地点）of one of the most outstanding spectacles in the world. Each day thousands in their seats in the stadium and millions in their chairs at home watch excitedly as men and women from almost every nation in the world attempt to run faster, jump higher and longer, lift heavier and heavier weights and throw further and further. They are all competing for that ultimate prize: an Olympic gold medal. Some only just fail by hundredths of a second or fractions of millimeter but are content with a silver or bronze. Most are extremely happy just to be there and in so doing agree with the other motto of the Games which says that it is not winning that is important but taking part.

However, as the Olympics reach the end of the 20th century and look forward to the 21st, it seems as if this second ideal is no longer a realistic one for our competitive world. Much as we are happy to see the medals won, especially if they are won by our *compatriots*（同胞）being broken. We all want to witness that moment in history when something is achieved for the very first time. Although we pretend that the Olympics are still the last preserves of the amateur ideal, we know that to be a world-class athlete now is a full-time activity. It is not only the intensive training given to potential champions by the super-powers, but many athletes are paid now. Since 1982, the International Olympic Committee has allowed money from appearances and advertising to be kept for the competitor until he or she retires and even used for training purposes and expenses.

Are we pushing the athletes too hard? Can we expect the athlete to live to the ideal of the Games without the help of the science and technology? Indeed, how much further can the human body go? Records continue to be broken but increasingly by smaller and smaller margins. Will we reach the stage of seeing someone run the fastest, jump the highest and throw the furthest that it is humanly possible to do? Is it too late to go back to the pure ideals of the ancient Games or is it just another part of our life that is increasingly dominated by technology?

57. It is implied in the passage that competitors at the Olympics is willing to _____.
    [A] entertain the spectators in the stadium and at home
    [B] perform better than anyone else does in the field
    [C] come as close as possible to the fastest time
    [D] do more than just participate

58. According to the passage, the second part of the motto of the Olympic Games _____.
    [A] will be dropped in the 21st century   [B] does not satisfy the general public
    [C] has been overtaken by the first motto   [D] is too idealistic

59. Non-competitors desire most strongly to see _____.
    [A] their countrymen and women win gold medals   [B] a world record being broken
    [C] athletes perform to the best of their ability   [D] an Olympic record being broken

60. The International Olympic Committee _____.
    [A] prevents amateurs from entering the Games
    [B] makes athletes pay to enter the Games
    [C] lets athletes be paid to enter the Games
    [D] lets athletes use the money earned from commercials

61. What can we infer from the last paragraph?
    [A] It will become more difficult to break records.
    [B] The Olympic ideals will be followed.
    [C] We must force athletes to train harder.
    [D] Athletes can continue to break records without resorting to drugs or technology.

答案与解析

Exercise 1

Passage One

【文章大意】
    洗钱业的迅速发展产生很多负面影响。本文首先围绕洗钱业的定义、洗钱的方法及洗钱的不良后果展开论述，最后指出了导致洗钱业发展迅速的原因及相应的解决办法。

52. 选[D]。事实细节题。由文章第一段第一句"Money laundering has been one of the world's fastest growing in-

dustries over the past decade…"可知,过去十年中,洗钱业的发展极为迅速,[D] 选项内容与原文一致。

53. 选[A]。语义理解题。由下文可知,money-laundering 是一种非法活动,那么它们当然是 the world's financial authorities(世界金融组织)这种正义性的组织所要打击消灭的对象,由此可以推断出 stamp out 应该能表达出"打击,消灭"这一含义,[A] 符合要求,为本题答案。stamp … out 意为"根除…"。

54. 选[C]。事实细节题。文章第二段最后一句指出 As good cash business …,其中的 they 指代的即是上句中的 Laundromats,由此可知黑手党购置并经营大量的自动洗衣店是因为它们可以为赃款披上合法收入的外衣,故答案为[C]。

55. 选[D]。事实细节题。文章第三段第二句指出 …moving the money from the scene of the crime (A) to a remote location (B),ideally in another country,preferably a bank account,if possible one that is anonymous,即把钱从犯罪现场(A)转移到一个遥远的地方(B),最理想的是转移到另一个国家,最好存入一个银行账户,尽可能存入匿名账户,故答案为[D]。

56. 选[C]。事实细节题。文章最后一段指出全球市场的自由化和外汇管制的放松是洗钱业迅速发展的主要原因,而洗钱业迅速发展的表现就是洗钱活动有了更多的渠道及有更多的机会隐藏赃款来源,故答案为[C]。

Passage Two

【文章大意】

本文是一篇人物报道。本文主要讲述了 1991 年诺贝尔经济学奖获得者 Ranald Coase 获奖时的情形,同时也介绍了其代表作及代表作的主要内容,还有他的贡献。在 Ranald Coase 获奖的时候,他的学校及诺贝尔委员会根本不知道他在哪里,是一个记者找到他告诉了他这个消息。和其他诺贝尔经济学奖获得者一样,Ranald Coase 的最佳作品是几十年前出版的。

57. 选[B]。篇首处常考。文章首段提到 Ronald Coase 在诺贝尔奖颁奖当天并没有守在电话旁等待消息,而是去了 Tunisia(突尼斯),并且他还是通过路透社记者得知获奖这一消息的,由此可推断 Ronald Coase 对获得诺贝尔奖一事并不是太热衷,故答案为[B]。

58. 选[C]。特殊标点处常考。第二段首句中冒号后面的内容是对前面内容的解释说明。his best work published decades ago 表明 Mr. Coase 获得诺贝尔奖的时间比获奖作品的发表时间晚了好几十年,由此可知,typical prize-winner 想要表达的是通常最终获得诺贝尔奖的人都要等待很长时间,故答案为[C]。

59. 选[A]。观点处常考。文章第三段只是说明企业并不是通过在现货市场交易彼此的服务从而将企业家、管理人员及工作人员联系在一起的,但没有具体指出 in that way 指的是哪种方式,通过本段倒数第二三句可知,in that way 指的就是以 contract(合同)的方式将企业家、管理人员及工作人员联系在一起,故答案为[A]。

60. 选[C]。举例处常考。文章第五段指出 the train-operators 要想通过农民的土地还有另一种方法,即 the train-operators 付钱购买通过农民土地的权利。Mr. Coase 举出此例是为了说明只要财产权能够被买卖,不管资源最初是如何分配的,它们都可以一样的被使用。由此可知,如果 the train-operators 为通过农民的土地付钱,即:the train-operators 购买了通过农民土地的权利,那么农民们就无权再阻止火车通过它们的土地了,故答案为[C]。

61. 选[B]。观点处常考。本文主要讲 1991 年诺贝尔经济学奖获得者 Ranald Coase 获奖时的状况和特征,以及他的代表作及其主要内容和他的贡献,故答案为[B]。文中虽然有提到 50 多年后,现代的理论家才意识到 Ronald Coase 将公司看成是一个互利的合同关系网的正确性,但是这只是文章的一部分,不足以概括全文,故[A] 错;[C] 也只是文章的一部分,文章并没有全面论述 Ronald Coase 的理论,故[D] 错。

Exercise 2

Passage One

【文章大意】

纹身并不是个陌生的话题,但并非所有的人都尝试过这种经历,这篇文章便讲述了有关纹身方面的内容。作者介绍了纹身时所用的仪器、纹身的过程(首先纹出图案的轮廓,然后上色,最后进行消毒处理)。要想美就得付出代价,纹身并不是件令人愉快的事。同时在纹身之前也得考虑好,因为去掉纹身更是件痛苦且困难的事情。作者也介绍了两种去纹身的办法,但都不能完全令人满意且耗时、费钱。

52. 选[D]。事实细节题。文章首段第二句指出特殊的电子器具上带有细小针头是为了能够 reproducing the approved drawing(画出既定图案),而这也是 fine needles 的作用,故答案为[D]。

53. 选[A]。事实细节题。文章第二段第四句指出填充颜色所需时间比打轮廓要长,并且因为大多数人只能忍受半个小时的针扎过程,所以 a major tattoo can take a number of visits to complete(一个大的纹身需要多次才能完成),这就意味着一个大面积的纹身需要纹身着多次去纹身师那里进行纹身,故答案为[A]。

54. 选[C]。事实细节题。文章第二段倒数第二句中的不定式短语 to prevent infection 虽然作分句的主语,但同样也表明它是 treated with an antiseptic cream and covered with a dressing 的目的,由此可知 a dressing 在纹身过程中的作用就是防止纹过身的皮肤发生感染,答案为[C]。

55. 选[C]。事实细节题。由第三段第三句"Removing a tattoo, if it can be done at all, has to be by one of two methods, neither of them pleasant or even completely satisfactory"可知,除去纹身是件很困难的事,即便能有一两种办法,也都不能令人满意,而且十分痛苦,选项[C]是原文"... neither of them pleasant or even completely satisfactory"的同义转述。

56. 选[D]。观点态度题。本文主要讲述了纹身方面的问题。第一、二段主要介绍了纹身的过程,第三段主要说明纹身不容易消除,第四段则主要说明一个纹身师对纹身的看法。整篇文章中作者并没有对是否应该纹身及纹身的好坏进行评论,他只是在客观的陈述事实,由此可推断作者对纹身采取中立态度,故答案为[D]。

Passage Two

【文章大意】

相信大家都知道奥林匹克运动会上有这样一句座右铭——重在参与。然而"重在参与"这一观点在目前充满竞争的社会已经不太现实了。奥运会在不断地变化着,起先是为业余选手而设的,但现在成了专业选手竞技的场所。在历届的奥运会中,运动员打破了一个又一个世界记录,创造了无数的奇迹。人体的极限究竟有多大?考虑到这个问题,人们也便意识到打破世界记录将会越来越困难。

57. 选[D]。推理判断题。第一段末句指出绝大多数运动员赞成重在参与,而第二段首句却提到在 20、21 世纪之交的时候,it seems as if this second ideal is no longer a realistic one for our competitive world(重在参与的精神在这个竞争的社会已经变得不切实际了)。由此可推断出运动员们参加奥运会想要做的不仅仅只是参与,他们还要想方设法赢得比赛,故答案为[D]。

58. 选[D]。事实细节题。第二段首句指出 ... it seems as if this second ideal is no longer a realistic one for our competitive world(重在参与的精神在这个竞争的社会已经变得不切实际了),换句话说就是 the second ideal 太理想化了,故答案为[D]。

59. 选[A]。事实细节题。题干中的 non-competitors(非竞争者)指的就是观看运动员比赛的人。第二段第二句中的"Much as we are happy to see the models won, especially if they are won by our compatriots being broken"表明他们最希望看到的就是自己的同胞赢得奖牌,[A]中的 their countrymen and women 为 compatriots(同胞)的同义转述。

60. 选[D]。事实细节题。第二段末句指出自 1982 年以来,国际奥委会允许参赛者在退休之前取得出场费和广告费,甚至允许他们将这些费用用以训练及训练费用开支,故答案为[D]。选[C]的同学可能将出场费简单理解为参加比赛获得的出场费,但是出场费并不仅仅局限于此,它也有可能是运动员参加商业活动所获得的报酬,故不选[C]。

61. 选[A]。推理判断题。由最后一段中的 Records continue to be broken but increasingly by smaller and smaller margins(运动员们不断的打破记录,但是新旧记录之间的差距却越来越小)可以推断出以后运动员们要打破记录将会越来越难,故答案为[A]。

阅读理解巅峰练习

Test 1

Part II Reading Comprehension（Skimming and Scanning）（15 minutes）

Is College Really Worth the Money?

The Real World

More and more college students are mortgaging their futures to meet soaring tuition costs and other college expenses. They're facing a one-two punch at graduation: hefty student loans and smothering credit card debt — not to mention a job market that, for now anyway, is dismal.

"We are forcing our children to make a choice between two evils," says Elizabeth Warren, a Harvard Law professor and expert on bankruptcy. "Skip college and face a life of diminished opportunity, or go to college and face a life shackled by debt."

Don't think this Catch-22 only traps those shelling out big bucks for schools like Harvard or Yale. The eight in ten paying for a public college or university are also in for sticker shock. For the past two decades, tuition at these schools has zoomed far above inflation. Last year, the annual tuition and fees at four-year public colleges averaged $4,081 (room and board added another $5,582). That was a leap from the previous year of 9.6 percent — six times the rate of inflation, then less than 2 percent. This year, the increase at certain schools was even more dramatic. Tuition at the University of Virginia and the University of California rose nearly 30 percent, and at the University of Arizona it jumped by 40 percent.

For some time, colleges have insisted their steep tuition hikes are needed to pay for cutting-edge technologies, faculty and administration salaries, and rising health care costs. Now there's a new *culprit*（肇事者）: shrinking state support. Caught in a severe budget crunch, many states have sharply scaled back their funding for higher education.

One of those states is California, and Janet Burrell's family is feeling the pain. A bookkeeper in Torrance, Burrell has a daughter at the University of California at Davis. Meanwhile, her sons attend two-year colleges because Burrell can't afford to have all of them in four-year schools at once.

Meanwhile, even with tuition hikes, California's community colleges are so strapped for cash they dropped thousands of classes last spring. The result: 54,000 fewer students.

Collapsing Investments

Many families thought they had a surefire plan: Even if tuition kept skyrocketing, they had invested enough money along the way to meet the costs. Then a funny thing happened on the way to Wall Street. Those investments collapsed with the stock market. Among the losers last year: the wildly popular "529" plans — federal tax-exempt college savings plans offered by individual states, which have attracted billions from families around the country. "We hear from many parents that what they had set aside declined in value so much that they now don't have enough to see their students through," says Penn State financial aid director Anna Griswold, who witnessed a 10 percent increase in loan applications last year. Even with a market that may be slowly recovering, it will take time, perhaps several years, for people to recoup their losses.

Nadine Sayegh is among those who didn't have the luxury of waiting for her college nest egg to grow back. Her father had invested money toward her tuition, but a large chunk of it vanished when stocks went south. Nadine was then only partway through college. By graduation, she had taken out at least $10,000 in loans, and her mother had borrowed even more on her behalf. Now 22, Nadine is attending law school, having signed for yet more loans to pay for that. "There wasn't any way to do it differently," she says, "and I'm not happy about it. I've sat down and calculated how long it will take me to pay off everything. I'll be 35 years old. " That's if she's very lucky: Nadine based her calculation on landing a job right out of law school that will pay her at least $120,000 a year.

The American Council on Education has its own calculation that shows how students are more and more dependent on loans. In just five years, from 1995 to 2000, the median loan debt at public institutions rose from $10,342 to $15,375. Most of this comes from federal loans, which Congress made more tempting in 1992 by expanding eligibility (home equity no longer counts against your assets) and raising loan limits (a dependent undergraduate can now borrow up to $23,000 from the federal government).

But students aren't stopping there. The College Board estimates that they also borrowed $4.5 billion from private lenders in the 2000-2001 academic year, up from $1.5 billion just five years earlier.

For lots of students, the worst of it isn't even the weight of those direct student loans. It's what they rack up on all those plastic cards in their wallets. As of two years ago, according to a study by lender Nellie Mae, more than eight out of ten undergrads had their own credit cards, with the typical student carrying four. That's no big surprise, given the in-your-face marketing by credit card companies, which set up tables on campus to entice students to sign up. Some colleges ban or restrict this *hawking* (兜售), but others give it a boost. You know those credit cards *emblazoned* (用…装饰) with a school's picture or its logo? For sanctioning such a card — a must-have for some students — a college department or association gets payments from the issuer. Meanwhile, from freshman year to graduation, according to the Nellie Mae study, students triple the number of credit cards they own and double their debt on them. As of 2001, they were in the hole an average $2,327.

A Wise Choice?

One day, Moyer sat down with his mother, Janne O'Donnell, to talk about his goal of going to law school. Don't count on it, O'Donnell told him. She couldn't afford the cost and Moyer doubted he could get a loan, given how much he owed already. "He said he felt like a failure," O'Donnell recalls. "He didn't know how he had gotten into such a mess. "

To be sure, suicides are exceedingly rare. But despair is common — and it sometimes leads students to rethink whether college was worth it. In fact, there are quite a few jobs that don't require a college degree, yet pay fairly well. On average, though, college graduates can expect to earn 80 percent more than those with only a high school diploma. Also, all but two of the 50 highest paying jobs (the exceptions being air traffic controllers and nuclear power reactor operators) require a four-year college degree. So foregoing a college education is often not a wise choice.

Merit Mikhail, who graduated last June from the University of California, Riverside, is glad she borrowed to get through school. But she left Riverside owing $20,000 in student loans and another $7,000 in credit card debt. Now in law school, Merit hopes to become a public-interest attorney, yet she may have to postpone that goal — which bothers her. To handle her debt, she'll probably need to start with a more lucrative legal job.

Like so many other students, Mikhail took out her loans on a kind of blind faith that she could deal with the consequences. "You say to yourself, 'I have to go into debt to make it work, and whatever it takes later, I'll manage.'" Later has now arrived, and Mikhail is finding out the true cost of her college degree.

1. Many college students have to undertake college tuition with a large amount of money, but their future is full of hope.

2. Last year, the increased rate of annual tuition and fees at four-year public colleges far exceeded the rate of inflation.

3. That Burrell's son has to attend two-year colleges is to some extent due to California's shrinking state support to higher education.

4. The decrease of students in California's community colleges put these colleges on the verge of bankruptcy.

5. Many parents can't rely on their previous investment to support their children's college tuition and fees, because _____ , according to Anna Griswold.

6. It will take Nadine _____ to pay off her loans if everything is advantageous to her.

7. Credit cards companies take _____ strategy to entice students to sign up for credit cards.

8. The article suggests that continuing a college education is _____ for students even though they are faced with financial problems.

9. According to the passage, after paying off her debt, Merit may pursue her goal to be _____ .

10. Mikhail applied for her loans on a kind of _____ that she could satisfy a debt.

Part IV Reading Comprehension (Reading in Depth) (25 minutes)
Section A

The dog, called Prince, was an intelligent animal and a slave to Williams. From morning till night, when Williams was at home, Prince never left his sight, practically ignoring all other members of the family. The dog had a number of clearly defined duties, for which Williams had patiently trained him and, like the good pupil he was, Prince lived for the chance to demonstrate his abilities.

When Williams wanted to put on his boots, he would murmur "Boots" and within seconds the dog would drop them at his feet. At nine every morning, Prince ran off to the general store in the village, returning shortly not only with Williams' daily paper but with a half ounce packet of Williams' favorite tobacco, John Rhiney's Mixed. A gun-dog by breed, Prince possessed a large soft mouth specially evolved for the safe carrying of hunted creatures, so the paper and the tobacco came to no harm, never even showing a tooth mark.

Williams was a railwayman, an engine driver, and he wore a blue uniform which smelled of oil and oil fuel. He had to work at odd times —"days", "late days" or "nights". Over the years Prince got to know these periods of work and rest, knew when his master would leave the house and return, and the dog did not waste this knowledge. If Williams overslept, as he often did, Prince barked at the bedroom door until he woke, much to the annoyance of the family. On his return, Williams' slippers were brought to him, the paper and tobacco too if previously undelivered.

A curious thing happened to Williams during the snow and ice of last winter. One evening he slipped and fell on the icy pavement somewhere between the village and his home. He was so badly shaken that he stayed in bed for three days; and not until he got up and dressed again did he discover that he had lost his wallet containing over fifty pounds. The house was turned upside down in the search, but the wallet was not found. However, two days later — that was five days after the fall — Prince dropped the wallet into Williams' hand. Very muddy, stained and wet through, the little case still contained fifty-three pounds, Williams' driving license and a few other papers. Where the dog had found it no one could tell, but found it he had and recognized it probably by the faint oily smell on the worn leather.

47. Prince could take back the paper and the tobacco safely because he had _____.

_____

48. The dog barked to remind Williams to get up for work, which made Williams' family feel _____.

_____

49. Williams did not realize his loss for several days because he had no occasion to _____.

_____

50. Williams got his wallet back on _____ after he slipped.

_____

51. What helped the dog find the wallet probably?

_____

Section B

Passage One

What is sports violence? The distinction between unacceptable viciousness and a game's normal *rough-and-tumble* (混战) is impossible to make, or so the argument runs. This position may appeal to our inclination for legalism, but the truth is most of us know quite well when an act of needless savagery has been committed, and sports are little different from countless other activities of life. The distinction is as apparent as that between a deliberately aimed blow and the arm failing of losing his balance. When a player balls his hand into a fist, when he drives his helmet into an unsuspecting opponent in short, when he crosses the boundary between playing hard and playing to hurt — he can only intend an act of violence.

Admittedly, rough acts in sports are difficult to police. But here, too, we find reflected the conditions of everyday life. Ambiguities in the law, confusion at the scene, and the reluctance of witnesses cloud almost any routine assault case. Such uncertainties, however, have not prevented society from arresting people who strike their fellow citizens on the street.

Perhaps our troubles stem not from the games we play but rather from how we play them. The 1979 meeting be-

tween hockey(曲棍球)stars from the Soviet Union and the National Hockey League provided a direct test of two approaches to sport — the emphasis on skill, grace, and *finesse*(技巧)by the Russians and the stress on brutality and violence by the NHL. In a startling upset, the Russians embarrassed their rough-playing opponents and exploded a long-standing myth: that success in certain sports requires excessive violence.

Violence apologists cite two additional arguments. First, they say, sports always have been rough; today things are no different. But arguments in America's Old West were settled on Main Street with six guns, and early cave-dwellers chose their women with a club. Civilizing influences ended those practices; yet we are told sports violence should be tolerated. The second contention is that athletes accept risk as part of the game, and, in the case of professionals, are paid handsomely to do so. But can anyone seriously argue that being an athlete should require the acceptance of unnecessary physical abuse? And, exaggerated as it may seem, the pay of professional athletes presumably reflects their abilities, not a payment against combat injuries.

"Clearly we are in deep trouble,"says perplexed former football player AL DeRogatis. "But how and why has it gotten so bad?"

52. According to the author, the distinction between violent acts and non-violent ones in sports is _____.

[A] impossible to make [B] not very clear in any circumstances

[C] too obvious to escape observation [D] not very difficult to make if enough attention is paid to

53. A sports violence "apologist" probably thinks that _____.

[A] violence in sports is a rare occurrence [B] violence in sports is not necessary

[C] athletes are paid enough for their injuries [D] professional athletes enjoy violence

54. In the last paragraph the author indicates that _____.

[A] nothing can be done about violence in sports

[B] football players are concerned about violence in sports

[C] violence in sports is worse now than it ever was

[D] athletes are confused about what should be permitted in sports

55. According to the author, _____.

[A] the personalities of athletes produce violent confrontations

[B] athletes should not have to accept unnecessary physical abuse

[C] athletes salaries are already too high

[D] athletes need higher salaries to compensate for their injuries

56. In the author's opinion _____.

[A] violence in sports is illegal [B] finesse is more important than aggression

[C] athletes should not be injured in sports [D] violence in sports is not necessary

Passage Two

A metaphor is a poetic device that deals with comparison. It compares similar qualities of two dissimilar objects. With a simple metaphor, one object becomes the other: My love is a rose. Although this does not sound like a particularly rich image, a metaphor can communicate so much about a particular image that poets utilize them more than any other type of figurative language. The reason for this is that poets compose their poetry to express what they are experiencing emotionally at that moment. Consequently, what the poet imagines love to be may or may not be our perception of love. Therefore, the poet's job is to enable us to experience it, to feel it the same way that the poet does. We should be able to nod in agreement and say, "Yes, that's it! I understand precisely where this guy is coming from. "

Let's analyze this remarkably unsophisticated metaphor concerning love and the rose to see what it offers. Because the poet utilizes a comparison with a rose, first we must examine the characteristics of that flower. A rose is spectacular in its beauty, its petals are velvety soft, and its aroma is wonderfully soothing and pleasing. It's possible to say that a rose is actually a veritable feast to the senses: the visual, the tactile and the aural, (more commonly known as the senses of sight, touch and sound). The rose's appearance seems to border on perfection, each petal seemingly symmetrical in form. Isn't this the way one's love should be? A loved one should be a delight to one's senses and seem perfect. However, there is another dimension added to the comparison by using a rose. Roses have thorns. This is the comprehensive image the poet wants to communicate; otherwise he would have presented a daisy or a mum to his audience as the ultimate representation of love. But he didn't, instead he wanted to convey the idea that roses can be treacherous.

So can love, the metaphor tells us. When one reaches out with absolute trust to touch the object of his or her affection, ouch, a thorn can cause great harm! Be careful, the metaphor admonishes: love is a feast to the senses, but it can overwhelm us, and it can also hurt us. It can prick us and cause acute suffering. This is the poet's perception of love. This is his admonition. What is the point? Just this: it took almost fourteen sentences to clarify what a simple metaphor communicates in only five words! That is the artistry and the joy of the simple metaphor.

57. The main idea of this passage is that _____.
　[A] poetic devices are necessary for poets
　[B] poetry must never cater to the senses
　[C] the metaphor always uses words that create one specific image
　[D] the metaphor is a great poetic device

58. It can be inferred that a metaphor is _____.
　[A] a type of figurative language　　　　[B] the only poetic device
　[C] not precise enough　　　　　　　　　[D] a type of flower in a poem

59. According to the passage, thorns _____.
　[A] protect the rose from harm　　　　　　[B] reduce the ability to love another
　[C] add a new element to the image of love　[D] are just more images to compare to a love

60. The author uses the example of the rose to demonstrate _____.
　[A] that love has two sides to it
　[B] its efficiency for representing the duality of love
　[C] how it can show the beauty of love
　[D] that love is not just beauty but also contains thorns

61. The author believes that a metaphor's main strength is its _____.
　[A] precision　　　　　　　　　　　　　　[B] enlightenment
　[C] efficiency　　　　　　　　　　　　　　[D] beauty

答案与解析

Part II

【文章大意】
　　越来越多的学生用他们的前途作抵押，来支付不断飙升的学杂费。然而，繁重的学生贷款以及信贷债务，再加上不景气的就业市场使得大学生们遭受重创。一方面，学费逐年上涨，州政府的资助却不断缩减，许多学生无法继续学业；另一方面，家长们纷纷将钱投资到孩子的学费上，却发现他们的投资因股票市场而失败。摆在眼前的现实让人们不得不开始思考：上大学到底值不值？

1.【定位】根据题目中的关键信息 college students，undertake，future 以及出题顺序可将搜索范围定位在第一个小标题 The Real World 下。
　【解析】[N]。通过阅读小标题下的内容可以发现题目出处为小标题 The Real World 下第一段。由该段第二句中的 a job market that, for now anyway, is dismal 可知，大学生的前景不容乐观，题目中 but 后陈述的内容与原文矛盾，故答案为[N]。

2.【定位】根据题目中的关键信息 last year，rate，inflation 可将搜索范围定位在小标题 The Real World 下第三段第四五句。
　【解析】[Y]。第五句的主语 that 指代的是上句中所说的"去年四年制大学每年的学费高达$4,081"这一情况，由此可知第五句中的 That was a leap from the previous year of 9.6 percent 表明去年的学费增长率比前一年9.6％的增长率还要高，是 the rate of inflation 的6倍多，这就说明学费增长率比通货膨胀率要大的多，题目与原文事实相一致，故答案为[Y]。

3.【定位】根据题目中的关键信息 Burrell's son，two-year colleges，California 可将搜索范围定位在小标题 The Real World 下倒数第二段。
　【解析】[Y]。该段第一句中的 those states 指的是那些 scaled back their funding for higher education（逐渐减少高等教育投资）的州，由该句可知，California 也在减少高等教育投资。而该段举出 Burrell 因负担不起两个孩子的学费,他的儿子只能读两年制大学的例子就是为了证明 California 减少对高等教育投资所带来的问题,题目是对原文正确的推断,故答案为[Y]。

4.【定位】根据题目中的关键信息 California's community colleges 在可将搜索范围定位在小标题 The Real World 下最后一段。

【解析】[NG]。该段指出一个事实:California's community colleges 去年因为资金问题不得不裁减上千个班级,导致生源减少了 54,000 人。但是并没有说生源的减少就会使这些学校濒临破产的境地,题目在原文中找不到依据,故答案为[NG]。

5.【定位】根据题目中的关键信息 investment,Anna Griswold 可将搜索范围定位在小标题 Collapsing Investments 下第二段倒数第二句。

【解析】what they had set aside declined in value。该句 so…that 句型中的 that 引导结果状语从句,由此可知造成"they now don't have enough to see their students through"的这一结果的原因就是 what they had set aside declined in value,题目中的主句与该句 that 引导的结果状语从句是同义表达。

6.【定位】根据题目中的关键信息 Nadine,pay off 可将搜索范围定位在小标题 Collapsing Investments 下第二段倒数一、二句。

【解析】13 years。结合倒数一二句可知,如果 Nadine 毕业时能够立即找到工作,且年薪为 12 万美元,那么她就可以在 35 岁时还清所有贷款,根据倒数第三句可知 Nadine 现在 22 岁,由此可知如果一切都顺利的话,Nadine 可以用 13 年时间还清贷款。

7.【定位】根据题目中的关键信息 credit card companies,entice,sign up 可将搜索范围定位在小标题 Collapsing Investments 第五段第四句。

【解析】in-your-face marketing。该句中 given 引导的条件状语从句说明了 more than eight out of ten undergrads had their own credit cards…并不奇怪的原因:信用卡公司采取 in-your-face marketing(面对面直销)的方式,在校园设立专柜诱使学生使用。

8.【定位】根据题目中的关键信息 college education 可将搜索范围定位在小标题 A Wise Choice?下第二段最后一句。

【解析】a wise choice。句首的 So 表明 foregoing a college education…是一种观点,前两句是在证明这一观点的正确性。通过该句可知,文章作者认为"放弃大学教育并不是明智之举",而继续大学教育则是十分明智的。

9.【定位】根据题目中的关键信息 Merit 可将搜索范围定位在小标题 A Wise Choice?下倒数第二段。

【解析】a public-interest attorney。该段最后两句指出,Merit 的目标是成为 a public-interest attorney,但是她现在必须推迟实现这一目标,因为她必须先从 a more lucrative legal job 开始以 handle her debt,由此可推知如果 Merit 还清了债务,她很可能会开始追求自己成为 a public-interest attorney 的目标。

10.【定位】根据题目中的关键信息 Mikhail 可将搜索范围定位在小标题 A Wise Choice?下最后一段。

【解析】blind faith。该段第一句指出 Mikhail 申请取得贷款时,对自己有一种 blind faith(盲信),认为她可以成功还清贷款,题目与该段第一句是同义表达。

Part IV

Section A

【文章大意】

本文主要讲述了一只名叫 Prince 的狗的一些优点。Prince 非常善解人意,在主人 Willams 要穿鞋时只要说声"Boots",Prince 就会帮他把鞋叼到他的跟前,每天早上 Prince 都会跑去商店为 Williams 买当日的报纸以及烟草;Prince 会在 Williams 睡过头时叫醒他,并在他出车归来时为他叼来拖鞋、报纸和烟;Prince 还曾帮助 Williams 找回了钱包。

47.【定位】根据题干中的关键信息 take back the paper and the tobacco 可将搜索范围定位在第一段最后一句。

【解析】a large soft mouth。该句中的连词 so 表明 the paper and the tobacco came to no harm,never even showing a tooth mark 是一种结果,导致该结果产生的因素是 Prince possessed a large soft mouth。题干中的 take back the paper and the tobacco safely 对应原文中的 the paper and the tobacco came to no harm,题干中的 had 对应 possessed,故答案为 a large soft mouth。

48.【定位】根据题干中的关键信息 get up,family 可将搜索范围定位在第二段倒数第二句。

【解析】annoyed / upset。该句指出如果 Williams 睡过了头,Prince 就会朝着他的卧室吠叫,直到他起床,但是它的吠叫却 much to the annoyance of the family(使 Williams 的家人烦恼)。题干中的系动词 feel 提示所填词应为形容词,所以应将原文中的 annoyance 改写为其形容词 annoyed 或 annoyed 的同义词 upset。

49.【定位】根据题干中的关键信息 his loss 可将搜索范围定位在最后一段。

【解析】feel in his pockets。题干中的 his loss 指的是 Williams 丢失钱包的事。该段指出 Williams 因滑倒摔得很严重,不得不在床上躺了 3 天。直到他 got up and dressed again(病好后穿衣服时),他才发现自己丢了钱包。由此可知,William 的钱包是放在他的衣服口袋中的。他事先不知道自己丢钱包是因为之前他卧病在床,没有机会(have no occasion)摸口袋(feel in his pockets)。

50.【定位】根据题干中的关键信息 got his wallet back 可将搜索范围定位在最后一段倒数第三句。

【解析】the sixth day。该句指出在 Williams 摔倒 5 天后 Prince dropped the wallet into Williams' hand。five days after the fall 指的即是 on the sixth day after the fall。题干中的介词 on 很明显是要求说明 Williams 在哪一天找回了他的 wallet,故答案为 the sixth day。

51.【定位】根据题干中的关键信息 helped the dog find the wallet 可将搜索范围定位在最后一段最后一句。

【解析】The faint oily smell on the worn leather。该句指出 Prince 或许是根据 the faint oily smell on the worn leather 而认出那就是 Williams 遗失的钱包。

Section B

Passage One

【文章大意】

本文主要讨论了球场上出现的暴力行为。文章首先提出了球场暴力的问题,指出什么是球场暴力,接下来分析了球场暴力的特点及其产生的根源。

52. 选[D]。事实细节题。文章首段第二句指出 The distinction between…, or so the argument runs(想要区分比赛中的恶意相向与正常的混战是不可能的事情),但该句句末的 or so the argument runs 表明这种观点并不是作者的观点,而该段第四句 The distinction is as apparent as that… 则清楚地表达了作者的观点,即如果加以注意,体育暴力与非暴力是不难区分的,故答案为[D]。

53. 选[C]。推理判断题。第四段主要指出了体育暴力拥护者的两种论据:体育一直以来都是粗暴的,现在也是如此;运动员们认为冒险是比赛的一部分,并且职业运动员会因其冒险精神而取得丰厚的报酬,[C] 与拥护者们的第二个论据相一致,故为答案。

54. 选[C]。事实细节题。文章结尾特别指出 AL DeRogaits 是一名 former football player(前足球运动员),它旨在表明 AL DeRogaits 对以前及现在的赛场上暴力情况的观点态度。整句话的时态为一般现在时,这就说明 AL DeRogaits 是在对现在赛场上的暴力进行评论,由反问句"how and why has it gotten so bad?"可以推断,现在的赛场暴力比以前的要严重,故答案为[C]。

55. 选[B]。事实细节题。第四段倒数第二句的反问句形式说明作者认为作为一名运动员不应该接受不必要的身体攻击,故答案为[B]。

56. 选[D]。观点态度题。文章第三段作者以苏联及美国曲棍球联盟之间的一次比赛为例,旨在说明取得成功并不一定需要暴力;第四段最后两句话及最后一段表明体育暴力是没有必要的,故答案为[D]。

Passage Two

【文章大意】

文章深入浅出地解释了比喻这种修辞手法的运用原理。第一段解释什么是比喻,以及诗人为什么要用比喻。第二、三段分析比喻的目的和功能。最后总结指出,一个简单的比喻能够产生强大的艺术感染力。

57. 选[D]。主旨大意题。经过对一个简单隐喻的详尽分析后,作者在篇尾对隐喻这种修辞手法的艺术感染力发出了由衷的赞叹,故答案为[D]。[A] 不言自明,无须详细地论证。[B] 显然与文中的例子及相关阐述相矛盾。[C] 不是隐喻定义的核心,也不是文章的主要内容。

58. 选[A]。事实细节题。由文章首段第四句 a particular image that poets utilize them more than any other type of figurative language(诗人使用它的频率比其他任何的修辞手法都要多)可知,隐喻是 figurative language(修辞手法)的一种,故答案为[A]。

59. 选[C]。推理判断题。本文探讨的是隐喻的创作手法,因此应着重理解本体和喻体在艺术作品中的意义,thorns 是 rose 形象的一部分,所以其喻体也应该是 rose 的喻体"爱"的一部分。因此[C] 正确。[A]、[B] 和[D] 不符合文中对 thorn 的寓意的解释,即"爱也可以具有危险性"。

60. 选[B]。观点态度题。文章末段倒数第二句指出 it took almost fourteen sentences to clarify what a simple meta-

phor…(隐喻能够只用5个词就表达出将近14个句子才能表达清楚的意思),这明显是在说明隐喻具有很高的语言效率,故答案为[B]。本文的目的不是就事论事,其目的应归结于隐喻对艺术创作手法的重要性这个主旨,而[A]、[C]和[D]均不符合。

61. 选[C]。推理判断题。文章末段最后总结性的两句即表达出作者对隐喻的效率的赞叹。

Test 2

Part II Reading Comprehension (Skimming and Scanning) (15 minutes)

Don't Waste Our Oceans

For too long, marine life has been largely open for the taking by anyone possessing the means to exploit it. Rapid advances in technology have meant that the ability and power of vessels and equipment used to exploit marine life now far outweigh nature's ability to maintain it. If left unchecked, this will have far-reaching consequences for the marine environment and for people who depend on it. Ocean life comes in an incredible array of shapes and sizes — from microscopic plankton to the largest of the great whales. Yet many species have been, or are being, driven towards extinction through devastating human impacts. The key threats facing our ocean creatures include:

Industrial Fishing

Many marine ecologists think that the biggest single threat to marine ecosystems today is over-fishing. Our appetite for fish is exceeding the oceans' ecological limits with devastating impacts on marine ecosystems. Scientists are warning that over-fishing results in profound changes in our oceans, perhaps changing them forever. Not to mention our dinner plates, which in future may only feature fish and chips as a rare and expensive delicacy.

• The Fish Don't Stand a Chance

More often than not, the fishing industry is given access to fish stocks before the impact of their fishing can be assessed, and regulation of the fishing industry is, in any case, woefully inadequate. The reality of modern fishing is that the industry is dominated by fishing vessels that far out-match nature's ability to replenish fish. Giant ships using state-of-the-alt fish-finding sonar can pinpoint schools of fish quickly and accurately. Ships are fitted out like giant floating factories — containing fish processing and packing plants, huge freezing systems, and powerful engines to drag enormous fishing gear through the ocean. Put simply: the fish don't stand a chance.

• Ocean Life Health Check

Populations of top predators, a key indicator of ecosystem health, are disappearing at a frightening rate, and 90 percent of the large fish that many of us love to eat, such as tuna, swordfish, marlin, cod, halibut, skate, and flounder — have been fished out since large-scale industrial fishing began in the 1950s. The depletion of these top predator species can cause a shift in entire oceans ecosystems where commercially valuable fish are replaced by smaller, plankton-feeding fish. This century may even see bumper crops of jellyfish replacing the fish consumed by humans.

These changes endanger the structure and functioning of marine ecosystems, and hence threaten the livelihoods of those dependent on the oceans, both now and in the future.

• Fisheries Collapse

The over-exploitation and mismanagement of fisheries has already led to some spectacular fisheries collapses. The cod fishery off Newfoundland, Canada collapsed in 1992, leading to the loss of some 40,000 jobs in the industry. The cod stocks in the North Sea and Baltic Sea are now heading the same way and are close to complete collapse. Instead of trying to find a long-term solution to these problems, the fishing industry's eyes are turning towards the Pacific — but this is not the answer. Politicians continue to ignore the advice of scientists about how these fisheries should be managed and the need to fish these threatened species in a sustainable way.

Bycatch

Many fisheries catch fish other than the ones that they target and in many cases these are simply thrown dead or dying back into the sea. In some trawl fisheries for shrimp, the discard may be 90 percent of the catch. Other fisheries kill seabirds, turtles and dolphins, sometimes in huge numbers.

Estimates vary as to how serious a problem bycatch is. Latest reports suggest that around eight percent of the total global catch is discarded, but previous estimates indicated that around a quarter of which might be thrown overboard. Simply no one knows how much of a problem this really is.

The incidental capture, or bycatch, of mammals, sea-birds, turtles, sharks and numerous other species is recognized to be a major problem in many parts of the world. This figure includes non-target species as well as targeted fish species that cannot be landed because they are, for instance, undersized. In short, anywhere between 6. 8 million and 27 million tonnes of fish could be discarded each year, reflecting the huge uncertainties in the data on this important issue. The scale of this mortality is such that bycatch in some fisheries may affect the structure and function of marine systems at the population, community and ecosystem levels. Bycatch is widely recognized as one of the most serious environmental impacts of modern commercial fisheries.

- **The Victims**

　　Different types of fishing practices result in different animal species being killed as bycatch: nets kill dolphins, porpoises and whales, longline fishing kills birds, and bottom trawling devastates marine ecosystems.

　　It has been estimated that a staggering 100 million sharks and rays are caught and discarded each year. Tuna fisheries, which in the past had high dolphin bycatch levels, are still responsible for the death of many sharks. An estimated 300,000 cetaceans (whales, dolphins and porpoises) also die as bycatch each year, because they are unable to escape out of nets. Birds dive for the bait planted on long fishing lines, swallow it (hook included) and are pulled underwater and drowned. Around 100, 000 albatrosses are killed by longline fisheries every year and because of this, many species are facing extinction.

　　Bottom trawling is a destructive way of "strip-mining" the ocean floor, harvesting the species that live there. As well as the target fish species, this also results in bycatch of commercially unattractive animals like starfish and sponges. A single pass of a trawl removes up to 20 percent of the seafloor fauna and flora. The fisheries with the highest levels of bycatch are shrimp fisheries: over 80 percent of a catch may consist of marine species other than the shrimp being targeted.

- **Technology**

　　Many technical fixes exist to reduce bycatch. Turtle exclusion devices are used in some shrimp fisheries to avoid killing turtle species. In the case of longline fisheries, the process of setting the hooks can be changed and bird-scaring devices employed which radically cut the numbers of birds killed. To avoid dolphins being caught in nets, other devices can be used. Pingers are small sound-emitting and dolphin-deterring devices that are attached to nets, but they are not always effective. Escape hatches (consisting of a widely spaced metal grid, which force the cetacean up and out of the net) have also been used.

　　Although these devices may have a role to play, they cannot address the whole problem. Such devices need continual monitoring to check how well they work and assess any potential negative effects they may have. Realistically they will probably only be used in areas with well-developed fishery management and enforcement agencies.

　　On a global level, probably the only effective way to address the problems of bycatch is to control fishing effort. This will be best achieved through the creation of marine reserves. Nonetheless, in the case of highly mobile species such as seabirds and cetaceans, the only effective way of preventing bycatch is to discontinue using particularly damaging fishing methods.

Fish Farming

　　Aquaculture (fish and shellfish farming) is often put forward as the future of the seafood industry. But the shrimp aquaculture industry is perhaps the most destructive, unsustainable and unjust fisheries industry in the world. Mangrove clearances, fishery destruction, murder and community land clearances have all been widely reported.

　　The salmon farming industry also proves farming is no solution — it takes approximately 4kgs of wild caught fish to produce 1 kg of farmed salmon.

Defending Our Oceans

　　Fundamental changes need to be made in the way our oceans are managed. This means that we must act to make sure that human activities are sustainable, in other words that they meet human needs of current and future generations without causing harm to the environment. Accordingly, governments must set aside 40 percent of our oceans as marine reserves. Marine reserves can be defined as areas of the ocean in which the exploitation of all living resources is prevented, together with the exploitation of non-living resources such as sand and gravel and other minerals.

1. People can exploit marine life at will as long as they possess _____ to do it.
　　[A]technology　　　　　　[B]means　　　　　　　[C]vessels　　　　　　[D]giant ships
2. Devastating human impacts on marine life may cause _____.

[A]the simplification of marine species   [B]the extinction of many marine species

[C]the transformation of marine species   [D]the reduction of marine species

3. How many jobs lost in the Canada fisheries collapses in 1992?

   [A]27 million.   [B]6.8 million.   [C]40,000.   [D]300,000.

4. What can we know about the cod stocks in the North Sea and Baltic Sea from the passage?

   [A]They have collapsed.   [B] They are the same with the cod stocks in Canada.

   [C] They are close to collapse.   [D] They are faced with difficulty.

5. How many shrimp of the catch in trawl fisheries are discarded?

   [A]20%.   [B]90%.   [C]80%.   [D]40%.

6. The victims of longline fishing are _____.

   [A]dolphins   [B]birds   [C]marine ecosystems   [D]sharks

7. The marine animal that used to suffer great bycatch in tuna fisheries is _____.

   [A]dolphin   [B]shark   [C]starfish   [D]shrimp

8. Each year, an estimated 300,000 cetaceans die as bycatch because of their disability to _____.

9. To avoid killing turtle species in shrimp fisheries, _____ are used.

10. Both the exploitation of non-living resources and _____ are forbidden in marine reserves.

Part IV Reading Comprehension (Reading in Depth) (25 minutes)

Section A

The earliest frontiersmen were hunters, trappers and traders. Primarily they roamed over the Appalachian and Ohio valleys __47__ for valuable furs. Many were of French descent, explaining the use of the word "rendezvous" to describe their annual meetings with both other frontiersmen and Native Americans, to whom they traded and sold their goods. Though not very numerous, these __48__ pioneers established a tradition of adventure and rough life that characterized all of the __49__ frontier movements. Facing rampant disease, as well as unknown lands and futures, many of these men became famous for their daring exploits.

Eventually, as the land in the Appalachians became more well known, families began settling there, building communities with the *omnipresent* (无所不在的) log cabin. Communities were established not __50__ for social reasons, but because it was more __51__ to combine the efforts of large groups of people to perform the tasks necessary for frontier life.

Technological advances and discoveries, especially those related to __52__, pushed settlement further west during the 19th century. The invention of the steamboat, as well as the growing __53__ of the covered wagon and railroads brought settlers to the prairie lands of the Midwest. Here, without forests to tap for resources, settlers often lived in houses made of sod, or earthen blocks.

The final great push west was __54__ by the discovery of gold in California in 1848. Once again, adventures and speculators packed up their bags and headed west, this time to "strike it rich". Perhaps more than any other frontier movement, the "gold rush", which has __55__ countless movies and books, __56__ the spirit of adventure and risk that marked all of them.

[A] searching	[B] advantage	[C] succeeding	[D] important	[E] original
[F] sparked	[G] practical	[H] transportation	[I] science	[J] symbolized
[K] predominance	[L] generated	[M] simply	[N] particularly	[O] spawned

Section B

Passage One

Radio and cinema had one novelty in common: they were forms of communication which dispensed with the written word, except for the captions in silent films. The written word has gone hand in hand with civilization from the beginning. Now, theoretically, an illiterate could be as well-informed about the world as the best-read man. Reading might have been expected to decline as a result, but this did not happen. Perhaps the habit was too inbred. Besides, primary education, now almost universal in Europe, made literacy also universal. Far from declining, the written, or rather the printed word, triumphed as never before. Newspapers, which had greatly increased their circulation during the World War I, continued to do so after it. In Great Britain, which carried the process furthest, the Press by 1930 ranked twelfth among British industries, ahead of shipbuilding. Newspapers now counted their readers by millions where they had previously counted by thousands. They had bigger headlines, shorter paragraphs, simpler writing. They derived their incomes mainly from advertisements, not from the half-pennies paid by readers. The decisive figure was the proprietor — Northcliffe and Beaverbrook in Great Britain, Hugenberg in Germany — not the editor. Nearly all the great newspapers were conservative in character, and often conservative in allegiance. They were among the most materialistic elements in a materialistic age. Nevertheless, they provided more news than had been provided by even the most esteemed newspaper of a staider past.

The newspapers, like the cinema and usually the radio, expressed popular culture, and observers talked as though this were the only culture which now existed. The flood of the message was supposed to have submerged the standards of previous times, but this was far from being the case. There was also a middle culture and a high culture — the distinctions between them resting on levels of sophistication (middlebrow and highbrow), not on class. The middlebrow culture was the least interesting, a repetition of past patterns interspersed with lamentations against anything new, either above or below. Those who condemned James Joyce or Picasso also disapproved of the cinema. These middlebrows felt more menaced than before, hence the intolerance which contrasted oddly with their professions of liberalism. Original artists and thinkers were constantly harassed. The works of three great British writers — Joyce, D. H. Lawrence, T. E. Lawrence — came under the legal ban of pornography. The organizer of an art exhibition learned to expect, in England, a visit from the police.

57. The author cites the situation of newspapers in order to _____.

    [A] make the popularity of newspapers known to the public

    [B] prove reading will not decline under the pressure of radio and cinema

    [C] make people familiar with the business of newspaper

    [D] show the newspapers make great profit from its low cost

58. The capital which supports the operation of a newspaper is from _____.

    [A] the owners   [B] the readers

    [C] the advertisers   [D] the conservatives

59. What does the author say about popular culture?

    [A] It was much more popular than any earlier culture.

    [B] It did not push out the older culture.

    [C] It carried the older culture with it and changed its character.

    [D] It vulgarized and lowered the level of the old culture.

60. According to the passage, we can know that the middlebrow _____.

    [A] would have the possibility of being improved if they like

    [B] criticized new things which are either earlier or later than the time it was in

    [C] is more complicated than the highbrow

    [D] should change their mind with the development of history

61. What does the author think of middlebrow culture?

    [A] He didn't think much of it.   [B] He thinks it has room for development.

    [C] He thinks it will disappear as time passed on.   [D] He thinks it advocates illegal behavior.

Passage Two

The origin of the almighty dollar is in what is now the Czech Republic. In 1519, a silver mine near the town of Joachimstal (literally "Joachim's valley", from the German Tal, meaning valley) began minting a silver coin called, unimaginative, the Joachimstaler. The coin, which was circulated widely, became better known by its clipped form, the taler. In Dutch and Low German, the initial consonant softened to become daler. English adopted this form, eventually changing its spelling to the modern dollar.

In the American colonies, there was no standard currency. The coin that was in widest use was the Spanish Peso, known also as "Pieces of Eight" because it could be divided into eight pie-like pieces. The English colonists informally assigned the name dollar to this coin. In 1785, when the Continental Congress established U. S. currency, they adopted dollar as name for the standard unit of currency, at the suggestion of Governeur Morris and Thomas Jefferson, because the term was widely known and was not associated with any form of official English currency. Jefferson also coined the term disme, from the French dixieme, for a tenth of a dollar. Pronounced deem, it eventually became dime.

The origin of the "$" sign has several folkloric stories attached. One says that Thomas Jefferson invented it, perhaps as a sort of monogram for TS. Jefferson was the first to use the symbol in relation to the U. S. dollar, but this story is fanciful. Another says that originally it was U superimposed over an S, for U. S. of course. Eventually the base of the U eroded due to poor printing technology, leaving an S with two lines through it. Another says that it is a variant of a figure eight that appeared on the Spanish Peso, standing for the pieces of eight. This last is close to the truth, but not quite there.

The Spanish royal family used on its escutcheon, two pillars representing the Pillars of Hercules in Gibraltar and Morocco crossed by an unfurled banner reading "Plus Ultra". This symbol appeared on the Peso, and looked much like the modern $ sign. It was adopted as a symbol for the Peso in the American colonies, and was transferred to the dollar. "

The U. S. was the first nation to adopt an official currency named the dollar. In 1797, the Bank of England began minting "dollar" coins as bank-issued currency. Other nations that have opted the name dollar for their currency have done so in emulation of either the U. S. or this short-lived Bank of England practice.

62. What does the phrase "clipped form" (Line 3, Para. 1) mean?

   [A] A silver coin.   [B] Old German coin.

   [C] Another name of the same thing.   [D] A shortened form of a long name.

63. Which one of the following is still in question?

   [A] Thomas Jefferson invented "$" sign for U. S. dollars.

   [B] The origin of the dollar is in the Czech Republic.

   [C] Spanish Peso was used widely in old American colonies.

   [D] The British central bank has once issued coins named dollars.

64. Why did Governeur Morris and Thomas Jefferson suggest using dollar as the name of U. S. currency?

   [A] The paper dollar was already been widely used in the country.

   [B] Dollar has never been used by British government.

   [C] Dollar has the association with the colony days.

   [D] Most Americans knew dollar is a term for currency.

65. We can infer from the passage that _____.

   [A] both U. S. and England have used dollar as the name of their official currency

   [B] the Bank of England used "dollar" coins as currency for just a short period of time

   [C] the origin of the "$" sign of the dollar is quite unimaginable

   [D] there are few countries in the world that have adopted an official currency named the dollar

66. The title of the article may well be _____.

   [A] The Birthplace of the Almighty Money   [B] Why People Love $

   [C] The Origin of Dollar   [D] Thomas Jefferson and the U. S. Dollar

答案与解析

Part II

【文章大意】

    本文主要讲述了人类在捕捞海洋生物的工作中对海洋以及海洋生物造成的危害。20 世纪 50 年代大规模的捕捞业开始发展,由于过渡捕捞和管理不善导致一些捕捞业瘫痪,并且到目前为止人类所发明的装置也无法有效地防止误捕。控制捕捞的最好办法就是创建海上禁捕区,文章最后呼吁人们保护海洋环境。

1.【定位】根据题目中的关键信息 exploit marine life,possess 可将搜索范围定位在第一段。

   【解析】选[B]。该段第一句指出长期以来,任何人只要是 possessing the means to exploit it,都可以大量的获取海洋生物,这就表明 exploit marine life 的条件是要有 means,故答案为[B]。

2.【定位】根据题目中的关键信息 devastating human impacts 可将搜索范围定位在第一段。

　　【解析】选[B]。该段倒数第二句中的 through ... human impacts 表明 devastating human impacts 是许多海洋物种已经或正面临 extinction 的主要原因,故答案为[B]。

3.【定位】根据题目中的关键信息 Canada, fisheries collapses, 1992 可将搜索范围定位在小标题 Fisheries Collapse 下。

　　【解析】选[C]。该段第二句指出 1992 年加拿大纽芬兰岛鳕鱼业的崩溃致使 the loss of some 40,000 jobs in the industry(工作岗位减少了 40,000 个),故答案为[C]。

4.【定位】根据题目中的关键信息 North Sea, Baltic Sea 可将搜索范围定位在小标题 Fisheries Collapse 下。

　　【解析】选[C]。该段第三句指出 North Sea 和 Baltic Sea 的 cod stocks 的发展趋势和 Canada 一样,也将近完全 collapse。[C]是原文的细节再现,故为答案。

5.【定位】根据题目中的关键信息 shrimp, trawl fisheries 可将搜索范围定位在小标题 Bycatch 下第一段。

　　【解析】选[B]。该段第二句指出,在某些网虾业中,the discard may be 90 percent of the catch,也就是说在捕捞上来的虾总量中,有 90 percent 被 discarded,故答案为[B]。

6.【定位】根据题目中的关键信息 victims, longline 可将搜索范围定位在小标题 The Victims 下第一段。

　　【解析】选[B]。该段主要指出了不同的捕捞方法对不同动物的伤害,其中 longline fishing 能够 kills birds,故答案为[B]。

7.【定位】根据题目中的关键信息 tuna fisheries 可将搜索范围定位在小标题 The Victims 下第二段。

　　【解析】选[A]。该段第二句中的定语从句表明 in the past(过去)在 tuna fisheries 中,经常遭受 bycatch 的是 dolphin,题目中的时态与该定语从句的时态一致,故答案为[A]。

8.【定位】根据题目中的关键信息 300,000 cetaceans 可将搜索范围定位在小标题 The Victims 下第二段。

　　【解析】escape out of nets。该段第三句指出据估计每年有 300,000 cetaceans 死于 bycatch,因为它们无法 escape out of nets,题目句子结构与原文相似,故答案为 escape out of nets。

9.【定位】根据题目中的关键信息 avoid killing turtle species 可将搜索范围定位在小标题 Technology 下第一段。

　　【解析】turtle exclusion devices。题目句子结构与该段第二句相似,由此可知本题答案即为该句的主语 turtle exclusion devices。

10.【定位】根据题目中的关键信息 marine reserves 可将搜索范围定位在小标题 Defending Our Oceans 下。

　　【解析】the exploitation of all living resources。由该段最后一句中的定语从句 in which the exploitation ... 可知,marine reserves 要求禁止 the exploitation of all living resources 和 the exploitation of non-living resources,题目将这种并列关系用 both ... and ... 结构表现出来,由此可知答案为 the exploitation of all living resources。

Part IV

Section A

【文章大意】

　　本文主要讲述的是美国边远居民的生活发展情况。第一段讲述的是最初的边远地区居民的生活方式构成,第二段说明边远地区越来越受人们的关注,并且纷纷向更边远的地区迁移,第三段则是说明科技的发展促进了边远地区文明的进步,第四段指出最大的进步是 19 世纪的"加利福尼亚大发现"以及"淘金热",这使得西部那些偏远地区不断发展起来。

【词性分析】

名　词:advantage(优势,利益);original(原物,原作);transportation(运输,运送);science(科学,理科);predominance(优势,主导作用)

动　词:searching(搜索,寻找);succeeding (成功);indicating(指示,表明);sparked(触发,引起);symbolized(象征,代表);generated(生产,引起);spawned(产卵,产生)

形容词:searching(透彻的,有观察力的);succeeding(以后的,随后的);important(重要的);original(最初的,独创的);practical(实际的,实用的)

副　词:simply(只是,仅仅);particularly(独特地,显著地)

47.选[A]。分析句子结构可知_____for valuable furs 在句中充当状语,故所填词很可能为动词的现在分词。备选项中的现在分词经常与 for 搭配使用的是[A] searching(搜索,寻找)。

48. 选[E]。根据上下文语义可知,these _____ pioneers 指的就是本段首句中的 the earliest frontiersmen,所以所填词应与 earliest 构成语义复现关系,故选[E] original(最初的)。

49. 选[C]。空前定冠词及空后名词提示所填词应为形容词。结合第 48 小题分析可知,tradition of adventure and rough life 是由最早的 pioneers 建立的,而他们形成的传统当然会对后来者及后来者的行为产生影响,故答案为[C] succeeding(以后的、随后的)。

50. 选[M]。分析句子结构可知所填词很可能为副词,备选项中只有[M] simply(只是,仅仅)和[N] particularly(独特地,显著地)符合要求。该句中的 not…but 意为"不是…而是…",连接并列成分,由 but 后的形容词比较级 more 可知,所填词用在句中应能表明 social reasons 并不是 communities 建立的唯一理由,故答案为[M] simply(只是,仅仅)。

51. 选[G]。空前形容词比较级 more 提示所填词应为形容词。备选形容词中在语义上符合语境的只有[D] important(重要的)和[G] practical(实际的,实用的),但整句话并没有涉及到 social reasons 和 to combine the efforts of large groups of people 哪个更为重要,故答案为[G] practical(实际的,实用的)。

52. 选[H]。空前的短语 related to 提示所填词应为名词。下句中的 steamboat,covered wagon 和 railroads 提示所填词应为[H] transportation(交通运输)。

53. 选[K]。空前形容词及空后介词提示所填词应为名词。备选项中的名词从语义上来看只有[B] advantage(优势,利益)和[K] predominance(优势,主导作用)符合句意。advantage 的英文解释为"something that may help one to be successful or to gain a favorable result",predominance 的英文解释为"the one which is powerful, noticeable, or important, or largest in number",通过比较二者的含义可知答案为[K] predominance(优势,主导作用)。

54. 选[F]。空前系动词及空后介词 by 提示所填词应为动词的过去分词。介词 by 提示本句主要讲的是 the discovery of gold 与 the final great push west 的关系。西部大开发的产生很明显是由 the discovery of gold 引起的,故答案为[F] sparked(发动,引起)。

55. 选[O]。空前助动词提示所填词应为动词的过去分词。which 引导定语从句修饰 the "gold rush"。本题的选择可以根据考生掌握的知识来解答,现在有很多以"淘金热"为素材的书籍及电影,也就是说 the "gold rush"为无数的电影及书籍提供了素材,故应选[O] spawned(引起,产生)。

56. 选[J]。分析句子结构可知,所填词为动词,在句中作谓语。将选项中的动词带入原文中可知,最符合句意的为[J] symbolized(象征,代表)。

Section B

Passage One

【文章大意】

　　广播和电影的发展并没有使阅读衰落,本文以报纸发行量的增加论证了这一点。文章第一段主要涉及了阅读不会衰落的原因以及与报纸相关的一些信息;第二段主要讲报纸所代表的文化并不能淹没所有的文化。

57. 选[B]。推理判断题。文章第一段第七句指出 Far from declining, the written, or rather the printed word, triumphed as never before(书面语或者说是印刷字不但没有衰落反而取得了前所未有的成功),紧接着说明报纸继一战之后 continued to do so(销量持续攀升)。报纸属于 the printed word 的一部分,所以作者提出报纸的情况就是为了证明书面语言并不会随着广播和电影的发展而衰落,故答案为[B]。

58. 选[C]。事实细节题。文章第一段倒数第五句涉及到报纸的收入来源。该句指出报纸 derived their incomes mainly from advertisements(主要的收入来源是广告),即 advertisers(广告商)所付的广告费支持着报纸的正常运转,故答案为[C]。

59. 选[B]。推理判断题。文章第二段第二句中的 this was far from being the case(事实却不是如此)表明尽管代表通俗文化的报纸有广泛的影响,但其并不能 submerged the standards of previous times(埋没以往时代的标准),由第三句中的 There was also a middle culture and a high culture…可知 the standards of previous times 指的即是旧文化的标准,故答案为[B]。

60. 选[B]。推理判断题。文章第二段第五句中的 James Joyce or Picasso 和 the cinema 分别代表旧时期的文化和新时期的文化,由此可推断第四句中的 against anything new, either above or below 指的是 the middlebrow culture 批评反对一切新时期和旧时期的新文化,above or below 指的是时间上的早晚,故答案为[B]。

61. 选[A]。观点态度题。由文章第二段第四句中的 The middlebrow culture was the least interesting 可知作者并不十分推崇 middlebrow culture,故答案为[A]。

Passage Two

【文章大意】
　　美元现在已是世界通用货币,美元的代表符号为＄,本文主要讲述了美元及其符号＄的由来。文章第一段主要从语音上讲述 dollar 的形成;第二段主要讲 dollar 成为美国正式的货币名称;第三段主要讲美元符号＄的由来;第四段主要讲＄在西班牙所具有的含义;第五段主要与 dollar 的流行有关。

62. 选[D]。事实细节题。文章首段第三句中的 the taler 是 its clipped form 的同位语,通过上下文语义联系可知 clipped form 前的 its 指代上句中出现的银币名称 the Joachimstaler,对比 taler 和 Joachimstaler 可发现 taler 是 Joachimstaler 的缩写形式,故答案为[D]。

63. 选[A]。事实细节题。文章第三段主要是关于＄符号的起源。该段指出有关＄符号的起源有好几个民间传说,其中一个就是 Thomas Jefferson 发明了该符号,但第二句末的 but this story is fanciful(但是这个传说并不真实),由此可知 Thomas Jefferson 发明了＄符号这一说法是值得怀疑的,故答案为[A]。[B]、[C]、[D]都是文中明确提到的内容。

64. 选[D]。事实细节题。文章第二段第四句指出 1795 年,大陆会议确定了美国的货币,在总督 Morris 和 Thomas Jefferson 的建议下,采用 dollar 作为货币单位的标准,莫里斯和杰弗逊提出这一建议的原因是因为 the term was widely know and was…,[D]是其中的原因之一,故为答案。[B]是对 was not associated…的错误理解。

65. 选[B]。事实细节题。文章第二段第四句中的…was not associated with any form of official English currency 说明 dollar 这个名称与英国任何形式的官方货币没有任何关系,故[A]错;文章最后一段最后一句话 Other nations …this short-lived Bank of England practice 表明英国银行使用 dollar 作为货币名称只持续了很短时间,[B]表述与原文一致,故为答案,而由该句同样可判断[D]错误;文中只指出＄这个货币符号带有民间传说的色彩,但并没有说它的起源令人费解,故[C]错。

66. 选[C]。主旨大意题。文章第一段主要是关于 dollar 的起源地及从语言方面介绍了 dollar 的发展过程;第二段主要是关于 Morris 和 Thomas Jefferson 对 dollar 成为货币名称的贡献;第三段主要是关于"＄"符号起源的一些民间传说;末段主要是关于不同的国家对 dollar 的使用,综合上面的分析可知,本文主要是与 dollar 的起源有关,故答案为[C]。

第三篇

综 合 测 试

第27－36天

Part 3

短文改错巅峰讲座

改错题是大学英语六级考试的传统题型之一,与完型填空一起作为二选一题型出现,文章长度大约在 250—280 词之间,分值比例为 10%。每篇文章一般包含 10 处错误,每行不超过 1 处错误,而且不会出现标点符号错误和纯粹的单词拼写错误。

Lecture 1　　第一讲　15 种常考错误类型

改错题要求考生根据对文章的理解,运用语篇、语法和词汇知识,辨认文章中出现的语言错误并加以改正,每个错误的改正仅限于一个单词,一般有以下三种更改形式:

1. 改正(correction):将文中错词用斜线"/"划去,然后在其后面对应的下划线上填入正确的词,表示替换该错词。

2. 删除(delete):将文中错词用斜线"/"划去,在其后面对应的下划线上也划一斜线"/",表示该错词应被删除。

3. 增添(add):在短文中需要添加新词的两个词之间加"∧"号,表示有遗漏,然后在下划线上填入被遗漏的词。

【例 1】

Television is rapidly becoming the literature of our periods. Many of the arguments having used for the study of literature as a school subject are valid for ∧ study of television.	time/times/period ———— the

总体而言,改错题的错误类型涵盖词汇用法、语法知识和篇章理解三大方面。具体来说,主要包括以下几种错误:

一、上下文语义矛盾

所谓的"上下文语义矛盾"是指文章前后所表达的意思不一致,甚至正好相反,即根据上下文的内容,应该是表达肯定或积极意义的地方,却误用了表达否定或消极意义的词;或是与此相反,应该是表达否定或消极意义,却误用了表达肯定或积极意义的词。

要识别这类错误,考生必须从宏观上把握全文,注意上下文语义上的衔接与连贯,而不能孤立地看待每个单词或句子。

【例 2】
(05-12-S3)

Initial impressions are vital and a badly presented CV could mean acceptance, regardless of what's in it.	S3. _____

【解析】前面提到 initial impressions(第一印象)非常重要,那么 badly presented(外表很差的)简历不管内容如何,肯定是会被拒绝,而不会被接受,原文中 acceptance 导致了上下文语义矛盾,应将其改为 rejection。

二、缺漏和赘述

一般来说,缺漏或赘述所涉及到的词大都为介词、冠词、代词或连词。赘述可能还涉及到双主语现象或把相近或相同意义的词语叠加在一起的现象。

要识别这类错误,考生应注意以下几点:

1. 熟悉常用介词、冠词、代词和连词的用法。

2. 注意修饰成份中是否有两个意思相同或相近的词,确认其中一个是否多余。

3. 如果句子已有主语,就不能在同一谓语前加上另外的代词或名词,否则便是双主语现象。

【例3】   (05-12-S1)

We've seen it all: CVs printed on pink paper, CVs that are 10 pages long and CVs with silly mistakes in first paragraph.	S1. _____

【解析】first 在这里作为序数词,修饰 paragraph,表示"第一段",而序数词前应加定冠词 the,故应在 in 和 first 之间加上 the。

【例4】   (05-12-S8)

If you are sending your CV electronically, check the formatting by sending it to yourself first. Keep up the format simple.	S8. _____

【解析】分析上文可知,keep 在此处的含义应该是"保持",是及物动词,后面可以接形容词充当宾补,keep the format simple 意为"保持格式简洁"。而 keep up 意为"(使…)保持或继续下去",后面可以跟名词,但不能接形容词充当宾补,因此应将原文中的 up 去掉。

三、逻辑关系混乱

改错题对逻辑关系的考查主要集中在句子之间的关系上,如因果、转折、条件、让步等关系。具体体现在句子间使用的连接词上,其中以因果、转折连接词的误用最为常见。

要识别这类错误,考生应注意以下几点:

1. 结合上下文仔细推敲,准确把握前后的逻辑关系。始终牢记文章中各个句子并不是孤立地堆砌在一起,而是相互联系的。

2. 熟悉表示各种逻辑关系的常用连接词。

【例5】   (03-9-S7,S8)

When U. S. soldiers came home before World War II, for example, they dreamed of buying houses and starting families. But there was a tremendous boom in home building.	S7. _____ S8. _____

【解析】士兵回家应该是战后,故应将 before 改成 after。前一句说二战后返家的士兵都梦想购买房屋和建立家庭,后一句说出现了建造房屋的热潮,显然前后应该是因果关系,而不是转折关系,故应将 But 改为 So。

四、主谓不一致

英语中谓语动词必须与主语一致,即主语的人称和数决定动词的形式,这通常被称为主谓一致关系。主谓一致方面的错误具体体现在两者"数"上的不一致,从而牵涉到与数相关的"形"上的不一致。改错题中,主语、谓语间有时会插入其他成份,如定语、同位语,这些成份往往会对识别错误构成干扰。

要识别这类错误,考生应注意以下几点:

1. 从形式上判断。规则名词看字形,不规则名词要熟记,单、复数同形的名词可借助句中其他线索,如从句修饰语的主动词或并列句的主动词是单数还是复数。

2. 从含义上判断。有些集合名词既可表示单数概念,也可表示复数概念,因此谓语动词的"数"要根据句子的上下文含义判定。很多情况下,概念上的一致是一条行之有效的原则。

3. 熟练掌握主谓一致方面的语法知识和习惯用法。如:either, neither 等词作主语时,谓语动词按习惯用法应为单数。

4. 注意寻找谓语动词的主语或逻辑主语,不要受分隔成份的干扰。尤其要注意定语从句中的谓语动词,其逻辑主语应是关系词前面的先行词。

【例6】   (02-6-S5)

Descriptions written by eighteenth-century travelers of the poor of Mexico City, and the enormous contrasts that was to be found there, …	S5. _____

【解析】此处 that 引导的是定语从句,用来修饰先行词 contrasts,因此从句谓语应与 contrasts 保持一致,故应将 was 改为 were。

五、平行结构错误

平行结构要求各部分采用相同的形式,改错题中经常会出现平行结构的连接词误用或是平行结构中某一部分与其他部分在形式上不统一的错误。

要识别这类错误,考生应注意以下几点:

1. 找到平行结构的连接词,根据上下文判断连接词的使用是否正确。
2. 明确平行结构由哪几部分组成,对照其形式是否一致。

【例7】   （05-12-S7）

Restrict yourself to one or two pages, and listing any publications or referees on a separate sheet.	S7. _____

【解析】and 连接平行结构,其前后部分的形式应该保持一致。and 前面的句子 restrict yourself…是祈使句,and 后面的句子也应该用祈使句,故应将 listing 改为 list。

六、时态语态错误

时态和语态错误主要包括:动词各种时态形式的误用、主动语态和被动语态的误用、被动语态中系动词的遗漏等。这方面的错误不只是限于谓语动词,还经常会涉及非谓语动词。

要识别这类错误,考生应注意以下几点:

1. 根据上下文所用的时态判断句子的时态是否正确。
2. 找到动词的主语或逻辑主语,弄清楚它们之间的关系。
3. 注意主语和谓语动词之间的分隔成份,不要受到这些成份的干扰。
4. 看动词后面是否有宾语,如果有宾语,则多半应为主动语态。

【例8】   （05-12-S9）

Do not send a photo unless specifically requested. If you have to send one, make sure it is one taking in a professional setting, rather than a holiday snap.	S9. _____

【解析】根据上文可知,one 代替前面的 photo,其后的分词短语充当 one 的后置定语,表示"被拍的照片",故应将 taking 改为 taken。

七、非谓语动词误用

非谓语动词包括不定式、分词和动名词,它不存在人称和数的变化,但具有各种时态形式,并有主动、被动之分。改错题中非谓语动词的误用主要包括:非谓语动词同谓语动词相混淆、非谓语动词发生的时间与谓语动词发生的时间的先后顺序相混淆、非谓语动词三种形式互相混淆、现在分词与过去分词作定语时的相互混淆等。

要识别这类错误,考生应注意以下几点:

1. 哪些动词之后只可接动词不定式作宾语,哪些只可接动名词,哪些又两者皆可接。
2. 非谓语动词的逻辑主语和句子的主语是否一致。如果不一致,则需要在非谓语动词前加上逻辑主语。
3. 现在分词和过去分词都可以放在其所修饰的名词之后,作后置定语。当所修饰的名词是分词所表示的动作的主体时,用现在分词;当所修饰的名词是分词所表示的动作的受体时,用过去分词。
4. 某些动词的现在分词与过去分词可用作形容词,但意思不同。现在分词作形容词时意为"令人有…的感觉",它的主语一般为事物。过去分词作形容词时意为"(人)有…的感觉"。如:surprising"令人惊讶的",surprised"惊讶的,诧异的";exciting"令人高兴的",excited"激动的,兴奋的"。

【例9】   （05-12-S4）

Here are a few ways to avoid end up on the reject pile.	S4. _____

【解析】动词 avoid 后面通常接动名词充当宾语,意为"避免做某事",故应将 end 改为 ending。

八、介词误用

介词在句中不能单独使用,而必须和另外的词一起构成短语后才可以充当独立的句子成份。改错中介词的误用,主要是指介词与其他各类词的搭配错误。

要识别这类错误,考生应注意以下几点:

1. 平时多积累、总结介词的用法。
2. 注意动词与介词、名词与介词、形容词与介词等习惯搭配中的介词。
3. 注意 at best, in brief, on (an/the) average 等固定短语中的介词。

【例10】　　　　　　　　　　　　　　　　　　　　　　　　　　(05-12-S5)

CVs with flowery backgrounds or pink paper will stand out upon all the wrong reasons.	S5. _____

【解析】此处是说,简历中带有花边或用粉红色的纸印简历是错误的做法,而且你的简历会因为这些错误显得更加突出。表示因为某种原因,应该用介词 for,而不能用介词 upon。

九、代词误用

代词用来代替其他实义词或意义。代词的误用主要包括:代词与其所指代的对象不符、反身代词的误用、it 的误用、代词的单复数误用等。

要识别这类错误,考生应注意以下几点:

1. 掌握各类代词的基本用法,包括人称代词、物主代词、反身代词、不定代词以及代词的各种格。
2. 明确代词在文中所指代的对象,不受各种插入语的干扰。
3. 记住一些特殊用法的代词,如 it 可作形式主语和形式宾语,one、that 和 those 可以用来代替前面提到的名词等。

【例11】　　　　　　　　　　　　　　　　　　　　　　　　　　(04-1-S2)

The fast-growing population's demand for food, they warned, would soon exceed their supply, leading to widespread food shortages and starvation.	S2. _____

【解析】此处是说,迅速增长的人口对食物的需求很快将超过"食物"的 supply(供应),因此 supply 前面的代词应与 food 保持一致,故应将 their 改为 its。

十、名词误用

名词的误用主要包括:可数名词单复数的混淆、可数名词与不可数名词的混淆、单复数同形的名词的误用、名词的所有格误用等。

要识别这类错误,考生应注意以下几点:

1. 注意名词前表示数量概念的修饰语和名词后的谓语等线索,判断名词的单复数形式。
2. 一般来说,单数可数名词前必须有冠词,否则就应该是复数形式。
3. 熟悉常见的表示数量概念的短语,牢记其修饰的是可数名词还是不可数名词。常见的修饰可数名词的短语有:a number of, many, few, a few;常见的修饰不可数名词的词或短语有:much, little, a little, an amount of, a great/good deal of;常见的既可以修饰可数名词又可以修饰不可数名词的词或短语有:a lot/lots of, plenty of, a quantity/ quantities of。
4. 熟悉名词两种名词所有格('s 所有格和 of 所有格)的用法。一般来说,有生命意义的名词所有格既可用 's 又可用 of 表示,无生命意义的名词所有格必须用 of 表示;词尾有 s 的复数名词所有格加 ',词尾没 s 的复数名词所有格加 's;复合名词或名词短语的所有格在最后一个词上加 's。
5. 熟悉双重所有格的用法。当 a(n), this, these, that, some, any, no… 等与名词所有格修饰同一名词时,两者不能同时放在该名词前面,要用双重所有格表示,即 a (this, that…)＋名词＋of＋名词所有格,如 a daughter of Mrs. Brown's。

【例12】　　　　　　　　　　　　　　　　　　　　　　　　　　(04-1-S10)

There is no guarantee that plant breeders can continue to develop new, higher-yielding crop, but most researchers see their success to date as reason for hope.	S10. _____

【解析】crop 是可数名词,其前有两个形容词充当其定语,且根据句意,此处应该不是表示一种农作物,故应将 crop 改为 crops。

十一、冠词误用

冠词的误用主要包括:单数可数名词前遗漏不定冠词、不可数名词前加不定冠词、特殊类别名词前冠词的误用、固定短语中冠词的误用等。

要识别这类错误,考生应注意以下几点:

1. 分清名词的可数与不可数。

2. 分清名词的泛指与特指。一般表示特指时,名词前加定冠词;表示泛指时,名词用复数或加不定冠词。

3. 熟悉特殊类别的名词前定冠词的用法。一般专有名词前一定要加定冠词,三餐前和球类名词前不加冠词。

4. 熟悉带有定冠词或不定冠词的固定短语。比如 a number of 和 an amount of 意为"大量的…",后面分别接可数名词复数和不可数名词。a number of… 作主语时谓语动词用复数形式,an amount of… 作主语时谓语动词用单数形式;the number of 和 the amount of 意为"…的数量",后面分别接可数名词的单数形式或复数形式和不可数名词,充当主语时谓语动词均为单数形式。

【例 13】
(05-1-S1)

Doctor Brundtland, head of the WHO, says a number of leprosy cases around the world has been cut by ninety percent during the past then years.

S1. ＿＿＿＿＿＿＿

【解析】根据句意及谓语的单数形式(has been cut)可知,此处讲的是 leprosy 病例的数量,所以应将 a 改成 the。

十二、形容词、副词误用

形容词、副词的误用主要包括:形容词原级误用成副词原级或副词原级误用成形容词原级、不可分级的形容词或副词误用了比较级或最高级结构、形容词或副词比较级和最高级的混淆等。

要识别这类错误,考生应注意以下几点:

1. 搞清形容词或副词在句中充当的成份及其所修饰的词语,判断是否存在误用情况。形容词修饰名词,在句中充当定语、表语或补语;副词修饰形容词、动词或整个句子,在句中充当状语。

2. 熟悉某些特殊形式的比较级和最高级,比如 good-better-best, little-less-least 等。

3. 熟悉常见的比较结构,如 as…as 同级比较、the more…, the more…等。

4. 了解一些本身含有比较意义的形容词,如 superior,senior 等,这些词没有比较级和最高级形式,表示比较时也不与 than 连用,而与 to 连用。

【例 14】
(05-12-S2)

A good CV is your passport to an interview and, ultimate, to the job you want.

S2. ＿＿＿＿＿＿＿

【解析】此处是说,一份好的简历是取得面试机会的通行证,而最终将成为获得一份好工作的通行证。显然形容词 ultimate 应改为副词 ultimately,在句中充当状语。

十三、关系词误用

名词性从句和定语从句中都需要一个用来引导从句的关系词,改错题中经常会出现这种关系词的误用现象。

要识别这类错误,考生应注意以下几点:

1. 熟悉引导各种从句常用的关系词及其用法。引导名词性从句的关系词主要有:that, whether, if, who(ever),whom(ever), whose, what(ever),which(ever), when, where, why, how;引导定语从句的关系词主要有:that, which,who, whom, whose, when, where, why。

2. 注意容易混淆的几对关系词的区别:what 和 that; which 和 that; which 和 as; which 和 whose; who 和 whom 等。

【例 15】
(05-1-S7)

Instead, patients can take that is called a multi-drug therapy.

S7. ＿＿＿＿＿＿＿

【解析】分析句子结构可知,take 后面接的是宾语从句,that 引导宾语从句时,只起引导作用,不充当成份,而此处需要一个能在从句中充当主语的关系词,故应将 that 改为 what。

十四、易混词误用

英语中有很多易混的近义词、同义词、近形词和同根词,如 consist(包括,由…组成)与 compose(组成)、forbid(禁止)与 prohibit(禁止)、arise(出现、起来)与 rise(上升、站起)等。这类词的误用也是改错题中常见的一种错误类型。

要识别这类错误,考生应注意以下几点:

1. 平时注意对这些易混词的积累。
2. 记忆单词时,多注意同根词在用法上的区别,如 sleep 和 asleep、affect 和 effect 等。
3. 仔细阅读每一个单词,从其词性、含义、用法三方面全面考虑其使用是否恰当。

【例 16】　　　　　　　　　　　　　　　　　　　　　　　　　　　　　(05-1-S4)

The disease mainly effects the skin and nerves.	S4. _____

【解析】根据句意,此处是说疾病对皮肤和神经造成影响,而 effect 作动词时意为"实现,达到",作名词时才表示"影响",因此应将 effect 改为 affect。

十五、词性误用

改错题中常见的词性误用主要包括形容词和名词之间的误用、连词和副词之间的误用以及前面提到的形容词和副词之间的误用,这种误用现象经常出现在平行结构中。

要识别这类错误,考生应注意以下几点:

1. 注意平行结构各部分之间形式的一致性,如要为名词就均为名词,要为形容词就均为形容词。
2. 分清句子的语法结构,判断各部分应该采用的词性。

【例 17】　　　　　　　　　　　　　　　　　　　　　　　　　　　　　(04-1-S6)

Most experts believe …, although feeding 10 billion people will not be easy for politics, economic and environmental reasons.	S6. _____

【解析】本句中 and 连接的三个并列的单词共同修饰 reasons,故三个单词的词性应保持一致,故应将名词 politics (政治,政治学)改为形容词 political (政治的)。

Exercise　　　即讲即练

It is necessary to have a break among college and post graduation. As we know, high school is the place to learn basic knowledge, college is for advanced training in special area, but postgraduate education requires us to make research. Although research can not be separated with experiments and production experience, post graduation should be connected with aboratories and workshops. If we have a break, we can decide on the better research subject, that will help us make most effective study. The world of classroom, the lecture, the discussion, the book, and study desk is not a real world. It is only a reflection, and no matter what clear, cannot show life like it really is. Only when we combine what we learn with the real life production, can what we have learned become richer and meaningful.

However, being away from school can give us a chance to think about life, society, rightness and wrongness, and many of the other concepts that so confuse the young.

In practice we can develop our attitudes and our ideas slowly but naturally. New and often radical ideas are thrown at the students lacked experience or tests so that they can't possibly do justice on them. They skim over the surface and reject or accept without any examination. To make our education fuller and grow both in body and mind, it is necessary to have a break before we

1. _____

2. _____
3. _____

4. _____

5. _____
6. _____

7. _____
8. _____

9. _____
10. _____

made our further study after graduation.

【答案与解析】

1. among — between。介词误用。between 指两者之间，among 指三者或三者以上之间。

2. Although — Since 或 Because。逻辑关系混乱。分析句意可知，分句与主句之间应是因果关系，所以连词应该是表因果关系的 Since 或 Because。

3. with — from。介词误用。separate 通常与介词 from 搭配使用，separate from… 意为"与…分离"。

4. that — which。关系词误用。根据语法知识可知，that will help… 是一个定语从句。但 that 引导的定语从句只能是限制性定语从句，其引导的定语从句与它所修饰的先行词之间不能有逗号，所以应将关系代词 that 改为 which。

5. what — how。易混词误用。what 作形容词时，应修饰名词，所以应将 what 改为副词 how 来修饰形容词 clear。

6. like — as。易混词误用。like 作介词时后面只能跟名词或名词性短语，不能跟句子。而与 like 同义的 as 可以作连词，连接一个句子，所以应将 like 改为 as。

7. and ∧ meaningful — more。平行结构错误。连词 and 连接并列成份，其前的形容词比较级提示其后的形容词同样也应用比较级，所以应在 meaningful 前加 more，使其与 richer 形式一致。

8. However — Moreover。逻辑关系混乱。结合上一句可知，本句与上一句不是转折关系，而应是递进关系，以进一步说明理论与实践相结合的好处，所以应将 However 改为 Moreover。

9. lacked — lacking。非谓语动词误用。分析句子结构可知 lacked experience or tests 应作 students 的后置定语，所以不应用过去分词 lacked，而应用现在分词 lacking。

10. on — to。介词误用。do justice 通常与介词 to 搭配使用，意为"公平地对待某人"。所以应将 on 改为 to。

Lecture 2　第二讲　4 步巧做改错题

改错题不但要求考生有扎实的语言基础，而且要求考生有较强的语篇理解能力以及利用上下文进行逻辑推理的能力。在具体的解题过程中，可以采取如下解题步骤：

第一步：分句阅读，改正明显的错误

通读文章，无错误的行略读而过，有错误的行稍停考虑，看是否有比较明显的错误，如一时无法作出判断，则继续阅读，不要停顿过久。这一步的目的主要是改正一些比较明显的错误，了解文章结构和大意，为后面的逐行分析打下基础。

第二步：逐行分析，排查错误

现在开始主要针对错误所在行进行分析：先从动词、句法的角度判断；确定无句法错误后，再考虑用法、搭配和近形近义方面的错误；考虑了上述两种可能后，再着重从语篇角度寻找有无上下文语义方面的错误，注意连接性词语和有反义词的词，注意标有题号的各行与上行或下行相临处的错误。

第三步：疑难之处，反复推敲

经过以上的步骤，还有判断不出来的，应在做完其他题目后，在对全文有了更深入、更完整的理解的基础上进行反复推敲，除了再次从词法、句法和语篇的角度进行仔细分析外，这时宜着重从介词及一些简单而易被忽视的语法角度的"细微处"多加考虑。

第四步：通读全文，核对检验

做完所有题目后，再通读改后的全文，检验全篇是否语意通顺，所做改正是否能使句子符合语法要求并使上下文语义连贯，是否按照所规定的形式改正错误。

【例】

(新 06-12)

The National Endowment for the Arts recently released the results of its "Reading at Risk" survey, which described the movement of the American public away from books and literature and toward television and electronic media. According to the

survey, "reading is on the decline on every region, within every
ethnic group, and at every educational level."

62. _____

The day the NEA report released, the U.S. House, in a tie
vote, upheld the government's right to obtain bookstore and library
records under a provision of the USA Patriot Act. The House proposal would have barred the federal government from demand library records, reading lists, book customer lists and other material
in terrorism and intelligence investigations.

63. _____

64. _____

These two events are completely unrelated to, yet they echo
each other in the message they send about the place of books and
reading in American culture. At the heart of the NEA survey is the
belief in our democratic system depends on leaders who can think
critically, analyze texts and writing clearly. All of these are skills
promoted by reading and discussing books and literature. At the
same time, through a provision of the Patriot Act, the leaders of our
country are unconsciously sending the message that reading may
be connected to desirable activities that might undermine our
system of government rather than helping democracy flourish.

65. _____

66. _____
67. _____

68. _____

Our culture's decline in reading begin well before the
existence of the Patriot Act. During the 1980s' culture wars, school
systems across the country pulled some books from library shelves
because its content was deemed by parents and teachers to be
inappropriate. Now what started in schools across the country is
playing itself out on a nation stage and is possibly having an
impact on the reading habits of the American public.

69. _____

70. _____

71. _____

62. on — in。survey 在上文中出现过,故前面加 the 是正确的;on the decline 是固定搭配,意为"在下降",符合文意。介词 on 与 region 搭配,显然不恰当,故将 on 改为 in。

63. report ∧ released — was。分析句子结构可知,the U. S. House(美国议院)为句子主语,upheld(支持,赞成)为谓语,the day the NEA report released 是一个时间状语从句,从句的主语 report 与谓语动词 release(发布,发表)之间应该是被动的关系,故应在 report 和 released 之间添加系动词 was。

64. demand — demanding。bar…from doing sth. 为习惯搭配,意为"禁止或阻止…做某事",故应将 demand 改为 demanding。

65. to — /。unrelated to…为习惯搭配,意为"与…无关",to 为介词,后面须接名词。根据此处句意,如采用添加名词的改法,只能添加词组 each other,而这与改错题只限于改动一个词的命题规律不符,故本题的改正方法应该是将介词 to 删掉。

66. in — that。本句为介词短语提前引起的倒装句,系动词 is 被提到主语 the belief 的前面,倒装形式没有错误。本句中同时出现两个动词,系动词 is 在主句中作谓语,因此 depends 应该是从句中的谓语,our democratic system depends on leaders … clearly 是 the belief 的同位语,引导同位语从句应该用 that,故应将 in 改为 that。

67. writing — write。writing 与 think 和 analyze 是由 and 连接的三个并列的动词,且三个动词都位于情态动词 can 之后,故都应使用动词原形,故应将 writing 改为 write。

68. desirable — undesirable。be connected to 为固定用法,意为"与…有关",其后一般接名词。此处的定语从句 that might undermine our system of government rather than helping democracy flourish 修饰名词 activities,根据从句中的 undermine(损坏,破坏)及 rather than helping (而不是帮助)可知,这些活动(activities)应该是消极的,desirable(可取的,有利的)与原文语义不符,故将 desirable 改为 undesirable。

69. begin — began。decline in 为习惯用法,意为"在某方面有所下降";well 可以表示程度,意为"相当地,充分地",well before 意为"早在…之前",符合语意。而 before … 表示句中的动作已经发生,因此动词应使用过去式,故应把 begin 改为 began。后面两句中使用的过去时态也提示此处应用过去式。

70. its — their。because 引导原因状语从句,从句中的主语 content(内容)为不可数名词,且本句描述的是过去发生的事,故从句中的 was 单复数形式和过去时态都正确。此处的 its 对应的是主句中的 some books,二者在语义上矛盾,故应将 its 改为 their。

71. nation — national。本句的主语为由 what 引导的从句,故谓语为 is,主谓一致正确;play out 为固定搭配,意为"放出,展示",符合句意;介词 on 与 stage 搭配也正确。nation 是名词,意为"国家,民族",而此处表示"在全国范围的舞台上展示",故应将名词 nation 改为形容词 national。

Exercise　　　即讲即练

The way people hold to the belief which a fun-filled, pain-free life equals with happiness actually reduces their chances of ever attaining real happiness. If fun and pleasure are equal to happiness, then pain must be equal to unhappiness. But in fact, the opposite is true: much often than not things that lead to happiness involve some pain.

As result, many people avoid the very attempts that are the source of true happiness. They fear the pain inevitably brought by such things like marriage, raising children, professional achievement, religious commitment, and self-improvement.

Ask a bachelor what he resists marriage even though he finds dating to be less and less satisfying. If he is honest, he will tell you that he is afraid of making a commitment. For commitment is in fact quite painful. The single life is full with fun, adventure, excitement. Marriage has such moments, and they are not its most distinguishing features.

Couples with infant children are lucky to get a whole night's sleep or a three-day vacation. I don't know any parent who would choose the word "fun" to describe raising children. But couples who decide to have children never know the joys of watching a child grow up or of playing with a grandchild.

Understanding and accepting that true happiness has nothing to do with fun is one of the most liberating realizations we can ever come to. It could liberate time: now we can devote more hours to activities that can genuine increase our happiness.

1. _____
2. _____
3. _____
4. _____
5. _____
6. _____
7. _____
8. _____
9. _____
10. _____

【答案与解析】

1. which — that。关系词误用。分析句子结构可知 belief 与 reduces 之间的内容显然是作 belief 的同位语从句,所以应将关系代词 which 改为 that。

2. with — /。介词误用。equal 作动词时为及物动词,后跟宾语时不需加介词,所以应将 with 删除。

3. much — more。形容词误用。通常与 often than not 搭配使用的是 more,more often than not 意为"时常"。

4. As ∧ result — a。缺漏。"as a result"是固定搭配,意为"结果"。

5. like — as。介词误用。such 通常与 as 搭配使用,such…as…意为"例如,像…"

6. what — why。关系词误用。下句中的 he will tell you that…提示本句中 ask 的直接宾语应该是 a bachelor 为什么不结婚,所以 ask 的宾语从句应该由 why 引导。

7. full —filled 或 with — of。介词误用或词性误用。表示"充满"的含义时,通常与 with 搭配使用的是 fill,根据语法知识可知,fill 在本句中应使用被动语态 filled;通常与 full 搭配使用的介词通常是 of。

8. and — but。逻辑关系混乱。本句首先肯定了婚姻中确实存在 such moments(令人痛苦的时刻),接着说 they are not its…(这些痛苦不是最容易识别的特点)。由此可知,二者前后明显存在对比关系,所以关系连词应用转折连词 but。

9. to ∧ have — not。上下文语义矛盾。本句中的否定词 never 提示没有孩子的夫妻体会不到看着孩子长大或同孙子玩耍的乐趣,所以在由 who 引导的定语从句中应在 to 前加 not 使其变成否定句,这样才能符合本句语境。

10. genuine — genuinely。词性误用。分析句子结构可知,geniune 在此处应该是修饰动词 increase,故应将其改为相应的副词 genuinely(真正地)。

Lecture 3　　第三讲　6 大精准纠错秘诀

要做好改错题,平时打好扎实的语言基础,掌握丰富的词汇用法、固定搭配及句法知识是必需的。此外,掌握一些实用的纠错秘诀,将有助于考生在考试时更加快速准确地找到并改正错误。

秘诀一：错误以改动一词为原则

每行最多只能改动一处,即在一个词上进行改动。可以是增词、减词、改词,但无论是何种改动,只能是增加一词,减少一词或把一个词改成另一个词。没有错误的一行只需打勾表明正确而无需改动。

【例 1】　　　　　　　　　　　　　　　　　　　　　　　　　　　　　　　　　　　　　　(05-1-S8)

This modern treatment will cure leprosy in 6 to 12 months, depend on the form of the disease.	S8. ＿＿＿＿＿＿

【解析】此处是说,这种现代治疗方法治愈 leprosy 的疗程在 6—12 月之内,具体时间取决于疾病的形式。正确表达后半句的含义可以用非限制性定语从句 which depends on …和现在分词短语 depending on…作状语。但是如果用非限制性定语从句表达就要增加一个词还要改动一个词,违背了改错题的更改原则,因此此处应将 depend 改为 depending。

秘诀二：改正以一个层次为原则

改错题中,在对原文中的某个词进行改动时,注意只能在一个层次上进行改动。要么改变词义,要么改变词性,要么改变形式,而不能既改变了词义又改变了词性,或是既改变了词性又改变了形式。

【例 2】　　　　　　　　　　　　　　　　　　　　　　　　　　　　　　　　　　　　　　(05-1-S3)

She says efforts are continuing to complete end the disease.	S3. ＿＿＿＿＿＿

【解析】此处是说,她表示继续努力最终会完全消灭这种疾病。end 为动词,其修饰语应用副词,故应将形容词 complete 改为副词 completely。表示"完全地"尽管也可以用 entirely,但这样改动则既改变了词性又改变了形式,违背了改错题中只在一个层次上进行改动的原则。

秘诀三：添加或删除的词一般为虚词

改错题中需要添加或删除的词一般都是冠词、代词、介词、连词、助动词等虚词,而动词、名词、形容词等实词则不要轻易添加或删除,否则会改变句子原意。

【例 3】　　　　　　　　　　　　　　　　　　　　　　　　　　　　　　　　　　　　　　(05-1-S6)

This alliance guarantees that all leprosy patients, even they are poor, have a right to the most modern treatment.	S6. ＿＿＿＿＿＿

【解析】此处是说,即使病人很穷,也有权利接受最现代化的治疗。even 是副词,不能用来引导从句,故应在 even 后面加上连词 if 或 though。

秘诀四：实词一般是改变形式

在改错过程中,对实词的处理一般只是改变它的形式,很少会将其改换成另一个实词,更不能随便添加或删除。

【例 4】　　　　　　　　　　　　　　　　　　　　　　　　　　　　　　　　　　　　　　(05-12-S10)

The rule here is to keep it factual and truthful—exaggerations usually get find out.	S10. ＿＿＿＿＿＿

【解析】get 在此相当于系动词 be,get done 相当于 be done,故应将 find 改为 found。

秘诀五：句子原意要保持不变

一般来说，改错题应遵循保持句子原意的原则，即不能改变文章或作者所要表达的意思，包括其语气和上下文的逻辑关系，只能对短文中的用词错误、语法错误、行文逻辑错误进行改正。

【例5】　　　　　　　　　　　　　　　　　　　　　　　　　　　　　(04-1-S9)

Elsewhere, rice experts in the Philippines are producing a plant with few stems and more seeds.	S9. _____

【解析】and 连接并列结构，其前后的形式应保持一致。and 后用的比较级 more，其前面也应该用比较级，故应将 few 改成 fewer。需要注意的是，尽管将 more 改成 many 也可以保证并列结构的前后形式一致，但却无法表达出原文想要表达的比较含义，无法保证上下文语义的连贯。

秘诀六：小心局部通顺陷阱

有时孤立地分析某个句子，其可能结构正确、语义通顺，但如果联系上下文，将其放到整个语篇当中考虑，就会发现其实该句中存在不合逻辑的地方。因此，一定要警惕局部通顺的陷阱，结合语篇进行全面分析。

【例6】　　　　　　　　　　　　　　　　　　　　　　　　　　　　　(05-12-S6)

Get someone to check for spelling and grammatical errors, because a spell-checker will pick up every mistake.	S6. _____

【解析】从原因状语从句本身看，并没有什么语法错误，语义也比较通顺，但联系主句内容则会发现，此处表达不合逻辑。因为主句是说需要找个人来检查拼写和语法错误，那么肯定是因为 a spell-checker"无法"检查出所有的错误，因此应在 will 和 pick 之间加上 not。

Exercise　　　　　即讲即练

Last year's economy should have won the Oscar for the best picture. Growth in gross domestic product was 4. 1 percent; profits soar; exports flourished; and inflation stayed around 3 percent for the third year. So why so many Americans give the picture a lousy B rating? The answer is jobs. The macroeconomic situation was good, and the microeconomic numbers were not. Yes, 3 million new jobs were there, but not enough of them were temporary, good jobs paying enough to support a family. Job security was rampant. Even as they announced higher sales and profits, corporations acted as if they were in a tailspin, cut 516,069 jobs in 1994 alone, almost as much as in the recession year of 1991.

Yes, unemployment went up. But over 1 million workers were so discouraged that they left the labor force. More than 6 million who wanted full-time job were only partially employed; and another large group was neither unqualified or sheltered behind the euphemism of self-employment. We lost a million good manufacturing jobs between 1990 and 1995, continuing the trend has reduced the blue-collar work force from about 30 percent in the 1950s to about half that today. White-collar workers found out they were no longer immune. For the first time, they were let go in numbers virtually equal to those for blue-collar workers. Many resorted to temporary work with lower pay, fewer benefits but less status. All that in a country where people meet for the first time would say, "What do you do?"

1. _____

2. _____

3. _____

4. _____

5. _____

6. _____

7. _____

8. _____

9. _____

10. _____

【答案与解析】

1. soar — soared。时态错误。本句的分号提示 Growth…4.1 percent, profits soar, exports flourished 等是并列关系，其他分句都是过去时态，所以 soar 也应改为过去式 soared。

2. and — but。逻辑关系混乱。本句前半句说宏观经济情况是好的，后半句说微观的经济情况却并不好。两个分句明显存在对比关系，所以关系连词应使用转折连词 but。

3. temporary — permanent。上下文语义矛盾。结合上句可知，本句中的 not enough of them were…属于 microeconomic（微观经济）形式。既然上句已经指出了微观经济形式不容乐观，那么本句中的 not enough of them were…也应表示新工作的形式不容乐观，只有将 temporary 改写为其反义词 permanent 才能使句子的逻辑关系成立。如果通过在 temporary 采用否定词 not 使本句逻辑关系成立，那么其后的 good 也应加否定词 not，这样就违背了改错只改动一词的原则，而且也会使句子表达啰嗦。

4. security — insecurity。上下文语义矛盾。根据下句中的 cutting 516,069 jobs in 1994 可知，人们的工作并没有受到很好的保障，所以应将本句中的 security 改为 insecurity。

5. cut — cutting。非谓语动词误用。分析句子结构和含义可知，此处 cut 并不是和 were 并列充当从句的谓语，而应该是充当伴随状语，动词 cut 与其逻辑主语 they 之间是主动关系，故应将 cut 改为其现在分词形式 cutting。

6. much — many。易混词误用。much 修饰的是不可数名词，但 jobs 是可数名词，所以应将 much 改为 many。

7. up — down。上下文语义矛盾。如果只阅读了上文内容，可能很容易就会认为 unemployment went up 是正确的，但是通过下文中的 over 1 million workers…（100 多万工人因为太失望所以脱离了劳动力大军）和转折连词 but 可知应将 up 改为 down。

8. neither — either。平行结构错误。根据句意可知本句并没有否定含义，所以应将否定标志 neither 改写为 either，以与 or 构成固定搭配 either…or…。

9. trend ∧ has — that / which。缺漏。分析句子结构可知，has reduced…today 应为 trend 的后置定语，虽然也可将 has reduced 改写为现在分词 having reducing 的形式，但是这样就违背了改错只改动一词的原则，故应在 trend 和 has 之间添加引导词 that/which。

10. but — and。逻辑关系混乱。分析句子结构可知 lower pay, fewer benefits, less status 都是 with 的宾语，与 with 一起充当伴随状语。lower pay, fewer benefits, less status 都是 temporary work 的不足之处，所以 less status 与 fewer benefits 根本不存在对比关系，而是并列关系，故应将 but 改写为 and。

短文改错巅峰练习

Exercise 1

Despite the wave of industrial development that has swept much of East Asia in recent decades, the country of 80 million remains extremely poor, mismanaged and still was predominantly agrarian. But the Philippines do play a visible role in the global economy, thanks largely to a single export commodity—its people. According to the government, 1 million Filipinos will go abroad as contract workers this year. "The Philippines has already surpassed Mexico as largest source of migrant labor in the world," says Manolo I. Abella, a migration specialist at the International Labor Office in Geneva. In all, about 8 million Filipinos—an astounded one tenth of the country's citizens—currently work overseas to support families back home. They remit more than $7 billion annually, according to the government, and that's only official transfers. A recent Asian Development Bank report put the real figure in the $14 billion to $21 billion range—a sum that dwarfs both foreign direct investment and aid flowing into the country, and amounts 32 percent of GNP. In the past, the Philippines is shamed by its inability to create enough good jobs to keep its people at home. But hard economic reality has shifted the sentiment. Today, in a move which countries like Indonesia and Bangladesh are likely to emulate itself, the government takes the position that, like it or not, the overseas workers constitute nation's biggest comparative advantage in an increasingly borderless world. And so Manila makes it easy for its citizens to immigrate, and works hard, through its embassies, to see that their rights as foreign workers are protected.

62. _____
63. _____

64. _____

65. _____

66. _____

67. _____
68. _____

69. _____
70. _____

71. _____

Exercise 2

The biggest problem facing Chile as it promotes itself as a tourist destination is that it is at the end of the earth. It is too far southern to be a convenient stop on the way to anywhere else and is much further than a relatively cheap half-day's flight away from the bigtourist markets. Chile, therefore, is having to fight hard to attract tourists, to convince travellers that it is worthwhile coming halfway round the world to visit.

Like all South American countries, Chile sees tourism as a valuable earner of foreign currency, although it has been far more serious than most in promoting its image abroad. Relatively stable politically within the region, it has benefited from the problems

62. _____
63. _____

64. _____

suffering in other areas. In Peru, guerrilla in recent years has dealt a heavy blow on the tourist industry.

More than 150,000 people are directly involved in Chile's tourist sector, an industry earns the country's more than $ 950 million each year. The state-run National Tourism Service, in partner with a number of private companies, is currently running a worldwide campaign, takes part in trade fairs and international events to attract visitors to Chile. Chile's great strength as a tourist destinationis its geographical diversity. From the parched Atacama Desert in the north to the Antarctic snowfields of the south, it is more than 5000km long. With the Pacific on one side and the Andean mountains on the other, Chile boasts in natural attractions. Its beaches are not up to Caribbean standards and resorts, such as Vina del Mar are generally clean and unspoilt and have a high standard of service.

65. _____
66. _____

67. _____

68. _____
69. _____

70. _____
71. _____

答案与解析

Exercise 1

62. was — /。赘述。poor, mismanaged 和 agrarian 都可以作 remains 的表语,所以系动词 was 在此多余。

63. do — does。由破折号后的 its 可知,本句的主语 the Philippines 应为单数名词,所以谓语动词也应相应地使用第三人称单数,故应将 do 改为 does。

64. as ∧ largest — the。缺漏。最高级 largest 前应该加上定冠词 the。

65. astounded — astounding。形容词误用。astounded 表示"使…大吃一惊",而此处明显是想表达 800 万的菲律宾人出国工作是非常令人吃惊的,表示"令人吃惊的"应是 astounding,故应将 astounded 改为 astounding。

66. and — but。逻辑关系混乱。本句前一分句指出出国打工的人每年往国内汇款 more than $ 7 billion,但后一句指出真正的数字是 in the $14 billion to $21 billion range,这就说明 $ 7 billion 并不是很多,所以本句中两个分句的连接词应该用转折关系连词 but,故应将 and 改为 but。

67. amounts ∧ 32 — to。缺漏。amounts"总计,等于",为不及物动词,后接宾语时须借助于介词 to,故应在 amounts 后加介词 to。

68. is — was。时态错误。本句状语 in the past 提示谓语动词应用一般过去式,故应将 is 改为 was。

69. which — that。关系词误用。此处 a move 后面的从句是用来解释说明 a move 的,从句中不缺少任何成份,应该是一个同位语从句,故引导词应改为 that。

70. itself — /。赘述。分析本句句子成份可知,emulate"仿效"的宾语为 move,所以应将 itself 删除。

71. immigrate — emigrate。易混词误用。immigrate 指移居入境,指的是外国人移入一国的过程,而本文主要是讲菲律宾人出国打工,所以菲律宾居民应是向外国移民,故应用"emigrate"来表达这一移出过程。

Exercise 2

62. southern — south。易混词误用。south 和 southern 都有形容词性,都可以指"南方的",但 southern 比较抽象,通常表示能让人联想到南方,或是南方气息;而本句主要是讲 Chile 地理位置偏南,所以应用具体的表示方向的形容词 south,故应将 southern 改为 south。

63. further — farther。易混词误用。当 further 作形容词时,一般强调在程度上的"更进一步";而本句指的是距离上远,所以应用形容词 farther,故应将 further 改为 farther。

64. worthwhile — worth。易混词误用。worthwhile 的主语 it 应该是形式主语;而在本句中 it 明显指代的是 Chile,所以应用 worthwhile 的同义词 worth 替换,worth 的主语可以是物,故应将 worthwhile 改为 worth。

65. suffering — suffered。非谓语动词误用。the problems 与 other areas 之间明显是被动关系,故应将 suffering 改为 suffered。

66. on — to。介词误用。deal blow to sth. 是固定搭配,意为"给…打击",故应将 on 改为 to。

67. industry ∧ earns — which /that。缺漏。分析句子结构可知,an industry…作 Chile's tourist sector 的同位语,所以 earns…就是 an industry 的定语从句,由此可知在 industry 和 earns 中缺少了引导定语从句的关系词,故应

添加 which 或 that。

68. partner → partnership。易混词误用。partner 特指"具体的伙伴",而本句强调的是 National Tourism Service 与 a number of private companies 的伙伴关系,所以应将 partner 改为 partnership。in partnership with 意为"与…的伙伴关系"。

69. takes → taking。非谓语动词误用。本句主要是讲 National Tourism Service 目前正加入了 worldwide campaign 之中,takes part in trade fairs and international events… 正是加入 worldwide campaign 的方式,所以 takes part… 在句中应作状语,故应将 takes 改为非谓语动词 taking。

70. in → /。赘述。boasts(拥有)为及物动词,后面应直接跟宾语,所以应将介词 in 删除。

71. and → but。逻辑关系混乱。本句的前一分句指出 Chile 的海岸标准比不上 Caribbean,这是在讲 Chile 的劣势,后一分句指出 Chile 的旅游胜地非常 clean and unspoilt,并且 have a high standard of service,这明显是在讲 Chile 的优势。两个分句之间明显存在对比性,所以分句连接词应用转折关系连词,故应将 and 改为 but。

完型填空巅峰讲座

第三章

完型填空是大学英语六级考试的传统题型之一,改革前后没有明显变化,仍然是与改错题一起作为二选一题型出现。其文章长度一般在 250—300 词之间,共包括 20 个空白,每个空白为一题,每题有四个选项。考试时间为 15 分钟,分值比例为 10%。

Lecture 1   第一讲 5 大常见考查重点

完型填空的空白处所删去的词既有实词也有虚词,它的目的是测试考生各个层面上的语言理解能力和语言综合运用能力。具体来讲,其考查重点主要包括以下几项:

一、对上下文语义的理解

完型填空题首先考查的就是考生对上下文语义的理解,它要求考生在充分理解上下文的基础上,填入一个符合上下文语境的词,从而使文章意思完整。

【例 1】   (07-6-69)

【原文】	【选项】
But a ___69___ of the past year in disaster history suggests that modern Americans are particularly bad ...	[A] review [B] reminder [C] concept [D] prospect

【解析】本题考查对上下文语义的理解。空后的 the past year in disaster history 决定了答案只能为[A] review(回顾),其他三项均不能使语义通顺。

二、对上下文逻辑关系的把握

除了理解文中各个句子的含义,完型填空题还要求考生能够把握前后句子之间的逻辑关系,并能根据前后的逻辑关系选择正确的连接词,从而使上下文形成合理的衔接。

【例 2】   (05-6-70)

【原文】	【选项】
At present, Cyclops costs $ 50, 000. ___70___, Mr. Kurzweil and his associates are preparing a smaller but improved version that will sell for less than half that price.	[A] Likewise [B] Moreover [C] However [D] Though

【解析】本题考查对上下文逻辑关系的把握。空前说目前 Cyclops 价值 50,000 美元;空后说 Mr. Kurzweil 和他的同事们正在开发一种价格更便宜、性能却更好的产品,前后明显形成转折关系,故答案为[C] However。

三、对词语习惯搭配的掌握

词语的习惯搭配是完型填空的考查重点之一,主要包括动词短语、名词短语、形容词短语、介词短语等习惯性搭配以及英语中一些常用的固定句式。

【例 3】   (07-6-62)

【原文】	【选项】
Historically, humans get serious about avoiding disasters only after one has struck them. ___62___ that logic, 2006 should	[A] To [B] By [C] On [D] For

have been a breakthrough year for rational behavior.

【解析】本题考查对习惯搭配的掌握。by that logic 是习惯搭配,意为"按照那个逻辑"。

四、对近义、近形词的辨别

英语中有很多近义或近形的易混词语,有些词语在意义上十分相近,但用法上却存在细微区别;有的词语在词形上十分相近,词义却大相径庭。完型填空题中经常会涉及到这些近义或近形词的辨别,这就需要考生不但能够充分理解上下文的意思,还要对这些近义或近形词有比较扎实的掌握。

【例4】 (07-6-63)

【原文】	【选项】	
With the memory of 9/11 still ___63___ in their minds, Americans watched hurricane Katrina, the most expensive disaster in U.S. history, …	[A] fresh [C] apparent	[B] obvious [D] evident

【解析】本题考查对近义词的辨别。the memory of 9/11 still fresh 表示"9/11 的记忆依然清晰",[A] fresh 可以用来表示"(记忆)犹新",其他三个词虽都有"明显"的含义,但通常都不能用来修饰 memory。

五、对句子语法结构的分析

完型填空题对语法结构的考查主要集中在对结构词(即代词、冠词、介词、连词等语法结构关系词)的考查,以及对虚拟语气、定语从句及状语从句和倒装句的考查上。另外,除了在题目中直接考查对语法结构的掌握以外,完型填空的所有题目中都贯穿着对考生理解句子语法结构能力的考查。

【例5】 (07-6-76)

【原文】	【选项】	
They have got the walls to ___76___ they were before Katrina, more or less.	[A] which [C] what	[B] where [D] when

【解析】本题考查对句子语法结构的分析。空前的 to 在此处表示方位,空格处所填词应能引导地点状语从句,故答案为[B] where。

Exercise　　　即讲即练

Though it is a mere one to three percent of the population, the upper class ___1___ at least 25 percent of the nation's wealth. This class has two segments: upper upper and lower upper. Basically, the upper upper class is the "old rich"—families that have been wealthy for several generations—an aristocracy of ___2___ and wealth. A few are known across the nation, such as the Rockefellers, and the Vanderbilts. Most are not ___3___ to the general public. They have no ___4___ to the rest of the community, ___5___ their income from the investment of their inherited wealth. By ___6___, the lower upper class is the "new rich". ___7___ they may be wealthier than some of the old rich, the new rich have been ___8___ to make their money like ___9___ else beneath their class. Thus their status is generally lower than that of the old rich, who

1. [A] possesses [B] demands [C] obtains [D] attains
2. [A] beginning [B] birth [C] infancy [D] foundation
3. [A] visible [B] seen [C] obvious [D] apparent
4. [A] connection [B] association
   [C] communication [D] relation
5. [A] pulling [B] extracting [C] drawing [D] making
6. [A] comparison [B] contrast [C] contrary [D] difference
7. [A] Although [B] Because [C] Therefore [D] However
8. [A] greedy [B] indifferent
   [C] unconcerned [D] uninterested
9. [A] nobody [B] everybody
   [C] somebody [D] anybody
10. [A] hand [B] thumb
    [C] finger [D] toe
11. [A] want [B] like [C] tend [D] hate
12. [A] Notwithstanding [B] Although
    [C] However [D] Whatever
13. [A] train [B] study
    [C] cultivate [D] nurture

have not found it necessary to lift a __10__ to make their money, and who __11__ to look down upon the new rich. __12__ its wealth is acquired, the upper class is very rich. They have enough money and leisure time to __13__ an interest in the arts and to __14__ rare books, paintings, and sculptures. They generally live in exclusive areas, __15__ to exclusive social clubs, communicate with each other, and marry their own kind—all of which keeps them so __16__ from the masses that they have been called the out-of-sight class. More than any other class, they tend to be __17__ of being members of a class. They also __18__ an enormous amount of power and influence here and abroad, as they __19__ many top government positions and control multinational corporations. Their actions __20__ the lives of millions.

14. [A] collect   [B] gather
    [C] assemble   [D] amass
15. [A] stick   [B] cling
    [C] attach   [D] belong
16. [A] distant   [B] far
    [C] removed   [D] remote
17. [A] aware   [B] conscious
    [C] sensitive   [D] sensible
18. [A] demand   [B] control
    [C] direct   [D] command
19. [A] seize   [B] retain
    [C] hold   [D] maintain
20. [A] influence   [B] affect
    [C] move   [D] manage

【答案与解析】

【文章大意】

本文的主要内容是关于上层阶级的两个组成部分。上层阶级拥有至少 25% 的国家财富,他们又分为老牌的富翁和新贵,接下来文章讲到了这两类人群各自的生活习惯,职业特征以及对国家和社会的影响力。

1. 选[A]。本题考查对上下文语义的理解。所填词应该表明 the upper class 与 25 percent of the nation's wealth 之间的关系。本句大意是尽管 the upper class 只占总人口的 1%—3%,但是他们的财富却占整个国家财富的 25%,选项中的动词只有[A] possesses(占有,拥有)符合句意。

2. 选[B]。本题考查对上下文语义的理解。破折号之间的内容 families that have been wealthy for several generations(连续几代人都很富有的家庭)表明 the "old rich" 是靠继承上一代的财富才变得富有的,由此可推测 the "old rich" 家族的人所拥有的财富是与生俱来的,故应选[B] birth(出生)。

3. 选[A]。本题考查对上下文语义的理解。由本句中的 most 与上句中的 a few 之间的对比可知,两个句子之间存在对比关系。上句说 A few are known across the nation(有一些富人全国闻名),那么本句肯定就是说大多数富人都是不出名的,即大多数富人都是不太能引起 the general public(普通大众)注意的。[A] visible 含有"引起公共注视的,令人瞩目的"含义,故为本题答案。

4. 选[D]。本题考查对词语习惯搭配的掌握。四个选项中与 to 搭配使用的只有[D] relation(关系),have a relation to sth. 意为"与…有关,有来往"。[A] connection、[B] association、[C] communication 通常都与 with 搭配使用。

5. 选[C]。本题考查对上下文语义的理解。所填词与 the income 构成动宾搭配,且与 from 结构同现,符合这两个条件的只有[C] drawing,当其宾语与钱有关时,意为"提款,取钱,获得…"。[A] pulling"拉;拖"后面跟与钱有关的名词时,通常需与 down 搭配使用,pull down 意为"获得钱作为报酬";[B] extracting"拔出,提取",extract …from…意为"从…中提炼出…",与此处语义不符;[D] making"制造",它后面通常会直接跟 money,如 make some money 意为"赚钱"。

6. 选[B]。本题考查对上下文逻辑关系的把握。上文提到 upper upper class is the"old rich"(上层阶级是老牌的富翁),而本句指出 the lower upper class is the "new rich"(上层阶级的底层是新贵),old 和 new 构成反义词复现,所以两者是相反的意思,并且所填词与 by 搭配,所以只能选[B] contrast"对照,对比"。by contrast 意为"相反,相对照而言"。[A] comparison"比较",by comparison 意为"比较而言,比较之下",不适合本句;[C] contrary"相反,反面"通常与 on 搭配使用,on the contrary 意为"相反";[D] difference"差异"通常不与 by 搭配使用。

7. 选[A]。本题考查对上下文逻辑关系的把握。下句句首的 Thus 提示上句所说的情况是造成下句所说的新贵比老牌富翁地位低的原因。由上文可知老牌富翁地位之所以高是因为他们 have no relation to the rest of the community(与普通大众没有联系),这就间接地说明了新贵的地位低是因为他们与普通大众有联系,并会像所有的普通大众一样渴望赚钱,故第 8 小题应选[A] greedy(渴望的,贪婪的),第 9 小题应选[B] everybody。

8. 选[A]。本题考查对上下文语义的理解。分析见第 7 小题。

9. 选[B]。本题考查对近形词的辨别。分析见第 7 小题。

10. 选[C]。本题考查对词语习惯搭配的掌握。lift a finger（通常用于否定句）意为"举手之劳，出一点儿力"；其他的三个词[A] hand；[B] thumb"拇指"；[D] toe"脚趾"都没有这样的搭配。

11. 选[C]。本题考查对上下文语义的理解。空格前的 who 指代的是 the old rich，由 look down upon the new rich 可知老牌富翁往往看不起那些新贵们，故应选[C] tend to do sth. 意为"往往，倾向于"。want to do sth. 意为"想要做…"，like to do sth. 意为"喜欢做…"，瞧不起无所谓想要与否或是喜欢与否；而 hate to do sth. "讨厌做…"则与文意相反。

12. 选[C]。本题考查对上下文逻辑关系的把握。空格所在的分句说的是老牌富翁财富的获得，后一个分句说他们很富有，前后两个分句之间不存在逻辑上的转折关系，所以排除[A] Notwithstanding"虽然，尽管"与[B] Although "虽然，尽管"。[C] However"不管用何种方法"，引导让步状语从句，符合语境，说明"不管老牌富翁的财富是如何获得的，他们都很富有"；[D] Whatever"无论怎样的，无论哪一种"，也引导让步状语从句，但不符合此处语境。

13. 选[C]。本题考查对上下文语义的理解。根据四个选项的提示可推测，本句的含义很可能是表示那些老牌富翁有足够的金钱和时间去培养兴趣。[A] train"培训，训练"，指训练、培养技能，宾语不能是 interest；[B] study"研究"，与 interest 不搭配；[D] nurture"养育，教育"，同样不能与 interest 搭配；[C] cultivate"培养（兴趣等）"正符合语境，故为本题答案。

14. 选[A]。本题考查对近义词的辨别。四个选项均有"收集"之意，但用法上有区分：[A] collect"收集"指作为一个爱好或为学习而收集；[B] gather"聚集，使聚在一起；采集"；[C] assemble 指为了一定的目的召集到一起成为一组或整体；[D] amass"积聚（尤指财富）"。此处指的是作为爱好而收集 rare books, paintings, and sculptures（罕见的书画和雕塑），故答案为[A] collect。

15. 选[D]。本题考查对上下文语义的理解。四个选项均可以与 to 搭配使用，但语义上有区分：[A] stick"粘住"，stick to 意为"坚持"；[B] cling"附着，紧贴"，cling to 意为"紧抓住，坚持，依靠"；[C] attach"贴上，系上"，attach…to…意为"把…贴在…上"；[D] belong"属于"，belong to 意为"属于"。句中的 they 指 the upper class，他们与 exclusive social club 应该是从属关系，故答案为[D]。

16. 选[A]。本题考查对近义词的辨别。由后面的解释 out-of-sight class 可知本句指的是上层阶级疏远大众，被称之为"看不见的阶级"，故选[A] distant。因为 distant 不但可以表示"距离远"，还可以表示"关系远的，疏远的，冷漠的"，例如：distant relations"远亲"。[B] far 则只能表示空间距离远；[C] removed"远离的，与…无关的"；[D] remote"遥远的，偏僻的"，含有不易到达的意思，不能修饰 them。

17. 选[B]。本题考查对词语习惯搭配的掌握。首先从是否能与介词 of 搭配使用上来看，可以将[C] sensitive、[D] sensible 排除。[A] aware"知道的，意识到的"，be aware of 意为"意识到，明白"；[B] conscious"有知觉的"，be conscious of 意为"内心上注意的或敏感的，留心的、意识到的"。根据本句的语义可以判断[B] conscious 更符合句意。

18. 选[D]。本题考查对词语习惯搭配的掌握。所填词与 power and influence 语义场同现，而且这种权力与影响力是国内与国外的，所以可推测本句话的意思是"上层阶级在国内和国外都掌握着巨大的权力和影响力"，故答案为[D] command"掌握，支配"。[A] demand"要求"，[B] control"控制，支配"，[C] direct"指导，指挥"都不能与 power 和 influence 同时搭配使用。

19. 选[C]。本题考查对词语习惯搭配的掌握。四个选项中，通常后面可以跟 position 作宾语的动词为[C] hold"占据，拥有"，hold position 指"占据职位"，如：held the governorship for six years"担任了六年的州长"。[A] seize"抓住，夺取"，[B] retain"保留"，[D] maintain"维持，维修"均不能与 position 搭配。

20. 选[B]。本题考查对近义词的辨别。[A] influence 指"通过说服、举例等对行动、思想、性格等产生不易觉察到的、潜移默化的影响"。[B] affect 指"产生的影响之大足以引起反应"，着重"影响"的动作，有时含有"对…产生不利影响"的意思；[C] move"感动"；[D] manage"管理，控制"。对比四个选项中动词的含义可知，最符合本句句意的为[B] affect。

Lecture 2　第二讲　4 种常见题目类型

一、语义衔接题

　　语义衔接题要求考生根据上下文语义的要求，在空白处填入合适的词，使上下文语义通顺。这类题的四个选项大多是以近义词、反义词、近形词的形式出现。

【例1】

【原文】	【选项】
In A. D. 63, Pompeii was seriously damaged by an earthquake, and the locals immediately went to work ___68___, in the same spot—until they were buried altogether by a volcano eruption 16 years later.	[A] revising [B] refining [C] rebuilding [D] retrieving

【解析】语义衔接题。空后的 in the same spot 提示,当地人是想在原来的地方重建 Pompeii,故答案为[C] rebuilding。

二、惯用衔接题

惯用衔接题要求考生根据某些习惯搭配或固定句式的要求,在空白处填入合适的词,使前后形成合理的搭配关系。这类题的选项多为介词。

【例2】

【原文】	【选项】
But it turns ___72___ that in times of crisis, our greatest enemy is ___73___ the storm, the quake or the…	[A] up [B] down [C] over [D] out

【解析】惯用衔接题。It turns out that…为固定句式,意为"结果是…,原来是…"。

三、结构衔接题

结构衔接题要求考生根据上下文语法结构的需要,在空白处填入合适的词,使句子的语法结构完整。这类题的选项多为引导从句的关系代词或关系副词。经常涉及到的语法结构有名词性从句、定语从句、强调句型、虚拟语气、倒装等。

【例3】

【原文】	【选项】
But it may be all ___78___ can be expected from one year of hustle(忙碌). Meanwhile, New Orleans officials have…	[A] but [B] as [C] that [D] those

【解析】结构衔接题。分析句子结构可知,所填词应为定语从句的引导词,先行词为 all,所填词应在从句中充当主语,故答案为[C] that。

四、逻辑衔接题

逻辑衔接题要求考生根据上下文因果、转折、并列等逻辑关系的要求,在空白处填入正确的衔接词语,使上下文形成合理的逻辑衔接。这类题的选项多为 because, however, so, or 等逻辑关系衔接词。

【例4】

【原文】	【选项】
"This is the first time that blind people have ever done individual studies ___79___ a product was put on the market," Hingson said.	[A] after [B] when [C] before [D] as

【解析】逻辑衔接题。按照逻辑,studies(研究)肯定是发生在产品 put on the market(上市)之前,而且前文也明确提到这种新机型还处在研发之中,故答案[C] before。

Exercise　　　即讲即练

Television is now playing a very important part in our life. But television, like other things, has both advantages and disadvantages. Do the former overweigh the latter?

In the first ___1___, television is not only a convenient source of entertainment, but also a (n) ___2___ cheaper one. For a family of four, for example, it is more ___3___ as well as cheaper to sit comfortably at home, with almost unlimited entertainment ___4___, than to go out in ___5___ of other sorts of entertainment ___6___. They do not have to pay for expensive seats at the theater, the cinema, or the opera, only to discover, perhaps, that the show is ___7___. All they have to do is ___8___ a button, and they can see plays, films, operas, and shows of every kind, not to ___9___ political discussions and the ___10___ exciting football match. Some people, ___11___, maintain that this is precisely where the danger lies. The television viewer ___12___ no initiative. He makes no choice and exercises no judgment. He is completely ___13___ and has everything presented to him without any effort ___14___ his part.

Television, it is often said, keeps one ___15___ about current events, allows one to ___16___ the latest developments in science and politics, and offers an endless ___17___ of programs which are both instructive and ___18___. The most distant countries and the strangest customs are brought right into one's sitting room. ___19___ here again there is a danger. We get so used to looking at it, so dependent on its sparkling pictures ___20___ it begins to dominate our lives.

1. [A] position　　[B] action　　[C] place　　[D] point
2. [A] comparatively　　　　[B] completely
   [C] absolutely　　　　　　[D] essentially
3. [A] easy　　　　　　　　[B] comfortable
   [C] convenient　　　　　　[D] inexpensive
4. [A] assessable　　　　　　[B] adaptable
   [C] approachable　　　　　[D] available
5. [A] need　　　　　　　　[B] exploration
   [C] hunt　　　　　　　　[D] search
6. [A] somewhere　　　　　　[B] anywhere
   [C] elsewhere　　　　　　[D] nowhere
7. [A] fascinating　　　　　　[B] interesting
   [C] disappointing　　　　　[D] touching
8. [A] press　　[B] dial　　[C] bang　　[D] knock
9. [A] talk　　[B] mention　　[C] state　　[D] declare
10. [A] modern　　[B] latest　　[C] last　　[D] latter
11. [A] moreover　　　　　　[B] therefore
    [C] whereas　　　　　　　[D] however
12. [A] makes　　　　　　　[B] does
    [C] takes　　　　　　　　[D] performs
13. [A] positive　　　　　　　[B] passive
    [C] dull　　　　　　　　[D] boring
14. [A] on　　[B] with　　[C] by　　[D] in
15. [A] announced　　　　　[B] acquainted
    [C] instructed　　　　　　[D] informed
16. [A] follow　　　　　　　[B] search
    [C] trace　　　　　　　　[D] chase
17. [A] selections　　　　　　[B] series
    [C] chains　　　　　　　[D] strings
18. [A] astonishing　　　　　[B] accommodating
    [C] entertaining　　　　　[D] overwhelming
19. [A] Thus　　[B] While　　[C] Yet　　[D] Still
20. [A] as　　[B] what　　[C] which　　[D] that

【答案与解析】

【文章大意】
　　本文的主要内容是关于电视的利弊。文章开始就提到电视在我们的生活中扮演着很重要的角色,它有利有弊,接着说明了电视对我们的生活带来的便利,最后作者点明了其中潜在的危险——电视已经在某种程度上开始主宰我们的生活。

1. 选[C]。惯用衔接题。in the first place 意为"首先,第一点"。
2. 选[A]。语义衔接题。句中的形容词比较级 cheaper 提示所填副词也应该含有比较的意味,四个选项中的副词只有[A] comparatively"比较地"符合要求。[B] completely"完全地"和[C] absolutely"完全地,绝对地"没有比较的含义;[D] fairly"相当地",不能修饰比较级。
3. 选[C]。语义衔接题。as well as 连接并列成份,其后的 cheaper 提示所填词不能与它同义,所以可以排除[D] inexpensive"不贵的";本句真正的主语是 to sit comfortably at home,所以所填词不可能是[B] comfortable"舒服的",否则会使句子表达的含义出现重复啰嗦的语病;[A] easy 的比较级是 easier,而不是 more easy。本题答案为[C] convenient。
4. 选[D]。语义衔接题。本题的选择可以根据四个选项的语义来判断,[D] available"可得到的,可利用的",with

unlimited entertainment available 意为"有无限的娱乐可以享受",符合语境。既然是 unlimited entertainment(无限的娱乐),就不应该是[B] measurable;娱乐也不是可估价的,故[A] assessable 错误;[C] valuable 应该作为前置定语修饰 valuable entertainment。

5. 选[D]。语义衔接题。[A] need"需要",in need of 意为"需要";[B] exploration"探险,探索",in exploration of"探索";[C] hunt"猎取,搜索,搜寻",它构成的短语通常是 on the hunt (for),意为"正在寻找";[D] search"寻找",in search of 意为"寻找,寻求"。比较各选项语义,可知答案为[D] search。

6. 选[C]。语义衔接题。根据四个选项可以初步推测本句的意思是看电视比"到别处去寻找其他娱乐方式要方便和便宜",[C] elsewhere(在别处),指离开家到其他的地方去。[A] somewhere"某处",[B] anywhere"无论何处",[D] nowhere"到处都无",均不符合题意。

7. 选[C]。语义衔接题。only to 意为"不料却,没想到会…"是对前面所叙述事情的转折,说明一种意料之外的事情。本句的前半句指出在家看电视的好处就是不必花很多钱去剧院、影院和戏院看电影或戏剧,所以所填词就应该是表示在家看电视的缺点,四个选项中符合要求的只有[C] disappointing"令人失望的"。[A] fascinating"迷人的",[B] interesting"有趣的",[D] touching"感人的",均不符合题意。

8. 选[A]。语义衔接题。[A] press"按键或按钮",press the button"按按钮",符合题意。[B] dial"打电话时拨号",[C] bang"重击,猛击,猛撞",[D] knock"敲击",均不能用在本句中。

9. 选[B]。惯用衔接题。not to mention 为固定搭配,意为"更不用说",故答案为[B] mention。

10. 选[B]。语义衔接题。根据常识可知,我们通常看足球比赛都是看最新的,故答案为[B] latest"最新的,最近的"。[A] modern"现代的,时髦的",[C] last"最后的,上一个",[D] past"过去的",都与句意不符。

11. 选[D]。逻辑衔接题。上文一直在强调电视的优点,而本句却说"有些人认为这是危险所在",由此可知本句是对上文的转折,所以应选表转折关系的副词[D] however。

12. 选[C]。惯用衔接题。take…initiative 为固定搭配,意为"占据主动,采取主动行为"。

13. 选[B]。语义衔接题。上文指出 The television viewer takes no initiative(看电视的人从不采取主动行为),He makes no choice and exercises no judgment(他从不选择自己想要的,也不作出任何判断),由此可推测这种人应该是"被动的",所以答案为[B] passive。[C] dull"迟钝的,呆滞的",从本句语义上看虽然符合本句句意,但是与上下文衔接不当,故可排除。

14. 选[A]。惯用衔接题。on one's part 为固定搭配,意为"就某人来说,出自某人一方"。in part 意为"部分地",其他的介词与 part 都不能构成固定搭配。

15. 选[D]。语义衔接题。keep sb. informed 意为"使某人知道,随时告知情况",所以[D] informed(见多识广的)符合题意。[A] announced"宣布,宣告";[B] notified"正式的官方通知";[C] reformed 是 informed 的形近词,意为"改革"。

16. 选[A]。语义衔接题。[A] follow 意为"密切注意,以了解明白事情的过程、进展",符合本句要求,为本题答案,本句的意思是"电视使我们了解科学和政治的最新发展"。[B] search"探索,寻求,寻找",[C] trace"探索,回溯,追踪",[D] chase"追捕,追击",都不符合句意。

17. 选[B]。惯用衔接题。a series of 为固定搭配,意为"一系列",本句的意思是"提供一系列看不完的电视节目"。[A] selections"选择,选集",[C] chain"(一连串)连结在一起的一系列事物",[D] string"(一串,一行)串在一起的物体",都不符合句意。

18. 选[C]。语义衔接题。分析句子结构可知,所填词与 instructive 都是在讲 programs 的好处,四个选项中只有[C] entertaining"有趣的,愉快的"符合本文所说的 programs 的好处,为本题答案。[A] astonishing"令人吃惊的",[B] accommodating"乐于助人的",[D] overwhelming"压倒性的",均不符合句意。

19. 选[C]。逻辑衔接题。上一句讲的是电视的好处,而本句话锋一转指出电视的危害,所以所填词应该是表示转折关系的连词。[C] Yet"然而"多用于句子开头表示转折,为本题答案。[A] Thus 表示结果关系;[B] While"虽然,然而"为连词,只能用于复合句中;[D] Still"仍然"语义与本句不符。

20. 选[D]。结构衔接题。so…that 为固定句型,that 引导结果状语从句,符合句意。

Lecture 3　第三讲　6 大快速解题技巧

解答完型填空题的关键在于能否迅速排除干扰选项、准确找到上下文中的"照应关系",而要想做到这一点,掌握一定的技巧和方法是十分必要的。

技巧一：代入选项排除明显的干扰

如果不能很有把握地直接选出某一道题的答案,可以先利用排除法将各选项代入空白处,排除明显不符题意的选项,从而缩小选择的范围。具体来讲,可以利用如下线索:

1. 判断所填词在句中充当什么成份,应是什么词性,从而排除干扰选项。
2. 利用上下文的时态、语态和语气排除不符合要求的干扰选项。
3. 利用名词的数来判断各选项是否符合句子要求。
4. 寻找与空白处构成搭配的词语,从而排除不能与其搭配的选项。
5. 将各选项代入空白处将句子译成汉语,排除明显不能使句子通顺的选项。

【例1】 (07-6-75)

【原文】	【选项】	
So what has happened in the year that ___75___ the disaster on the Gulf Coast?	[A] ensued	[B] traced
	[C] followed	[D] occured

【解析】语义衔接题。分析句子结构可知,此处需要一个及物动词,在 that 引导的定语从句中充当谓语动词。[A] ensued(接着发生)和[D] occurred(发生)均为不及物动词,故首先排除。[C] followed(跟着,接着),为及物动词,符合句意。

技巧二：寻找固定搭配或习惯用法

运用词汇间的搭配关系经常可以无需理解上下文而直接确定答案。即使确定不了答案,也往往可以排除一些明显不符合搭配关系的选项,缩小选择范围,提高答案的准确率。

【例2】 (05-6-80)

【原文】	【选项】	
"Most manufacturers believed that having the blind was like telling disabled people to teach other disabled people. In that ___80___, the manufacturers have been the blind ones."	[A] occasion	[B] moment
	[C] sense	[D] event

【解析】语义衔接题。由空前的介词 in 可以排除[A]、[B]两项,因为 occasion(场合)和 moment(时刻)一般都不与介词 in 连用。此处是说,制造商请盲人参与检测,就像是在告诉残疾人去教其他残疾人,从那种意义上说,制造商就是盲人。in that sense 为习惯搭配,意为"从那种意义上说"。in that event 意为"如果那种情况发生",尽管搭配正确,但不符合此处语义要求。

技巧三：理清空格所在句子结构

理清句子的语法结构对解答完型填空题来说尤其重要。这不仅仅限于直接考查语法结构的题目,在解答那些不是针对语法结构而设置的题目时,考生也必须仔细分析每个句子的语法结构,从而理解句子的含义和上下文之间的逻辑关系,最终在空白处填入正确的词。

【例3】 (07-6-71)

【原文】	【选项】	
We know more than we ___71___ did about the dangers we face. But it turns...	[A] never	[B] ever
	[C] then	[D] before

【解析】分析句子结构可知,本句中包含一个 than 引导的比较状语从句,比较对象是我们现在对所面临危险的了解和我们过去对所面临危险的了解,从句中的谓语动词 did 代替的是实义动词 knew,所填词应为副词,修饰动词 did,表示"过去"的概念,故答案为[B] ever(曾经)。

技巧四：寻找复现或共现关系

完型填空的文章是一个意义相关联的语篇,围绕一个话题论述,因此在行文中词语的重复、替代、复现和同现现象是不可避免的。根据这个原则,某一个空格所对应的答案很可能就是在上下文中复现或同现的相关词,考生可以根据这些词之间的有机联系来确定答案。所以,解题时应联系上下文寻找相关线索,如某一个词的原词、指代词、同义词、近义词、上义词、下义词和概括词等。

【例4】

【原文】	【选项】
His machine, Cyclops, has a camera that scans any page, interprets the print into sounds, and then delivers them orally in a robot-like ___66___ through a speaker.	[A] behavior [B] expression [C] movement [D] voice

【解析】语义衔接题。空前的 sounds(声音)和 orally(口头地)和空后的 speaker(扬声器)与所填词构成语义场共现,由此可推知答案为[D] voice(说话声)。

技巧五:熟悉常用的逻辑关系词语

只有明确文章结构,了解段与段之间、句与句之间的逻辑关系,才能加深对文章的理解,从而在空白处填入正确的词语,这就要求考生熟悉和掌握一些常用的逻辑关系词语。

常用的逻辑关系词语包括:

逻辑关系	常用连接词语
并列	and, as well as, both…and, not only…but(also), neither…nor
转折	but, however, whereas, while, yet, still, instead, nevertheless, notwithstanding, on the other hand, not…but, rather than
选择	or, nor, or else, otherwise, either…or
递进	besides, also, even, moreover, likewise, furthermore, what's more, in addition
解释	that is (to say), in other words
时间	when, whenever, as, since, till, until, before, after, once, the moment(/day/instant/minute/second), every time, no sooner…than, hardly…when, then, meanwhile, subsequently, afterward, later
比较或对比	(not) as…as, not so…as, (not) such…as, (not) the same as, than, in contrast, on the contrary
条件	if, unless, providing(/provided) that, as(/so) long as, on condition that, suppose(/supposing) that, in case, only if, if only
因果	because, since, as, now that, seeing that, considering that, in that, for, thus, so, therefore, hence, consequently, accordingly, as a result, so that
让步	though, although, even if(/though), as, while, whatever, wherever, whoever, however, no matter…, whether…or

技巧六:利用文章和段落的主题句

为了使考生更易于理解文章内容,出题者在设计完型填空试题时,总是保留一个完整的或是大半个完整的表达主旨的句子,而这样的句子往往位于文章的开头。因此,考生应充分利用文章开头来了解文章的主旨。另外,段落的首句也往往是该段的主题句。所以,考生也要学会利用段首句提供的信息,把握文章的结构和行文思路。

Exercise

即讲即练

Skyrocketing salaries, foreign workers, and raids on other corporations for talents are all becoming part of ___1___ as usual for many technology-based corporations today. These ___2___ are not cold-blooded; they have simply become necessary for ___3___ in the current technology explosion, which has caused a ___4___ shortage of qualified talents. This shortage will only increase as the world continues to move online.

Is there a better way to get talented employees

1. [A] profession   [B] commerce
     [C] trade   [D] business
2. [A] schemes   [B] tactics
     [C] plots   [D] tricks
3. [A] survival   [B] existence
     [C] living   [D] standing
4. [A] significant   [B] major
     [C] important   [D] large
5. [A] firing   [B] meeting
     [C] facing   [D] hiring

without __5__ under-qualified college graduates and paying for extensive training to get them up to par? There is. Your company can __6__ in education.

It's easier __7__ you think locally, not globally. Find a __8__ college or university that offers a major in your company's field and build a __9__ with it.

Starting small is a good idea. Call the college, talk to the __10__ department head, and offer your company's assistance. Offering the school a chance to train students __11__ your company's software or hardware __12__ that there will be more people trained in the use of these products. __13__ adds to your company's market share and potential employee __14__, and enhances its public image. __15__ may qualify your company for tax deductions, which can help increase its bottom __16__.

What's the next step? __17__ those better-educated college students into employable talents by becoming a (an) __18__ site for the school. Internships offer companies a chance to __19__ the education of students through real-world experience while __20__ out prospective employees without incurring huge expenses.

6. [A] cooperate　　　　　[B] invest
　　[C] wade　　　　　　　[D] involve
7. [A] except　　[B] if　　[C] lest　　[D] than
8. [A] small　　　　　　　[B] native
　　[C] famous　　　　　　[D] local
9. [A] relation　　　　　　[B] association
　　[C] relationship　　　　[D] connection
10. [A] appropriate　　　　[B] respectable
　　[C] respectful　　　　　[D] appreciative
11. [A] with　[B] on　[C] for　　[D] in
12. [A] represents　　　　　[B] means
　　[C] claims　　　　　　　[D] proclaims
13. [A] Those　[B] These　[C] This　[D] Such
14. [A] bank　[B] store　[C] number　[D] pool
15. [A] Donations　　　　　[B] Dedication
　　[C] Assistance　　　　　[D] Cooperation
16. [A] raw　[B] margin　[C] line　[D] border
17. [A] Change　[B] Transfer　[C] Turn　[D] Shift
18. [A] experiment　　　　　[B] internship
　　[C] exercise　　　　　　[D] training
19. [A] further　　　　　　[B] support
　　[C] continue　　　　　　[D] finance
20. [A] testing　　　　　　[B] examining
　　[C] sifting　　　　　　　[D] selecting

【答案与解析】

【文章大意】

本文的主要内容是关于公司如何找到合适而又合格的人才。文章开始就说新形势的发展使得公司里的合格人才缺乏,接着作者对这个问题提出了合理的解决方法,那就是企业为学生提供实习的机会,学校把优秀的学生输送到企业去实习,这样造成一种双赢的局面。

1. 选[D]。语义衔接题。由四个选项可知本题主要是区别各个表示"商业"的名词。[A] profession"职业",指"需受过特殊教育和训练的脑力劳动者的职业";[B] commerce"商业,贸易",特指国与国之间的商业往来;[C] trade"买卖或货物交换",特指国内外之间的贸易;[D] business"经济,商业",含义很广,通常指"生意,行业",表示"为图利(常指为个人谋利)而做的工作"。综合整篇文章可知,本文并不与国内外或国与国之间的经济来往有关,故可排除[A] profession、[B] commerce 和[C] trade。

2. 选[B]。语义衔接题。空前的指示形容词 these 提示,these _____ 指代的应是上句中的 skyrocketing salaries, foreign workers, raids on other corporations for talents,它们都是目前公司为了发展而采取的一些策略,故答案为[B] tactics"策略,手段"。[A] schemes"诡计,方案",[C] plots"阴谋,秘密计划",[D] tricks"诡计,窍门"都含有贬义,与句中的表语 not cold-blooded 抵触,所以均应排除。

3. 选[A]。语义衔接题。本分句中的 they 指代的是 skyrocketing salaries, foreign workers, raids on other corporations for talents,公司采取这些策略当然是为了公司的生存及发展,故答案为[A] survival"生存"。[B] existence"存在",强调存在的静态状态;[C] living"生存,生活",live in 指人生活在某地,后面的宾语不能是 the current technology explosion;[D] standing"站立",stand in 意为"位于···中",明显不符合句意。

4. 选[B]。语义衔接题。which 引导定语从句,修饰 technology explosion,众所周知 technology explosion(科技爆发)即科技的迅速发展会导致 qualified talents(人才)严重紧缺。所以应选[B] major"非常严重的",该词除了名词"专业"及形容词"大量的"的含义,还有"非常严重的"含义。[A] significant "有意义的,重大的"和[C] important"重要的",不能修饰 shortage;[D] large 只能修饰平均尺寸、长度、数量或数额,也不能修饰 shortage。

5. 选[D]。语义衔接题。下句中的 There is 说明本句提出的问题是有解决方法的,根据下文可知,该解决方法就是公司与能提供他们所需要人才的学校建立联系,并向该学校提供相应的帮助,这样做的目的就是该校学生毕业后,公司可以不用花费大量的时间和金钱对他们进行培训,他们就可以直接上岗。由此可推断出本句问的问题就是有没有更好的方法能使公司不雇用 under-qualified college graduates(能力还达不到要求的大学毕业生)及花费大量的金钱培训他们。故答案为[D] hiring"雇用"。

6. 选[B]。语义衔接题。根据第5小题的分析可知,公司与能提供他们所需要人才的学校建立联系及提供相应的帮助都属于公司为教育投资的范畴,故答案为[B] invest"投资",invest in"投资"。[A] cooperate"与某人合作",须与 with 搭配;[C] wade"跋涉",wade in"插手",含有贬义;[D] involve in"密切关联,牵连,和…直接有关",不符合文意。

7. 选[B]。结构衔接题。句中虽有比较级但没有两者的比较关系,我们可以初步排除 than。如将[A] except"只是,要不是" 和 [C] lest"惟恐,以免,免得"放入句中,句子逻辑混乱。[B] if 用在句中时,本句意为"如果从当地着手而不是从全球范围考虑,那么事情就非常简单了",[B] if 在此起到委婉建议的作用,故为本题答案。

8. 选[D]。语义衔接题。根据第7小题的分析可知,本文提倡的是 think locally,所以如果选择能向公司提供所需要人才的学校,也应该从公司所在地考虑,故答案应为[D] local"当地的,本地的"。

9. 选[C]。语义衔接题。如果公司从当地选择好了一个能给它提供所需要人才的学校,那么当然公司就应该与该学校建立起一定的关系。[A] relation"关系,联系",不如[C] relationship"友好关系"确切;[B] association"协会,联合",表示"与…有关联"时通常用的短语是 in association with;[D] connection"联系",同 relation,不带有感情色彩。结合上面的分析可知,答案应为[C] relationship。

10. 选[B]。语义衔接题。本段建议公司打电话到学校与负责相关专业的系主任联系。[A] appropriate"合适的",不用于修饰人;[B] respectable"可敬的,有名望的",符合此处语意;[C] respectful "尊重人的,有礼貌的",语义不符;[D] appreciative"有欣赏力的",逻辑虽符,但放在此处语义不符。

11. 选[D]。惯用衔接题。由空格后的 your company's software or hardware 可知此处指的是在公司软件或硬件方面的培训,故应选[D] in,train in 意为"在某方面培训"。[A] train with"用…培训,结交",显然不符合语境。本题也可用同义复现的技巧。从句中的"be more people trained in the use of these products"复现了 train in。

12. 选[B]。语义衔接题。此题主要从辨析词义入手:[A] represents"显示,呈现";[B] means"意思是,意味着";[C] claims"主张";[D] proclaims"宣布,声明"。通过各单词词义的对比可知答案为[B] means。本句意为"公司为学校提供培训学生使用该公司软件或硬件的机会,这意味着会有更多的人受用使用公司的产品"。

13. 选[C]。结构衔接题。本句的谓语动词 adds 为第三人称单数,这就决定了主语也应是单数名词,故可排除[A] Those 和[B] These;[D] Such 指这样的人或物;只有[C] This 可指代上文提到的事,故答案为[C] This。

14. 选[D]。语义衔接题。公司为学生提供培训机会将增加公司市场份额和人才库存。[D] pool 指集中备用的物资(如钱、物、工人等),符合本句句意,故为本题答案。

15. 选[A]。语义衔接题。根据常识可知,本句谓语 qualify your company for tax deductions(使公司有资格减免税费)的主语应是[A] Donations"捐资",而且与前文中出现的 invest in education 照应。[B] Dedication"贡献,奉献",[C] Assistance"帮助"和[D] Cooperation"合作"都不符合文意。

16. 选[C]。惯用衔接题。tax deduction 说明此处的选项也与经济有关,故选[C] line,因为只有 bottom line 能与前面提到的词构成语义场同现,bottom line 指"账本底线,盈亏一览结算线",在财务报表中用此线标明净收益或净损失。本句句意为"捐资使公司有资格减免税费,这有助于提高公司的利润"。

17. 选[C]。语义衔接题。分析句子结构可知,所填词在句中应能与 into 搭配使用,所以排除[B] Transfer 与[D] Shift。[A] Change"改变",change into"使改变",指从一种状态变为另一种状态;[C] Turn"变化,变成",turn into"使变成",符合此处语境,指把这些受过良好教育的学生变成可聘用的人才;[B] Transfer"调动,转移",transfer to 意为"调动,转移";[D] Shift"转换,转变",shift to 意为"转换,移动,转变"。

18. 选[B]。语义衔接题。下句指出,internships(实习期)为公司提供了一个…机会,所以根据上下文语义联系可知,本题应选[B] internship。本句句意为"通过让学生到公司实习,把这些受过良好教育的学生变成可聘用的人才"。

19. 选[A]。语义衔接题。上文提到公司为学校提供培训,学生有使用该公司软件或硬件的机会,这是公司参加教育活动之一,那么提供实习机会应是之二了,是进一步的教育,所以应选[A] further"促进,增进"。[B] support "支持",后面应该直接跟 the students;[C] continue"继续",语义不符;[D] finance"负担经费",宾语应直接为人。

20. 选[A]。惯用衔接题。所填词能与 out 搭配使用,四个选项中只有[A] testing 符合,test out"考验,考察";[B] examining"检查,调查,考试"是及物动词,不与 out 搭配;[C] separating"分离,分散",与 from 搭配;[D] selecting "选择",同样为及物动词,不与 out 搭配。本句句意为"同时公司不需花费巨资就可充分考查可能成为公司雇员的学生"。

完型填空巅峰练习

Exercise 1

The term "quality of life" is difficult to define. It __62__ a very wide scope such as living environment, health, employment, food, family life, friends, education, material possessions, leisure and recreation, and so on. __63__ speaking, the quality of life, especially __64__ seen by the individual, is meaningful in terms of the degree __65__ which these various areas of life are available or provide __66__ to the individual.

As activity carried __67__ as one thinks fit during one's spare time, leisure has the following __68__ : relaxation, recreation and entertainment, and personal development. The importance of these varies according to the nature of one's job and one's lifestyle. __69__, people who need to __70__ much energy in their work will find relaxation most __71__ in leisure. Those with a better education and in professional occupations may __72__ more to seek recreation and personal development (e. g. __73__ of skills and hobbies) in leisure.

The specific use of leisure __74__ from individual to individual. __75__ the same leisure activity may be used differently by different individuals. Thus, the following are possible use of television watching, a __76__ leisure activity, a change of experience to provide __77__ from the stress and strain of work; to learn more about what is happening in one's environment; to provide an opportunity for understanding oneself by __78__ other people's life experiences as __79__ in the programs.

Since leisure is basically self-determined, one is able to take __80__ his interests and preferences and get __81__ in an activity in ways that will bring enjoyment and satisfaction.

62. [A] composes   [B] consists
     [C] covers   [D] constitutes

63. [A] Basically   [B] Frankly
     [C] Primarily   [D] Generally

64. [A] when   [B] as   [C] while   [D] which

65. [A] to   [B] as   [C] of   [D] in

66. [A] satisfaction   [B] information
     [C] respect   [D] admiration

67. [A] out   [B] through
     [C] away   [D] off

68. [A] effects   [B] operations
     [C] functions   [D] features

69. [A] However   [B] Thus
     [C] Nevertheless   [D] Yet

70. [A] provide   [B] hire
     [C] exercise   [D] exert

71. [A] preferable   [B] desirable
     [C] obtainable   [D] perfect

72. [A] tend   [B] prefer   [C] enjoy   [D] oblige

73. [A] training   [B] promotion
     [C] nurturing   [D] cultivation

74. [A] varies   [B] differs   [C] changes   [D] alters

75. [A] Still   [B] Yet   [C] Even   [D] So

76. [A] correct   [B] adequate
     [C] precise   [D] proper

77. [A] separation   [B] escape
     [C] flight   [D] isolation

78. [A] contrasting   [B] comparing
     [C] matching   [D] measuring

79. [A] portrayed   [B] described
     [C] related   [D] narrated

80. [A] after   [B] on   [C] with   [D] to

81. [A] involved   [B] participated
     [C] attended   [D] employed

Exercise 2

There were many theories about the beginning of drama in ancient Greece. The __62__ most widely accepted today is based on the assumption that drama __63__ from ritual. The argument for this view goes as follows. In the beginning, human being viewed the __64__ forces of the world—even the seasonal changes __65__ unpredictable, and they sought through various means to control these __66__ and feared powers. Those measures which appeared to bring the desired results were then retained and repeated until they __67__ into fixed rituals. Eventually stories arose which explained or __68__ the mysteries of the rites. As time passed some rituals were abandoned, __69__ the stories, later called myths, __70__ and provided material for art and drama.

Those who believe that drama evolved out of __71__ also argue that those rites contained the seed of theater __72__ music, dance, masks, and costumes were almost always used. __73__ , a suitable site had to be provided for performances and when the entire community did not participate, a clear __74__ was usually made between the "acting area" and the "auditorium". In addition, there were performers, and, since considerable importance was __75__ to avoiding mistakes in the enactment of rites, religious leaders usually assumed that task. __76__ masks and costumes, they often impersonated other people, animals, or supernatural beings, and mimed the desired __77__ —success in hunt or battle, the coming rain, the revival of the Sun—as an actor might. Eventually such dramatic __78__ were separated from religious activities.

Another theory traces the theater's origin from the human's __79__ in storytelling. According to this view tales (about the hunt, war, or other feats) are gradually __80__ , at first through the use of impersonation, action, and dialogue by a __81__ and then through the assumption of each of the roles by a different person.

62. [A] other 　　　　[B] another
　　[C] few 　　　　　[D] one

63. [A] developed 　　[B] transformed
　　[C] evolved 　　　[D] came

64. [A] natural 　　　[B] personal
　　[C] actual 　　　　[D] individual

65. [A] as 　　　　　　[B] of
　　[C] for 　　　　　 [D] on

66. [A] unseen 　　　　[B] unknown
　　[C] dangerous 　　[D] harmful

67. [A] settled 　　　[B] reached
　　[C] changed 　　　[D] hardened

68. [A] veiled 　　　　[B] retreated
　　[C] exposed 　　　[D] displayed

69. [A] and 　　　　　 [B] when
　　[C] but 　　　　　 [D] so

70. [A] persisted 　　[B] continued
　　[C] endured 　　　[D] deserted

71. [A] story 　　　　[B] myth
　　[C] ritual 　　　[D] mystery

72. [A] if 　　　　　　[B] hence
　　[C] unless 　　　　[D] because

73. [A] Secondly 　　　[B] Furthermore
　　[C] Similarly 　　[D] Generally

74. [A] section 　　　[B] cut
　　[C] line 　　　　　[D] division

75. [A] attached 　　 [B] put
　　[C] placed 　　　 [D] stressed

76. [A] Making 　　　　[B] Having
　　[C] Wearing 　　　[D] Dressing

77. [A] affect 　　　　[B] effect
　　[C] impact 　　　　[D] result

78. [A] interpretations [B] illustrations
　　[C] representations [D] expressions

79. [A] care 　　　　　 [B] curiosity
　　[C] interest 　　　[D] keenness

80. [A] formed 　　　　[B] elaborated
　　[C] finished 　　　[D] appeared

81. [A] leader 　　　　[B] person
　　[C] performer 　　 [D] narrator

答案与解析

Exercise 1

【文章大意】

　　本文的主要内容是关于生活质量。文章首先说生活质量涵盖很广并给出了生活质量的一个常见的定义，接下来提到了休闲活动对人们的重要意义以及各种不同的休闲方式的选择，最后作者说休闲是一种完全自主的行为，只要满足了自己的兴趣和意愿，就能给人带来乐趣和满足。

62. 选[C]。语义衔接题。本句主语 it 指代 quality of life，它与后面列举的 living environment，health，employment，food 等是上下义词复现关系，因此应该选[C] covers"包括，包含，涉及"。[A] composes"组成"，用于 be composed of"由…组成"结构；[B] consists"由…组成，在于"，表示"组成"时需与 of 连用，consist of 意为"由…组成"；[D] constitutes"组成"，应该是下义词在前，上义词在后，与本句的位置正好相反。

63. 选[D]。语义衔接题。[A] Basically"基本上，主要地"；[B] Frankly"坦率地"；[C] Primarily"主要地"；[D] Generally"一般地，通常地"。本句是从一般的意义上叙述"the quality of life"，所以应选[D] Generally，generally speaking 意为"一般来说"。

64. 选[B]。结构衔接题。空格所在部分是对 the quality of life 的进一步说明，是定语从句，所以空格处需填一个引导定语从句的词，首先排除[A] when 和[C] while。[B] as 和[D] which 都能引导非限制性定语从句，as 引导的非限制性定语从句可以放在句首、句中，也可以置于句尾，而 which 引导的非限制性定语从句只能放在句尾。这里的非限制性定语从句是插在句中的评述，所以应该用 as，另外当 as 后有 is 或 was＋过去分词构成的被动语态时，is 或 was 可省略，本句 as 后正是省略了助动词 is。

65. 选[A]。惯用衔接题。分析句子结构可知，which 引导的定语从句修饰 the degree，因为 which 引导定语从句时，也在句子中充当一定的成分，可能为主语或宾语。在这个定语从句中 which 只能是充当介词宾语。四个选项中的介词通常与 available 搭配使用的只有[A] to。

66. 选[A]。语义衔接题。分析整句话可知，or 连接的两个并列分句其实是在叙术生活质量是 meaningful(有意义的)的两个方面：一个方面是生活的各个领域可以达到一定的程度；另一个方面就是生活的各个领域能够提供给个人 _____。因此，所填词应该能够说明生活质量是 meaningful 的，故答案为[A] satisfaction"满足感"。

67. 选[A]。语义衔接题。四个选项均可与 carry 搭配，但语义不同：[A] carry out"进行，开展活动等"；[B] carry through"完成，进行到底"；[C] carry away"使倾倒，使游动失去控制"；[D] carry off"运走，夺走"。本句中 carried 的宾语是 activity，故答案应为[A] out。

68. 选[C]。语义衔接题。relaxation，recreation and entertainment，and personal development"放松、娱乐和个人发展"是休闲活动的三个功能，所以答案为[C] functions"功能，作用"。[A] effects"效果，影响"；[B] operations"运转，操作"；[D] features"特点，特征。"

69. 选[B]。逻辑衔接题。本题的选择应建立在 70 题的基础之上。该题各选项的含义分别为[A] provide"供应，提供"；[B] hire"雇用，租用"；[C] exercise"训练，行使，使用"，多指使用、行使权力；[D] exert"发挥，使用，尽力"。因动词宾语为 energy，所以动词最好使用[D] exert，以与 energy 构成语义场共现，exert one's energy 意为"消耗精力"。现在再来分析此题。上一句指出休闲活动的功能的重要性是因人而异的，而本句指出需要将大量精力投入到工作中的人会觉得放松。两个句子之间明显存在一种递进关系，故答案为[B] Thus。

70. 选[D]。语义衔接题。分析见上题。

71. 选[B]。语义衔接题。所填词由 most 修饰，同时又修饰 relaxation，首先排除[A] preferable"更好的，更可取的"，因为它本身就有比较的意味，因此没有比较级或最高级；[B] desirable"值得要的，合意的"，most desirable"最合意的"，符合消耗精力过多的人对 relaxation 的需求，故为答案。[C] obtainable"能得到的"，与本句句意相违背，因为把大量精力用于工作的人很难有 relaxation(放松)的时间；[D] perfect"完美的，理想的"，也没有比较级与最高级。

72. 选[A]。语义衔接题。所填词被后面的副词 more 修饰，表示"更…"。[B] prefer"偏爱，更喜欢做"，本身就是比较，不能再用比较级来修饰；[C] enjoy"喜欢"，enjoy doing"喜欢做"，不能跟不定式；[D] oblige"迫使"，搭配为 be obliged to do sth. 意为"不得不做某事"，这三个词从语法上都不符合本句要求，而[A] tend"往往是，倾向于"，tend more to do sth. "更倾向于做某事"，符合本句语法及语义要求。

73. 选[D]。语义衔接题。所填词的逻辑宾语是 skills and hobbies，结合四个选项可知本处可能要表达"技能与爱好的培养"。[A] training"训练，培养"，指通过别人的训练、教导或练习惯于一种行为或表现方式；[B] promotion"促进，发扬"；[C] nurture"养育，教育"；[D] cultivation"培养"，如培养爱好、习惯等，是自己完成的行为，故答案为[D] cultivation。

74. 选[A]。语义衔接兼惯用衔接题。下句中的 the same leisure activity may be used differently by different individuals 表明不同的人在 the specific use of leisure(休闲活动的特殊用途上)是不同的，故答案为[A]varies"变化，不同"，vary from…to…，意为"在…到…之间变化"。[B]differs"不同"，differ from 意为"不同于，和…不同"，介词 from 的宾语通常是表示具体的事物，而不是表示范围的事物，本句中 from 的宾语是 individual to individual，它表示的是一种范围，故不选[B]；[C]changes"改变，变化"，change from…to…"从…变成…"，语义上与本句不符；[D]alters"改变"，不能与 from 搭配。

75. 选[C]。逻辑衔接题。本句是对前一句的进一步说明，所以应该用表示进一步说明、加强语气的副词。[C]even "甚至"是表递进关系的副词，为本题答案。

76. 选[D]。语义衔接题。本句在列举电视作为一种休闲活动的可行性，所以所填词要表达"适当的"的意思，说明 "电视是一种很好的休闲活动"。分析四个选项，只有[D]proper"适当的，好的"符合题意。[A]correct"正确的" 与[C]precise"精确的"均不能用来形容 leisure activity；[B]adequate"足够的，适当的"，强调数量足够，或者能力 胜任，且 adequate 是以元音音素开头，不定冠词应该用 an 而不是 a，故不选。

77. 选[B]。语义衔接题。本句主要是讲看电视的可行性用途。所填词所在的短语是看电视的用途之一：能够帮助 人们减轻工作压力。[A]separation"分离，分开"，虽然能与 from 连用，但是意思不确切；[B]escape"逃避，逃 离"，指"逃避现实，从忧虑、担心和不愉快中得到暂时的解脱"，符合本句句意；[C]flight"逃走，飞行"与[D]isolation"隔绝，隔离"均不符合句意，故答案为[B]escape。

78. 选[B]。语义衔接题。所填词所在的短语是讲看电视的用途之一：可以通过与其他人的生活经历比较而更好地 理解自己的生活。[A]contrasting"使与…对比，对照"，主要是指不同点的比较；[B]comparing"比较"，找出其中 的相似点和不同点；[C]matching"匹配"；[D]measuring"测量，衡量"，故答案为[B]comparing。

79. 选[A]。语义衔接题。分析句子结构可知，as _____ in the programs 在句中作 other people's life experiences 的后置定语。所以 the programs 与 other people's life experiences 的关系就是 the programs(电视节目)能够描述 或展现 other people's life experiences(其他人的生活经历)。[A]portrayed"描绘，用图画来描绘或表现"；[B]described"描写，形容"，特指口头描述或书面描述；[C]related"讲述，叙述或告诉"；[D]narrated"叙述，讲述，讲述 一个事件"。文中指的是"电视节目(用图像)所描绘的"，故答案为[A]portrayed。

80. 选[D]。语义衔接题。四个选项均可与 take 搭配：[A]take after"长得像"；[B]take on"呈现出，担任"；[C]take up"开始从事"；[D]take to"沉溺于，养成…的习惯"。空格前 one 泛指人，人与 interest and preference 之间的 关系用 take to 说明最合适，故答案为[D]to。本句意为"既然休闲本质上是由自己决定的，那么我们就可以沉溺 于我们自己的兴趣和爱好中"。

81. 选[A]。惯用衔接题。本题考查的是四个选项中哪一个符合 get … in 结构。[A]involved"陷入"，get involved in 意为"卷入，陷入，参与"；[B]participated"参加"是不及物动词，没有被动语态；[C]attended"从事，参加"，不能用 于 get … in 这样的结构；[D]employed"雇用，使用"，get employed"被雇用"。从语法及语义上来看，只有[A]involved 符合要求，故为本题答案。

Exercise 2

【文章大意】

本文的主要内容是关于戏剧起源的不同观点。文章开始就提到关于戏剧如何起源最为人们广泛接受的观点 是戏剧起源于典礼仪式，接着进一步说持有这种观点的人们认为类似的典礼仪式也是剧院的雏形，最后说另一种 观点认为剧院起源于人类对讲故事持有的浓厚兴趣。

62. 选[D]。语义衔接题。由本句中的副词最高级 most 以及本句谓语动词的单数形式可知所填词应是单数形式，具 有唯一性，指代上句中的 many theories 中的一种理论。选项中能起到这一作用的只有[D]one，用在此处是为了 避免重复上句提到的名词。

63. 选[C]。语义衔接题。结合选项可推测本句的大体含义为：其中一个人们普遍接受的理论是戏剧是从仪式演化 而来。[A]developed "发展，开发"，指把潜在的因素引向完善；[B]transformed"转变，转化"，强调改变形状；[C]evolved "演变，演化"，一种事物演变成另一种更复杂、更好的事物，强调变化过程的复杂；[D]came"来自"，没有演化的含义。由此可知[C]evolved 符合语境，而且根据第二段"those who believe that drama evolved out of …"中 evolve 的复现可以判断答案。

64. 选[A]。语义衔接题。破折号后的 even the seasonal changes 起进一步说明的作用，_____ forces of the world 与 the seasonal changes 是上下义词复现关系，故答案为[A]natural，natural force 意为"自然力量"。[B]personal "个人的"；[C]actual"真实的"；[D]individual"个人的"，这三个选项均与 the seasonal changes 相矛盾。

65. 选[A]。惯用衔接题。此处是考查固定搭配 "view … as …"，意为"把…看作…"，故答案为[A]as，其他选项都不符合搭配。

66. 选[B]。语义衔接题。分析句子结构可知,these _____ and feared powers 指代的是 and 前的分句中的 the _____ forces of the world。根据上一小题的分析可知,最初人们把世界上的自然力量也看作是不可预知的,这就说明他们对自然力量不了解,故答案为[B] unknown "不知道的,未知的"。因而,可排除选项 [C] dangerous "危险的"和 [D] harmful "有危害的";[A] unseen 意为"未见过的,看不见的"。

67. 选[D]。语义衔接题。本句的主语 those measures 指的是上句中的用来控制那些未知的、令人害怕的自然力量的 various means。主句中的谓语 were retained and repeated 表明与 fixed rituals 相比,这些方法还在变化中,还没有最终稳固下来。选项中的动词能表达事物由不稳固到稳固这一过程的只有[D] hardened "稳固,稳定"。[A] settled "安放在牢固的位置或地点,建立";[B] reached "达到;延伸";[C] changed "改变",及物动词,在此处应用被动语态。

68. 选[A]。语义衔接题。所填词与动词 explained 由 or 连接,形成相对选择关系,即与 explain 反义复现,同时宾语是 mysteries "神秘性",故答案为[A] veiled "掩盖,遮盖"。[B] retreated "撤退,退却",与 mysteries 不搭配;[C] exposed "暴露,使…被看见",[D] displayed "陈列,显示",与 explain 不形成选择关系。

69. 选[C]。逻辑衔接题。根据"…and provided materials for art and drama"可知,the stories 没有被 abandoned,最终存活下来,所以此处应用转折连词,故答案为[C] but。

70. 选[A]。语义衔接题。根据上题的分析可知此空大意应是"保留",与 abandoned 构成反义复现。[A] persisted "保持,坚持",符合文意。[B] continued "继续,连续";[C] endured "忍受,承受";[D] deserted "放弃,遗弃"。

71. 选[C]。语义衔接题。本句中的副词 also 提示 Those who believe that drama evolved out of _____ 应是指第一段中的那些认为 drama evolved from ritual 的人,所以所填词应是 ritual 的原词复现,故答案为[C] ritual。

72. 选[D]。逻辑衔接题。music, dance, masks 和 costumes 都是 theater 的 seed,所以才会说 those rites 包含了戏剧的因素,因此所填词应是表因果关系的副词,故答案为[D] because。

73. 选[B]。逻辑衔接题。上句是讲 rite 和 theater 的相似因素,而 a suitable site had to be provided for performances 同样也是 rite 和 theater 共同需要的,因此本句是讲 rite 和 theater 的另一个相似因素,所以应选表递进关系的副词,故答案为[B] Furthermore "此外,而且"。

74. 选[D]。语义衔接题。由时间状语从句 when the entire community did not participate 可知,如果观众没有参与,那么观众所处的位置只能称之为 auditorium,这就与 acting area "演出区"是有区别的,所以所填词应该是能表示"区别"的含义,故答案为[D] division "区分,区别"。

75. 选[A]。惯用衔接题。由 avoiding 可知空格后的 to 是介词,各选项中能与介词 to 搭配使用的只有[A] attached "附上…的",attach importance to 意为"重视,认为…重要"。

76. 选[C]。语义衔接题。由后文的 impersonate 与 mime "模仿"可知,此处讲的不是 mask 与 costumes 的制造,故排除选项 [A] making。因此本题关键在于区分动词 wear, have, dress 作"穿戴"时的不同用法和含义。[B] have 表示"穿着"时必须和 on 搭配,构成词组 have on ≈ to wear;[C] wear "穿衣,佩戴饰物",强调状态;[D] dress "给…穿衣",宾语应该是人,故答案为[C] wear。

77. 选[B]。语义衔接题。句中的破折号表明破折号之间的内容是对 the desired _____ 的解释说明,success in hunt or battle, the coming rain, the revival of the Sun 都是一种舞台效果,所以所填词应为[B] effect "效果,作用"。[A] affect "影响"极易与 effect 混淆,它是动词,所以不能用在本句中。

78. 选[C]。语义衔接题。上文出现的 performance, impersonate, mime 提示这里指的是最终这些戏剧性的表演从宗教活动中分离出来。从词义辨析入手[A] interpretations "演出,演奏",是指一个表演者对歌曲、舞蹈、音乐或角色的有特色的、个人的独到处理和艺术加工;[B] illustrations "图解";[C] representations "(戏剧等的)演出,扮演";[D] expressions "表达",故答案应为[C] representations,与 performance 同义复现。

79. 选[C]。惯用衔接题。所填词与 in 结构同现,符合条件的只有[C] interest,interest in 意为"对…感兴趣"。[A] care 常与 for 或 about 搭配,care for 意为"喜欢",care about 意为"关心";[B] curiosity 应和 about 搭配,意为"对…好奇";[D] keenness 与 on 搭配,意为"对…渴望"。

80. 选[B]。语义衔接题。本段的主题句 Another theory traces… 表明另一理论来源于人类对"讲故事"的兴趣。本分句想表达的是:根据这种观点,故事首先是以 impersonation, action 和 dialogue 的形式来 _____ tales。impersonation "扮演"、action "表演"和 dialogue "独白"是用表演的形式表达 tales,所以所填词应含有表达的含义,故答案为[B] elaborated "详述(用更长的篇幅或更多的细节表达)"。

81. 选[D]。语义衔接题。通过对上一题的分析可知,所填词应是能表达 elaborate the tales(讲故事)的人,故答案为[D] narrator "讲述者,叙述者"。

汉译英巅峰讲座

汉译英共包括 5 个句子,句子长度大约在 15—30 词之间。句子的一部分已用英文给出,要求考生根据全句意思将汉语部分译成英语,译文必须符合英语的语法结构和表达习惯。

Lecture 1　第一讲　13 大必熟常考考点

六级考试汉译英部分主要测试考生对英语中基础语法以及重点句式、短语和词汇的掌握和运用。具体而言,包括以下知识要点:

一、虚拟语气

虚拟语气强调说话人的主观愿望和假想情况。针对汉译英的特点,复习时应注意以下几点:

1. 熟悉 if 引导的虚拟条件句的主从句谓语形式。

2. 注意主从句时间概念不一致的混合虚拟句。如条件句是表示对过去的假设,而主句则是表示对现在事实或将来可能造成的影响。

3. 掌握一部分表示建议、主张、命令等概念的词语。由于本身隐含说话人的主观愿望,这类词语后面接的主语从句、宾语从句、同位语从句的谓语动词往往采用"(should)＋动词原形"的形式。

4. 熟悉能引起虚拟语气的某些介词、介词短语和连词。如 lest, in case, otherwise, without, but for 等。

5. 掌握 would rather, wish, as if, it's time that 等句型中虚拟语气的运用。

(新 06-12-72)

【例1】

72. If you had _____ (听从了我的忠告,你就不会陷入麻烦).

【答案】followed my advice/suggestion, you would not have put yourself in trouble.

【解析】本题考查对虚拟语气的掌握。表示对过去事实的虚拟,if 条件句中谓语动词用 had done 的形式,主句中谓语动词用 would have done 的形式。put (oneself) in trouble 表示"(某人)陷入麻烦"。

二、非谓语动词

这是语法部分的重中之重,复习时应注意以下几点:

1. 根据非谓语动词同其所修饰的名词或逻辑主语的一致关系,确定使用主动语态或被动语态,然后考虑采用现在分词或过去分词。

2. 非谓语动词同主句谓语动词动作发生的先后关系。动作正在进行的用现在分词进行式,同时发生或不分先后发生的用现在分词一般式或过去分词;在主句谓语动词之前发生的用现在分词完成式、不定式完成式;发生在主句谓语动词之后的多用不定式一般式。

3. 有些动词既可接名词作宾补又可接不定式作宾补。动名词强调动作正在进行或当时的状态,不定式强调过程,如 see, watch, hear 等;动名词表示动作已经发生,不定式表示动作还没发生,如 remember, forget, regret 等。

4. 独立主格结构。当非谓语动词带有自己的逻辑主语,即其逻辑主语与句子的主语不一致时,这种结构我们就称其为独立主格结构。一般说来,在句子中没有连接词的情况下,逗号是不能连接两个句子的,其中一部分要么是非谓语动词短语,要么就是独立主格结构。

5. 表状态多用分词;表目的多用不定式。

【例2】

73. With tears on her face, the lady ＿＿＿＿＿＿＿＿＿＿（看着她受伤的儿子被送进手术室）.

【答案】watched her injured son being sent into the surgery.

【解析】本题考查对动名词作宾补用法的掌握。动词 watch/see 后面既可以接不定式作宾补，也可以接动名词作宾补。本句是表示女士当时看到儿子被送进手术室时的情形，因此应该用动名词充当宾补；而动词 send 与其逻辑主语 son 是动宾关系，故此处应该用动名词的被动式。

三、倒装结构

倒装表示强调或突出，分为全部倒装和部分倒装。复习时应注意以下几点：

1. 能引导倒装的否定词或短语。如 hardly, scarcely, rarely, in no case, under no circumstances 等。
2. 部分倒装和全部倒装的区别。部分倒装是指将助动词提前构成倒装；全部倒装则是将主谓完全倒装。
3. as 在倒装结构中的用法及意义。as 引导让步状语从句时，必须将 as 所在句子的表语部分提前引起部分倒装。
4. if 条件句的倒装。if 引出的条件句，可将 should 等助动词提前，将 if 省略，构成部分倒装。
5. not until…引起的倒装句式。
6. hardly…when 和 no sooner…than 结构中的倒装。

【例3】
（710 分样卷-76）

76. The customer complained that no sooner ＿＿＿＿＿＿＿＿＿＿（他刚试着使用这台机器，它就不能运转了）.

【答案】had he tried to use the machine than it stopped working

【解析】本题考查对倒装结构的掌握。no sooner…than 或 hardly…when 表示"刚一…就…"，主句要求用过去完成时，从句要求用一般过去时，如将 no sooner 提前，则其后句子要求部分倒装。

四、强调句型

强调句型的基本结构是：It is/was＋被强调成分＋that/who＋其他成分。汉译英时要注意根据所给汉语意思判断需要强调的成分，以及句子应该采用何种时态。

【例4】
（新 06-12-76）

76. ＿＿＿＿＿＿＿＿＿＿（直到截止日他才寄出）his application form.

【答案】It was not until the deadline (that) he sent out/posted

【解析】本题考查对强调句型以及 not…until 句型用法的掌握。根据所给汉语意思，本句是要强调时间状语，故最好用强调句型来表达。强调 until 引导的时间状语时，要将 not 和 until…一起放到被强调的位置。根据句意，句子的动作应该是发生在过去，故本句应采用一般过去时。本句恢复成正常语序为：He didn't sent out/post his application form until the deadline.

五、时态和语态

英语中一共有 16 种时态，最常用的 5 种时态是一般现在时、现在进行时、一般过去时、一般将来时和现在完成时。六级考试中出现最多的考点是将来完成时、现在完成时、过去完成时和完成进行时。针对这一题型，考生要注意抓住句子中的时间状语，是表示现在、将来还是过去？是短暂性时间还是延续性时间？

虽然语态问题不单独作为一个重要考查点，但也是汉译英中所涉及到的重要知识点之一，而且常常是考生容易忽略的一点，需引起重视。

【例5】
（07-6-86）

86. The problems of blacks and women ＿＿＿＿＿＿＿＿＿＿（最近几十年受到公众相当大的关注）.

【答案】have received great attention from the public in the recent decades / have been paid great attention by the public in the recent decades

【解析】本题考查对时态的掌握。时间状语"最近几十年"一般用 in the recent decades 来表达，该时间状语决定本句应采用现在完成时。此处的"受到…关注"既可以用主动语态表达，也可以用被动语态表达。

【例6】

84. It is absolutely unfair that these children _____ (被剥夺了受教育的权利).

【答案】be deprived of their rights to receive education
【解析】本题考查对虚拟语气和被动语态的掌握。与表示重要性、必要性、公平性等含义的形容词(如 important, necessary, unfair, advisable 等)相连的名词性从句一般要采用虚拟语气,其谓语动词用 should do 的形式,should 常常省略。deprive sb. of…表示"剥夺某人(某项权利,机会等)",本句中表示"被剥夺"应该用被动语态。

六、it 充当形式主语或宾语

为了使句子结构更加清晰、对称,经常会用 it 代替不定式、动名词短语或从句在句中充当形式主语,而将真正的主语置于句子后面。当动名词或不定式充当动词宾语时,后面又跟有宾语补足语时,须用 it 充当形式宾语,而将真正的宾语(动名词或不定式)置于宾补之后。

【例7】

75. The workmen think _____ (遵守安全规则很重要).

【答案】it very important to comply with/follow the safety regulations
【解析】本题考查对 it 充当形式宾语用法的掌握。it 在这里充当形式宾语,真正的宾语是后面的不定式短语。

七、各类从句

英语中各类从句,尤其是定语从句和状语从句,是汉译英的考查重点之一,复习时应注意以下几点:
1. 从句的引导词。从句用什么词来引导,引导词在句中充当什么成分,这些在翻译时应仔细考虑。
2. 从句的语序。要注意宾语从句的语序应该是陈述语序,有时还可能会涉及到句子的倒装问题。
3. 从句的时态。注意主句和从句时态的一致问题。

【例8】

88. The prevention and treatment of AIDS is _____ (我们可以合作的领域).

【答案】the field where we can cooperate /the field in which we can cooperate
【解析】本题主要考查对定语从句的掌握。领域通常用 the field 表示,"我们可以合作的"作 the field 的定语,引导词可以用 where 也可以用 in which,"合作"通常用 cooperate 表示。

【例9】

91. Please come here at ten tomorrow morning _____ (如果你方便的话).

【答案】if it is convenient for you
【解析】本题主要考查对 if 引导的条件状语从句的掌握。"你方便的话"通常用 it is convenient for you。

八、对比和比较

as…as 同级比较、含有比较级的结构(如 no more than, more…than 等)在六级翻译考试中也经常出现。另外,while, whereas 表示两种情况的对比或比较的用法,考生也需要予以注意。

【例10】

88. Since my childhood I have found that _____ (没有什么比读书对我更有吸引力).

【答案】nothing is more attractive to me than reading
【解析】本题考查对比较结构的掌握。attractive"有吸引力的"为多音节词,比较级形式为 more attractive;"对…有吸引力"用 be attractive to sb. 来表示。汉语中的一些动宾结构在英语中常用动名词表示,比如唱歌 singing,跳舞 dancing,开车 driving 等,因此"读书"用 reading 表示。

【例11】

90. The more you explain, _____ (我愈糊涂).

【答案】the more confused I am

【解析】本题考查对句型 the more…，the more… 的掌握。the more…，the more 表示"越…，就越…"。表示"糊涂"应用 confused 或 puzzled。注意该句型中前后句都应用陈述语序。

九、情态动词

除了掌握一些情态动词的基本用法以外，汉译英中尤其要注意的是情态动词表示推测的用法。表示肯定推测谓语用 must do /must have done 的形式；表示否定推测，谓语用 can't do /can't have done 的形式；表示可能性推测，谓语用 might do /might have done 的形式。

【例 12】 （四级 06-12-90）

90. Some psychologists claim that people ＿＿＿＿＿＿＿＿（出门在外时可能会感到孤独）.

【答案】might feel lonely when they are far from home

【解析】本题考查对情态动词 might 表推测用法的掌握。解答此题时应注意不要混淆了 lonely 和 alone 的语义及用法：lonely 强调主观上感到孤独和寂寞，常在句中作表语或定语；alone 强调客观上独自一人，在句中作表语或状语。"出门在外"也可以用 when they are traveling 表达。

十、祈使句

祈使句常用于表示命令、要求、建议、鼓励等，一般要求以动词原形开头，句首或句尾常会加上 please。六级汉译英题中往往要求考生能够根据句子要表达的意思，使用正确的祈使句形式进行表达。

【例 13】 （四级 07-6-90）

90. To make donations or for more information, please ＿＿＿＿＿＿＿＿（按以下地址和我们联系）.

【答案】contact us at the following address

【解析】本题考查对祈使句的掌握。空格前的 please 提示该句应为祈使句，因此应以动词原形开头。"与某人联系"一般用动词 contact，"以下地址"通常表达为 following address，介词 at 与其一起构成介宾短语。

十一、并列结构

either…or…，not only…but also，but…and…，neither…nor… 等连接的并列结构往往也是翻译重点考查的内容之一。翻译时要注意并列成份形式上的一致性。

【例 14】

I was advised ＿＿＿＿＿＿＿＿（或者打电话，或者写信给该旅店预订房间）.

【答案】either to telephone or to write the hotel for reservations

【解析】本题考查对 either…or…用法的掌握。either…or…用于连接并列成份，表示"或者…或者…"，本句中连接的是并列的不定式结构。

十二、主谓一致

这类考题灵活性大，需要根据实际情况判定谓语动词的单复数形式。复习时应注意以下几点：

1. 一部分具有生命意义的集合名词作主语时谓语动词多采用复数形式，如 people，poultry，militia 等。

2. 用 and 连接的成份表单一概念时谓语动词用单数。

3. 主语中含有某些连词，如 as well as，besides，in addition to 等时，谓语动词的数同这些连词前面的名词保持一致。

4. 就近原则。not only…but also…，either…or… 等短语连接并列主语时，谓语动词采用就近原则，即与和其相近的名词的数保持一致。

【例 15】

John, as well as his parents, ＿＿＿＿＿＿＿＿（正在前往机场的路上）at that time.

【答案】was on his way to the airport
【解析】本题考查对主谓一致原则和时态的掌握。as well as 表示"也,还",连接并列主语时,其后的谓语动词与其前面的部分一致,故本句中谓语应与 John 保持一致,即用单数形式。由时间状语 at that time(那时,当时)可知,本句应采用一般过去时态。

十三、重点句式和短语

六级考试大纲中涉及到的词汇、短语和一些重点的句式结构也是六级翻译测试的重点。考生在平时复习时应注意积累,并有针对性地做一些专项训练。

【例 16】 (07-6-85)

85. Our years of hard work are all in vain, _____(更别提我们所花费的大量金钱了).

【答案】not to mention the large sum of money we have spent / let alone the large sum of money we have spent
【解析】本句考查对短语 not to mention 或 let alone 用法的掌握。表示"更别提…,更不要管…"常用 not to mention 或 let alone。由于"大量金钱"有限定语"我们所花费的",所以 large sum 前面应该用"the"而不是"a"。

【例 17】 (新 06-12-75)

75. I prefer to communicate with my customers _____(通过写电子邮件而不是打电话).

【答案】via / by email instead of telephone
【解析】本题考查对介词 by 或 via 以及短语 instead of 用法的掌握。表示通过某种方式,可以用 by 或 via;表示"代替…,而不是…"常用介词短语 instead of。

Exercise 即讲即练

1. _____(不要再相信这个演讲者), since the remarks he made in his lectures are never compatible with the facts.
2. The manager ordered that it was imperative that _____(这项工程在下周一之前完工).
3. It annoyed him that no sooner _____(他刚上车,就发现自己忘记带钱包了).
4. The influence of the nation's literature, art and science _____(正引起越来越广泛的关注).
5. Newspapers must not only provide for the reader the facts, pure, unprejudiced, objectively selected facts, _____(而且还要提供解释,即这些事实的含义).
6. As I looked at the carpet, I wished that it could speak, since it _____(一定目睹了许多有趣的事) in the past decade.
7. One major hazard of space travel is _____(存在于地球大气层之外的辐射).
8. People who live in the countryside or in the mountains, _____(他们的眼睛不断地调整以看远处的物体), seldom have to wear glasses in early or middle life.
9. The more he explains it, _____(我越觉得这个计划难以实施).
10. The workmen think _____(遵守安全规则很重要).
11. It is advisable that _____(这些项目尽早完工).
12. _____(直到所有的证据摆在他面前他才承认) his crime.
13. Only after the accident _____(他才让人对他的车进行了仔细的检查).
14. Although oriental ideas of woman's subordination to man prevailed in those days, _____(她还是敢以平等的地位与男人交往).
15. Some fish would therefore not have been caught, since no baited hooks would have been available to trap them, _____(这就导致低估了过去的鱼量).

【答案与解析】

1. 【答案】Don't trust the speaker any more
   【解析】本题考查对祈使句的掌握。祈使句一般以动词原形开头,表达了一种命令。any more 常用于否定句和疑问句末,意为"再也不…,不再…",注意不能用 no more 表示此意,不要将二者混淆。

2. 【答案】the project be completed before the next Monday

　　【解析】本题考查对虚拟语气的掌握。有些表示重要性、必要性或某种意愿的形容词如 essential, important, necessary, imperative, advisable, desirable 等，当 it 充当形式主语，这些词充当表语时，后面 that 引导的主语从句的谓语动词用 should do 的形式，should 常常省略。

3. 【答案】had he got on the bus than he found he forgot to take the wallet with him

　　【解析】本题考查对 no sooner…than 句型的掌握。no sooner…than 和 hardly(scarcely)…when 都表示"刚一…就…"，注意其中连词的区别。该句型有两个特点：一是主句中一般使用过去完成时，而从句中一般使用一般过去时；二是 no sooner 或 hardly(scarcely)位于句首时，则要求句子采用部分倒装。本句中 no sooner 位于句首，故句子应用倒装。另外注意，表示"忘记做某事"时应用"forget to do sth."。

4. 【答案】is capturing more and more widespread attention /is arousing wider and wider attention

　　【解析】本题考查对主谓一致用法的掌握。本句主语为 The influence of the nation's literature, art and science，但其中心词为 the influence，所以谓语应该用第三人称单数 is。

5. 【答案】but also supply interpretation, the meaning of the facts

　　【解析】本题考查对并列结构及同位语的掌握。not only…but also…意为"不仅…而且…"。"即这些事实的含义"很明显是"解释"的同位语，用来进一步解释说明"解释"的含义。英语中当同位语与前面的词关系比较松散时，两者之间常用逗号隔开(表示略有停顿)。

6. 【答案】must have witnessed many interesting events

　　【解析】本题考查对情态动词的掌握。"must have ＋动词过去分词"用于肯定句中，表示对过去情况较有把握的、肯定性的推测，意为"一定…，准是…，肯定…"。

7. 【答案】the radiation that exists beyond Earth's atmosphere

　　【解析】本题考查定语从句的掌握。本句表语的中心词为 radiation(辐射)，"存在于地球大气层之外"应是修饰 radiation 的定语从句。

8. 【答案】where the eyes are constantly adjusting themselves to objects at a distance

　　【解析】本题考查对地点状语从句的掌握。分析句子结构可知，所翻译的成份应该是复合句中的地点状语从句，所以用 where 作引导词，表示"在那儿…"。

9. 【答案】the more I find this plan difficult to put into practice

　　【解析】本题考查对比较结构以及"put into practice"用法的掌握。比较结构"the more…，the more…"表示"越…，就越…"，也可在 more 的位置上放相应的形容词或副词的比较级。put into practice 意为"实行，实施，实现"。

10. 【答案】it very important to follow the safety regulations

　　【解析】本题考查对 it 作形式主语的掌握。it 作宾语从句中的形式主语，真正的主语是不定式 to follow the safety regulations。

11. 【答案】these programs be completed as early as possible

　　【解析】本题考查对虚拟语气及被动语态用法的掌握。有些表示重要性、必要性或某种意愿的形容词如 essential, important, necessary, imperative, advisable, desirable 等，当 it 充当形式主语，这些词充当表语时，后面 that 引导的主语从句的谓语动词用 should do 的形式，should 常常省略。另外注意本句应该用被动语态。

12. 【答案】Not until he was showed all evidence did he confess /It was not until he was showed all evidence that he confessed

　　【解析】本题考查对 not…until 句型的掌握。not…until 意为"直到…时，才…"，为了起到强调作用，经常将 not until 提前引起句子部分倒装。另外，本句也可以使用强调句型，要注意不要和倒装的用法相混淆。

13. 【答案】did he have his car inspected carefully

　　【解析】本题考查对倒装句的掌握。after the accidents 是一个介词词组，Only 与其连用作状语放在句首时，句子应部分倒装。have sth. done 意为"让某事被做"。

14. 【答案】she did dare to meet with man on equal basis

　　【解析】本题考查对强调句式的掌握。译文中的"还是敢"提示所要翻译的句子是强调句式。英语中，特别是祈使句或肯定句中，需要强调谓语动词时，须在谓语动词前加上助动词 do, does 或者 did，用以加强语气，意为"还是，确定"。

15. 【答案】leading to an underestimate of fish stocks in the past

　　【解析】本题考查对非谓语动词的掌握。"导致"也可使用动词 cause，但 cause 通常是引起某件事情发生，而 lead to 则是导致某种结果的产生，"低估了过去的鱼量"是一种结果，故应使用短语 lead to 表示"导致"。

Lecture 2　第二讲　7大汉译英高分要诀

　　阅卷统计显示,有相当一部分考生在词汇方面并没有多大障碍,但却仍然没能写出准确地道的译文,究其原因,主要有以下几点:这些考生只注重汉语意思的表达,而没有明白题目考查的重点;忽略了整个句子的结构和语法需要,单从句子的汉语意思出发;忽略了英语的表达习惯,只按照汉语的顺序直译出来。

　　针对以上问题,考生除了掌握必要的词汇以外,还要了解一些实用有效的避错秘诀,才能使自己的译文更加准确地道,最终博得高分。

要诀一: 首先要明确考查要点

　　前面第一讲中已经提到,每道汉译英题都有其考查重点,下笔翻译前要通读整个句子,思索该句子的考查重点是什么,明确出题人的意图之后再进行有针对性地翻译,这样才能写出准确地道的译文。

(07-6-82)

【例1】

82. The auto manufacturers found themselves ＿＿＿＿＿＿＿＿ (正在同外国公司竞争市场的份额).

【答案】competing against foreign companies for market share
【解析】本题考查对现在分词作宾补用法的掌握。明确了这一考查要点,就可以很容易给出正确的译文。表示"与…竞争"一般用 compete against… 表达,注意介词 against 的用法。

要诀二: 理清句子结构再下笔

　　由于是补全句子,所以所给译文不仅要清楚地表达出括号内汉语的意思,还必须符合整个句子的结构需要。因此,在下笔翻译前考生要判断该句是简单句还是复杂句,分清句子的主干和修饰成份,然后根据结构需要给出正确的译文。

(07-6-83)

【例2】

83. Only in the small town ＿＿＿＿＿＿＿＿ (他才感到安全和放松).

【答案】can he feel safe and relaxed
【解析】本题考查对倒装结构的掌握。当"only＋状语成份"位于句首时,句子结构要求部分倒装,故将情态动词 can 提到主语 he 的前面。如果在翻译之前没有理清句子结构,则很容易将本句译成正常语序。

要诀三: 不要受汉语语序影响

　　英语和汉语在语序的安排上存在很大差别,考生平时要注意培养英语的逻辑思维,汉译英时不要一味地按照汉语的顺序生搬硬套,要根据英语的语言习惯正确安排语序。

【例3】

Nobody thinks it advisable that the government ＿＿＿＿＿＿＿＿ (停止那条公路的建设).

【答案】(should) stop the construction of the road
【解析】本题考查对虚拟语气的掌握。advisable 意为"可取的",与其连用的名词性从句中的谓语动词要用 should do 的形式,should 常常省略。翻译本题时要注意根据英文表达习惯调整语序,如果按照汉语的语序直接译成 stop the road's construction 就不符合英文的表达习惯。

要诀四: 用词要简洁规范

　　汉译英时用词要简洁,译文以表达清楚为宗旨,译文中多余的词不但不能增强语言的表现力,反而使语言显得累赘,使表达显得不够清晰,因此汉译英时要尽量避免重复啰嗦。另外,用词要规范,尽量使用书面语言,避免使用成语、俚语和过于生僻的词语,也不要堆砌华丽的辞藻。

(新06-12-75)

【例4】

75. I prefer to communicate with my customers ＿＿＿＿＿＿＿＿ (通过写电子邮件而不是打电话).

【答案】via /by email instead of telephone

【解析】本题考查对介词 by 或 via 以及短语 instead of 用法的掌握。表示通过某种方式,可以用 by 或 via;表示"代替…,而不是…"常用介词短语 instead of。需要注意的是,汉语中虽然有"写"和"打",但按照英语习惯可不必将其译出,如果译成 by writing email instead of making a telephone,不但不能准确地表达出汉语意思,反而会使表达显得累赘而且不够地道。

要诀五:用词要准确贴切

汉译英时用词除了要简洁规范以外,还要能够准确贴切地表达出所给汉语的意思。考生在翻译某个汉语词汇时,往往会在脑子里浮现出不止一个英文单词,但是一般来说,这些英文单词中只有一个是最符合此处的表达需要的,这就要求考生结合语境进行反复斟酌,从而选择出最能够准确地表达出此处汉语意思的词汇。

【例5】

Human behavior is mostly a product of learning ＿＿＿＿＿＿＿＿(然而,动物的行为主要依靠本能).

【答案】while animal behavior depends mainly on instinct /whereas the behavior of an animal depends mainly on instinct

【解析】本题考查对表示对比或相反情况的连接词的掌握。while 或 whereas 都可以作为连词,表示前后的一种对比或相反的情况,意为"然而"。注意此处不要用 however,尽管 however 也可以译成汉语的"然而",但 however 表示的是一种强烈的转折关系,而不能强调前后情况的对比。

要诀六:结合全句进行核查

翻译完成后,要通读全句,进行全面核查,这是不可缺少的一个重要环节。主要涉及以下几项内容:标点符号、大小写、单复数使用是否正确;译文与汉语是否完全对应,是否有多译或漏译单词的情况;译文时态与已给出的英文部分的时态是否一致、与所给汉语时态是否一致;译文与已给出的英文部分连在一起是否通顺、是否符合英语表达习惯。

要诀七:注意合理分配时间

由于汉译英只有 5 分钟的时间,所以要合理分配各题时间,切忌在某一题上花费太长的时间,而最后耽误了其他几道题的翻译,或是最后由于时间紧张而出现单词拼写、单复数、大小写、标点等方面的失误。平时训练时,要注意控制时间,培养良好的翻译习惯。

Exercise　　　　　　　即讲即练

1. ＿＿＿＿＿＿＿＿(要想帮助朋友解决困扰他的问题), a man should be equipped with the kind of knowledge required.

2. Understanding the cultural habits of another nation, especially one containing ＿＿＿＿＿＿＿＿(像美国那么多不同元素的), is a complex task.

3. The gloves were really too small, and ＿＿＿＿＿＿＿＿(只有撑着才能设法戴上).

4. Only ten to twenty percent of cold viruses are transmitted by carriers ＿＿＿＿＿＿＿＿(他们通过打喷嚏、咳嗽将病毒喷入空气中).

5. How strange it is that ＿＿＿＿＿＿＿＿(他小时候养成的习惯仍然伴随着他).

6. She didn't think the failure was her fault. Instead, ＿＿＿＿＿＿＿＿(她宁愿把它归结于运气不好).

7. To apply for this position, a man ＿＿＿＿＿＿＿＿(要具备相当娴熟的专业技能).

8. The longer you have got along with him, ＿＿＿＿＿＿＿＿(你就越会觉得他是一个值得信任的人).

9. The most important point of his speech was ＿＿＿＿＿＿＿＿(我们必须全心全意为人民工作).

10. We object to the idea that ＿＿＿＿＿＿＿＿(动用武力解决国际争端).

11. More than two hundred years ago ＿＿＿＿＿＿＿＿(美国脱离了大英帝国,成为一个独立的国家).

12. Hardly ＿＿＿＿＿＿＿＿(他几乎还没有安顿下来就把房子卖了)and left the country.

13. Some doctors suggest that those who feel lonely ＿＿＿＿＿＿＿＿(最好养些小家畜作为宠物).

14. ＿＿＿＿＿＿＿＿(接受教育是提升地位的主要途径)in a culture that generally stresses achievement, skillful-

ness, and upward mobility.

15. _____(开始看起来模糊不清或者乱七八糟的事情) might well become clear and organic a third time.

【答案与解析】

1. 【答案】To help a friend solve the problem troubling him
   【解析】本题考查对不定式用法的掌握。不定式短语可以在句子中充当状语,表示"以便,为了,要想"。

2. 【答案】as many different substances/elements as the United States
   【解析】本句考查对"as…as…"同级比较结构的掌握。as…as表示"和…一样的","元素"通常用substances或elements表示。

3. 【答案】it was only by stretching them that I managed to get them on
   【解析】本题考查对强调句型的掌握。强调的成分为本句的状语only by stretching them。"戴上(帽子、手套等)"通常用短语"get on"表示。

4. 【答案】who spray the viruses into the air through/by sneezing and coughing
   【解析】本题考查对定语从句的掌握。本句所给出的汉语中的"他们"指的就是carriers,所以可用who引导的定语从句修饰先行词carriers。

5. 【答案】the habit he developed in his childhood still clings to him
   【解析】本题考查对主语从句的掌握。How strange it is that中的it是形式主语,真正的主语是that引导的主语从句,How strange在句首表明本句是一个含有主语从句的感叹句。

6. 【答案】she would rather attribute it to bad luck
   【解析】本题考查对惯用搭配"attribute…to…"的掌握。attribute…to…意为"把…归因于…";"宁愿"通常用"would rather"表达。

7. 【答案】should be equipped with the proficient professional skills
   【解析】本题考查对被动语态的掌握。be equipped with表示"具备…,配备…",注意介词的搭配。

8. 【答案】the more you will find him a reliable man
   【解析】本题考查对the more…, the more…句式的掌握。"the＋more…, the＋more…"表示"越…,就越…",注意"the＋more"要位于两个分句的句首,具体用哪一个形容词的比较级要根据句子的具体结构和含义而定。

9. 【答案】that we should do all work whole-heartedly for the people
   【解析】本题考查对表语从句的掌握。所填句位于主句中的系动词之后,在句中充当表语,由从属连词that引导。

10. 【答案】it is military force that should be resorted to in settling international disputes
    【解析】本题考查对强调句型的掌握。分析句子可知,所翻译的部分强调的是"动用武力",所以需用强调句型来表达。强调句型的基本结构为:It is/was ＋ 被强调成分＋that ＋句子的其它成分。本句中,所强调的部分是military force。

11. 【答案】America broke away from the British Empire and became an independent country
    【解析】本题考查对惯用搭配"break away"的掌握。break away意为"脱离,放弃,突然离开"。

12. 【答案】had he had time to settle down when he sold the house
    【解析】本题考查对倒装句的掌握。hardly(scarcely)…when句型有两个特点:一是主句中一般使用过去完成时,而从句中一般使用一般过去时;二是hardly(scarcely)位于句首时,句子应部分倒装。本句中hardly位于句首,故句子应用倒装语序。

13. 【答案】had better keep some small domestic animals as pets
    【解析】本题考查对不带to的动词不定式的掌握。在had better, would rather/sooner…than…, would just as soon, might just as well, cannot(help) but…等之后,都必须接动词原形。

14. 【答案】To acquire education is a principal way of gaining status
    【解析】本题考查对不定式的掌握。To acquire education在句子中作主语。注意所填句子开头字母要大写。

15. 【答案】What seems confusing or fragmented at first
    【解析】本题考查对主语从句的掌握。关系代词what引导seems confusing or fragmented at first构成主语从句,意为"…的事情"。

Lecture 3　　　　**第三讲　7 大汉译英常用方法**

　　翻译需要大量的实践练习,这一点是毋庸置疑的,但同时,掌握一定的翻译技巧也是必需的。有效的技巧不但可以帮助我们提高译文的准确性,而且也可以加快我们翻译的速度,为考试节约时间。

　　翻译的技巧五花八门,下面我们针对六级考试翻译题的特点介绍几种在汉译英单句翻译中常用的技巧:

方法一:词义引申法

　　汉译英过程中,有时会遇到一些无法找到对等含义的英语词汇而无法确切体现该语境意义的情况,这就需要运用词汇的引申含义进行表达。

【例1】

The manager asked me to keep him ＿＿＿＿＿＿＿＿＿(了解计划的进展情况).

【答案】informed of how the plan is going on

【解析】利用 how 的引申含义表达"进展情况"。本题考查对过去分词作宾补用法的掌握。本句是表示"让某人了解某事",这里的"了解"是指通过别人而了解,故应该用 inform(告知),而不能用 understand 或 know。inform sb. of sth. 意为"告知某人某事",此处的 him 与 inform 之间是被动的关系,故应该用 inform 的过去分词形式充当宾补。另外,这里的"进展情况"强调的是计划随时的进展情况,因此用"the situation of the plan"就不如用 how the plan is going on 表达得确切。

方法二:词性转换法

　　由于英语和汉语的语言结构和表达方式不同,因此在很多时候,我们找不到意思对等词性又对等的词汇或短语,这时就必须根据英语的表达习惯,对汉语的词性进行相应的转换。

【例2】

The writer ＿＿＿＿＿＿＿＿＿(如此专心致志地写作)that he forgot to tap the ashes from his cigar.

【答案】was so absorbed in his writing

【解析】汉语中的副词"专心致志地"转换成了英语中的形容词"absorbed",汉语中的动词"写作"转换成了英语中的名词"writing"。本题考查对 so…that 句型和短语 be absorbed in (doing) sth. 的掌握。so…that 意为"如此…,以致于",引导结果状语从句。be absorbed in (doing) sth. 意为"全神贯注于…,专心于…"。

方法三:成分转译法

　　由于英语和汉语的语言结构和表达方式不同,因此在将汉语译成英语时,如果完全按照汉语的结构和句子成份直译过来,往往无法译出通顺地道的译文,这就要求我们在汉译英时,根据英语的表达习惯,适当转换句子的成份。

【例3】

It is universally acknowledged ＿＿＿＿＿＿＿＿＿(狗的嗅觉敏锐).

【答案】that dogs have an acute sense of smell

【解析】汉语中的主语"嗅觉"转译成英语中的宾语"sense of smell",汉语中的表语"敏锐"转译成英语中的定语"acute"。本题考查对主语从句的掌握。句中的 it 是形式主语,需要翻译的部分是句子真正的主语。

方法四:反译法

　　由于语言表达习惯不同,汉语中的肯定形式,有时候需要用英语的否定形式来表达。同样,汉语中的否定形式,有时候也可能需要用英语中的肯定形式来表达,关键是要符合英语的表达习惯。

【例4】

She ＿＿＿＿＿＿＿＿＿(对我们的警告充耳不闻)and got lost.

【答案】turned a deaf ear to our warnings

【解析】将汉语中的否定短语"充耳不闻"转译成了英语中的肯定短语"turn a deaf ear to"。本题考查对短语 turn a deaf ear to 的掌握。turn a deaf ear to sth. 意为"对…置若罔闻或充耳不闻"。and 后面的 got 提示此处应该用一般过去时态。

方法五：倒置法

英汉两种语言的表达习惯不同，自然在语序上也有很大差别。汉语中，往往习惯将定语和状语等修饰成份置于被修饰语之前；而英语中，定语和状语后置的情况则较多。因此，在汉译英时，要根据英语的表达习惯适当调整语序。

【例5】 (四级 06-12-87)

> 87. Specialists in intercultural studies say that it is not easy to _____ (适应不同文化中的生活).

【答案】adapt oneself to life /living in different cultures
【解析】定语"不同文化中的"后置。本题考查对短语 adapt (oneself) to 的掌握。adapt to 意为"适应"，在主语不明确的情况下，adapt 后通常要用反身代词 oneself 泛指所有人。to 在此处是介词，后须接名词短语(life in different cultures)或动名词短语(living in different cultures)。

方法六：增译法

增译法是指根据英语的表达习惯，在翻译时增加某些词汇或短语。汉语强调意合，而英语则更强调形合。因此，在将汉语译成英语时，经常需要添加连词、物主代词、介词或冠词等，以使句子的表达符合英语作为形合语言的特点，以保证译文语法结构的完整。

【例6】 (四级新 06-6-89)

> 89. The professor required that _____ (我们交研究报告) by Wednesday.

【答案】we (should) hand in our research report
【解析】增译了物主代词 our。本题考查对虚拟语气的掌握。表示要求、命令、建议等含义的动词如 require, urge, suggest 等后面接的宾语从句通常用虚拟语气，从句的谓语动词用"(should)＋原形动词"。"递交,提交"应该用短语 hand in。

方法七：省译法

省译法与增译法相反，它是指在翻译时省去一些词语不译出来。汉语中为了保证句子的平衡、气势和表达完整，常常会出现某些词语的重复现象或结构类似、含义相近的词语连用的现象。因此，在将汉语译成英语时，原文中含义重复的词语只需译出一个，以保证译文的简洁，避免累赘。

【例7】 (四级新 06-6-88)

> 88. _____ (为了挣钱供我上学), Mother often takes on more work than is good for her.

【答案】In order to finance my education
【解析】省译了"挣钱"。本题考查对不定式作目的状语的掌握。不定式短语经常位于句首充当目的状语。in order to 或 so as to 可以起到突出强调该目的的作用，但 so as to 一般不用在句首。"挣钱供…"还可以用 support 表示。

Exercise 即讲即练

1. You know that _____ (只要两个箱子加起来不超过 40 公斤), that's all right for the American air flight.
2. Martin Luther King, the great Black leader in the movement against racial discrimination, _____ (为世界和平作出了贡献而被授予诺贝尔和平奖).
3. Alone in a deserted house, he was _____ (忙于科研工作以致于感觉不到孤单).
4. The company was charged _____ (未能履行事先签订的合同).
5. The new government was accused of failure to _____ (实现其降低失业率的承诺).
6. The man was left on an isolated island, _____ (在那里呆了半年之久).

7. The footballer scored with such velocity _____ (以致于对方守门员没有机会将球扑出门外).

8. Being inquisitive by nature, _____ (一看到不同寻常的事情他总是忍不住要问题).

9. John couldn't have known the news _____ (否则他早就发出申请了).

10. _____ (我父亲原打算去巴黎度假), but his flight was delayed by the sudden heavy fog.

11. People who live in the countryside or in the mountains, _____ (他们的眼睛不断地调整以看远处的物体), seldom have to wear glasses in early or middle life.

12. The customer complained that no sooner _____ (他刚试着使用这台机器,它就不运转了).

13. _____ (看着他的朋友在遭受病痛的折磨), he felt very sad.

14. Many traditional Chinese believe _____ (前额高表示智慧高).

15. Children between the age of 2 and 11 cannot comprehend the difference between commercials and television, _____ (所以他们无法抵御商业电视广告的诱惑手段).

【答案与解析】

1.【答案】as long as the two cases don't exceed 40 kg

　【解析】利用 the two cases 的引申含义表达"两个箱子加起来"。通常在看到"加起来",一般会想到使用动词 plus 或动词词组 add to 来表达,但如果使用动词或动词词组则会使条件状语从句中包含一个主从复合句,这样就会使句子显得累赘。本题考查对 as long as 用法的掌握。as long as 意为"只要",引导条件状语从句。

2.【答案】was awarded the Nobel Prize for peace for his contribution to world peace

　【解析】汉语中的动词"作出了贡献"转换成了英语中的名词"contribution"。本题考查对惯用搭配"be awarded…for…"的掌握。be awarded…for…意为"因为…而被授予…"。

3.【答案】so busy with his research work that he didn't feel lonely

　【解析】汉语中的谓语"忙于"转译成英语中地表语"busy"。本题考查对"so…that…"结构的掌握。so…that…意为"如此…以致于…",that 引导结果状语从句。

4.【答案】with failure to fulfill the contract signed in advance

　【解析】汉语中的否定短语"未能",转译成了英语中的肯定短语"with failure to"。本题考查对 charge 的搭配以及其他一些短语用法的掌握。charge sb. with sth. 意为"以某事指控或控告某人",另外 accuse…(of)也表示"控告或指控",注意不同的介词搭配。failure (fail) to do sth. 常用于表示"未能做成某事",因为是紧跟在介词 with 之后,所以应用 failure to do sth。

5.【答案】fulfill its promise to reduce the unemployment rate

　【解析】宾语"承诺"前置。本题考查对惯用搭配的掌握。fulfill promise 意为"实现承诺";the unemployment rate 意为"失业率"。

6.【答案】where he stayed for as long as half a year

　【解析】增译了主语 he。本题考查对非限制性定语从句的掌握。先行词 island 在主句中充当地点状语,故定语从句应该用关系副词 where 来引导。表示"长达…之久",用"as long as+时间"。

7.【答案】that the goalkeeper didn't have the chance of saving the goal

　【解析】省译了"对方"、"门外"。本题考查对"such…that…"的掌握。such…that…意为"如此…以致于…"。

8.【答案】he could not help asking questions whenever he saw something unusual

　【解析】利用 whenever 的引申含义表达"一遇到"。本题考查对时间状语从句和惯用搭配"can't help doing"的掌握。连词 whenever 引导时间状语从句,表示"无论何时"。can't help doing sth. 意为"忍不住做某事"。

9.【答案】otherwise he would have sent his application

　【解析】增译了物主代词 his。本题考查对虚拟语气用法的掌握。前半句中 couldn't have known 是对过去情况的否定推测,后面的"否则"表示对过去的一种假设,即"如果不是那样的话",相当于一个 if 引导的虚拟条件句,故后面的句子应用虚拟语气,谓语动词用 would have done 的形式。

10.【答案】My father had intended to go to Paris for a holiday

　【解析】汉语中的动词"度假"转换成了英语中的介词短语"for a holiday"。本题考查对过去完成时用法的掌握。当 plan, intend, decide, mean 等含有"计划或打算"意义的动词用于过去完成时态时,常表达"原本想要做某事,但实际上却没有实现"的含义。

11.【答案】where the eyes are constantly adjusting themselves to objects at a distance

　【解析】定语"远处的"后置。本题考查对地点状语从句的掌握。分析句子结构可知,所翻译的成份应该是复合句中的地点状语从句,所以用 where 作引导词,表示"在那儿…"。

12.【答案】had he tried to use the machine than it stopped working

　　【解析】汉语中的否定短语"不运转",转译成了英语中的肯定短语"stopped working"。本题考查对倒装句及 no sooner…than…用法的掌握。具有否定意义的副词放在句首时,一般采用倒装句(谓语前置)。这类表示否定意义的词有 never, seldom, scarcely, little, few, not, hardly, 以及 not only…but (also), no sooner…than, hardly…when scarcely…when 等等。no sooner…than…意为"刚…就一…"。

13.【答案】Watching his friend suffering the illness

　　【解析】省译了"折磨"。本题考查对现在分词用法的掌握。现在分词 watching 在此充当句子的状语,表示原因。watch 后面既可以接动名词作宾补,也可以接不定式作宾补,动名词强调动作和当时的状态,不定式则强调过程和结果。此处是表示正在遭受痛苦,强调当时的状态,故应该用现在分词 suffering。

14.【答案】that high forehead is indicative of great mental power

　　【解析】汉语中的动词"表示"转换成了英语中的形容词"indicative"。本题考查对宾语从句的掌握。that 引导宾语从句的情况十分普遍,在 believe, think, suppose, presume 等动词之后,that 也可省略。be indicative of 意为"指示性的,可表示的"。

15.【答案】so they cannot defend themselves against the persuasive techniques of commercial television advertising

　　【解析】增译了反身代词 themselves。本题考查对惯用搭配"defend…against…"的掌握。defend…against… 意为"抵挡,抵御…以免于"。persuasive techniques 意为"诱惑性的、善说服性的手段",用于此处最为合适。

汉译英巅峰练习

Exercise 1

82. Many photographers prefer to take pictures at dusk, _____(那时他们可利用落日的特殊效应).

83. Great writers are those who not only have great thoughts but also express these thoughts in words _____(强烈地影响我们的思想和情感).

84. _____(迄今为止主管一直没有时间做详细地研究), but he gave us an idea about his plan.

85. The police blamed the accident on the driver _____(试图超车).

86. Researchers speculate that genes may determine the strength of the immune system, _____(这对于解释为什么传染病可以遗传有帮助).

Exercise 2

82. Our research has focused on a drug _____(药力强大足以改变大脑化学物质组成).

83. Alcohol abuse is the most serious drug problem in the United States today. Nevertheless, Dr. Chavetz believes that _____(如果控制得当，酒是利大于弊的).

84. Under no circumstances is it unacceptable _____(车祸后试图逃逸).

85. If you had not run the red light, _____(事故就不会发生了).

86. Jack was sure that _____(钱包肯定是让一个店员给拾去了), but it was not returned to him.

Exercise 3

82. Only after his wife left him _____(他才意识到她对他有多么重要).

83. _____(除非政府提供更多的资金), the hospital will have to close.

84. AIDS _____(据说对当地妇女构成了最大的健康威胁)in the past decade.

85. _____(无论谈判双方可能达成什么协议)will only be temporary.

86. The nuclear science should be developed _____(对人类有益而不是有害的).

答案与解析

Exercise 1

82. 【答案】when they can take advantage of the special effects of the setting sun

【解析】本题考查对时间状语从句的掌握。引导时间状语从句的连词最常见的有：when, as, while, before, after, till, until, (ever) since, as soon as 等。take advantage of 意为"利用"。

83. 【答案】which appeal powerfully to our minds and emotions

【解析】本题考查对定语从句的掌握。which引导的定语从句作后置定语,修饰先行词 words。appeal to 意为"吸引,影响,请求,呼吁"。

84. 【答案】The supervisor didn't have time so far to go into it at length

【解析】本题考查了对惯用用法的掌握。so far 意为"到目前为止,迄今为止";at length 意为"详细地,最后地"。

85. 【答案】who had attempted to overtake the car before him

【解析】本题考查对定语从句的掌握。who引导定语从句,修饰其前的 driver。要注意的是所翻译部分的谓语动词的时态。很显然,司机超车的动作发生在警察责备他的动作之前,所以要用过去完成时。

86. 【答案】which could help explain why an infectious disease could have a hereditary link

【解析】本题考查对非限制性定语从句的掌握。分析句子结构可知所要翻译的部分应是修饰前面整个句子,而能修饰整个句子的定语从句最常用的是 which 引导的非限制性定语从句。

Exercise 2

82.【答案】which is so powerful as to be able to change brain chemistry

【解析】本题考查对定语从句和"so… as to…"用法的掌握。which 引导定语从句修饰先行词 drug。so… as to… 意为"如此…以致于…"。

83.【答案】if properly controlled, alcohol can do more good than harm

【解析】本题考查对省略了成份的条件状语从句的掌握。if 引导条件状语从句,因该条件状语从句的主语与主句的主语 alcohol 是一致的,所以可将条件状语从句的主语和谓语省略。do more good than harm 意为"利大于弊"。

84.【答案】to attempt to escape after the car accident

【解析】本题考查对不定式作真正主语的掌握。分析句子结构可知,所翻译部分在句中作真正主语,所以应用不定式短语。attempt to do sth. 意为"试图做某事"。

85.【答案】the accident would not have happened

【解析】本题考查对虚拟语气的掌握。根据句意,此处表示对过去事实的假设,因此 if 条件句的谓语动词应该用过去完成时,主句谓语动词应该用过去将来完成时。

86.【答案】the wallet must have been found by one of the shop assistants

【解析】本题考查对 must 表示推测用法的掌握。情态动词 must 常用于表示肯定推测,意为"一定,必然"。表示对现在或将来事实的肯定推测时,用 must do 的形式;表示对过去事实的肯定推测时,用 must have done 的形式。本题很明显是表示对过去事实的推测。

Exercise 3

82.【答案】did he realize how important she is to him

【解析】本题考查对倒装句式的掌握。"only＋状语"位于句首时,句子要部分倒装。另外,注意宾语从句要用陈述语序。

83.【答案】Unless the government agrees to provide extra money

【解析】本题考查对连词 unless 用法的掌握。unless 表示"除非…否则…",相当于"if… not",常用于引导条件状语从句。

84.【答案】is said to have been the greatest healthy challenge to the local women

【解析】本题考查对被动语态和不定式完成式用法的掌握。表达"据说",考生比较习惯用 It is said that…, it 为形式主语,that 从句为句子的真正主语。但本句中没有采用形式主语,而是将叙述的主体 AIDS 作为句子的主语,因此应该采用 is said to do 的句式。而根据后面的时间状语 in the past decade 可知,此处应用不定式的完成式。

85.【答案】Whatever agreement the two parties may reach in the negotiation

【解析】本题考查对主语从句的掌握。表示"无论什么",可以用 no matter what,也可以用 whatever。但需要注意的是,no matter what 只能用于引导状语从句,而不能引导主语从句,因此本句只能用 whatever。另外,需要注意 agreement 应该紧跟在 whatever 之后。

86.【答案】to benefit the people rather than harm them／to benefit the people instead of harming them

【解析】本题考查对不定式和短语 rather than 的掌握。此处应该用不定式充当主语补足语。rather than 意为"而不是",用于连接并列成份。另外,这里也可以用 instead of 来表达。

综合测试巅峰练习

Test 1

Part V Error Correction(15 minutes)

A severe shortage of drivers could hurt the U. S. economy, which relies heavily on trucking. Those in the industry say openings number in the thousands, if only tens of thousands. The shortage is likely to end soon. The government estimates the number of truck drivers will raise 19% from 2002 to 2012, making driving one of the fastest-growing occupation during those 10 years. Trucking companies are trying to fill jobs by offering drivers cash bonuses and prizes such as boats and vacations to refer fellow drivers their firms. Base pay is rising, and trucking companies are guaranteeing drivers much time at home. Firms are offering generous 401 (k), stock option and health care packages and other perks. Truck stops now have massage therapists and Wi-Fi computer technology.

Still, the number of drivers is woefully inadequate. It's not just an issue of recruiting. Retaining drivers has become constant headache: The turnover rate at large trucking companies was 116% in the second quarter, according to the American Trucking Associations. "I define this the most serious problem the industry has," says Duff Swain, President of Trincon Group, a transportation consulting firm in Columbus, Ohio. Companies he has been speaking to recently say 10% of their trucks are idle because they can't find enough drivers. It goes way beyond trucking. Trucks carried more than three-quarters of the goods that travel in the USA in 2003. If there aren't enough drivers to haul the nation's production, the economy runs the risk of stumbling. Plus, if drivers can be found only by raising pay and benefits, those costs could be passed along and eventually could show up in higher consumer prices.

62. _____

63. _____

64. _____

65. _____

66. _____

67. _____

68. _____

69. _____

70. _____

71. _____

Part VI Translation (5 minutes)

72. _____(直到 19 世纪末和 20 世纪初) that the State was willing to remove a yuong child from direct supervision of careless parents.

73. _____(生活在偏远山村), the girl has never seen the computer.

74. It has been estimated that _____(人类吸收的多达 10%的蛋白) comes from the oceans.

75. The more you read, _____(你越觉得自己的知识少).

76. Most analysts agree _____(记者一定要对事件敏感) such as fairness, balance, and accuracy.

答案与解析

Part V

62. only — not。上下文语义矛盾。openings number in the thousands 指的是"职位空缺数量有几千",相对于 tens of thousands 来说,the thousands 数量较少,所以应将 only 改为 not。if not tens of thousands 意为"如果不是有几万个"。

63. likely — unlikely。上下文语义矛盾。由下段首句中的 the number of drivers is woefully inadequate 可知,卡车司机缺乏的情况不可能很快结束,故应将 likely 改为否定形式 unlikely。

64. raise — rise。易混词误用。raise 含有"抬高,提高"之意,它强调动作的姿态,所以应用它的同义词 rise 替换,它表示"事物由低到高的变化",符合本句中卡车司机数量增加的含义,故应将 raise 改为 rise。

65. occupation — occupations。名词单复数误用。名词性词组中 one of... 后的名词应用复数形式,所以应将 occupation 改为 occupations。

66. drivers ∧ their — to。缺漏。货车运输公司给员工提供现金红利、发放奖金以及给予假期,这些措施都是为了留住卡车司机,同下文中的 retaining 意思相同,所以 refer 在本句中就应该含有"使注意…,引导…的注意力",故应在 drivers 与 their 之间增加介词 to,refer sb. to sth. 在文中意为"使某人的注意力集中到某物上"。

67. much — more。上下文语义矛盾。and 前的分句 Base pay is rising(基本工资正在上涨)是相对于过去的基本工资而言的,所以后一分句也应是相对于过去情况而言。既然是与过去情况的比较,那么就应该使用比较级,故应将 much 改为 more。

68. become ∧ constant — a。缺漏。constant 前应加上不定冠词 a,泛指 headache。

69. this ∧ the — as。缺漏。define 在作"把…解释成,说明…"时应加介词 as 连接宾语,故应在 this 和 the 之间添加 as。

70. travel — travelled。时态错误。时间状语 in 2003 以及主句的谓语动词 carried 表明定语从句的谓语也应用一般过去式,故应将 travel 改为 travelled。

71. production — products。易混词误用。production 指产品时,侧重于产品产量,而本句明显不是侧重于产量,而是侧重于产品,故应将 production 改为 products。

Part VI

72. 【答案】It was not until the late nineteenth and early twentieth centuries
【解析】本句考查对 not…until 句型以及强调句型的掌握。not…until 意为"直到…才…",而强调句的固定结构为 it was＋被强调成分(可以是主语、宾语、状语、间接宾语,但不能是谓语)＋that＋其他成分。

73. 【答案】Living in a remote village
【解析】本句考查对现在分词用法的掌握。根据主语 the girl 与"生活"的逻辑关系确定使用主动语态。现在分词 living…在句中充当句子的状语。

74. 【答案】as much as 10% of human protein intake
【解析】本句考查对 it 充当形式主语的掌握。it 在这里充当形式主语,真正的主语是 that 所引导的句子。

75. 【答案】the less you feel your knowledge is
【解析】本题考查对 the more…, the more… 句式的掌握。"the＋比较级…,the＋比较级…"表示"越…,就越…",注意"the＋比较级"要位于两个分句的句首,具体用哪一个词的比较级要根据句子的具体结构和含义而定。

76. 【答案】that journalists must remain sensitive to issues
【解析】本题考查对宾语从句的掌握。that 引导宾语从句,在从句中不充当任何成份,可省略。be sensitive to…为固定短语,意为"对…灵敏,敏感"。

Test 2

Part V Cloze(15 minutes)

A major reason for ___62___ in the animal world is territory. The male animal establishes an area. The size of the area is sufficient to provide food for him, his ___63___ and their offspring. Migrating birds, for example, ___64___ up

62. [A] attack [B] conflict
[C] invasion [D] quarrel
63. [A] friend [B] mate
[C] neighbor [D] opponent

the best territory in the order of "first come, first __65__ " The late arrivals may acquire larger territories, but less food is __66__ , or they are too close to the __67__ of the enemies of the species. __68__ there is really insufficient food or the danger is very great, the animal will not mate. In this way, the members of the species which are less fit will not have __69__ .

When there is conflict __70__ territory, animals will commonly use force, or __71__ of force, to decide which will stay and which will go. It is interesting to note, however, that animals seem to use the __72__ amount of force necessary to drive away the __73__ . There is usually no killing. In the case of those animals which are __74__ of doing each other great harm, there is a system for the __75__ animal to show the winning animal that he wishes to __76__ . When he shows this, the __77__ normally stops fighting. Animals especially birds, which can easily escape from conflict seem to have no obstacle against killing, equally no mechanism __78__ submission. The defeated bird simply flies away. However, if two doves are __79__ in a cage, and they start fighting, they will continue to fight until one kills the other. We all think of the dove as a __80__ of peace and, in its natural habitat, it is peaceful. But the "peace" mechanism does not __81__ in a cage.

64. [A] break　　　[B] divide
　　[C] speak　　　[D] make
65. [A] occupied　[B] served
　　[C] seated　　　[D] manipulated
66. [A] admissible　[B] accessible
　　[C] agreeable　　[D] available
67. [A] caves　　　[B] habitats
　　[C] nests　　　[D] houses
68. [A] Hence　　　[B] Therefore
　　[C] However　　[D] Provided
69. [A] offspring　[B] children
　　[C] spouses　　[D] kids
70. [A] regarding　[B] beneath
　　[C] beyond　　　[D] over
71. [A] a proof　　[B] a show
　　[C] evidence　　[D] an example
72. [A] minimum　　[B] maximum
　　[C] scarce　　　[D] sufficient
73. [A] offspring　[B] mate
　　[C] intruder　　[D] neighbor
74. [A] able　[B] capable　[C] fond　[D] likely
75. [A] lost　[B] losing　[C] won　[D] winning
76. [A] conquer　[B] submit　[C] overwhelm　[D] defeat
77. [A] successor　　[B] winner
　　[C] intruder　　[D] loser
78. [A] by　[B] for　[C] about　[D] lined
79. [A] stationed　[B] placed　[C] deposited　[D] lined
80. [A] indication　[B] gesture
　　[C] sign　　　　[D] symbol
81. [A] apply　　　[B] function
　　[C] revolve　　[D] imply

Part VI Translation (5 minutes)

82. _____ (虽然我们试图集中注意力听讲座), we were distracted by the noise from the next room.

83. They had to eat a hasty meal, or _____ (他们有可能就来不及听音乐会了).

84. I believe China's economic success should be seen _____ (与其说是威胁，不如说是机遇).

85. I could hear nothing but the roar of the airplane engines _____ (飞机引擎的噪音淹没了其他的声音).

86. _____ (他原本可以用较好的措辞表达想法), but I find what he said makes a lot of sense.

答案与解析

Part V

> 【文章大意】
> 　　本文主要与动物世界里的领地争端有关。文章第一段指出动物是怎样划分领地的；第二段则指出动物解决领地争端的方法。

62. 选[B]。语义衔接题。通读文章可知，本文的内容主要是与动物世界里的领地争端有关。文章第二段首句中的 conflict 提示所填词应是 conflict 的同义复现，故答案为[B] conflict。

63. 选[B]。语义衔接题。本空前的 him 指的是 the male animal。由连词 and 的特点可知，him，his _____ 与 their

offspring 应是并列关系,所以这三者应构成语义场共现,故答案为[B] mate"配偶"。

64. 选[B]。语义衔接题。四个选项都可以与 up 搭配使用,所以本题可以从语义辨析入手判断答案。[A] break, break up 意为"打破,破碎,结束,分裂";[C] speak, speak up 意为"大声说";[D] make, make up 意为"弥补,虚构,缝制,整理,包装"。这三者的意思明显不符合句意,故可排除。而[B] divide, divide up 意为"分割",在句中指"分割领土",符合原文,故为答案。

65. 选[B]。惯用衔接题。结合原文及选项可知,first come, first _____ 是一个谚语,所填词应为 served, first come, first served 意为"先到先得",故答案为[B] served。

66. 选[D]。语义衔接题。本句是讲后到者有许多的不利情况,所以所填词所在的分句应是讲后到者没有很多食物可以吃,故所填词应能表达"没有足够的食物"这一含义。备选项中只有[D] available"可利用的"符合要求,故为答案。[A] admissible"可容许的,可接纳的";[B] accessible"易接近的,可到达的";[C] agreeable"使人愉快的,适合的"。

67. 选[B]。语义衔接题。根据四个选项中各词的意思可知本分句是想表达"后到者太过接近它们敌人的住处"。the enemies of the species 比较概括,所以表达 the enemies of the species 的居住环境的词也应是一个概括、笼统的词,只有选项[B] habitats"(动植物的)生活环境,栖息地"符合题意。[A] caves"洞穴",通常是穴居动物的栖息地,[C] nests"鸟巢",通常是鸟类的栖息地,[D] houses"房屋",通常是人的居住地,这些词都太过具体,故均排除。

68. 选[D]。语义衔接题。分析主句与从句之间的关系可知,there is really insufficient food or the danger is very great 是 the animal will not mate 的条件,所以所填词应能引导条件状语从句,故答案为[D] Provided"倘若"。

69. 选[A]。语义衔接题。本句中的定语从句 which are less fit 指的是上句所说的"没有足够的食物以及处于极大危险之中"的鸟类。这些鸟类 not mate(不交配)的结果就是,它们会没有后代。本段第二句已经指出鸟类的后代用 offspring 表示,所以所填词应是 offspring 的原词复现,故答案为[A] offspring。

70. 选[D]。惯用衔接题。本句要表达的含义是"当动物之间在领地上有冲突"的含义,故答案为[D] over。

71. 选[B]。语义衔接题。通读整句话可知,本句主要是讲动物通常会使用武力来决定谁去谁留。[A] a proof, a proof of force"武力证明";[C] evidence, evidence of force"武力证据";[D] an example, an example of force"武力的例子"。无论从短语本身还是从句意上都不符合逻辑,故可排除。[B] a show, a show of force"武力展示"符合句意,故为答案。

72. 选[A]。语义衔接题。由下句 There is usually no killing 可知,虽然动物之间会使用武力解决领地争端,但是武力却不会造成死亡,这就说明动物们使用武力的目的只是赶走入侵者,而不是杀死入侵者,所以它们使用的武力应该是能赶走入侵者的最小武力,故本题答案为[A] minimum"最小"。

73. 选[C]。语义衔接题。通读整段话可知,本段主要与动物如何解决领地争端有关。所以本句中的 drive away(赶走)的宾语应是指"入侵某种动物领地的其他动物",由此可知答案应为[C] intruder"入侵者"。

74. 选[B]。语义衔接题。所填词应能与 of 构成搭配,所以应排除[A] able 和[D] likely,二者都是与 to 搭配使用;[C] fond, be fond of 意为"喜欢,爱好",明显不符合句意,故也可排除,[B] capable, be capable of 意为"有能力……",符合句意,故为答案。

75. 选[B]。语义衔接题。由上文可知,在一场武力比试中,通常"失败"的一方要向获胜方表示屈服,故答案为[B] losing。

76. 选[B]。语义衔接题。分析整句话可知,that 引导的宾语从句中的 he 指代的是失败方,而失败方应该顺从、屈服于获胜方,故[B] submit"服从,顺从"符合题意。

77. 选[B]。语义衔接题。由上两题的分析可知,当失败方向获胜方屈服,那么"获胜方"就应该停止战斗,故[B] winner 符合题意。

78. 选[B]。语义衔接题。通过对比阅读本句和上一句可知,本句中的 mechanism 和上一句中的 system 都是指一种失败者能够表示屈服的机制。所以本题的介词应该选用 for,以表示 mechanism 的内容,故答案为[B]。

79. 选[B]。语义衔接题。上句讲鸟类一般不会被杀,因为失败的鸟通常会飞走,而本句却说鸽子一旦开始争斗,那么它们就会一直等到一只鸽子杀死另一只鸽子之后才会停止争斗,但发生这种情况有一个前提,即: two doves are _____ in a cage. 很明显,这个前提就是,鸽子不能自由飞走,它们被关在了笼子里。[A] stationed"驻扎,配置",[C] deposited"存放,堆积",[D] lined"排成一队"都无法体现"关"这一动作,故可排除。而[B] placed"放置"则能体现"关"这一动作,故为本题答案。

80. 选[D]。惯用衔接题。根据常识可知,鸽子是和平的象征,"象征"通常用"symbol"表示,故答案为[D] symbol。[A] indication"指示,迹象,暗示";[B] gesture"姿势,手势";[C] sign"标记,符号"。

81. 选[A]。语义衔接题。文章提到关在笼子里的两只鸽子自相残杀这一事实是为了说明"和平"机制适用于动物们在自然的条件下解决争端时采用,而并不适用于当它们被关在笼子里时,所以所填词应含有"适用"的含义,故答案为[A] apply"适用于"。

Part II

82. 【答案】Although we tried to concentrate on the lecture

【解析】本题考查对让步状语从句的掌握。让步状语从句主要由 although,though,even though,while,whereas 等连词引起,表示"尽管,虽然"。

83. 【答案】they would be too late for the concert

【解析】本题考查对情态动词的掌握。would 为情态动词,后面接动词原形,表示对某种情况较有把握的、肯定的推测,意为"有可能"。be late for 意为"迟到"。

84. 【答案】more as an opportunity than a threat

【解析】本题考查对比较级结构"more…than…"的掌握。"more…than…"意为"与其说是…不如说是…"。

85. 【答案】which drowned all other sounds

【解析】本题考查对定语从句的掌握。which 引导定语从句,修饰前面的 the roar,注意从句中的谓语动词应该用过去式,保持时态一致,并且应与 the roar 一致。

86. 【答案】He might have used better words to express his ideas

【解析】本题考查对虚拟语气的掌握。might have done 常表示"原本可以做…,但实际上没有做…"的含义,是对过去事实的假设。

第四篇 短文写作

第37－42天

Part 4

第一章 短文写作巅峰讲座

六级写作要求考生根据规定的题目和所提供的提纲、情景、图片或图表等,写出一篇不少于 150 词的短文,其考试时间为 30 分钟,所占分值比例为 15%。

Lecture 1　　第一讲　3 种常见出题方式

六级写作着重测试考生用文字评论和说明事物的能力,因此体裁以说明文和议论文居多,偶尔也会涉及到应用文(多为书信)。六级写作的题材主要涉及两类内容:一类是关于大学生的学习、校园生活及对未来的工作、人生等问题的态度和看法;另一类是与日常生活息息相关或贴近社会变化、发展和进步的热点话题。

从历年真题来看,其出题方式主要有以下三类:

一、提纲式文字

这类出题方式一般会给出作文的英文题目以及两到三点的中文提纲(偶尔也可能是英文提纲),提纲大致规定了各主体段落的主题,要求考生根据该主题制定各段落主题句,然后围绕所制定的主题句展开段落,最后对文章主题进行总结。

【例 1】 (05-6)

> **Directions:** *In this part, you are allowed 30 minutes to write a short essay entitled **Say No to Pirated Products**. You should write at least 150 words following the outline given below:*
>
> 1) 目前盗版的现象比较严重
> 2) 造成这种现象的原因及危害
> 3) 我们应该怎么做?
> 可能用到词汇:
> 盗版 piracy(n.)
> 盗版产品 pirated products
> 知识产权 intellectual property rights
> 侵犯版权 infringe sb's copyright; copyright infringement

二、提纲式图表

这类出题方式一般会给出作文的英文题目以及一个或几个图片或图表,并在图片或图表的下方给出两到三点的中文提纲,要求考生用文字描述图片或图表的内容,解释图表所反映出来的某种趋势或问题,然后分析导致该趋势或问题的原因或其带来的后果和影响。

【例 2】 (06-6)

> **Directions:** *For this part, you are allowed 30 minutes to write a short essay entitled **Traveling Abroad**. You should write at least 150 words based on the chart and outline given below:*

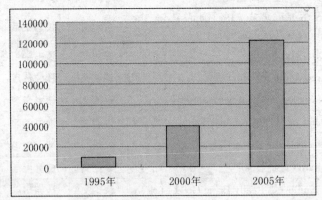

Number of people in City X traveling abroad in 1995, 2000 and 2005

1) 近十年来×市有越来越多的人选择出境旅游

2) 出现这种现象的原因

3) 这种现象可能产生的影响

三、情景式

这类出题方式的作文一般都属于应用文文体,且以信函居多。一般会给出一个特定的情景,要求考生根据该情景撰写一封书信或其他某种形式的应用文。

【例3】   (05-12)

Directions: *For this part, you are allowed 30 minutes to write a letter to a company declining a job offer. You should write at least 150 words following the outline given below:*

1) 对公司提供职位表示感谢

2) 解释为何不能接受所提供的职位

3) 希望予以谅解,并表示对公司的良好祝愿

附:

综合以上各方面的分析,为了让考生对六级作文有更深入的了解,准确把握六级作文的出题规律,现将近十年的六级作文试题列表分析如下:

考试时间	主题或题目	体裁	题材	出题方式
2007.06	Should One Expect a Reward When Doing a Good Deed?	议论文	社会热点	提纲式文字
新 2006.12	The Importance of Reading Classics	说明文	读书学习	提纲式文字
2006.12	The Celebration of Western Festivals	说明文	社会热点	提纲式文字
2006.06	Traveling Abroad	说明文	社会热点	提纲式图表
2005.12	A Letter Declining a Job Offer	应用文	职场工作	情景式
2005.06	Say No to Pirated Products	说明文	社会热点	提纲式文字
2005.01	Your Help Needed	应用文	校园生活	提纲式文字
2004.06	A Letter to the Editor of a Newspaper	应用文	日常生活	提纲式文字
2004.01	Reduce Waste on Campus	说明文	校园生活	提纲式文字
2003.09	Reading Preference	说明文	读书学习	提纲式图表
2003.06	Changes in the Ownership of Houses	说明文	日常生活	提纲式图表
2003.01	It Pays to Be Honest	议论文	日常生活	提纲式文字
2002.06	Student Use of Computers	议论文	读书学习	提纲式图表

考试时间	主题或题目	体裁	题材	出题方式
2002.01	A Letter to the University President About the Canteen Service on Campus	应用文	校园生活	情景式
2001.06	A Letter to a Schoolmate	应用文	读书学习	情景式
2001.01	How to Succeed in a Job Interview	说明文	社会热点	提纲式文字
2000.06	Is a Test of Spoken English Necessary?	议论文	读书学习	提纲式文字
2000.01	How I Finance My College Education	说明文	读书学习	提纲式文字
1999.06	Reading Selectively or Extensively?	议论文	读书学习	提纲式文字
1999.01	Don't Hesitate to Say "No"	议论文	日常生活	提纲式文字
1998.06	Do "Lucky Numbers" Really Bring Good Luck?	议论文	社会热点	提纲式文字
1998.01	My View on Fake Commodities	说明文	社会热点	提纲式文字

Lecture 2　　第二讲　5 大写作评分标准

六级写作部分所占分值比例为 15%,标准分满分为 106.5。阅卷评分按照满分 15 分计算,评分标准共分五个等级:2 分、5 分、8 分、11 分和 14 分。

阅卷人员根据阅卷标准对照样卷进行评分,先就总体印象划定作文等级,然后根据具体情况对分数进行适当调整。若认为与某一分数等级相似,即定为该分数;若阅卷过程中发现该作文稍优或稍劣于该分数,则可加 1 分或减 1 分。各分数档的评判标准如下:

2 分:条理不清,思路紊乱,语言支离破碎或大部分句子均有错误,且多数为严重错误。

5 分:基本切题,表达思想不清楚,连贯性差,有较多的严重语言错误。

8 分:基本切题,有些地方表达思想不够清楚,文字勉强连贯,语言错误相当多,其中有一些是严重错误。

11 分:切题,表达思想清楚,文字连贯,但有少量语言错误。

14 分:切题,表达思想清楚,文字通顺,连贯性较好,基本上无语言错误,仅有个别小错。

在总体作文评分原则的指导下,六级作文的评分强调五项标准,即内容切题、表达清楚、文字连贯、句式多变和语言规范。

一、内容切题

文章要结构完整、内容充实(包含提纲、图表、图画和题目要求的所有信息)、主题突出、上下文内容统一。

二、表达清楚

文章要具有清晰的层次和充分有力的论证。中西方文化差异造成英语和汉语在思维方式和文字表述方式上的截然不同:汉语中多出现概括描述,而英文表述更注重事实论证。所以,写英语作文不要过多地进行心理、环境描写,而是要用理由和实例来说明问题或论证自己观点的正确性。

三、文字连贯

语言表达要流畅,能使用恰当的连接词,使前后语句意思连贯,逻辑性强,不相互矛盾,不东拉西扯。

四、句式多变

为避免文章平淡、呆板,可使用不同的句式,如强调句、倒装句、否定句等。长短句要合理相间:用短句表达有力的结论;用长句体现严密的逻辑关系。

五、语言规范

用词要准确,并能表现出足够大的词汇量。所用语言符合英语的表达习惯并且语法错误较少。不出现有语法错误的句子和不合理的断句;正确使用平行结构。

第三讲 3 大写作高分要素

一、结构清晰

要写出一篇相对成功的文章,首先要树立一个框架意识,结构要完整,主题要明确,各段详略必须得当,段与段的衔接要自然流畅。否则即使语言运用得再好,也很难得高分。

【例 1】 (00-1)

> **Directions:** *For this part, you are allowed 30 minutes to write a composition on the topic* **How I Finance My College Education**. *You should write at least 120 words, and base your composition on the outline(given in Chinese) below:*
>
> 1)上大学的费用(tuition and fees)可以通过多种途径解决
> 2)哪种途径适合于我(说明理由)

【5 分作文】

College students can get their tuition and fees in various ways. They can get it from their parents. They can earn money after class to get it. If they study hard, the school will give some students scholarships.

My parents can give me some money. I will earn money after class to pay *others*(the rest). I think that is the suitable way for me.

I don't like *apply* (applying for) loans from school. I will study hard to try to get scholarships from school. I have won the first-class scholarships for two years. I like *do* (doing) part-time jobs such as a tutor. I can solve my tuition and fees and make *well* (good /better) use of time. Many students also pay tuition and fees through other *method* (methods).

【点评】

本文之所以只得到 5 分,除了出现一些语法错误(斜体部分)之外,在很大程度上是因为结构问题。

首先,文章框架不合理。本文虽然也是三段式的安排,但第二段明显与第三段陈述的是同一主题,应该合为一段。

其次,文章结构不完整。提纲虽只给出两点,但一开始就交代解决上大学费用的途径显得有些突兀,应在第一段前给出该问题出现的背景,这样结构才比较完整。

再次,主题有些偏离。第二、三段只是简单陈述自己喜欢哪种方式、不喜欢哪种方式,而没有充分地阐释理由,而且还出现个别与主题不相关的句子,如文章结尾一句。

最后,文章的连贯性很差。第一段中列举了三种解决上大学费用的途径,但给人一种信息堆砌之感,缺少必要的衔接;第二段和第三段逻辑顺序比较混乱,条理不清,整段的内容显得杂乱无章,缺少必要的衔接。

【7 分作文】

The new tuition policy is adopted. College students must afford their tuition and fees for themselves. They must pay an average sum of 2,500 yuan each year as tuition. They must pay many fees. For example, they must pay for their accomodation. They must pay for their diseases.

College students can get their tuition and fees in various ways such as *parents, part-time jobs, scholarships and loans* (asking for them from parents, doing part-time jobs, winning scholarships and applying for loans).

My family can't afford *my all* (all my) expenses at college. But my family is not poverty-stricken. I have no right to seek help from the loan programs. And I wish to practice self-reliance. Then I offer instruction as a tutor. It helps a lot financially and I make great progress in study. I have won the first-class scholarships for two years.

【点评】

本文整体结构还算完整,语法错误(斜体部分)也不算太多,语言的运用方面也还可以,但却只拿到了 7 分,究其原因,主要还是结构问题。

首先,文章的连贯性较差。第一段介绍背景,但各句之间缺少必要的衔接,没有从背景很好地过渡到交学费这一问题;第三段无论从主题句的创作还是理由的陈述方面都欠缺逻辑性和条理性,导致文章不够连贯,主题不够突出。

其次,各段详略安排不当。第一段作为背景出现,其目的只是引出主题,不需要详细阐述;而第二段是针对所给提纲的第二点进行论述,是文章的主要内容之一,应该展开说明,但本文第一段有六句话,第二段却只有一句话,明显是主次颠倒,详略安排不当。

【10 分作文】

　　Nowadays, if we want to go to college, we'll have to pay a big sum of money. It's a problem to many students. Many ways are available to solve this serious problem.

　　First, you can ask your parents for help. Second, you can do part-time jobs to make money. In addition, you can *apply* (apply for) a bank loan. Finally, *we* (you) can get scholarships from the school.

　　For me, I prefer a bank loan. *My reasons of choice* (My reasons for this choice /The reasons why I choose this) can be listed as follows: First of all, my parents are not *very rich* (rich enough) to *afford me* (afford my tuition and fees). Secondly, if I do some part-time jobs, I'll not have enough time to study. In addition, I think I can get a good job in the future to pay back the loan.

【点评】

　　本文虽出现一些语法错误(斜体部分),句式上也比较单一,显得有些拘谨,也没有什么出彩的亮点,但却也能够得到 10 分,主要原因如下:

　　首先,文章框架合理——典型的三段式文章。

　　其次,结构比较完整——包含提纲中所列要点,并交代背景,引出现象和问题。

　　再次,时刻围绕主题——通篇都围绕主题展开论述,没有多余的与主题不相关的内容。

　　第四,段落衔接自然——文中标下划线的部分均起到了很好的衔接作用,使整篇文章条理清楚,过渡自然,形成一个意义连贯、形式统一的整体。

　　第五,各段详略得当——首段简单交代背景,第二、三段分别针对提纲中所给出的两点展开论述,主题阐述充分,详略得当。

二、句式多变

　　一篇高分作文,除了结构清晰外,还要在语言上做到句式多变、丰富多姿。真正的优秀文章应做到长短句搭配合理,主动被动合理运用,适当穿插倒装、强调、比较等特殊句式,并能够确保各句之间紧密衔接,从而使文章错落有致、行文流畅并体现出语言功底。

【例2】　　　　　　　　　　　　　　　　　　　　　　　　　　　　　　　　(99-6)

Directions: *For this part, you are allowed 30 minutes to write a composition on the topic* **Reading Selectively or Extensively?** *You should write at least 120 words, and base your composition on the outline (given in Chinese) below:*

1)有人认为读书要有选择
2)有人认为应当博览群书
3)我的看法

【8 分作文】

　　People all know that reading is very important. But people have different opinions towards how to read. Some people say we should read selectively, and other people believe that we should read extensively.

　　Some people think that reading selectively is very important. First, some books are harmful and not *worthy* (worth) reading. Second, after work people do not have enough time to read extensively.

　　Some people think that people should read extensively. Now, different branches of knowledge are closely related. If one wants to make great achievements, he will have to read books *not only in his own field of study but also other fields* (concerning not only his own field of study but also other fields of study). Reading extensively can give us experience, and broaden our horizon.

　　I think we should read both selectively and extensively. As to bad books, we should never read them. As for good books, we should read as extensively as we can.

【点评】

　　本文在结构安排上没有问题,通篇看来,也没有出现什么严重的语法错误(斜体部分),之所以只拿到 8 分,主要是因为句式比较单一,文章显得毫无生气。

　　首先,长短句搭配不够合理。文章中所用句式比较简单,而且有些雷同,缺少能够体现出语言功底的特色长句,没能很好地将长短句合理搭配使用。首段的引言部分显得苍白无力,除第三段以外,其余各段中无论是主题句还是扩展句的句式都比较简单,甚至有些重复。

　　其次,没能很好地运用被动。首段开头句使用主动语态表达该语意,一方面不太符合书面语的文体风格,另一方面给人过于平淡的感觉,如果改成被动结构 It is widely accepted that…就会使句子的表达更加贴切。

　　第三,缺少倒装强调等特色句式。整篇文章中几乎没有使用任何有特点的句式,显得句式单一、平淡无味。

　　最后,句与句之间衔接不够紧密。虽然本文从整体上看行文还算流畅,但很多句子之间只做到了意义上连贯,形式上缺少必要的连接。如第三段对两点理由的陈述,既与主题句没有很好的衔接,两点理由之间也没有适当的过渡。

【12分作文】

Nowadays, it is generally accepted that reading is of *quite* (much) importance. But when it comes to how to read, there has sprung up a heated discussion as to whether we should read selectively or read extensively.

Some people are in favor of the idea of reading selectively. First, they believe that it is not how much one reads but what he reads that really counts. In addition, since one's time and *effort* (efforts) are limited, *we* (he) should read books that are suited to *our* (his) interests and needs.

However, those who insist on reading extensively argue that it is through reading extensively that one can broaden his horizon. Only when one reads widely can he really make remarkable achievements in his study.

In my opinion, we should read selectively on the basis of reading extensively. For one thing, by reading widely we can keep ourselves well informed of as much knowledge as possible. For another, without selection, reading may become aimless and blind, which makes reading ineffective. Therefore, we should combine selective reading with extensive reading.

【点评】

本文虽出现个别语法错误(斜体部分),但结构清晰,句式多变,行文流畅,不失为一篇优秀的作文。

首先,长句短句错落有致。本文中句式多样,各段长短句搭配合理,如首段中第一句话简洁明了引出事实背景,然后通过 when it comes to…句型自然过渡到要讨论的主题。文中对长句的运用,体现了作者较强的语言功底。

其次,主动被动运用合理。本文首句使用被动结构 it is generally accepted that…引出普遍存在的事实,恰当准确,符合书面语的文体风格。而文中其他地方尽管没有更多地运用被动语态,但也是从实际的表达需要出发,并不影响本文的整体效果。

再次,倒装强调穿插得当。文中穿插了倒装、强调等特色句式,起到了突出强调、增加气势的作用。

最后,句与句之间衔接紧密。本文无论从意思上还是形式上都非常连贯,过渡自然,连接词运用恰当准确,整篇文章给人感觉逻辑清晰,浑然一体。

三、出现亮点

在保证结构清晰、句式多变的前提下,如果能够在语言的运用方面花些心思,设计一到两个能让考官眼前一亮的亮点,如遣词用语准确地道、适当运用修辞手法、恰当使用警句格言、开头结尾突破常规等,这势必会给你的作文锦上添花,对作文取得高分起到"点睛"的作用。

【例3】 (98-6)

Directions: *For this part, you are allowed 30 minutes to write a composition on the topic **Do "Lucky Numbers" Really Bring Good Luck?** You should write at least 120 words, and base your composition on the outline (given in Chinese) below:*

1)有些人认为某些数字会带来好运
2)我认为数字和运气无关…

【10分作文】

Some people say that "lucky numbers" can bring them good luck. They believe that lucky numbers make them feel safe or energetic and so they can deal with problems better.

However, others don't believe that numbers have any connection with good luck. They think *such idea* (such kind of idea /such an idea) is only a superstitious belief. In fact, numbers are only numbers. Luck is only luck. There is no *relations* (relationship) between them.

So far as I am concerned, "lucky numbers" have nothing to do with good luck. If lucky numbers really worked, we would not fail anything. Numbers can never bring good luck to a person at all and our fortune is in our own hands. Therefore, everyone can have good fortune only if he tries his best.

【点评】

本文结构比较清晰,句式变化也还可以,语法错误也很少(斜体部分),但从整篇文章来看缺少语言亮点。

首先,遣词用语缺乏特色。全文在用词方面缺乏深度和特色,几乎都是一些过于大众化的单词,如 believe, think 等,不能给人留下深刻的印象。

其次,没有恰当运用修辞。全文未运用任何恰当的修辞手法。

再次,没有使用警句格言。全文未出现任何警句或格言。

最后,开头结尾平淡无奇。开头结尾均没有出现有特色的句式,无法激起阅卷老师的兴奋点。

【14分作文】

Some people say that some numbers will bring them good luck. Take 8 for example. The Chinese pronunciation of the number "8" has almost the same sound as that of the Chinese character "发", which means making a fortune. Therefore, many Chinese people spare no money to get their telephone number or car number to include this number "8". They believe without any doubt that the number will bring them money.

However, others don't believe that numbers have any connection with good luck. They think such kind of idea is only an ignorant and superstitious belief. They will say: How can you ever have any good luck simply because of some lucky numbers, even if you don't work hard, don't have good opportunities and don't get along well with those people around you?

So far as I am concerned, I agree with the latter. Obviously, such belief is only a kind of superstition. Perhaps it holds true for some cases, but often it does not. Numbers can never bring good luck to a person at all and our fortune is in our own hands. Therefore, everyone can have good fortune only if he tries his best. Let's always remember "Opportunities are only for the prepared mind" and "No pains, no gains."

【点评】

本文之所以能够得到14分,除了结构清晰、句式多变以外,还有很多语言亮点。

首先,遣词用语准确地道。如第一段第四句中 spare(吝惜,节约)一词就用得很准,形象地刻画出这类人的心态。紧接着第五句中的 without any doubt(不假思索)的使用也非常恰当,提醒读者不假思索地相信幸运数字是缺乏辩证思维的。另外,最后一段中的 hold true 也是典型的英语表达方式,显现出本文用语的地道。

其次,适当运用修辞手法。第二段第三句运用反问使问题的答案不言自明,观点的表达更加有力。而该句中三个 don't 构成排比,更加强了气势,使论证达到高潮。

再次,恰当使用警句格言。本文的最后以两句谚语作为结束,运用恰到好处,又突显出作者的文采。

最后,开头结尾突破常规。开头运用例证为主题提供充分验证,说服力很强。结尾用谚语收尾,使人眼前一亮。

Lecture 4　　第四讲　5类作文行文思路

从写作类型上来看,提纲式命题作文和提纲式图表作文主要可分为:现象解释型、对比选择型、问题解决型、观点论证型四大类;而应用文则以信函为主,包括建议信、拒绝信、投诉信等,另外偶尔也会涉及到倡议书、演讲辞或通知等。

一、问题解决型

问题解决型作文通常要求考生从试题的提示性文字、图表或图画入手,描述提示性文字、图表或图画所反映出的问题,提出解决方案或应对措施。

其基本结构是:首先引出要解决的问题及其严重性或必要性,并简要分析其产生的原因;然后提出解决问题的办法或措施;最后表明自己的态度,提出建议并展望前景。

1. 行文思路一

Topic	标题
首段(描述问题段) ① Recently, there has been a discussion about 总述该问题. / Nowadays, it has become a common phenomenon 总述该问题. ② 危害一/原因一. ③ Additionally, 危害二/原因二. ④Therefore, it is high time that 解决该问题.	**首段(描述问题段)** ① 引出问题,指出问题的现状 ② 问题主要危害一/原因一 ③ 问题主要危害二/原因二 ④ 表达解决该问题的必要性或紧迫性
中间段(说明方法段) ⑤ The following ways can be adopted to 解决该问题. / Some effective measures have been taken to 解决该	**中间段(说明方法段)** ⑤ 承上启下,引出该问题的解决办法或决定因素 ⑥ 具体阐述解决办法一/决定因素一

问题. /Many a factor plays an important role in <u>解决该问题</u>. ⑥ Firstly/First of all, <u>方法一/因素一</u>. ⑦ Secondly/In addition, <u>方法二/因素二</u>. ⑧ Thirdly/Besides/Moreover, <u>方法三/因素三</u>. ⑨ Only through these ways/Only in this way <u>该问题才能够解决</u>.	⑦ 具体阐述解决办法二/决定因素二 ⑧ 具体阐述解决办法三/决定因素三(也可以不包括这一点) ⑨ 总结以上方法或因素,强调其必要性(也可不包括这一点)
结尾段(总结观点段) ⑩ It is no doubt that <u>解决该问题的意义</u>. ⑪As for me, <u>"我"的建议或看法</u>. ⑫<u>总结观点</u>.	**结尾段(总结观点段)** ⑩承上启下,强调解决该问题的意义 ⑪阐述"我"的建议或看法 ⑫总结观点,发出呼吁或作出展望

【例1】　　　　　　　　　　　　　　　　　　　　　　　　　　　　　　　　　　(04-1)

Directions: *For this part, you are allowed 30 minutes to write a composition on the topic **Reduce Waste on Campus**. You should write at least 150 words according to the outline given below in Chinese:*
　　1)目前有些校园内浪费现象严重
　　2)浪费的危害
　　3)从我做起,杜绝浪费

【思路点拨】本题属于提纲式文字命题。提纲第1点指出目前校园内浪费现象严重,提纲第2点要求分析这种现象造成的危害,提纲第3点则要求阐述自己应该如何来做,由此可判断本文应为问题解决型作文。
　　根据所给提纲,本文应包含以下内容:提出校园内浪费现象严重,指出浪费的危害性;说明杜绝浪费的方法,如人走关灯,节约用水等;总结全文,从我做起,呼吁大家养成节约的习惯。

【参考范文】

Reduce Waste on Campus

　　① Recently, there has been a discussion about waste on campus. ② It is obvious that a great loss of precious resources, such as water and electricity have been caused by waste. ③ Additionally, our waste adds much burden to our parents and society. ④ Therefore, it is high time that more attention was paid to solve this problem. (描述问题段)

　　⑤ The following ways can be adopted to reduce waste on campus. ⑥ Firstly, we should stop wasting water when we bath, or clean faces, or wash clothes and dishes. ⑦ Secondly, in our daily life, we must learn to be economical and only buy what we really need. ⑧ Thirdly, we should turn off the light when leaving dorms or classrooms so as to save electricity. ⑨ Only through these ways can waste on campus be eliminated in the near future. (说明方法段)

　　⑩ It is no doubt that reduction of waste is of significance to our whole society. ⑪As for me, the cultivation of good habit of thrift is most important for all of us. ⑫ Every college student should join in the efforts to combat the waste on campus. (总结观点段)

2. 行文思路二

Topic	标题
首段(描述问题段) ① Nowadays it is generally accepted that <u>总述问题</u>. ② <u>具体表现一</u>. ③ <u>表现二</u>.	**首段(描述问题段)** ① 总述问题的现状 ② 问题具体表现一 ③ 问题具体表现二
中间段(说明原因段) ④ There are many reasons accounting for <u>该问题</u>. / It should be paid attention to that <u>该问题</u> is bringing great damage. ⑤ On one hand/For one thing, <u>原因一/危害一</u>. ⑥ On the other hand/For another, <u>原因二/危害二</u>. ⑦ Therefore, it is high time that <u>解决该问题</u>.	**中间段(说明原因段)** ④ 承上启下,引出该问题的原因/危害 ⑤ 具体阐述原因一/危害一 ⑥ 具体阐述原因二/危害一 ⑦ 承上启下,说明解决问题的必要性

结尾段(说明方法段)	结尾段(说明方法段)
⑧ Many a way can be adopted to 解决该问题. / Many a factor plays an important role in 解决该问题. ⑨ Firstly /First of all, 方法一 /因素一. ⑩ Secondly / In addition, 方法二 /因素二. ⑪ Thirdly /Besides /Moreover, 方法三 /因素三. ⑫ Only through these ways / Only in this way 该问题才能够解决.	⑧ 承上启下,引出问题解决办法或决定因素 ⑨ 具体阐述解决办法一 /决定因素一 ⑩ 具体阐述解决办法二 /决定因素二 ⑪具体阐述解决办法三 /决定因素三(也可以不包括这一点) ⑫用倒装句小结解决问题的根本途径(也可用其他句式)

【例2】
(05-6)

Directions: *In this part, you are allowed 30 minutes to write a short essay entitled **Say No to Pirated Products**. You should write at least 150 words following the outline given below:*

1)目前盗版的现象比较严重
2)造成这种现象的危害
3)我们应该怎么做?
可能用到词汇:
盗版 piracy(n.)
盗版产品 pirated products
知识产权 intellectual property rights
侵犯版权 infringe sb's copyright; copyright infringement

【思路点拨】本题属于提纲式文字命题。提纲第1点要求描述一种不良社会现象,提纲第2点要求分析这种现象造成的危害,提纲第3点则要求提供解决方法,由此可判断本文应为问题解决型作文。

根据所给提纲,本文应包含以下内容:描述目前盗版现象的猖獗程度;说明盗版对正版生产者及顾客造成的危害;从政府和顾客两方面提出解决问题的举措。

【参考范文】

Say No to Pirated Products

　　① Nowadays it is generally accepted that piracy is becoming more and more of a problem in China. ② Almost any product, such as tape, CD and hi-tech device can be copied. ③ Shortly after a newly-developed product is put on the market, people will unsurprisingly find its pirated counterparts in the stores.(描述问题段)

　　④ It should be paid attention to that piracy causing great harm. ⑤ On one hand, pirated products often cost far less than the original ones, so they enjoy unbeatable advantage in price in spite of their relatively poor quality, and the original ones, on the contrary, sell poorly. ⑥ On the other hand, take a long-term view, pirated products may also have negative impacts on customers since those legitimate producers' enthusiasm may be greatly hurt as a result of money loss. ⑦ Therefore, it is high time that we solved this problem as soon as possible.(说明原因段)

　　⑧ Many a way can be adopted to reduce the piracy phenomenon. ⑨ First of all, it is the duty of the government to call on everyone to fight the battle against piracy. ⑩ In addition, as customers, we should develop our consciousness to resist pirated products. ⑪ Thirdly, strict laws and decrees are of great importance. ⑫ Only in this way can this problem be solved radically.(说明方法段)

3. 行文思路三

Topic	标题
首段(描述问题段)	**首段(描述问题段)**
① Nowadays it is generally accepted that 总述该问题. ② 表现一 /作用一. ③ Additionally, 表现二 /作用二. ④ Therefore, how to 总述该问题 is worth paying more attention to.	① 引出问题,指出问题的现状 ② 表现一 /作用一 ③ 表现二 /作用二 ④ 表达解决该问题的必要性或紧迫性
中间段(说明方法段)	**中间段(说明方法段)**
⑤ The following ways can be adopted. /Some effective measures have been taken to 解决该问题. /Many a	⑤ 承上启下,引出该问题的解决办法或决定因素 ⑥ 具体阐述解决办法一 /决定因素一

factor plays an important role in 解决该问题. ⑥ First-ly /First of all, 方法一 /因素一. ⑦ Secondly /In addition, 方法二 /因素二. ⑧ Thirdly /Besides /Moreover, 方法三 /因素三.	⑦ 具体阐述解决办法二 /决定因素二 ⑧ 具体阐述解决办法三 /决定因素三
结尾段(总结观点段)	**结尾段(总结观点段)**
⑨ As for me /As far as I am concerned, "我"的建议或看法. ⑩ "我"的理由一. ⑪ Besides /In addition, "我"的理由二. ⑫总结观点.	⑨ 承上启下,引出"我"的建议或看法 ⑩ 阐述"我"的理由一 ⑪ 阐述"我"的理由二 ⑫ 总结观点,发出呼吁或作出展望

【例3】 (00-1)

Directions: *For this part, you are allowed 30 minutes to write a composition on the topic* **How I Finance My College Education?** *You should write at least 120 words, and base your composition on the outline (given in Chinese) below:*

1)上大学的费用(tuition and fees)可以通过多种途径解决

2)哪种途径适合我(说明理由)

【思路点拨】本题属于提纲式文字命题。提纲第1点要求从几个方面说明如何解决上大学的费用问题,提纲第2点要求阐述"我"自己的选择,由此可以判断本文应为问题解决型作文。

根据所给提纲,本文应包含以下内容:描述解决上大学费用这一问题的紧迫性;具体阐述可以通过哪些途径来解决学费问题;表明"我"的选择及理由。

【参考范文】

How I Finance My College Education?

① Recently, there has been a discussion about how to finance college education. ② The solution to this problem is quite important for college students to finish education smoothly. ③ Additionally, it is also necessary for us college students to find ways to release our parents' burden. ④ Therefore, it is high time that more attention was paid to solving this problem. (描述问题段)

⑤ The following ways can be adopted to pay all kinds of expenses in college. ⑥ First of all, we can find a part-time job, for example, as a tutor, to support ourselves. ⑦ In addition, by studying hard some of us can gain academic scholarship. ⑧ Besides, for those students from poor families, applying for a student loan is quite a good choice. (说明方法段)

⑨ As for me, a part-time job is a wise choice. ⑩ Since my parents can afford most of my expenses in college, I only need make some money for my changes by doing a part-time job. ⑪Besides, it can help not only support myself financially but increase my chances to practise in society. ⑫All in all, we should choose a suitable way to finance our college education so that we can finish our education smoothly. (总结观点段)

Exercise 即讲即练

作文一

Directions: *For this part, you are allowed 30 minutes to write a composition on the topic* **The Bad Effects of Fake Diplomas.** *You should write at least 150 words, and base your composition on the outline given in Chinese below:*

1)目前假文凭现象比较严重

2)这种现象所带来的危害

3)我们应该怎么做

The Bad Effects of Fake Diplomas

作文二

Directions: *For this part, you are allowed 30 minutes to write a composition on the topic* **How to Keep Fit**. *You should write at least 150 words, and base your composition on the outline given in Chinese below:*

1) 健康的身体对我们很重要
2) 如何才能拥有健康的体魄

How to Keep Fit

_____

_____

【参考范文】

作文一

【思路点拨】

本题属于提纲式文字命题。提纲第1点要求描述一种不良现象,提纲第2点要求分析这种现象造成的危害,提纲第3点则要求提供解决方法,由此判断本文应为问题解决型作文。

根据所给提纲,本文应包含以下内容:描述目前假文凭现象十分普遍的现状;说明假文凭对雇主及有真才实学的人造成的危害;阐述我们该如何解决问题。

【参考范文】

How to Keep Fit

There has been a serious epidemic of fake diplomas in some big cities recently. Obviously, its appearance and development involve two parts: the demander and the supplier. People who do not have the necessary diploma to get a desire job naturally think of this short cut, especially when there are so many profit-driven people making fake diplomas so easily available. (描述问题段)

The victims of fake diplomas are first of all employers, who pay high salaries but do not get real talents. By and by, his business will suffer, and people who have genuine diplomas are also hurted greatly for the decreasing opportunities of job hunting. Thus, actually this phenomenon may encourage people to cheat instead of acquiring a degree honestly. (说明原因段)

To combat the epidemic, we should stop putting ever more emphasis on the academic background of the job applicators or promotion candidates. Instead, practical ability and individual personality should be recognized as important factors. Besides, effective measures supported by advanced IT technology should·be introduced and taken to help employers distinguish genuine diplomas from fake ones. Once the demand disappears, the supply will be gone too. (说明方法段)

作文二

【思路点拨】

本题属于提纲式文字命题。提纲第1点要求阐述健康的重要性,提纲第2点要求说明如何才能保持身体健康,由此判断本文应为问题解决型作文。

根据所给提纲,本文应包含以下内容:描述阐述健康的重要性;说明保持身体健康有哪些方法;总结全文。

【参考范文】

The desire for good health is universal. In our competitive society it is important to maintain good health. On one hand, people with good health can do work with full confidence and their progress in work in turn contributes to their health and happiness. On the other hand, a sick person is usually not interested in everything around him and therefore he loses many opportunities to become successful. (描述问题段)

The methods to keep us fit vary. Firstly, in the morning, you can get up early, go outdoors, breathe the fresh air, and do physical exercises. If you don't have much time allocated to do these things, you can try to walk to your office instead of riding a bike or taking a bus. Besides, you should always keep to an balanced diet which provides you with necessary nutrients and enhances your immunity. Finally, you have to take a routine physical check-up. (说明方法段)

Health is the most valuable possession a person expects in his life. Try every means to keep fit is my advice to those people who want to live a happy life in this beautiful world. (总结观点段)

二、现象解释型

　　现象解释型作文通常要求考生从试题的提示性文字、图表或图画入手,描述提示性文字、图表或图画中反映出的现象,对该现象进行解释说明,分析其原因并加以评论。

　　其基本结构是:首先描述现象并说明其现状;然后分析这种现象的原因或相关因素;最后提出建议或总结观点。

1. 行文思路一

Topic	标题
首段(描述图表段) ① From the chart/graph/table/picture, we learn that 总述社会现象/事实现象, which has aroused the great/common concern. ② What impresses us most is 图表中重点数据. ③ There are many reasons accounting for 现象或变化.	**首段(描述图表段)** ① 概括图表所反映的总体现象 ② 描述图表中最能体现出现象变化的重点数据,要具有一定概括性 ③ 过渡句,引出下文对原因的分析,也可放在下段开头
中间段(说明原因段) ④ First of all/To begin with, 原因一. ⑤ What is more/Moreover, 原因二. ⑥ 进一步说明原因二. ⑦ In addition/Besides, 原因三. ⑧ Therefore/As a result, 总结原因导致的结果.	**中间段(说明原因段)** ④ 导致现象的原因一 ⑤ 导致现象的原因二 ⑥ 进一步说明原因二(也可对原因一进行展开说明) ⑦ 导致现象的原因三 ⑧ 总结以上原因所导致的结果,重申主题
结尾段(总结观点段) ⑨ As to me/As far as I am concerned, "我"的观点. ⑩ For one thing/On one hand, 影响一/问题一. ⑪ For another/On the other hand, 影响二/问题二. ⑫ Thus/In brief/To conclude, 总结观点.	**结尾段(总结观点段)** ⑨ "我"对现象的思考或看法(对现象趋势、可能带来影响或存在问题的评述,具体内容根据提纲) ⑩ 可能带来的影响一/存在问题一 ⑪ 可能带来的影响二/存在问题二 ⑫ 总结全文,重申观点,提出建议或展望

【例 4】　　　　　　　　　　　　　　　　　　　　　　　　　　　　　　　　　　　　　(06-6)

> **Directions:** *For this part, you are allowed 30 minutes to write a short essay entitled* **Traveling Abroad.** *You should write at least 150 words based on the chart and outline given below:*
>
> *Number of people in City X traveling abroad in 1995, 2000 and 2005*
>
>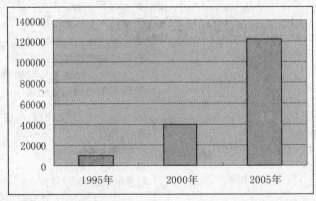
>
> 1)近十年来×市有越来越多的人选择出境旅游
> 2)出现这种现象的原因
> 3)这种现象可能产生的影响

【思路点拨】本题属于提纲式图表命题。提纲第 1 点要求描述近十年来 X 市出现的一种现象,提纲第 2 点要求指出这种现象产生的原因,提纲第 3 点要求分析这种现象可能产生的影响,由此可判断本文应为现象解释型作文。

　　根据所给提纲,本文应包含如下内容:简要描述图表中所反映的近十年来 X 市选择出境旅游的人数情况,以及旅游人数的变化情况;对导致该变化的原因进行分析;说明"我"对该现象的理解,以及该现象造成的影响,总结全文。

【参考范文】

Traveling Abroad

① From the chart, we learn that there has been a sharp rise in the number of people traveling abroad in X city in the past decade, which has aroused the greatest concern. ② What impresses us most is in 1995 the number of people traveling abroad was only about 10,000, which increased to nearly 40,000 in 2000, and by 2005, the number had reached over 120,000, which was more than ten times as many as ten years ago. ③ There are many reasons accounting for this phenomenon. (描述图表段)

④ First of all, China's opening policy has been implemented for many years, which has created more chances for people to go abroad. ⑤ What is more, it is due to the increase of people's incomes in X city. ⑥ People are better off many times than before and can afford a trip abroad. ⑦ In addition, the increase has also a lot to do with the development of travel industry. ⑧ As a result, it becomes an unavoidable trend for more and more Chinese people to travel abroad. (说明原因段)

⑨ As far as I am concerned, from the changes reflected in the table, we can predict that the number of individuals going out of the country will boost. ⑩ On one hand, the increasing number of people traveling abroad will further promote the exchanges in economy and culture between X city and other cities in the world. ⑪On the other hand, this phenomenon will also bring more opportunities for the development of X city and other Chinese cities. ⑫To conclude, it is no doubt that the further development of tourism will be beneficial to both the individual and the society. (总结观点段)

2. 行文思路二

Topic	标题
首段(描述图表段) ① According to the chart/graph/table/ picture, it is clear that 图表/图片内容总概括. ② The chart/ graph/table/picture shows 图表数据一, while 图表数据二.	**首段(描述图表段)** ① 概括图表/图片所反映的总体现象 ② 具体描述图表/图片数据
中间段(说明原因段) ③ Many reasons contribute to 现象概括. ④ First of all/To begin with, 原因一. ⑤ What is more/Moreover, 原因二. ⑥ In addition/Besides, 原因三. ⑦ As a result, 段落总结句.	**中间段(说明原因段)** ③ 过渡句,引出下文对原因的分析(也可放在上段结尾) ④ 导致现象的原因一 ⑤ 导致现象的原因二 ⑥ 导致现象的原因三 ⑦ 总结以上原因所导致的结果,重申主题(根据实际情况,有时也无需总结句)
结尾段(总结观点段) ⑧ As to me/As far as I am concerned, "我"的选择或看法. ⑨ First of all, 理由一. ⑩ Besides, 理由二. ⑪ To conclude, 段落总结句.	**结尾段(总结观点段)** ⑧ "我"的个人选择或看法 ⑨ 支持看法的理由一 ⑩ 支持看法的理由二 ⑪重申观点,总结全文

【例5】　　　　　　　　　　　　　　　　　　　　　　　　　　　　　　　　　　(03-9)

Directions: *For this part, you are allowed 30 minutes to write a composition on the topic **Reading Preferences**. You should write at least 150 words, and base your composition on the table and the outline given below:*

Reading Preference of Students in an American University in 2002

Categories of Books	Percentage of Book Circulation in the Library
Popular Fiction	65.90%
General Notifications	18.20%
Science/Technology/Education	10.80%
Art/Literature/Poetry	5.10%

1) 根据上表, 简要描述美国某大学学生借阅图书的分布情况
2) 你对于这些学生阅读偏爱的评论
3) 你通常喜欢阅读哪一类书籍? 说明理由

【思路点拨】本题属于提纲式图表命题。提纲第 1 点要求描述图表所反映的现象, 提纲第 2 点要求对这种现象作出评论和分析, 提纲第 3 点要求陈述自己的观点, 由此可判断本文应为现象解释型作文。

根据所给提纲, 本文应包含以下内容: 简要描述图表中的反映出来的美国某大学学生借阅图书的具体情况, 总结出学生阅读的偏爱; 对导致该阅读偏爱的原因进行分析; 说明"我"的读书偏好, 并给出理由, 总结全文。

【参考范文】

Reading Preference

① According to the chart, it is clear that college students vary in reading preference. ② The chart shows the percentage of book circulation of popular fictions and general nonfictions in an American university library has accounted for 65.9% and 18.2% respectively, while the circulation of science /technology /education books and art /literature /poetry books is 10.8% and 5.1% respectively. (描述图表段)

③ Many reasons contribute to this reading preference. ④ To begin with, popular fictions usually possess more appealing plots than other types of books do, and so many readers are attracted by popular fictions. ⑤ That is to say, thanks to its appealing plot, popular fictions attract more people than other types of books do. ⑥ Moreover, popular fictions and general nonfictions are easier to be understood. ⑦ In addition, science and art books demand certain knowledge in special field of study. ⑧ As a result, more students tend to choose popular fictions and general nonfictions. (说明原因段)

⑨ As to me, I think I'm in favor of books of science and technology. ⑩ First of all, in order to deepen what I'm learning, I need read more books relevant to my major and observe the new development in science and technological circles. ⑪ Besides, these books can also broaden my vision. ⑫ To conclude, college students should choose books according to their interests and needs. (观点总结段)

3. 行文思路三

Topic	标题
首段(描述现象段)	**首段(描述现象段)**
① <u>总体现象</u> has been brought into focus. /<u>总体现象</u>, which has aroused great concern. ② <u>现象表现或变化</u>. ③ In addition, <u>进一步阐述现象</u>.	① 开门见山, 直接点题 ② 阐述现象的具体表现或变化 ③ 进一步阐述现象, 强化主题
中间段(说明原因段)	**中间段(说明原因段)**
④ There are many reasons accounting for this phenomenon. /The factors <u>影响该现象</u> are varied. ⑤ Among all these reasons /factors, <u>原因一</u> plays a very important role. ⑥ <u>阐述原因一</u>. ⑦ What is more /Moreover, <u>原因二</u>. ⑧ In addition /Besides, <u>原因三</u>. ⑨ Therefore, <u>重申该现象</u>.	④ 承上启下, 引出下文对现象原因的分析 ⑤ 列举原因一 ⑥ 进一步阐述原因一 ⑦ 列举原因二 ⑧ 列举原因三(也可以只阐述两点原因) ⑨ 由原因再次引出现象(此句可有可无)

结尾段(总结观点段)	结尾段(总结观点段)
⑩ As to me/As far as I am concerned, 我的观点. ⑪For one thing, 具体的看法/理由一. ⑫For another, 进一步说明看法/理由二. ⑬To conclude/In a word, 观点总结.	⑩ "我"对现象的思考或看法(可能是个人选择或是对现象趋势或影响的评述) ⑪ 具体说明自己的看法或陈述理由一 ⑫ 进一步说明自己的看法或陈述理由二 ⑬ 重申观点,总结全文,提出建议或作出展望

【例6】

(06-12)

Directions: *For this part, you are allowed 30 minutes to write a short essay entitled* **The Celebration of Western Festivals.** *You should write at least 150 words following the outline given below:*

1)现在国内有不少人喜欢过西方的某些节日
2)产生这种现象的原因
3)这种现象可能带来的影响

【思路点拨】本题属于提纲式文字命题。提纲第1点指出目前社会上出现的一种现象,提纲第2点要求分析产生这种现象的原因,提纲第3点要求分析这种现象可能带来的影响,由此可判断本文应为现象解释型作文。

根据所给提纲,本文应包含以下内容:描述国内许多人喜欢过西方节日这一普遍现象;说明产生这种现象的原因;分析这种现象可能带来的影响。

【参考范文】

The Celebration of Western Festivals

① The popularity of western festivals in China has been brought into focus. ② Nowadays, a growing number of people in China are immersed in the thrilling atmosphere of the upcoming Christmas. ③ In addition, some people even give as high status to Christmas as they give to the Spring Festival. (描述现象段)

④ The reasons for this phenomenon are varied. ⑤ Among all these reasons, western culture plays a very important role. ⑥ Younger age groups are exposed to western culture and festivals through learning English. ⑦ Moreover, some western festivals provide relaxing and comfortable atmosphere, which attracts a larger number of Chinese young people. ⑧ Besides, many businessmen view foreign festivals as golden opportunities to make money, who desperately try to boost the atmosphere of foreign festivals. ⑨ Therefore, more and more Chinese people are celebrating foreign festivals. (说明原因段)

⑩ As far as I am concerned, these western festivals have to some extent weakened our home-grown festivals' crucial roles in Chinese traditional culture. ⑪ Furthermore, they are exerting strong influence on young people's traditional values and thoughts. ⑫ In a word, we shouldn't be immersed too much in the western festivals but ignore Chinese traditional festivals. (总结观点段)

Exercise　　　　　　即讲即练

作文一

Directions: *For this part, you are allowed 30 minutes to write a composition on the topic* **Why Living off Campus Is Popular?** *You should write at least 150 words, and base your composition on the outline given in Chinese below:*

1)大学生选择校外租房住宿较普遍
2)校外租房住宿的原因
3)我的看法

Why Living off Campus Is Popular?

_____

_____

作文二

Directions: *For this part, you are allowed 30 minutes to write a composition on the topic* **Why Are Electric-bicycles So Popular in China?** *You should write at least 150 words, and base your composition on the outline given in Chinese below:*

1) 近年来越来越多的人开始使用电动自行车
2) 产生这种现象的原因
3) 这种现象可能带来的影响

Why Are Electric-bicycles So Popular in China?

_____

_____

【参考范文】

作文一

【思路点拨】

本题属于提纲式文字命题。提纲第 1 点指出目前大学生选择校外租房住宿十分普遍的现象,提纲第 2 点要求分析产生这种现象的原因,提纲第 3 点要求阐述"我"的观点,由此可判断本文应为现象解释型作文。

根据所给提纲,本文应包含以下内容:描述大学生选择择校外租房住宿这一普遍现象;说明产生这种现象的原因;阐述"我"对此现象的看法。

【参考范文】

Why Living off Campus Is Popular?

Nowadays living off-campus enjoys great popularity among college students. Why, then, do students do so when they are provided with very modern apartments and good services on campus? The reasons can be listed as follows. (描述现象段)

First, living off-campus can relieve the student from time consuming and energy consuming trivialities. Since people from different places have different personalities, habits, and interests, etc., some students think that it is difficult to adapt themselves to those different habits. Secondly, living off-campus can offer them a lot of freedom. Freed from the regulations of the university, they can do whatever they want in whatever time they like. For example, they can stay up late, reading books or surfing on the Internet. Lastly, living off-campus can give them more privacy. (说明原因段)

I think living off-campus has both its benefits and shortcomings. If we live off campus we will not have the chance to experience the rich and colorful collective life on campus. Away from our classmates, we will not have the chance to learn how to communicate with those who have divergent opinions. (总结观点段)

作文二

【思路点拨】

本题属于提纲式文字命题。提纲第 1 点指出目前社会上出现的一种现象,提纲第 2 点要求分析产生这种现象的原因,提纲第 3 点要求分析这种现象可能带来的影响,由此可判断本文应为现象解释型作文。

根据所给提纲,本文应包含以下内容:描述近年来越来越多的人开始使用电动车这一普遍现象;说明产生这种现象的原因;分析这种现象可能带来的影响。

【参考范文】

Why Are Electric-bicycles So Popular in China?

There have been more and more electric-bicycles on the road in recent years. They dash on wide highways or move slowly through lanes. Whether you are in a city or in a rural area, you can see electric-bicycle riders here and there. There has been a trend towards the replacement of bicycles by electric-bicycles. (描述现象段)

Why are electric-bicycles so popular in China? First of all, electric-bicycles run faster than bicycles. They provide people with the easiest and cheapest form of transportation. The second reason is the fact that China is a developing country, and most people can't afford a car, although they are wealthier than before. Last but not least, powered by electricity, electric-bicycles have the advantage of pollution-free . This advantage contributes enormously to the popularization of electric-bicycles. (说明原因段)

However, the increasing number of the electric-bicycles may cause more traffic accidents, since there haven't existed the lanes for electric-bicycles only on the roads, and they share the same lanes with bicycles. In my opinion, some measures should be taken to ensure the securities of the electric-bicycles riders and the proper orders of the roads. (总结观点段)

三、对比选择型

对比选择型作文的标志十分明显,非常容易识别,其要求比较明确,富有针对性。即直接要求考生比较两种观点或两种做法,进而表明自己对问题或事物的态度或观点,也就是作出选择。

其基本结构是:首先对要评论的事物或现象进行整体介绍;然后陈述两种不同的观点或做法及其理由;之后表明自己的观点或结论。

1. 行文思路一

Topic	标题
首段(提出观点段) ① When it comes to 事物/问题, there is no complete agreement among people. ② Some people take it for granted 一种观点. ③ However, others maintain 另一种观点.	**首段(提出观点段)** ① 开宗明义,表明对某事/问题人们各有不同的看法 ② 一部分的看法 ③ 另一部分人的看法
中间段一(对比论证段一) ④ Those people who hold the former opinion believe 观点一理由一. ⑤ In addition, 观点一理由二. ⑥ Therefore, 总结观点一.	**中间段一(对比论证段一)** ④ 阐述支持观点一的理由一 ⑤ 阐述支持观点一的理由二 ⑥ 总结段落,重申观点一(此句可有可无)
中间段二(对比论证段二) ⑦ However, still others advocate the latter opinion because they hold 观点二的理由一. ⑧ Besides, they argue that 观点二的理由二. ⑨ So, 总结观点二.	**中间段二(对比论证段二)** ⑦ 阐述支持观点二的理由一 ⑧ 阐述支持观点二的理由二 ⑨ 总结段落,重申观点二(此句可有可无)
结尾段(总结观点段) ⑩ Weighing up these two arguments, "我"的看法. ⑪For one thing, 个人看法的依据一. ⑫For another, 个人看法的依据二. ⑬Taking above-mentioned factors into consideration, we/I may reasonably conclude that 重申观点.	**结尾段(总结观点段)** ⑩ 表明"我"对该问题的个人倾向或看法 ⑪ 个人看法的依据一 ⑫ 个人看法的依据二 ⑬ 总结全文,重申个人看法

【例7】　　　　　　　　　　　　　　　　　　　　　　　　　　　　　　　　(99-6)

Directions: *For this part, you are allowed 30 minutes to write a composition on the topic **Reading Selectively or Extensively?** You should write at least 120 words, and base your composition on the outline (given in Chinese) below:*

1)有人认为读书要有选择

2)有人认为应当博览群书

3)我的看法

【思路点拨】本题属于提纲式文字命题。提纲第1点和提纲第2点分别提出了两种截然相反的看法,提纲第3点要求考生表明自己的立场和看法,由此可判断本文应为对比选择型作文。

根据所给提纲,本文应包含以下内容:简明扼要地提出对于读书人们的两种不同的看法:应有选择地读书和应博览群书;分别说明支持两种观点的理由;表明"我"赞成哪种观点,说明理由。

【参考范文】

Reading Selectively or Extensively?

① When it comes to the question whether we should read selectively or extensively, there is no complete agreement among people. ② Some people take it for granted that we should read selectively. ③ However, others think that extensive reading outweighs selective reading. (观点提出段)

④ Those people who hold the former opinion believe that by selective reading we can get information and knowledge we really need more quickly and efficiently. ⑤ In addition, reading selectively can save them much time and enable them have enough time to digest what they have read. ⑥ Therefore, whenever we read, we should se-lect what we read. (对比论证段一)

⑦ However, still others advocate the latter opinion because they hold that extensive reading can extend their range of knowledge and broaden their vision. ⑧ Besides, they argue that only by reading extensively can people get a general view about the world. (对比论证段二)

⑨ Weighing up these two arguments, I think, for a collgege student, reading selectively is more reasonable. ⑩ For one thing, without selection, reading may become aimless and blind, which make, reading inefficient. ⑪ For another, books of low quality may do harm to the youths who are lack of enough ability to tell the truth from the false. ⑫ Taking above-mentioned factors into consideration, I may reasonably conclude that we college students should read selectively. (总结观点段)

2. 行文思路二

Topic	标题
首段(提出观点段) ① Different people have different views on 看法/问题. ② Some prefer 一种看法/观点. ③ Others tend to 另一种的看法/观点. ④ As to me, I agree to the first/second opinion.	**首段(提出观点段)** ① 开门见山,直入主题,表明对某事人们各有不同的看法 ② 一部分人的看法 ③ 另一部分人的看法 ④ "我"的倾向(同意哪种观点)
中间段(对比论证段) ⑤ Of course, "我"不赞同观点的合理性. ⑥ For example, 支持其合理性的例子. ⑦ But in my opinion, "我"不赞同观点的不足. ⑧ The following reasons can account for my argument.	**中间段(对比论证段)** ⑤ 承认"我"所不赞同的看法有一定合理性 ⑥ 举例说明"我"不赞同观点的合理性,支持第⑤句 ⑦ 转折指出这种观点的不足 ⑧ 承上启下,引出下文对"我"所持观点的理由的阐述
结尾段(总结观点段) ⑨ Firstly, 支持观点的理由一. ⑩ A good example to illustrate is 支持理由一的例子. ⑪ In addition/Moreover/What's more, 支持观点的理由二. ⑫ To conclude/From the foregoing, 重申观点.	**结尾段(总结观点段)** ⑨ 支持观点的理由一 ⑩ 举例说明理由一 ⑪ 支持观点的理由二 ⑫ 总结全文,重申"我"的观点

【例8】 (00-6)

Directions: *For this part, you are allowed 30 minutes to write a composition on the topic* **Is a Test of Spoken English Necessary?** *You should write at least 120 words and you should base your composition on the out-line (given in Chinese) below:*

1)很多人认为有必要举行英语口语考试,理由是…

2)也有人持不同意见

3)我的看法和打算

【思路点拨】本题属于提纲式文字命题。提纲第1点和提纲第2点指出对于英语口语考试存在两种不同的观点,提纲第3点要求阐述"我"对这一考试的看法和打算,由此可判断本文应为对比选择型作文。
根据所给提纲,本文应包含以下内容:提出对口语考试的两种不同的观点;表明"我"赞同哪种观点并说明原因;总结"我"的观点并表明自己的打算。

【参考范文】

Is a Test of Spoken English Necessary?

① Different people have different views on the test of spoken English. ② Some prefer to have such a test. ③ Others tend to decline any kind of tests of spoken English. ④ As to me, I agree to the first statement. (提出观点段)

⑤ Of course, a test of spoken English is very difficult to handle and the test time is not long enough to fully display participants' ability to speak in English. ⑥ For example, if a candidate draws a topic which he or she is not familiar with, it is hard to show his or her command of spoken English. ⑦ But in my opinion, without such a test, some people may not have motivation to practise spoken English. ⑧ The following reasons can account for my argument.（对比论证段）

⑨ Firstly, such a test enhances college students' awareness of the importance of spoken English. ⑩ A good example to illustrate is that several years ago, college students only stressed reading and writing skills, ignoring to build up listening and speaking ability. ⑪ In addition, a certificate of such a test will make job-hunting easier. ⑫ From the foregoing, I think a test of spoken English is of necessity.（总结观点段）

3. 行文思路三

Topic	标题
首段（提出观点段） ① When asked about/When it comes to **事物/问题**, different people will offer different opinions. ② Some people take it for granted that **观点一**. ③ In their opinion, **观点一的理由一**. ④ Besides, **观点一的理由二**.	**首段（提出观点段）** ① 开宗明义，表明对某事人们各有不同的看法 ② 提出观点一 ③ 阐述观点一的理由一 ④ 阐述观点一的理由二
中间段（对比论证段） ⑤ However, others hold **观点二**. ⑥ They maintain **观点二的理由一**. ⑦ And **观点二的理由二**.	**中间段（对比论证段）** ⑤ 提出观点二 ⑥ 阐述观点二的理由一 ⑦ 阐述观点二的理由二
结尾段（总结观点段） ⑧ Weighing up these two arguments, **"我"的观点**. ⑨ For one thing /On one hand, **理由一**. ⑩ For another /On the other hand, **理由二**. ⑪For instance, **举例说明理由二**. ⑫Therefore, as stated above, **总结全文**.	**结尾段（总结观点段）** ⑧ 表明"我"的倾向或观点（赞成观点一或观点二） ⑨ "我"的理由一 ⑩ "我"的理由二 ⑪举例说明理由二（此句可有可无，也可将其移到第⑩句前说明观点一） ⑫综上所述，再次强调"我"的观点

【例9】　　　　　　　　　　　　　　　　　　　　　　　　　　　　　　　　　　(98-6)

Directions: *For this part, you are allowed 30 minutes to write a composition on the topic Do "Lucky Numbers" Really Bring Good Luck? You should write at least 120 words and you should base your composition on the outline (given in Chinese) below:*

1)有些人认为某些数字会带来好运
2)我认为数字和运气无关

【思路点拨】本题属于提纲式文字命题。提纲第1点要求说明某些人的观点，提纲第2点要求说明我对这种观点持反对意见，由此可知，本文要求考生在比较两种观点的基础上表明自己的观点，由此可判断本文应为对比选择型作文。

　　根据所给提纲，本文应包含以下内容：人们对于幸运数字各有看法；对比论证命运与幸运数字是否有关；论证"我"认为命运与幸运数字无关，总结全文。

【参考范文】

Do "Lucky Numbers" Really Bring Good Luck?

① When it comes to lucky numbers, different people will offer different opinions. ② Some people take it for granted that lucky numbers have nothing to do with their luck. ③ In their opinions, lucky numbers themselves are given certain meaning for the purpose of application of mathematics. ④ Besides, all the numbers are equal, they never decide your fate and affect your luck.（提出观点段）

⑤ However, others hold that lucky numbers really bring good luck to them. ⑥ They maintain that some superstars and famous persons have their own lucky numbers to bless themselves. ⑦ And lucky numbers make them feel peaceful or energetic and hence they can tackle problems better.(对比论证段)

⑧ Weighing up these two arguments, I am for the former one. ⑨ For one thing, if lucky numbers really worked, we would not fail anything. ⑩ For another, lucky numbers can never change the objective reality and make miracles. ⑪ For instance, patients are cured by experienced doctors but not by lucky numbers. ⑫ Therefore, as stated above, we should work hard instead of depending on lucky numbers to bring us a happy life.(总结观点段)

Exercise　　　　　即讲即练

作文一

Directions: *For this part, you are allowed 30 minutes to write a composition on the topic* **Is Watching Movies More Enjoyable Than Reading Fiction?** *You should write at least 150 words, and base your composition on the outline given in Chinese below:*

1)有些人认为读小说更有趣
2)另一些人认为看电影更加享受
3)我的看法

Is Watching Movies More Enjoyable Than Reading Fiction?

_____

_____

作文二

Directions: *For this part, you are allowed 30 minutes to write a composition on the topic* **Styles of Living**. *You should write at least 150 words, and base your composition on the outline given in Chinese below:*

1)有些人愿意和父母居住在一起
2)有些人想自己独立居住
3)我的看法

Styles of Living

_____

_____

【参考范文】

作文一

【思路点拨】

本题属于提纲式文字命题。提纲第1点和提纲第2点分别指出了两种人的观点,提纲第3点要求阐述"我"对此的看法,由此可判断本文应为对比选择型作文。

根据所给提纲,本文应包含以下内容:分别指出人们的两种观点:读小说更好与看电影更好;对比论证这两种观点;表明"我"的观点并说明原因。

【参考范文】
Is Watching Movies More Enjoyable Than Reading Fiction?

Billions of dollars are spent on entertainment every year in every country in the world. Much of this money is spent on either movies or fictional books, as these two types of entertainment are found to be most enjoyable by the masses. Which, however, is more enjoyable?(提出观点段)

Some people find reading fictional books more enjoyable. For one reason, books are available whenever there is time and wherever you are. For another, when reading a fictional book, one is able to let his /her imagination run wild. Everything from the setting to the character descriptions is left up to the reader's mind, and therefore can be quite enjoyable.(对比论证段一)

Others hold that movies are more interesting. Movies allow the viewer to be completely engrossed in the plot.

There is no need for thinking, as everything is presented to you in a straightforward form, and one never has to ponder what a place or a person looks like.（对比论证段二）

As far as I'm concerned, in a society where we want everything faster, better and more exciting, perhaps movies are a more relevant medium. However, both have its advantages, and we should make good use of them.（总结观点段）

作文二

【思路点拨】

本题属于提纲式文字命题。提纲第1点和提纲第2点分别提出了截然相反的观点,提纲第3点要求阐述"我"的立场和看法,由此可判断本文应为对比选择型作文。

根据所给提纲,本文应包含以下内容:简明扼要地提出人们对于生活方式的两种不同的看法:和父母住在一起与独立居住;对比论证这两种观点;表明"我"赞成哪种观点,说明理由。

【参考范文】
Styles of Living

After graduating from the college, most of the young people begin to choose their own life styles. Some people enjoy living together with their parents, while others prefer to live separately.（提出观点段）

Those people who hold the former opinion think that living with parents, they can take better care of their parents and vice versa. Meanwhile, they can turn to their parents for help if they get into trouble or have some difficulties.（对比论证段一）

However, still others advocate the latter opinion because they cherish the idea to be independent of their parents, seek more freedom and wish to have a place of their own, in which they can do what they like. Bedsides, they don't want to be overprotected by their parents but long for chance to face the society by themselves.（对比论证段二）

As to me, I like an independent life style in spite of the fact I love my parents. Different generations have different life styles and values. Living separately , each generation can enjoy different value. In addition, by leading an independent life , I can train my character and develop my own ability to deal with things encountered in my life.（总结观点段）

四、观点论证型

观点论证型作文一般要求考生根据题目所给论点,按照提纲要求,通过摆事实、讲道理的方式对该论点进行论证。

其基本结构是:首先提出要论证的论点;然后提供论据对其进行论证;最后表明自己的立场和看法。

1. 行文思路一

Topic	标题
首段（提出观点段） ① It is well known that 论点. ② The truth is deep and profound. ③ 正确性表现. ④总结论点.	**首段（提出观点段）** ① 开门见山,直接提出观点 ② 进一步强调观点的正确性 ③ 阐述观点正确性的表现 ④ 重申论点
中间段（论证观点段） ⑤ Many remarkable factors/reasons contribute to this argument. ⑥ First of all, 论据一. ⑦ What's more/Moreover, 论据二. ⑧ For example, 支持论据二的事例. ⑨ In addition/Besides, 论据三.	**中间段（论证观点段）** ⑤ 承上启下,引出对观点的论证 ⑥ 列举论据一 ⑦ 举例说明论据一（也可举例说明论据二或三） ⑧ 列举论据二 ⑨ 列举论据三
结尾段（总结观点段） ⑩ All mentioned above tell us that 重申观点. ⑪Therefore, there is no denying that 正确态度或做法. ⑫In short, 总结全文.	**结尾段（总结观点段）** ⑩ 承接上文,重申观点 ⑪ 指出应该采取的态度或做法 ⑫ 总结全文,再次强调观点的正确性和重要性

【例10】 (99-1)

Directions: *For this part, you are allowed 30 minutes to write a composition on the topic* **Don't Hesitate to Say "No"**. *You should write at least 120 words, and base your composition on the outline (given in Chinese) below:*

1）别人请求帮忙时,在什么情况下我们会说"不"
2）为什么有些人在该说"不"的时候不说"不"
3）该说"不"时不说"不"的坏处

【思路点拨】 本题属于提纲式文字命题。提纲第1点和第2点提出了一种论点,即:该说"不"的时候就要说"不";提纲第3点要求说明该说"不"时不说"不"的坏处,即从反面论证该观点,由此可判断本文属于观点论证型作文。

根据所给提纲,本文应包含如下内容:提出该说"不"时要说"不"的论点;列举该说"不"时不说"不"的坏处,从反面论证观点的正确性;总结并重申观点,提出建议或希望。

【参考范文】

Don't Hesitate to Say "No"

①It is well known that we should not hesitate to say "No" on many occasions. ②The truth of it is self-evident. ③No one can deny that when we are unable to offer help, we should say "No". ④Therefore, a direct reply "No" should be frequently used to avoid misunderstandings among us. (提出观点段)

⑤Many remarkable reasons contribute to this argument. ⑥First of all, if you agree to unreasonable requests, it will spoil your principles of doing things and it may also do harm to other people. ⑦For example, a personnel official who offer a job to his unqualified friend makes the employment system unfair. ⑧What's more, if you cannot keep your promise in that the request is beyond your ability, you will be considered dishonest. ⑨Besides, some people who help their criminal friends to cover the fact or to escape from being punished will receive well-deserved punishment. (论证观点段)

⑩All mentioned above tell us that sometimes say "Yes" without hesitation may make things much worse. ⑪Therefore, there is no denying that it will do harm to ourselves as well as others if we promise to do something we should say "No" or cannot do. ⑫In short, we should say "No" firmly to unreasonable requests. (总结观点段)

2. 行文思路二

Topic	标题
首段(提出观点段) ①论点背景. ②It is true that 论点. ③No one can deny 正确性表现. ④Therefore, 重申论点.	**首段(提出观点段)** ① 交代与论点相关的背景、现象或观点 ② 提出本文论点 ③ 阐述观点正确性的表现 ④ 重申论点
中间段(论证观点段) ⑤Many remarkable factors/reasons contribute to this argument. ⑥First of all, 论据一. ⑦For example, 支持论据一的事例. ⑧What's more/Moreover, 论据二. ⑨In addition/Besides, 论据三.	**中间段(论证观点段)** ⑤ 承上启下,引出对观点的论证 ⑥ 列举论据一 ⑦ 举例说明论据一(也可举例说明论据二或三) ⑧ 列举论据二 ⑨ 列举论据三
结尾段(总结观点段) ⑩All mentioned above tell us that 重申观点. ⑪Therefore, there is no denying that 正确态度或做法. ⑫In short, 总结全文.	**结尾段(总结观点段)** ⑩ 承接上文,重申观点 ⑪ 指出应该采取的态度或做法 ⑫ 总结全文,再次强调观点的正确性和重要性

【例 11】

Directions: *For this part, you are allowed 30 minutes to write a composition on the topic* **It Pays to Be Honest**. *You should write at least 150 words according to the outline given below in Chinese:*

1) 当前社会上存在许多不诚实的现象

2) 诚实利人利己,做人应该诚实

【思路点拨】本题属于提纲式文字命题。提纲第 1 点指出当前社会中的一种不良现象,提纲第 2 点则针对该现象提出一种论点,由此可判断本文应为观点论证型作文。

根据所给提纲,本文应包含以下内容:由不良现象引出论点:诚实利人利己;阐述诚实的积极作用,证明论点;重申观点,总结全文。

【参考范文】

It Pays to Be Honest

①Nowadays there still exist many dishonest phenomena, such as cheating, overcharging, making and selling fake commodities, etc., which ruin our normal life. ②It is true that being honest is not only beneficial to others but also to oneself. ③No one can deny honesty is a traditional virtue of Chinese people. ④Therefore, we should value honesty highly.(提出观点段)

⑤Many remarkable reasons contribute to this argument. ⑥First of all, honesty can make our society more stable. ⑦For example, Singapore, which is a society of trustworthiness and integrity, has a comparatively low criminal rate. ⑧What's more, honesty can make our life easier and more harmonious. ⑨Besides, only honest people can be truly respected by others and can make more friends over a long period of time.(论证观点段)

⑩All mentioned above tell us that being honesty is of benefit to both the state and the individual. ⑪Therefore, there is no denying that we should foster the spirit of honesty and let the dishonesty has no place to stay in our society. ⑫In a word, laying stress on honesty will become the public morals in our society.(总结观点段)

3. 行文思路三

Topic	标题
首段(提出观点段) ①论点, which has been generally accepted. ②论点含义. ③The truth of it is deep and profound.	**首段(提出观点段)** ① 开门见山,直接提出观点(常为谚语或格言) ② 阐释论点的含义 ③ 强调论点正确性
中间段(论证观点段) ④There are numerous examples supporting this argument. /Many remarkable examples contribute to this argument. ⑤A case in point is 例证一. ⑥This is close to suggest 例证一的道理. ⑦For another example, 例证二. ⑧Moreover, 例证三.	**中间段(论证观点段)** ⑤ 承上启下,引出对观点的论证 ⑥ 例证一 ⑦ 例证一蕴涵的道理(换种方式表达论点) ⑧ 例证二 ⑨ 例证三
结尾段(总结观点段) ⑨Judging from the evidence offered, we might safely draw the conclusion that 重申观点. ⑩But one thing we have to notice is 需要注意的问题. ⑪In short, 总结全文.	**结尾段(总结观点段)** ⑩ 承接上文,重申观点 ⑪ 指出需要注意或考虑的问题 ⑫ 总结全文,再次强调观点的正确性和重要性

【例 12】

Directions: *For this part, you are allowed 30 minutes tow rite a composition on the topic* **Practice Makes Perfect**. *You should write at least 100 words and you should base your composition on the outline (given in Chinese) below:*

1) 怎样理解"熟能生巧"

2) 例如:在英语学习中…

3) 又如…

【思路点拨】本题属于提纲式文字命题。提纲第 1 点要求阐述"熟能生巧"这一谚语,提纲第 2 点和提纲第 3 点要求举例论证该谚语的正确性,由此可判断本文应为观点论证型作文。

根据所给提纲,本文应包含以下内容:阐释"熟能生巧";举例说明该谚语在英语学习中以及其他方面的应用;重申论点,强调其正确性和重要性。

【参考范文】

Practice Makes Perfect

①"Practice makes perfect", is a proverb full of logic, which has been generally accepted. ②It tells us that if we practice unfamiliar things again and again, we'll be able to perform it perfectly. ③The truth of it is deep and profound. (提出观点段)

④Many remarkable examples contribute to this argument. ⑤A case in point is in order to learn English well, we need extra practice, such as reading English books, going to English corners, or communicating with foreigners. ⑥This is close to suggest people can grasp English only if they follow the saying "practice makes perfect". ⑦For another example, if we want to be skilled in using the computer, we also need to practice using it. ⑧Moreover, in other areas of your life, practice is also necessary, and we can hardly do things well without practice and preparation. (论证观点段)

⑨Judging from the evidence offered, we might safely draw the conclusion that continuous practice and great efforts will lead to final success. ⑩But one thing we have to notice is we should have a right theoretical direction before we put something into practice. ⑪In short, we must apply theories to practice in order to achieve our goals. (总结观点段)

Exercise   即讲即练

作文一

Directions: *For this part, you are allowed 30 minutes to write a composition on the topic **Green Olympics**. You should write at least 150 words, and base your composition on the outline given in Chinese below:*

1)现在社会上出现很多环境污染和精神污染的现象,"我"对"绿色奥运"的看法

2)为什么要提倡"绿色奥运"

3)提倡绿色奥运,从自己做起

Green Olympics

_____

_____

作文二

Directions: *For this part, you are allowed 30 minutes to write a composition on the topic **Learning from Experience**. You should write at least 150 words, and base your composition on the outline given in Chinese below:*

1)提出从经验中学习知识的观点

2)从经验中学习知识的重要性

3)总结观点

Learning from Experience

_____

_____

【参考范文】

作文一

【思路点拨】

本题属于提纲式文字命题。提纲第 1 点要求阐述"我"对"绿色奥运"看法,提纲第 2 点和提纲第 3 点要求举例论证为什么要提倡"绿色奥运",提纲第 3 点要求总结观点,由此可判断本文应为观点论证型作文。

根据所给提纲,本文应包含以下内容:阐释"我"对"绿色奥运"的看法并提出观点;举例说明提倡"绿色奥运"的重要性;重申论点,总结全文。

【参考范文】

Green Olympics

Olympic Games, as we all know, is a historic sports meeting. "Green Olympics" is one of the three themes of Beijing 2008 Olympic Games. At present, people's life is being flooded with exhaust gas from automobile, blue film, waste water and so on. Owing to these phenomena, we should advocate "Green Olympics", and I am positive of this point. (提出观点段)

Two possible reasons are as follows. Firstly, environmental protection benefits people's health. In terms of increasing number of trashes around us, such as white plastic bags, one-off cups and chopsticks, it is sensible of disposing of them reasonably. Secondly, environmental protection is crucial to our country, and even to the world, because we live under the same sky; pollution is not just the matter of a country, but the whole world. Only if the entire environment gets improved, the society, even the whole world, can be more harmonious. (论证观点段)

In conclusion, as college students and the young generation, we should try our best to advocate "Green Olympics". Then the 2008 Olympic Games will be a green and unique Olympics. (总结观点段)

作文二

【思路点拨】

本题属于提纲式文字命题。提纲第1点要求提出从经验中学习知识的观点,提纲第2点要求论证从经验中学习知识的重要性,提纲第3点要求总结观点,由此可判断本文应为观点论证型作文。

根据所给提纲,本文应包含以下内容:提出从经验中学习知识的观点;论证从经验中学习知识的重要性;重申论点,强调其正确性和重要性。

【参考范文】

Learning from Experience

There has been much talk recently about whether we should learn from books or we should learn from experience. Some people think that learning from experience is more important while others hold the opposite opinion. Personally, I side with the former, in the belief that experience is the best teacher. (提出观点段)

At first, experience is the source of knowledge, understanding as well as meaning. Nowhere can the importance of learning from experience be described so vividly and accurately as in the old saying—"Nothing ever becomes real till it is experienced". Besides, unlike the theories recorded in books, experiences can apply to practical use. When we are at work, what we need is the experience of practical application instead of the abstract theories in our books. (论证观点段)

Taking all these into account, we can draw a conclusion that learning from experience is such an important means to acquire knowledge. Always remember the old saying given by Einstein—"The only source of knowledge is experience". (总结观点段)

五、应用文

应用文所涉及的内容多种多样,但大部分都与日常生活比较贴近。六级写作中的应用文以各类信函为主,具体包括:建议信、抱怨信、求职信、求学信、拒绝信、道歉信、感谢信、祝贺信、邀请信、求职推荐信、求学推荐信、索取信等,另外,演说辞、倡议书、海报、景点介绍和日程安排等校园生活及日常生活中常用到的应用文体,考生也必须熟悉并掌握其基本写法。

1.建议信行文思路

Topic	标题
Date	日期和称呼
Dear _____,	①写信的原因
①I am very pleased to know that _____.	②引出考生的建议
②It _____. ③In my opinion, _____.	③表述建议内容
④On one hand, _____ ⑤On the other hand, _____.	④提出建议的理由一

⑥As to _____ , I suggest _____ . ⑦If _____ . ⑧It is unnecessary for you to ____ _____ . ⑨In addition, _____ . ⑩I am sure _____ . ⑪Please inform me _____ . ⑫I am looking forward to _____ . Sincerely yours, Signature	⑤建议的理由二 ⑥具体到某一方面的建议内容 ⑦供被建议人选择的条件 ⑧建议内容的另一方面 ⑨其他的建议 ⑩对建议内容所作的承诺 ⑪希望对方回复 ⑫表达本人的愿望 信件结尾与签名

【例13】 (01-6)

Directions: *For this part, you are allowed 30 minutes to write a letter. Suppose you are Zhang Ying. Write a letter to Xiao Wang, a schoolmate of yours who is going to visit you during the weeklong holiday. You should write at least 150 words according to the suggestions given below in Chinese:*

1）表示欢迎
2）提出对度假安排的建议
3）提醒应注意的事项

【思路点拨】本题要求写一封建议信。根据所给提纲,本文应包含以下内容:点明写信的缘由,表明对朋友的思念之情;具体阐述建议的内容,包括对度假活动的具体建议以及注意事项;要求对方告知决定以及表达盼望之情。

【参考范文】

A Letter to a Schoolmate

January 20，2002

Dear Wang,

①I am delighted to learn that you will visit me for a week during this National Day. ②It has been several years since we departed last time, and I am looking forward to your visit. ③In my opinion, Nanjing is your best choice for this holiday. ④On one hand, there are many places of interest and historical sites in Nanjing. ⑤On the other hand, Nanjing is a cultural center with various artistic and musical performances.

⑥As to the famous sites, I suggest that you should visit the Confucius Temple and Dr. Sun Yat sen's Mausoleum. ⑦If you are interested in parks, the Xuanwu Lake Park will be your best choice. ⑧It is unnecessary for you to bring anything except your sweaters since it is a little chilly in the evening. ⑨In addition, as there will be many people at the railway station, you should not leave your belongings unattended! ⑩I am sure you will enjoy your visit in Nanjing.

⑪Please inform me once you have made your decision. ⑫I am looking forward to seeing you soon.

Sincerely yours,
Zhang Ying

2. 抱怨信行文思路

Topic	标题
Date	日期和称呼
Dear _____ , ①I am _____ . ② Here I am writing to you to call your attention to some problems about _____ . ③For one thing, _____ . ④For another, _____ . ⑤Besides, _____ . ⑥_____ . ⑦So it is urgent to take measures to _____ _____ . ⑧I do hope _____ . ⑨Thank you very much. Sincerely yours, Signature	①写信人的身份 ②表述抱怨内容 ③说明存在问题之一 ④说明存在问题之二 ⑤说明存在问题之三 ⑥说明事物的重要性 ⑦点明解决问题的紧迫性 ⑧表达本人的愿望 ⑨信件结尾的常用语 信件结尾与签名

【例14】　　　　　　　　　　　　　　　　　　　　　　　　　　　　　　(02-1)

Directions：*For this part, you are allowed 30 minutes to write a composition on the topic* **A Letter to the University President about the Canteen Service on Campus**. *You should write at least 120 words and you should base your composition on the outline（given in Chinese）below:*

假如你是李明，请你就本校食堂的状况给校长写一封信，内容应涉及食堂的饭菜质量、价格、环境、服务等，可以是表扬，可以是批评建议，也可以兼而有之。

【思路点拨】本题要求写一封抱怨信或建议信，根据命题要求，本文应包含以下内容：简单介绍自己，指出不满的地方；具体说明存在的问题或提出具体建议；表达自己的祝愿。

【参考范文】

A Letter to the University President
about the Canteen Service on Campus

Jan. 12, 2002

Dear Mr. President,

　　①My name is Li Ming. ②I am a junior from the Civil Engineering School. ③I venture to write you a letter about the canteen service on campus.

　　④The focus of the complaint is the poor quality and high price of the food. ⑤For one thing, the rice is so hard, the steam bread too cold, and vegetables overcooked. ⑥For another, the price of the food is so high that many of us go out to dine. ⑦Honestly speaking, the canteen service is a little better than before. ⑧But the cooking staff need to do the cooking more carefully. ⑨Besides, the cost needs to be reduced to lower the price.

　　⑩All in all, there is still much room for improvement. ⑪I do hope the service will be much improved very soon. ⑫Thank you for your time and kind consideration.

Sincerely yours,

Li Ming

3. 求职信行文思路

Topic	标题
Date	日期和称呼
Dear _____ ,	①直接表达自己想申请报纸等登出的职务
①I would like to apply for the position of _____ advertised/posted in _____. ②I have attached a copy of my resume for your consideration. ③I believe my qualifications are ideal match for your requirements	②告知随信附详细简历
	③强调自己符合要求，加强印象
④I am a major in _____. ⑤I will graduate on _____ from _____. ⑥In addition to the required courses, I have _____. ⑦My internship/working at spare time in _____ as _____ provided me the opportunity to _____. ⑧I believe my education and experience _____. ⑨You will find me to be _____.	④介绍自己大学期间专业
	⑤介绍教育背景一
	⑥介绍教育背景二
	⑦介绍相关经历
	⑧表明信心
	⑨加强对方对自己的信心
⑩I would appreciate your time in reviewing my enclosed resume and if there is any additional information you require, please contact me. ⑪I would welcome an opportunity to meet with you for a personal interview. ⑫I can be reached by telephone between _____ and _____.	⑩希望被考虑
	⑪争取面谈机会
	⑫告知对方自己的联系时间
Sincerely yours, Signature	信件结尾与签名

【例15】

Directions： *For this part, you are allowed 30 minutes to write a letter to Jin Bian Attorney-at-law to apply for a position of legal secretary. You should write at least 150 words according to the suggestions given below in Chinese:*

1) 申请法律秘书职务
2) 说明自己的专业
3) 请求面谈

【思路点拨】 本题要求写一封求职信。根据所给提纲，本文应包含以下内容：点明写信的缘由：申请秘书一职；介绍自己的教育经历和专业能力；提出期望，争取面试。

【参考范文】

An Application Letter

January 19, 2007

Dear Mr. Jin Bian,

①I would like to apply for the position of legal secretary advertised in *Today's Youth Daily*. ②I have attached a copy of my resume for your consideration. ③I believe my qualifications are ideal match for your requirements.

④I am a major in economic law. ⑤I will graduate on July 1st, 2007 from Peking University. ⑥In addition to the required courses, I have studied English and Accounting as my second and third major. ⑦My working at spare time in TL company as legal secretary provided me the opportunity to sharpen my skills. ⑧I believe my education and experience will enable me to perform better than other candidates who lack working experience. ⑨You will find me to be reliable and efficient.

⑩I would appreciate your time in reviewing my enclosed resume and if there is any additional information you require, please contact me. ⑪I would welcome an opportunity to meet with you for a personal interview. ⑫I can be reached by telephone between 3 p.m. and 10 p.m..

Sincerely yours,

Wang Li

4. 求学信行文思路

Topic	标题
<div align="right">Date</div>Dear _____ , ①I have read the annual prospectus issued by your school and found that it has the best graduate program of _____. ②I am greatly interested in the program and hope that I could do my Doctor/Master degree under your instruction. ③I am _____ at the _____ Department of _____ _____ University. ④During _____, I took such courses as _____. ⑤And I have passed all the required courses with satisfactory marks. ⑥Also, I have learned _____ is supremely important to my work. ⑦I am especially proficient in _____. ⑧Besides, I was a major member of several campus clubs including _____. ⑨Two of my former professors and the present dean of our Department have kindly written letters of recommendation for me, as enclosed with/attached to this letter. ⑩I would be very grateful if you could send me the necessary forms and any information about financial aid in your program. ⑪I look forward to hearing from you soon. <div align="right">Sincerely yours, <u>Signature</u></div>	日期和称呼 ①介绍自己获悉对方学校的信息 ②表达自己申请该校就读的愿望 ③开始介绍自己的情况 ④⑤⑥具体介绍自己大学期间的学习、所学的专业和其他课程及特长 ⑦⑧进一步介绍自己的其他能力 ⑨提及自己已获得教授的推荐，争取对方学校的信任 ⑩再一次发出请求，并表达自己的感激之情 ⑪结束语 信件结尾与签名

【例 16】

Directions： *For this part, you are allowed 30 minutes to write an application letter to a University of America for your Master degree in Electrical Engineering Department. You should write at least 150 words* following the outline given below：

1）表达申请攻读硕士学位的心愿
2）自己的情况简介
3）表达对申请学校、专业、教授的看法

【思路点拨】本题要求写一封求学信。根据所给提纲，本文应包含以下内容：点明写信的缘由：申请研究生学位；介绍在校期间的情况及相关情况；表达申请心愿。

【参考范文】

An Application Letter For Further Study

January 4，2007

Dear Professor William，

①I have read the annual prospectus issued by your school and found that it has the best graduate program of Engineering Science. ②I am greatly interested in the program and hope that I could do my Master degree research under your instruction.

③I am working at the Electrical Engineering Department of Wuhan University. ④During my four-year study here, I took such courses as Electrical Technology and Engineering Science. ⑤And I have passed all the required courses with satisfactory marks. ⑥Also, I have learned the spirit of cooperation is supremely important to my work. ⑦I am especially proficient in spoken and written English. ⑧Besides, I was a major member of several campus clubs including Flyer's Disciples and Technology Association.

⑨Two of my former professors and the present dean of our Department have kindly written letters of recommendation for me, as enclosed with this letter.

⑩I would be very grateful if you could send me the necessary forms and any information about financial aid in your program. ⑪I look forward to hearing from you soon.

Sincerely yours，

Li Ming

5. 拒绝信行文思路

Topic	标题
Date	日期和称呼
Dear _____，	①对某事表示感谢，为拒绝埋下伏笔
①Thank you very much for _____. ②I/We would like to accept _____ but I/we cannot due to _____. /I am/We are so sorry that I/we cannot _____ due to _____.	②委婉地表达拒绝之意，引出下文要解释的原因
③I/We decline it because _____. ④What's worse/What's more, _____. ⑤At least, _____. ⑥On account of all these factors, you can understand why it is not possible for me/us to _____. ⑦I hope this does not cause you too much inconvenience.	③陈述拒绝原因一 ④陈述拒绝原因二 ⑤进一步说明原因二 ⑥总结原因，正式拒绝对方 ⑦表达希望：没有给对方带来不便
⑧If _____, I/we will _____. ⑨I/We do appreciate your _____. ⑩And I/we wish _____.	⑧提出补救措施/方案 ⑨向对方表示谢意 ⑩表达对对方的美好祝愿
Sincerely yours，Signature	信件结尾与签名

【例 17】

(05-12)

Directions： *For this part, you are allowed 30 minutes to write a letter to a company declining a job offer. You should write at least 150 words following the outline given below：*

1）对公司提供职位表示感谢
2）解释为何不能接受所提供的职位
3）希望予以谅解，并表示对公司的良好祝愿

【思路点拨】本题要求写一封拒绝信。根据所给提纲,本文应包含以下内容:对公司提供职位表示感谢;解释为何不能接受所提供的职位;希望予以谅解,并表示对公司的良好祝愿。

【参考范文】

A Letter Declining a Job Offer

Dec. 24, 2005

Dear Ms. White,

①Thank you very much for offering me the Sales Associate position with your company. ②I would like to accept the offer but I cannot due to the following reasons.

③I decline it because I have accepted another opportunity that is more in line with my skills and career goals. ④What's more, two hours' commute to your building is really a burden on me. ⑤That's because there is no direct bus leading there. ⑥On account of all these, you can understand why it is not possible for me to accept your offer. ⑦I hope this does not cause you too much inconvenience.

⑧If possible, I will work hard for our future cooperation. ⑨I do appreciate your kindness to discuss the details of the position with me and give me time to consider your offer. ⑩And I wish that your company would continue success.

Sincerely yours,

Nancy Lewis

6. 道歉信行文思路

Topic	标题
Date	日期和称呼
Dear _____, ①I am excessively sorry to say/tell you that _____. ②Now, I am writing you this letter to show my deep regret. ③Please accept my sincere apology with gratitude. ④I fear you are displeased at _____. ⑤I hope you will understand me and excuse me for _____. ⑥I will be very grateful if you are kind to listen to my explanation. ⑦The reason for my _____ was that _____. ⑧I had no way out because _____. ⑨Therefore it's not in my power to _____. ⑩In addition, I want to suggest _____. ⑪I shall be obliged if you will kindly write and tell me when and where you _____. ⑫We may meet again and I hope to see you soon.	①直接表达自己不能实现先前的承诺或约定 ②表达歉意 ③诚恳希望对方能接受道歉 ④⑤表达出自己的心情,并请求对方原谅 ⑥过渡句,引出道歉的原因 ⑦说明失约的原因 ⑧表达出自己当时的处境和情况 ⑨总结自己道歉的原因 ⑩提出补救措施 ⑪约定下次的时间和地点 ⑫再次表达下次见面的愿望
Sincerely yours, Signature	信件结尾与签名

【例18】

Direction: *For this part, you are allowed 30 minutes to write a letter to the headmaster of your previous high school who has invited you to give a speech to your schoolmates, to explain, for your failure to do this. You should write at least 150 words, and your composition should include the following:*

1)由于不能按计划做演讲向校方道歉

2)解释推迟计划的原因

3)建议下次做演讲,并约定下次演讲的时间

【思路点拨】本题要求写一封道歉信。根据所给提纲,本文应包含以下内容:表达歉意;详细解释原因;提出弥补建议。

【参考范文】

An Apology Letter to the Previous Headmaster

January 24, 2007

Dear Mr. Smith,

①I am excessively sorry to tell you that I couldn't make the speech on how to study English language in China as planned. ②Now, I am writing you to show my deep regret. ③Please accept my sincere apology with gratitude. ④I fear you are displeased at my being unable to making a speech. ⑤I hope you will understand me and excuse me for being absent.

　　⑥I will be very grateful if you are kind to listen to my explanation. ⑦The reason for my absence was that I had already arranged to do something else. ⑧I had no way out because the thing I need to do was very urgent. ⑨Therefore, it's not in my power to comply with your request.

　　⑩In addition, I want to suggest that I give another speech at the end of this term. ⑪I shall be obliged if you will kindly write and tell me when and where you will arrange the lecture for students. ⑫We may meet again and I hope to see you soon.

Sincerely yours,

Li Ming

7. 感谢信行文思路

Topic	标题
<div align="right">Date</div>　Dear ＿＿＿＿＿＿＿＿, ①I am now writing these few lines to express my sincere thanks for ＿＿＿＿＿＿＿. ②I'd like you to know how much your ＿＿＿＿＿＿ meant to me. ③You have a positive genius for ＿＿＿＿＿＿. ④I not only enjoyed ＿＿＿＿＿, but also ＿＿＿＿＿. ⑤I shall ever remember ＿＿＿＿＿ as ＿＿＿＿＿. 　　⑥I ＿＿＿＿＿. ⑦I hope to have the opportunity to express my gratitude to you face to face. ⑧I will feel very honored and pleased if you have time to ＿＿＿＿＿. ⑨Would you kindly let me know ＿＿＿＿＿ ＿＿＿＿? ⑩I am looking forward to seeing you! 　　⑪I repeat my thanks again for your ＿＿＿＿＿. ⑫Please give my kind regards to your ＿＿＿＿＿. <div align="right">Yours truly, Signature</div>	日期和称呼 ①直接表达为何事表示谢意 ②表达出自己非常珍惜对方的付出／礼物 ③给对方一定的赞美 ④⑤表达对方的情意对自己的影响。 ⑥介绍自己的近况 ⑦表达出自己希望有回报的机会 ⑧对方的回应是自己的荣幸 ⑨询问对方什么时候有空 ⑩提出希望见面的愿望 ⑪再次表达感谢 ⑫最后表达真挚的祝福 信件结尾与签名

【例19】

Directions: *For this part, you are allowed 30 minutes to write **A Letter of Gratitude** expressing your thanks for your friend's kindness. You write at least 150 words and base your composition on the outline (given in Chinese) below:*

1)简单说明事因

2)表示感谢并希望有回报机会

【思路点拨】本题要求写一封感谢信。根据所给提纲,本文应包含以下内容:说明为何事而感谢对方;表达真诚谢意;提出希望有回报的机会。

【参考范文】

A Letter of Gratitude

June 7, 2007

Dear Li Ying,

　　①I am now writing these few lines to express my sincere thanks for your parcel last Friday, with English books and tapes which are helpful to my study. ②I'd like you to know how much they meant to me. ③You have a positive genius for studying English. ④I not only enjoyed the English books, but also those tapes. ⑤I shall ever remember them as one of the most important things in my life.

　　⑥I will not be very busy in the following days. ⑦I hope to have the opportunity of reciprocating. ⑧I will feel very honored and pleased if you have time to make me a call. ⑨Would you kindly let me know what time you are at convenience? ⑩I am looking forward to seeing you soon!

　　⑪I repeat my thanks again for your parcel. ⑫Please give my kind regards to your family.

Yours truly,

Wang Ning

8. 祝贺信行文思路

Topic	标题
Date	日期和称呼
Dear _____ ,	①获悉值得祝贺的消息
①I was delighted to learn that _____ . ②This happy event in your life prompts me to reply at once and, in my own peculiar way , to attempt to offer you my hearty congratulations and good wishes. ③It is really good news to _____ . ④And I feel very happy for you.	②表达自己的祝贺
	③评价所获消息
	④表达自己的心情
	⑤对被祝贺人的评价
⑤You are really _____ . /You must be very _____ _____. ⑥I know this is _____ . ⑦It is _____ you richly deserve.	⑥说明被祝贺人成功的原因或一直以来的愿望
	⑦说明被祝贺人值得获得这样的成功或幸福
⑧With your _____ , I am sure that you will _____ _____. ⑨I hope _____ . ⑩Again, please accept my sincere congratulations.	⑧表达对对方的信心
	⑨表达自己的愿望
	⑩再次表示祝贺
⑪Best wishes for you!	⑪表达自己真诚的祝福
Sincerely yours,	信件结尾与签名
Signature	

【例20】

Directions: *For this part, you are allowed 30 minutes to write **A Letter of Congratulation** expressing your congratulation on your Aunt's marriage. You should write at least 150 words and base your composition on the outline (given in Chinese) below:*

1)得知你姑姑结婚的消息特写信表示祝贺

2)表达你的喜悦之情以及希望能够当面祝贺

【思路点拨】本题要求写一封祝贺信。根据所给提纲,本文应包含以下内容:得知姑姑结婚的消息而非常高兴;表达对姑姑的真诚祝愿;提出希望有机会当面祝贺。

【参考范文】

A Letter of Congratulation

January 1, 2007

Dear Aunt Anny,

①I was delighted to learn that you will get married next month. ②This happy event in your life prompts me to reply at once and, in my own peculiar way , to attempt to offer you my hearty congratulations and good wishes. ③It is really good news to all our family and your friends. ④And I feel very happy for you.

⑤You must be very excited to face this wonderful event. ⑥ I know this is what you have been longing for. ⑦It is a gift from God you richly deserve.

⑧With your happiness, I am sure that you will be the most beautiful bride that day. ⑨I hope I will have time to go back to express my congratulation face to face. ⑩Again, please accept my sincere congratulation.

⑪Best wishes for you!

Sincerely yours,

Mary

9. 邀请信行文思路

Topic	标题
Date	日期和称呼
Dear _____ ,	①开门见山提出事件(活动)的地点和时间
①_____ . ②It would be pleasant /honored to have you here. ③Will you join us /give me the pleasure of your company?	②表达邀请愿望
	③正式发出邀请
④During the _____ time, we will have lots activities /points you will be interested in. ⑤First, _____ .	④开始介绍活动的内容
	⑤具体介绍要举行的活动内容一
⑥Second, _____ .	⑥具体介绍要举行的活动内容二

⑦I know/believe that you will be very interested _____. ⑧_____. ⑨Also/In addition, _____. ⑩The _____ would not be complete without you! ⑪Since the _____ will begin _____, is it possible for us to meet _____? ⑫We do hope you can come.

Sincerely yours,

Signature

⑦引出受邀请人参加的理由

⑧受邀请人被希望参加的理由一

⑨受邀请人被希望参加的理由二

⑩总结受邀请人参加的必要性

⑪提出具体约定时间和地点

⑫再一次发出邀请

信件结尾与签名

【例21】

Direction：*For this part, you are allowed 30 minutes to write a letter to one of your best friends to invite him/her to take part in your birthday party. You should write at least 150 words, and base your composition on the outline give below:*

1）交待生日宴会的时间和地点

2）介绍宴会中的活动内容

3）阐述被邀请人必须参加的必要性

【思路点拨】本题要求写一封邀请信。根据所给提纲，本文应包含以下内容：举办宴会的时间和地点，正式发出邀请；介绍宴会的内容安排；强调被邀请人参加的必要性。

【参考范文】

An Invitation Letter

June 7, 2007

Dear Jack,

①Next Saturday, June 16, is my birthday and my parents will hold a birthday party for me in our house. ②It would be pleasant to have you here. ③Will you join us?

④During the party time, we will have lots of activities you will be interested in. ⑤First, we can have a good chitchat about anything under the sun. ⑥Second, we can also sing the beautiful popular songs we like and cut the birthday cake.

⑦I believe that you will be very interested in this occasion. ⑧First, you are my best friends and my parents want to meet you too. ⑨Second, we haven't seen each other for a long time and I am eager to see you. ⑩The party would not be complete without you!

⑪Since the birthday party will begin at 7：30 p.m., is it possible for us to meet at the seven o'clock, Saturday evening in our house? ⑫We do hope you can come.

Sincerely yours,

Tan Liang

10. 推荐信行文思路

Topic

Date

To Whom It May Concern,

①It affords me much pleasure to recommend _____ to you. ②During his/her _____ in _____ he/she was my _____. ③As his/her _____ I found him/her _____.

④His/Her performance in the _____ was outstanding. ⑤First, he/she had been/taken _____ and showed great talents in _____. ⑥In addition, he/she has a very pleasant personality. ⑦He/She has developed a strong _____, and working with him/her is always _____. ⑧I can state that he/she has all the qualities of being _____.

⑨Therefore, I here recommend him/her to you with all my heart. ⑩Your favorable consideration of his/her application will be most appreciated. ⑪I am sure that his/her future conduct will prove worthy of your confidence. ⑫If further information about his/her qualification is needed, please feel free to contact with me.

Sincerely yours,

Signature

Title

标题

日期和称呼

①直接表达自己很乐意推荐某人

②介绍自己和被推荐人的关系

③简单介绍自己对被推荐人的看法

④过渡句，开始引出被推荐人的各种优势

⑤被推荐人学业和工作方面的优势

⑥被推荐人的人格魅力

⑦介绍被推荐人的能力

⑧总结自己对被推荐人的评价

⑨竭力推荐被推荐人

⑩希望对方接受被推荐的愿望

⑪给予对方接受被推荐人的信心

⑫再次表达推荐的愿望

信件结尾与签名及写信人的头衔

【例22】

Directions: *For this part, you are allowed 30 minutes to write **A Letter of Reference** for your former colleague John Smith. You should write at least 150 words and base your composition on the outline (given in Chinese) below:*

　1)你曾是约翰·史密斯的部门主管
　2)介绍他在公司时的优秀表现并极力举荐他

【思路点拨】本题要求写一封推荐信,根据所给提纲,本文应包含以下内容:自己与约翰. 史密斯的关系;约翰. 史密斯的优点和优秀表现;极力推荐约翰. 史密斯并希望对方接受他。

【参考范文】

Reference for John Smith

June 11, 2007

To Whom It May Concern,

①It affords me much pleasure to recommend John Smith, one of my former colleagues, to you. ②During his work in A. N. Y Company, he was my assistant. ③As his direct leader, I found him a most reliable and effective member of the sales team.

④His performance in the work was outstanding. ⑤First, he had been professional and efficient in his approach to work and showed great talents in sales. ⑥In addition, he has a very pleasant personality. ⑦He has developed a strong teaming spirit, and working with him is always pleasing and encouraging. ⑧I can state that he has all the qualities of being an excellent sales man.

⑨Therefore, I here recommend him to you with all my heart. ⑩Your favorable consideration of his application will be most appreciated. ⑪I am sure that his future conduct will prove worthy of your confidence. ⑫If further information about his qualification is needed, please feel free to contact with me.

Sincerely yours,

Penny Farthing

Managing Director

11. 索取信行文思路

Topic	标题
Date	日期和称呼
Dear ＿＿＿＿＿＿,	①简单介绍自己的情况.
①I ＿＿＿＿＿＿. ② I am in great need of /deeply interested in ＿＿＿	②表明自己需要的资料
＿＿＿＿. ③I would appreciate you sending me ＿＿＿＿＿＿.	③正式发出请求
④Here are some reasons why I am in so desperate need of ＿＿＿	④过渡句,引出理由
＿＿＿. ⑤ For one thing, ＿＿＿＿＿＿. ⑥For another, ＿＿＿＿＿＿.	⑤阐述需要资料的理由一
⑦Therefore, I would like to apply hereby to you for ＿＿＿＿＿＿.	⑥阐述需要资料的理由二
⑧I shall be much obliged if you will be so kind as to let me have ＿＿＿	⑦总结需要该资料的理由。
＿＿＿＿. ⑨If this is not a convenient time for you, please feel free to suggest another time. ⑩If you prefer, you can call me at ＿＿＿＿＿＿.	⑧提出自己希望拿到资料的时间
	⑨考虑给对方一个时间,以表示礼貌
⑪I am looking forward to your response at your earliest convenience.	⑩提供一个方便的联系方式
⑫Thanks again for your kind consideration.	⑪再一次发出请求
Sincerely yours,	⑫再次表示自己的感谢
Signature	信件结尾与签名

【例23】

Directions: *For this part, you are allowed 30 mintutes to write a letter to the director of your college to ask for a new diploma you received there. You should write at least 150 words and base your composition on the outline (given in Chinese) below:*

　1)简单介绍自己
　2)你急需毕业证书的原因
　3)告诉对方你需要的时间和联系方式

【思路点拨】本题要求写一封索取信。根据所给提纲,本文应包含以下内容:简要介绍自己;说明索要资料的内容及原因;说明你需要的时间和联系方式。

【参考范文】

A Request Letter

February 24, 2007

Dear Director of Foreign Economy and Trades,

①I am Li Ming, a graduate of the Department of Foreign Economy and Trades. ②I am in great need of another diploma because I lost my original one owing to my home suffering a serious flood last summer. ③I would appreciate you sending me that after checking my academic records kept in the university.

④Here are some reasons why I am in so desperate need of the diploma. ⑤For one thing, I am going to be interviewed for a very attractive position in a foreign-invested enterprise and this enterprise thinks much of the academic background of its personnel. ⑥For another, an original diploma is of vital importance to any graduate because it concerns a person's future career. ⑦Therefore, I would like to apply hereby to you for a new diploma.

⑧I shall be much obliged if you will be so kind as to let me have the new copy of diploma at the end of this month. ⑨If this is not a convenient time for you, please feel free to suggest another time. ⑩If you prefer, you can call me at the number 83851090.

⑪I am looking forward to your response at your earliest convenience. ⑫Thanks again for your kind consideration.

Sincerely yours,

Li Ming

12. 演说辞行文思路

Topic	标题
Dear _____,	日期和称呼
①It is a great honor for me to stand here and give my speech.	①表达自己的心情
②To begin with, let me introduce myself. My name is _____.	②作一下简单的自我介绍
③As some of you may know, I am _____.	③进一步介绍自己的情况
④As for the position of _____, I find I am qualified.	④说明竞选职位,引出自己所具备的条件
⑤Firstly, I _____. ⑥Secondly, I _____.	⑤所具备的条件一
⑦Thirdly, I am good at _____.	⑥所具备的条件二
	⑦所具备的条件三
⑧Looking into the future, I will try my best to serve my _____ if I am lucky enough to be the _____.	⑧展望未来,作出承诺(当选后会做些什么)
⑨On one hand, I, with my co-workers, will _____.	⑨承诺一
⑩On the other hand, I will _____. ⑪In addition, I will _____.	⑩承诺二
	⑪承诺三
⑫I wish all of you the best and thank you all for listening. Thank you!	⑫演说结束语

【例24】

Directions: *For this part, you are allowed 30 minutes to write a campaign speech in support of your election to the post of chairman of the student union. You should write at least 150 words following the outline given below in Chinese:*

1)你认为自己具备了什么条件(能力、性格、爱好等)可以胜任学生会主席的工作

2)如果当选,你将为本校同学做些什么

【思路点拨】本题要求写一篇演说辞。根据所给提纲,本文应包含以下内容:点明竞选职位;指出自己所具有的优势及能力;提出当选后的目标。

【参考范文】

A Campaign Speech

Dear fellow students,

①It is a great honor for me to stand here and give my speech. ②To begin with, let me introduce myself. My name is Huck, a junior from the English Department. ③As some of you may know, I am the monitor of Class 4,

Grade Two.

④As for the position of president of the students' union, I find I am qualified. ⑤Firstly, I have gained a lot of experience and received wide praise from my classmates for my job as monitor. ⑥Secondly, I am a warm-hearted boy and always ready to help others, quick to react to the needs of my fellow students. ⑦Thirdly, I am good at organizing activities and have held a number of English corners and debate contests.

⑧Looking into the future, I will try my best to serve my fellow students if I am lucky enough to be the president of the students' union. ⑨On one hand, I, with my co-workers, will invite more famous professors to give lectures and speeches. ⑩On the other hand, I will organize more activities to enhance the understanding of each other. ⑪In addition, I will open more channels for our students to voice their opinions and their needs.

⑫I wish all of you the very best and thank you all for listening. Thank you!

13. 倡议书行文思路

Topic	标题
Date	日期和称呼
Dear _____ ,	①直接表达写信目的
①I am writing this letter to call on _____ to _____ .	②开始引出问题出现的背景
②As some of you may know, _____ . ③In fact, _____ .	③进一步阐述问题的现状
④It is necessary for us to _____ . ⑤On one hand, _____ . ⑥On the other hand, _____ . ⑦However, _____ . ⑧So, it is high time _____ . ⑨Firstly, _____ . ⑩Secondly, _____ .	④关注解决问题的必要性
	⑤解决问题很必要的理由一
	⑥解决问题很必要的理由二
	⑦进一步表达问题需要解决的紧迫性
⑪If you are willing to _____ , please _____ .	⑧发出号召,提出解决办法
⑫Join us in the action and extend _____ into a spirit that dares any possible difficulties.	⑨解决办法一
	⑩解决办法二
Thank you!	⑪联系方式
Sincerely yours, Signature	⑫书信结尾语,发出号召,增加感染力

【例25】 (05-1)

Directions: *For this part, you are allowed 30 minutes to write an open letter on behalf of the students' union asking people to give help to a student who is seriously ill. You should write at least 150 words following the outline given below:*

1) 对病人的简单介绍:目前的病情和家庭情况

2) 目前的困难:无法继续承担医疗费用,需要护理

3) 希望捐助,联系方式

【思路点拨】本题要求写一封倡议书。根据所给提纲,本文应包含以下内容:点明写信的目的;介绍病人情况,指出需要大家关注解决的问题和困难;倡议捐助,并提供联系方式。

【参考范文】

Your Help Needed

June 15, 2007

Dear friends,

①I am writing this letter to call on all the students in our university to do something for Lucy. ②As some of you may know, Lucy, a lovely girl student from Class Two, Grade One has been seriously ill. ③In fact, she has been suffering from hepatitis, which is very dangerous.

④It is necessary for us to show our love and help to her now. ⑤On one hand, Lucy is now in urgent need of operation to have her liver transplanted. ⑥On the other hand, she needs great care. ⑦However, her family is too poor to afford the expenses, which totaled 120,000 yuan. It is impossible for her family to raise such a large sum of money in such pressing time. ⑧So, it is high time for us to help Lucy out of danger, and let's do whatever we can to save our fellow student's life. ⑨Firstly, we can raise money to help her out. ⑩Secondly, we can also help her through many other ways, such as taking care of her and chatting with her.

⑪If you are willing to give her a hand, please contact us at the number 233564 in the daytime and 233331 at night. ⑫Join us in the action and extend our love into a spirit that dares any possible difficulties. Thank you!

Sincerely yours,

Students' Union

14. 海报行文思路

Topic	标题
①Under the auspices of _____ , _____ ____ will be held /organized _____ . ②_____ _____ . ③This activity aims _____ . ④The arrangements are as follows:　⑤This activity includes /is arranged _____ . ⑥_____ . ⑦_____ . ⑧_____ ____ .　⑨Anyone who _____ is welcomed warmly. ⑩Those interested are expected _____ . ⑪Please _____ . ⑫Looking forward to your active participation.	可以直接用 Poster 作为标题（Topic）或根据海报内容撰写标题,注意要简洁明快　①交代活动主办单位或活动时间、地点　②概括描述活动内容　③交代活动的主要目的　④引出活动具体安排或主要特点　⑤总述活动安排　⑥ 描述活动具体安排一/特点一　⑦ 描述活动具体安排一/特点二　⑧ 描述活动具体安排一/特点三　⑨交代参加活动的条件　⑩交代参加活动的方式　⑪交代联系或咨询方式　⑫发出号召,增加感染力　最后落款给出主办单位或组织机构名称

【例26】

Directions: *For this part, you are allowed 30 minutes to write a poster recruiting volunteers. You should write at least 150 words following the outline given below:*

1)校学生会将组织一次暑假志愿者活动,现招募志愿者

2)本次志愿者活动的目的、活动安排等

3)报名条件及联系方式

【思路点拨】本题要求写一张招募志愿者的海报。根据所给提纲,本文应包含以下内容:交代为什么要招募志愿者;介绍活动的目的及具体安排;说明报名条件及方式,鼓励参加。

【参考范文】

Volunteers Needed

①Under the auspices of the Students' Union of our school, a volunteer activity will be organized during the summer holidays. ② The volunteer team will go to the rural areas to give poor children computer and English lessons. ③This activity aims to provide a platform to show and prove the students' abilities, and broaden the students' horizon. ④The arrangements are as follows:

⑤This activity is arranged to last 20 days or so. ⑥It is planned to begin on July 10. ⑦The team members will be arranged to go to different country primary schools. ⑧Your main task is to teach children how to use a computer and learn English well.

⑨Anyone who has good English and computer knowledge is welcomed warmly. ⑩Those interested are expected to come to the office of the Students' Union to fill in an application form. ⑪Please contact Liqiang at 62511123 for further information. ⑫Looking forward to your active participation.

The Students' Union

15. 景点介绍行文思路

Topic	标题
Ladies and Gentlemen /Dear _____, ①Welcome to _____. ②To begin with, _____. ③It's my pleasure to _____. ④The following is schedule of _____. ⑤The first spot we are going to visit _____. ⑥The next sight to look around is _____. ⑦In addition, _____. ⑧As a matter of fact, _____. ⑨During your visit, _____. ⑩There is no doubt that _____. ⑪I hope that _____. ⑫If any of you have questions, please feel free to ask me at any time.	①向听众表示欢迎 ②作一简单的自我介绍 ③点明自己的任务 ④开始介绍景点游览安排 ⑤景点一 ⑥景点二 ⑦景点三 ⑧突出重点,如参观的重点地方或日程中的重点活动 ⑨具体特点,如该地方或活动的具体特点 ⑩进一步阐述其特点或影响 ⑪向听众表示良好祝愿 ⑫惯常结束语

【例 27】

Directions: *For this part, you are allowed 30 minutes to write a composition entitled **A Brief Introduction to a Tourist Attraction**. You should write at least 150 words according to the following guidelines:*

Your role: a tour guide

Your audience: a group of foreign tourists

Your introduction should include:

1) Some welcoming words

2) The schedule for the day

3) A description of the place the tourists will be visiting (e. g. a scenic spot or a historical site, etc.)

You should make the introduction interesting and the arrangements of the day clear to everybody.

【思路点拨】本题要求写一篇景点介绍。根据所给提纲,本文应包含以下内容:致欢迎词;介绍一天的行程安排;描述景点特点。

【参考范文】

A Brief Introduction to a Tourist Attraction

Ladies and Gentlemen,

①Welcome to China and thank you for your trusting our travel agency. ②To begin with, I would like to introduce myself: I am the tourist guide from China Travel Service and my name is Lisa. ③It's my pleasure to be your guide.

④The following is schedule of the day. ⑤The first spot we are going to visit is the Great Wall, the grandest fortification in ancient China. ⑥The next sight to look around is the Ming Tombs, which is one of the best-preserved tombs for 13 emperors in Ming Dynasty more than one thousand years ago. ⑦In addition, in the afternoon, we will go for the Summer Palace, the royal park for Chinese ancient emperors.

⑧As a matter of fact, the Great Wall we will visit is the most complete and best preserved section. ⑨During your visit, you will enjoy a magnificent view of continuous mountains, green trees and blooming wild flowers. ⑩There is no doubt that you will not regret your tour.

⑪I hope that you will enjoy your day. ⑫If any of you have questions, please feel free to ask me at any time.

16. 日程安排行文思路

Topic	标题
Ladies and Gentlemen /Dear _____, ①Welcome to _____. ②To begin with, _____. ③It's my pleasure to _____. ④Now to share the schedule with you, _____. ⑤_____. ⑥_____. ⑦In addi-	①向听众表示欢迎 ②作一简单的自我介绍,如姓名、身份或所代表的组织 ③表达自己的荣幸 ④日程的总体安排 ⑤具体活动安排一

tion,＿＿＿＿＿＿＿.	⑥具体活动安排二
⑧ Please keep in mind that ＿＿＿＿＿＿. ⑨There is no doubt that ＿＿＿＿＿. ⑩If any of you have questions, please feel free to ask me at any time.	⑦具体活动安排三
	⑧提醒听众要注意的事项：如出发时间
	⑨阐述理由
	⑩习惯结束语
⑪I hope that ＿＿＿＿＿. ⑫Thank you very much for your attention.	⑪向听众表示良好祝愿
	⑫向听众致谢

【例28】

Directions: *For this part, you are allowed 30 minutes to write a composition entitled* **A Visit to a Campus**. *You should write at least 150 words according to the following guidelines:*

Your role：the president of a university

Your audience：a visiting delegation from other universities

Your introduction should include：

1) Some welcoming words

2) The schedule for the day

3) A description of the place you will visit at the campus

You should make the introduction interesting and the arrangements for the day clear to everybody.

【思路点拨】本题要求写一篇日程安排。根据所给提纲，本文应包含以下内容：对访问代表团表示欢迎；介绍一天的安排(校园参观路线、吃饭安排等等)。

【参考范文】

A Visit to a Campus

Ladies and Gentlemen,

① Welcome to our university, one of the best known universities all over the country. ② To begin with, I'd like to introduce myself. I am Thomas Wilson, president of the university. ③ It is my pleasure to take the opportunity to address you here.

④Now to share the schedule with you, you will be shown around the campus this morning. ⑤You will set out half an hour after the ceremony. ⑥At 10:00, you will visit our teaching building, modern library, the new gym and the canteen. ⑦In addition, you will have a free lunch in the canteen at 12:00.

⑧Please keep in mind that the library is one of the most important places on campus. ⑨There is no doubt that your visit to the library will be very fruitful. ⑩If any of you have questions, please feel free to ask me at any time.

⑪I hope that you will have a nice day. ⑫Thank you very much for your attention.

Exercise

即讲即练

作文一

Directions: *For this part, you are allowed 30 minutes to write a letter to the chief librarian, Sun Jianmin, to offer your suggestions. You should write at least 150 words according to the outline given below:*

最近,你们当地的图书馆无论是在服务方面还是在硬件设备方面都在进行改进,给图书馆负责人写一封建议信,信中应包含以下内容：

1)对图书馆进行改进一事表示欢迎

2)提出你对图书馆改进的建议

A Letter to the Librarian

＿＿＿＿＿＿＿＿＿＿＿＿＿＿＿＿＿＿＿＿＿＿＿＿＿＿＿＿＿＿＿

＿＿＿＿＿＿＿＿＿＿＿＿＿＿＿＿＿＿＿＿＿＿＿＿＿＿＿＿＿＿＿

作文二

Directions: *For this part, you are allowed 30 minutes to write a letter of complaint to the manager of the post office, explaining the situation and giving your suggestions for improvement. You should write at least 150 words according to the outline given below:*

假如你是冯芳,你觉得邮局寄来的电话账单有问题,于是打电话询问此事。可是接待人员非常没有礼貌,请你就邮局礼貌问题给邮局经理写一封抱怨信。

A Letter to the Manager of the Post Office

_____

_____

作文三

Directions: *For this part, you are allowed 30 minutes to write a letter to the general manager of a company for a position of personal secretary. You should write at least 150 words according to the outline given below:*

1)申请个人秘书职务
2)说明自己的专业
3)请求面谈

An Application Letter

_____

_____

作文四

Directions: *For this part, you are allowed 30 minutes to write an application letter to Boston University for your Master degree in Applied Physics. You should write at least 150 words according to the outline given below:*

1)表达申请攻读硕士学位的心愿
2)简单介绍自己的情况
3)表达自己对所申请的学校、专业以及教授的看法

A Letter of Application

_____

_____

作文五

Directions: *For this part, you are allowed 30 minutes to write a poster about a football match between Chinese National Team and Brazilian National Team. You should write at least 150 words according to the outline given below:*

中国国家队和巴西国家队近期将举行一场足球友谊赛,旨在促进两国友谊。该海报要点如下:

该足球赛很精彩,很值得观看。届时将有很多足球明星到场。

足球比赛比赛时间:周日(十一月十一号)下午2:00

地点:省体育场

届时将评选最幸运观众。

Poster

_____

_____

作文六

Directions: *For this part, you are allowed 30 minutes to write a letter to your pen friend who will visit your city, to explain for your failure to meet him at the airport. You should write at least 150 words according to the outline given below:*

1）因不能按计划接笔友而向其道歉

2）解释不能接笔友的原因

3）提出解决措施

An Apology Letter to a Pen Friend

_____

_____

【参考范文】..

作文一

【思路点拨】

　　本题要求写一封建议信。根据所给提纲,本文应包含以下内容:点明写信的缘由,表明自己对图书馆进行改进一事的支持;具体阐述建议的内容并说明理由;表示感谢,并表达自己的愿望。

【参考范文】

A Letter to the Librarian

Aug. 8, 2007

Dear Sun,

　　I am glad to hear that the library is to take some measures to make improvements in its service and facilities. So I am writing to offer my proposals. As far as I am concerned, our library should do its best to purchase the latest publications and make sure it has a full set of classical works and reference books. On one hand, libraries play a vital role in the education and entertainment of the general reader. On the other hand, the quality of the library books reflects people's spiritual outlook.

　　As to the facility, I suggest the library connect the Internet via computers. In that way, the library will expand its services to a larger number of readers. It is unnecessary for the citizens to go out to the library to read. I am sure the improvements will be welcomed by the citizens.

　　Please inform me if I can do anything for you. I will highly appreciate your consideration of my proposals.

Sincerely yours,

Liu Xiaoqian

作文二

【思路点拨】

　　本题要求写一封抱怨信。根据命题要求,本文应包含以下内容:简单介绍自己,并指出不满的地方;具体说明存在的问题,并提出改进意见;表达自己的祝愿。

【参考范文】

A Letter to the Manager of the Post Office

Oct. 10, 2007

Dear Manager,

　　I am a customer of your post office. Here I am writing to call your attention to some problem about the deplorable attitude of one of your staff member.

　　Yesterday I received my telephone bill for the previous month from you and thought there were some errors in calculation: I had been overcharged for two overseas calls. However, when I called your Complaints Department, the girl who answered my phone was very rude. For one thing, she interrupted me continually. For another, she even said that it is I myself that made the fault.

Complaints Department is of great significance in the post office, for it reflects the quality of your services directly. So, it is urgent to take measures to improve the services and management there. I do hope the girl in question should be disciplined and she can make a formal apology to me.

An early response will be appreciated.

Sincerely yours,

Feng Fang

作文三

【思路点拨】

本题要求写一封求职信。根据所给提纲,本文应包含以下内容:点明写信的缘由:申请秘书一职;介绍自己的教育经历和专业能力;提出期望,争取面试。

【参考范文】

An Application Letter

July 5, 2007

Dear Manager,

In reply to your advertisement in *China Daily*, I beg to apply for the post of personal secretary in your company. I have attached a copy of my resume for your consideration. I am fully confident that I am the right person for the job.

I major in English. In addition to the required courses, I have studied Economic Law as my second major. Actually, I have worked as the private secretary in an insurance company for two years and gained many experiences. I believe my education and work experiences will combine to produce an excellent work performance. You will find me to be reliable and efficient.

I would appreciate your time in reviewing my enclosed resume and if there is any additional information you require, please contact me. I would welcome an opportunity to meet with you for a personal interview. I can be reached at 89765678 at anytime.

Yours sincerely,

Mary

作文四

【思路点拨】

本题要求写一封求学信。根据所给提纲,本文应包含以下内容:点明写信缘由:申请研究生学位;介绍在校期间的情况及其他相关情况;表达申请心愿。

【参考范文】

A Letter of Application

Sep. 10, 2007

Dear Professor Richard,

I have read the annual prospectus issued by your school and found that it has the best graduate program of Applied Physics. I should like to further my studies in Physics Department of your university.

I will graduate and get my BS degree from the Physics Department of Tsinghua University. During my college study there, I took such major courses as Applied Physics, Math, and some courses like English and drawing. And I have passed all the required courses with satisfactory marks. Also I have learnt the teamwork spirit, which, I believe, is supremely important to my work. I am very excellent in spoken and written English. Besides, I was a major member of computer club.

One of my former professors and the present dean of our Department have kindly written letters of recommendation for me, as enclosed with this letter.

I will appreciate it very much if you could send me the Graduate Application Forms, the Application Form for Scholarships /Assistantships, a detailed introduction to the School of Physics, and other relevant information. I look forward to hearing from you soon.

Sincerely yours,

Li Hua

作文五

【思路点拨】

　　本题要求写一张足球比赛的海报。根据命题要求,本文应包含以下内容:交代足球比赛的时间、地点以及比赛双方身份;介绍该足球比赛的目的及特点;鼓励大家积极购票观看。

【参考范文】

Poster

　　Under the auspices of the General Administration of Sport of China, a football match between Chinese National Team and Brazilian National Team will be held in the Province Stadium at 2:00 p.m. next Sunday on November 11. The football match aims to promote the friendship between the two countries, and meanwhile improve the football skill of the Chinese football player.

　　The football match is really worth watching. First, it seldom has such an opportunity to see Chinese National Team to compete with Brazilian National Team, a supreme one in the football field. Second, a lot of famous football stars will be there and you can see your idol with your own eyes. In addition, the match-holder will choose a lucky audience who will be given a pleasant surprise.

　　Anyone who wants to watch the football match, especially the football fans should be quick. Please contact the Sports Group for tickets. A school bus will be made available. The goers are expected to gather on the cement ground in front of Dormitory No. 3 at 7:00 sharp p.m. on the given day.

　　Looking forward to your active participation.

Sports Group

作文六

【思路点拨】

　　本题要求写一封道歉信。根据所给提纲,本文应包含以下内容:真诚地表达歉意;详细解释失约原因;提出补救措施。

【参考范文】

An Apology Letter to a Pen Friend

May 28, 2007

Dear John,

　　I do apologize for having to send you this letter about my failure to meet you at the airport as planned. Now, I have to express my deep regret. However, I sincerely hope you can accept my apology with gratitude.

　　I am afraid that you will be displeased at my failure to meet you at the airport. But I still hope you will understand me and excuse me for my absence.

　　I will be very grateful if you are kind to listen to my explanation. The reason for my absence is that your flight will arrive early in the morning, and I have a very important exam at the same time. And I had no way out. So it's not in my power to meet your request.

　　However, I can have my sister pick you up. By the way, as you have never seen her I must tell you home to identify her: She is of 165cm tall and has a long hair. In addition, she will wear a white skirt and carry a *China Daily* in hand.

　　Hope we can meet soon.

Sincerely yours,
Alice

Lecture 5　　第五讲　6 种灵活句式变换

　　使用的句式不同,表达的效果就不同。一篇文章中如果反复使用同一句式,文章就会显得单调无味,毫无生气。因此要注意句式的变化,避免单一重复。

一、长句与短句的变换

　　长句含有许多修饰语,适合表达复杂的思想,解释观点或理论,描写细致的事物;短句比较简洁、明快、有力,适合陈述重要的事实或想法。在实际写作中,一味地采用长句或短句都是不可取的,要长短句交替使用,以简单句为基础,配以适当的并列句和复合句。简单句可长可短,一般要加些附属成分,如分词短语、不定式短语、介词短语或副词短语等。

1. 短句变长句

在平时写作时,考生要注意前后句子之间是否存在联系,善于发现各简单句之间的关联,用恰当的连接词将简单句连接起来,组成准确地道的复杂长句,增加文章的气势。

【例 1】

【原文】	【优化】
Teenagers are pressured by school work. They are also encouraged by their peers. Under such circumstances, they resort to smoking. But sometimes they feel a little guilty.	Pressured by school work and encouraged by their peers, teenagers often resort to smoking, though they feel a little guilty sometimes.

【分析】原文中包含四个短句,语意显得不够连贯。我们将前两个短句改写成用 and 连接的两个并列的分词短语,充当句子的状语,同时将后两句合并成一个包含由 though 引导的让步状语从句的主从复合句。

2. 长句变短句

写作中句子的长短应根据表达的需要,有话则长,无话则短。短句不仅指句子长度较短,也指句子内部结构精炼,简洁是一个重要的原则。用词累赘是写作的大忌。

【例 2】

【原文】	【优化】
A basic reason for divorce is that some people are not really ready for marriage, perhaps because they are still establishing themselves in their careers and haven't had enough time to get to know themselves and many members of the opposite sex, but family pressures make them feel that something is wrong with them since they are not married, and so they marry too soon.	A basic reason for divorce is that some people are not really ready for marriage. As they are still establishing themselves in their careers, they haven't had enough time to get to know themselves and many members of the opposite sex. However, family pressures make them feel that something is wrong with them since they are not married. So they marry too soon.

【分析】原文中只包含一个长句,冗长而复杂,表面上看衔接紧密,但是读完却让人感到喘不过气,理解起来也很困难。究其原因,主要是因为在一个意群结束时没有适当断句,勉强用连词接上,导致句子缺乏层次感,语意表达模糊。优化后的段落则解决了这一问题。

二、主动与被动的变换

什么时候用被动,什么时候用主动,主要是由陈述对象决定的。英语写作中特别强调陈述对象的一致性,因此考生在选择主动和被动时一定要慎重。

1. 主动变被动

1)不需要体现动作的执行者

【例 3】

【原文】	【优化】
We should advise people to protect their own interests and not to be led astray by false advertisements.	People should be advised to protect their own interests and not to be led astray by false advertisements.

【分析】本句并不强调动作的执行者"we",因而使用被动语态将会使表达更贴切。

2)需要强调动作的承受者

【例 4】

【原文】	【优化】
The employees elected Mr. Li chairman of the committee last week.	Mr. Li was elected chairman of the committee by the employees last week.

【分析】原句也没有什么错误,但如果要强调是"Mr. Li"被选为主席,就应该使用被动语态。

3)保持陈述对象的一致,以求行文通顺

【例5】

【原文】	【优化】
Computers may help scientists in analyzing data and do-ing complex calculation, while engineers make use of some computers in designing a plane, or a spaceship.	Computers may help scientists in analyzing data and doing complex calculation, while some computers are made use of by engineers in designing a plane, or a spaceship.
【分析】原句中主句的主语是 computers，从句的主语则是 engineers，而 computers 变成了宾语，为了避免陈述对象混乱，保证行文的通顺，应该将从句改为被动句。	

2. 被动变主动

　　1) 需要体现动作的执行者

【例6】

【原文】	【优化】
Now how to improve their English is paid more attention to by college students.	Now college students pay more attention to how to im-prove their English.
【分析】本句是想表达"大学生越来越关注该如何提高英语水平"的含义，因此句子是要体现"college students"的行为，因此应该采用主动语态。	

　　2) 保持陈述对象的一致，以求行文通顺

【例7】

【原文】	【优化】
If we don't know how the wastes should be used, we can sell them to the recycling station.	If we don't know how to use the wastes, we can sell them to the recycling station.
【分析】原句中 if 引导的从句中的宾语从句的被动语态导致 if 从句中前后陈述对象混乱，影响了句意的明晰和语言的流畅。	

三、非谓语动词与从句的变换

　　非谓语动词包括：动词不定式、动名词、现在分词和过去分词。使用非谓语动词可以在有限的空间内表达更多的信息，使句子结构紧凑、逻辑严谨。

【例8】

【原文】	【优化】
It must be realized that people should be cautious when they decide which books they should choose to read since if they read bad books, it will be time-wasting and harmful.	It must be realized that people should be cautious when deciding which books to read since reading bad books is time-wasting and harmful.
【分析】原句中的时间状语从句改为现在分词短语作状语，if 条件从句改为动名词短语作主语，句子结构变得更加紧凑，简洁明了。	

四、松散句与掉尾句的变换

　　松散句指的是"把主要信息放在前面，辅助信息放在后面"的句式，常用来自然有序地陈述观点或罗列事实；掉尾句则指的是"把辅助信息放在前面，主要信息放在后面"的句式，常用于强调或起到修饰作用。

　　文章中绝大多数句子都是松散句，但正是由于这个缘故，偶尔使用掉尾句便会起到强调突出的效果，但注意不要频繁使用，以免使文章的意思表达显得不够直接明了。

【例9】

【原文】	【优化】
Some students don't like having roommates. Because ev-ery person has his or her own way, they think several people living together causes some unpleasantness. We have the chance to adjust the subtle relationships.	Some students don't like having roommates. They think several people living together causes some un-pleasantness because every person has his or her own way. We have the chance to adjust the subtle relation-ships.

【分析】本段话中第二句使用了掉尾句,将原因状语从句放到了主句的前面,但此句并不是要强调原因,而是要表达一些同学的看法,因此应该将该句改为松散句,这样才符合句子的表达需要。

【例10】

【原文】	【优化】
That living together offers an excellent chance of cooperation is one incomparable advantage. Planning a party single-handedly may be a boring and difficult job. Our roommates' help make it enjoyable and easy. We may do anything perfectly, combining every member's wit and talent together.	One incomparable advantage is that living together offers an excellent chance of cooperation. Planning a party single-handedly may be a boring and difficult job. Our roommates' help make it enjoyable and easy. Combining every member's wit and talent together, we may do anything perfectly.

【分析】本段中第一句使用了掉尾句,将从句放到了主句的最前面,但此句是要说明与别人合住的"One incomparable advantage"是什么,而且作为段首句,应该清楚直接,因此应该将该句改为松散句,将句子的主要部分放到最前面。而本段中最后一句使用的是松散句,将分词短语放到了句子主干结构之后,这样表达未能突出作者的意图,因此应将该句改为掉尾句,把分词短语提到句首。

五、强调句的变换

写作中,常使用强调句来达到突出重点的目的。强调句的基本结构是:It is / was + 被强调部分 + that / who + 句子其他成份。另外,英语中还经常会使用助动词 do / does / did 对谓语动词进行强调。

【例11】

【原文】	【优化】
Parents and other family members' money mainly support us.	It is parents and other family members' money that mainly support us.

【分析】改成强调句以后,句子的主语得到了突出,句意的表达更加有力。

六、倒装句的变换

句子成份在句子中都有一定的位置,但有时可以把某些句子成份前后倒置,以达到突出强调的目的或起到某种修饰作用。

英语中倒装分为全部倒装和部分倒装。部分倒装在写作中比较常用,经常由否定词提前或"only + 状语"提前引起。

【例12】

【原文】	【优化】
I think that by sticking to one job one can accumulate a lot of experience in it, which in turn will further improve his work.	I think that only by sticking to one job can one accumulate a lot of experience in it, which in turn will further improve his work.

【分析】状语前加上 only 并位于句首引起了句子倒装,突出了这种措施的必要性,句意的表达更加有力。

Exercise　　即讲即练

作文一

Directions: *For this part, you are allowed 30 minutes to write an essay entitled Selfishness in Dormitory Life.*

You should write at least 150 words following the outline given below:

1)大学寝室里自私自利的现象比较普遍

2)分析出现这种现象的原因

3)"我"对自私自利的看法

Selfishness in Dormitory Life

①Recently, people have brought selfishness in university dormitories into focus. ②Some students never care about their roommates' needs. ③Some students never offer any help to their roommates. ④Some others even interrupt others' normal daily life. ⑤They speak loudly, turn on the loudspeakers and telephone at midnight and have other bad-mannered behaviors. (描述现象段)

⑥There are many reasons that can account for this phenomenon. ⑦First, many students are the only children in their families. ⑧They are the apples of their parents' eye. ⑨Their parents and grandparents have spoiled them and they are used to being satisfied. ⑩Therefore, they hardly pay any attention to others' feelings initiatively. ⑪Second, many students is not accustomed to collective life. ⑫They do not understand mutual respect and mutual help are keys to harmonious dormitory life. ⑬So they have no idea how they should get along with others in the dormitories. (说明原因段)

⑭As far as I am concerned, selfishness can erode youngsters' mind. ⑮Selfishness can also undermine their all-round development. ⑯We can create a healthy atmosphere for the dormitory life and the future social life when we become respectful and helpful to each other. (总结观点段)

要求:请按照下面的提示对左栏的作文进行优化改写。
1. 对句①中的语态进行优化。
2. 将句②、句③合成一句。
3. 通过介词 by 将句④、句⑤合成一句。
4. 用非谓语动词代替句⑥中定语从句。
5. 利用 as(作为)将句⑦、⑧合为一句。
6. 对句⑨中的语态进行优化。
7. 用非限制性定语从句改写句⑪和句⑫。
8. 将 how 引导的宾语从句改成不定式结构。
9. 将句⑭、句⑮合成一句。
10. 将句⑯改成掉尾句,并改成倒装句。

Selfishness in Dormitory Life

_____

_____

作文二

Directions: _For this part, you are allowed 30 minutes to write an essay entitled_ **Should Students Be Skeptical about What's Taught?** _You should write at least 150 words following the outline given below_:

1)怀疑精神是一种可贵的学术精神。大多数中国学生在课堂上缺乏怀疑精神,不敢挑战权威的学习方法是不可取的
2)阐明持有此种观点的理由

Should Students Be Skeptical about What's Taught?

①It is well known that skepticism is a valuable spirit in academic. ②But most Chinese students always believe that teachers are truth-holders in class and their authority is unquestionable, for which they fear voicing their own opinions and do not dare defy the authority of teachers. ③This way to learn knowledge is not advisable. (提出观点段)

④For one thing, teachers are human beings. ⑤They are not perfect and do make mistakes. ⑥So if students accept teachers' opinion unquestioningly, it will do great harm to their study. ⑦For another, students will be eager to seek the truth when doubts come. ⑧They will resort to reference books. ⑨They can also turn to teachers for further arguments. ⑩What's more, when they have fun in learning, their interest in what is taught will grow and interest is the best teacher. (论证观点段)

⑪All mentioned above tell us that we should encourage students to adopt a skeptical attitude in class. ⑫By challenging the authority and generating their own ideas students can develop their creativity and gain academic independence. (总结观点段)

要求:请按照下面的提示对左栏的作文进行优化改写。
1. 将句②分解成两个句子。
2. 用 it 作形式主语改写句③。
3. 通过介词 as(作为)将句④、句⑤合成一句。
4. 用非谓语动词短语将句⑥改写成简单句。
5. 将句⑦改写成掉尾句,用 either…or 将句⑧、句⑨合并,并通过 by 与句⑦合为一句。
6. 将句⑩改写成掉尾句。
7. 对句⑪中的语态进行优化。
8. 将句⑫改成倒装句。

Should Students Be Skeptical about What's Taught?

_____

_____

【参考范文】

作文一

Selfishness in Dormitory Life

①Recently, people have brought selfishness in university dormitories into focus. ②Some students never care about their roommates' needs. ③Some students never offer any help to their roommates. ④Some even interrupt others' normal daily life. ⑤They speak loudly, turn on the loudspeakers and telephone at midnight and have other bad-mannered behaviors. (描述现象段)

⑥There are many reasons that can account for this phenomenon. ⑦First, many students are the only children in their families. ⑧They are the apples of their parents' eye. ⑨Their parents and grandparents have spoiled them and they are used to being satisfied. ⑩Therefore, they hardly pay any attention to others' feelings initiatively. ⑪Second, many students is not accustomed to collective life. ⑫They do not understand mutual respect and mutual help are keys to harmonious dormitory life. ⑬So they have no idea how they should getalong with others in the dormitories. (说明原因段)

⑭As far as I am concerned, selfishness can erode youngsters' mind. ⑮Selfishness can also undermine their all-round development. ⑯We can create a healthy atmosphere for the dormitory life and the future social life when we become respectful and helpful to each other. (总结观点段)

Selfishness in Dormitory Life

Recently, <u>selfishness</u> in university dormitories <u>has been brought into focus.</u> <u>Some students</u> never <u>care</u> about their roommates' needs <u>or offer</u> any help to their roommates. <u>Some others</u> even interrupt others' normal daily life <u>by speaking</u> loudly, <u>turning</u> on the loudspeakers <u>and telephoning</u> at midnight and other bad-mannered behaviors. (描述现象段)

There are many reasons <u>accounting for</u> this phenomenon. First, many students, <u>as the only children in their families</u>, are the apples of their parents' eye. They <u>have been spoiled and are used to being satisfied.</u> Therefore, they hardly pay any attention to others' feelings initiatively. Second, many students is not accustomed to collective life, <u>who do not understand</u> mutual respect and mutual help are keys to harmonious dormitory life. So they have no idea <u>how to get</u> along with others in the dormitories. (说明原因段)

As far as I am concerned, selfishness can erode youngsters' mind <u>and may well</u> undermine their all-round development. <u>Only when</u> we become respectful and helpful to each other <u>can we</u> create a healthy atmosphere for the dormitory life and the future social life. (总结观点段)

作文二

Should Students Be Skeptical about What's Taught?

①It is well known that skepticism is a valuable spirit in academic. ②But most Chinese students always believe that teachers are truth-holders in class and their authority is unquestionable, for which they fear voicing their own opinions and do not dare defy the authority of teachers. ③This way to learn knowledge is not advisable. (提出观点段)

④ For one thing, teachers are human beings. ⑤They are not perfect and also make mistakes. ⑥So if students accept teachers' opinion unquestioningly, it will do great harm to their study. ⑦For another, students will be eager to seek the truth when doubts come. ⑧They will resort to reference books. ⑨They can also

Should Students Be Skeptical about What's Taught?

It is well known that skepticism is a valuable spirit in academic. But most Chinese students always believe that teachers are truth-holders in class and their authority is unquestionable. <u>They fear</u> voicing their own opinions, <u>let alone defying</u> the authority of teachers. <u>It is not advisable to</u> learn knowledge by this way. (提出观点段)

For one thing, teachers, <u>as human beings</u>, are not perfect and <u>do make</u> mistakes. So <u>accepting teachers' opinion unquestioningly</u> does great harm to students. For another, <u>when doubts come, students will be eager to seek the truth</u>, <u>either by</u> resorting to reference books <u>or by</u> turning to teachers for further

turn to teachers for further arguments. ⑩What's more, their interest in what is taught will grow when they have fun in learning and interest is the best teacher. (论证观点段)

⑪All mentioned above tell us that we should encourage students to adopt a skeptical attitude in class. ⑫ By challenging the authority and generating their own ideas students can develop their creativity and gain academic independence. (总结观点段)

arguments. What's more, <u>when they have fun in learning, their interest in what is taught will grow</u> and interest is the best teacher. (论证观点段)

All mentioned above tell us that <u>students should be encouraged</u> to adopt a skeptical attitude in class. <u>Only by</u> challenging the authority and generating their own ideas <u>can students</u> develop their creativity and gain academic independence. (总结观点段)

Lecture 6   第六讲   5 大写作亮点设计

一篇优秀的作文,除了做到结构清晰、句式多变以外,往往还会出现一到两个让考官眼前为之一亮的亮点。这样的亮点设计会给你的作文大大增色,往往会给考官留下深刻的印象。

一、遣词用语准确贴切

1. 认真辨析同义词

由于英语词义范畴非常广泛,即便是同义词也只是某种程度上的近似,不可能在意义上完全对等。这就需要考生在选词时斟酌其含义的微妙差别,辨析同义词在具体语境中的不同用法。

【例1】

1. Everyone had special interest while reading so we could <u>choose</u> different books to read according to our personal interests.
2. Everyone had special interest while reading so we could <u>select</u> different books to read according to our personal interests.

【分析】choose 指的是"一般性的选择";而 select 则强调"在一定范围内挑选",此处明显用后者更为恰当。

2. 恰当使用限定词

用词准确从另外一个角度讲就是要使论述客观、适度,这就需要考生适当使用一些限定词,以避免观点的绝对化,从而提高说服力和可信度。

写作中常见的限定词有:may, maybe, perhaps, probably, mainly, generally, commonly, personally, comparatively, typically, usually, sometimes, often, most, mostly, nearly, almost, not necessarily, in general, at least, at most, may as well, had better, to some extent, to some degree, more often than not, for the most part 等。

【例2】

I don't agree to the first argument <u>to some extent</u>.

【分析】to some extent 意为"在某种程度上",表明观点的客观性,避免了绝对化,为自己留有余地。

3. 注意词语的习惯搭配

用词准确不但要求考生掌握具体单词的含义,还要熟悉词语的习惯搭配,一定要避免受汉语语意的干扰而出现错误。

【例3】

1. The traffic in many big cities is getting <u>more and more crowded</u>.
2. The traffic in many big cities is getting <u>heavier and heavier</u>.

【分析】汉语中我们可以说"交通拥挤",但英文中 traffic 和 crowded 是不能搭配的,因为 crowded 是表示街道、房间等地方挤满了人或东西,我们可以说"The street is crowded",但不能说"The traffic is crowded"。而要表达"交通拥挤",应该用 heavy 一词。

4. 避免生造词语

生编硬造词语是考生在写作中常犯的错误之一,主要表现为将汉语意思生译成英文,即所谓的"中国式英语"。

【例4】

> 1. To be <u>a three good student</u> is always a symbol of achievement for the Chinese students.
> 2. To be <u>an all-round student</u> is always a symbol of achievement for the Chinese students.

> 【分析】a three good student 在此是表示"三好学生",中国人都能看懂,但却令外国人费解,是典型的"中国式英语";而恰当的表达应该是"an all-round student",或用比较直白的方式将其译为"an excellent student in all aspects"。

5. 避免口语化

　　六级作文除个别应用文以外,基本都属于较正式的书面文体,因此在写作时要避免使用口语化的词汇,具体遣词时要注意以下几点:

　　1)避免使用缩写形式,比如 do not 不要写成 don't;it is 不要写成 it's。

　　2)避免使用方言俚语,比如 a whole' nother(完全不同的)或 flip side(另一面,反面)等。

　　3)避免使用非标准化的表述方式,比如 gonna, wanna 之类的口语。

　　4)尽量使用单词而不是短语,比如用 investigate 要优于用 look into;用 determine 要优于 make up one's mind。因为相对于单词来说,短语更加口语化,而且不够精练。

　　5)不要总使用常用的、口语色彩较浓的词汇,比如 many, about, do 之类的词。

【例5】

> 1. Many college students <u>are gonna</u> take part in CET-6.
> 2. Many college students <u>would like to</u> take part in CET-6.

> 【分析】be gonna 与 would like to 都可以表示"想要或打算…",但 be gonna 是口语中的非正式用法,不能出现在书面文体中。

6. 避免赘言啰嗦

　　考生在写作时要有意识地使用同义词、同根词或上、下义词来取代上文中出现过的词汇以避免重复和啰嗦,以求文采。

【例6】

> 1. With the publication of the novel, he became <u>famous</u> as the greatest writer living then, and he has been <u>more and more famous</u> as a major American author ever since. He is now also becoming <u>more and more famous</u> with Chinese readers.
> 2. With the publication of the novel, he became <u>famous</u> as the greatest writer living then, and his <u>reputation</u> as a major American author has been <u>on the increase</u> ever since. He is now also becoming <u>more and more popular</u> with Chinese readers.

> 【分析】第1段中表示"闻名"使用的都是同一个词"famous",给人感觉单调乏味,缺少文采;而第2段中则使用了"famous"、"reputation"和"popular"三个词性不同、意义接近的词来表达"闻名"的意思,而且"on the increase"和"more and more"表达的也是同样的意思,这样就避免了用语的重复,表达灵活生动,颇具文采。

二、遣词用语形象生动

　　文章的形象生动是由多方面因素决定的,遣词用语也是一个重要的方面。要做到选词形象生动,主要应注意以下几个方面:

1. 选用具体明确的词

　　在特定的语境下,要根据表"情"达"意"的需要,尽量选用含义比较形象具体的词来取代那些含义比较抽象的词,也就是要从一般趋于特定、由抽象趋于具体、由模糊趋于明确。

【例7】

> 1. No one <u>saw</u> the bank being broken into.
> 2. No one <u>witnessed</u> the bank being broken into.

> 【分析】see 表示"看,看见",意思比较抽象,范围较大;而 witness 则强调"亲眼目睹",描述的动作更为具体生动,更符合"目睹银行抢劫"这一具体的语境。

2. 利用不同的词类

英语和汉语在词性的运用上有很大区别,但很多考生往往受汉语思维的影响,经常完全依据汉语的词性对译英文,导致作文中出现多个谓语动词集结的错误或造出来的句子十分生硬死板。因此,考生在平时训练时一定要注意摆脱汉语思维的束缚,学会根据具体的语境活用不同的词类,这样才能写出地道生动的句子。

1) 抽象名词的使用

【例8】

1. They are written in plain language so that everyone can read when they want to entertain or relax themselves.
2. They are written in plain language so that everyone can read for entertainment or relaxation.

【分析】第2句中用抽象名词 entertainment 和 relaxation 代替了第1句中的动词 entertain 和 relax,将时间状语从句简化成介词短语,使句子表达更加简洁地道。

2) 形容词的使用

【例9】

1. Piracy has become a phenomenon that can be seen everywhere.
2. Piracy has become a prevailing phenomenon.

【分析】第2句中用具体的形容词 prevailing 代替了第1句中的定语从句,更加形象生动地描述了这种现象。

3) 介词短语的使用

【例10】

1. To start with, pirated products often cost much less than the original ones, so they enjoy unbeatable advantage in price though their quality is relatively poor.
2. To start with, pirated products often cost much less than the original ones, so they enjoy unbeatable advantage in price despite their relatively poor quality.

【分析】第1句中的让步状语从句并不强调动作,只是一种存在的事实;而第2句用介词短语"despite…"代替了该从句,句子结构更加简化,表达上更加体现出英语味道。

3. 动态动词的使用

要做到选词形象生动,还要注意选择具有动态意义的词,这些表示具体动作的动态动词往往比 be, there be, make, need 等静态动词更有活力,可以达到更好的写作效果。

【例11】

1. There are various answers among different groups of people.
2. Answers vary among different groups of people.

【分析】第1句中使用的 there be 句型属典型的静态表达;第2句中则使用了动词词组 vary,明显比第1句多了一分动态的生气。

4. 注意词语的感情色彩

英语中许多词带有自己的感情色彩,有褒义词、中性词和贬义词之分。选词时必须注意这种区分,否则会因褒贬失宜而造成用词不当,影响句子的准确表达。

另外,除了褒贬之分,词语还带有很多其他的感情色彩,如有的明快,有的凝重,有的有讽刺意味,有的带有幽默色彩。如能够恰当运用,无疑会使表达更加形象生动。

【例12】

I am firm, you are stubborn, he is pig-headed.

【分析】firm, stubborn 和 pig-headed 三个词都有"不轻易改变决定"的意思,firm 通常是褒义词,意为"坚定";stubborn 通常是中性词,意为"固执,执着";而 pig-headed 通常是贬义词,意为"顽固,僵化",使用时要注意根据具体的语境选择合适的词。

三、开头结尾突破常规

1. 开头的写法

文章的开头除了要表明主题外,还有一个重要的任务就是吸引阅卷老师的注意。因此,开头一定要具有与众不

同的吸引力,这样才能给阅卷老师留下深刻的印象。下面介绍几种实用有效的开头方式及常用句型:

1)现象法

所谓现象法,就是在文章开头就指出某种社会现象或问题。这种开头方式在六级写作中十分常见,主要应用于现象解释型作文和问题解决型作文。

【常用句式】

① Recently / Presently the phenomenon / issue / problem of… has been brought into focus / aroused public attention / become a heated topic / been in the limelight.

② With…, there arises a heated debate as to…

③ With the steady / rapid / amazing development of…, people begin to…

④ In the past… years, many… have been faced / troubled / confronted with…

⑤ Nowadays / Recently, one of the hottest / most popular topics / problems many people complain / concern / talk / discuss about is…

⑥ Nowadays, our society is witnessing more and more…

⑦ In the past… years, there has been a sharp / dramatic increase / growth / rise / decline in … According to an official report / survey / poll, …

⑧ In recent… years, … has experienced an alarming increase / growth / rise / decline in…

【例 13】

Nowadays, one of the hottest problems many people complain about now is piracy. Books, tapes, VCDs and other high-tech products have been pirated. For instance, when a new product comes onto market, most probably, its pirated version will soon show up in the market, too.

【分析】本段文字是关于如何解决盗版问题的文章开头,运用了现象法,段首句使用了句式⑤。

2)对立法

所谓对立法,就是引出人们对要讨论问题的不同看法和观点,然后提出自己的看法或者表明自己偏向哪一看法。这种开头方式一般用于有争议的主题,主要适用于对比选择型作文。

【常用句式】

① When asked…, a great / vast majority of people / most… say that… But I think / view quite differently. / But in my eyes / view, …

② When it comes to…, some people believe that…, but some others argue / claim that… (the opposite / reverse is true). There is probably some truth in both arguments / statements, but… (I tend to agree to / would prefer the former / latter.)

③ Now, it is commonly / generally / widely believed / held / acknowledged that…. They claim / believe / argue that … But I wonder / doubt whether…

④ Nowadays there is no agreement among people as to…. Some people focus on / advocate / favor… while others may think…. (From my point of view, …)

⑤ When faced with / In the face of… quite a few people claim that…, but other people argue…

⑥ There is much discussion / public debate / controversy nowadays as to the problem of…. Some people say that… Others hold that…

⑦ There is a general debate over the phenomenon of …. People who are against / object to it claim / hold …. But people who advocate it, on the other hand, claim / argue …

⑧ The value of this form of… is now being questioned by… /There is growing skepticism toward…

【例 14】

Nowadays there is no agreement among people as to the best measure of a country's success. Some people focus on rich economy while others may think the quality of life has nothing to do with money.

【分析】本段文字是关于什么是国家成功的标准的文章开头,运用了对立法,段首句使用了句式④。

3)观点法

所谓观点法,就是开门见山,直截了当地提出本文要论证的观点或要解决的问题。这种开头方式主要适于观点论证型作文和问题解决型作文。

【常用句式】

① Now there is a growing awareness /recognition of the necessity to…/ Now people are becoming increasingly a-ware/ conscious of the importance of…

② It is true that…. No one can deny …

③ …, which has been generally accepted. The truth of it is deep and profound / self-evident.

④ Now people in growing / significant numbers are beginning / coming to realize / accept / be aware that…

⑤ Nowhere in… / Never in history has the issue / change / idea of… been more evident / visible / popular / serious than in…

⑥ Perhaps / Maybe we should / it is time to rethink / reexamine / have a fresh look at the idea / value / attitude / wisdom / desirability that…

【例 15】

"Haste makes waste"—a proverb full of logic, <u>which has been generally accepted</u>. It tells us that we have to do some steady and down-to-earth work if we want to accomplish something. <u>The truth of it is deep and profound.</u>

【分析】本段文字是关于"欲速则不达"的文章开头,运用了观点法,段首句使用了句式③。

4) 比较法

所谓比较法,就是通过对过去、现在两种不同的倾向、观点进行比较,从而引出文章要讨论的观点。一般来说,对过去的观点都只是一笔带过,而将写作的重点放在现在的即文章要讨论的观点上。这种开头方式主要适用于观点论证型作文。

【常用句式】

① For years, …had been viewed as… But people are taking a fresh look now. With the growing / development of …, people…

② People used to think that… (In the past, …) But people don't share this view now.

③ It is a tradition / custom / practice / traditional way… But now / in recent decades things have changed.

【例 16】

<u>It is a custom</u> for the Chinese to get married with a person with the same family background, regardless of the fact they may actually do not love each other. <u>But in the recent decades things have changed.</u> Chinese young people now tend to consider love to be the only factor to decide whether they will get married with someone or not.

【分析】本段文字是关于中国人对待婚姻的观念发生改变的文章开头,运用了比较法,段首句使用了句式③。

5) 问题法

所谓问题法,就是先将要讨论的问题进行设问,然后在解答的过程中引出观点。这样开头的好处在于从一开始就能引起读者的兴趣,但需要注意的是,如果问题设计不好,就会导致首段中心不突出,主题句表达苍白等负面效果,因此使用时要慎重。这种开头方式主要适用于对比选择型作文和现象解释型作文。

【常用句式】

① Should /What…? Opinions of / Attitudes towards / Answers to… vary widely / greatly / from person to person. Some… are favor of / view / regard / think of…. Others believe / argue / claim…

② "Why do/ have…?" Many … often ask/ pose the question like this.

③ One of the basic/ hot topic facing our society is：What /Why…?

④ How do you think of the problem of…? In seeking answer to this question, …

⑤ Why is there a … in society? It is no easy task to identify the causes for it.

【例 17】

<u>"Why do we have to learn English while it may be useless after graduation?" Many college students often ask the question like this.</u> Surely it is because they haven't realized the importance of English. They do not know in the international communication, English is always the language to be used.

【分析】本段文字是关于大学生为什么要学英语的文章开头,运用了问题法,段首句使用了句式②。

6) 引用法

所谓引用法,就是在文章开头引用名人名言、箴言、谚语或有代表性的看法,来引出文章要论述的观点。这种方法通过引用切合主题的名言警句,一方面可以突出主题,另一方面也能为文章增加文采,容易给人留下深刻的印象。但是这种开头要求考生必须有一定知识储备,对所使用的名言警句等要运用自如。另外,所引用的名言警句一定要为中心服务,不能单纯为了增加文采而引用。这种开头方式主要适用于观点论证型作文。

【常用句式】

① One of the great /early writers /philosophers /scientists said /wrote /remarked, "…". If this is true / the case, then the present / current view / value / attitude / situation should make us wonder whether…/ ponder over…

② "…". The same idea / complaint / attitude is voiced / echoed / shared by…

③ "…". How often we hear / We are used to hearing / Many people have heard (such) statement / words / complaint like / as this / those.

④ There is a(n) old / popular saying / proverb which goes that…. The truth of it is profound and significant. / Under its simplified cover, a truth is ironically pointed out, that is, …

⑤ One great … had ever said / once remarked, "…". Now it still has a realistic / profound significance. / Now it is still working in our modern society. / Now more and more people share this belief. / The remark is still confirmed by people in today's society. / The remark has been shared by generations. / The view has been echoed by many…

【例 18】

There is an old proverb which goes that the grass is always greener on the other side of the valley. Under its simplified cover, a truth is ironically pointed out, that is, people are not contented with the already blessing situation. On the contrary, we always think that there are people around us who are much more fortunate than us. In fact, this kind of opinion is very dangerous.

【分析】本段文字是关于成功是靠运气还是靠努力奋斗的文章开头,运用了引用法,段首句使用了句式④。

2. 结尾的写法

文章的结尾一般篇幅不宜过长,但却也是决定文章成败的点睛之笔。面对堆积如山的试卷,阅卷老师的精力更多的是放在文章的开头、各段的过渡及文章的结尾。好的结尾,可以增添文章的效果和说服力,加深阅卷老师的印象。一篇文章的结尾是否能够产生最佳效果,关键是能否使用恰当的方法和优秀的句式有效地体现文章主题。

1) 总结法

所谓总结法,就是通过文章前面的讨论分析引出一段总结性的言论,重申文章的中心思想或总结自己的观点,作为全文的结束。这是一种最常见的结尾方式,主要用于观点论证型作文和对比选择型作文。

【常用句式】

① Given the factors that I have just outlined, it is wise to support the statement that…

② From what has been discussed above/ Judging from all evidence offered, we may safely/ undoubtedly draw/ come to/ arrive at the conclusion that …

③ Taking into account all these factors/ In view of the above-mentioned facts, we should draw/ come to/ arrive at the conclusion that…

④ All the available/ conclusive/ reliable/ striking evidence goes to show/ piles up to show that…

⑤ All the evidence/ analysis supports/ warrants an unmistakable/ fair conclusion that…

⑥ All the evidence/ analysis justifies/ confirms an unshakable/ sound view/ idea that…

⑦ All the available/ conclusive/ reliable/ striking evidence points to the fact/ lends support to the view that …

⑧ To sum up/ conclude, …/ The conclusion is self-evident. …

⑨ Weighing up these two arguments, I am for ….

⑩ Taking into account all these factors/ In view of the above-mentioned facts, I prefer …

【例 19】

To conclude, smoking is nothing but evil as it is so harmful to people. All smokers should be taught of the great harm of smoking and be persuaded out of smoking. More importantly, we should protect our children from the harm of smoking through education.

【分析】本段文字是吸烟有害健康的文章结尾,运用了总结法,段首句使用了句式⑧。

2) 后果法

所谓后果法，就是对所讨论的问题或现象可能会产生的后果作出预测或分析。这种后果可能是积极的，也可能是消极的，需根据文章主题而定。这种结尾方式主要适用于问题解决型作文和现象解释型作文。

【常用句式】

① Clearly/Obviously/No doubt, if we do not/cannot…/if we ignore/are blind to…, there is every chance/are chances that…/it is very likely that…

② Any person/nation/society who/which ignores/is blind to/fails to learn… would pay a heavy price.

③ Fortunately, however, more and more people come to realize the importance of… and improvement is in near future.

④ If we work on… from now on, in foreseeable future, we will not be perplexed/cursed/overwhelmed by the same dilemma/problem.

⑤ If we can solve the problem with no efforts spared, human being will not be caught/stuck in the same conditions.

⑥ There is no effective/easy solution/approach to the issue/problem of…, but… might be helpful/beneficial./But our commitment will be rewarded as long as we insist on assuming our responsibility on it.

⑦ Following these methods may not guarantee the success in…, but the pay-off will be worth the sweat we shed.

⑧ The effect that… will bring about are far-reaching.

【例20】

All these things come to one simple fact: people are always trying very hard to get a better life. Any nation which ignores the importance of developing its productivity and consequently improving the life of its people would have to pay a heavy price.

【分析】本段文字是关于要重视提高人们生活水平的文章结尾，运用了后果法，段首句使用了句式②。

3) 呼吁法

所谓呼吁法，就是在文章结尾敦促或呼吁读者作出努力，对某问题予以关注或采取行动。但是需要注意的是，不能空感口号，这样会使文章显得空洞，不伦不类。这种结尾方式主要适用于问题解决型作文。

【常用句式】

① It is high time that we…/It is ripe time for us to… in no half-hearted manner.

② It is essential/necessary/important/imperative that effective/quick/proper measures/actions/steps/remedies should be taken to…

③ If there is time to…, it is now.

④ To reverse the trend is not a light task, and it requires keen consciousness of…

⑤ There is no denying that considerable attention must be paid to the plight of…

⑥ We must call for an immediate action/method, because the current tendency of …, if permitted to develop at will, it will result in the destruction of …

⑦ Only when… all go into action can we…

【例21】

It is high time that we took some measures to protect our environment. Government should make a law to punish those polluting our environment, and the public should realize the importance of environmental protection.

【分析】本段文字是关于如何保护社会环境的文章结尾，运用了呼吁法，段首句使用了句式①。

需要注意的是，结尾一定要与主题相匹配，切忌谈一些与主题无关的内容。另外，除了以上方法，结尾也可采用引用法和提出建议法。而且在实际写作时，可以不必局限于一种方法，要根据实际情况将几种方法有效结合。

四、适当运用修辞手法

1. 比喻

六级写作中常用的比喻手法是明喻和暗喻。明喻要使用诸如 like, as 之类的比喻词。另外，as if, as though, as… as, similar to 等也可以表示明喻。暗喻一般不用比喻词，只是用 be 动词表示比喻对象的相似性。

【例22】

Working in big companies is similar to the role played by a screw in a big machine.
在大公司工作的人就像是大机器上的一颗螺丝钉。

【分析】本句运用了明喻的修辞手法,形象生动地描述了在大公司工作的情形。

2. 平行结构

平行结构指的是将结构相同或相似、意义并重、语气一致的语言成份并行排列的一种修辞手法。这种结构层次清晰、语意顺畅,能够起到加强语气、增强表达效果的作用。

【例23】

If you promise to help when you should say "No", you may in the end fail to keep your promise and lose your friend's trust. On the other hand, even if you have succeeded in fulfilling your friend's will, you may feel depressed because you must have put in too much energy or money. You may even become a criminal if you help to do something.

【分析】本段文字将三个结构相似的句子并行排行,三个句子层层深入,表现出很强的逻辑性。

3. 修辞问句

修辞问句以提问形式出现,却并不表示疑问,其目的是为了引起读者注意或表示强调。一般可分为设问和反问两种形式。

设问一般自问自答,答案紧随在问题之后;反问一般只问不答,答案就蕴含在问句当中。

【例24】

1. Will so-called lucky numbers really bring people good luck? I don't think so.
2. So far as the present situation is concerned, is it a good or bad thing to open the university campus for tourists? Different people have their own opinions.

【分析】以上两句话均运用了设问的修辞手法,答案紧随其后。

【例25】

1. Why not work together to put an end to such immoral behaviors?
2. Isn't it high time we eliminated fake commodities from the market?

【分析】以上两句话均运用了反问的修辞手法,答案即在问句之中。

4. 重复

重复主要起到强调、渲染和号召的作用。常见的重复方式主要有两种:同成分重复和同义重复。

【例26】

We, though different in colors, different in languages, and different in cultures, can bind together to fulfill any tough mission.

【分析】本句运用了同成分重复的修辞手法,起到了突出强调的作用。

5. 夸张

夸张是一种故意言过其实,或夸大或缩小事物的形象,突出事物的某种特征或品质,鲜明地表达思想情感的修辞方式。

【例27】

I have got a million reasons to object to your proposal.

【分析】本句运用了夸张的修辞手法,突出强调"理由非常充分"。

五、恰当使用警句格言

如果能在文章中恰当地引用一两句警句格言或名人名言,不但能起到支持和突出主题的作用,还会大大增加文章的文采,达到意想不到地表达效果。

【例28】

As an old Chinese saying goes, traveling ten thousand miles and reading ten thousand books is the top ideal for people. Travel does broaden our horizon. It enables us to appreciate beautiful scenery, value the culture and customs of a people and learn the history.

【分析】本段话是一篇文章的开头段,通过"traveling ten thousand miles and reading ten thousand books is the top ideal for people(行万里路,读万卷书)"人人认同的格言引出"旅游开阔视野"的主题,令人信服,且颇显文采。

Exercise 　　　即讲即练

作文一

Directions： *For this part, you are allowed 30 minutes to write an essay entitled* **Is Study Pressure Good for University Students?** *You should write at least 150 words following the outline given below:*

1)对于高校学习压力的影响,大学生的观点各不相同
2)你的观点,并说明原因
3)你的建议

Is Study Pressure Good for University Students?

①When it comes to whether study pressure is good for university students, there is no complete agreement among people. ②Some students think that too much pressure do harm to their study life. ③They think pressure may make them feel they are not free and have no enough place. ④In addition, too much pressure will do harm to their physical health. (提出观点段)

⑤However, others believe that pressure is a driving force that encourages them to work hard. ⑥They think that pressure does good because pressure can let them know their own ability and the reality, which make them have more force to solve difficulty. ⑦So they believe pressure can do more good than harm. (对比论证段)

⑧Personally, I am in favor with the latter opinion. ⑨Modern society is full of competition. ⑩If the students are not used to working under pressure, they will not gain a position in the society full of competition. ⑪Taking above-mentioned factors into consideration, I may reasonably conclude that pressure is good for university students. (总结观点段)

要求:请按照下面的提示对左栏的作文进行优化改写。

1. 用 harm 的另一种词性改写句②,避免重复,使表达更加生动。

2. 用同义短语代替句③中的 they think,避免重复;用同义词代替句③中的 place,使表达准确。

3. 用同义短语代替句④中的 too much pressure,避免重复。

4. 用 regard 改写句⑤,使表达更加生动。

5. 用同义词代替句⑥中的 think,避免重复;用同义词或短语代替句⑥中的 does good 避免重复,并使表达更加生动;用更加动态的动词或短语替换句⑥中的 make them have more force,使表达更加生动;用同义短语代替句⑥中的 know,使表达更加生动;用同义短语代替句⑥中的 solve,使搭配正确。

6. 用恰当的介词替换句⑧中的 with,使搭配正确。

7. 用同义短语代替句⑩中的 in the society full of competition,避免重复。

Is Study Pressure Good for University Students?

_____

_____

作文二

Directions： *For this part, you are allowed 30 minutes to write an essay entitled* **How to Make Friends.** *You should write at least 150 words following the outline given below:*

1)朋友对任何人都很重要,但是有的人认为结交朋友很难
2)"我"认为怎样才能交到朋友

①As we know, it is very miserable for a man to live alone in the world. ②In fact, there are many things in life we alone cannot do. ③Friends are people who are willing and ready to help us when we meet trouble and show sympathy for us if we are in misery. ④Therefore, it is necessary for us to know the ways by which we can make friends. (描述问题段)

⑤In order to make friends, first, we must think more of others than we think of ourselves and never judge a person by his appearance and clothes. ⑥Second, we must be honest, noble-minded and have a kind heart so that we can leave a favorable impression for others since other people observe us the same way as we observe them. (说明方法段)

⑦As far as I am concerned, all the splendor in the world is not worth of a good friend. ⑧A good friend can give me suggestions in my work and life. ⑨They can also do what he can to forward me in the path to success. ⑩All in all, friends are indispensable in our life. (总结观点段)

要求:请按照下面的提示对左栏的作文进行优化改写。

1. 用谚语"One man is not good enough to live alone in the world."改写句①。
2. 用同义词或短句代替句②中的 in fact 和 do,使表达更加生动。
3. 将句③中的形容词 willing 和 ready 改成其相应的副词,并将该句改写成一个含有平行结构的句子。
4. 将句④改写成一个简单句,避免赘言,使句子表达更加清晰。
5. 删去句⑤中多余的成分。
6. 适当改变句⑥主句中 and 前后部分的形式,使结构平行;用恰当的介词替换句⑥中 impression 后面的 for;删去句⑥中多余的成分。
7. 用 not only…but (also)…连接的平行结构改写句⑦和句⑧;删去句⑦中多余的成分。

How to Make Friends

_____
_____
_____
_____

【参考范文】

作文一

Is Study Pressure Good for University Students?

①When it comes to whether study pressure is good for university students, there is no complete agreement among people. ②Some students think that too much pressure do harm to their study life. ③They think pressure may make them feel they are not free and have no enough place. ④In addition, too much pressure will do harm to their physical health. (提出观点段)

⑤However, others believe that pressure is a driving force that encourages them to work hard. ⑥They think that pressure does good because pressure can let them know their own ability and the reality, which make them have more force to solve difficulty. ⑦So they believe pressure can do more good than harm. (对比论证段)

⑧Personally, I am in favor with the latter opinion. ⑨Modern society is full of competition. ⑩If the students are not used to working under pressure, they will not gain a position in the society full of competition. ⑪Taking above-mentioned factors into consideration, I may reasonably conclude that pressure is good for university students. (总结观点段)

Is Study Pressure Good for University Students?

When it comes to whether study pressure is good for university students, there is no complete agreement among people. Some students <u>argue</u> that too much pressure <u>is harmful to</u> their academic life. <u>In their opinion</u>, pressure may make them feel they are not free and have no enough <u>space</u>. In addition, <u>excessive tension</u> will do harm to their physical health. (提出观点段)

However, others <u>regard pressure as a driving force</u> that encourages them to work hard. They <u>hold</u> that pressure <u>is beneficial</u> because pressure can let them <u>be aware of</u> their own ability and the reality, which <u>give them</u> more power to <u>overcome</u> difficulty. So they believe pressure can do more good than harm. (对比论证段)

Personally, I am in favor <u>of</u> the latter opinion. Modern society is full of competition. If the students are not used to working under pressure, they will not gain a room <u>in the competitive society</u>. Taking above mentioned factors into consideration, I may reasonably conclude that pressure is good for university students. (总结观点段)

作文二

How to Make Friends

①As we know, it is very miserable for a man to live alone in the world. ②In fact, there are many things in life we alone cannot do. ③Friends are people who are willing and ready to help us when we meet trouble and show sympathy for us if we are in misery. ④Therefore, it is necessary for us to know the ways by which we can make friends.（描述问题段）

⑤In order to make friends, first, we must think more of others than we think of ourselves and never judge a person by his appearance and clothes. ⑥Second, we must be honest, noble-minded and have a kind heart so that we can leave a favorable impression for others since other people observe us the same way as we observe them.（说明方法段）

⑦As far as I am concerned, all the splendor in the world is not worth of a good friend. ⑧A good friend can give me suggestions in my work and life. ⑨They can also do what he can to forward me in the path to success. ⑩All in all, friends are indispensable in our life.（总结观点段）

How to Make Friends

There is an old proverb which goes that "One man is not good enough to live alone in the world." The truth of it is profound and significant. Indeed, there are many things in life we alone cannot preform. Friends are people who willingly and readily help us when we are in trouble and show sympathy for us when we are in misery. Therefore, it is necessary for us to know how to make friends.（描述问题段）

In order to make friends, first, we must think more of others than of ourselves and never judge a person by his appearance and clothes. Second, we must be honest, noble-minded and kind-hearted whereby to leave a favorable impression on others since other people observe us the same way as we do.（说明方法段）

As far as I am concerned, all the splendor in the world is not worth a good friend. A good friend can not only give me suggestions in my work and life, but do what he can to forward me in the path to success. All in all, friends are indispensable in our life.（总结观点段）

短文写作巅峰练习 第二章

Exercise 1

Directions: *For this part, you are allowed 30 minutes to write a composition on the topic:* **Talent Shows.** *You should write at least 150 words, and base your composition on the chart and the outline given in Chinese below:*

1) 近年来选秀节目层出不穷
2) 产生这种现象的原因
3) 我的看法

Talent Shows

_____

_____

_____

Exercise 2

Directions: *For this part, you are allowed 30 minutes to write a composition on the topic:* **How Can We Get to Know the World outside the Campus?** *You should write at least 150 words, and base your composition on the chart and the outline given in Chinese below:*

1) 时代在发展,当代大学生需要同社会接轨
2) 在校大学生了解社会的途径

How Can We Get to Know the World outside the Campus?

_____

_____

_____

Exercise 3

Directions: *For this part, you are allowed 30 minutes to write a letter of reference for your student Wang Wei. You should write at least 150 words according to the outline given below:*

1) 你曾是 Wang Wei 的老师
2) 点明写信缘由,介绍 Wang We 的学习表现及性格品质
3) 希望 Wang We 的申请被考虑

Reference for Wang Wei

_____

_____

_____

Exercise 4

Directions: *For this part, you are allowed 30 minutes to write a composition on the topic:* **Importance of Social Skills.** *You should write at least 150 words, and base your composition on the chart and the outline given in Chinese below:*

1) 人们需要掌握一定的社交技巧
2) 掌握社交技巧的重要性

Importance of Social Skills

_____

_____

Exercise 5

Directions: *For this part, you are allowed 30 minutes to write a composition on the topic:* **Is Income Gap a Good Thing?** *You should write at least 150 words, and base your composition on the chart and the outline given in Chinese below:*

1) 收入差距悬殊是当前社会的一种现象
2) 人们对此褒贬不一
3) 我的看法

Is Income Gap a Good Thing?

_____

_____

参考范文

Exercise 1

【思路点拨】

　　本题属于提纲式文字命题。提纲第 1 点要求指出目前社会上出现的一种现象,提纲第 2 点要求分析产生这种现象的原因,提纲第 3 点要求说明"我"个人的看法,由此可判断本文属于现象解释型作文。

　　根据所给提纲,本文应包含以下内容:描述近年来选秀节目层出不穷的现象;说明产生这种现象的原因;"我"个人对此的看法。

【参考范文】

Talent Shows

　　TV has been one medium of communication that has connected millions, and it is this link that makes talent shows on the tube amazingly influential. Young faces conveying disappointment or even overwhelming joy have become a common sight on as many channels as your remote allows you to surf. (描述现象段)

　　Why talent show is so popular nowadays? For one thing, while most of the ordinary people have long dreamed of being a star without knowing how, this kind of program enables everyone to take part in and have an opportunity to be a real star. For another, in terms of business, the increasing popularity of talent shows has helped the channels gain huge profits by way of advertising and promotions. As a result, more and more similar shows come into being to attract more eyeballs. (说明原因段)

　　As far as I am concerned, it is a wonderful feeling and a great way to relax by watching talent shows and see ordinary people like myself become famous. As long as talent shows are entertaining and inspiring us, it does make sense to keep and encourage them. (总结观点段)

Exercise 2

【思路点拨】

本题属于提纲式文字命题。提纲第1点要求阐述大学生需要同社会接轨的时代要求,提纲第2点要求分析大学生如何了解社会,由此判断本文属于问题解决型作文。

根据所给提纲,本文应包含以下内容:阐述当代大学生需要同社会接轨;分析大学生了解社会的途径有哪些;总结全文。

【参考范文】

How Can We Get to Know the World outside the Campus?

With the rapid development of our society, the campus is no longer an "Ivory Tower". We students must get in touch with the world outside the campus so that we can adapt ourselves to society more quickly when graduating. However, how can we get to know the society when studying in the campus? (描述问题段)

Firstly, we can keep ourselves informed by TV, radio broadcasts or newspapers in order to get a general knowledge of the society we are living in. In addition, we can turn to help to the friends or relatives who have work for several years, and they can give us some useful advice on what qualification we should bear before stepping into the society. Then, we can have a goal in mind without puzzling when graduating. Moreover, we can make good use of the vacations to find a part-time job, from which not only can we combine the knowledge with the practice, but learn many valuable experiences we can't obtain in the campus. (说明方法段)

Being a college student of modern society, we have to keep up with the development of the country, and also keep in contact with the society to be a useful person in the future. (总结全文段)

Exercise 3

【思路点拨】

本题要求写一封推荐信。根据所给提纲,本文应包含以下内容:自己与 Wang Wei 的关系;介绍 Wang Wei 的优点和优秀表现;极力推荐 Wang Wei 并希望对方接受。

【参考范文】

Reference for Wang Wei

July 30. 2007

To Whom It May Concern,

I take great pleasure in recommending Wang Wei, one of my favorite students, for admission into your distinguished graduate program. I got to know him personally when he was taking the course—Methodology of Management Research, a course I taught. To my knowledge, Wang Wei is a very excellent student.

His performance in the study was outstanding. Wang Wei showed great aptitude on my course and other courses. Undoubtedly, he got excellent scores on the courses and ranked among the top five of his class. He is not only strong in academics, but also in sports and social activities. He was the captain of the soccer team of North-western University (NWU) and led the team to play in the soccer league of our university for two successive years. He was also one of the main founders of the first academic club of NWU. I am confident that Mr. Caleb will contribute greatly to your program as well as he did in the NWU.

Therefore, I feel very delighted to recommend him to you with all my heart. He will improve he is the right person. Please don't hesitate to contact me if you need more information.

Sincerely yours,

Wang Xiaobin

Dean

Exercise 4

【思路点拨】

本题属于提纲式文字命题。提纲第1点要求阐述人们需要掌握一定的社交技巧,提纲第2点要求论证掌握社交技巧的重要性,由此可判断本文属于观点论证型作文。

　　根据所给提纲,本文应包含以下内容:阐述人们需要掌握一定的社交技巧;论证掌握社交技巧的重要性;重申论点,强调其正确性。

【参考范文】

Importance of Social Skills

　　Many smart people with the best education may fail as ordinary people. They do not fail for lack of knowledge, but rather, more often than not, for only one simple reason—the lack of social skills. Therefore, certain knowledge of social skills seems not only useful but necessary.(提出观点段)

　　To begin with, proper social skills were essential to one's future careers. In Chinese schools, we overemphasize academic achievements and neglect the development of social skills. After graduation, you may have great academic intelligence and still lack social intelligence—the ability to make friends, to be sensitive to the feelings of the others, to give and take criticism well. People with high social intelligence know how to build team work and take leadership, and they may be appreciated well by the boss and promoted quickly. Besides, gaining proper social skills can help to promote one's self-image and make many friends. When you get along with others in a polite and conversable manner, you may find yourself being liked and respected as well.(论证观点段)

　　Social intelligence is so important that we should develop such skills conscientiously. Like good manners, they can after all be learned. If we have academic and social intelligence, we must have a brighter and happier life.(总结观点段)

Exercise 5

【思路点拨】

　　本题属于提纲式文字命题。提纲第 1 点要求指出目前社会上出现的一种现象,提纲第 2 点要求说明人们对此现象持两种不同的观点,提纲第 3 点要求阐述个人对此现象的看法,由此可判断本文属于对比选择型作文。

　　根据所给提纲,本文应包含以下内容:描述当今社会出现贫富差距这一普遍现象;说明人们对此正反两方面的态度;阐述"我"对此现象的看法。

【参考范文】

Is Income Gap a Good Thing?

　　Now the income gap is getting wider and wider. In some privately owned firms, joint-ventures, or foreign-funded companies, an executive's yearly income is ten times or even a hundred times as much as an ordinary worker's. However, is income gap a good thing?(提出观点段)

　　Faced with this situation, people will undoubtedly have different opinions. Some believe that it benefits the social and economic development since driving force is often derived from the gap. In other words, the gap inspires people and gives a push to advancement. Others speak of its side effect: income gap is often the root of social unrest and also contrary to our country's principle.(对比论证段)

　　From my point of view, while it is true that the income may stimulate the social development to some extent, it causes trouble as well. An income gap that is too wide for most people to bear can neither contribute to the stability of a country nor promote its economic development. Therefore, while we are advocating the rapid development of our country, we should tolerate the narrow income gap but narrow the wide one.(总结观点段)

第五篇

巅 峰 预 测

第43－45天

Part 5

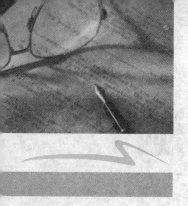

预 测 试 题 一

Part I Writing (30 minutes)

Directions: *For this part, you are allowed 30 minutes to write a composition on the topic:* **Brain Drain.** *You should write at least 150 words, and base your composition on the outline given in Chinese below:*

1)近年来中国人才流失的现象十分严重
2)产生这种现象的原因
3)你对此现象的看法

Brain Drain

_____

_____

Part II Reading Comprehension (Skimming and Scanning) (15 minutes)

Directions: *In this part, you will have 15 minutes to go over the passage quickly and answer the questions on Answer Sheet 1.*

For questions 1—4, mark

Y (for YES) if the statement agrees with the information given in the passage;

N (for NO) if the statement contradicts the information given in the passage;

NG (for NOT GIVEN) if the information is not given in the passage.

For questions 5—10, complete the sentences with the information given in the passage.

The Good Journalism:
Why Democracy Needs Investigative Journalism

In the 1970s, reporters played critical roles in revealing what became the most serious U. S. political scandal in the post-World War Ⅱ period. Washington journalists pursued the clues left at a petty burglary in the Watergate office building, following them all the way to the White House. The reportage led to congressional investigations and the ultimate resignation of President Richard Nixon.

The performance of the press during Watergate was held as the mirror that reflected the best that journalism could offer to democracy: holding power accountable. It became a trend in American newsrooms. The profession enjoyed high credibility in the years that followed, and a remarkable increase in journalism school enrollment occurred.

Almost three decades later, the situation has changed. Investigative journalism does not seem to be the brightest star in the *firmament* (太空) of American news. If the tone of the press was self-congratulatory in the post-Watergate years, pessimism about the state of American journalism is currently widespread. Observers have often argued that increasing media ownership concentration and the drive to sensationalize news coverage have *sapped* (侵蚀) the vigor that investigative reporting requires. Business pressures also deter investigative reporting. Its demands for a great deal of time, human and financial resources frequently conflict with profit expectations and production cost controls. Also, the fact that stories might result in expensive lawsuits makes news companies nervous about supporting investigations. Notwithstanding these factors, there has been no shortage of investigative stories produced in the past decade. Major urban newspapers in the United States have produced articles that have revealed corruption, injustice, and environmental mismanagement.

What Is Investigative Journalism?

Investigative reporting is distinctive in that it publicizes information about wrongdoing that affects the public interest. Denunciations result from the work of reporters rather than from information leaked to newsrooms.

While investigative journalism used to be associated with lone reporters working on their own with little, if any, support from their news organizations, recent examples prove that teamwork is fundamental. Differing kinds of expertise are needed to produce well-documented and comprehensive stories. Reporters, editors, legal specialists, statistical analysts, librarians, and news researchers are needed to collaborate on investigations. Knowledge of public information access laws is crucial to find what information is potentially available under "freedom of information" laws, and what legal problems might arise when damaging information is published. New technologies are extremely valuable to find facts and to make reporters familiar with the complexities of any given story.

Democracy and Investigative Journalism

Investigative journalism matters because of its many contributions to democratic governance. Its role can be understood in keeping with the Fourth Estate model of the press. According to this model, the press should make government accountable by publishing information about matters of public interest even if such information reveals abuses or crimes committed by those in authority. From this perspective, investigative reporting is one of the most important contributions that the press makes to democracy. It is linked to the logic of check and balances in democratic systems. It provides a valuable mechanism for monitoring the performance of democratic institutions as they are most broadly defined to include governmental bodies, civic organizations and publicly held corporations.

The centrality of the media in contemporary democracies makes political elites sensitive to news, particularly to "bad" news that often causes a public commotion. The publication of news about political and economic wrongdoing can trigger congressional and judicial investigations. In cases when government institutions fail to conduct further inquiries, or investigations are plagued with problems and suspicions, journalism can contribute to accountability by monitoring the functioning of these institutions. It can examine how well these institutions actually fulfill their constitutional *mandate* (要求) to govern responsibly in the face of press reports that reveal dysfunction, dishonesty, or wrongdoing in government and society. At minimum, investigative reporting retains important agenda-setting powers to remind citizens and political elites about the existence of certain issues.

Investigative journalism also contributes to democracy by nurturing an informed citizenry. Information is a vital resource to empower a vigilant public that ultimately holds government accountable through voting and participation. With the ascent of media-centered politics in contemporary democracies, the media have *eclipsed* (超越) other social institutions as the main source of information about issues and processes that affect citizens' lives.

Public Access

Access to public records and laws ensuring that public business will be conducted in open sessions is indispensable to the work of an investigative journalist. When prior *censorship* (审查制度) or defamation laws loom on the horizon, news organizations are unlikely to take up controversial subjects because of potentially expensive lawsuits. Consequently, democracies must meet certain requirements for investigative journalism to be effective and to provide diverse and comprehensive information.

The Ethics of Investigative Journalism

Every team of investigative reporters pursues a story under different circumstances, so creating an all-purpose ethical rulebook is problematic, though certain standards have become generally accepted. The legal implications of reporters' actions are, by far, more clear-cut than ethical issues. If the law approves it, it is legal; if it doesn't, it is not. Ethics, instead, deals with how to distinguish between right and wrong, with philosophical principles used to justify a particular course of action. Any decision can be judged ethical, depending on what ethical framework is used to justify it, and what values are prioritized. What journalists and editors need to determine is who will benefit as a result of the reporting.

If journalism is committed to democratic accountability, then the question that needs to be asked is whether the public benefits as a result of investigative reports. Whose interest does investigative journalism serve by publishing a given story? Does the press fulfill its social responsibility in revealing wrongdoing? Whose interests are being affected? Whose rights are being invaded? Is the issue at stake a matter of legitimate public interest? Or is individual privacy being invaded when no crucial public issue is at stake?

Most discussions about ethics in investigative journalism have focused on methodology, namely, is any method valid to reveal wrongdoing? Is deception legitimate when journalists aim to tell the truth? Is any method justifiable no matter the working conditions and the difficulties in getting information? Can television reporters use hidden cameras to get a story? Can journalists use false identities to gain access to information?

On this point, an important factor to consider is that the public seems less willing than journalists to accept any method to reveal wrongdoing. Surveys show that the public is suspicious of invasion of privacy, no matter the public relevance of a story. The public generally seems less inclined to accept that journalists should use any method to get a story. Such an attitude is significantly revealing in times when, in many countries, the credibility of the press is low. The press needs to be trustworthy in the eyes of the public. That is its main capital, but too often its actions further undermine its credibility. Therefore, the fact that citizens generally believe that journalists would get any story at any cost needs to be an important consideration. Exposes that rely on questionable methods to get information can further diminish the legitimacy and public standing of the reporting and the journalists.

Ethical issues are not limited to methods. Corruption is also another important ethical issue in investigative journalism. Corruption includes a variety of practices, ranging from journalists who accept bribes, or quash exposes, or pay sources for information. The harm to private citizens that might result from what's reported also needs to be considered. Issues of privacy usually come to the forefront, as investigative journalism often walks a fine line between the right to privacy and the public's right to know. It is usually assumed that privacy applies differently to public figures than to average citizens.

1. We can know from the first paragraph that Watergate _____.
   [A] was a serious political scandal　　　　[B] made Richard Nixon notorious
   [C] was unveiled by the U. S. congress　　[D] reflected what journalism could offer to democracy
2. What result did the high credibility of journalism bring to the journalism school?
   [A] Its size enlarged.　　　　　　　　　　[B] Its quality of teaching improved greatly.
   [C] Its management improved.　　　　　　[D] Its number of students increased greatly.
3. For how many years did investigative journalism keep its brightest role in American news?
   [A] More than 40 years.　　　　　　　　　[B] Less than 40 years.
   [C] More than 30 years.　　　　　　　　　[D] Almost 30 years.
4. Compared with the tone of the press in the post-Watergate years, the present tone of the American journalism seems to be _____.
   [A] pessimistic　　　　　　　　　　　　　[B] positive
   [C] self-congratulatory　　　　　　　　　[D] self-cognitive
5. Denunciations are caused by _____.
   [A] the information leaked to newsrooms　[B] the work of reporters
   [C] investigative reporting　　　　　　　[D] the teamwork of reporters
6. Investigative journalism is important because of its contributions to _____.
   [A] public interest　　　　　　　　　　　[B] the complexities of journalism
   [C] democratic systems　　　　　　　　　[D] democratic governance
7. By which way can a well-formed citizenry ultimately hold government accountable?
   [A] Voting and participation.　　　　　　[B] Monitoring government institutions.
   [C] Unearthing government's wrongdoing.　[D] Supporting investigative journalism.
8. Effective investigative journalism depends on the access to _____.
9. Since there is no all-purpose ethical rulebook, what journalists and editors need to do is to determine _____ from their reporting.
10. The public does not willingly accept the practice of revealing wrongdoing by _____.

Part III　Listening Comprehension (35 minutes)
Section A

Directions: *In this section, you will hear 8 short conversations and 2 long conversations. At the end of each conversation, one or more questions will be asked about what was said. Both the conversation and the questions will be spoken only once. After each question there will be a pause. During the pause, you must read the four choices marked* [A] *,* [B] *,* [C] *and* [D] *, and decide which is the best answer. Then mark the corresponding letter on **Answer Sheet 2** with a single line through the centre.*

11. [A] She would go home immediately after work.　　[B] She would go to a party.
　　[C] She would work overtime.　　[D] She would work early in the morning.
12. [A] She misplaced her class card for biology.　　[B] She arrived for registration too early.
　　[C] She missed registration.　　[D] The man can't spell her name.
13. [A] The situation looks better than it is.　　[B] The phone connection was bad.
　　[C] The woman ought to speak to Mary in person.　　[D] It is better to be courageous.
14. [A] Green.　　[B] Yellow.
　　[C] Light blue.　　[D] Brown.
15. [A] To call the police.　　[B] To send a faith healer.
　　[C] To see a counselor.　　[D] To keep quiet.
16. [A] The man can have his camera fixed here.　　[B] She will probably fix the man's camera herself.
　　[C] The man will buy a new camera.　　[D] The camera should have been brought in earlier.
17. [A] At a bookstore.　　[B] At a bank.
　　[C] At a club.　　[D] At a grocery store.
18. [A] Secretary and boss.　　[B] Husband and wife.
　　[C] Old classmates.　　[D] Doctor and patient.

Questions 19 to 21 are based on the conversation you have just heard.

19. [A] Daisy.　　[B] Fresh flowers.
　　[C] Whiskey.　　[D] Sherry.
20. [A] She could be between a half-hour and an hour late.
　　[B] She should be in the cocktail party on time.
　　[C] She could bring without present.
　　[D] She should be active in the cocktail party.
21. [A] For the celebration of New Year.
　　[B] For the celebration of the woman's friend's birthday.
　　[C] For the celebration of the man's friend's wedding.
　　[C] For the celebration of Christmas.

Questions 22 to 25 are based on the conversation you have just heard.

22. [A] Environment.　　[B] Transportation.
　　[C] Culture.　　[D] Weather.
23. [A] It was hot.　　[B] It was cool.
　　[C] It was warm.　　[D] It was surprisingly cold.
24. [A] September.　　[B] August.
　　[C] October.　　[D] November.
25. [A] Golden Gate Park.　　[B] Fishermen's Wharf.
　　[C] Cable car ride.　　[D] Disneyland.

Section B

Directions: *In this section, you will hear 3 short passages. At the end of each passage, you will hear some questions. Both the passage and the questions will be spoken only once. After you hear a question, you must choose the best answer from the four choices marked [A], [B], [C] and [D]. Then mark the corresponding letter on **Answer Sheet 2** with a single line through the center.*

Passage One

Questions 26 to 28 are based on the passage you have just heard.

26. [A] His father.　　[B] His mother.
　　[C] His brother.　　[D] His sister.
27. [A] Florist.　　[B] Tailor.
　　[C] Shoemaker.　　[D] Pageboy.
28. [A] They hated it.　　[B] They were fond of it.
　　[C] They were indifferent to it.　　[D] They criticized it.

Passage Two

Questions 29 to 31 are based on the passage you have just heard.

29. [A] To introduce some secrets of public speaking.
 [B] To inform people the bad symptoms of speech.
 [C] To tell people how to breathe in speech.
 [D] To show people how to speak to a group.
30. [A] To take deep breaths.
 [B] To drink alcohol.
 [C] To fight anxiety directly.
 [D] To practise a lot.
31. [A] It can make the speaker feel fresh.
 [B] It can help the speaker calm down.
 [C] It can make the speaker excited.
 [D] It can lift the speaker's blood pressure.

Passage Three

Questions 32 to 35 are based on the passage you have just heard.

32. [A] Excited.
 [B] Disappointed.
 [C] Satisfied.
 [D] Angry.
33. [A] The abstract of marketing message.
 [B] The exaggeration of marketing message.
 [C] The ambiguity of marketing message.
 [D] The animadversion of marketing message.
34. [A] Be credible.
 [B] Be faithful.
 [C] Be true.
 [D] Be honest.
35. [A] To tell marketers how to get the sale.
 [B] To tell the marketers how to advertise their products.
 [C] To tell the marketers how to communicate with consumers.
 [D] To tell the marketers how to make good products.

Section C

Directions: *In this section, you will hear a passage three times. When the passage is read for the first time, you should listen carefully for its general idea. When the passage is read for the second time, you are required to fill in the blanks numbered from 36 to 43 with the exact words you have just heard. For blanks numbered from 44 to 46 you are required to fill in the missing information. For these blanks, you can either use the exact words you have just heard or write down the main points in your own words. Finally, when the passage is read for the third time, you should check what you have written.*

Health care in Australia relies on private and public facilities: a predominantly private medical profession, private and public hospitals, and private and public health financing. Most (36)_____ health care is provided by private practitioners, who charge their patients directly and set their own (37)_____. Some is provided by the (38)_____ of health centers and public hospitals, who may also exercise their right to practise privately. Patients receive hospital care in either private or public hospitals. The choice is theirs, although most (39)_____ on the advice of their medical practitioners and their health insurance (40)_____. Medicare, the (41)_____ national health financing system, is funded in part by a special *levy*(征税) on income and in part by general (42)_____. It provides access to public hospital services and cash (43)_____ for medical treatment provided out of hospital by medical practitioners.

Under Medicare, public hospitals are funded by the federal and state governments. All permanent Australian residents have access, without direct charge, (44)_____. Private hospitals charge for their services and are funded from the revenue generated. (45)_____. Private health-insurance organizations offer a range of benefits to cover hospital charges. (46)_____.

Part IV　Reading Comprehension (Reading in Depth) (25 minutes)
Section A

Directions: *In this section, there is a short passage with 5 questions or incomplete statements. Read the passage carefully, then answer the questions or complete the statements in the fewest possible words on **Answer Sheet 2**.*

War games are commonly used by the military to evaluate strategies, explore scenarios and reveal unexpected weaknesses. American ships and aircraft have just begun two weeks of war games in the Gulf, prompting protests from Iran, and last week South Korea carried out an annual computerized war-game exercise.

Might war games deserve a greater role in business? Military analogies abound in the corporate world. Plenty of bosses look to Sun Tzu, an ancient Chinese general, for management tips. And in business, as in war, outcomes depend on what others do, as well as one's own actions. Yet many firms fail to think systematically about how rivals will react to their plans — and traditional planning does a poor job of taking competitors' responses into account, says John McDermott, head of strategy at Xerox, an office-equipment company. Corporate war games, which simulate the interactions of multiple actors in a market, provide a better way to do so.

Such games have two chief characteristics. First, players break into teams and take on the roles of fierce competitors (and sometimes other citizens, such as customers). Second, the games involve several turns, allowing competitors not just to draw up their own strategies but to respond to the choices of others. Their popularity is rising. Booz Allen Hamilton (BAH), a consultancy, is running 100 war games a year, up from around 50 three years ago. Open Options, a Canadian strategy consultancy, has been going since 1996 and its revenue doubled last year.

BAH introduces a quantitative element into its games, calculating the effect of each team's strategy on their company's profits and stock market value at the end of each turn. Open Options takes a further step. To help Xerox understand the market dynamics of the print and copy industry, it ran a one-day workshop in which teams from Xerox took the roles of the big companies in the market, itself included. Each team identified the things "their" company could do to change its strategy and drew up a list of its desired outcomes; these "preference trees" were shared with the other teams. The results were then pumped into Open Options' proprietary software tools, which played out interactions between the companies and produced a range of possible outcomes.

Mr McDermott says the game's predictive power was astonishing: one forecast, that a company would start to acquire a certain group of assets within the industry, came true within six months. By shedding light on areas where companies have different priorities, the concept of preference trees helps to highlight potential trade-offs, as well as competition. Open Options charges North American clients roughly $100,000 for an engagement.

47. According to the passage, many CEOs read military book to get _____.

_____

48. According to the passage, traditional corporate planning doesn't do well in _____.

_____

49. In war games a player is provided the chance to make reactions to _____.

_____

50. By _____, the company strategy's effect on his profits can be calculated.

_____

51. "Preference trees" refers to _____ of the companies, which help to highlight potential trade-offs and competition.

_____

Section B

Directions: *There are 2 passages in this section. Each passage is followed by some questions or unfinished statements. For each of them there are four choices marked [A], [B], [C] and [D]. You should decide on the best choice and mark the corresponding letter on **Answer Sheet 2** with a single line through the centre.*

Passage One

Questions 52 to 56 are based on the following passage.

Early intelligence tests were not without their critics. Man enduring concerns were first raised by the influential journalist Walter Lippman, in a series of published debates with Lewis Terman, of Stanford University, the father of IQ testing in America. Lippman pointed out the superficiality of the questions, their possible cultural biases, and the risks of trying to determine a person's intellectual potential with a brief oral or paper-and-pencil measure.

Perhaps surprisingly, the conceptualization of intelligence did not advance much in the decades following Terman's pioneering contributions. Intelligence tests came to be seen, rightly or wrongly, as primarily a tool for selecting people to fill academic or vocational niches. In one of the most famous remarks about intelligence testing, the influential Harvard psychologist E. G. Boring declared, "Intelligence is what the tests test." So long as these tests did what they were supposed to do (that is, give some indication of school success), it did not seem necessary or prudent to probe too deeply into their meaning or to explore alternative views of the human intellect.

Psychologists who study intelligence have argued chiefly about two questions. The first: Is intelligence singular, or does it consist of various more or less independent intellectual faculties? The purists — ranging from the turn-of-the-century English psychologist Charles Spearman to his latter-day disciples Richard J. Herrntein and Charles Murray — defend the notion of general intelligence. The pluralists — ranging from L. L. Thurstone, of the University of Chicago, who posited seven vectors of the mind, to J. P. Guilford, of the University of Southern California, who discerned 150 factors of the intellect — construe intelligence as composed of some or even many dissociable components.

The public is more interested in the second question: Is intelligence (or are intelligences) largely inherited? This is by and large a Western question. In the Confucian societies of East Asia individual differences in endowment are assumed to be modest, and differences in achievement are thought to be due largely to effort. In the West, however, many students of the subject sympathize with the view that intelligence is inborn and one can do little to alter one's intellectual birthright.

Studies of identical twins reared apart provide surprisingly strong support for the "heritability" of psychometric intelligence. That is, if one wants to predict someone's score on an intelligence test, the scores of the biological parents (even if the child has not had appreciable contact with them) are more likely to prove relevant than the scores of the adoptive parents. By the same token, the IQs of identical twins are more similar than the IQs of fraternal twins. And, contrary to common sense, the IQs of biologically related people grow closer in the later years of life.

52. Walter Lippman's idea about early intelligence tests by Lewis Terman is that _____.
   [A] the testing questions are good enough to show the testees' intellectual potential
   [B] the testing questions vary too much from one culture to another
   [C] the usability of the testing questions should be questioned
   [D] the testing questions are beyond of human being's reach

53. What does E. G Boring's remarks "intelligence is what the tests test" suggest?
   [A] Intelligence tests have come to be seen rightly or wrongly.
   [B] Intelligence tests have become primarily a tool for selecting people.
   [C] Intelligence tests have become an irritating test.
   [D] Intelligence tests can hardly justify one's intellect.

54. The author's attitude toward intelligence tests is of _____.
   [A] bias　　　　　　[B] neutralism　　　　　　[C] criticism　　　　　　[D] positivism

55. The divergence existing between the purists and the pluralists is that the purists _____.
   [A] think intelligence is inborn but the pluralists don't think so
   [B] don't think intelligence has other components but the pluralists think it has
   [C] think intelligence tests are useful in deciding one's IQ but the pluralists don't thinks so
   [D] think intelligence could be influenced by the environment but the pluralists don't think so

56. In the eyes of some western students, if one falls behind others, he would ascribe his failure to _____.
   [A] his lower inborn intelligence　　　　　　[B] his less effort
   [C] his disadvantaged life environment　　　　　　[D] his less concentrated attention

Passage Two

Questions 57 to 61 are based on the following passage.

When Oxford University raised the idea of establishing a business school six years ago, outraged Ionians unleashed volleys of Ciceronian oratory, arguing that the groves of academe should be out of bounds to commerce. How times have changed. Frustrated by the British government's reluctance to let the university charge real-world tuition fees, demoralized by mounting charges of elitism, with research and teaching stifled by inadequate state subsidies, the dons are realizing that capitalism might just be the key to their future. At the traditional 800-year-old institution, increasing numbers of them are calling for their university to be privatized.

That's a hugely controversial proposal in a country that still clings fiercely to the ideal of providing a free, state funded education to anyone who merits it. Prime Minister Tony Blair wants 50% of Britain's under-30s in fulltime education by 2006, and given his no new-taxes style, universities suspect they'll be responsible for finding a large proportion of the $15 million that will cost. Already Oxford is having trouble paying salaries sufficient to attract top teachers; a full Professor gets $68,400 roughly half the salaries of their U. S. counterparts. For Oxford, long the global epitome of top-drawer education, the question is whether the university's days as a bastion of world-class excellence might be over.

Lately the issue seems to have taken on a new urgency. Newspapers reported mini-scandal just last week that a 19-year-old deaf student, Anastasia Fedotova, failed to win place despite high exam scores. Chancellor of the Exchequer Gordon Brown criticized the admissions system as "more reminiscent of the old-boy network… than genuine justice in our society." This highlighted just how vulnerable Oxford remains to charges of elitism.

"More and more people are saying the only solution is independence," says classics professor Richard Jenkyns. In the end, Oxford may be hoping for some in-between solution. Since 1998 it has been pumping funds into a private company called ISIS Innovation, set up to commercialize researchers' discoveries. Of a total of 28 fledging spin-offs, all are still in business. While big payoffs are still a long way off, "that could quickly change," says managing director Tim Cook, "if one of them hits the jackpot." More immediately, Oxford bigwigs report that permission to charge the full cost of tuition will almost certainly be given in government report due this November. Oxford still isn't likely to let business interests run wild over its hallowed greensward. But it is learning that the academic freedom it so prizes can be preserved only at a price.

57. The passage is mainly about _____.

    [A] the future orientation of Oxford University

    [B] the financial and moral problems of Oxford University and the solution

    [C] the influence of government's policy on Oxford University

    [D] the purity of Oxford University in its field of academic research

58. The major reason for Oxford University's lack of funding according to the passage is that _____.

    [A] the idea of building of a business school has been rejected by the teachers

    [B] the government is reluctant to let it charge the students high tuition fees

    [C] it has to pay sufficient salaries to attract top teachers

    [D] the government can't afford the high research subsidies

59. The example that Anastasia Fedotova was rejected by Oxford University illustrates that the university _____.

    [A] has taken on a new urgency

    [B] holds a strong discrimination against the disabled

    [C] is in favor of a network of older applicants

    [D] puts too much emphasis on elitism

60. The phrase "hit the jackpot" in the fourth paragraph probably means"_____".

    [A] get out of business suddenly

    [B] be discovered accidentally by foresighted businessman

    [C] make a lot of money unexpectedly

    [D] prove to be very useful in daily life by chance

61. We can learn from the passage that _____.

    [A] Oxford University will gradually become a private university just as Harvard

    [B] Oxford University is beginning to think of commercial ways to collect money

    [C] the only solution to Oxford University's problems is being independent

    [D] the British government will offer Oxford University more subsidies

Part V Error Correction (15 minutes)

Directions: *This part consists of a short passage. In this passage, there are altogether 10 mistakes, one in each num-*

bered line. You may have to change a word, add a word or delete a word. Mark out the mistakes and put the corrections in the blanks provided. If you change a word, cross it out and write the correct word in the corresponding blank. If you add a word, put an insertion mark (∧) in the right place and write the missing word in the blank. If you delete a word, cross it out and put a slash (/) in the blank.

Example：

Television is rapidly becoming the literature of our ~~periods~~.
Many of the arguments ~~having~~ used for the study of literature as a
school subject are valid for ∧ study of television.

　　1.　_time/times/period_
　　2.　_____/_____
　　3.　_____the_____

For the last fifteen or twenty years the fashion in criticism or
appreciation of the arts have been used to deny the existence of
any valid criteria and to make the words "good" or "bad"
irrelevant, immaterial, and inapplicable. There is no such thing, we
are told, like a set of standards first acquired through experience
and knowledge and late imposed on the subject under discussion.
This has been a popular approach, for it relieves the critic of the
responsibility of judgment and the public by the necessity of
knowledge. It pleases those resentful of disciplines, it flatters the
empty-minded by calling him open-minded, it comforts the
confused. Under the banner of democracy and the kind of quality
which our forefathers did not mean, it says, in effect, "Who are
you to tell us what is good or bad?" This is same cry used so long
and so effectively by the producers of mass media who insist that
it is the public, not they, who decide what it wants to hear and to
see, and that for a critic to say that this program is bad and that
program is good is pure a reflection of personal taste. Nobody
recently has expressed this philosophy most succinctly than Dr.
Frank Stanton, the highly intelligent president of CBS television.
At a hearing before the Federal Communications Commission, this
phrase escaped from him under questioning: "One man's
mediocrity is another man's good program".

　　62.　_____
　　63.　_____
　　64.　_____
　　65.　_____
　　66.　_____
　　67.　_____
　　68.　_____
　　69.　_____
　　70.　_____
　　71.　_____

Part VI　Translation (5 minutes)

Directions: *Complete the following sentences on* **Answer Sheet 2** *by translating into English the Chinese given in brackets.*

72. The experiment cannot be satisfactory _____(因为他只能选用那些随机挑选的样本).
73. These findings _____(与国内其他地区的实际情况并不符合).
74. Only when you graduate _____(你才会意识到学校生活是多么美好).
75. It will be a shame for anyone visiting China _____(没去看长城).
76. Lighting can be used _____(不仅能营造气氛,还能突出房子的装饰), such as ornaments or pictures.

答案与解析

Part I

【思路点拨】

　　本题属于提纲式文字命题。提纲第1点指出目前社会上存在的一种现象,提纲第2点要求分析产生这种现象的原因,提纲第3点要求阐述个人对此现象的看法,由此可判断本文属于现象解释型作文。

　　根据所给提纲,本文应包含以下内容:描述中国近年来人才流失这一普遍现象;说明产生这种现象的原因;阐述个人对此现象的看法。

【参考范文】
Brain Drain

Brain drain is a delicate problem with which China is confronted. In the last ten years or so, a lot of scientists and technicians have swarmed into developed countries for further studies or research work, let alone numerous promising students. And there are no indications that they will be back to mother land before long. Our country has paid the expenses of training them but finally lose them.(描述现象段)

How did that come about? It is self-evident that their delay of coming back is due to those favorable working and living conditions abroad which are essential to research work. Sophisticated equipment makes it easier for one to gain academic achievements. Chinese competent scientists abroad are offered higher rewards and greater opportunities which contribute to their success in career.(说明原因段)

In my view, it's difficult to attract the scientists and the like back home, unless great importance is attached to the intellectual's deserving treatment and effective measures are taken to provide them with great opportunities, excellent pay and agreeable conditions.(总结观点段)

Part II

【文章大意】

本文讲述调查类新闻与民主的关系。文章首先介绍了在美国新闻业不景气的情况下,调查类新闻并未受到其影响,接着详细介绍了调查类新闻,其后讲述调查类新闻对民主的推动作用以及其获得公众的档案纪录维持其有效性,最后文章讲述了调查类新闻所牵涉到的道德问题。

1. 【定位】根据题目中的关键信息 the first paragraph 可将搜索范围定位在第一段。
   【解析】选[A]。第一段第一句指出 1970s,reporters 在揭露美国二战后的一段时间内的 most serious…political scandal 方面发挥了重要作用,紧接着举出了 Watergate 的史实,由此不难得知,Watergate 是一件 political scandal(政治丑闻),故答案为[A]。

2. 【定位】根据题目中的关键信息 high credibility of journalism,journalism school 可将搜索范围定位在第二段。
   【解析】选[D]。分析该段最后一句的句意可知,and 连接的两个分句之间存在隐含的因果关系,即:新闻学校学生数量 increase 是新闻业享有 high credibility 的结果,故答案为[D]。

3. 【定位】根据题目中的关键信息 brightest,American news 可将搜索范围定位在第三段。
   【解析】选[D]。该段第一句指出大约 three decades 之后,investigative journalism 的情形发生了改变,它不再是 the brightest star in…American news,这就说明在之前的 three decades,investigative journalism 一直在美国新闻中发挥着重大作用。由此可知,investigative journalism 的 brightest role 一直保持了大约 three decades。[D]为 three decades 的同义转述,故为答案。

4. 【定位】根据题目中的关键信息 post-Watergate years 可将搜索范围定位在第三段。
   【解析】选[A]。该段第二句提出了一种假设情况即:如果用 self-congratulatory 来形容水门事件后几年时间中新闻业的状况的话,那么目前美国新闻业的情况就是 pessimism。[A]pessimistic 是 pessimism 的形容词形式,故为答案。

5. 【定位】根据题目中的关键信息 Denunciations 可将搜索范围定位在小标题 What Is Investigative Journalism? 下第一段。
   【解析】选[B]。该段第二句中的…rather than…表明 denunciations 是由 the work of reporters 引起产生的,而不是 the information leaked to newsrooms 引起产生的,故答案为[B]。

6. 【定位】根据题目中的关键信息 Investigative journalism,important 及 contributions 可将搜索范围定位在小标题 Democracy and Investigative Journalism 下第一段。
   【解析】选[D]。该段第一句指出 Investigative journalism matters(调查类新闻非常重要),因为它对 democratic governance(民主管理)作出了许多 contributions,故答案为[D]。

7. 【定位】根据题目中的关键信息 citizenry 可将搜索范围定位在小标题 Democracy and Investigative Journalism 下第三段。
   【解析】选[A]。该段首句说调查类新闻报道对民主的另一个贡献是使民众消息灵通,紧接着后面一句话说 Infor-

mation is a vital resource to empower a vigilant public that ultimately holds government accountable through voting and participation,该句中的 a vigilant public 指的其实就是首句中的 an informed citizenry,由此可知该句主要表达了消息灵通的民众可以通过 voting and participation(选举与参与)最终使政府承担起责任。

8.【定位】根据题目中的关键信息 access 可将搜索范围定位在小标题 Public Access 下。

【解析】public records and laws。该段第一句话指出 Access to public records and laws …is indispensable to the work of an investigative journalist,明确了该句的主干成分就可以找出本题答案。

9.【定位】根据题目中的关键信息 ethical 及 what journalists and editors need to 可将搜索范围定位在小标题 The Ethics of Investigative Journalism 下第一段最后一句。

【解析】who will benefit。该段指出 ethics 不像法律,对对与错有明确的指示,采取不同的 ethical framework 及 values 作出的决定就是不同的,即没有 an all-purpose ethical rulebook(全能的道德规则手册),在这种情况下 journalists 和 editors 需要做的就是决定 who will benefit from the reporting(判断谁将会从报道中获益)。

10.【定位】根据题目中的关键信息 the public, accept the practice of revealing 可将搜索范围定位在小标题 The Ethics of Investigative Journalism 下第四段。

【解析】questionable methods。第三段指出了 revealing wrongdoing 的多种方法,如 deception,use hidden cameras,use false identities 等,但都不能在本题中一一列举出来,继续读第四段,在该段末句可以找出能够概括这些方法的短语,即 questionable methods。

Part III

Section A

11.

[A] She would go home immediately after work. [B] She would go to a party. [C] She would work overtime. [D] She would work early in the morning.	M: Do you think you could possibly work late this evening? I'm afraid there's some work we really must finish this evening. W: Work late? I suppose so, if you really think it's necessary. Q: What would the woman probably do?
【解析】行为活动题。女士话中的 I suppose so, if you really think it's necessary 表明如果男士认为有必要,她就会加班即 work overtime。	

12.

[A] She misplaced her class card for biology. [B] She arrived for registration too early. [C] She missed registration. [D] The man can't spell her name.	W: My name is Helen Ware. Can I get a class card for biology today? M: Oh, no. Registration for students whose last names begin with W doesn't start until tomorrow. Q: What has happened to the woman?
【解析】事实状况题。男士话中的 Registration for students whose last names begin with W doesn't start until tomorrow(名字以 W 开头的学生明天才开始注册)表明女士今天不能注册,言外之意就是女士来的 too early(太早了)。	

13.

[A] The situation looks better than it is. [B] The phone connection was bad. [C] The woman ought to speak to Mary in person. [D] It is better to be courageous.	W: I wasn't sure what Mary really thought of my suggestion just from our phone conversation. M: Yes, it would be better to talk about it face to face. Q: What does the man mean?
【解析】观点态度题。男士话中的 it would be better to talk about it face to face 是在建议女士同 Mary 当面谈一下自己的 suggestion,[C] 是原文的同义转述。in person 意为"亲自"。	

14.

[A] Green. [B] Yellow. [C] Light blue. [D] Brown.	W: At first I thought this cloth was yellow but now it looks green to me. M: You were right the first time. It's this blue light in the store that makes everything look different. Q: What color is the cloth in fact?

【解析】事实状况题。女士话中的转折连词 but 表明衣服实际的颜色并不是 yellow(黄色的),而是 green(绿色的)。

15.

[A] To call the police. [B] To send a faith healer. [C] To see a counselor. [D] To keep quiet.	W: Our next-door neighbors quarrel constantly and I can hardly stand it. Do you think there is anything we could do to help? M: I suppose if they wanted to talk to friends or neighbors about their problems it might help, but they don't. Their difficulties are so deeply seated that they should probably secure some sort of professional advice. Q: What does the man think the neighbors should do?

【解析】行为活动题。男士话中的 Their difficulties are so deeply seated…表明他们的邻居夫妻之间的关系已经不是仅凭向朋友或邻居倾诉就可以解决的,他们应该 secure some sort of professional advice(寻求专业意见)。[C] To see a counselor 是寻求 professional advice 的一种。

16.

[A] The man can have his camera fixed here. [B] She will probably fix the man's camera herself. [C] The man will buy a new camera. [D] The camera should have been brought in earlier.	M: I have this camera here that I bought about 12 months ago. But it suddenly doesn't work. W: Let me have a look at your sales slip, I am sorry, sir. Yours is expired. Q: What does the woman mean?

【解析】事实状况题。女士在看过男士的 sales slip(销售发票)之后对男士说他的发票已经 expired(过期了),不能免费给他修理,言外之意就是相机 should have been brought in earlier(应该早点被拿来修理)。

17.

[A] At a bookstore. [B] At a bank. [C] At a club. [D] At a grocery store.	W: We have several kinds of accounts, Mr. Brown. The best interest rate is for the customer club account, but you must maintain a monthly balance of $300. M: That will be fine. Q: Where did this conversation most probably take place?

【解析】地点场景题。根据关键信息 accounts,interest rate 和 a monthly balance of $300 可以判断对话发生在 bank。

18.

[A] Secretary and boss. [B] Husband and wife. [C] Old classmates. [D] Doctor and patient.	M: Well, I haven't seen you since our graduation. How are things going with you? W: Not bad. I'm my own boss now. Q: What is the relationship between the speakers?

【解析】身份关系题。由男士话中的 I haven't seen you since our graduation(自从毕业就没看到你)可知,二者曾经是 classmates(同学)。

Conversation One

【听力原文】	【答案解析】
W: How was the party last night at Wilson's house? M: It was very nice. I had a good time and met some very nice people. But where	19. What present will the woman plan to send to her friend?

are you off to in such a hurry?

W: I've been invited to a cocktail party at 5:30. I'm late, and I need to buy some gift to my friend. [19] **Do you know somewhere I can buy some fresh flowers?**

M: Over there. But you told me that if you're invited to a party, [20①] **you should plan to arrive between a half-hour and an hour late.** Why are you in such a hurry?

W: [20②] **A party — yes. But not a cocktail party. A cocktail party is generally set for specific hours,** say from 5:30 to 7:30.

M: What's a cocktail party like?

W: Alcoholic beverages and hors d'oeuvres.

M: Only that?

W: Yes, people usually don't get dinner on a cocktail party.

M: Why will you have such a party?

W: [21] **It's called by some of my colleagues to celebrate the New Year.**

M: To celebrate the New Year! Why not have a dinner party?

W: Dinner party is too formal for us. We just take it for relaxation.

M: What will you do after the cocktail party?

W: Perhaps some of us will go to a pub.

M: That's too strange to me. What do you do then at the pub?

W: Drink and chat.

M: You will stay there for the whole night?

W: Yes. Anyway, New Year is a special day.

M: You don't celebrate the New Year with your family?

W: No. I only celebrated New Year with my family when I was a little girl.

M: It's really funny to hear that. But I say you'd better get moving, or you'll be late for your cocktail party.

W: OK. Goodbye.

M: So long. Have a good time.

【解析】选[B]。细节题。由女士向男士提出的问题 Do you know somewhere I can buy some fresh flowers 可知，女士打算买 fresh flowers 作为礼物送给朋友。

20. What does the woman think she should do when she is invited to a cocktail party?

【解析】选[B]。推断题。对话中男士说女士曾告诉过他如果她被邀请去参加宴会，她会 arrive between a half-hour and an hour late，但是现在她却如此匆忙。女士话中的 not a cocktail party 表明 cocktail party 与一般的 party 不同。由此可推断，女士认为去参加 cocktail party 应该 on time(准时)。

21. What is the cocktail party for?

【解析】选[A]。细节题。对话中男士问女士为什么举办 cocktail party，女士回答说她的同事邀请她去 celebrate the New Year，由此可知，女士要参加的 cocktail party 是为了庆祝新年。

Conversation Two

【听力原文】

W: Hi, Xiao Wang, and welcome back. How is the West Coast?

M: Terrific. I had a wonderful time. It was really nice to get away from the city for a while.

W: What did you think of Los Angeles?

M: It was all right. I liked it better than I thought I would. It's very clean and spacious, and it's got lots of trees. [22] **The problem is transportation. The bus service is terrible, and, of course, they don't have a subway, so it's a little difficult to get around.** We had to rent a car.

W: And what did you see?

M: Oh, the usual thing. We took a drive around Hollywood and looked at the stars' home, and then we went to Universal Studios and Disneyland.

W: How did you like Disneyland?

M: It was great. We really enjoyed it. We took all the rides, some of them twice, and had lots of fun. I felt just like a kid again.

W: Was the weather good?

【答案解析】

22. What aspect did not Xiao Wang like about Los Angeles?

【解析】选[B]。细节题。对话开头处，男士提到 Los Angeles 比他预想的要好很多，但唯一美中不足的是 the transportation，那里的公交车服务太差，并且没有地铁，由此可知，Los Angeles 的 transportation 是男士不喜欢的地方，故答案为[B]。

23. How was the weather like in Los Angeles when Xiao Wang was there?

【解析】选[C]。细节题。对话中，男士提及 Los Angeles 的天气时说到，It was nice and warm in Los Angeles，故答案为[C]。

24. Which month was it when Xiao Wang was in San Francisco?

M: Oh, yeah. [23] It was nice and warm in Los Angeles and cool but comfortable in San Francisco.

W: Cool in San Francisco? That's surprising.

M: Yeah, it surprised us a bit, too. We didn't take any sweaters or anything. [24] But they say it's always like that in August. Anyway, I just loved it. It's probably the most beautiful town in the U. S. — all those hills, and the bay, and those charming old Victorian houses.

W: So, you liked it better than Los Angeles?

M: Oh, yes. There's much more to see and do. And because it's smaller than Los Angeles, it's a lot easier to get around. There are lots of buses and streetcars, and of course, the cable cars.

W: What did you like best?

M: Oh, I don't know. It's hard to say. I liked Golden Gate Park and Fishermen's Wharf. [25] But I guess, most of all, I liked the cable car ride— that was the most fun.

【解析】选[B]。推断题。对话中,男士提到 San Francisco 的天气是 cool but comfortable,由接下来男士话中的 But they say it's always like that in August 可知,San Francisco 在 August 时的天气总是 cool but comfortable 的,由此可以推断,男士在 San Francisco 的时候已经是八月份了。

25. Which of the following is of Xiao Wang's greatest favorite in San Francisco?

【解析】选[C]。细节题。对话结尾处,男士话中的 most of all, I liked the cable ride…表明在 San Francisco,他最喜欢的是 cable car ride。

Section B

Passage One

【听力原文】

Charlie Chaplin was born on April 16, 1889 in London. His parents were both entertainers. While they were by no means rich, they somehow provided Chaplin with a comfortable life.

Unfortunately, their happy life didn't last long. Chaplin's father's alcoholism was slowly destroying his marriage. Finally, it ended in divorce, but Hannah, Chaplin's mother, was invincible. Without her, Chaplin would have become just one more child lost in the poverty of Victorian London. Hannah often sat at the window watching the passersby and guessed their characters from the way they looked and behaved, spinning tales to delight Chaplin. [26] Chaplin took in her skills and went on to use them in his entire life. He had always believed, even in the worst times, that something special was locked away inside him. He courageously went to see one of the top theatrical agents. [27] With no experience at all, he was offered the part of the pageboy in a new production of "Sherlock Holmes". "Sherlock Holmes" opened on July 27, 1903 at the enormous "Pavilion Theatre". Chaplin seemed to change overnight. It was as if he had found the thing he was meant to do. In 1910, cinema was born. As Chaplin thought, people still believed it was a passing fashion and would never replace live shows. However, he kept hanging around for several weeks, and he watched and learned. He was determined to master this new medium. It offered him the chance of money and success and it would set him free from the unpredictability of live audiences.

Chaplin's first film, released in February 1914, was called "Making a Living". [28] Though it didn't satisfy Chaplin, the public liked it and distributors were demanding more and more Chaplin's films. In an incredibly short time, Chaplin became a very important man in motion pictures.

【答案解析】

26. Who made an indelible influence on Chaplin's career?

【解析】选[B]。推断题。文中提到,Chaplin 的母亲经常坐在窗前根据路人的相貌及行为方式猜测他们的性格,然后编些故事来逗 Chaplin 开心,Chaplin took in her skills and went on to use them in his entire life (Chaplin 汲取了母亲的这些技巧并受用终生),由此可推断 Chaplin 的母亲对他后来的演艺事业起到了重要作用,答案为[B]。

27. What was the role Chaplin was in "Sherlock Holmes"?

【解析】选[D]。细节题。文中提到,因为没有经验,Chaplin 只在新剧 Sherlock Holmes 中扮演了一个 pageboy(小听差) 的角色,答案为 [D]。

28. What was the audience's reaction to Chaplin's first film?

【解析】选[B]。细节题。文中提到 Chaplin 的第一部电影并没有令他自己满意,但是观众们却 liked it,[B] They were fond of it 是原文的同义转述。

Passage Two

【听力原文】	【答案解析】

【听力原文】

Speaking to a group is the number one fear among adults today, making it one of the most sought-after skills in the professional world. Why do some people seem like born speakers while you just feel so nervous when you have to give a speech? Well, [29] let me introduce a few secrets of public speaking.

Great speakers aren't born, but they're trained. Like great athletes, great speakers have coaches, learn techniques, and practise regularly to improve their skills.

Alcohol and drugs are not good ways to control anxiety. In fact, they often make us less effective. Knocking knees, shaky hands, a quivering voice and memory loss are reactions to anxiety, though most audiences don't notice these symptoms.

[30①] One of the best ways to control speech anxiety is to breathe. The symptoms caused by anxiety are due to our brains going into "fight" mode. When we think we're in danger, our brain sends a signal to our body in preparation to fight the danger or escape from it. Running from a presentation is not a good way to handle anxiety, so you have to stay and "fight" it. [30②] By taking deep breaths, you can help convince your brain you are not in danger. [31] Breathing will help lower your blood pressure and calm down.

Learning how to control speech anxiety is like learning how to throw a ball. You must learn how to do it, and then you have to practise what you've learned. Once you learn the proper techniques, it's just as simple as riding a bike.

【答案解析】

29. What is the main purpose of the passage?

【解析】选[A]。推断题。短文开头处首先提出问题，即 Why do some people seem like born speakers while you just feel so nervous when you have to give a speech，接着 the speaker 说明自己会 introduce a few secrets of public speaking，下文中的如何成为 great speakers 及如何控制 sepech anxiety 都属于 secrets 的一部分。由此可推断本文的主要目的即是 introduce some secrets of public speaking，答案为 [A]。

30. What is the way the speaker suggests to control speech anxiety?

【解析】选[A]。细节题。文中提到控制演讲恐惧的最有效的方法之一就是 to breathe(呼吸)，而结合下文中的 by taking deep breathes 可知作者所推荐的控制演讲恐惧的方法即是 to take deep breaths(深呼吸)，答案为[A]。

31. What effect does breathing can bring to the speaker?

【解析】选[B]。细节题。文中提到 breathing 能够 help lower your blood pressure(帮助降低血压)，并且还能帮助演讲者 calm down(平静下来)。[B] 是 breathing 的作用之一，为本题答案。

Passage Three

【听力原文】	【答案解析】

【听力原文】

Did you ever order something through the mail as a child? [32] The toy you ordered looked great in the advertisement. When the real thing came, it almost always was smaller, cheaper, and less fun than you expected. You learned: not to believe everything you read in an advertisement.

Kids grow into adults understanding that marketing is full of exaggeration. As a result, consumers instinctively believe that most marketing messages are overstated. [33] Marketers make the problem worse by claiming their products are the solution to every problem. We make claims that sound so great that they are not believable, even when they might be true. As a result, we create marketing messages that are dismissed or ignored.

If you are more honest than consumers expect, you are removing those consumers built-in disbelief. If their defense mechanisms are taken away, consumers may be more willing to listen to what you have to say. They may

【答案解析】

32. How will consumers feel when receiving the goods they ordered as mentioned in the very beginning?

【解析】选[B]。推断题。文中开头处提到要订购的 toy 在广告里 looked great(看起来非常好)，但实物却是 smaller, cheaper and less fun than you expected，由此可推断 consumers 收到订购的商品时会感到很 disappointed(失望)，答案为[B]。

33. What will make the marketing message unbelievable?

【解析】选[B]。细节题。文中提到商人 claiming their products are the solution to every problem(声称他们的产品能解决一切问题)，而消费者认为把产品宣扬得太好反而会使它们 not believable(不可信)。由此可知，商家对产品的 exaggeration 使消费者对 the marketing message 感到 unbelievable。

34. What does the speaker suggest the marketers to be?

【解析】选[D]。细节题。文中提到 being honest 能够避免使你听起来像是一个不诚实的商人，由此不难看

regard the rest of your message with a bit more interest than usual.

[34] Being honest helps you avoid sounding like a dishonest sales person. By admitting your product is not the perfect solution for everyone, you increase the chances that the right prospect will listen to you.

[35①] However, that does not mean you'll get the sale every time. It's just the first step. [35②] You should increase the chances so that the likely buyer will listen to more of your message. [35③] You still have to have a good product and the right message, and [35④] you must be communicating with the prospective customer.

出 being honest 正是 the speaker 建议 the marketers 要做的,另外根据整篇短文都是在讲 the marketers 应该 honest 也可以得出答案为[D]。

35. What is the purpose of the passage?

【解析】选[A]。主旨题。短文首先指出了 marketers 过分宣传他们的产品使消费者对其产品产生疑问,接着给出解决之法即, marketers 应该 be honest,但文中提到这只是 get the sale 的第一步, marketers 还应该 increase the chances、have a good product and the right message 及 communicating with the prospective customer,这些都有利于商人 get the sale,综合上面的分析可知本文的目的即是 tell the marketers how to get the sale。

Section C

【听力原文】

Health care in Australia relies on private and public facilities: a predominantly private medical profession, private and public hospitals, and private and public health financing. Most (36) primary health care is provided by private practitioners, who charge their patients directly and set their own (37) fees. Some is provided by the (38) staff of health centers and public hospitals, who may also exercise their right to practise privately. Patients receive hospital care in either private or public hospitals. The choice is theirs, although most (39) rely on the advice of their medical practitioners and their health insurance (40) status. Medicare, the (41) universal national health financing system, is funded in part by a special levy(征税) on income and in part by general (42) taxation. It provides access to public hospital services and cash (43) rebates for medical treatment provided out of hospital by medical practitioners.

Under Medicare, public hospitals are funded by the federal and state governments. All permanent Australian residents have access, without direct charge, (44) to public hospital accommodation and to inpatient and outpatient treatment by doctors appointed by the hospital concerned. Private hospitals charge for their services and are funded from the revenue generated. (45)Doctors treating patients in private hospitals charge them independently and the same benefits apply to such charges as in public hospitals. Private health-insurance organizations offer a range of benefits to cover hospital charges. (46)They also offer benefits for relevant services not covered by Medicare such as dental, physiotherapy and so on.

【答案解析】

36. 空后的名词提示所填词应为形容词。primary 意为"主要的"。

37. 空前的形容词提示所填词应为名词。fees 意为"费用"。

38. 空前的定冠词 the 及空后的介词 of 提示所填词应为名词。staff 意为"全体职员"。

39. 分析句子结构可知所填词在句中作谓语,故所填词应为动词,且能与 on 搭配。rely 意为"依靠"。

40. 分析句子结构可知 their 所修饰的中心词为 health insurance _____,故所填词应为名词。status 意为"情况,情形"。

41. 空前的定冠词 the 及空后名词短语提示所填词很可能为形容词。universal 意为"普遍的,通用的"。

42. 空前的形容词提示所填词应为名词。综合整句话可知,本句主要与 Medicare 的资金来源有关。taxation 意为"征税"。

43. 空前的并列连词 and 提示 cash _____ 应与 public hospital services 并列作 to 的宾语,故所填词应为名词。rebates 意为"回扣"。

44. 【Main Points】to public hospital accommodation and to impatient and outpatient treatment by doctors **assigned** by the hospital concerned

45. 【Main Points】**In private hospitals**, doctors **who treat** patients charge them independently and the same benefits apply to such charges as in public **ones**

46. 【Main Points】They also **provide** benefits for relevant services **which are** not covered by Medicare such as dental, physiotherapy and so on

Part IV

Section A

【文章大意】

本文是一篇说明文,围绕实战演习的商业用途及其价值这个话题进行了分析。第一段简单介绍了什么是实战演习,第二段则立刻引入话题,指出公司制定战略的传统方式存在的缺点,从而提出本文的主要观点,即实战演习能够帮助公司更好地理解自身与竞争对手的状况。第三段介绍了实战演习的两个特点;第四段介绍了两家提供实战演习服务的咨询公司策划的实战演习内容及其效果。

47. 【定位】根据题干中的关键信息 CEOs, military books 可将搜索范围定位在第二段第三句。

    【解析】management tips / management skills。题干中的 CEOs 对应文中的 bosses, military book 对应文中的 Sun Tzu(孙子兵法), 表目的的不定式短语 to get 对应文中表目的的介词 for, 所以原文中 for 的宾语即是本题答案。

48. 【定位】根据题干中的关键信息 traditional corporate planning 可将搜索范围定位在第二段倒数第二句。

    【解析】taking competitors' responses into account / considering rivals' reactions。题干中的 doesn't do well in 对应文中的 does a poor job of, 所以答案为 taking competitors' responses into account 或是它的同义转述 considering rivals' reactions。

49. 【定位】根据题干中的关键信息 player 可将搜索范围定位在第三段。

    【解析】other competitors' strategies。该段前半部分指出公司实战演习的两个特点, 其中第二个特点指出该种演习包括好几轮, allowing competitors not just to draw up their own strategies but to respond to the choices of others(竞争者们不仅能够策划自己的战略, 而且也能够对其他人的选择做出反应)。题干中的 make reactions to 与原文中的 respond to 对应, 故原文中 to 的宾语即是本题的答案出处。分析该句可知, the choices of others 指的即是竞争者对别的竞争者的策略作出的反应, 即 other competitors' strategies。

50. 【定位】根据题干中的关键信息 effect, profits 及 calculated 可将搜索范围定位在第四段第一句。

    【解析】introducing a quantitative element。该句指出 BAH 引进了 a quantitative element 到它的演习中, 用以计算 the effect of each team's strategy on their company's profits..., 由此可知 a quantitative element 是计算公司策略对公司利润的影响的方法, 故答案为 introducing a quantitative element。题干中的 the company strategy's effect on his profits can be calculated 是对原文 calculating the effect of each team's strategy on their company's profits 的同义转述。

51. 【定位】根据题干中的关键信息 Preference trees 可将搜索范围定位在第四段第四句。

    【解析】desired outcomes。该句中的指示代词 these 提示 preference trees 指代的是前一分句中的 desired outcomes。题干中的 refers to 意为"涉及, 提到"。

Section B

Passage One

【文章大意】

智力测试究竟能否真的说明一个人的智力潜能, 以及智力是单一结构还是由多个功能组成等疑问是研究智力的心理学家们争论的焦点, 本文主要对这些心理学家们争论的焦点进行了阐述。文章第一、二段主要阐述了智力测试是否有其必要性; 第三、四段主要阐述了心理学家们争论的两个问题; 第五段主要是举例说明智力具有遗传性。

52. 选[C]。推理判断题。文章首段最后一句指出 Lippman 认为 Lewis Terman 的观点存在不足之处: the superficiality of the questions(问题的肤浅性), their possible cultural biases(问题可能存在文化偏见), the risks of trying to...(仅通过简单的口试和笔试就决定一个人的智力潜力)。[C](问题的可用性应该受到质疑)是对 the superficiality of the questions 的延伸, 既然 Lippman 觉得 Terman 用于智商测试的问题太过肤浅, 那么就说明 Lippman 对这些问题的可用性持有怀疑态度, 故答案为[C]。

53. 选[D]。推理判断题。综合文章第一二段可知, 这两段主要是与人们对 intelligence tests 的功能的质疑有关, E. G. Boring 的评论 Intelligence is what the tests test(智力只不过是智力测试的结果罢了)出现在这一语境之中明显表明 E. G Boring 认为 intelligence tests 不能真正的显示出人的真实智商, 故答案为[D]。

54. 选[C]。观点态度题。文章第一二段主要与 intelligence tests 有关。结合文章第一段中的 Early intelligence tests were not without their critics 以及第二段最后一句 So long as these tests did what they were supposed to do... 可以推知作者认为这些 intelligence tests 具有不足之处, 是应该受到批判的, 故答案为[C]。

55. 选[B]。事实细节题。文章第三段主要是关于研究智力的心理学家们所争论的第一个问题, 即: Is intelligence singular, ...?(智力是单一的还是由其他各种独立的功能组成?)。通过阅读该段可发现 the purists(纯化论者) defend the notion of a single overarching "g"(认为智力是单一的), 而 the pluralists(多元论者)则认为 intelligence as composed of...(智力是由多种独立成分构成的), 综合上面分析可知, the purists 和 the pluralists 的分歧点就在于二者对智力的组成成分的不同看法, [B] 正好说明了这一点, 故为本题答案。

56. 选[A]。事实细节题。文章第三段主要是关于研究智力的心理学家们所争论的第二个问题, 即: Is intelligence (or are intelligence) largely inherited?(智力是否很大程度上是天生的?)。该段最后一句指出许多西方研究智力的学者都认为智力是 inborn(天生的), 人很难改变。由此可以推断, 在这些研究者看来, 如果一个人在某方面落后于其他人, 他肯定会把自己失败的原因归结于自己的天资不如别人, 故答案为[A]。

Passage Two

【文章大意】

牛津大学是世界顶级学府, 但却面临着资金短缺及精英主义日益攀升的危机, 本文围绕这两重危机进行了详细论述。文章第一段即指出牛津大学所面临的危机以及牛津大学所要采取的解决办法; 第二段指出牛津大学的解决办法与该国的教育观点相违背;第三段用实例证明牛津大学精英主义的不堪一击;第四段指出牛津大学为解决资金短缺问题所采取的具体办法。

57. 选[B]。主旨大意题。文章第一、二段指出由于政府及精英统治论的影响,Oxford University 面临着资金短缺的问题;第三段指出了因高人一等的优越感而导致的招生制度的缺陷:一个 19 岁的聋哑学生尽管考试分数很高但最终还是没有被批准入学,此 mini-scandal 属于 moral problem 的范畴;第四段给出了相应的解决方法:independence,选项[B] 的内容是对全文的概括总结,故为答案。

58. 选[B]。事实细节题。由文章第一段第三句可知,Oxford University 的研究和教学遇到 inadequate state subsidies(政府补助短缺)的阻碍,即 Oxford University 面临着资金短缺的问题,由本句前半部分可知,造成资金短缺的原因而就是 government's reluctance to let the university charge real-world tuition fees,选项[B] 为它的同义转述,故为答案。

59. 选[D]。推理判断题。文章第三段最后一句中的 this 指代的是财政大臣的评论,该句表达的意思是:财政大臣的评论突出显示了 how vulnerable Oxford remains to charges of elitism(牛津大学的精英主义不堪一击),而从财政大臣的评论中可以推断 Anastasia Fedotova 被拒绝是牛津大学受 elitism 的影响,由此可以看出 elitism 在牛津大学的重要性,故答案为[D]。

60. 选[C]。推理判断题。条件状语从句 if one of them hits the jackpot 是对 that could quickly change 作出的假设,所以此题的关键是理解 that 的所指。分析整句话可知,that 指代的是 big payoffs are still a long way off(还很久才能实现高盈利)。所以高盈利能够迅速实现的条件是 one of them hits the jackpot,由此可以推断 hits the jackpot 应与 money 有关,故答案为[C]。hit the jackpot 意为"意外地获得一大笔钱"。

61. 选[B]。事实细节题。文章第四段第三句指出,自 1998 年开始,牛津大学就开始向 ISIS Innovation 投入资金,为了 commercialize researchers' discoveries(使研究人员的发现商业化),由此不难发现牛津大学正试图通过商业手段改善其资金短缺的问题,故答案为[B]。[A]、[D] 文中没有提到;[C] 与文中的 Oxford may be hoping for some in-between solution 相违背。

Part V

62. have — has。主谓不一致。本句主语为 the fashion,是单数名词,所以谓语动词也应相应的用单数,故应将 have 改写为 has。

63. like — as。介词误用。such…as… 为固定搭配,故应将 like 改写为 as。

64. late — later。易混词误用。late 应改写为 later,以与 and 连接的前一分句中的副词 first 相对应。

65. by — of。介词误用。relieves 通常与 of / from 搭配使用,意为"减轻…,消除…",此处为了与 and 前面的 of 对称,应将 by 改为 of。

66. him — them。代词误用。"the ＋ 形容词"通常表示一类人,所以用代词指代这一类人时应使用表复数的代词,故应将 him 改写为 them。

67. is ∧ same — the。缺漏。the same 表示"唯一,独一无二"的概念,故应在 is 与 same 之间加上定冠词 the。

68. decide — decides。主谓不一致。what 引导的宾语从句中 it 指代的即是 the public,由此可知本句中 the public 表示的是单数概念,故应将 decide 改写为 decides。it is … who 是强调句型。

69. pure — purely。形容词与副词误用。pure 应改写为 purely,以修饰谓语动词 is。

70. most — more。形容词比较级与最高级混淆。此处表示两者之间的比较,故应将 most 改写为 more。

71. from — /。及物动词与非及物动词混淆。escape 在作"被某人情不自禁地说出来"讲时,是及物动词;而只有在作"逃跑"讲时,才是不及物动词。本句明显表达的意思是"被 Dr. Frank Stanton 情不自禁说出来",故应将 from 删除。

Part VI

72.【答案】because he has to use the selection of specimens chosen at random
【解析】本题考查对原因状语从句的掌握。because 引导原因状语从句,表示"原因是…"。at random 意为"随机地、胡乱地"。

73.【答案】are at odds with what is going on in the rest of the country
【解析】本题考查对惯用搭配 be at odds with… 的掌握。be at odds with… 后面可接 sb. ,意为"与某人有分歧";也可以接 sth. ,意为"与…有差异,相矛盾"。

74.【答案】will you realize how colorful the school life is
【解析】本题考查对倒装句式的掌握。"only＋状语"位于句首时,要求将助动词提前,使句子部分倒装。另外注意宾语从句要用陈述语序。

75.【答案】not to see the Great Wall
【解析】本题考查对不定式的掌握。在本句中 it 是形式主语,指代 not to see…。

76.【答案】not only to create an atmosphere, but also to highlight features of the house
【解析】本题考查对并列结构和不定式的掌握。"not only…but also…"连接两个并列成分,意为"不仅…而且…"。不定式 to creat…和 to highlight…充当目的的状语。

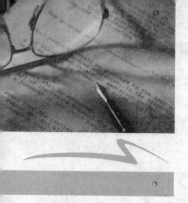

预 测 试 题 二

Part I Writing (30 minutes)

Directions: *For this part, you are allowed 30 minutes to write a composition on the topic:* ***Are Prizes a Good Thing?*** *You should write at least 150 words, and base your composition on the outline given in Chinese below:*

1) 竞赛中奖品的好处
2) 奖品的弊端
3) 我的看法

Are Prizes a Good Thing?

Part II Reading Comprehension (Skimming and Scanning) (15 minutes)

Animal Factories

Every year billions of animals are raised and killed for human consumption. In the U.S. alone, more than 10 billion land animals are slaughtered annually. (Billions more fish are raised and killed in fish "farms" or are taken from oceans, rivers, and lakes.)

Like all animals, farmed animals have the ability to experience pleasure and pain. Unfortunately, farmed animals endure tremendous amount of pain and suffering for unnecessary human use and consumption.

Currently, few legal protections exist for farmed animals. The federal Animal Welfare Act does not apply to animals used in agriculture and many states have enacted laws that specifically exempt farmed animals from portions of state anti-cruelty statues. The Humane Slaughter Act requires that all animals slaughtered in federally inspected meat processing plants be rendered unconscious to the process of slaughter. However, this law is poorly enforced and does not cover chickens and turkeys, nor does it cover kosher, ritual, or home slaughter.

The only other federal law that addresses welfare of animals raised for food or food production is the "28-hour law", which generally requires that livestock being transported across state lines be humanely unloaded into *pens* (牛、羊圈) for food, water, and at least 5 hours of rest every 28 hours. The effectiveness of this law is questionable, however; because there is some question as to whether it applies to transportation in large trucks as opposed to rail, and because most fanned animals in the U.S. are transported by truck, the law is rarely, if ever, enforced. Moreover, 28-hour time limit is sadly inadequate to protect the welfare of transported farmed animals and lags far behind international initiatives that call for time limits of between 8 and 12 hours.

Unlike family farms of the past, most animals used in agriculture today are part of high-production factory farms that treat animals as little more than machines.

In factory farms, animal suffering exists on an almost unimaginable scale. Thousands of animals are confined in extremely small spaces to maximize production. They are subjected to painful damages such as debarking, toe removal, dehorning, and castration, without benefit of pain relief. They are denied the ability to engage in natural behaviors. They frequently die during transport in overcrowded trucks. Once arriving at the slaughterhouse, they may have their throats cut or be boiled alive while still conscious.

Here's a look at how some animals are treated as they are turned into food and other products for human use:

Cattle

More than 40 million cattle and calves are slaughtered annually in the United States. Some beef cattle are raised on the range while others are raised in crowded feed lots.

Whether raised on the range or on the feed lot, when large enough, cattle are crammed into metal trucks and taken to slaughter. On the way to the slaughterhouse, cattle may travel for hours in sweltering temperatures with no access to water.

Animals who become weak and unable to stand due to broken legs or illness are called "downers" by the meat industry. Downer animals are electrically prodded, dragged with chains, or left to die without food or water.

Pigs

In the United States more than 120million pigs are slaughtered for human consumption each year.

Factory-farmed pigs are raised in crowded pens enclosed inside of huge barns. The air in these structures is filled with eye and lung-burning ammonia created from the waste collected below the floors.

Breeding *sows* (母猪) spend their lives in metal pens so small that they cannot even turn around. Without adequate space and freedom of movement, these sows often develop fixed behavior — repetitive movements that serves no practical purpose and that indicate psychological distress — such as head bobbing and rail biting.

At the slaughterhouse pigs are stunned (often inadequately) and hung upside down. Their throats are then cut, and they are bled to death. If workers fail to kill a pig with the knife, the pig is carded on the conveyer belt to the next station, where it may be boiled alive.

Poultry

Every year more than 9.8 billion chickens, turkeys, and ducks are raised and slaughtered for human consumption in the United States. Most of these animals are chickens.

Crowded and unable to express natural behavior, chickens often excessively peck each other. Instead of providing adequate space for the chickens, farmers have them "debeaked" — cutting off the sensitive top portion of the beak with a mechanical blade.

Chickens raised to become meat have been genetically altered to grow abnormally large. As a result, many broiler chickens' bones are unable to support the weight of their muscle tissue, causing them to limp in pain or become totally crippled.

At the slaughterhouse, chickens are hung upside down by the feet and attached to a moving rail while still conscious. The birds missed by the mechanical neck-slicing blade and boiled alive are called "redskins" by the industry.

Egg-laying Chickens

Almost all of the more than 400 million egg-laying hens in the United States are confined to "battery" cages — tiny prisons roughly 16 by 18 inches wide. Five or six birds are crammed into each cage, and the cages are piled in tall rows. The overcrowding causes serious injury, or even death.

Hens are forced to produce 10 times the amount of eggs that they would produce naturally. When egg production slows down, farmers use "forced molting" to shock the hens into losing their feathers and prematurely starting a new laying cycle. This "forced molting" includes starving and denying water to the hens for several days during which many hens die. To keep hens from pecking each other, farmers "debeak" the hens. Debeaking is a painful procedure whereby the hen's sensitive upper beak is sliced off with a hot blade. Male chicks — by-products of laying hen production — are thrown into plastic bags to slowly suffocate or are ground into animal feed while still alive.

Dairy Cows

About half of the 10 million dairy cows in the United States are kept in some type of confinement system.

Dairy cows are forced to produce 10 — 20 times the amount of milk they would naturally need to suckle their calves. This intensive production of milk is extremely stressful. As a result, dairy cattle "burn out" at a much younger age than their normal lifespan.

In order to continue to produce milk, a cow must have a calf each year. Calves would normally stay with their mothers for a year or more. However, on the dairy farm, calves are immediately removed from their mothers so that the milk can be sold for human consumption. Calves are sold to the beef or veal industry, or become replacements for "burned out" dairy cows.

Other Farmed Animals

Other animals are used in agriculture in large numbers:

Sheep are raised for both food and fiber. About 3 million were slaughtered to make meat in the U.S. in 2004. Sheep also suffer enormously in the wool industry. Lambs may have their tails chopped off and be *castrated* (阉割) without an *esthetic* (麻醉药). In Australia (from where 80 percent of all wool comes) ranchers perform an operation called "mulesing", where large strips of skin are carved off the backs of animals' legs. This procedure is performed to produce scarred skin that won't harbor fly *larvae* (幼虫), so that the rancher can spend less time caring for the sheep. The clipping of sheep at most wool ranches can be a brutal procedure, as workers are encouraged to clip as quickly as possible. As a result, an estimated 1 million Australian sheep die every year from exposure. Sheep who are no longer useful for their wool are sent to crowded feedlots and then transported to the slaughterhouse.

Goats are also increasingly exploited in the U.S. to produce milk, meat, and fiber. More than 2 million goats are currently used in meat and milk production, and more than 600,000 goats were slaughtered in 2004.

1. The purpose of this article is to draw more and more concerns about the poor welfare of farmed animals.
2. The Humane Slaughter Act applies to animal slaughter done at home but is poorly implemented.
3. The "28-hour law" is slightly effective in protecting the welfare of transported farmed animals but follows the international calls for time limits of animal transportation.
4. Over 40 million cattle and calves are inadequately stunned to death in the U.S. every year.
5. At the slaughterhouse it may happen that pigs are boiled alive in the scalding tank when the workers _____.
6. The chickens' beaks are always cut off by farmers so that they cannot _____.
7. To increase egg production, farmers force hens to begin a new cycle of egg-laying ahead of their regular cycle by using _____.
8. Dairy cows live much shorter than their natural lifespan due to _____.
9. On the dairy farm calves are taken away at once after their birth so that their mothers' milk can be saved for _____.
10. In order to spend less time caring for sheep, Australian ranchers cut large strips of skin off the backs of sheep's legs to _____.

Part III　Listening Comprehension (35 minutes)

Section A

11. [A] Near an art gallery.　　　　　　　　　　[B] In front of a library.
　　[C] At a stoplight.　　　　　　　　　　　　[D] Outside a bookstore.
12. [A] He has missed three fourths of his two classes.　[B] He couldn't attend his classes because of illness.
　　[C] He failed in the exam.　　　　　　　　　[D] He attended no classes at all.
13. [A] She wants to quit her job.　　　　　　　　[B] She wants to apply for a promotion.
　　[C] She wants to transfer to another department.　[D] She wants to get a salary rise.
14. [A] The professor spoke too fast.
　　[B] The professor spoke with a strong accent.
　　[C] The professor's lecture notes were too complicated.
　　[D] The professor's presentation was not convincing enough.
15. [A] She doesn't like either of them.　　　　　[B] John copied it from Jim.
　　[C] Jim copied it from John.　　　　　　　　[D] One of the compositions is the copy of the other.
16. [A] A waitress.　　　　　　　　　　　　　　[B] A nurse.
　　[C] A secretary.　　　　　　　　　　　　　[D] A telephone operator.
17. [A] $240.　　　　　[B] $250.　　　　　　　[C] $290.　　　　　[D] $200.
18. [A] He is going to watch the play.　　　　　　[B] He is going to do some work.
　　[C] He is going to watch TV.　　　　　　　　[D] He is going to have a rest.

Questions 19 to 21 are based on the conversation you have just heard.

19. [A] From her friends.　　　　　　　　　　　[B] From TV advertisement.
　　[C] From advertisement leaflets.　　　　　　[D] From newspaper advertisement.
20. [A] Because her previous salary was too low.　　[B] Because her previous boss disliked him.
　　[C] Because her previous company was closed down.　[D] Because she disliked her previous job.

21. [A] The woman's previous company was a joint venture.

    [B] The woman's salary in her new company is 1,500 dollars a month.

    [C] The woman will start to work in the new company the next Monday.

    [D] The woman will be better paid in the new company.

Questions 22 to 25 are based on the conversation you have just heard.

22. [A] Because she is lonely.   [B] Because she loves to protect a pet.

    [C] Because she thinks dogs are good companions. [D] Because she just lost one dog.

23. [A] How old the dog is.   [B] What kind of companion he needs.

    [C] What personality the dog is.   [D] What environment the dog lives in.

24. [A] Between 6 to 8 weeks.   [B] Between 4 to 6 weeks.

    [C] Between 8 to 12 weeks.   [D] Between 6 to 10 weeks.

25. [A] Adopting a dog.   [B] Giving up the idea of having a dog.

    [C] Buying dogs and cats at the same time.   [D] Asking for another one's opinion.

Section B

Passage One

26. [A] It can't offer evidence to prove who used it.   [B] It can provide more information to the criminal.

    [C] It can help the criminal hide the corpus delicti. [D] It can help the criminal get away from the police.

27. [A] Because he stole money from the bank.   [B] Because he joined in illegal gambling.

    [C] Because he cheated his customer.   [D] Because he often made computer errors.

28. [A] The ones who receive high education.   [B] The ones who have perfect knowledge of computer.

    [C] The ones who know the psychology of criminals. [D] The ones who are proficient at tracing down criminals.

Passage Two

29. [A] Spending is largely driven by a comparative or competitive process.

    [B] Spending is to some extent driven by consumers' own willing.

    [C] Spending is to use lest money to buy most things.

    [D] Spending is to buy the most competitive things.

30. [A] The development of society.   [B] The development of city.

    [C] The married women's entry into workforce. [D] The convenience of shopping outside.

31. [A] The crimes and violence in the society.   [B] The lifestyles of the rich and upper middle class.

    [C] The relationship among all kind of people. [D] The custom of present consumption.

Passage Three

32. [A] 48.   [B] 49.   [C] 46.   [D] 47.

33. [A] The Arctic Circle.

    [B] The area between the Pacific Ocean and the Canadian Rockies.

    [C] The Atlantic Ocean.

    [D] The Antarctic Circle.

34. [A] 8.2 million dollars.   [B] 7.2 million dollars.

    [C] 6.2 million dollars.   [D] 9.2 million dollars.

35. [A] Alaska has less population than most of the states.

    [B] Alaska was purchased from French.

    [C] Alaska achieved statehood in 1912.

    [D] The size of Alaska is twice as large as Texas.

Section C

All that we really need to plot out the future of our universe are a few good (36)_____ . This does not mean that we can sit down today and (37)_____ the future course of the universe with anything like certainty. There are still too many things we do not know about the way the universe is put together. But we do know exactly what (38)_____ we need to (39)_____ in our knowledge, and we have a (40)_____ good idea of how to go about getting it.

Perhaps the best way to think of our present (41)_____ is to (42)_____ a train coming into a switch-yard. All of the switches are set before the train arrives, so that its path is completely determined. Some switches we can see, others we cannot. There is no (43)_____ if we can see the setting of a switch: (44)_____. At the unseen switches, however, there is no such certainty about it. (45)_____. The unseen switches are the true decision points in the future and what happens when we arrive at them determines the entire subsequent course of events.

When we think about the future of the universe, we can see out "track" many billions of years into the future, but after that there are decision points to be dealt with and possible fates to consider. (46)_____.

Part IV　Reading Comprehension (Reading in Depth) (25 minutes)
Section A

Urbanization is the process by which large numbers of people become permanently concentrated in relatively small areas, forming cities.

The definition of what __47__ a city changes from time to time and place to place, but it is most usual to explain the term as a matter of *demographics* (人口统计学). The United Nations has recommended that countries regard all places with more than 20,000 __48__ living close together as urban.

Whatever the __49__ definition is, it is clear that the course of human history has been marked by a process of __50__ urbanization. It was not until the *Neolithic period* (新石器时代), __51__ 10,000 years ago, that humans were able to form permanent settlements. Even 5,000 years ago the only such settlements on the globe were small, semi-permanent villages of peasant farmers, towns whose size was __52__ by the fact that they had to move whenever the soil nearby was __53__. It was not until the time of __54__ antiquity that cities of more than 100,000 existed, and even these did not become common until the sustained population __55__ of the last three centuries. In 1800 less than 3 percent of the world's population was living in cities of 20,000 or more; this had increased to about 25 percent by the mid-1960s and to about 40 percent by 1980. It is estimated that, by this __56__, about half the world's population will be urban in the year 2000.

[A] roughly	[B] constitutes	[C] numerical	[D] classical	[E] immigrants
[F] explosion	[G] inhabitants	[H] measure	[I] consists	[J] exhausted
[K] accelerated	[L] accurately	[M] modern	[N] pace	[O] limited

Section B

Passage One

In general, our society is becoming one of giant enterprises directed by a bureaucratic management in which man becomes a small, well-oiled cog in the machinery. The oiling is done with higher wages, well-ventilated factories and piped music, and by psychologists and "human-relations" experts; yet all this oiling does not alter the fact that man has become powerless, that he does not wholeheartedly participate in his work and that he is bored with it. In fact, the blue-and the white-collar workers have become economic puppets who dance to the tune of automated machines and bureaucratic management.

The worker and employee are anxious, not only because they might find themselves out of a job; they are anxious also because they are unable to acquire any real satisfaction or interest in life. They live and die without ever having confronted the fundamental realities of human existence as emotionally and intellectually independent and productive human beings.

Those higher up on the social ladder are no less anxious. Their lives are no less empty than those of their subordinates. They are even more insecure in some respects. They are in a highly competitive race. To be promoted or to fall behind is not a matter of salary but even more a matter of self-respect. When they apply for their first job, they are tested for intelligence as well as for the right mixture of submissiveness and independence. From that moment on they are tested again and again — by the psychologists, for whom testing is a big business, and by their superiors, who judge their behavior, sociability, capacity to get along, etc. This constant need to prove that one is as good as or better than one's fellow-competitor creates constant anxiety and stress, the very causes of unhappiness and illness.

Am I suggesting that we should return to the pre-industrial mode of production or to nineteenth century "free enterprise" capitalism? Certainly not. Problems are never solved by returning to a stage which one has already outgrown. I suggest transforming our social system from a bureaucratically managed industrialism in which maximal production and consumption are ends in themselves into a humanist industrialism in which man and full development of his potentialities — those of love and of reason — are the aims of all social arrangements. Production and consumption should serve only as means to this end, and should be prevented from ruling man.

57. By "a well-oiled cog in the machinery" the author intends to render the idea that man is _____.

　　[A] an unimportant part in comparison with the rest of society, though functioning smoothly

　　[B] a necessary part of the society though each individual's function is negligible

　　[C] a humble component of the society, especially when working smoothly

　　[D] working in complete harmony with the rest of the society

58. Unemployment is what the worker and employee worry, but they also worry that _____.

　　[A] they are faced with the fundamental realities of human existence

　　[B] they are deprived of their individuality and independence

　　[C] they don't own the genuine satisfaction or interest in life

　　[D] they are unable to acquire new jobs

59. From the passage we can infer that real happiness of life belongs to those _____.

　　[A] who are higher up in their social status

　　[B] who prove better than their fellow-competitors

　　[C] who could keep far away from this competitive world

　　[D] who are at the bottom of the society

60. To solve the present social problems the author suggests that we should _____.

　　[A] take the fundamental realities for granted

　　[B] enable man to fully develop his potentialities

　　[C] offer higher wages to the workers and employees

　　[D] resort to the production mode of our ancestors

61. The author's attitude towards bureaucratically managed industrialism might best be summarized as one of _____.

　　[A] tolerance　　　　　　　　　　　　[B] suspicion

　　[C] approval　　　　　　　　　　　　[D] dissatisfaction

Passage Two

　　Increasingly, over the past ten years, people — especially young people — have become aware of the need to change their eating habits, because much of the foods they eat, particularly processed food, are not good for the health. Consequently, there has been a growing interest in natural foods: foods which do not contain chemical additives and which have not been affected by chemical fertilizers, widely used in farming today.

　　Natural foods, for example, are vegetables, fruit and grain which have been grown in soil that is rich in organic matter. In simple terms, this means that the soil has been nourished by unused vegetable matter, which provides it with essential vitamins and minerals. This in itself is a natural process compared with the use of chemicals and fertilizers, the main purpose of which is to increase the amount — but not the quality — of foods grown in commercial farming areas.

　　Natural foods also include animals which have been allowed to feed and move freely in healthy pastures. Compare this with what happens in the mass production of poultry: there are battery farms, for example, where thousands of chickens live crowded together in one building and are fed on food which is little better than rubbish. Chickens kept in this way are not only tasteless as food; they also produce eggs which lack important vitamins.

　　There are other aspects of healthy eating which are now receiving increasing attention from experts on diet. Take, for example, the question of sugar. This is actually a nonessential food! Although a natural alternative, such as honey, can be used to sweeten food if this is necessary, we can in fact do without it. It is not that sugar is harmful in itself. But it does seem to be addictive: the quantity we use has grown steadily over the last two centuries and in Britain today each person consumes an average of 200 pounds a year! Yet all it does is to provide us with energy, in the form of calories. There are no vitamins in it, no minerals — and no fiber.

　　It is significant that nowadays fiber is considered to be an important part of a healthy diet. In white bread, for example, the fiber has been removed. But it is present in unrefined flour and of course in vegetables. It is interesting to note that in countries where the national diet contains large quantities of unrefined flour and vegetables, certain diseases are comparatively rare. Hence the emphasis is placed on the eating of whole-meal bread and more vegetables by modern experts on "healthy eating".

62. Which of the following is in accordance with people's "eating habits" as mentioned in the first paragraph?

    [A] To eat organic food.　　　　　　　　　　[B] To eat foods grown in soil.

    [C] To eat food containing additives.　　　　　[D] To eat natural meat.

63. The advantage of using unused vegetable matter to provide nourishment to the soil is that _____.

    [A] the unused vegetable matter can guarantee the food output

    [B] the unused vegetable matter can guarantee the quality of food grown in the soil

    [C] the unused vegetable matter can make the soil more nourished

    [D] the unused vegetable matter can guarantee the health of the soil

64. Battery chickens cannot be called "natural food" because _____.

    [A] they live in crowded conditions　　　　　　[B] they are tasteless

    [C] their eggs have no vitamins　　　　　　　[D] they are not allowed to move about and eat freely

65. What does "nonessential food" (Line 2, Para. 4) mean, according to the passage?

    [A] Sugar is valueless at all.　　　　　　　　[B] Sugar is not indispensable to people's diet.

    [C] Sugar is not important in nourishment.　　　[D] Sugar is not beneficial to people's health.

66. What is the effect of fiber according to the passage?

    [A] It can help people lose weight.　　　　　　[B] It can prevent some kind of disease.

    [C] It can be transformed into calories.　　　　[D] It can help people absorb the food more easily.

Part V　Cloze (15 minutes)

There was a time when parents who wanted an educational present for their children would buy a typewriter, a globe or an encyclopedia set. Now those __67__ seem hopelessly old fashioned: this Christmas, there were a lot of __68__ computers under the tree. __69__ that computers are their key to success, parents are also frantically insisting that children __70__ taught to use them on school as early as possible.

The problem for schools is that when it __71__ computers, parents don't always know best. Many schools are __72__ parental impatience and are purchasing hardware without __73__ educational planning so they can say, "Ok, we've moved into the computer age." Teachers __74__ themselves caught in the middle of the problem between parent pressure and __75__ educational decisions.

Educators do not even agree __76__ how computers should be used. A lot of money is going for computerized educational materials __77__ can be taught __78__ with pencil and paper. Even those who believe that all children should __79__ to computer warn of potential __80__ to the very young.

The temptation remains strong largely because young children __81__ so well to computers. First graders have been __82__ willing to work for two hours on math skills. Some have an attention span

67. [A] items　　　[B] toys　　　[C] sets　　　[D] series

68. [A] private　　[B] children　[C] school　　[D] personal

69. [A] Given　　　　　　　　[B] Provided
    [C] Convinced　　　　　　[D] Believed

70. [A] are　　　　　　　　　[B] be
    [C] are being　　　　　　[D] were

71. [A] talks about　　　　　[B] comes to
    [C] turns to　　　　　　[D] mentions

72. [A] ignorant of　　　　　[B] blaming
    [C] yielding to　　　　　[D] improving

73. [A] reason　　[B] sound　　[C] hard　　[D] some

74. [A] relied on　[B] relaxed　[C] freed　　[D] found

75. [A] wise　　　[B] clever　　[C] slow　　[D] enough

76. [A] on　　　　[B] with　　　[C] to　　　[D] among

77. [A] however　[B] where　　[C] what　　[D] that

78. [A] equally　　　　　　　[B] the same way
    [C] just as well　　　　　[D] not as well

79. [A] be open　　　　　　　[B] have access
    [C] look　　　　　　　　[D] turn

80. [A] approaches　　　　　[B] exposures
    [C] dangers　　　　　　[D] laziness

81. [A] adopt　　　　　　　　[B] keep
    [C] adapt　　　　　　　　[D] devote

82. [A] watched　　　　　　　[B] seen
    [C] told　　　　　　　　[D] taught

83. [A] High　　　　　　　　[B] Not every
    [C] No　　　　　　　　　[D] Any

of 20 minutes.

____83____ school, however, can afford to go into computing, and that creates ____84____ another problem: a division between the have's and have-not's. Very few parents ask ____85____ computer instruction in poor school districts, ____86____ there may be barely enough money to pay the reading teacher.

84. [A] already [B] of course
   [C] in addition [D] yet
85. [A] for [B] against
   [C] to buy [D] to use
86. [A] in that [B] in any case
   [C] although [D] where

Part VI Translation (5 minutes)

87. Persistent efforts are needed _____ (为了完成很重要但令人讨厌的任务).

88. After six months' work on the project, _____ (我终于感到有了一些发展).

89. _____ (货品中有圣诞树), flowers, candles, turkeys and toys.

90. Not only _____ (他们不仅进行了音乐表演), but they also gave a brief introduction to the history of Western brass instruments.

91. _____ (一直到所有的要求遭到拒绝之后) did they decide to go on strike.

答案与解析

Part I

【思路点拨】

本题属于提纲式文字命题。提纲第 1 点和提纲第 2 点要求指出竞赛中奖品的利与弊,提纲第 3 点要求阐述"我"对奖品的看法,由此可判断本文应属于对比选择型作文。

根据所给提纲,本文应包含以下内容:分别指出奖品的利与弊;表明"我"的观点并说明原因。

【参考范文】

Are Prizes a Good Thing?

More and more competitions are held nowadays with desiring prizes that can be a medal standing for honor or just an opportunity you have long dreamed of. Are prizes a good thing? (提出观点段)

Some people hold that competitions with prizes can bring people's initiative into full play. Encouraged by a strong desire to win a prize, one will go all out to seek his greatest success. Consequently, the best achievements will be obtained in a game with awards. (对比论证段一)

Others believe that a prize does not always lead to desirable results. For example, a competitor who cannot overcome the temptation of a prize is likely to take a stimulant, and the hopeless competitor sees nothing but the prize, which might cause improper behavior. (对比论证段二)

In my opinion, prizes are a good thing. The remedy for its bad effects lies in moral education of competitors. This will help them better understand the slogan: "Friendship — first, and competition — second". Then, prizes will play a better part in any contest. (总结观点段)

Part II

【文章大意】

本文讲述和列举了一些农场饲养的动物在饲养、运输、屠宰过程中所遭受的种种残忍的对待。文章通过对细节的描述以及指出动物保护法令的实施不力,呼吁人们关注和改善动物目前的悲惨境遇。

1. **【定位】**题干中的关键信息 the purpose of this article 提示本题与文章主旨有关,故应定位于整篇文章。

   【解析】[Y]. 结合文章的开篇内容及各个小标题可知,文章谈到了各种动物所遭受的虐待,其目的当然是为了引起更多的人关注动物们的遭遇。

2. **【定位】**根据题干中的关键信息 the Humane Slaughter Act 可将搜索范围定位在第三段。

   【解析】[N]. 该段第三句指出 The Humane Slaughter Act requires…(无痛屠宰法规定肉食品加工厂中的屠宰行为要在被屠宰的动物处于无意识的状况下才能进行),由该句中的 plants(工厂)可知,the Humane Slaughter Act 适用于 meat processing 而不是在 home 中发生的屠宰动物的行为。该段最后一句表明该法律并没有被很好的执行,由此可知,题干前半部分与原文相悖。

3.【定位】根据题干中的关键信息 28-hour law 可将搜索范围定位在第四段。

　　【解析】[N]。该段最后一句指出 28-hour time limit is sadly inadequate to protect the welfare of transported farmed animals and lags far behind international initiatives that call for time limits of between 8 and 12 hours(28 小时的时限对于保护运输中的农场动物的健康显然是不够的,而且该时间远远落后于国际上号召的 8—12 小时时限),题干的后半部分内容显然与原文不符。

4.【定位】根据题干中的关键信息 40 million 可将搜索范围定位在小标题 Cattle 下。

　　【解析】[NG]。该段第一句指出美国每年有 40 million 的牛与牛犊被屠宰,但题干中涉及到牛与牛犊被以什么方式屠宰,所以应将搜索范围扩展到下面几段中。阅读后可发现,在小标题 Cattle 下并没有讲这 40 million 是如何被屠宰的,题干表述内容在文中找不到依据。

5.【定位】根据题干中的关键信息 pigs、boiled 及 workers 可定位于小标题 Pigs 最后一段。

　　【解析】fail to kill them with the knife。该段最后一句指出 If workers fail to kill a pig with the knife, that pig is carded on the conveyer belt to the next station, where it may be boiled alive(如果工人们没能用刀子杀死猪,那么这只猪就会被放在传送带上送到下一个地方,在那里它们会被用开水活活烫死),答案应从该句中的条件从句中寻找。

6.【定位】根据题干中的关键信息 chickens 及 beaks 可将搜索范围定位在小标题 Poultry 或 Egg-laying Chickens 下。

　　【解析】peck each other。小标题 Poultry 下第二段指出因为生长环境拥挤及无法进行自然活动,chickens often excessively peck each other,所以 farmers have them "debeaked"(农民们就会切去它们的嘴尖),该段说明农民们 cut off(切去)鸡的嘴尖是为了使 chickens 不能再 peck each other。小标题 Egg-laying Chickens 下第二段 To keep hens from pecking each other, farmers "debeak" the hens 同样说明了 "debeak" 是为了使 chickens 不能再 peck each other。

7.【定位】根据题干中的关键信息 hens 及 eggs 可将搜索范围定位在小标题 Egg-laying Chickens 下第二段。

　　【解析】forced molting。该段第二句指出 When egg production slows down, farmers use "forced molting" to shock the hens into losing their feathers and prematurely starting a new laying cycle(当鸡蛋产量下降时,牧场主们就会采用"强制换毛"的方法使母鸡换掉旧羽毛,提前开始新一轮的产蛋期),题干内容是原文的同义转述。

8.【定位】根据题干中的关键信息 dairy cows 及 lifespan 可将搜索范围定位在小标题 Dairy Cows 下第二段。

　　【解析】the intensive production of milk。该段指出 the intensive production milk 给奶牛带来了非常大的负担,结果就造成了 dairy cattle "burn out" at a much younger age than their normal lifespan(奶牛在它们的自然寿命结束之前就过早死亡)。

9.【定位】根据题干中的关键信息 calves 及 milk 可将搜索范围定位在小标题 Dairy Cows 下最后一段。

　　【解析】human consumption。该段第三句指出在 dairy farm(乳牛场),小牛一出生就被送走,这样 the milk can be sold for human consumption(牛奶就可以出售,以供人类消费)。

10.【定位】根据题干中的关键信息 Australia ranchers 可将搜索范围定位在小标题 Other Farmed Animals 下第二段。

　　【解析】produce scarred skin that won't harbor fly larvae。该段第六句指出 This procedure is performed to produce…so that the rancher can spend less time caring for the sheep,其中的 this procedure 指的就是上句中的 mulesing,题干内容是该句话的同义转述。

Part III

Section A

11.

[A] Near an art gallery. [B] In front of a library. [C] At a stoplight. [D] Outside a bookstore.	M: Stop for a minute. I want to look at this display in the window. W: I see some books are on sale. Let's go inside and see if we can find something on art. Q: Where are they standing?
【解析】地点场景题。女士话中的 I see some books are on sale(我看到一些书正在出售)及 Let's go inside(我们进去吧)表明他们现在 outside a bookstore(在书店的外面)。	

12.

[A] He has missed three fourths of his two classes. [B] He couldn't attend his classes because of illness. [C] He failed in the exam. [D] He attended no classes at all.	W: Tom, I've been told you've missed six out of eight times in two different classes! M: Oh, come on. Those classes are really boring! Q: What's the matter with Tom?

【解析】事实状况题。女士话中的 you've missed six out of eight times in two different classes 表明,男士落下了 three fourths of his class(四分之三的课程)。

13.

[A] She wants to quit her job. [B] She wants to apply for a promotion. [C] She wants to transfer to another department. [D] She wants to get a salary rise.	M: Miss Green, why should you want to put in for a transfer? W: Well, I don't like the office and the staff. I'm a-fraid of you. So I don't want to go on. Q: What does Miss Green want to do?

【解析】事实状况题。由男士话中的反义疑问句 why should you want to put in for a transfer(你为什么申请调动部门)可知,女士想要 transfer to another department(换部门)。

14.

[A] The professor spoke too fast. [B] The professor spoke with a strong accent. [C] The professor's lecture notes were too complicated. [D] The professor's presentation was not convincing enough.	W: The presentation made by Professor Jackson was too complicated to understand. M: Well, I think he didn't speak slowly enough for us to take notes. Q: What is the man's complaint?

【解析】事实状况题。男士话中的 ...he didn't speak slowly enough for us to take notes 表明 Professor Jackson 说得太快,以至于他们都作不了笔记,由此可知他在抱怨 Professor Jackson 讲课时 spoke too fast。

15.

[A] She doesn't like either of them. [B] John copied it from Jim. [C] Jim copied it from John. [D] One of the compositions is the copy of the other.	M: Don't you think John and Jim are telling the truth? W: It doesn't seem likely. It would be hard to write two compositions so much alike unless one of them was copying from the other. Q: What seems to be the woman's opinion?

【解析】观点态度题。女士话中的 unless one of them was copying from the other(除非其中一人抄袭另一人的作文)表明她认为 John 和 Jim 其中一个人是在抄袭另一个人的作文,否则他们不可能写出这么相像的作文,也就是说 one of the compositions is the copy of the other(两篇作文中有一篇是在抄袭另一篇)。

16.

[A] A waitress. [B] A nurse. [C] A secretary. [D] A telephone operator.	M: Anne, my morning meeting may last longer than planned, would you call my wife and tell her I won't have lunch at home? W: Yes, sir. If anyone calls while you're out, I'll take the message. Q: What do you think is the woman's profession?

【解析】身份关系题。根据男士交代给女士的任务 call my wife and tell her... 和女士的回答 If anyone calls..., I will take the message 可以判断女士应该是一名 secretary。

17.

[A] $240. [B] $250. [C] $290. [D] $200.	M: How much is the rent? W: It's two hundred dollars a month unfurnished or two hundred and fifty dollars furnished. Utilities are forty dollars extra. Q: How much will it cost the man to rent a furnished apartment, including utilities?

【解析】数字信息题。由女士话中的 two hundred dollars a month unfurnished... 可知,没有装修的公寓月租金为 $200,装修过的公寓月租金为 $250,另外还要交纳 $40 的公用设施费用,所以如果男士要租一个带有公共设施的 furnished apartement,每月总共需付租金 $290。

18.

[A] He is going to watch the play. [B] He is going to do some work. [C] He is going to watch TV. [D] He is going to have a rest.	W: Aren't you going to watch the play in the theatre? M: Well, I have a lot of work to do. I would if I had the time. Q: What is the man going to do?

【解析】行为活动题。男士话中的 I have a lot of work to do 表明他不能去剧院看戏,因为他需要 do some work。

Conversation One

【听力原文】	【答案解析】
W: Good morning, sir. It's very nice to meet you. I've come for an interview. M: I see. Good morning. Take your seat, please. W: Thank you. I received your letter yesterday, and you told me to come this morning for an interview. M: Oh, so you are Miss Smith, and [19] you are one of the applicants to have answered our advertisement in the paper for an assistant account. Yes, we are having a vacancy, and I am expecting you. W: Thank you very much, sir. Nice office here. I suppose your company's business is very good. M: Well, not bad. May I see your reference materials? Frankly speaking, I'm quite satisfied with your qualifications since you have six years' experience in office work. I consider you the right person for this position. By the way, what company are you working with now? W: Well, I am out of job for the time being. I used to work in a Chinese firm whose boss was the sole proprietor. [20] But two months ago the boss went back to China with his family, so the firm was closed down. M: Does it mean that you can come here to work any time on call if we hire you? W: That's right. By all means. M: I think you understand that we'll have to take you on a three-month probation first. W: Of course, I understand. I'll do my best, and I think I can do a good job. By the way, what is the salary? M: One thousand and five hundred dollars a month to start with, and in three months' time your salary would be adjusted. And a year from now, you will have two weeks' annual leave. W: That's great. And when shall I start to work?	19. Where did Miss Smith get the information about the job vacancy? 【解析】选[D]。细节题。对话开头部分,在女士作完介绍之后,男士说女士是 one of the applicants to have answered our advertisement in the paper ...,由此可知,女士(Miss Smith)是从报纸上的招聘广告中得知男士公司的招工需求的,故答案为[D]。 20. Why is the woman applying for a new job? 【解析】选[C]。细节题。对话中女士提到她现在 out of job(没有工作),因为两个月前她的老板同家人回中国了,so the firm was closed down,由此可知,女士现在找工作是因为她先前的公司 closed down,故答案为[C]。 21. Which of the following is true according to the talk you've just heard? 【解析】[C]。细节题。对话结尾处,男士问女士对 start working on Monday 有没有意见,由女士的回答 I think it's the best 可知,女士同意下周一上班,故答案为[C]。由女士话中的 ... whose boss was the sole proprietor 可知[A] 选项错误;对话中男士说女士在试用期刚开

M: Let's see — today is Friday. [21①] You may start working on Monday. What do you say to it?

W: [21②] I think it's the best. Thank you very much, sir.

M: Good luck to you.

始的工资是 one thousand and five hundred dollars，但在试用期内工资会有变化，故[B]选项错误；[D]在对话中没有提到。

Conversation Two

【听力原文】

M: Hi, Alice. I hear that you are planning to have a dog in your house. Is that true?

W: Yeah. But I am not so sure now. [22] I'd love to have one because I think dogs are good companions.

M: Sure. I think most people have had a dog or wanted one as their companion at some time in their lives. [23] If you are thinking of buying a dog, you should first decide what sort of companion you need and whether the dog is likely to be happy in the surroundings you can provide.

W: So, what's your advice?

M: Specialist advice is available to help you choose the most suitable breed of dog. But in part, the decision depends on common sense. Most breeds were originally developed to perform specific tasks. So, if you want a dog to protect you or your house, for example, you should choose a breed that has the right size and characteristic.

W: I have not decided yet, you know. I just thought dogs are lovely and they will do things you want them to do.

M: That's half true. You must be ready to devote a good deal of time to train the dog when it is young and give it the exercise it needs throughout its life. Dogs are demanding pets. [24] The best time to buy a baby-dog is when it is between 6 and 8 weeks old so that it can transfer its affection from its mother to its master. If baby dogs have not established a relationship with the human being until they are over three months old, their strong relationship will always be with dogs. They are likely to be too shy when they are brought out into the world to become good pets.

W: Thank you so much for bring such valuable advice, Tom. [25] I think I am readier than before to have my own dog now.

【答案解析】

22. Why does the woman want to have a dog?

【解析】选[C]。细节题。由对话开头部分，女士话中的 I'd love to have one because I think dogs are good companions 可知，女士想要养狗是因为狗是人类的 good companions（好伙伴），故答案为[C]。

23. Which of the following should be taken into consideration when a person decides to adopt a dog?

【解析】[B]。细节题。对话中，男士提醒女士，如果她要考虑买狗的话，应该首先 decide what sort of companion you need and whether the dog is likely to be happy…，[B] 为考虑的因素之一，故为答案。

24. How old is the perfect age for a dog when it can easily transfer its affection from its mother to its master?

【解析】[A]。细节题。对话中，男士提到买小狗的最佳时间是狗出生后 6 至 8 周，这样小狗就能够将它对母亲的感情转移到它主人身上，故答案为[A]。

25. What do you think the woman is going to do?

【解析】选[A]。推断题。对话一开始，女士就说她想养一只狗，但是还不确定是否要养，但对话结尾处女士说她认为自己已经 readier than before to have my own dog now,（下定决心要养一只狗了），由此可推测，女士将会 adopt a dog，故答案为[A]。

Section B

Passage One

【听力原文】

In many businesses, computers have largely replaced paper work, because they are fast and don't make mistakes. As one bank manager said that unlike humans, computers never have a bad day, and they are honest. Many banks put advertisements in the newspaper showing that their business bills are untouched by human hands and therefore safe from human temptation. Obviously, computers have no reason to

【答案解析】

26. What is the disadvantage of computer in regard to computer criminals?

【解析】选[A]。推断题。文中提到，即使抓到了电脑罪犯也很难惩治他们，因为没有目击证人也没有证据，通过上下文可知，造成这种局面的一个重要因素就是 computer（电脑）无法记住利用它作案的人，言外之意就是电脑 can't offer evidence

steal money. But they also have no conscience, and a growing number of computer crimes show that they can be used to steal.

Computer criminals don't use guns and even if they are caught, it is hard to punish them because there are no witnesses and often no evidence. [26] A computer cannot remember who used it. It simply does what it is told to do. One clerk at a New York City Bank used a computer to steal more than one and a half million dollars in just four years. No one noticed this, because he moved money from one account to another. Each time a customer he had robbed questioned the amount in his account, the clerk claimed a computer error, then replaced the missing money from someone else's account. [27] This clerk was caught only because he was gambling. When the police broke up an illegal gambling operation, his name was put in the record.

Most computer criminals have been minor employees, but police wonder if this is true. As one official says that he has a feeling that there are more crimes out there than they are catching. What they are seeing is also poorly done. [28] He wonders what the real experts are doing — the ones who really know how a computer works.

to prove who used it(不能提供证据证明是谁利用它犯罪),这正是电脑的一个缺点,答案为[A]。

27. Why was the clerk at a New York City Bank arrested by the police?

【解析】选[B]。细节题。文中提到,New York City Bank 的一名员工利用职务之便,在四年的时间里从银行盗取了 150 万美元,但是直到警方根据他们破获的一起非法赌博案件中有他的名字而将其逮捕之后,他从银行非法盗窃钱财的事情才被揭发出来,也就是说 the clerk at a New York City Bank 最先是因为参加 illegal gambling(非法赌博)才被捕的,答案为[B]。

28. What does "experts" refer to in this passage, according to the police official?

【解析】选[B]。细节题。短文结尾处提到 one official说他 wonders what the real experts are doing — the ones who really know how a computer works(很奇怪那些真正的专家在做什么——那些真正知道电脑是如何运行的人),由此可知,one official 所说的 experts 在本短文中指的就是 the ones who really know how a computer works,[B]是原文的同义转述,为本题答案。

Passage Two

【听力原文】

Social comparison and its dynamic manifestation — the need to "keep up" — have long been part of American culture. [29] The term is "competitive consumption" — the idea that spending is in large part driven by a comparative or competitive process in which individuals try to keep up with the norms of the social group with which they identify a "reference group". Although the term is new, the idea is not. What's new is the redefinition of reference groups. Today's comparisons are less likely to take place between or among households of similar means. Instead, the lifestyles of the upper middle class and the rich have become a more salient point of reference for people throughout the income distribution. One reason for this shift is the decline of the neighborhood as a focus of comparison. Economically speaking, neighborhoods are relatively homogeneous groupings. In the 1950s and 60s, when Americans were keeping up with the Joneses down the street, they typically compared themselves to other households of similar incomes. [30] But as married women entered the workforce in larger numbers — particularly in white-collar jobs — they were exposed to a more economically diverse group of people, and became more likely to gaze upward. Neighborhood contacts correspondingly declined, and the workplace became a more prominent point of reference. Moreover, as people spent more time on the family room couch, television became more important as a source of consumer information. Because [31] television shows are so heavily skewed

【答案解析】

29. What does the term "competitive consumption" mean, according to the passage?

【解析】选[A]。细节题。文中开头处提到了 competitive consumption(竞争性消费)是指人们的消费 in large part driven by a comparative or competitive process(在很大程度上受到比较或竞争过程的影响),[A]是原文的同义转述,为本题答案。

30. Which of the following contributes to the decline of neighborhood contacts?

【解析】选[C]。细节题。文中提到在 1950s 和 60s,美国人通常会把自己与有着相同收入的家庭做比较,但是随着已婚妇女进入劳动大军——尤其是那些白领工作,她们能够见到更多不同经济层次的人,并且也更有可能朝经济处于上层的群体看齐,correspondingly(从而)导致了 neighborhood contacts decline,故答案为[C]。

31. What do television shows lay particular stress on, according to the passage?

【解析】选[B]。细节题。文中提到 television shows are so heavily skewed to the "lifestyles of the rich and upper middle class"(电视大力宣扬富有和中上层的人生活方式),题干中的

to the "lifestyles of the rich and upper middle class", they inflate the viewer's perceptions of what others have, and by extension what is worth acquiring what one must have in order to avoid being "out of it".

lay particular stress on 是 heavily skewed to 的同义转述,由此可知电视节目大力宣扬 lifestyles of the rich and upper middle class,故答案为[B]。

Passage Three

【听力原文】

[35①] Alaska is the largest of the states in size and the second smallest in population. [32] Nearly everything about this 49th state is big. Its Mount McKinley is higher than any other peak in North America. Its Yukon River is one of the longest navigable waterways in the world.

Alaska is a land of spectacular contrasts, smoking volcanoes and *frozen tundra*（冻原）, hot springs and *ice floes*（浮冰）, *creeping glaciers*（冰川）and virgin forests. This vast, raw, and rough land thrusts a chain of volcanic islands more than a thousand miles southwest into the Bering Sea. Reaching beyond the International Date Line, the land area originally spanned four time zones. [33] It stretches northward far into the Arctic Circle, and to the south, its Panhandle extends for miles between the Pacific Ocean and the Canadian Rockies.

The Stars and Stripes have flown over Alaska since March 30, 1867, [34] [35②] when the vast land was purchased from Russia for 7.2 million dollars. In 1959, Alaska became the first new state since [35③] New Mexico and Arizona had achieved statehood in 1912.

The state is so large that it increased the area of the United States by a fifth. [35④] Alaska is more than twice the size of Texas. About a third of the vast area is forested, and glaciers cover more than 28,800 square miles.

The name Alaska comes from the Aleut word "alaxsxaq", meaning "object toward which the action of the sea is directed", that is, the mainland. Its nicknames are the Land of the Midnight Sun and America's Last Frontier. It was once labeled "Seward's folly" and "Seward's icebox" in ridicule of the secretary of state who negotiated the purchase of what was considered a burden.

【答案解析】

32. How many states had been established in the United States before Alaska?

【解析】选[A]。推断题。文中提到几乎所有关于 this 49th state 的东西都是大的,根据短文首句话可知 this 49th state 指的就是 Alaska,由此可知 Alaska 是美国成立的第 49 个州,言外之意就是在 Alaska 成立之前美国已有 48 个州,故答案为[A]。

33. Where does Alaska reach southward?

【解析】选[B]。细节题。文中提到 Alaska 向北延伸到 the Arctic Circle(北极圈),向南延伸数里直至 the Pacific Ocean and the Canadian Rockies(太平洋和洛基山脉)之间的区域,故答案为[B]。

34. How much money did the United States spend in buying Alaska from Russia?

【解析】选[B]。细节题。文中提到 1867 年 3 月 30 日,美国以 7.2 million dollars 的价钱从俄国手中买下 Alaska 这片土地,故答案为[B]。

35. Which of the following about Alaska is true, according to the passage?

【解析】选[A]。细节题。短文一开始就指出 Alaska 的面积是美国最大的,人口却是美国的倒数第二,言外之意是 Alaska 的人口比绝大多数州的人口都少,故答案为[A]。文中提到 Alaska 是美国于 1867 年从 Russia(俄国)买来的,故[B]选项错;文中提到 New Mexico 和 Arizona 于 1912 年建州而不是 Alaska 于 1912 建州,故[C]错;文中提到 Alaska 的大小是 Texas 的两倍多,而不是只有两倍,故[D]错。

Section C

【听力原文】

All that we really need to plot out the future of our universe are a few good (36)measurements. This does not mean that we can sit down today and (37)outline the future course of the universe with anything like certainty. There are still too many things we do not know about the way the universe is put together. But we do know exactly what (38)information we need to (39)fill in our knowledge, and we have a (40)pretty good idea of how to go about getting it.

【答案解析】

36. 空前的形容词 a few 及 good 提示所填词应为复数可数名词。measurements 意为"测量"。

37. 空前的并列连词 and 提示所填词应与 sit down 并列,充当句子的谓语,故所填词应为动词。outline 意为"画出轮廓"。

38. 分析句子结构可知,所填词在从句中作 need 的宾语,故所填词应为名词。information 意为"信息"。

Perhaps the best way to think of our present (41)situation is to (42)imagine a train coming into a switchyard. All of the switches are set before the train arrives, so that its path is completely determined. Some switches we can see, others we cannot. There is no (43)doubt if we can see the setting of a switch: (44)we can say with confidence that some possible futures will not be realized and others will. At the unseen switches, however, there is no such certainty about it. (45)We know the train will take one of the tracks leading out but we have no idea which one. The unseen switches are the true decision points in the future and what happens when we arrive at them determines the entire subsequent course of events.

When we think about the future of the universe, we can see out "track" many billions of years into the future, but after that there are decision points to be dealt with and possible fates to consider. (46)The goal of science is to reduce the vagueness at the decision points and find the true road that will be followed.

39. 空前的不定式符号 to 及空后的介词提示所填词应为动词,且能与 in 搭配使用。fill 意为"填满、提供"。

40. 空前的不定冠词 a 及空后的名词提示所填词应为形容词。pretty 意为"相当好的"。

41. 空前的形容词提示所填词应为名词。situation 意为"形式,情况"。

42. 空前不定词 to 及空后名词提示所填词应为及物动词的动词原形。imagine 意为"设想,想象"。

43. 空前形容词 no 提示所填词应为名词。doubt 意为"疑问,怀疑"。

44. 【Main Points】we can **confidently** say that some possible futures will be **unrealized but** others will

45. 【Main Points】We know the train will take **one track which leads** out but we **don't know** which one

46. 【Main Points】The goal of science is to reduce the vagueness at the decision points and find the true road **we should follow**

Part IV

Section A

> 【文章大意】
>
> 　　本文主要讲述城市的定义与其演变过程。第一段讲述城市化的一般定义,第二段则从统计学上对城市化进行定义,第三段从历史上对城市的形成和演变过程进行具体的说明,同时还对城市的变化趋势进行预测。

> 【词性分析】
>
> 名　词:immigrants(移民);explosion(爆发,爆炸);inhabitants(居民);measure(方法,标准);modern(现代人,有思想的人);pace(速度)
>
> 动　词:accelerated(加速);constitutes(组成);measure(测量,测试);consists(组成);exhausted(用光,耗尽);pace(踱步,缓慢的走);limited(限制)
>
> 形容词:numerical(数字的,用数字表示的);classical(古典的,传统的);exhausted(耗尽的,疲惫的);accelerated(加快的);modern(现代的,现代化的);limited(有限的)
>
> 副　词:roughly(大约地,粗略地);accurately(精确地,正确地)

47. 选[B]。所填词作 what 引导的宾语从句的谓语,故所填词应为动词。主句的时态提示所填词应为一般现在时。备选项中符合此要求的为[B] constitutes(组成)和[I] consists(组成),但[I] consists 通常需与 of 搭配才表示"由…组成",并且它的主语应是复数或集体名词,故可排除。答案为[B] constitutes(组成)。

48. 选[G]。空前数词提示所填词应为复数名词,备选项中的复数名词只有[E] immigrants(移民)和[G] inhabitants(居民)。本句主要是讲 the United Nations 建议将有着 20,000 _____ 的地区看作是城市。结合全文可知,本文所讲的 urbanization 没有涉及到移民问题,所以可将[E] immigrants 排除,故答案为[G] inhabitants(居民)。

49. 选[C]。空前定冠词及空后名词提示所填词应为形容词。本文首段对 urbanization 的定义都是从人口数量出发的,所以联系上下文可以判断本句的 Whatever the _____ definition is 是对上段内容的总体概括,因此 _____ definition 应该是与数字有关的定义,故答案为[C] numerical(数字的,用数字表示的)。

50. 选[K]。空前介词及空后名词提示所填词应为形容词。备选项中的形容词从语义上来看可以初步确定[K] accelerated(加速的)和[M] modern(现代化的)符合要求。但空前的 a process of 提示"_____ urbanization"应是一个表示动态发展的城市化,故答案为[K] accelerated(加速的)。

51. 选[A]。分析句子结构可知所填词应为副词,备选项中的副词有[A] roughly(大约地,粗略地)和[L] accurately(精确地,正确地)。从常理来看,[A] roughly 更符合事实情况。

52. 选[O]。空前系动词及空后介词提示所填词应为动词的过去分词。上句指出到新石器时代人们才可以建立 permanent settlement,而本句则指出即使是 5,000 年以前这样的 permanent settlement 也只是 small, semi-permanent villages of peasant farmers。很明显在这 5,000 年的时间里肯定是某种原因阻碍了 permanent settlements 的发展,本句给出了阻碍它发展的原因,故所填词应该含有"阻碍,限制"之意,故答案为[O] limited(限制)。

53. 选[J]。空前系动词提示所填词可能为形容词或动词的过去分词。由第 52 小题的分析可知,这里阻碍 permanent settlement 发展的原因肯定是消极的。根据常理可知,人们要迁移是因为 the soil nearby 不再能满足他们的需求了,备选项中只有[J] exhausted(用光,耗尽)符合句意要求。

54. 选[D]。空前介词及空后名词提示所填词应为形容词。此处句意为:直到_____,才有了超过十万人口的城市。备选项中的形容词,最合适本处语境的是[D] classical(古典的,传统的),classical antiquity 指的是"18 世纪末 19 世纪初的一段时间"。

55. 选[F]。分析句子结构可知,所填词应为名词。备选项中的名词通常与 population 搭配使用的为[F] explosion(爆炸,爆发)。population explosion 意为"人口大爆炸"。

56. 选[H]。空前形容词提示所填词应为名词。分析上句可知,该句中的 this 指的是"生活在城市中的人口数量占总人口数量的百分比"。该句分别指出 mid-1960s 和 by 1980 这两个时期城市人口数量的百分比是为给本句中"估计到 2000 年世界会有一半的人口住在城市里"提供一种可能性的依据,所以根据上下文的语义联系可以推测 by this _____ 应表示"按这种标准",故答案为[H] measure(方法,标准)。

Section B

Passage One

【文章大意】

在注重生产和消费的现代化社会中,人的地位变得十分渺小。本文讲述的就是现代化社会的不足之处。文章第一段指出社会是一个由官僚政治管理的庞大企业,人的地位则十分低下;第二三段指出不论处于社会下层还是社会上层的人都有其担心之事;第四段中作者提出自己的观点。

57. 选[A]。事实细节题。文章第一段第一句提到 enterprises 时用了修饰词 giant,而用 small, well-oiled cog 来修饰 human,由 giant 与 small 之间的鲜明对比可以看出,human 在注重工业化的社会里显得十分渺小。而该段第二句中的 all this oiling does not alter the fact… 同样说明了这一点,[A]的表述内容与原文一致,为本题答案。

58. 选[C]。事实细节题。文章第二段第一句指出工人和被雇佣者的担心不仅是因为他们会 find themselves out of a job(失业),而且还是因为 they are unable to acquire any real satisfaction or interest in life(他们不会从生活中感受到任何真正的满足或兴趣),[B]为原文中第二个原因的同义转述,故为本题答案。

59. 选[C]。推理判断题。文章第三段末句指出一个人不断的证明自己和竞争对手一样甚至更加优秀导致了 anxiety and stress(忧虑和压力),而它们即是 unhappiness and illness(不幸和疾病)的原因,由此可推断出这三者之间的关系:竞争导致 anxiety and stress 产生,而 anxiety and stress 又导致 unhappiness and illness 产生,由此关系可知,如果一个人没有生存在竞争如此激烈的社会中,他就会感到幸福,故答案为[C]。

60. 选[B]。推理判断题。题干中的 the present social problems 指的是在由官僚政治统治管理的工业社会中,人的地位越来越低。作者在最后一段第四句对解决这一问题的方法提出了建议,即将社会体系由官僚政治统治的工业主义转变成 a humanist industrialism,在该体系下,人及他的 full development of potentialities 是所有社会安排的目的,由此可推断,要想改变现在的社会问题,就应该能使人充分发挥其潜能,故答案为[B]。

61. 选[D]。观点态度题。文章第一段最后一句 the blue-and the white-collar workers…,第二段最后一句 They live and die without…,第三段最后一句 This constant need to prove…及最后一段作者为改变当前社会问题而提出建议都表明作者对 bureaucratically managed industrialism 是不满的,故答案为[D]。

Passage Two

【文章大意】

本文是一篇提倡健康饮食的文章。文章第一段提出这样一个事实:越来越多的人开始注重健康饮食;第二三段主要介绍了什么是天然食物;第四五段主要介绍了健康饮食的其他方面。

62. 选[C]。事实细节题。第一段中出现的 eating habits 指的是人们在意识到 natural foods 的重要性以前的饮食习惯。由该段最后一句对 natural foods 的解释可知,在人们意识到 natural foods 的重要性以前,通常吃的是 foods…chemical additives 和 food … been affected by chemical…等,[C]属于其中的一种,故为答案。

63. 选[B]。推理判断题。文章第二段末句中的 This 指土壤由 unused vegetable matter 提供养料,这与用 chemicals and fertilizers 提供养料不同。文中指出用 chemicals and fertilizers 给土壤提供养料的目的是增加产量,而不是提高质量。由二者的对比可知,用 unused vegetable matter 给土壤提供养料能保证产品质量,故答案为[B]。

64. 选[D]。事实细节题。文章第三段首句指出那些 have been allowed to feed and move freely in healthy pastures 的动物才属于 natural foods,言外之意就是没有饮食及行动自由的动物不属于 natural foods。被饲养在 battery farms 中的鸡没有饮食及行动自由,所以它们不属于 natural foods,故答案为[D]。

65. 选[B]。推理判断题。文章第四段第三句中的 This 指的是 sugar,由第四句中的 we can in fact do without it 可知,sugar 不是饮食中不可缺少的。由此可知 nonessential food 指的是糖不是饮食中不可缺少的,故答案为[B]。

66. 选[B]。推理判断题。文章最后一段第三句指出 fiber 存在于 unrefined flour 和 vegetables 中,而第四句接着指出在大量食用 unrefined flour and vegetables 的国家,certain diseases are comparatively rare,由此可推断 unrefined flour 和 vegetables 中含有的 fiber 可以起到防止某种疾病产生的作用,故答案为[B]。

Part V

【文章大意】

目前,家长们十分重视孩子们的计算机教育,有些学校也迫于家长的压力,在没有切实可行的教学计划的情况下就购买计算机,对学生进行计算机教学。当涉及到计算机时,会有两个问题产生:一是父母们并不是十分了解计算机教学;二是并不是所有的学校都有能力购买计算机,实行计算机教学。

67. 选[A]。语义衔接题。空前的代词 those 提示所填词应该能囊括上句提到的 a typewriter,a globe 和 an encyclo-pedia set。[B] toys 专指玩具;[C] sets 指一套或一组东西;[D] series 表示丛书。这几个词都可以指代某种东西,但过于具体。[A] items 常用来指一组事物或某一清单中的一项、一条内容,根据上述分析,items 在本文中应指代一组事物,故答案为[A] items。

68. 选[D]。语义衔接题。根据上文可知,_____ computers 是现在父母送给子女的具有教育性的礼物。既然是父母送给子女的礼物,就不可能是[C] school;[B] children 后直接跟 computers 不符合语法规范;[A] private 和 [D] personal 都含有"私有的、个人的"意思,但它们的用法有差别:前者强调"归私人所有";而后者主要强调"个人的,个人用的",personal computer 意为"个人计算机",故答案为[D] personal。

69. 选[C]。结构衔接题。结合主句大意可知 computers are their key to success 是父母们的一种观念,故四个选项从意义上可首先排除[A] Given 和[B] Provided。而如果选[D] believed 的话,那么就表明 parents 和 believe 之间是被动关系,这明显不符合语法规范,故可将其排除;convince 意为"使相信,说服",常用于句型 convince sb. of sth. 和 convince sb. ＋that 从句,此处为过去分词作状语,表被动,故[C] Convinced 符合要求。

70. 选[B]。结构衔接题。insist 常用的句型是 insist ＋that(从句),表达两种意思:一是"坚持认为(说)",从句应该用陈述语气;二是"坚决要求,坚决主张",从句应该用虚拟语气,动词应该用"should＋动词原形"的形式,通常 should 可省。本句是表达父母们的一种主张,故动词应用"should＋动词原形"的形式,答案为[B] be。

71. 选[B]。惯用衔接题。从语法搭配上可排除[A] talks about 和[D] mentions,因这二者的主语通常是表示"人"的名词,it 在本句中明显指代的不是"人"。由主句 parents don't always know best 可知从句表达的是"当涉及到计算机的问题",英语中常用搭配 when it comes to… 表示"当说到…,当涉及到…"这一含义,故[B] comes to。

72. 选[C]。语义衔接题。and 连接的后一分句中的 without… 表明学校购买计算机时并没有充分准备好,由此可知,学校是在 parental impatience 的压力下购买计算机的。[C] yielding to"屈服于,让步于"符合句意,故为答案。

73. 选[B]。语义衔接题。通过 72 小题的分析可知,without _____ educational planning 表明学校在没有切实可行的教育计划时就购买了计算机,[A] reason 为名词,不能修饰名词;[C] hard 意为"艰难的",不符合句意要求; [B] sound 和[D] some 相比较而言,[B] sound 更符合句意,它在本句中意为"可靠的,合理的"。

74. 选[D]。结构衔接题。四个选项都为动词,表明所填词应在句中作谓语,这就表明 themselves 是所填词的宾语,而 caught in the middle of the problem 则只能作宾语补足语,四个选项中的动词具有"动词＋宾语＋宾补(分词、形容词、副词、名词、介词短语或 to be)"这一用法的只有[D] found。

75. 选[A]。惯用衔接题。英语中通常用 wise 修饰 decision 来表示"明智的决定",故答案为[A] wise。

76. 选[A]。惯用衔接题。四个选项中除[D] among 外都可以与 agree 搭配使用。[A] on,agree on 意为"就…取得一致意见";[B] with,agree with 意为"与…意见一致,与…相符",后既可以跟表示人的名词或人称代词,也可以跟表示意见、看法的名词或 what 引导的从句;[C] to,agree to 意为"同意某一建议或安排并参与执行"。根据上文可知,家长、学校、教师对计算机的问题意见不一,通过表递进关系的副词 even 可知,本句要表达的是教育学家们甚至对怎么使用计算机没有达成一致意见。结合上面的分析可知,[A] on 符合要求。

77. 选[D]。结构衔接题。分析句子结构可知,本句需要一个引导定语从句的关联词,[A] however 和[C] what 都不能引导定语从句,故可排除;[B] where 虽然能引导定语从句,但其先行词应是地点名词,故也可排除;[D] that 用在句中指代先行词 materials,故为答案。

78. 选[C]。语义衔接题。空后的 with pencil and paper 表示的是不同于 computerized(计算机化)教学方式的另一种教学方式:用纸和笔教学。误选[A] equally 和[B] the same way 的同学通常是因为它们能与介词 with 搭配使用,但却忽略了 with pencil and paper 在句中充当的是方式状语。通过上下文语义可知,本处表达的应是使用计算机教学的效果和使用纸和笔教学的效果是一样的,[C] just as well 符合句意,故为答案。

79. 选[B]。语义衔接题。本句中的副词 Even 以及主句的谓语 warn of 提示定语从句要表达的是"一些教育学家认为所有孩子都应该接触结算机"。四个选项中的词或短语都能与 to 搭配使用,但意义上有所差别:[A] be open, be open to 意为"对…开放";[B] have access, have access to 意为"有机会进入,接近,了解";[C] look, look to 意为"照顾,照料";[D] turn, turn to 意为"转向,求助于"。结合上面的分析可知[B] have access 最符合句意。

80. 选[C]。语义衔接题。结合 79 小题的分析可知,warn of 的主语为"那些认为孩子们应该有机会接触计算机的教育学家"。warn of 提示"孩子们接触计算机也存在着潜在的_____",很明显,所填词应为[C] dangers。

81. 选[C]。语义衔接题。所填词应能与介词 to 搭配使用,[A] adopt 为及物动词,故可首先将其排除。[B] keep, keep to 意为"坚持,保持,不离开";[C] adapt, adapt to 意为"适应";[D] devote, devote to 意为"致力于"。结合句意可知[C] adapt 最符合要求。本句的隐含意义为"当人们还在讨论要不要对孩子进行计算机教育的时候,孩子们已经很好的适应了计算机,这就导致了继续投入并使用计算机这种诱惑愈演愈烈。"

82. 选[B]。结构衔接题。[C] told 和[D] taught 通常没有 told doing 或 taught doing 的用法,故可首先排除;[A] watched 和[B] seen 都既可以跟 to do 形式也可以跟 doing 的形式,但[A] watched 侧重于"观看比赛、电视"等动态的事物,而[B] seen 侧重于"看到",强调看到的结果,willing to work…是"看到"的结果,故答案为[B] seen。

83. 选[B]。语义衔接题。上文提到很多学校迫于压力都买了计算机,实行计算机化教育,本句中的转折连词 however 提示本句的情况与上文提到的情况相反,即:有些学校却买不起计算机,开展不了计算机化教育。故所填词应该选择带有否定含义的词,[B] Not every 和[C] No 初步符合要求,但上文已经提到有很多学校都买了计算机,所以不能选择表示全部否定的否定词[C] No,而应选择表示部分否定的否定词[B] Not every。

84. 选[D]。结构衔接题。结合 83 小题的分析可知,并不是所有的学校都能买得起计算机并实行计算机教学,and 起进一步陈述的作用,that 指代前一分句所说的情况。[D] yet 的用法归纳起来有以下几点:一是用在否定句中,意为"还(没有)";二是用在疑问句中,意为"已经";三是意为"仍然,还在,还得";四是与比较级连用,意为"更加";五是和 another 或 more 连用,意为"还有"。本题明显是使用了 yet 的第五个用法,故答案为[D] yet。

85. 选[A]。语义衔接题。本句大意是在贫困地区,很少有父母要求学校进行计算机指导。[B] against 明显不符合句意;[C] to buy 和[D] to use 都不能与 instruction 搭配;[A] for, ask for 意为"要求,请求"符合句意。

86. 选[A]。结构衔接题。本句前半句大意为"在贫困地区,几乎没有家长要求计算机教学",后半句大意为"在这些贫困地区可能连读物都没钱买"。很明显,后半句是前半句的原因,故答案为[A] in that。in that 是从属连词,用在这里引导状语从句表示原因,相当于 because。[B] in any case 意为"不管怎样"。

Part VI

87. 【答案】in order to finish important but unpleasant tasks

【解析】本题考查对 in order to 用法的掌握。in order to 意为"为了…",引导目的状语从句。

88. 【答案】at last I feel I'm getting somewhere

【解析】本题考查对固定短语 get somewhere 的掌握。get somewhere 意为"有所进展、进步",类似的固定表达还有 get nowhere(没有进展、一无是处)。

89. 【答案】Among the goods are Christmas trees

【解析】本题考查对倒装句的掌握。当介词短语位于句首时,句子应采用倒装。"介词短语+be+主语"构成倒装,并且已成为一种固定的表达方式。介词短语 Among the goods 在句中实为表语成分。

90. 【答案】did they present a musical performance

【解析】本题考查对倒装以及 not only…but also 用法的掌握。当表示否定的词语位于句首时,句子应采用倒装。类似表示否定的词语还有 not, never, seldom, rarely, scarcely, hardly, little 等。"not only…but also…"连接并列成分,意为"不仅…而且…"。

91. 【答案】Not until all the demands had been turned down

【解析】本题考查对 not…until 句型的掌握。not…until 意为"直到…时,才…"。将 not…until 置于句首时,句子应采用倒装结构。

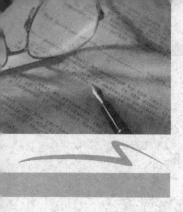

预 测 试 题 三

Part I　Writing（30 minutes）

Directions: *For this part, you are allowed 30 minutes to write a composition on the topic:* **Power Shortage**. *You should write at least 150 words, and base your composition on the outline given in Chinese below:*

1）目前许多城市出现电力供应紧张的现象
2）发生这种现象的原因
3）我们该采取什么样的应对措施

Power Shortage

Part II　Reading Comprehension（Skimming and Scanning）（15 minutes）

Cooperative Education

Cooperative Education is a planned learning process, which integrates classroom studies with supervised work assignments. These assignments may vary in length, depending upon the company's needs, the university's guidelines, and the availability of students. Students completing these assignments typically graduate with a year or more of experience in their major field as well as a diploma.

In What Way Will My Company Benefit?

Companies co-op for varying reasons, but those companies serious about making a long-term investment through their cooperative education programs do so for the following advantages:

- Lower labor costs: Fringe benefits often consume 25 to 35 percent of personnel costs. These costs can be minimized by utilizing co-op students in appropriate positions.

- Lower recruitment costs: Most companies spend more money than they realize on recruitment. Hours allocated for interviewing and direct dollars spent for travel to campuses are expensive. But perhaps the biggest hidden cost is hiring someone because he or she "looks good on paper". Looking like a productive worker on paper and being a productive worker are sometimes two different things. Co-op students are known quantities since company personnel have already worked with them.

- Improved employee retention: When hired after graduation, cooperative education students generally remain with initial employers longer than traditional students. Job expectations of co-op students are more realistic because of exposure to the real work environment. This employee retention also decreases long-term recruitment costs.

- Improved work performance: The breadth and depth of knowledge co-op students gain during their work periods enable them to begin at a higher level of responsibility and productivity than inexperienced graduates.

What Types of Jobs Are Applicable to Co-op?

Because most universities include a wide range of majors, virtually all white collar, managerial, professional and/or technical jobs are applicable to co-op.

What Kinds of Job Roles Can Be Assigned?

- Assistant to a position: When a company is growing, but is unsure of future growth, a co-op student is an excellent "hedge" to free a manager, planner, or other personnel to pursue critical matters. Using cooperative education in this manner allows a company a year or more to determine whether a company's growth is permanent or temporary. If permanent, then a permanent position may be created after the co-op cycle. If temporary, the co-op position can be deleted after the work cycle is completed.

● Project work: The "TO DO" list seems ever growing in many companies. Most workers are too busy keeping the company operating to do that needed statistical report, quality control study, layout experiment, comparison study, inventory check or the vital market study. These activities are excellent projects to co-op students.

● Trainee: Among companies that co-op mainly for recruiting purposes, the job role most frequently assigned to beginning co-op students is trainee. This position differs from the assistant position because more independent work assignments are required.

What Types of Structures Are Available?

Alternating Structure: Nationwide, this is probably the most popular approach. Students work a term and alternate the next term with academic study. This process is continued until work sessions are completed. To organize this structure within a company's payroll and personnel systems, most companies create a full-time co-op position. One full-time position requires two co-op employees. For example, student "A" works the fall semester. Student "B" works the spring semester while student "A" takes academic courses.

This popular method allows companies the opportunity to view two prospective employees for future human resource needs.

Consecutive Structure: In the consecutive structure, the student works a full year and then returns to finish studies. For jobs requiring students to move, this is the most economical and convenient structure. Since the student will work 2 to 3 straight semesters, the student moves only once rather than many times as in the alternating structure, perhaps the consecutive structure's greatest advantage is optimal continuity and completion of in-depth projects.

Parallel Structure: This is another popular work pattern. This structure permits companies to employ one or more students on a part-time basis. The students may at the same time take a limited number of courses. This structure doubles the number of prospective employees a company may examine (assuming full-time positions divided in half). However, the structure also doubles the amount of training and administrative work.

What to Include in Job Descriptions

A job description should be created for each work session, and each work session should be progressively more complex.

The main purposes for cooperative education job descriptions are to develop guidelines, avoid incorrect assumptions, and encourage productivity. The company, student and university should agree and understand the expectations of the student for each work period. Companies will be employing sophomore or junior students, not graduates. Scaling down the current job description into appropriately numbered sessions helps the work supervisor develop realistic student worker capabilities as well as provide psychological security to the student. When the company, student, and university plan for and expect progressive responsibility and productivity, teamwork, pride, and positive working relationships develop among the three parties.

Where Should a Company Set Salary?

Because companies must operate using economic soundness, special care should be devoted to determining pay for cooperative education students. The first session salary should be as high as possible to attract quality applicants; however, a company must leave itself room to increase its wages matching to job description and responsibilities developed for subsequent work sessions. The last work session salary should be strategically set to allow a company to hire the student upon graduation if so desired. A sufficient salary differential should exist between the final work session co-op salary and the permanent job salary if it is to be attractive to the student upon graduation. While determining salaries, companies should remember cooperative education graduates nationwide begin at a higher salary than non-experienced graduates do.

The guidelines to follow when setting salary are:

● Set beginning salary high enough to attract quality students, but

● Set final salary low enough to allow for an attractive permanent job salary, and

● Plan for salary progression between each work session.

Are Co-op Students Entitled to Fringe Benefits?

Fringe benefits, if any, are determined strictly by each company. Following are some of the fringe benefits most frequently asked about by both employers and students.

Paid Holidays: These can be awarded with or without pay, but companies need to determine this prior to interviewing students and should set a policy to avoid misunderstanding.

Insurance: Companies should be sure students have or will be provided health insurance. Many universities will have "insurance available to students". To protect the company, some policies on insurance requirements should be set.

Seniority: Those companies that utilize cooperative education as a recruiting tool include time accumulated during co-op sessions when calculating seniority. This is a definite incentive to a prospective employee who was a co-op student at that company.

Travel Expenses: When companies are located many miles (as defined by each company) from the university campus, some pay mileage to and from the university campus.

Management: Key Points to Remember Are

- Select and Develop Skilled Work Supervisors. These people are critical components of a co-op program. They must have skill in human relations and be willing to work with and to develop students.

- Work with Multiple Schools. When your company becomes familiar with cooperative education, consider working with additional schools. This will increase both the pool of student applicants and the variety of majors from which you may choose.

- Develop and Revise Job Descriptions. Changes in responsibilities are inevitable within any organization. Evaluating each job description and appropriately revising it prior to hiring another co-op student is an excellent procedure.

- Determine and Update Salary Schedules. Update cooperative education base salaries each fiscal year when other personnel salaries are updated. This should be a relatively simple procedure to begin and would keep the company economically competitive.

- Develop Working Relationships with University Personnel. Develop and maintain an open relationship with the university Cooperative Education Director and departmental instructors in your co-op students' majors. These relationships could lead to student field trips to your company and to university visits by company personnel, both of which are excellent advertising and public relations tools for your organization.

Conclusion

As we progress into the new century, more and more companies are utilizing cooperative education programs for recruiting purposes. Cooperative education workers are known quantities.

1. Cooperative education is a useful form utilized by companies as a labor-recruiting tool.
2. Co-op programs can help the company recruit productive employees, which can lower company's recruitment costs.
3. Half of the co-op students are less likely to hop from job to job than traditional students.
4. Project work that other employees are not able to do can be assigned to co-op students.
5. In co-op programs, _____ is generally favored by companies in terms of working structure.
6. In _____, the students move less frequently than that in the alternating structure.
7. When setting salary, companies should bear in mind that there should be a _____ between each work session.
8. Applicants often show their focus on fringe benefits including _____.
9. In order to have more students and more majors to choose, co-op companies are advised to cooperate with _____.
10. By updating cooperative education base salaries each fiscal year, co-op companies may _____.

Part III　Listening Comprehension (35 minutes)

Section A

11. [A] In the book department.　　　　　　　[B] In the record department.
　　[C] In the marketing department.　　　　　[D] In the sales department.
12. [A] Because he likes feeling completely free.　[B] Because he likes to see the changes in climate.
　　[C] Because he is interested in talking with people.　[D] Because he likes feeling the ground under his feet.
13. [A] That he can't sleep at night.
　　[B] That he can't find a quiet place to study.
　　[C] That he can't narrow down his research topic.
　　[D] That he can't find enough information for his research paper.

14. [A] Travel by train.   [B] Travel by plane.
     [C] Drive by himself.   [D] Hitchhike.

15. [A] Boss and employee.   [B] Classmates.
     [C] Teacher and student.   [D] Father and daughter.

16. [A] In a fashionable dress store.   [B] On a fashion show.
     [C] In a shopping mall.   [D] On a recent fair.

17. [A] She fears for the coming examination.   [B] She doesn't want to leave her classmates.
     [C] She is afraid she will not find a job.   [D] She wants to continue her study.

18. [A] To travel abroad together with the man.   [B] To study English further.
     [C] To learn a foreign language from some immigrants.   [D] To teach English to some immigrants.

Questions 19 to 21 are based on the conversation you have just heard.

19. [A] Reading some books.   [B] Writing some essays.
     [C] Learning some practical research methods.   [D] Doing some research work.

20. [A] In West.   [B] At home.
     [C] At abroad.   [D] In the U. S.

21. [A] Her university.   [B] Dr. Spencer.
     [C] Chinese government.   [D] Dr. Wilson.

Questions 22 to 25 are based on the conversation you have just heard.

22. [A] It is difficult to get a certification of the health profession.
     [B] It is constantly breaking new ground.
     [C] It is beneficial to anyone who like both nursing and traveling.
     [D] It usually needs five years to get a diploma.

23. [A] Six.   [B] Three.
     [C] Five.   [D] Four.

24. [A] She loves to travel.   [B] She loves to be different.
     [C] She loves to challenge.   [D] She loves to meet people.

25. [A] Contracting some infectious diseases.   [B] Working while others are enjoying themselves.
     [C] Facing the patients all the time.   [D] Keeping learning.

Section B

Passage One

26. [A] To establish their own kingdoms.   [B] To escape from other groups' attack.
     [C] To have a comfortable living environment.   [D] To develop their own culture.

27. [A] It is still a feudal society.   [B] Its tourism develops rapidly.
     [C] It still locates in the north of China.   [D] It is still underdeveloped.

28. [A] Buddhist.   [B] Christianism.
     [C] Taoism.   [D] Catholicism.

Passage Two

29. [A] The purity of wastewater.   [B] The recycle of wastewater.
     [C] Good management practices.   [D] Proper treatment with wastewater.

30. [A] Sanitation promotion.   [B] The nutrition of food.
     [C] The consciousness of people.   [D] The abundance of water resource.

31. [A] In 1979.   [B] In 1899.
     [C] In 1989.   [D] In 1968.

Passage Three

32. [A] Canadian and American newspapers.   [B] Italian and Greek newspapers.
     [C] French and American newspapers.   [D] British and Kansas newspapers.

33. [A] *A Farewell to Arms*.   [B] *The Sun Also Rises*.
     [C] *For Whom the Bell Tolls*.   [D] *The Old Man and the Sea*.

34. [A] In 1964.　　　　　　　　　　　　[B] In 1958.
    [C] In 1954.　　　　　　　　　　　　[D] In 1914.
35. [A] He liked hunting for animals.　　　[B] He liked fighting against soldiers.
    [C] He liked sports.　　　　　　　　　[D] He liked bullfight.

Section C

Social customs and ways of behaving change. Things which were (36) _____ impolite many years ago are now (37) _____. Just a few years ago, it was an impolite (38) _____ for a man to smoke on the street. No man who thought of himself as being a (39) _____ would make a fool of himself by smoking when a lady was in a room.

Customs also (40) _____ from country to country. Does a man walk on the left or the right of a woman in your country? Or does it not matter? What about table manners? Should you use both hands when you are eating?

The Americans and the British not only speak the same language but also share a large number of social customs. For example, in both America and England, people shake hands when they meet each other for the first time. Also, most Englishmen will open a door for a woman or (41) _____ their seats to a woman, and so will most Americans. In England and America, (42) _____ is important both. That is, if a dinner (43) _____ is for 7 o'clock, (44) _____.

The important thing to remember about social customs is (45) _____. There is an old story about a man who gave a formal dinner party. When the food was served, one of the guests started to eat his peas with a knife. The other guests were amused or shocked, but the host calmly picked up his knife and began eating in the same way. (46) _____.

Part IV　Reading Comprehension (Reading in Depth) (25 minutes)
Section A

Medical science is doing all it calls to extend life and is succeeding brilliantly. Living conditions are so much better, so many diseases can either be prevented or cured that life expectation has increased enormously. No one would deny that this is a good thing — provided one enjoys perfect health. But is it a good thing to extend human suffering, to prolong life, not in order to give joy and happiness, but to give pain and sorrow? As an extreme example, take the case of a man who is so senile that he has lost all his faculties. He is in hospital in an unconscious state with little chance of coming round, but he is kept alive by artificial means for an indefinite period. Everyone, his friends, relatives and even the doctors agree that death will bring relief. Indeed, the patient himself would agree — if he were in a position to give choice to his feelings. Yet everything is done to perpetuate what has become a meaningless existence.

The question of *euthanasia* (安乐死) raises serious moral issues, since it implies that active measures will be taken to terminate human life. And this is an exceedingly dangerous principle to allow. But might it not be possible to compromise? With regard to senility, it might be preferable to let nature take its course when death will relieve suffering. After all, this would be doing no more than was done in the past, before medical science made it possible to interfere with the course of nature.

There are people in Afghanistan and Russia who are reputed to live to a ripe old age. These exceptionally robust individuals are just getting into their stride at 70. Cases have been reported of men over 120 getting married and having children. Some of these people are said to be over 150 years old. Under such exceptional conditions, who wouldn't want to go on living forever? But in our societies, to be 70 usually means that you are old; to be 90 often means that you are decrepit. The instinct for self-preservation is the strongest we possess. We cling dearly to life while we have it and enjoy it. But there always comes a time when we'd better die.

47. It would be much better for a person to live as long as possible only if he (she) _____.

_____ _____ _____ _____ _____ _____ _____ _____ _____ _____

48. Extended life supported by artificial means does not always make the person feel _____.

_____ _____ _____ _____ _____ _____ _____ _____ _____ _____

49. What does the phrase "to let nature take its course" mean in the second paragraph?

_____ _____ _____ _____ _____ _____ _____ _____ _____ _____

50. Euthanasia is a word used to describe a fact that human life _____.

_____ _____ _____ _____ _____ _____ _____ _____ _____

51. What attitude does the author hold toward euthanasia?

_____ _____ _____ _____ _____ _____ _____ _____ _____

Section B

Passage One

The scattering of galaxies, the habits of macromolecules, and the astounding abundance of stars are forcing those who ponder such matters to a further adjustment of their concept of the place and function of man in the material universe.

In the history of the evolving human mind, with its increasing knowledge of the surrounding world, there must have been a time when the philosophers of the early tribes began to realize that the world was not simply anthropocentric — centered on man himself. The geocentric concept then became common doctrine. It accepted a universe centered on the earth. This first adjustment was only mildly deflationary to the human ego, for man appeared to surpass all other living forms.

The second adjustment in the understanding of man's relation to the physical universe, that is, the abandonment of the earth-center theory, was not generally acceptable until the sixteenth-century Copernican revolution soundly established the heliocentric concept — the theory of a universe centered on the sun. Man is a stubborn adherent to official dogma; eventually, however, he accepted the sun as the center not only of the local family of planets, but also of the sidereal assemblage, and he long held that view.

Then, less than forty years ago, came the inescapable need for a third adjustment. This shift has deeply punctured man's pride and self-assurance, for it has carried with it the knowledge of the appalling number of galaxies.

The "galactocentric universe" suddenly puts the earth and its life near the edge of one great galaxy in universe of millions of galaxies. Man becomes peripheral among the billions of stars of his own Milky Way; and, according to the revelations of paleontology and geochemistry, he is recent and apparently ephemeral in the unrolling of cosmic time. We cannot restore geocentrism or heliocentrism. And since we cannot go back to the cramped but comfortable past, we go forward and find there is more to the story.

The downgrading of the earth and sun and the elevation of the galaxies is not the end of this progress of scientific pilgrims through philosophic fields. The need for another jolting adjustment now appears — not wholly unexpected by workers in science, nor wholly the result of one or two scientific revelations.

Our new problem concerns the spread of life throughout the universe. As unsolicited spokesmen for all the earthly organisms of land, sea, and air, we ask the piquant question: Are we alone?

52. The passage is mainly about _____.

[A] how the universe develop as time passed on   [B] people's developing knowledge about the universe

[C] the component of the universe   [D] the theories related to the universe

53. What does "geocentric" (Line 3, Para. 2) mean, according to the passage?

[A] The universe in which man is the most important.   [B] The universe which is related to the earth.

[C] The universe which centered on the sun.   [D] The universe in which earth is the center.

54. What did man think of Copernican's the sun-center theory at first, according to the passage?

[A] They advocated it.   [B] They thought it absurd.

[C] They showed enthusiastic about it.   [D] They compared it with the former theory.

55. People didn't believe that _____ before the adjustment from the sun-center universe to the galactocentric universe happened.

[A] there are numbers of galaxies in the universe   [B] the universe is composed of macromolecules

[C] the galactocentric universe can form   [D] their pride and self-assurance could be shocked

56. What will it talk about if the passage continues?

[A] Whether it is reasonable for man to represent all the creature on earth.

[B] Whether there is creature as man somewhere in the universe.

[C] Whether the universe will develop or not.

[D] Whether man will be lonely.

Passage Two

At the moment the second plane was slamming into the south tower, President Bush was being introduced to the second-graders of Emma E. Booker Elementary in Sarasota, FLA. When he arrived at the school he had been whisked into a holding room: National Security Adviser Condoleezza Rice needed to speak to him. But he soon appeared in the classroom and listened appreciatively as the children went through their reading drill. As he was getting ready to pose for pictures with the teachers and kids, Chief of Staff Andy Card entered the room, walked over to the President and whispered in his right ear. The President's face became visibly tense and serious. He nodded Card left and for several minutes the President seemed distracted and somber, but then he resumed his interaction with the class. "Really good readers, whew!" he told them. "These must be sixth-graders!"

Meanwhile, in the room where Bush was scheduled to give his remarks, about 200 people, including local officials, school personnel and students, waited under the hot lights. Word of the crash began to circulate; reporters called their editors, but details were sparse — until someone remembered there was a TV in a nearby office. The President finally entered, about 35 minutes later, and made his brief comments. "This is a difficult time for America," he began. He ordered a massive investigation to "hunt down the folks who committed this act". Meanwhile the bomb dogs took a few extra passes through Air Force One, and an extra fighter escort was added. But the President too was going to have trouble getting home. Even as the President spoke, the second front opened. Having hit the country's financial and cultural heart, the killers went for its political and military muscles. David Marra, 23, an information-technology specialist, had turned his BMW off an I395 exit to the highway just west of the Pentagon when he saw an American Airlines jet swooping in, its wings wobbly, looking like it was going to slam right into the Pentagon: "It was 50ft off the deck when he came in. It sounded like the pilot had the throttle completely floored. The plane rolled left and then rolled right. Then he caught an edge of his wing on the ground." There is a helicopter pad right in front of the side of the Pentagon. The wing touched there, then the plane cart wheeled into the building.

57. What did President Bush convey by saying "These must be sixth-graders"?

   [A] The pupils are six-graders in fact.

   [B] Even if the sixth-graders cannot have so good reading level.

   [C] The teacher is so good that his students are so excellent.

   [D] The second-graders' reading level is laudable.

58. What was President Bush doing when he heard the news about crash from Card?

   [A] He was painting a picture with the teachers and children.

   [B] He was preparing to be photographed with the teachers and children.

   [C] He was making a speech to the teachers and children.

   [D] He was listening carefully to the children reading.

59. How might the 200 people response when they first knew the crash?

   [A] They were panic-stricken.

   [B] They were calm.

   [C] They were eager for President Bush's comment.

   [D] They showed great concern about the safety of the president.

60. The phrase "the second front" (Line 7, Para. 2) refers to _____.

   [A] the second frontispiece of the financial and cultural heart

   [B] the second forward part of the plane

   [C] the second attack toward the financial and cultural heart of the U. S.

   [D] the second place where the financial and cultural heart locates

61. David Marra was _____ according to the passage.

   [A] a survivor of the crash   [B] a witness of the crash

   [C] a succor after the crash   [D] a police officer

Part V   Error Correction (15 minutes)

We are living in what we call the second great change in the state of man. The first is the change from pre-civilized to civilized societies. The first five hundred thousand years or so of man's existence on the earth were relatively eventful.

Comparing with his present condition, he puttered along in an astonishing stationary state. There may have been changes in language and culture which are not reflected in artefacts, but if there was, these changes are lost to us. The evidence of the artefacts, therefore, is conclusive. Whatever changes they were, they were almost unbelievably slow. About ten thousand years ago, we begin to perceive an acceleration in the rate of changes. This becomes very noticeable five thousand years ago as the development of the first civilization. The details of this first great change are probably past our recovery.

However, we did know that it depended on two phenomena: the development of agriculture and the development of exploitation.

Agriculture, which is the domestication of crops and livestocks and the planting of crops in fields, gave man a secure surplus of food from the food producer. In a hunting and fishing economy it seems to take the food producer all his time to produce enough food for himself and his family. The moment we have agriculture, with its superior production of this form of employment of human resources, the food producer can produce more food than he and his family can eat.

62. _____

63. _____

64. _____

65. _____

66. _____

67. _____

68. _____

69. _____

70. _____

71. _____

Part VI Translation (5 minutes)

72. It is interesting _____ (把英国的法制同美国的相对比).

73. Many people cherish time very much, so it's very necessary that _____ (时间应得到合理规划).

74. The students as well as the teacher _____ (出席了会议).

75. As the president drew up, _____ (人群中爆发出热烈的掌声).

76. _____ (我本可以轻易通过考试), but I made too many stupid mistakes.

答案与解析

Part I

【思路点拨】

本题属于提纲式文字命题。提纲第1点要求描述当前电力供应紧张的现象,提纲第2点要求分析出现这种现象的原因,提纲第3点则要求提供解决方法,由此可判断本文属于问题解决型作文。

根据所给提纲,本文应包含以下内容:描述当前许多城市电力供应紧张的现象;分析出现这种现象的原因;阐述我们该如何解决问题。

【参考范文】

Recently, every morning when I wake up, I find my air-conditioner automatically turned off. I didn't understand why at first, but soon I learned that there is a great shortage of electricity supply in our city—my air-conditioner turned off because of a power failure at midnight. (描述问题段)

With the rapidly developing industry and the ever increasing population, demand for electricity supply is soaring. Besides, summers in recent years are much hotter than before, so most working places and households have air-conditioners on, which consume additional electricity. (说明原因段)

Faced with such a hard nut, we have to find ways to crack it. Above all, there is surplus of electricity supply in western areas of China, so cities thirsty for electricity may ask for remote help. Then, we should remember to save electricity in daily life. Set your air-conditioners at 27℃ and you won't feel less comfortable than when they are at 26℃. In fact, some factories already shift their working hours to avoid the peak time of electricity-consuming. This is also a way out, isn't it?(说明方法段)

Part II

【文章大意】

　　本文讲述合作教育给企业和学生所带来的益处。首先从公司角度讲述其所得到的好处;其次介绍适合学生从事的工作以及公司所选用的工作结构模式、工作描述以及工资的设定;接着介绍了学生所能享受的福利待遇,最后对公司的管理提出几点建议。

1. 【定位】根据题干内容可知,本题考查的是全文的主旨,故应定位于整篇文章。

【解析】[Y]。结合文章各个小标题可知,文章主要讲的是合作教育的种种好处,目的在于说明它为企业提供了一种更好的员工招募方式。

2. 【定位】根据题干中的关键信息 lower company's recruitment costs 可将搜索范围定为在小标题 In What Way Will My Company Benefit?下的第三段。

【解析】[Y]。该部分是 cooperative education programs 的一个优点。本段先指出没有 cooperative education programs 的公司会面临的问题是:spend more money than they realize on recruitment,hiring someone because he or she "looks good on paper"。而根据下文可知 he or she "looks good on paper"指的是公司招聘的生产效率低的员工,而在 co-op education programs 帮助下的公司则不会出现这种情况,由此可知 co-op education programs 能够帮助公司 recruit productive employees(招聘到生产效率高的员工)。

3. 【定位】根据题干中的关键信息 hop from job to job 可将搜索范围定位在小标题 Is What Way Will My Company Benefit?下的第四段。

【解析】[NG]。该段首句指出 when hired after graduation. Cooperative education students generally remain with initial employers longer than traditional students,由此可知原文只是说合作教育培养的学生在最初的公司待的时间比传统学校的学生长,即他们跳槽的可能性较小,但并未提及具体的比例。

4. 【定位】根据题干中的关键信息 project work 可将搜索范围定位在小标题 What Kinds of Job Roles Can Be Assigned?下的第二段。

【解析】[N]。该段第二句指出大多数工人 too busy keeping the company operating to do…(大多数工人都忙着使公司运转以至于没有时间作统计报告、质检调查等工作),由此可知这些工作只是大多数工人没有时间做,而不是 not able to do(没有能力做)。

5. 【定位】根据题干中的关键信息 working structure 可将搜索范围定位在小标题 What Types of Structures Are Available?下。

【解析】the alternating structure。该部分分别介绍了三种不同的结构:Alternating Structure,Consecutive Structure,Parallel Structure,在介绍第一种结构 Alternating Structure 时,文章使用了最高级 this is probably the most popular approach,这就说明 alternating structure 是最受欢迎的一种结构。

6. 【定位】根据题干中的关键信息 move less frequently 以及 the alternating structure 可将搜索范围定位在小标题 What Types of Structures Are Available?下。

【解析】consecutive structure。该部分提到在 consecutive structure 下学生会连续工作 2 至 3 个学期,所以他们 moves only once(只会离开一次);而在 alternating structure 下学生 work a term;在 parallel structure 下只是 on a part-time basis,可以离去上课,所以学生离开次数比在 alternating structure 下的次数少的是 consecutive structure。

7. 【定位】根据题干中的关键信息 setting salary 及 work sessions 可将搜索范围定位在小标题 Where Should a Company Set Salary?下。

【解析】salary progression。该部分第一段指出在 the first work session 时,薪资水平应该 as high as possible to attract quality applicants,在接下来的 work sessions,公司在设置薪资水平时应该给自己留有余地以使薪资水平能符合 job description 和 responsibilities 的发展,而在最后一个 work session 时,薪资水平应该能使公司所要雇佣的学生满意。也就是说公司设置薪资水平在不同的 work session 应该有所不同,应是逐渐增长的,即 between each work session,都应有个 salary progression,这一点可以在本部分最后一句得到验证。

8. 【定位】根据题干中的关键信息 fringe benefits 可将搜索范围定位在小标题 Are Co-op Students Entitled to Fringe Benefits?下。

【解析】paid holiday,insurance,seniority and travel expenses。该标题下的各个点就是应聘者最经常关注的 fringe benefits 的内容。

9. 【定位】根据题干中的关键信息 co-op companies are advised 可将搜索范围定位在小标题 Management: Key Points to Remember Are 下。

【解析】multiple schools。该部分指出,当公司对合作教育熟悉以后就应该考虑 working with additional schools,这

既有助于增加 the pool of student applicants,也有助于 the variety of majors from which you may choose,由此可知如果公司想要有更多的机会来选择学生或专业,那么它们就应该 work with multiple schools(跟多个学校合作)。

10.【定位】根据题干中的关键信息 updating…base salaries 可将搜索范围定位在小标题 Management: Key Points to Remember Are 下。

【解析】become economically competitive。该部分第四段最后一句指出 This…would keep the company economically competitive,该句即为本题答案出处。

Part III

Section A

11.

[A] In the book department.	M: How long have you been working here, Miss Jones?
[B] In the record department.	W: Nearly two years, sir, but not all the time in the book department. I was in the record department for ten months.
[C] In the marketing department.	
[D] In the sales department.	Q: Where does Miss Jones work at present?

【解析】地点场景题。由女士话中的 I was in the record department for ten months 的过去时态可知,女士曾经在 record department 工作了十个月,但现在她在 the book department 工作。

12.

[A] Because he likes feeling completely free.	W: I like getting to different places fast by plane. I enjoy seeing the sudden changes in social atmosphere and climate.
[B] Because he likes to see the changes in climate.	
[C] Because he is interested in talking with people.	M: Well, I'm afraid I'd rather travel by car or by train. I like feeling the ground under my feet.
[D] Because he likes feeling the ground under his feet.	Q: Why does the man like to travel by train?

【解析】事实状况题。男士话中的 I like feeling the ground under my feet 表明,他喜欢乘坐火车或开车出去旅行的原因是他 likes feeling the ground under his feet。

13.

[A] That he can't sleep at night.	W: Have you had any luck finding a topic for your research paper?
[B] That he can't find a quiet place to study.	
[C] That he can't narrow down his research topic.	M: No, Prof. Grant told us to write about anything in cultural anthropology. For once I wish she had not given us so much of a choice.
[D] That he can't find enough information for his research paper.	Q: What seems to be the man's problem?

【解析】事实状况题。男士通过虚拟语气 I wish she had not given us so much of a choice 表明,Prof. Grant 所给的论文选择范围太宽泛,他 can't narrow down his research topic(没办法确定自己论文研究的主题)。

14.

[A] Travel by train.	W: Do you like hitchhiking?
[B] Travel by plane.	M: I used to like it. It is cheap. But now I prefer to travel by plane.
[C] Drive by himself.	
[D] Hitchhike.	Q: What does the man like to do now?

【解析】行为活动题。男士话中的转折连词 but 所引导的句子表明,他现在喜欢的旅行方式与以前不同了,现在他 prefer to travel by plane(更喜欢乘飞机旅行)。

15.

[A] Boss and employee.	W: I'm really sorry about my mistake. I hope you'll forgive me.
[B] Classmates.	M: Of course, but only if you can improve your work. If you can't, I'm afraid you'll get the pink note.
[C] Teacher and student.	
[D] Father and daughter.	Q: What's the relationship between the two speakers?

【解析】身份关系题。由男士话中的 you'll get the pink note(被辞退)可知他是女士的 boss(上司),即两人是 boss 和 employee 的关系。get the pink note ≈ get fired,意为"接到辞职信,被辞退"。

16.

[A] In a fashionable dress store.	M: Where did you buy such a sweater? It looks good on you.
[B] On a fashion show.	W: Oh, thank you. I bought it on last fashion show.
[C] In a shopping mall.	
[D] On a recent fair.	Q : Where did the woman buy her sweater?

【解析】地点场景题。女士话中的 I bought it on last fashion show 表明,她的 sweater(毛衣)是在上次的 fashion show(时装表演会)上买的。

17.

[A] She fears for the coming examination.	W: I'm scared of graduation. I don't think we're all going to find a job.
[B] She doesn't want to leave her classmates.	
[C] She is afraid she will not find a job.	M: Come on! I'm sure there'll some good chances for us.
[D] She wants to continue her study.	Q : Why is the woman scared of graduation?

【解析】事实状况题。由女士话中的 I don't think we're all going to find a job(我想我们毕业后不是都能找到工作的)可知,她担心她 will not find a job(找不到工作),所以才害怕毕业。

18.

[A] To travel abroad together with the man.	M: Well, Katherine, the school year is almost over. We are planning to travel abroad. Would you like to go with us?
[B] To study English further.	
[C] To learn a foreign language from some immigrants.	W: I'm afraid I can't. I'm going to teach English to some immigrants in summer holidays.
[D] To teach English to some immigrants.	Q : What is Katherine going to do this summer?

【解析】行为活动题。由女士话中的 I'm going to teach English to some immigrants 可知,暑假期间她要 teach English to some immigrants(给一些移民讲英语)。

Conversation One

【听力原文】

W: Good morning, Dr. Wilson.

M: Hi, Li, haven't seen you for some time. What have you been busy with recently?

W: [19] Writing my essays.

M: That's good. [20①] Do you find the courses here helpful to your future career at home?

W: Yes, very much. I've learnt a lot, not only some cutting edge knowledge, but also practical research methods.

M: Great!

W: But I haven't been able to do any practical research work, which is directly relevant to my future career.

M: You mean, you want to join some research group here?

W: Exactly. You know Dr. Spencer's research, I mean, the techniques used in his research can also be applied to my work at home. If I could do some practical work and get some working experience, it would be easy for me to start my research at home.

M: I understand what you mean. But you're staying here for only one year, aren't you?

W: Yes, but I can extend my stay, 6 months or a year?

M: Well … er … [20②] What type of visa do you have?

W: J-1.

【答案解析】

19. What has the woman been busy doing recently?

【解析】选[B]。细节题。对话开头处,男士问女士最近在忙些什么,女士回答说她最近一直在忙于 writing essays(写论文),故答案为[B]。

20. Where is the woman studying, according to the conversation?

【解析】选[C]。推断题。由对话开头处男士话中的 Do you find the courses here helpful to your future career at home 及对话中间男士话中的 What type of visa do you have 等可知,女士应该是在国外学习,但具体地点文中没有

M: You know your IAP-66 is valid for a maximum period of one year. If you have a J-1 visa and plan to stay for more than one year, you must renew your IAP-66.

W: Yes, that's what I want, to renew my IAP-66.

M: Who's going to support you?

W: Dr. Spencer said if I work for him, he'll …

M: Wait, wait. I remember now. [21①] You're sponsored by your government, aren't you?

W: Yes.

M: [21②] Then you need to get permission for an extension of stay from the Chinese Embassy.

W: Should I?

M: Yes, according to the agreement between the two governments.

W: I'll try.

M: If your government says OK, I have no objection.

W: OK. I see. Thank you for your advice.

M: You're always welcome.

W: Good-bye.

提到,故答案为[C]。

21. Who is the supporter of the woman's studying, according to the conversation?

【解析】选[C]。推断题。由对话结尾处男士话中的 You're sponsored by your government 可知,女士的学习是由 government 提供支持的,接着,再由男士话中的 Then you need to get permission … from the Chinese Embassy 可知,女士是 Chinese,由此可推断女士的学习是由 Chinese government 提供支持的,故答案为[C]。

Conversation Two

【听力原文】

M: What made you want to become a nurse?

W: Nursing is a job in which you can make a difference and I wanted to do something that was worthwhile.

M: What training and skills did you need?

W: You are always training and learning. [22] The health profession is constantly breaking new ground and so you are constantly learning new skills—took a three-year diploma course in Manchester. The course combined classroom theory with working on the wards, putting your theory into practice as it were. [23] To qualify for the course I needed to pass exams in English, math and three other subjects. Biology is helpful but not essential.

M: What are you doing now?

W: [24①] I decided to travel and see some of the world and am at present working in Sydney, Australia as a community nurse.

M: Is nursing an easy profession to travel with?

W: Yes, I have had no difficulty in finding work when travelling. Nursing is a profession that transfers worldwide. [24②] It has given me a great opportunity to visit some fantastic places and still do the job I love.

M: What do you really enjoy about your job?

W: Feeling that I'm doing something that makes a difference. I get to meet some fantastic people, patients, medical staff, teachers and students. I get to learn about some fascinating subjects and am constantly learning new skills and expanding my experience and knowledge.

M: What do you really hate about your job?

【答案解析】

22. What does the woman think of the health profession?

【解析】选[B]。细节题。对话开头处,女士提到护士工作需要不断地学习和接受训练,因为她认为 the health profession is constantly breaking new ground(健康业总是会开辟出新天地),故答案为[B]。

23. To qualify for the nurse course, how many exams should the woman pass?

【解析】选[C]。细节题。女士提到要通过护士课程、取得资格证,她需要 pass exams in English, math and three other subjects,而 biology 不是必修课程,由此可知女士需要通过5门考试,故答案为[C]。

24. What kind of person is the woman like, according to the conversation?

【解析】选[A]。推断题。女士提到她以前就下决心要 travel and see some of the world,所以她现在会在 Sydney 做一名社区护士,并且还提到护士这一职业给她提供 a great opportunity to visit some fantastic places,由此可推断,女士除了喜欢护士这一职业外,还十分喜欢旅游,故答案为[A]。

25. What does the woman think is bad about being a nurse?

【解析】选[B]。推断题。对话结尾处,男士问女士护士工作的缺点,女士回答说 Working night shifts and weekends can be a real pain though(上夜班和周末加班确实是一件痛苦的事情),加夜班时生物钟就会变得十分紊乱,而别人在参加聚会

W: I don't really hate anything. [25] Working night shifts and weekends can be a real pain though. Your body clock can get really messed up on nights and it can be hard knowing everyone is out partying while you are working.

的时候她却在上班,这令她很难受,由此可以推断,对女士而言,护士工作的不足之处就是别人在休息、娱乐时她却必须忙于工作,故答案为[B]。

Section B

Passage One

【听力原文】

The Thai people originally lived in the north of China, [26] but they were regularly attacked by other groups from the north, and they moved further south until they finally established kingdoms in the territory that has become present-day Thailand.

Now, a new theory has evolved. It holds that the Thai, which included a subgroup known as the Dai, were an ethnic group that spread over Yunnan Province in southern China, Burma, Laos, and the north of Thailand.

The more China has modernized, the more earnest it has become about conducting research of this kind and using it to plan for the development of Dai-Thai culture. The Thai people in China, formerly known as the Dai nationality, number around 1.2 million. They are concentrated in Yunnan Province, in areas like the Xishuanbana prefecture, the Linchang prefecture, the Dahong prefecture and the reaches of the Mekong and Red rivers.

The Thai-Dai has direct ethnic and cultural relations with northern Thailand. The cultures of both areas are very similar. That's why some Chinese scholars have a deep interest in the field of Thai-Dai ethnic history and Thai-Dai comparative cultural studies. [27①] After the 1950s, Dai society was transformed from a local feudal society into a part of regular Chinese society, and a new epoch began. [27②] Modern education, culture, medical treatment, transport, telecommunication, and tourism development arrived rapidly, especially in the last 20 years.

Such developments have influenced Dai society and culture deeply. For example, the Dais now speak Chinese and read Chinese scripts as well as use their own ethnic language. [28] They still have their Buddhist faith and their ethnic identity. They still enjoy their own ethnic housing, dress, food, folk and lifestyles. But they also face new and strange challenges—globalization, social change, tourism and economic development.

【答案解析】

26. Why did the Thai people moved southward?

【解析】选[B]。细节题。短文一开始就提到 the Thai people 起初居住在中国北部地区,但是他们 regularly attacked by other groups from the north(经常受到其他北部民族的侵袭),所以他们 moved further south(向南迁移),由此可知 the Thai people 向南迁移是为了 escape from other group's attack(躲避其他民族的侵袭),故答案为[B]。

27. What is the Dai society now like, according to the passage?

【解析】选[B]。细节题。文中提到 20 世纪 50 年代后 Dai society 就由封建社会转变成中国现代社会的一部分,那里的 modern education, culture, medical treatment, transport, telecommunication 和 tourism 的发展都很迅速,由此可知 the Dai society 的 tourism(旅游业)develops rapidly,故答案为[B]。

28. What faith do the Dais embrace?

【解析】选[A]。细节题。短文结尾处明确提到 the Dais 仍然信奉 Buddhist(佛教)和 ethnic identity(民族统一性),故答案为[A]。

Passage Two

【听力原文】

As freshwater becomes increasingly scarce due to population growth, and probably, climate change, the use of wastewater in agriculture, groundwater recharge and in other areas will increase. In some cases, wastewater is the only water resource available to poor, subsistence level farming communities. Although there are benefits to using wastewater in agriculture—including health benefits such as better nutrition and food security for many households, uncontrolled use of wastewater frequently is associated with

【答案解析】

29. What can lower the negative health impact caused by uncontrolled use of wastewater?

【解析】选[C]。细节题。文中提到经常使用 wastewater 会对人体产生消极影响,但可以通过实行 good management practices 使这种消极影响最小化,故答案为[C]。

30. Which of the following measures can be

significant negative human health impacts. [29] These health impacts can be minimized when good management practices are carried out.

Guidelines for the safe use of wastewater in agriculture lie in how to keep a balance between maximizing public health benefits and still allowing for the beneficial use of scarce resources. Guidelines need to be adaptable to the local social, economic and environmental conditions. [30] In order to reduce the negative effects on human health, we should take the concrete measures including sanitation promotion, provision of adequate drinking water, and other primary health-care measures. It is expected that these measures will contribute to the better usage of wastewater.

[31] WHO published *Guidelines for the Safe Use of Wastewater in Agriculture* in 1989. These guidelines have had a major impact on the rational reusage of wastewater in countries worldwide. The WHO guidelines for the safe use of wastewater in agriculture are currently under revision with expected publication in the near future.

taken to reduce the negative effects of wastewater on human health?

【解析】选[A]。细节题。文中提到，为了减轻 wastewater 对人体的消极影响，我们应该采取具体措施，包括 sanitation promotion，provision of adequate drinking water 和 other primary health-care measures，由此可知 sanitation promotion 是其中一项措施，故答案为[A]。

31. When was the *Guidelines for the Safe Use of Wastewater in Agriculture* published?

【解析】选[C]。细节题。文中提到 WHO (世界卫生组织)于 1989 年颁布了 *Guidelines for the Safe Use of Wastewater in Agriculture*(《农业用废水安全使用指南》)，故答案为[C]。

Passage Three

【听力原文】

Ernest Hemingway, born in Illinois, started his career as a writer in a newspaper office in Kansas City at the age of seventeen. Before the United States entered the First World War, he joined a volunteer ambulance unit and served as an ambulance driver. Serving at the front, he was wounded, was decorated by the Italian Government, and spent considerable time in hospitals. [32] After his return to the United States, he became a reporter for Canadian and American newspapers and was soon sent back to Europe to cover such events as the Greek Revolution.

[33] During the twenties, Hemingway became a member of a group of expatriate Americans in Paris, which he described in his first important work, *The Sun Also Rises.* Equally successful was *A Farewell to Arms,* the study of an American ambulance officer's disillusionment in the war. Hemingway used his experiences as a reporter during the civil war in Spain as the background for his most ambitious novel, *For Whom the Bell Tolls.* Among his later works, the most outstanding is his short novel, *The Old Man and the Sea,* which tells about an old fisherman's journey, his long and lonely struggle with a fish and the sea, and his victory in defeat. [34] *The Old Man and the Sea* was such a great success that he was awarded the Nobel Prize for Literature in 1954. No doubt Hemingway has made one of the greatest influences on American literature in the 20th century.

[35] Hemingway himself was a great sportsman; he liked to portray soldiers, hunters and bullfighters. His straightforward prose and his spare dialogue are particularly effective in short stories.

【答案解析】

32. Who did Hemingway work for after he returned to the United States?

【解析】选[A]。细节题。文中明确提到，在 Hemingway 回到美国之后，他 became a reporter for Canadian and American newspapers(成为加拿大和美国报纸的一名记者)，故答案为[A]。

33. Which book describes Hemingway's life in Paris?

【解析】选[B]。细节题。文中提到在 Hemingway 20 多岁的时候，他成为一名被放逐到巴黎的美国人，他在他的第一部重要的作品 *The Sun Also Rises*(《太阳照常升起》)中描述了这段在 Paris 的生活，故答案为[B]。

34. When did Hemingway get the Nobel Prize for Literature?

【解析】选[C]。细节题。文中提到 Hemingway 因作品 The Old Man and the Sea 于 1954 年获得诺贝尔文学奖，答案为[C]。

35. What kind of person was Hemingway like, according to the passage?

【解析】选[C]。细节题。短文结尾处提到 Hemingway 是一个很好的 sportsman (运动家)，由此可知 Hemingway 很 like sports (喜欢运动)，故答案为[C]。

Section C

【听力原文】	【答案解析】
Social customs and ways of behaving change. Things which were (36)considered impolite many years ago are now (37)acceptable. Just a few years ago, it was an impolite (38)behavior for a man to smoke on the street. No man who thought of himself as being a (39)gentleman would make a fool of himself by smoking when a lady was in a room. Customs also (40)differ from country to country. Does a man walk on the left or the right of a woman in your country? Or does it not matter? What about table manners? Should you use both hands when you are eating? The Americans and the British not only speak the same language but also share a large number of social customs. For example, in both America and England, people shake hands when they meet each other for the first time. Also, most Englishmen will open a door for a woman or (41)offer their seats to a woman, and so will most Americans. In England and America, (42)promptness is important both. That is, if a dinner (43)invitation is for 7 o'clock, (44) the dinner guest either arrives close to that time or calls to explain his delay. The important thing to remember about social customs is (45)not to do anything that might make other people feel uncomfortable, especially if they are your guests. There is an old story about a man who gave a formal dinner party. When the food was served, one of the guests started to eat his peas with a knife. The other guests were amused or shocked, but the host calmly picked up his knife and began eating in the same way. (46)It would have been bad manners to make his guests feel foolish or uncomfortable.	36. 空前的系动词 were 和空后的形容词 impolite 提示所填词应为形容词或动词的过去分词形式或副词。considered 意为"认为,考虑"。 37. 空前的系动词 are 提示所填词应为形容词或动词的过去分词形式。根据本句中的两个时间状语 many years ago 和 now 的对比可知,本句主要是讲以前人们认为是 impolite 的事,而现在的人们不那样认为了。acceptable 意为"可接受的"。 38. 空前的形容词 impolite 和空后的介词 for 提示所填词应为名词。由本句的真正主语 to smoke on the street 可知表语 an impolite _____ 应表达吸烟是一种不礼貌的行为。behavior 意为"行为"。 39. 空前的不定冠词 a 提示所填词应为单数名词。gentleman 意为"绅士"。 40. 分析句子结构可知,所填词在句中作谓语,由上下文时态可知本文是一般现在时,再根据主语 Customs 可知所填词应为动词原形。differ 意为"不同于"。 41. 空前的并列连词 or 提示所填词应与 open 并列,都在句中作谓语,故所填词应为动词原形。根据 or 前分句中的 open a door for a woman 可知,本句与大多数英国男士对女士的绅士行为有关,故所填词可能表达英国男士会为女士"让座"的含义。offer 意为"提供,让"。 42. 空后的系动词 is 提示所填词应为名词。下句中的 That is(也就是说)表明该句是对上一句的解释说明,由下句中出现的时间 7 o'clock 可知,所填词可能与时间有关。promptness 意为"守时,准时"。 43. 空前的不定冠词 a 和空后的系动词 is 提示所填词应为单数名词。invitation 意为"邀请"。 44. 【Main Points】the dinner guest **should** arrive **near** that time or calls to explain his **lateness** 45. 【Main Points】not to do anything that might make other people **uncomfortable**, especially **your guests** 46. 【Main Points】It would have been **impolite** to make **the** guests feel foolish or uncomfortable

Part IV

Section A

【文章大意】
本文的主要内容是关于生命质量和生命长度之间的比较问题。第一段举了一个极端的例子,说明在牺牲生命质量的前提下延长生命的长度,带来的是痛苦和悲伤;第二段指出安乐死引发了很多道德问题,而作者认为衰老死亡是很自然的事情;第三段举出了阿富汗人和俄罗斯人的例子说明有质量的生活才是快乐的生活。

47.【定位】根据题干中的关键信息 It would be much better for a person… 可定位在第一段第三句。

　　【解析】enjoys perfect health。题干中的 It would be much better…是该句中 No one would deny…的同义转述,题干中的 only if ≈ provided。由此可知答案为 enjoys perfect health。

48.【定位】根据题干中的关键信息 artificial means 可定位在第一段倒数第四句。

【解析】joyful and happy。题干中的 artificial means 与首段倒数第四句对应,由此可知题干中的 Extended life supported by artificial means 表示的是人的寿命是靠医疗措施人为延长的,与人的自然寿命相违背。而通过该段第四句中的 But is it a good thing… 可知人为延长寿命只会给人带来 pain and sorrow,并不会带来 joy and happiness。根据题干的语法要求可知 joy 和 happiness 应转换成与其分别对应的形容词。

49.【定位】根据题干中的关键信息 to let nature take its course 可定位在第二段第三句。
【解析】To let people die naturally。第二段中,作者讲到安乐死带来的一些道德上的思考时讲到"…it might be preferable to let nature take its course when death will relieve suffering",由其中的 when death will relieve suffering 可推知 let nature take its course 的意思是 let people die naturally(让人自然死亡)。

50.【定位】根据题干中的关键信息 euthanasia 可定位在第二段第一句。
【解析】is terminated by taking active measures。根据原文 it implies that active measures will be taken… 可知,euthanasia 暗含之意即是:active measures will be taken to terminate human life,题干将 human life 作为同位语从句的主语,故所填内容应使用被动语态,答案为 is terminated by taking active measures。

51.【定位】根据题干的要求可知,本题的定位应是整篇文章。
【解析】Positive。文章第一段中作者谈到如果人们能健康快乐,那么活着就有意义,否则,只有承受痛苦和悲伤,由此说明安乐死的必要性。另外通过"death will bring release"以及"be preferable to let nature take its course…"等也可看出作者认为 euthanasia 很有必要,故可知作者对 euthanasia 的态度是 positive(积极的)。

Section B

Passage One

【文章大意】

人类对于宇宙的认识主要经历了几个阶段,本文主要围绕各个阶段人们对宇宙的认识而展开,阐述了关于宇宙的观念的调整。文章第一二段主要是关于人们第一次观念的调整;第三四段分别是关于第二次观念调整和第三次观念调整;第五段主要讲观念调整的必然性;第六七段初步涉及了最新一次的观念调整。

52.选[B]。主旨大意题。文章前六段以时间为序分别说明人类在不同的历史时期对 universe 的认识,人们最先认为宇宙是以人类为中心,之后又认为宇宙是以地球为中心,而到了 16 世纪,则认为宇宙是以太阳为中心的,在距今不到 40 年的时候,人们又认为宇宙是以成千上万个星系为中心的,文章最后一段又提到了一个新的 adjustment。由此可知,本文主要与人们对 universe 的不断认识有关,故答案为[B]。

53.选[D]。事实细节题。文章第二段第二句指出 The geocentric concept…(以地球为中心的观点开始成为主要学说),第三句指出 It accepted a universe…(它认为宇宙是以地球为中心的)。联系上下文可知第三句中的 it 指 geocentric concept,由此可知,geocentric concept 与"宇宙是以地球为中心"的理论有关,故答案为[D]。

54.选[B]。推理判断题。文章第三段末句中 however 后的句子表明人们最终接受了 Copernican 的理论,由 however 可知,前半句是想表达人们最初并不同意 Copernican 的理论,Man is a stubborn adherent…就是指人们最初顽固的认为先前的理论是正确的,由此可推断,人们肯定会一度认为 Copernican 的理论是错误的,故答案为[B]。

55.选[A]。推理判断题。题干中的 the adjustment from the sun-center universe to the galactocentric universe 指的就是文章中的 the third adjustment。文章第四段末句指出 This shift has deeply punctured…(这一转变深深的刺痛了人类的自尊心及自信),因为 it has carried with it the knowledge of the…(它承载着一个事实:宇宙中有无数个星系)。由此可推断在 the third adjustment 发生以前,人类并不知道宇宙中有无数个星系,故答案为[A]。

56.选[B]。推理判断题。文章最后一段首句指出我们的新问题与 the spread of life throughout the universe(宇宙中生命的延续有关),结合第二句中的问题 Are we alone 的隐含意:宇宙中是否也存在与人类一样的生命呢?可推断,如果文章继续下去,那么内容应该与宇宙中是否存在与人类一样的生命有关,故答案为[B]。

Passage Two

【文章大意】

本文是以 9·11 事件为背景,对美国当时的情况进行了描述。文章第一段主要讲撞机事件发生时,美国总统正在做的事情;第二段主要讲美国针对撞机事件所采取的措施以及目击者对撞机过程的描述。

57.选[D]。推理判断题。文章第一段首句指出在第二架飞机撞向南面的高塔时,布什正被 introduced to the second-graders of Emma E. Booker Elementary,而结合该段末句中的 These must be six-graders 可推断,布什是想说这些二年级孩子的阅读水平足以达到六年级的水平,这其实是在赞美孩子们的阅读水平高,故答案为[D]。

58. 选[B]。事实细节题。文章第一段第四句指出，当 Card 走近布什，在他右耳边低语时，布什正 getting ready to pose for pictures with the teachers and kids(准备摆好姿势和师生们合影)，由下文可知，Card 是在告诉他 crash 的事。[B] 中的 being prepared…是原文 getting ready to…的同义转述，故为答案。

59. 选[A]。推理判断题。文章第二段第二句指出，在人们急切地希望得知关于 crash 的消息时，那大约 200 多人中一开始竟没有人想到他们可以通过旁边办公室的 TV 获得消息，由此可以推断出，刚开始时，这些人很有可能因为突然听到 crash 的消息而变得惊慌失措，故答案为[A]。

60. 选[C]。语义理解题。文章第二段第八句指出即使是在布什进行演讲的时候，the second front opened。第九句前半句的完成时态及后半句的一般过去时表明第八句中的 the second front 指的是袭击分子对美国的经济文化中心进行的第二次袭击，故答案为[C]。

61. 选[B]。推理判断题。文章第二段倒数第四句中提到当 David Marra 看到 an American Airlines jet swooping…时，他急忙掉转车头朝高速公路的 I395 出口开去，再结合下文 David Marra 对飞机袭击过程的描述可以推断出他是 crash 事件的 witness(目击者)，故答案为[B]。

Part V

62. eventful — uneventful。上下文语义矛盾。第二段第一句话指出与人类现在的情况相比,50 万年前的人类度过了一个非常平静的时期,该句话是承接第一段末句而言的。既然人类经历过的 50 万年时间是一个非常平静的时期,那么他们的生活就不会有太多的变故,故应将 eventful 改写为 uneventful。

63. Comparing — Compared。非谓语动词误用。主句的主语 he 和动词 compare 的关系应是被动的关系,如果用完整的句子应是 If he was compared with how he was in his present condition,故应将 Comparing 改写为 Compared。

64. astonishing — astonishingly。词性误用。此处是表示"一种令人感到惊讶的静止状态",astonishing 修饰的是形容词 stationary,而不是名词 state,故应将其改为副词形式 astonishingly。

65. was — were。主谓不一致。转折连词 but 前的分句已明确表示语言和文化的变化没有反映在人造物中,这就说明 but 后的分句是虚拟语气,故应将 was 改写为 were。

66. therefore — however。逻辑关系错误。上句指出"…我们无从知晓这些变化",而本句则说"人造物留下了确凿的证据"。两句之间明显存在转折关系,故应将 therefore 改写为 however。

67. as — with。介词误用。as 作介词表示"作为",用在本句中语义不通,故应将 as 改写为 with,表示"随着"。

68. past — beyond。介词误用。本句想表达的是我们无法恢复第一次大变化的详情。past 和 recovery 不搭配,故应将 past 改写为 beyond,beyond recovery 表示"无法恢复"。

69. did — do。时态错误。虽然 that 引导的宾语从句的时态是过去时态,但此处却是表示我们现在了解的情况,故应用一般现在时态,故应将 did 改为 do,助动词 do 在这里表示强调。

70. livestocks — livestock。名词单复数误用。livestock 是集体名词,故应将 livestocks 改写为 livestock。

71. production — productivity。易混词误用。production 作"产品"讲时,侧重于产品产量,但本句明显不是侧重于产品的产量,而是侧重于生产力,故应将 production 改写为 productivity"生产力"。

Part VI

72. 【答案】to contrast the British legal system with the American one
【解析】本题考查对惯用搭配 contrast…with…和不定式的掌握。contrast…with…意为"把…和…相对比、对照"。句首的 It 是形式主语,不定词 to 引导的部分才是真正的主语。

73. 【答案】time be manipulated properly
【解析】本题考查虚拟语气及被动语态用法的掌握。当 it 充当形式主语,而表示重要性、必要性或某种意愿的形容词如 essential,important,necessary,imperative,advisable,desirable 等充当表语时,后面 that 所引导的主语从句的谓语动词用 should do 的形式,should 常省略。另外注意本句应该用被动语态。

74. 【答案】were present at the meeting
【解析】本题考查对主谓一致的掌握。当"名词＋as well as＋名词"出现在句中时,谓语动词应与第一个名词一致,类似词语还有 with,together with,along with 等。be present at meeting 意为"出席会议"。

75. 【答案】the crowd broke into loud applause
【解析】本题考查对短语 break into sth. 的掌握。break into sth. 意为"突然开始(笑、唱等)"。

76. 【答案】I could have passed my examination easily
【解析】本题考查对情态动词 could 的掌握。could have done 一般表示过去可能完成而未完成的动作。

预 测 试 题 四

Part I Writing (30 minutes)

Directions: *For this part, you are allowed 30 minutes to write a letter to your neighbor Mr. Wang about the noise in the evening. You should write at least 150 words according to the outline given below:*

假如你是 *Li Juan*,你的邻居每天晚上练习弹奏乐器,让你不能入眠。请就此写一封抱怨信。

A Letter to My Neighbor

_____

_____

Part II Reading Comprehension (Skimming and Scanning) (15 minutes)

Learning Styles and Success in School

College is different from high school. Graduate school is unlike college. Entering any new environment brings novel challenges and distractions. Moreover, each step of the learning process is usually accompanied by more and harder work. Though you obviously learned to negotiate and succeed at your last educational stop, you may find there is some readjusting to do now. This is especially true for adult returning students and students beginning a new, more advanced, or more specialized field of study. By expanding on your current learning skills, you will better meet the challenges ahead. We hope that the following will provide useful information and tools to make this next educational step a success.

Learning Styles: What Are They?

There are many types of learning styles. Often, these types coincide with our personality style. Each of us has a different style or combination of styles. Though the majority of us have the capacity to use most modes, we tend to rely on or prefer certain styles. Hopefully, these are the styles that have brought us success in the past. If this is not the case, it may be helpful to reassess one's approach. We all learn differently but we can all learn effectively. It is important to understand your own learning style and use it to your best advantage in the classroom.

Eyes or Ears

Do you remember best what is said to you or what you read? Do you prefer television or newspapers as your source of news?

Some people learn best by reading. They need to see something to remember it. Others learn best by listening. Information sticks once they hear it.

If you have a visual style, you may have difficulty with an instructor who believes telling people what to learn and know is enough. Instructors who rely heavily on class discussion will also cause you some angst. Handouts, reading assignments, and writing information on the blackboard are most helpful to you.

On the other hand, if you have an auditory style, you may be in trouble with an instructor who writes a lot and assigns reading that is not discussed in class. Class discussions and study groups are a better way for you to learn.

Movement

Does it help you to rewrite your notes or take notes as you read?

Some people's learning is enhanced by motoric movement. In other words, they learn as they write notes in class. Or when they are reading an assignment, they remember the content best if they take notes as they read. Sometimes the act of highlighting important information that is read works in the same way.

Group or Solitary

Do you find you remember more when you study in a group or alone?

Some people draw their energy from the outside world, that is, interacting with other people, activities, or things. This is often called extraversion. Others prefer to gain their energy from their own internal ideas, emotions, or impressions. Some people call this introversion.

If you tend to be more extroverted, you communicate freely and like to have other people around. Thus, working in groups and talking material over with others helps you understand and process new ideas more fully and completely. You may be impatient and distracted working on your own. A class that is less varied and not as action-oriented may be a particular challenge. You like instructors who are active, energetic, and enthusiastic. You also prefer a more friendly and personal approach. In addition, you probably find larger classes exciting.

If you are more introverted, you probably work contentedly alone and don't mind working on one project for a long time without interruption. As such, you may be quiet in the classroom and dislike classes with a lot of oral presentations and group interaction and work. Sometimes having to communicate with others is hard. You work best if you read lessons over or write them out before discussion, think before participating, and ask questions before completing tasks or exercises. You like classes that require being thoughtful and introspective. You may dislike a professor with a more personal style of attention and closeness. A quiet and tactful style works best for you. Smaller classes are your preference.

Practical or Innovative

Do you like to follow an established way of doing things? Or would you rather follow your inspirations?

Some people prefer to take information in through their five senses, taking note of what is actually there. They want, remember, and trust facts. They are sometimes called practical types. Others prefer to take information in through a "sixth sense", focusing on what might be. These people like to daydream and think about what might be in the future. One could call them innovative.

If you are a practical type, you probably like an established, routine way of doing things. You prefer using skills you already know rather than new ones. Taking note of details, memorizing facts, and reaching a conclusion step by step is your ideal. You learn best if you have clear directions to follow. Films, audiovisuals, hands-on exercises, and envisioning practical examples are most helpful. You learn best when instructors are factual and thorough, working out details in advance and showing you why things make sense.

If you are more innovative, you probably like to solve new problems. You may dislike doing the same thing repeatedly and may be impatient with routine details. You may also find yourself daydreaming during factual lectures. You work best when you can see the big picture, have independence and autonomy, and incorporate new approaches into your work. You like enthusiastic instructors who indicate challenges, point out future benefits, and let you figure out your own way.

Thinking or Feeling

Do you respond more to people's thoughts or feelings?

Some people prefer to organize information in a logical, objective way. They respond more easily to people's thoughts and are more analytical. If you are such a person, emotions play less of a part in your life, decisions, and interactions with others. You work best if you can organize and outline a subject, know your objectives and goals, get to the task, and receive rapid feedback. You are most motivated when you can see a logical rationale for studying certain material or working on a particular project. You probably prefer teachers who are task-focused, logical, well-organized, less emotional, and who offer feedback.

Other people prefer to organize and structure information in a personal, value-oriented way. If this sounds familiar, you are likely to be very aware of other people and their feelings. You prefer harmony. You probably learn best if you can identify with what you are doing and have an emotional connection to it. You like an environment with little competition and with opportunity to respond more personally. You probably prefer teachers who are personable, friendly, and easy to work with. You also like a teaching style that is positive, tells you why what you are doing is valuable, and supports your personal goals.

Open-ended or Closure-driven

Do you like to get things settled and finished? Or would you rather leave things open for alterations?

Some people prefer to live a planned and organized life. They go on vacation and plan out all of their activities before they go. Other people like to be more open-ended, living more spontaneously and flexibly.

If you need closure, you probably work best when you can plan your work and follow that plan. You like to get things finished and do not like to be interrupted. In an effort to complete a task, however, you may make decisions too quickly. You learn best if you can stick to a routine and follow a specific time frame and precise guidelines. You probably prefer instructors who are structured, timely, precise, and organized. You also like specific performance guidelines.

For those who are more open-ended, you probably like change and undertaking many projects at once. You may have trouble making decisions and may postpone unpleasant jobs. You probably learns best if you can be original, physically active, and spontaneous. You gravitate towards instructors who are more open, creative, spontaneous, and informal. You dislike deadlines and too much direction, wanting to follow your own path.

1. This article aims to recommend some useful learning styles to make one's college life a success.
2. Generally, students have different learning styles because they have their own personality style.
3. Visual style students tend to perform less actively in discussions held in the class.
4. Introverted students prefer to attend smaller class and enjoy classes in which they have chances to communicate.
5. Those who pay more attention to what may happen in the future and know something through a six sense are called _____.
6. Those people who are practical type would rather use _____ to do things than the ones they are not familiar with.
7. Well-organized and less-emotional professors will play a more important role in teaching students who are _____ with their own objectives and goals.
8. Those who respond more to people's feelings prefer to organize and structure information in _____.
9. Closure-driven learners may learn best when they can follow _____.
10. Open-ended people unwillingly meet the deadlines, have difficulty in making decisions and may _____.

Part III Listening Comprehension (35 minutes)

Section A

11. [A] Mr. Brown's assistant.
    [C] Mr. Thompson's secretary.
    [B] Mr. Thompson's wife.
    [D] Mr. Brown's wife.
12. [A] Because he is leaving for a holiday for several days.
    [C] Because he has to meet another important customer.
    [B] Because he can not reach Mr. Johnson.
    [D] Because he will have a meeting for several days.
13. [A] Tomorrow morning.
    [C] This morning.
    [B] This afternoon.
    [D] Tomorrow afternoon.
14. [A] Jane did not wish to marry so early.
    [C] Jane thought Jack was too ambitious.
    [B] Jane thought Jack was too idle.
    [D] Jane thought Jack was too young.
15. [A] She is encouraging the man to begin his new business.
    [B] She is blaming the man for his mismatch.
    [C] She is trying to comfort the man's broken heart.
    [D] She is blaming the man for his indecision in his business.
16. [A] A grocery store.
    [C] A cookie store.
    [B] A fruit store.
    [D] A grain store.
17. [A] Central air conditioning and a TV set.
    [C] A balcony and two bathrooms.
    [B] A dishwasher, air conditioning and two bathrooms.
    [D] A study room and a swimming pool.
18. [A] At the supermarket.
    [C] At the department store.
    [B] In a wine factory.
    [D] At a grocery store.

Questions 19 to 21 are based on the conversation you have just heard.

19. [A] In the man's salon.
    [C] On the street.
    [B] In the interview room.
    [D] At a supermarket.
20. [A] About 25 minutes.
    [C] Less than 25 minutes.
    [B] More than 25 minutes.
    [D] 25 minutes.

21. [A] Soft green.　　　　　　　　　　[B] Blue.
　　 [C] Pink.　　　　　　　　　　　　[D] Red.

Questions 22 to 25 are based on the conversation you have just heard.

22. [A] His subconsciousness.　　　　　　[B] Some aliens.
　　 [C] His imagination.　　　　　　　[D] People in real life.

23. [A] John Nash.　　　　　　　　　　[B] Russell Crowe.
　　 [C] Nash's friend.　　　　　　　　[D] Crowe's doctor.

24. [A] He is mentally ill.　　　　　　　[B] He takes himself seriously.
　　 [C] He is an actor.　　　　　　　　[D] He is a graduate.

25. [A] He was quite alerted.　　　　　　[B] He was enlightened.
　　 [C] He was mentally ill.　　　　　　[D] He was in a movie.

Section B

Passage One

26. [A] The education officials.　　　　　[B] The head of the faculty.
　　 [C] The staff of the faculty.　　　　[D] The faculty and the students.

27. [A] The student making apology to the faculty.
　　 [B] The student being kicked out of school.
　　 [C] The student getting a failing grade in his assignment.
　　 [D] The student being looked down on.

28. [A] Inform the student's parents in writing.
　　 [B] Inform the student and the person in charge of the department.
　　 [C] Inform the head of the faculty.
　　 [D] Ask the student to perform additional assignments.

Passage Two

29. [A] It was set up in 1908.　　　　　　[B] Its origin is not clear.
　　 [C] Its ceremony was first held in Virginia.　[D] It is promoted by a nun.

30. [A] Five.　　　　　　　　　　　　[B] Seven.
　　 [C] Six.　　　　　　　　　　　　[D] Four.

31. [A] Because he had no time on that day.
　　 [B] Because it is too hurried for him to prepare the service well.
　　 [C] Because that day was not a lucky day.
　　 [D] Because he was asked to delay the service.

Passage Three

32. [A] They hold a positive attitude towards it.
　　 [B] They think it is against the traditional belief.
　　 [C] They think it is the result of the development of society.
　　 [D] They are indifferent to it.

33. [A] Because the child is the one who is the hope of our society.
　　 [B] Because the child is the one who can carry on the family name.
　　 [C] Because the child is the one who can make them happy.
　　 [D] Because the child is the one who is the new workforce of the family.

34. [A] The modernization drive.　　　　[B] The open-door policy.
　　 [C] The entry into WTO.　　　　　[D] The influence of TV.

35. [A] Their children.　　　　　　　　[B] The social security system.
　　 [C] Themselves.　　　　　　　　[D] Their savings.

Section C

　　In common sense, a myth is fiction — something which is untrue. Scholars of (36)_____ define myth as a special kind of story which tries to (37)_____ some aspects of the world around us.

A (38)_____ of definitions of myths might be (39)_____ by the following paraphrase: myths are stories, usually about gods and other supernatural beings. Some of them are (40)_____, prescientific, and (41) _____ to explain the natural world. As such, they are usually functional and are the science of primitive people. The terms legend and folktale are sometimes used (42)_____ with myth. Technically, however, these are not the same. Here are some (43)_____ on the differences.

First, a myth is a story from the past. It may explain the origin of the universe and of life, or it may express its culture's moral values in human terms. Myths concern (44)_____. Although myths are religious in their origin and function, they may also be the earliest form of history, science, or philosophy. A folktale, then, is a story that is purely fictional in plot and has no particular location in either time or space. However, despite its elements of fantasy, (45)_____.

Second, a legend is a story from the past about a subject that was, or is believed to have been historical. Legends concern people, places, and events. Usually, the subject is a saint, a king, a hero, a famous person, or a war. (46) _____.

Part IV Reading Comprehension (Reading in Depth) (25 minutes)
Section A

Not long ago, a woman living alone in the west of England was disturbed by the sound of a thief in her room. She screamed, and the thief ran away. The incident was reported to the police. They found an article of clothing in the kitchen of the woman's home and sent it to Forensic Science Laboratory in London.

Scientist at the laboratory, on examining the clothing, found tiny shreds of a certain unusual metal which then had only one use. It was used in the manufacture of jet-engine rotors. That put the police in mind of one particular man. He worked as rotor grinder in a factory near the woman's home. He was the man all right. And that is what meant by trace evidence.

There is nothing new about trace evidence, as any reader of detective stories knows. That, after all, was what Sherlock Holmes was looking for through his magnifying glass. What is new is the way forensic scientists find it, and use it to help track down criminals.

A thief who broke into a church in the north of England was caught because traces of wax, found on his clothes, had come, not from household candles, but the sort of candle used only in churches. A man who kicked a girl in the face was found to have in the toe of his boot trace of white powder.

Although scientists from the laboratory occasionally visit the scene of a crime, the evidence as a rule comes to them, sometimes in the form of stained or torn clothing, or sometimes in the form of weapons used to commit a crime.

One of the points they look for is "fiber transference". "That means the transfer of fibers from one's clothes to another one's clothes." One of the laboratory's senior staff said. "That would help us to establish the degree of contact between two people. We have to go over every inch of a piece of clothing, picking up tiny shreds of fibers to see if they match what we're looking for."

47. The _____ on an article of clothing left by the thief was provided as a clue for police to track down the thief in the west of England.

_____

48. Besides the way forensic scientists find it, the newness of trace evidence lies in its _____.

_____

49. The examples in the fourth paragraph are used to prove that _____ plays an important role in tracking down criminals.

_____

50. What is useful in making sure two people's degree of contact?

_____

51. Who plays an important role in finding the criminals, according to the passage?

_____

Section B

Passage One

William Schopf was a professor at UCLA in the 1980s when he found what he took to be fossilized microbes in a chert — a rock made of grains of quartz — from a site in Western Australia. Since the chert was 3.5 billion years old, it appeared that Schopf's fossils came from far earlier than any other life form found.

Not only were the fossils very old, but they were also surprisingly complex. Some of Schopf's fossils seemed to be filaments made up of rows of separate cells. Schopf argued that they were photosynthetic blue-green algae.

Now Martin Brasier of the University of Oxford is reinterpreting Schopf's evidence. He starts not with the fossils, but with a careful study of the rocks around them. As a result of these studies, Brasier and his colleagues point to evidence that no oxygen-producing photosynthesis could have occurred there, and from the makeup of the rock they infer that the temperature at which the chert was formed was above 200 degrees Celsius — too hot for life.

In early versions of their critique, Brasier and his colleagues doubted that there was any organic matter in the fossils at all. Since then Schopf has used a new technique to show that the structures identified as fossils are rich in organic molecules. But "organic", a chemical term that applies more or less to all molecules with carbon in them, isn't the same as "biological". Most organic molecules are produced by living creatures, but that need not always have been the case. Brasier argues that a hydro-thermal vent could have produced organic molecules from carbon monoxide and hydrogen. Schopf is scornful of this idea, seeing it as "exceedingly implausible". "Non-biological organic matter has never been found in the geological record ever," Schopf says. "I'd be delighted if there were such a thing, but you do have to have some criteria to say this is biological and this is not. And they don't have any criteria."

As to the filament-like structures, Brasier sees them as part of the fabric of the quartz. He argues that the structures come in different forms, only some of which look like algae. Some look like no bacteria ever seen, and some appear to be branched — a no-no for primitive blue-green algae. Schopf says that Brasier has mistaken folded filaments for branched ones. He puts the confusion down to a lack of experience with the microscopes used to study such structures. But not everyone who has seen the samples agrees with Schopf's explanation.

52. If the fossils were proved to be photosynthetic blue-green algae, _____.
  [A] the chert would have had great value of researching
  [B] the photosynthesis would have existed earlier than human life
  [C] the present speculation about the time of the origin of life would have not been right
  [D] William Schopf would have been the pioneer among researchers who studied fossils

53. Why did Martin Brasier say that the fossils could not be photosynthetic blue-green algae?
  [A] Because there is no proper equipment to prove it.
  [B] Because the temperature at which the chert formed is too high for algae to live.
  [C] Because the oxygen-producing photosynthesis did not exist in the chert.
  [D] Because he put much attention to the rocks around the fossils.

54. According to Schopf, _____.
  [A] "organic" is the same as "biological" in geology　　　[B] "organic" is the same as "carbon" in molecules
  [C] non-biological organic matter has never existed　　　[D] a hydrothermal vent is exceedingly implausible

55. What may lead to the question whether the fossils are photosynthetic blue-green algae, according to Schopf?
  [A] The lack of experience with the microscopes used to study the structures of the algae.
  [B] The lack of evidence that there could not be creature in the chert.
  [C] The lack of equipment to make clear that the fossils are part of the fabric of the quartz.
  [D] The lack of knowledge about the geological record.

56. What is the author's attitude towards the argument between the two scientists?
  [A] Enthusiastic.　　　　　　　　　　　　　[B] Objective.
  [C] Ironic.　　　　　　　　　　　　　　　　[D] Amused.

Passage Two

Recently McDonald's announced that it was changing its cooking oil — reducing trans-fatty acids 48% and increasing polyunsaturated fats 167%. It is a good thing. More important, it's a step in the right direction for the fast-food industry.

McDonald's, Burger King and the rest rely heavily on fatty acids to fry their wares. This is not entirely bad. Fatty acids are the building blocks of dietary fats, an essential part of the human diet. Dietary fats contain a mixture of saturated and unsaturated fatty acids. Saturated fats carry a full quota of hydrogen atoms in their chemical structure and are associated with increases in LDL cholesterol (the bad kind), whereas unsaturated fats can bring that number down.

It gets a little confusing when you start talking about trans-fatty acids. In the old days, fast-food fried products were cooked primarily in animal fats, which are generally saturated and bad for your heart. Under pressure from consumers, many fast-food chains switched to unsaturated vegetable oils. But vegetable oils tend to be less stable and turn rancid more quickly than animal fats. So many outlets switched again, turning to vegetable oils that have been hydrogenated — a process that fills open slots in unsaturated fat molecules with hydrogen atoms, allowing vegetable oils to stay fresh longer while still cooking up fries that are crisp and tasty.

For the fast-food industry, these partially hydrogenated oils were doubly beneficial: the companies got a cheap product with a long shelf life while giving customers the vegetable oils they demanded, hydrogenated ones though. For the eating public, however, the result was quite the opposite. That's because hydrogenated fats contain a kind of hydrogen bond that is as bad as the hydrogen bond in saturated fats — maybe even worse, according to CNN dietitian Liz Weiss, an expert on family nutrition. While saturated fats raise LDL cholesterol, trans fats appear to both raise bad (LDL) cholesterol and lower the good (HDL) cholesterol.

McDonald's oil change will make its fried foods better for the hearts of the 46 million US customers who eat there every day, but it will not turn any of those dishes into health foods. Fries cooked in the new oil will have precisely the same caloric content and will do nothing to trim a growing waistline. So eat fries from time to time if you must, but don't super-size them. Better still, try the salads.

57. Which of the following is beneficial to human beings, according to the passage?

[A] Trans-fatty acids.　　　　　　　　　[B] Fat molecules.

[C] Hydrogen atoms.　　　　　　　　　 [D] Unsaturated fats.

58. Animal fats which are used in frying food are harmful to people's health, because it may _____.

[A] lead to the increase of LDL cholesterol 　[B] put pressure on people's heart

[C] lead to food poisoning　　　　　　　 [D] lead to indigestion

59. The vegetable oils are not practical for fast-food industry until they are hydrogenated because _____.

[A] they go bad quickly　　　　　　　　 [B] they have open slots

[C] they need hydrogen atoms　　　　　　[D] they contain saturated fats

60. What does "shelf life" (Line 2, Para. 4) mean, according to the passage?

[A] The length of time a shelf may last.

[B] The length of time a document will be serviceable to users.

[C] The length of time a product may be stored.

[D] The length of time a product may become rotten.

61. What is the author's attitude toward McDonald's new announcement?

[A] Positive.　　　　　　　　　　　　　[B] Critical.

[C] Objective.　　　　　　　　　　　　 [D] Passive.

Part V Cloze (15 minutes)

The German concept of self requires a wide area of privacy, which is often __62__ and regimented. Doors, hedges, fences: these __63__ features of a German home reflect an __64__ on privacy, __65__ is widespread throughout German life. The sense of privacy is reflected not just in a house but also in a small apartment. In German houses, doors are __66__ shut between rooms to suggest the need for __67__ space and individual privacy. The ideal German house has an __68__ hall that leads visitors into the house __69__

62. [A] impressive　　　　　　[B] casual

[C] depressive　　　　　　　[D] formal

63. [A] essential　　　　　　　[B] physical

[C] symbolic　　　　　　　　[D] mechanical

64. [A] appeal　　　　　　　　[B] influence

[C] emphasis　　　　　　　　[D] observation

65. [A] it　　　[B] who　　　[C] that　　　[D] which

66. [A] firmly　[B] loosely　[C] closely　[D] wholly

67. [A] partial　　　　　　　 [B] personal

[C] independent　　　　　　 [D] transparent

showing specific rooms and __70__ the family's privacy. It is an __71__ to be invited into a German home; this does not __72__ happen to foreigners, who are usually viewed with __73__. Pieces of furniture are heavy and placed far apart, __74__ personal space is maintained during conversation. Formal interactions—not __75__, happy-go-lucky conversations—are common.

Good German neighbors are quiet. Do not intrude, keep the sidewalk clean, and __76__ the flowers nicely. They do not drop __77__ for a chat. Time periods for noise (even running water) are often __78__. Sometimes Germans are not allowed to use their running water after nine o'clock at night. The formality of personal space and social distance is maintained by outside doors that are split, __79__ only at waist height. The outdoors are very important to Germans. Gardens, lawns, and balconies are used often for dining as well as for gardening; __80__ are made as private as possible. It is possible to live in the same German neighborhood for years without having a __81__ with one's neighbors.

68. [A] entrance　　　　　[B] assembly
　　[C] discussion　　　　[D] warming-up
69. [A] without　[B] while　[C] before　[D] except
70. [A] destroying　　　　[B] hampering
　　[C] spoiling　　　　　[D] corroding
71. [A] hospitality　　　　[B] embarrassment
　　[C] interference　　　　[D] honor
72. [A] invariably　　　　[B] frequently
　　[C] similarly　　　　　[D] undoubtedly
73. [A] confidence　　　　[B] gratitude
　　[C] mystery　　　　　[D] suspicion
74. [A] such that　[B] in that　[C] so that　[D] since that
75. [A] released　[B] relaxed　[C] intensive　[D] rejoiced
76. [A] tend　[B] consider　[C] attend　[D] breed
77. [A] out　　[B] off　　[C] by　　[D] down
78. [A] subscribed　　　　[B] prescribed
　　[C] described　　　　[D] inspired
79. [A] having opened　　[B] opening
　　[C] being opened　　　[D] to be opened
80. [A] such　[B] those　[C] these　[D] they
81. [A] participation　　　[B] involvement
　　[C] commitment　　　[D] relationship

Part VI Translation (5 minutes)

82. _____ (她全力倾注于自己的事业), so she had no time to care about her marriage.
83. You know I have a disease _____ (这种病折磨我九年了).
84. _____ (一被任命为最高统帅之后), he took the stern measures expected of him.
85. _____ (我口袋里只不过有五美元), so it's really a problem for me to buy the dress.
86. Although I'm a foreigner in German, _____ (我可以毫不费力地表达了自己的意思).

答案与解析

Part I

【思路点拨】

　　本题要求写一封抱怨信。根据命题要求,本文应包含以下内容:简单介绍自己,指出不满;具体提出存在的问题;提出具体建议或要求。

【参考范文】

A Letter to My Neighbor

Nov 8, 2007

Dear Mr. Wang,

　　I am your neighbor. I am writing to complain about the noise you made while you practiced your musical instruments every night.

　　To be frank, the music you play is not pleasant to listen to in the evening. Besides, I find I cannot settle down to do anything I want and it difficult to stay in the house. I invent any excuse to go out for the evening to be away from the terrible noise. What's more, your noise has a bad effect on me that I can't fall asleep, so I feel very sleepy in the daytime.

　　As you have known, sleep is very important to a person's health. So I am not prepared to put up with the situation anymore. I think it is high time you realized your responsibilities as a member of the community, and I must warn you that unless you do something about the situation, I will be forced to take legal action. I really appreciate it if you would and could do something about my complaint!

Thank you very much.

Yours sincerely,

Wu Min

Part II

【文章大意】

本文讲述了学习风格与学业之间的关系。文章讲述不同的个性、不同的做事方式以及不同类型的人选择什么样的学习风格以及在什么样的老师指导下会有所表现,目的是为刚入校的大学生提供一些信息以帮助他们选择适合自己的学习风格,在学业上有所成就。

1. 【定位】题干中的关键信息 This article aims to 提示本题与文章的主旨有关,故应定位于整篇文章。

 【解析】[N]。结合文章各个小标题可知,文章谈到了学习风格以及什么类型的人有什么样的学习风格,文章只是在陈述事实,为刚入学的大学生提供信息,并没有推荐学习方式。

2. 【定位】根据题干中的关键信息 learning styles 可将搜索范围定位在小标题 Learning Styles: What Are They?下。

 【解析】[NG]。该部分第一句指出有不同的学习风格,通常情况下 these types coincide with our personality style (学习风格与人的性格相符),但并未提及两者之间存在因果关系。

3. 【定位】根据题干中的关键信息 visual style students 可将搜索范围定位在小标题 Eyes or Ears 下的第三段。

 【解析】[Y]。该段指出如果你采用 visual style 的学习风格,那么主要依赖于课堂讨论来讲课的讲师就会 cause you some angst(使你忧虑不已),由此可推测,采用视觉类学习风格的学生不喜欢参加课堂讨论,因此他们的表现就会不积极。

4. 【定位】根据题干中的关键信息 introverted 可将搜索范围定位在小标题 Group or Solitary 下的第四段。

 【解析】[N]。结合本段第二句 As such, you may be quiet in the classroom and dislike classes with a lot of oral presentations and group interaction and work 及最后一句 Smaller classes are your preference 可知,内向的人喜欢小班上课,但不喜欢集体交流与集体作业。

5. 【定位】根据题干中的关键信息 sixth sense 可将搜索范围定位在小标题 Practical or Innovative 下的第二段。

 【解析】innovative types。该段倒数第二句中的 these people 指的是上一句中的 others,即喜欢用 sixth sense(第六感)来获得信息的人,这种人通常会把精力放在 what might be in the future(将来会发生什么事情)上,人们通常称这种类型的人为 innovative(创新)的人。

6. 【定位】根据题干中的关键信息 practical type 可将搜索范围定位在小标题 Practical or Innovative 下的第三段。

 【解析】skills they already know。该段第一二句指出,如果你属于 practical type,你或许会喜欢 an established, routine way of doing things(一种已知的、按部就班的做事方式),并且你 prefer using skills you already know rather than new ones,题干内容是第二句话的同义转述。

7. 【定位】根据题干中的关键信息 less-emotional 可将搜索范围定位在小标题 Thinking or Feeling 下的第二段。

 【解析】analytical。该段第一二句指出有的人喜欢有条理地、客观地整理信息,他们对其他人的想法反应得很快,也具有 more analytical(更强的分析能力),最后一句指出这样的人更喜欢 teachers who are task-focused, logical, well-organized, less emotional and who offer feedback。由此可推测 Well-organized and less-emotional professors(做事有条理、很少感情用事的老师)可能更受有目标、有分析能力(analytical)的学生的欢迎。

8. 【定位】根据题干中的关键信息 respond more to people's feeling 可将搜索范围定位在小标题 Thinking or Feeling 下的第三段。

 【解析】a personal, value-oriented way。该段第一句指出 other people 更喜欢以 a personal, value-oriented way 来整理信息,而根据下句可知,other people 指的就 be very aware of other people and their feelings(非常顾及别人感受)的人。由此可知,对别人的感觉回应较多的人更倾向于以 a personal, value-oriented way 来组织整理信息。

9. 【定位】根据题干中的关键信息 closure-driven 可将搜索范围定位在小标题 Open-ended or Closure-driven 下的第三段。

 【解析】a specific time frame and precise guidelines。该段第四句指出如果 you can stick to a routine and follow a specific time frame and precise guidelines,你就可以 learn best,而这句里的 you 指的就是本段第一句中

need closure 的人,也就是 Clusure-driven learners,题干是原文的同义转述。

10.【定位】根据题干中的关键信息 open-ended 可将搜索范围定位在小标题 Open-ended or Closure-driven 下的第四段。

　　【解析】postpone unpleasant jobs。由该段第二句话 you may have trouble making decisions and may postpone unpleasant jobs 即可找出本题的答案,本句中的 you 就是 open-ended people。

Part III

Section A

11.

[A] Mr. Brown's assistant.	M: This is Mr. Brown speaking. I'd like to speak to Mr. Thompson, please.
[B] Mr. Thompson's wife.	W: I'm sorry. Mr. Thompson will not be in the office for the whole day.
[C] Mr. Thompson's secretary.	
[D] Mr. Brown's wife.	Q: Who is the woman probably?

【解析】身份关系题。由女士话中的 Mr. Thompson will not be in the office for the whole day(Mr. Thompson 今天一整天都不在办公室)可推测,她很可能是 Mr. Thompson 的 secretary(秘书)。

12.

[A] Because he is leaving for a holiday for several days.	W: Mr. Smith, would you care to make another appointment with Mr. Johnson?
[B] Because he can not reach Mr. Johnson.	M: Unfortunately, I'm leaving town for a meeting rather unexpectedly, and I may be gone for several days.
[C] Because he has to meet another important customer.	Q: Why can't Mr. Smith make another appointment with Mr. Johnson?
[D] Because he will have a meeting for several days.	

【解析】事实状况题。由男士话中的 I'm leaving town for a meeting… 可知,他 will have a meeting for several days(要去参加一个为期几天的会议),所以不能与 Mr. Johnson 见面。

13.

[A] Tomorrow morning.	M: I'd like to have a talk with the manager about something urgent. Could you arrange it for me?
[B] This afternoon.	W: I'll check the schedule. Ur, today and tomorrow morning are all booked up. Will tomorrow afternoon be OK?
[C] This morning.	
[D] Tomorrow afternoon.	Q: When can the man talk to the manager?

【解析】数字信息题。女士话中的反义疑问句 Will tomorrow afternoon be OK 表明经理 tomorrow afternoon 有时间,如果男士愿意,他可以在明天下午与经理面谈。

14.

[A] Jane did not wish to marry so early.	W: Hi, Jack. I heard you've broken up with Jane. What happened? I thought you two were made for each other.
[B] Jane thought Jack was too idle.	M: Well, you never know. I'm ready for a commitment and want to settle down, but Jane says she wants to pursue her career while she's still young.
[C] Jane thought Jack was too ambitious.	
[D] Jane thought Jack was too young.	Q: Why did Jack break up with Jane?

【解析】事实状况题。男士话中的转折连词 but 引导的转折句表明 Jane 的态度与他不同,男士已经准备好要和 Jane 结婚了,但 Jane 却说她想 pursue her career while she's still young(趁她年轻的时候努力工作),言外之意就是 Jane 不想 marry so early(太早结婚)。

15.

[A] She is encouraging the man to begin his new business. [B] She is blaming the man for his mismatch. [C] She is trying to comfort the man's broken heart. [D] She is blaming the man for his indecision in his business.	W: Mike, I don't know what to say, but cheer up! There's plenty of fish in the sea and you'll find your soul mate, your perfect match! M: Yeah, but it's hard to forget her at the moment. You know, we were together for almost five years. Q: What is the woman doing in the conversation?

【解析】行为活动题。女士话中的 cheer up 和男士话中的 but it's hard to forget her at the moment 表明男士现在正在为与女友分手的事伤心,由此可知女士是在 comfort the man's broken heart(安慰正在伤心的男士)。

16.

[A] A grocery store. [B] A fruit store. [C] A cookie store. [D] A grain store.	M: I hear that your mother runs a store. What kind of store? W: Well, it sells food, like bread, eggs, soft drinks, rice, sugar and cookies. Things that people buy every day. Q: What kind of store does the woman's mother run?

【解析】事实状况题。由女士话中的 it sells food, like bread, eggs, soft drinks, rice, sugar and cookies 可知,她的母亲开的是一家 grocery store(杂货店)。

17.

[A] Central air conditioning and a TV set. [B] A dishwasher, air conditioning and two bathrooms. [C] A balcony and two bathrooms. [D] A study room and a swimming pool.	W: Mr. White, are there any amenities which you would like to have in the apartment? For example, a dishwasher, a balcony or a swimming pool? M: I would definitely like to have a dishwasher, and with summers like there, central air! A balcony is not that important. Oh, yes, and two bathrooms would be nice. Q: What does the man want in the apartment?

【解析】事实状况题。由男士的话可知,他对公寓的要求是要有 dishwasher(洗碗机)及 central air(空调),two bathrooms,而 balcony(阳台)可有可无。

18.

[A] At the supermarket. [B] In a wine factory. [C] At the department store. [D] At a grocery store.	M: We've got enough food to feed a small army. Let's go over to the check-out stand. W: OK. But just let me pick up a bottle of wine and some cooking oil before we go. Q: Where does the conversation probably happen?

【解析】地点场景题。由对话中的关键信息 food, the check-out stand(收银台),a bottle of wine 及 cooking oil(食用油)可推测,对话可能发生在 supermarket(超市)。

Conversation One

【听力原文】	【答案解析】
W: Hello. I'm Dorothy Johnson with BBC's "Fashion Today". In New York City, no self-respecting woman would be caught dead without perfectly manicured hands. The reason, hundreds of women drop in nail bars all designed to have you buffed, polished now and out in a time frame that fits perfectly within your lunch hour. Well, the finger phenomenon has come to London and [19①] I'm here to check it out. How long does a manicure take? M: A quick manicure is twenty-five minutes, which is really for a very quick manicure and not a luxurious treatment. [20] It should be done in	19. Where did this interview probably take place? 【解析】选[A]。推断题。结合女士话中的 I'm here to check it out 和男士话中的 This is where we have a lot of office workers around here 以及对话结尾处女士的问话 What's the most popular nail colour in your salon 可知,对话可能发生

twenty-five minutes, and it shouldn't take any longer and certainly not any less. So, in a standard manicure, you'll have attention paid to the cuticle for the shape. This is what we call the "lunch time manicure". [19②] This is where we have a lot of office workers around here, so they need to come in at their lunch break to be able to achieve their manicure, or after work.

W: What are the most fashionable shapes at the moment for nails?

M: The oval is coming back in!

W: Really?

M: Yes, the square has been around now for about twelve months. It has been predominantly square, short and square and neat.

W: What are the fashions in terms of colours?

M: Colours at the moment, we've got a lovely choice, because all the pastels are in. [21] All the soft blue, soft pink, soft green, the lilacs, those are the most popular shades at the moment. Everybody loves those.

W: [19③] What's the most popular nail colour in your salon?

M: Still French manicure, I think, obviously, because there is no limitation on coordinating colour with outfits. And if you're having a lot of changes, then obviously the French manicure is so easy to go with.

在 the man's salon,故答案为[A]。

20. How much time does it need to finish a quick manicure, according to the man?

【解析】选[D]。细节题。男士提到快速修指甲需要 25 分钟时间,并且 it shouldn't take any longer and certainly not any less(不应该比 25 分钟时间长,也不能比 25 分钟时间短),由此可知,快速修完指甲的标准时间是 25 分钟,既不能多也不能少,故答案为[D]。

21. Which of the following colours is one of the most popular nail colours?

【解析】选[A]。细节题。男士提到,目前最流行的各种修甲颜色为 soft blue, soft pink, soft green, the lilacs, soft green 属于其中一种,故答案为[A]。

Conversation Two

【听力原文】

W: In the film version of your life, Russell Crowe, who plays your part, sees people who really aren't there. Did aliens speak to you?

M: When I began to hear voices I thought of the voices as from something of that sort.

W: What would they say to you?

M: Well, [22] you see it's really my subconscious talking. It was really that night because I know.

W: [23] I once read an article about you and it described you like this: "John Nash, an arrogant guy."

M: Yeah. That is a word that has been used.

W: Your arrogance back then was said to be monumental. "You don't know crap," you would say to some of your fellow graduate students. "How could you?" Accurate?

M: Well, I think the first one is probably invented but the second one might be accurate.

W: And you took yourself quite seriously and your work.

M: Well, [24] of course I took myself seriously.

W: What happened when you went into the mental illness?

M: Now, [25] you know that it's mental illness if you're coming out of that reality. It's like the movie you see, at first the signals in the newspaper, the codes, and all this is the true reality which has been discovered.

W: But when you are in that reality you are in that reality, and you don't realize that you are schizophrenic.

M: You're not mentally ill, you're rather extra-normally aler-

【答案解析】

22. Where did the strange voices the man heard come from?

【解析】选[A]。推断题。对话开头处,女士问男士听到的那些声音是否对他说了什么,男士回答说那些声音只不过是来自于他的 subconscious talking,也就是说,那些奇怪的声音来自于男士的 subconsciousness(潜意识),故答案为[A]。

23. Who is the man?

【解析】选[A]。细节题。女士提到她曾经读到过一篇关于男士的一篇文章,it described you like this: "John Nash, an arrogant guy",由此可知男士 John Nash,故答案为[A]。

24. What kind of person is the man like?

【解析】选[B]。细节题。女士描述男士时说他对他本人和工作的要求十分严格,男士说 of course I took myself seriously,故答案为[B]。

25. What didn't the man realize when he went into his mental illness?

【解析】选[C]。细节题。对话结尾处,女士问男士在他患有精神病时发生了什么事,男士回答说 you know that it's mental illness if you're coming out of that reality,言外之意就是当你患精神病的时候,你就会把那时所看、所想的事情当作是事实,但当时你并不会意识到自己患有精神病,而当你好了之后,你才会意识到那时你患有精神病,由此可知,当男士患有精神病的时候,他并没

ted to hidden truths. You're enlightened, you're exceptionally enlightened.

有意识到自己 mentally ill,故答案为[C]。

Section B

Passage One

【听力原文】

Academic dishonesty is an offense against the university. A student who has committed an act of academic dishonesty has failed to meet a basic requirement of satisfactory academic performance. Thus, academic dishonesty is not only a basis for disciplinary action, but also relevant to the evaluation of the student's level of performance.

The faculty and administration recognize the necessity of maintaining an academic environment in which each student is evaluated on the basis of his own performance. [26] The maintenance of such an environment requires that both faculty and students be aware of the nature and consequences of academic dishonesty.

Each instructor should familiarize himself with the procedures regarding preparation and supervision of examinations in his department and the guidelines relating to procedures for handling cases of academic dishonesty. Early each term, the instructor should inform the class of any expectations unique to the course.

The instructor determines the grade to be awarded to a student and, in making that determination, may take into account academic dishonesty on the part of the student. [27] When there has been academic dishonesty, the instructor may award a failing grade in the assignment or a failing grade in the course. The instructor may also require the student to perform additional assignments. Before assigning a grade affected by academic dishonesty, the instructor must make a reasonable effort to discuss the matter with the student. [28] When a grade is affected by academic dishonesty, the instructor must inform in writing both the student and the person in charge of the department.

【答案解析】

26. Who should do his duty for the maintenance of an honest academic environment?

【解析】选[D]。推断题。文中提到 the maintenance of such an environment(维持这样一个学术氛围)需要 both faculty and students(学院和学生)都意识到 the nature and consequences of academic dishonesty(学术造假的本质和后果)。由上文可知 such an environment 指的就是一种 each student is evaluated on the basis of his own performance(根据学生自己的表现来评定学生成绩)的学术氛围,这样的学术氛围才是 an honest academic environment(良好的学术氛围)。综合上面的分析可知,要建立一个良好的学术氛围,faculty 和 students 都应该尽到自己的职责,故答案为[D]。

27. What result can academic dishonesty lead to, according to the passage?

【解析】选[C]。细节题。文中提到,教师在给学生评定成绩时应考虑到该学生是否有 academic dishonesty(学术造假)行为,如果有,教师可以 award a failing grade in the assignment of a failing grade in the course(给学生的作业或课程评为不及格),故答案为[C]。

28. What should an instructor do when a student's grade is affected by academic dishonesty?

【解析】选[B]。细节题。文中提到,当学生的分数确实受到 academic dishonesty 的影响时,the instructor 应该以书面形式通知 the student 和 the person in charge of the department(学生所在系的负责人),故答案为[B]。

Passage Two

【听力原文】

On the third Sunday in June, fathers all across the United States are given presents, treated to dinner or otherwise made to feel special. [29] The origin of Father's day is not clear. Some say that it began with a church service in West Virginia in 1908. Others say the first Father's Day ceremony was held in Vancouver, Washington.

Regardless of when the first true Father's Day occurred, the strongest promoter of the holiday was Mrs. John Bruce Dodd of Spokane, Washington, who was then Sonora Louise Smart. She thought of the idea for Father's Day while listening to a Mother's Day sermon in 1909.

【答案解析】

29. What do we know about Father's Day?

【解析】选[B]。细节题。文中提到 the origin of Father's Day is not clear(人们不知道父亲节的起源),有人说它始于 1908 年的西弗吉尼亚的一次教会活动,也有人说第一次庆祝 Father's Day 是在温哥华·华盛顿,故答案为[B]。

30. How many children did William Smart

Sonora wanted a special day to honor her father, William Smart. [30] Smart, who was a Civil War veteran, was widowed when his wife died while giving birth to their sixth child. Mr. Smart was left to raise the newborn and his other five children by himself on a rural farm in eastern Washington State.

After Sonora became an adult she realized the selflessness her father had shown in raising his children as a single parent. In 1909, Mrs. Dodd approached her own minister and others in Spokane about having a church service dedicated to fathers on June 5, her father's birthday. [31] That day was too soon for her minister to prepare the service, so he spoke a few weeks later on June 19th. From then on, the State of Washington celebrated the third Sunday in June as Father's Day. Children made special desserts or visited their fathers if they lived.

In 1966 President Lyndon Johnson signed a presidential proclamation declaring the 3rd Sunday of June as Father's Day and put the official stamp on a celebration that was going on for almost half a century.

have?

【解析】选[C]。细节题。文中在介绍 Sonora 的父亲 William Smart 时提到，他的妻子在 giving birth to their sixth child(生第六个孩子)的时候去世了，Mr. Smart 只得自己抚养 the newborn(新生儿)和 his other five children，由此可知 Smart 有 six children，故答案为[C]。

31. Why didn't Sonora's minister give a church service on June 5?

【解析】选[B]。细节题。文中提到，Mrs. Dodd 请她的牧师和其他人在 June 5 那天做礼拜以庆祝他父亲的生日，但是 June 5 对她的牧师来说太 soon(仓促了)，他无法 prepare the service well，故答案为[B]。

Passage Three

【听力原文】

The nation's younger generation is rapidly losing traditional family values and replacing them with independent, carefree lifestyles that delay parenthood. [32] Some 60 percent of urban residents in the northern city of Tianjin look favorably on "dink"—double income, no kids couples, according to a recent survey by the city's women's federation.

[33] This is contrary to the typical Chinese belief that newlyweds need to have a child as soon as possible to carry on the family name, as well as to have someone to care for them after retirement. About 64 percent of the respondents said it was "understandable" and "acceptable" not to have a child, though most were not dinks themselves. The respondents were all above 18 years old and were randomly selected from 600 urban families in Tianjin.

Sociologists say the trend mirrors changes in the Chinese values system. Usually, the most frequently heard blessing to a newlywed couple is "may you have a child soon," and the child-bearing ability is essential to be considered for a good wife. [34] With the country's modernization drive, however, more couples now place a higher value on career development and the quality of life. A son or daughter would be an intruder in their carefree lifestyle.

[35] Most respondents expressed confidence that the state's social security system would ensure well-being during retirement. A respondent said that the days were gone when you had to rely on your own kids for financial support. Li Yin, who began her research on dinks more

【答案解析】

32. What do most of urban residents in Tianjin think of "dink"?

【解析】选[A]。推断题。文中提到，在天津，60％的城市居民 look favorably on "dink"(认为"丁克家庭"不错)，言外之意就是天津的大多数城市居民对 dink 持有的态度是 positive(积极的)，故答案为[A]。

33. Why should a family have a child, according to the typical Chinese belief mentioned in the passage?

【解析】选[B]。细节题。文中提到 dink 与传统信仰相悖，中国传统信仰认为新婚夫妇应该尽早生子，以便 to carry on the family name 及 have someone to care for them after retirement，言外之意就是每个家庭要有孩子的原因是孩子可以 carry on the family name 和照顾他们的父母，由此可知延续家族的姓氏是其中原因之一，故答案为[B]。

34. What contribute to the shift of Chinese values system, according to the passage?

【解析】选[A]。细节题。文中提到，在国家的 modernization drive(现代化的驱动)下，越来越多的夫妻更加重视 career development(事业的发展)和 the quality of life(生活质量)，由此可知造成中国人价值体系转变的一个原因就是 modernization drive，故答案为[A]。

35. What will most respondents rely on after retirement, according to the survey?

【解析】选[B]。推断题。文中提到，大多数的 respondents 表达了他们对 the state's social security system(社会保障体系)非常有信心，认为该体系能够保障他们退休后的 well-being(富足生活)，言外之意

than 10 years ago once said that the people who choose not to have a child are mostly hedonists. They value individuality and the quality of married life more than parenthood.

就是他们退休后可以依靠 social security system 过上富足的生活,故答案为[B]。

Section C

【听力原文】

In common sense, a myth is fiction—something which is untrue. Scholars of (36) mythology define myth as a special kind of story which tries to (37) interpret some aspects of the world around us.

A (38) collection of definitions of myths might be (39) framed by the following paraphrase: myths are stories, usually about gods and other supernatural beings. Some of them are (40) explanatory and prescientific, and (41) attempt to explain the natural world. As such, they are usually functional and are the science of `primitive people. The terms legend and folktale are sometimes used (42) interchangeably with myth. Technically, however, these are not the same. Here are some (43) guidelines on the differences.

First, a myth is a story from the past. It may explain the origin of the universe and of life, or it may express its culture's moral values in human terms. Myths concern (44) the powers that control the human world and the relationship between those powers and human beings. Although myths are religious in their origin and function, they may also be the earliest form of history, science, or philosophy. A folktale, then, is a story that is purely fictional in plot and has no particular location in either time or space. However, despite its elements of fantasy, (45) a folktale is actually a symbolic way of presenting the different means by which human beings cope with the world in which they live.

Second, a legend is a story from the past about a subject that was, or is believed to have been historical. Legends concern people, places, and events. Usually, the subject is a saint, a king, a hero, a famous person, or a war. (46) A legend is always associated with a particular place and a particular time in history.

【答案解析】

36. 空前的介词 of 和空后的动词 define 提示所填词应为名词。本句中 define 的宾语 myth 提示 Scholars of _____ 是本句的主语,可能是研究神学的学者。mythology 意为"神学"。

37. 空前的不定式 to 和空后的名词提示所填词应为动词原形。interpret 意为"解释,说明"。

38. 空前的不定冠词空后的介词 of 提示所填词应为名词。collection 意为"收集"。

39. 空前的系动词 be 和空后的介词 by 提示所填词应为动词的被动形式。framed 意为"限定框架"。

40. 空前的系动词 are 和空后的并列连词 and 提示所填词应为形容词或动词的过去分词形式,与 prescientific 并列。explanatory 意为"解释性的,说明性的"。

41. 空前的并列连词 and 和空后的不定式短语 to explain 提示所填词应为动词原形,与句中的另一谓语动词 are 并列。

42. 分析句子结构以及空前的 used 可知,所填词应为副词。interchangeably 意为"可交替地"。

43. 空前的形容词 some 和空后的介词 on 提示所填词应为复数名词。下文提到了 legend, folktale 的区别,并分别以 first, second 并列开来,由此可推测 Here are some (43) _____ an the differences 是下面两段的总起句,很可能表达"区分这两个词的指导,参考"的意思。guidelines"指导"。

44. 【Main Points】the powers **which master** the human world and the relationship between **the** powers and **human**

45. 【Main Points】a folktale **in fact** is a symbolic way of presenting the different means by which **human** cope with the world **where** they live

46. 【Main Points】A legend is always **related to** a particular **place and time** in history

Part IV

Section A

【文章大意】

本文主要讲述了科学家利用在犯罪现场发现的细微痕迹和证据追查凶手的故事。文章开始就举了一个例子,说的是科学家通过受害者屋内的一块布上留有不同寻常的金属碎屑破获了一起案件;接着又举了好几个例子,讲述的都是研究人员通过犯罪现场的证据追查犯罪嫌疑人,文章的最后提到了"纤维转移"的概念,也就从衣服间相互转移的纤维入手,来确定两个人之间的接触程度,可以帮助破案。

47.【定位】根据题干中的关键信息 in the west of England 以及 an article of clothing 可定位在第一段最后一句。

【解析】tiny shreds of a certain unusual metal。由首段末句 They found an article of clothing… 及第二段首句 …found tiny shreds of a certain unusual metal 可知,警察是根据小偷遗落在女士厨房中的布片上的 tiny shreds of certain unusual metal 找到小偷的。

48.【定位】根据题干中的关键信息 the way forensic scientists find it 可定位在第三段最后一句。

【解析】being used to help track down criminals。根据上文可知,末句中的 it 指代的即是 trace evidence,由此可推断 trace evidence 的新奇之处在于 the way forensic scientists find it 和 forensic scientists use it to help track down criminals,因此对 forensic scientists use it to…进行改写即可得出答案。

49.【定位】根据题干中的关键信息 in the fourth paragraph 可定位在第四段。

【解析】trace evidence。该段指出盗窃教堂的贼被抓是因为警方发现了他衣服上的 traces of wax,而踢了女孩脸部的男人被抓则是因为他鞋尖上的 traces of white powder。根据文章可知,traces of wax 及 traces of white powder 都属于 trace evidence,故答案为 trace evidence。

50.【定位】根据题干中的关键信息 degree of contact 可定位在最后一段第四句。

【解析】Fiber transference。本题的解题关键在于弄清楚该句里的 that 的所指,综合整段内容不难发现,that 指代的是本段句首的 fiber transference。

51.【定位】根据题干中的关键信息 according to the passage 可知本题的定位应是整篇文章。

【解析】The forensic scientists。通读全文可知,在破获各种案件当中 forensic scientists 起到了重要作用。

Section B

Passage One

【文章大意】

本文是一篇学术论文,主要围绕 William Schopf 和 Martin Brasier 的不同观点而展开。文章第一二段主要与 William Schopf 发现的一种微生物化石有关;第三段主要讲 Martin Braiser 的异议;第四五段主要讲 William Schopf 和 Martin Braiser 之间的争辩。

52.选[C]。推理判断题。文章第一段最后一句指出 Schopf 发现的这些化石很有可能是 came from far earlier than any other life form found(比所有已发现生命的存在时间都要早),第二段最后一句指出 Schopf 认为这些化石是 photosynthetic blue-green algae(能进行光合作用的蓝绿藻),综合上面的分析可推测,如果那些化石真被证明是 algae 的话,那么 algae 就会是世界上最早生存的生物,这就说明以前关于生命最早起源的推测并不正确,故答案为[C]。

53.选[B]。事实细节题。文章第三段末句指出 Brasier 通过对岩石组成成分的研究得知,the chert 形成时的温度在 200 摄氏度以上,too hot for life(对生命体来说温度太高),这就表明那些化石不可能是能进行光合作用的海藻,由此可知 Brasier 提出他的观点的理由就是 the chert 形成时的温度太高不适合海藻存活,故答案为[B]。

54.选[A]。观点态度题。文章第四段第三句指出 But "organic"…isn't the same as "biological",该段倒数第二句则指出 Schopf 的观点:Non-biological organic matter has never been found in the geological record ever(地质记录史上从未发现过非生物有机体),由此可知,Schopf 认为在地质方面 organic 与 biological 是一样的,故答案为[A]。

55.选[A]。事实细节题。通读整篇文章可知,Braiser 与 Schopf 争论的焦点就是 Schopf 发现的 fossils 是否就是能进行光合作用的蓝绿藻,文章在最后一段倒数第二句提到了 Schopf 的观点。他认为造成这种迷惑的原因在于 a lack of experience with the microscopes used to study such structures,[A]为原文的细节再现,故为答案。

56.选[B]。观点态度题。文章首先指出 Schopf 发现了一种化石,接着描述了 Schopf 与 Braiser 之间对于该化石是否为能进行光合作用的蓝绿藻进行的争论,但作者并没有在文章中掺杂进任何自己的观点,所以可以说作者对 Schopf 和 Braiser 之间的争论始终保持着客观的态度,故答案为[B]。虽然文章最后一句中的 not everyone…是表达观点的句子,但该观点是看过化石的人的观点,而不是作者的观点。

Passage Two

【文章大意】

本文主要是关于快餐行业改换其食用油以满足消费者的需求。第一段为本文的主旨段,说明快餐行业所使用的食用油的变化;第二三段主要是介绍用来炸食品的食用油的成分;第四段主要是讲改换食用油对快餐行业以及消费者的好处;第五段作者提出自己的观点:少吃油炸食品。

57.选[D]。事实细节题。文章第二段最后一句指出饱和脂肪酸的化学结构中的氢原子达到了饱和状态,会增加人体内低密度脂蛋白胆固醇的含量,对人体有害,但是 unsaturated fats can bring that number down,由此可知 unsaturated fats 对人体是有利的,故答案为[D]。文章第一段第一句指出 McDonald's 宣布要减少 48% 的trans-fatty acids(反式脂肪酸),这就说明 trans-fatty acids 对人体不利,故[A]错;[B]、[C]虽然在文中有提到,但是并没有说明它们是否对人体有利,故错误。

58. 选[A]。推理判断题。文章第三段第二句指出以前主要用 animal fats 来油炸食品,这些 animal fats 大部分都是 saturated(饱和的),而通过第二段最后一句 Saturated fats…are associated with increases in LDL cholesterol 可知,饱和脂肪酸能够增加人体内 LDL 胆固醇的含量,由此可知,之所以说 animal fats 对人体有害,是因为它们能够增加人体内 LDL 胆固醇的含量,故答案为[A]。

59. 选[A]。事实细节题。文章第三段第四句指出 vegetable oils 的缺点,即:less stable and turn rancid more quickly (相对不稳定并且很容易就坏掉),该段第五句中描述了一种能改变该缺点的方法,即:将植物油 hydrogenated,由此可知,如果植物油不被 hydrogenated,那么它们对快餐行业来说就不适用,因为它们很容易就会变坏,故答案为[A]。

60. 选[C]。语义理解题。文章第三段中指出 vegetable oils 很容易变坏,而氢化后的 vegetable oils 则能保存较长时间,所以快餐公司使用氢化后的植物油是由于氢化后的植物油有较长的保质期,由此可以推断 shelf life 与某一产品的保质期有关,故答案为[C]。

61. 选[C]。观点态度题。题干中 McDonald's new announcement 指的即是 McDonald's 宣布改变其所使用的食用油。文章最后一段首句首先指出 McDonald's 改换后的食用油使其油炸食品对 4600 万的美国食用者的心脏来说要好一点,但该句接着以转折连词 but 连接分句表明改换食用油并不能说明这些食品就是健康食品。由此可知,作者的这种先扬后抑的写作手法表明 McDonald's 的新决定既有优点又有不足,即作者持客观的态度看待 McDonald's 的决定,故答案为[C]。

Part V

【文章大意】

德国人十分重视保护隐私,不论是房屋外面的门、树篱、栅栏还是屋里面的房门都显示了德国人对自我空间以及个人秘密的重视。在人际交往方面,德国人也十分注意保护自己的隐私,邻里之间甚至几年都不会有任何往来。

62. 选[D]。语义衔接题。单从本句语义上无法判断出正确选项,所以应从整篇文章着手。通读文章可发现第二段第六句中的 The formality of personal space 提示德国人对自我空间的要求是非常刻板的,而 personal space 属于 privacy,由此可知所填词应该与 formality 处于同一语义场中,备选项中符合此要求的只有[D] formal "刻板的,拘泥于形式的"。

63. 选[B]。语义衔接题。冒号后的 these 明显表明 _____ features 是对 Doors, hedges, fences 的归纳总结,doors,hedges,fences 都是实体,所以所填词应含有"实体的"之意,备选项中符合此要求的只有[B] physical "实体的,物质的"。

64. 选[C]。语义衔接题。所填词应能与介词 on 搭配使用,故可首先排除[A] appeal "吸引力";其余三个选项都可以与介词 on 搭配使用,所以只能根据文章整体意思判断正确选项。通读整篇文章可知,本文主要在讲德国人对 privacy 的重视,而 doors,hedges,fences 等实体特征正反映了德国人对 privacy 的重视,备选项中能表达这一含义的只有[C] emphasis "重视"。

65. 选[D]。结构衔接题。结合四个选项可知,本题考查对定语从句引导词的掌握。先行词 privacy 以及空前逗号提示所填词应为[D] which。[C] that 引导定语从句时其前不能用逗号隔开,[B] who 引导的定语从句通常修饰"人"。

66. 选[A]。语义衔接题。四个选项都是副词,因此在推断本句大意时可暂时将其含义忽略。本句主干大意为:在德国人的房屋内,房间与房间之间的门也是关着的,所填副词应选用[A] firmly "牢固地,稳固地"以起到进一步强调"shut"这一动作的作用。[D] wholly "完全地,统统"虽然也是程度副词,而且在意义上也适合本句,但 wholly 强调的是"范围",与本句要求强调"门被关"的程度不一致,故可排除;[B] loosely "宽松地,松散地",[C] closely "接近地",不符合本句语境,故也可排除。

67. 选[B]。语义衔接题。根据 and 后的 individual 可知,所填词应与 individual 并列,且处于同一语义场中,备选项中符合此要求的只有[B] personal "个人的"。[A] partial "部分的",[C] independent "独立的",[D] transparent "透明的"都不符合句意,故可排除。

68. 选[A]。语义衔接题。由空后的定语从句 that leads visitors into the house 可知,an _____ hall 是可以使客人经过它进入房屋的地方。客人由外面进入房屋所经过的地方很明显应是 entrance hall(门廊),故答案为[A] entrance "入口,进入"。[B] assembly "集合,会议",assembly hall "会议厅";[C] discussion "讨论",discussion hall "洽谈处";[D] warming-up,warming-up hall "准备活动厅"。

69. 选[A]。语义衔接题。本文主要讲德国人对 privacy 的重视,在这一大的语境之下可知,德国人房屋里的 an entrance hall 的作用就是为了保护他们的 privacy,即不让来访的客人看到他们的 specific rooms,所以所填词应含有否定含义,备选项中只有[A] without "不,没有"符合要求。

70. 选[C]。语义衔接题。结合前面的分析可知,本分句是讲门廊能够保护 the family's privacy,即能使 the family's

privacy 不被破坏,备选项中能使本分句在意义上符合逻辑的只有[A] destroying"破坏"和[C] spoiling"损坏"。但[A] destroying 强调的是"物质上的破坏";而[C] spoiling 强调的是"精神上的损坏",本句中的 privacy 提示应选[C] spoiling。

71. 选[D]。语义衔接题。空前不定冠词 an 提示所填词第一个音节应为元音音素,故可首先将[A] hospitality"好客,盛情"排除;[B] embarrassment"困窘,阻碍",[C] interference"冲突,干涉"都带有消极的感情色彩,很明显不符合本文的语境,故可排除。答案只能为[D] honor"荣幸",用在句中表明"被邀请到德国人家里做客是一种荣幸",这也从侧面表明了德国人通常不邀请人到家里做客。

72. 选[B]。语义衔接题。本分句的主语 this 指代的是上句所说的"被邀请到德国人家里做客"这一事情。由本句特意提出的 foreigners 可知,上句着重强调的"be invited to a German home"的客人是德国人。结合上句可知,既然德国人甚至不经常邀请本国人到家里做客,那么更不用说是 foreigners 了,由此可知"德国人邀请人到家里做客"这一事情更不会经常发生在外国人身上了,所以所填词应是频率副词,故答案为[B] frequently"经常地"。

73. 选[D]。语义衔接题。who 引导的定语从句可以表明德国人对 foreigners 的态度,这种态度直接导致了"德国人不经常邀请外国人到家里做客"这一结果,由此可推测德国人对 foreigners 的态度肯定是不好的,故所填词在本句中应能表示消极含义,备选项中有消极含义的只有[D] suspicion"怀疑"。[A] confidence"自信",[B] gratitude"感激",[C] mystery"神秘,神秘的事物"都不含有消极的意义,故可排除。

74. 选[C]。结构衔接题。分析本句句意可知,Pieces of furniture are heavy and placed far apart 是为了 personal space is maintained during conversation,备选项中能引导目的状语从句的只有[C] so that"为了"。[A] such that,通常不独立使用,经常会以"such +名词或名词性词组+that"结构出现;[B] in that"由于,因为",引导原因状语从句;[D] since that"从…以后"。

75. 选[B]。语义衔接题。所填词与空后的 happy-go-lucky"逍遥自在的,随遇而安的"是并列关系,都用来修饰 conversations。由此可知,所填词应与 happy-go-lucky 处于同一语义场中,备选项中只有[B] relaxed"不拘束的,不严格的"符合此要求。

76. 选[A]。语义衔接题。结合四个选项的含义可知,所填词应能表达"照料"之意,所填词的宾语为 flowers,故答案为[A] tend"照料"。[B] consider"考虑",通常指照顾某人的感受,[C] attend"照顾",特指照顾病人,[D] breed"养育",通常指养育新一代。

77. 选[C]。惯用衔接题。空前 drop 与四个选项中的副词都能构成固定搭配,本题答案的选择可以根据四个动词组的意义来确定,[A] out,drop out"放弃",[B] off,drop off"逐渐减少",[C] by,drop by"顺便拜访(某人)",[D] down,drop down"放下"。根据空后的 for a chat 可知动词组应选 drop by,故答案为[C] by。

78. 选[B]。语义衔接题。下一句中的 Germans are not allowed to use their running water… 提示德国人的 time periods for noise(允许制造噪音的时间段)是受到规定和限制的,例如,使用 running water 的时间只能在晚上 9 点以前,9 点以后就不能再使用了。备选项中含有"规定,限制"含义的为[B] prescribed"规定,命令"。

79. 选[B]。语义衔接题。所填词和 spilt 都作 are 的表语,表明 outside doors 的状态,故答案为[B] opening。[A] having opened 和[D] to be opened 的时态与原文不符,[C] being opened 的语态与该句不符。

80. 选[D]。语义衔接题。空前的分号表明所填词所在的句子应与上一分句是并列关系,所以根据并列关系可知,所填词应能指代上一分句提到的主人在阳台上 dining 和 gardening 的行为,并且所填词在该分句中作主语,所以所填词应是名词,备选项中既是名词也能指代上一句的 dining 和 gardening 这些行为的只有[D] they。

81. 选[D]。惯用衔接题。备选项中的名词能与 with 搭配使用的只有[D] relationship"关系"。[A] participation"参与"和[B] involvement"包含,牵连"通常与 in 搭配使用;[C] commitment"许诺"通常与 to 搭配使用。

Part VI

82. 【答案】She devoted herself to her career
　　【解析】本题考查对固定短语 devote…to… 的掌握。devote…to… 意为"献身于…,致力于…"。

83. 【答案】that is tormenting me for nine years
　　【解析】本题考查对定语从句和时态的掌握。that 引导的定语从句修饰前面的 disease,注意主谓一致(应用单数形式)。从 have 可知现在"我"还有这种病,即这种病对人的影响一直在发生,所以应用现在进行时。

84. 【答案】Once appointed supreme commander
　　【解析】本题考查对过去分词的掌握。主语 he 与"任命"是被动关系,所以句子应采用被动语态,而"任命"与"行动"差不多是同时发生的,故也用一般过去时。Once appointed… 在句中充当状语。

85. 【答案】I have no more than five dollars in my pocket
　　【解析】本题考查对比较结构的掌握。no more than 意为"只不过…",主要是表达数量之少。

86. 【答案】I have no difficulty(in) making myself understood
　　【解析】本题考查对固定短语 have no difficulty (in) doing sth. 的掌握。have no difficulty(in) doing sth. 意为"做…并不困难",in 常常可以省略。

预测试题五

Part I Writing (30 minutes)

Directions: *For this part, you are allowed 30 minutes to write a composition on the topic*: **The Challenge to the Only Child in the College Life**. *You should write at least 150 words, and base your composition on the outline given in Chinese below*:

1) 中国的独生子女们开始面临大学生活的挑战
2) 大学校园生活为何成为独生子女们的一大挑战
3) "我"的看法

The Challenge to the Only Child in the College Life

_____

Part II Reading Comprehension (Skimming and Scanning) (15 minutes)

A cooler planet

Scientists are cooking up solutions based on current technology that they say could dramatically turn down the heat of global warming over the next 50 years. Innovations such as cheaper wind power, gas-electric hybrid cars and gas cars that generate funds for climate change projects already are available. Introducing them across the nation could put a dent in the growth of greenhouse gases that are warming the planet, scientists say.

The concentration of carbon dioxide — a potent greenhouse gas — is likely to double before the end of the century, the United Nations says. Scientists say further warming is inevitable as greenhouse gas emissions climb but that the worse effects can still be avoided. "The question now is not 'whether to adapt?' but 'how to adapt?'" says a 2004 U. N. report on climate change. The solutions, say experts, must come from action by politicians, business people, scientists and individuals. Over the next century, power could be derived from sources that release less carbon dioxide into the atmosphere such as nuclear fusion, hydrogen fuel cells and more efficient combustion engines.

Scientists: Technology already exists

Technology is a crucial component to meet the challenge of global warming, say climate researchers and policy experts. "You need technology," says Elliot Diringer, international strategies director with the Pew Center on Global Climate Change. "There's no question about that. The question is, 'What is the most efficient way to not only generate the technology but get it deployed.'"

The Intergovernmental Panel on Climate Change, a U. N. body issuing regular assessments on the climate, says innovation has advanced faster than expected. It estimates technological improvements could reduce greenhouse gas emissions below 2000 levels within 20 years and avert even more risky levels of such concentrations. The IPCC has estimated that technological improvements could some time between 2010 and 2020 reduce greenhouse gas emissions to levels below those in the year 2000. "We need to move as fast as we can," Diringer says. "The longer we wait to take concerted action, the greater the impacts will be ... the more it will cost to achieve the reduction."

Technology with the greatest potential to reduce greenhouse gas emissions already exists, say Princeton University scientists Stephen Pacala and Robert Socolow in a 2004 study published in the journal Science.

Improving efficiency and conservation could reduce billions of tons in atmospheric emissions of greenhouse gases each year. Improvements such as efficient engineering, better gas mileage and new fuel sources for vehicles and power plants have the potential to halt growth of emissions by around 2050, according to the study.

"It is important not to become diverted by the possibility of revolutionary technology," the Princeton authors write in Science. "Humanity can solve the carbon and climate problem in the first half of this century simply by increasing what we already know how to do." The scientists picked seven actions that they say could make the climate stable by 2054. They focused on technology already in place that simply needs to be expanded a lot.

Cars are an easy target. Each gallon of gas burned gives off about 20 pounds of carbon dioxide into the atmosphere, according to the Environmental Protection Agency. That's a lot of carbon for the 2 billion cars that may be on the road by 2054, nearly four times the number today, the authors report. The Science article suggests that doubling the average fuel efficiency of cars from 30 miles per gallon today to 60, switching to wind-generated hydrogen fuels or halving the annual number of miles traveled per car to 5,000 could reduce carbon dioxide emissions. The savings would provide one-seventh of the total cuts needed to make U. S. emissions stable, the article states.

In addition, scientists are watching plenty of other technologies being developed to make emissions stable.

Carbon Storage

Burying carbon dioxide allows fossil fuel companies to continue pumping oil while reducing greenhouse emissions. The United Nations estimates by 2050 it should be possible to store half of the increasing global emissions in underground reservoirs at reasonable prices. The U. S. government already has started a test project at a West Virginia coal power plant. The energy company BP sends 1 million tons of carbon dioxide each year beneath the sands of the Sahara desert at one of its facilities in Algeria.

These carbon reducing projects send millions of tons of carbon dioxide gas into underground geologic formations such as gas beds now filled with water, natural gas or oil. The risks of such techniques include leakage of carbon dioxide from underground reservoirs that may endanger human life and the environment. Scientists are studying techniques to find which rock formations permanently store gases such as carbon dioxide.

Renewable Energy

Renewable power is a major facet of reducing global warming emissions, according to the United Nations.

Because most renewable energy sources — wind, ocean tides, solar, biomass fuel — emit less carbon dioxide into the atmosphere than they absorb, they do not add to climate change. The share of renewable in the world energy supply accounts for at least 14 percent of the total, the United Nations estimates.

The price of these renewable fuels and technology is plummeting as demand grows and hardware improves. "Green" tariffs, already introduced in some European countries, guarantee premium prices for energy derived from renewable sources. States such as New York and California also require utilities to generate a fraction of their energy supply from renewable.

Trading Carbon

Carbon emissions trading is designed to make global warming prevention affordable, according to the U. N. Convention on Climate Change. Under the Kyoto Agreement, participating countries agree to emit a certain amount of carbon. If a country cannot afford to meet its carbon emissions limit, it can buy "credits" from a country that has produced less than its allotted amount.

Although critics say there are significant problems under the Kyoto system, the United Nations says emissions trading allows countries gradually to eliminate carbon dioxide while preventing some economic hardships of reducing emissions growth.

Corporate action

Companies also are devising ways for businesses and individuals to offset greenhouse emissions. Oregon-based Climate Neutral Network says it will offer air travelers access to "Cool Class" air travel in which a portion of airline fares, negotiated through contracts with different companies are invested in ways to reduce greenhouse emissions.

1. Innovations such as cheaper wind power, gas-electric hybrid cars can be used to _____.

  [A]save energy [B]turn down the heat of global warming

  [C]end the growth of greenhouse gases [D]develop new technology

2. Before the end of the century, the concentration of carbon dioxide may become _____ as high as the present one.

  [A]two times [B]three times [C]four times [D]five times

3. What is the essential component in turning down global warming?

  [A]Law. [B]Technology. [C]Efficiency. [D]Conservation.

4. According to Diringer, the concerted action to reduce greenhouse gas emissions should _____.

[A]be taken with the help of technology   [B]be taken as soon as possible

[C]have greater impacts   [D]aim to achieve the reduction

5. How much carbon dioxide can one gallon of gas burned give off into the atmosphere, according to the Environment Protection Agency?

[A] About 40 pounds.   [B] About 60 pounds.

[C] About 30 pounds.   [D] About 20 pounds.

6. The number of cars on the road by 2054 is likely to be _____ as many as today's.

[A] nearly 2 billion   [B] nearly 2 times

[C] nearly 3 billion   [D] nearly 4 times

7. Once carbon dioxide leaks from underground reservoirs, _____will be confronted with danger.

[A]the climate   [B]human life and the environment

[C] underground geologic formations   [D]underground water

8. Renewable energy sources being beneficial to climate lies in the fact that the carbon dioxide they emit into the atmosphere is _____ they absorb.

9. According to the United Nations, about _____ of the total world energy supply goes to the renewable energy.

10. In spite of the problems under Kyoto Agreement, carbon emissions trading can reduce the cost of _____.

Part III Listening Comprehension (35 minutes)

Section A

11. [A] In a restaurant.   [B] In a fruit store.

     [C] In a supermarket.   [D] In a cafeteria.

12. [A] She is going on a tour of Harvard.   [B] She is going to pay an official visit to Harvard.

     [C] She is going do some research in Harvard.   [D] She is going to study in Harvard.

13. [A] She has been longing to attend Harvard University.

     [B] She'll consider the man's suggestion carefully.

     [C] She has finished her project with Dr. Garcia's help.

     [D] She'll consult Dr. Garcia about entering graduate school.

14. [A] A traffic guard.   [B] A sociologist.

     [C] A student.   [D] A salesperson.

15. [A] He lost his hearing forever.   [B] He regained his eyesight and hearing.

     [C] He was hit by a car.   [D] He saw a miracle from the paper.

16. [A] At 10:45.   [B] At 10:40.

     [C] At 10:55.   [D] At 11:00.

17. [A] She thinks they are overpriced.   [B] She thinks they are stolen ones.

     [C] She thinks they are in poor working condition.   [D] She thinks they should buy one.

18. [A] In a doctor's office.   [B] In an operating room.

     [C] In a professor's office.   [D] In a gymnasium.

Question 19 to 21 are based on the conversation you have just heard.

19. [A] They are irresponsible.   [B] They often divorce.

     [C] They are admirable.   [D] They get no pain from divorce.

20. [A] No means is effective to fix a marriage.   [B] Fixing a marriage is like changing a tire.

     [C] Fixing a marriage is not easy.   [D] Marriages can never be fixed.

21. [A] Understanding.   [B] Divorce.

     [C] Argument.   [D] Calmness.

Question 22 to 25 are based on the conversation you have just heard.

22. [A] An actress.   [B] A tour guide.

     [C] A student.   [D] A computer operator.

23. [A] Back pains.   [B] Mental pressure.

     [C] Neck problems.   [D] Stomachache.

24. [A] They only care about their work.

[B] They are forbidden to have a rest during working time.

[C] They sit by the desk too long and seldom do exercise.

[D] Their work time is too long that they have no time to rest.

25. [A] The place the woman can get a massage.

[B] The way the woman can get cured.

[C] The place the woman can learn massage.

[D] The proper job in which the woman can get rid of neck problems.

Section B

Passage One

26. [A] The student is eager to get rid of language anxiety.

[B] The student feels uncomfortable in a social setting.

[C] The student experiences a difficult campus life.

[D] The student is looked down on by his classmates.

27. [A] Teacher's tolerance.　　　　　　　　[B] Peer's friendliness.

[C] Less stressful language environment.　　[D] Parents' encouragement.

28. [A] People will speak foreign language fluently as long as they work hard.

[B] Speaking foreign language fluently can't be achieved easily.

[C] You should go overseas to learn foreign language.

[D] Speaking foreign language fluently can't be achieved by people with language anxiety.

Passage Two

29. [A] The decrease of workforce and the low employment rate.

[B] The low corporate profits and the high unemployment rate.

[C] The intense international situation and the high corporate profits.

[D] The pressure from outside and inside.

30. [A] The low employment rate.　　　　　　[B] The inflation.

[C] The low consumer prices.　　　　　　　[D] The changeable strategy.

31. [A] Because of the rapid growth in corporate capital spending.

[B] Because of the cuts in public works spending.

[C] Because of the high prices of commodity.

[D] Because of the improper market system.

Passage Three

32. [A] In 1940.　　　　　　　　　　　　　[B] In 1942.

[C] In 1927.　　　　　　　　　　　　　　[D] In 1946.

33. [A] Althea's coach.　　　　　　　　　　[B] Buddy Walker.

[C] Althea's parents.　　　　　　　　　　　[D] A white musician.

34. [A] The Civil War.　　　　　　　　　　　[B] The World War I.

[C] The War of Independence.　　　　　　[D] The World War II.

35. [A] Twice.　　　　　　　　　　　　　　[B] 4 times.

[C] 3 times.　　　　　　　　　　　　　　[D] 9 times.

Section C

The concept of an intelligent building was born in the United States at the end of this century. The first intelligent building was built in Hartford in the United States in 1984. China's intelligent building (36)＿＿＿＿ started in the 1990s, but its (37)＿＿＿＿ of fast development is (38)＿＿＿＿ to the world.

The intelligent building is a necessary product resulting from the information (39)＿＿＿＿, an intelligent degree of building increasing with the development of science and technology. The major (40)＿＿＿＿ of the development of today's world science and technology are the so-called four-Cs technologies. The four-Cs technologies are used in buildings to form a computer, an (41)＿＿＿＿ network in building so that the buildings are made "intelligent".

　　Intelligent buildings should be "investment-justified, highly (42)_____, and quite (43)_____. Convenient, quick and very safe space is provided through the optimized design of four elements of buildings-structure: system, service and management, and internal relations among them. (44)_____in expenditures, comfort in life, commercial activities and personal safety."

　　(45)_____, and, in combination with modern service and management methods, to provide safe and comfortable environment spaces for living, studying and working.

　　The house looks like an ordinary two-story building in appearance. Telephones, computers and family electric appliances are on-line to form a united communication operation platform and join its information web to the Internet. (46)_____, such as the washing machine, the food in the refrigerator, someone bursting into the house and so on.

Part IV Reading Comprehension (Reading in Depth) (25 minutes)

Section A

　　Throughout history humans have been directly or indirectly influenced by the oceans. Ocean waters serve as a source of food and valuable minerals, as a vast highway for commerce, and provide a place for both recreation and waste disposal. Increasingly, people are turning to the oceans for their food supply either by direct consumption or indirectly by harvesting fish that is then processed for livestock feed. It has been estimated that as much as 10% of human protein intake comes from the oceans. Nevertheless, the food producing potential of the oceans is only partly realized. Other biological products of the oceans are also commercially used. For example, pearls taken from oysters are used in jewelry, and shells and coral have been widely used as a source of building material.

　　Ocean water is processed to extract commercially valuable minerals such as salt, bromine, and magnesium. Although nearly 60 valuable chemical elements have been found dissolved in ocean water, most are in such dilute concentrations that commercial extraction is not profitable. In a few arid regions of the world, such as Ascension Island, Kuwait, and Israel, ocean water is desalinated to produce fresh water.

　　The shallow continental shelves have been exploited as a source of sands and gravels. In addition, extensive deposits of petroleum-bearing sands have been exploited in offshore areas, particularly along the Gulf and California coasts of the United States and in the Persian Gulf. On the deep ocean floor *manganese nodules*(锰结核), formed by the *precipitation*(沉淀)of manganese oxides and other metallic salts around a nucleus of rock or shell, represent a potentially rich and extensive resource. Research is currently being conducted to explore nodule mining and metallic extraction techniques. Ocean water itself could prove to be a limitless source of energy in the event that nuclear fusion reactors are developed, since the oceans contain great quantities of *deuterium*(氚).

　　The oceans also have become more important for recreational use, as each year more people are attracted to the sports of swimming, fishing, scuba diving, boating, and water skiing. Ocean pollution, meantime, has escalated dramatically as those who use the oceans for recreational and commercial purposes, as well as those who live nearby, have disposed of more and more wastes there.

47. Extracting chemical elements from sea water is not profitable because _____.

　　_____

48. People have been exploiting shallow continental shelves for _____.

　　_____

49. Manganese nodules as a potentially rich and extensive resource are located _____.

　　_____

50. Once the development of nuclear fusion reactors succeeds, limitless energy will be obtained from _____.

　　_____

51. Who should be responsible for the worsening ocean pollution according to the author?

　　_____

Section B

Passage One

　　The world now loses a language every two weeks, a rate unprecedented in history. Two lively and accessible new books, Andrew Dalby's *Language in Danger* and *The Power of Babel* by John McWhorter, map the intricate combination of politics, genocide, geography and economics that typically conspire in their demise — and ask whether we are losing a testament to human creativity that rivals great works of art.

Dalby and McWhorter take us on a fascinating and colourful spin through history, chronicling the rise of empires and crisscrossing the globe to take in the indigenous tribes of west Africa, Tasmania and the Amazon, tracking down itinerant healers in Bolivia, whale hunters off the coast of Germany, Russian immigrants in New York — in short, anyone who can cast light on the unique ways people communicate.

McWhorter likens linguistic change to Darwin's theory of evolution, arguing that languages, like animals and plants, inevitably split into sub-varieties, alter in response to environmental pressures and evolve new forms and useless features. In prose that is bold and compelling, he warns against seeing grammar as a repository of culture, arguing that it is more often formed by chance and convenience and does not reflect its speakers' world view any more than "a pattern of spilled milk reveals anything specific about the bottle it came from".

Rather than dissociating languages from the people who speak them, Dalby takes on the difficult but equally rewarding challenge of drawing out the distinct consciousness expressed by each tongue. As Babel becomes homogenized, surviving languages have fewer new words and ideas to draw on. Without Greek there would be no "wine-dark sea". We would not "bury the hatchet" if American Indians hadn't done it already.

Despite these differences, both authors agree that with each language we learn, our ability to comprehend the world is given fresh, new scope. The word for "world" in Yupik, an Eskimo-Aleut language of Alaska, encompasses weather, outdoors, awareness and sense, as compared with its European equivalents, which tend to refer to "people, a crowd, inhabitants".

Why are these languages disappearing? Globalization is an important reason, both authors argue. Dalby and McWhorter rewrite the script on language change from nearly opposite but equally intelligent perspectives, agreeing on the most significant point: if our rich linguistic heritage is not preserved, even English speakers may find themselves uncomfortably lost for words.

52. The two authors show in their books great concern about _____.
    [A] prejudices against minor languages
    [B] relationship between human creativity and languages
    [C] the extinction of language in world
    [D] the importance of English to the speakers of dead languages

53. What does McWhorter want to convey by citing the relationship between spilled milk and the bottle?
    [A] He wants to prove that grammar is formed intentionally and has some relationship with what the speaker wants to convey.
    [B] He wants to show that he doesn't think grammar is essential.
    [C] He wants to convey that spilled milk has to do with the bottle it came from.
    [D] He wants to say that the speaker's world is based on grammar but grammar can't reflect his world view.

54. In what perspective does Dalby compose his book *Language in Danger*?
    [A] He attributes the extinction of languages to the globalization.
    [B] He divides language into many smaller sub-varieties.
    [C] He associates languages with the people who speak them.
    [D] He separates grammar from the speaker's world view.

55. The example of the word "world" (Line 2, Para. 5) suggests that _____.
    [A] the Yupik-speaking people know more about nature than Europeans do
    [B] the Yupik-speaking people exclude the human factor from their world view
    [C] each language reveals the way of thinking is unique to its speakers
    [D] each language is capable of splitting into sub-varieties in a unique way

56. The writer of this passage holds _____ attitude toward McWhorter and Dalby.
    [A] an objective   [B] an ironical
    [C] a suspicious   [D] a favourable

Passage Two

Researchers from around the world gathered for the American Stroke Association's 25th International Stroke Conference in New Orleans recently to discuss better ways of dealing with strokes. The news out of the meeting was not good. According to a new study, the number of strokes — having declined in the 1960s and 1970s — is unexpectedly rising again. In 1999 alone there were 750,000 full-fledged strokes in the US and half a million transient ischemic attacks (TIAs), or mini-strokes. Although both numbers have doctors worried, the conference paid particular attention to the mini-strokes because of both the stealth of their damage and the dramatic effectiveness of timely treatment.

Mini-strokes result from temporary interruptions of blood flow to the brain. Unlike full strokes, they present symptoms lasting anywhere from a few seconds to 24 hours. Rarely do they cause permanent neurological damage, but they are often precursors of a major stroke.

"Our message is quite clear," says Dr. Robert Adams, professor of neurology at the Medical College of Georgia in Augusta, the conference moderator. "TIAs, while less severe than strokes in the short term, are quite dangerous and need a quick diagnosis and treatment as well as appropriate follow-up to prevent future injury."

Unfortunately, mini-strokes are greatly under-diagnosed. A study conducted for the National Stroke Association indicates that 2.5% of all adults aged 18 or older (about 4.9 million people in the US) have experienced a confirmed TIA. An additional 1.2 million Americans over the age of 45, the study showed, have most likely suffered a mini-stroke without realizing it. These findings suggest that if the public knew how to spot the symptoms of stroke, especially mini-strokes, and sought prompt medical treatment, thousands of lives could be saved and major disability could be avoided.

The problem is that the symptoms of a mini-stroke are often subtle and passing. Nonetheless, there are signs you can look out for:

- Numbness or weakness in the face, arm or leg, especially on one side of the body.
- Trouble seeing in one or both eyes.
- Confusion and difficulty speaking or understanding.
- Difficulty walking dizziness or loss of coordination.
- Severe headache with no known cause.

Along with these symptoms, researchers have identified some key indicators that increase your chances of having a full-blown stroke after a TIA: if you're over 60, have experienced symptoms lasting longer than 10 minutes, feel weak and have a history of diabetes.

If you experience any of the symptoms, your first call should be to your doctor. It could be the call that saves your life.

57. What does the word "news" (Line 2, Para. 1) refer to, according to the passage?

[A] Information about recent events or happenings, especially as reported by newspapers.

[B] Information about the amount of people who have experienced strokes.

[C] Information about how the International Stroke Conference is faring.

[D] Information about the new study's being badly conducted.

58. The 25th International Stroke Conference shows greater concern about _____.

[A] the better ways of dealing with strokes   [B] the symptoms of mini-strokes

[C] the mini-strokes   [D] the damage of mini-strokes

59. According to the study conducted for the National Stroke Association, _____ is of great importance if you are experiencing a mini-stroke.

[A] quick diagnosis   [B] the calmness

[C] instant pill   [D] prompt medical treatment

60. Which of the following is the symptom of a mini-stroke?

[A] A person is permanently disabled.   [B] A person suddenly falls over himself.

[C] A person cannot remember who he is forever.   [D] A person gets moderate headache.

61. Why could not the 1.2 million Americans, the object of the study conducted for the National Stroke Association, realize they have suffered a mini-stroke?

[A] Because the present medical technology is not developed enough to diagnose the mini-strokes.

[B] Because the symptoms of the mini-strokes are subtle and passing.

[C] Because mini-strokes are difficult to be diagnosed.

[D] Because they don't pay any attention at all.

Part V　Error Correction (15 minutes)

Fossils, remains or traces of prehistoric plants and animals, were buried and preserved in sedimentary rock, and trapped in organic matter. Fossils representing most lively groups have been discovered, as well as many fossils representing groups that were now extinct. Fossils range at age from 3.5-billion-year-old traces of blue-green algae to 10,000-year-old remains of animals preserved during the last ice age. Many factors can influence how the fossils are preserved.

62. ＿＿＿＿＿＿

63. ＿＿＿＿＿＿

64. ＿＿＿＿＿＿

65. ＿＿＿＿＿＿

66. ＿＿＿＿＿＿

Remains of an organism may be replaced by minerals, dissolved by an acidic solution to leave only their impression, or simply reducing to a more stable form. The fossilization of an organism depends on the chemistry of the environment and on the biochemical make up of the organism. As a result, not all organisms in a community can be preserved. Plants are most commonly fossilized through carbonization. In this process, the mobile oils in the plant's organic matter are leached out and the remaining matter is reduced to a carbon film. Plants having an inner structure of rigid organic walls what may be preserved in this manner, revealing the framework of the original cells.

67. ＿＿＿＿＿＿

68. ＿＿＿＿＿＿

69. ＿＿＿＿＿＿

Different types of fossils are found in different geological formations, depended on the prehistoric environment represented and the age of the rock. Older rocks are found on low, eroded continents near the edges of large oceans. Younger rocks are found more commonly there is active mountain building and volcanic activity.

70. ＿＿＿＿＿＿

71. ＿＿＿＿＿＿

Part VI　Translation (5 minutes)

72. The suggestion ＿＿＿＿＿＿(采纳新规则) came from the chairman.

73. I had been puzzled over the problem for over an hour without any result ＿＿＿＿＿＿(突然间解决方案在我脑中一闪).

74. ＿＿＿＿＿＿(在一定程度上), we are all responsible for the loss of the company.

75. Either Tim or his brothers ＿＿＿＿＿＿(必须把雪铲出去).

76. If they hadn't gone on vacation, ＿＿＿＿＿＿(他们家是不会被破门而入的).

━━━━━━ 答案与解析 ━━━━━━

Part I

【思路点拨】

　　本题属于提纲式文字命题。提纲第 1 点指出目前社会上出现的一种现象,提纲第 2 点要求分析产生这种现象的原因,提纲第 3 点要求阐述个人对此现象的看法,由此可判断本文属于现象解释型作文。

　　根据所给提纲,本文应包含以下内容:描述中国的独生子女们面临大学生活的挑战这一现象;说明大学校园生活为何成为独生子女们的一大挑战;阐述个人对此现象的看法。

【参考范文】

The challenge to the Only Child in the College Life

Now more and more sons and daughters from one-child families are attending universities. They distinguish themselves as a new social group. This new generation has obvious advantages since they are brought up in favorable family circumstances. But there also exist some weaknesses in the way they think behave, and in their sentiments and characters. Therefore, they have to face a great challenge during their college life. (描述现象段)

Though most of these college students are intelligent and fond of study, they may find things tough when meeting something unexpected. Besides, being the only child in the family, they may not be used to the collective life and also not good at looking after themselves. They feel weak at knowing how to conduct themselves in college and communicating with different people. As they have received excessive cares from their parents, to live independently is really a challenge for them. (说明原因段)

I think we college students should face these problems positively and try to adjust ourselves to college life and the society. I believe our future will be brighter! (总结观点段)

Part II

【文章大意】

本文谈论目前解决全球变暖问题的进展情况。文章从五个方面讲述了全球变暖问题:现有技术、二氧化碳气体的贮藏、可更新能源、二氧化碳交易以及共同努力,旨在说明全球变暖问题经过人类的共同努力以及科技的进步是可以解决的。

1. 【定位】根据题目中的关键信息 wind power,hybrid cars 可将搜索范围定位在第一段。
   【解析】选[B]。结合该段最后两句话可知,像 cheap wind power 这样的 innovations 能够被用来 put a dent(减少) the growth of greenhouse gas...,通过最后一句中的定语从句可知,innovations 减少了 the growth of greenhouse gases 能达到降低 the heat of global warming 的效果,故答案为[B]。

2. 【定位】根据题目中的关键信息 concentration of carbon dioxide 可将搜索范围定位在第二段。
   【解析】选[A]。该段首句指出到本世纪末之前,the concentration of carbon dioxide 可能会 double。double ≈ two times,故答案为[A]。

3. 【定位】根据题目中的关键信息 component 将搜索范围定位在小标题 Scientists: Technology already exists 下第一段。
   【解析】选[B]。该段第一句指出 technology 在 meet the challenge of global warming 方面是 a crucial component,题目中的 essential≈crucial,故答案为[A]。

4. 【定位】根据题目中的关键信息 Diringer,concerted action 可将搜索范围定位在小标题 Scientists: Technology already exists 下第二段。
   【解析】选[B]。该段最后两句中 Diringer 指出减少温室气体排放量的行动需 as fast as...can,因为等得越久,影响越大,费用也就越大,[B]是文中 as fast as...的同义转述,故为答案。

5. 【定位】根据题目中的关键信息 Environment Protection Agency 可将搜索范围定位在小标题 Scientists: Technology already exists 下第六段。
   【解析】选[D]。由该段第二句中的 Each gallon of gas...gives off about 20 pounds...carbon dioxide 可知答案为[D]。

6. 【定位】根据题目中的关键信息 2054 可将搜索范围定位在小标题 Scientists: Technology already exists 下第六段。
   【解析】选[D]。该段第三句中的 nearly four times the number today 为 the 2 billion cars 的同位语,由此可知,到 2054 年汽车的数量将会是现在的近 4 倍左右,故答案为[D]。

7. 【定位】根据题目中的关键信息 underground reservoirs 可将搜索范围定位在小标题 Carbon Storage 下第二段。
   【解析】选[B]。该段第二句指出掩埋 carbon dioxide 也存在危险,如一旦 carbon dioxide 从

8. 【定位】根据题目中的关键信息 renewable energy sources 及 absorb 可将搜索范围定位在小标题 Renewable Energy 下第二段。
   【解析】less than。该段首句指出因为大多数 renewable energy sources 如 wind,ocean tides 所排放的二氧化碳气体比吸收的要少得多,所以它们并不会引起气候变化,即它们对气候环境有利,题目是原文的同义转述。

9.【定位】根据题目中的关键信息 renewable 及 the United Nations 可将搜索范围定位在小标题 Renewable Energy 下第二段。

　　【解析】14 percent。该段最后一句可知,世界能源供应中,the share of renewable(可再生能源供应)占 14 percent。

10.【定位】根据题目中的关键信息 Kyoto Agreement 可将搜索范围定位在小标题 Trading Carbon 下。

　　【解析】global warming prevention。第一段首句即指出 Carbon emission trading 的目的就是 make global warming prevention affordable,结合最后一段可知,carbon emission trading 尽管存在一些不足,但是它还是能够起到减少 global warming prevention 费用的作用。

Part III

Section A

11.

[A] In a restaurant.	W: The pork I ordered was not fresh.
[B] In a fruit store.	M: Oh! I'm sorry to hear that. This is very unusual as we have
[C] In a supermarket.	fresh pork from the regular supplier every day.
[D] In a cafeteria.	Q: Where is the woman?

【解析】地点场景题。由女士话中的 The pork I ordered was not fresh(我点的猪肉不新鲜)可知,女士是在一家 restaurant(餐厅)就餐。

12.

[A] She is going on a tour of Harvard.	M: Excuse me, Miss, what are you going to do in Boston?
[B] She is going to pay an official visit to Harvard.	W: I'm a government-sent visiting scholar, going to Harvard University to do my research.
[C] She is going do some research in Harvard.	
[D] She is going to study in Harvard.	Q: What is the woman going to Boston to do?

【解析】行为活动题。由女士话中的 going to Harvard University to do my research 可知,她是作为 visiting scholar(访问学者)去 Boston(波士顿)do some research in Harvard(在哈佛大学做研究)。

13.

[A] She has been longing to attend Harvard University.	M: Hi, Melissa, how's your project going? Have you thought about going to graduate school? Perhaps you can get into Harvard.
[B] She'll consider the man's suggestion carefully.	
[C] She has finished her project with Dr. Garcia's help.	W: Everything is coming along really well. I have been thinking about graduate school. But I'll talk to my tutor Dr. Garcia first and see what she thinks.
[D] She'll consult Dr. Garcia about entering graduate school.	Q: What do we learn about the woman from the conversation?

【解析】事实状况题。男士问女士是否考虑过 going to graduate school(上研究生),女士话中的 But I'll talk to my tutor Dr. Garcia first and see what she thinks 表明,她想先 consult Dr. Garcia about graduate school(向 Dr. Garcia 咨询一下,看看他对女士读研有什么意见)。

14.

[A] A traffic guard.	W: I'm looking for a textbook for my sociology course. It's called
[B] A sociologist.	*American Society at the Cross-roads*. Do you have it?
[C] A student.	M: Yes, we do. You'll find it in section 24, on the top shelf.
[D] A salesperson.	Q: What's the woman's occupation probably?

【解析】身份关系题。女士说她正在 looking for a textbook for my sociology course(找社会学课本),由此可知女士应该是一名 student。

15.

[A] He lost his hearing forever.	M: Did you hear that Mike was able to see and hear again after he
[B] He regained his eyesight and hearing.	was struck by lightning?
[C] He was hit by a car.	W: I read about him in the paper this week. It was a miracle. He'd been
[D] He saw a miracle from the paper.	blind and lost hearing for about eight or more years.
	Q: What happened to Mike?

【解析】事实状况题。男士话中的反问句 Did you hear that Mike was able to see and hear again…? (你听说 Mike 自从被雷击后又能看见和听见了吗?)表明,Mike 现在 regain his eyesight and hearing(视力和听力都恢复了)。

16.

[A] At 10:45.	W: Excuse me. I wonder if the bus would come at all. It's already
[B] At 10:40.	10:45.
[C] At 10:55.	M: Oh, I'm afraid you've just missed the last one which left 5 mi-
[D] At 11:00.	nutes ago.
	Q: When should the woman have arrived to catch the last bus?

【解析】数字信息题。女士话中的 It's already 10:45 表明现在的时间是 10:45,而男士话中的 you've just missed the last one which left 5 minutes ago 表明 5 分钟前最后一班车已经发车了,由此可知女士应在 10:40 到达车站才能赶上最后一班车。

17.

[A] She thinks they are overpriced.	M: Look at the low prices on these used television sets. Something
[B] She thinks they are stolen ones.	is fishy. Don't you think so?
[C] She thinks they are in poor working	W: Well, there have been a lot of robberies recently. Some of the
condition.	stolen goods may have landed here.
[D] She thinks they should buy one.	Q: How does the woman feel about the television sets?

【解析】观点态度题。女士话中的 there have been a lot of robberies recently… 表明,她认为这些便宜的二手电视机很可能是 stolen ones(偷来的电视机)。

18.

[A] In a doctor's office.	M: I have an appointment to see Doc. Grant for a physical exam-
[B] In an operating room.	ination.
[C] In a professor's office.	W: Please have a seat. He is in surgery right now.
[D] In a gymnasium.	Q: Where did the conversation probably take place?

【解析】地点场景题。根据男士话中的 physical examination(体检)和女士话中的 Doc. Grant is in surgery right now(Doc. Grant 正在做手术)可推测,对话很可能发生在 a doctor's office(医生办公室)。

Conversation One

【听力原文】	【答案解析】
M: Dear audiences, today we talk about divorce and its effect on children. Our guest is Jennifer Benzes. Thank you for coming. Jennifer, do you mind saying something about your divorce?	19. What are famous people like in the eye of the woman?
	【解析】选[B]。推断题。对话中,女士提
W: No. I got divorced years ago. Even worse, I got divorced when I had small children.	到他们不像名人 who trade spouses like shoes(像换鞋子一样换配偶),言外之意就
M: Have you thought of the effect divorce may have on your chil-	是名人们 often divorce(经常离婚),故答案
dren? Their needs can be forgotten as parents are struggling to	为[B]。
reestablish their lives.	20. What does the woman think of fixing a
W: Of course, we have. We are definitely more aware of the impact	marriage?
on children. [19] After all we are not famous people who trade	【解析】选[C]。推断题。对话中女士提到
spouses like shoes. For most of us divorce is not entered into	fixing a marriage is not like changing a tire

lightly. We all suffer. Anyway, we try to comfort our children.

M: How?

W: We tell them we love them and will always do.

M: You haven't thought of saving the marriage?

W: Yes, we have. We would do anything to spare our children' pain. [20] But you know fixing a marriage is not like changing a tire. Family conflicts may take hold like a cancer.

M: [21①] Then divorce is the only way to get rid of it.

W: [21②] It's true with me. Others may succeed in fixing.

M: Yet most people believe a bad marriage is better for children than a divorce. According to a recent poll, more people today think parents should stay together for the sake of the children. What do you think?

W: I think the cost of staying together is worse than the benefits. Parents quarrelling and fighting all day may do more harm to their children.

M: What do you want society to do for you?

W: Understand us, not curse us. More importantly, they should help us share the loss and build a better future.

（修补一个即将破裂的婚姻并不像换轮胎），由此可推断，女士把修补婚姻同换轮胎这么容易的事做比较就是为了说明弥补一个破裂的婚姻并不像换轮胎那么 easy，故答案为[C]。

21. What does the woman apply to solving their family conflicts?

【解析】选[B]。细节题。对话中，女士提到 family conflicts（家庭冲突）会像癌症一样挥之不去，所以 the only way to get rid of it（解决家庭冲突的唯一方法）就是 divorce，故答案为[B]。

Conversation Two

【听力原文】

W: Doctor, my neck, shoulders and back hurt a lot these days. I cannot figure out why. You know, I am only 25. I never thought such problems would pursue me.

M: I see. Can you tell me what you do for a living?

W: [22] I am a computer operator working in a very modern office building. Is there anything wrong with that?

M: I am not sure, but probably you sit by the desk for so long and you seldom do exercise.

W: Yes, you are right. I usually sit for the whole morning or afternoon except for a cup of coffee. But I thought I was young, and I was in good shape.

M: Probably. [23] In the past only those who are over 40 may have neck problems, but situations have changed nowadays. Young people, especially those desk workers, are more likely to suffer from this disease. Occasionally they have chronic headaches and dizziness.

W: I see. [24] My neck problem is caused by my sitting for too long and insufficient exercise.

M: Yes, you are right. Besides, incorrect seating posture may bring lots of pressure to the neck and thus distort the natural curve of the spine.

W: Yes, I always keep my head stretched forward when I work. But how can I get rid of this disease?

M: During the early stages neck problems can be treated effectively by massaging. Experienced TCM doctors, or traditional Chinese medicine doctors, can reset displaced joints into right position.

W: Do you think massaging suits me?

M: Yes, I think so. Besides professional treatment, a warm bath or

【答案解析】

22. What is the patient?

【解析】选[D]。细节题。对话开头处，男士问女士作什么工作，女士回答说她是一名 computer operator，故答案为[D]。题干中的 What is the patient? 是对话中男士话中的…what you do for a living? 的同义转述。

23. What kind of health problem nowadays clings to the desk workers?

【解析】选[C]。细节题。对话中，男士提到以前只有 40 岁以上的人会有 neck problems，但现在年轻人，尤其是那些整天坐在办公桌前办公的人，more likely to suffer from this disease（更容易患有这种疾病），故答案为[C]。

24. What can we learn about the desk workers, according to the conversation?

【解析】选[C]。推断题。对话中，女士说她的 neck problem 是因为她 sitting for too long and insufficient exercise 而造成的。由对话开头部分可知，女士是一名 computer operator，是那些坐在办公桌前办公的人中的一员，因此她的情况能反映大多数 desk worker 的真实情况，[C] 中的 seldom do exercise 是 insufficient exercise 的同义转述，为本题答案。

25. What will the speakers talk about if the conversation continues?

shower is also helpful. When inflammation or other symptoms occur, you will have to take some prescribed drugs. From now on, remember to do exercise or move around every one or two hours when you work.

W: Thank you, doctor. [25] Can you recommend a place where I can get massage from an experienced TCM doctor? …

【解析】选[A]。推断题。对话结尾处女士问男士能否给她推荐 a place where I can get…，由此可推断，如果对话继续下去，说话者很可能会涉及女士去哪里可以得到按摩服务，故答案为[A]。

Section B

Passage One

【听力原文】

Many students have anxieties in English study. Researchers generally agree that language anxiety has a negative effect on learning a foreign language. [26] Language anxiety can lead to academic failure, being uncomfortable in a social setting, or a painful emotional experience. Anxious students tend not to do well academically in their grades and proficiency testing. In addition, anxiety may make students work harder to make up for a lack of linguistic ability in the language they are studying. But, they often achieve little out of the increased effort. In addition to the negative effect on academic achievement, language anxiety can cause a person to avoid classroom participation, communicating with others, or social interaction. Avoiding classroom participation and social interaction could remove the opportunity to get the assistance of teachers, peers, or native speakers that is needed to develop the language. Worse still, high levels of anxiety can lead to a lack of motivation and self-confidence.

Since language anxiety is harmful, what can be done to help reduce it and increase learning? [27] We can create a less stressful language environment and help students deal with anxiety. Here are a few other suggestions.

First, form a support or study group. This helps you share your thoughts as well as your frustrations. Thus, it will boost your confidence and allow you to learn from others.

Second, be realistic. [28] Learning takes time. It is impossible to learn to speak perfect English overnight. You need to develop ways to be more realistic and productive.

Third, keep a journal. In your journal, you can describe your feelings of inadequacy to find a more realistic and positive way to make progress.

【答案解析】

26. Which of the following is the negative effect language anxiety leads to?

【解析】选[B]。细节题。文中提到 language anxiety(语言焦虑)能够导致学生 academic failure(学业失败)、being uncomfortable in a social setting(在社会环境下感到不自在)、或是成为 a painful emotional experience(一种痛苦的情感经历)，[B] 是 language anxiety 所造成的负面后果之一，为本题答案。

27. What could help reduce student's language anxiety?

【解析】选[C]。细节题。文中提到 language anxiety 十分有害，对于如何能 reduce 语言焦虑的问题，接着又提到，我们可以 create a less stressful language environment and help students deal with anxiety(创造一个压力较小的学习环境帮助学生们缓解焦虑)，由此可知，less stressful language environment 可以帮助缓解 language anxiety，故答案为[C]。

28. What does the speaker think of learning foreign language?

【解析】选[B]。细节题。文中在给出如何克服 language anxiety 的三点建议时指出，学习外语的人应该 be realistic(现实一点)，因为 learning takes time(学习是需要时间的)，并且指出要想 overnight(在一夜之间)就能说一口流利的英语是不可能的，言外之意就是学习外语不可能 achieved easily(一蹴而就)，故答案为[B]。

Passage Two

【听力原文】

[29] Japan's economy is nearing crisis as falling prices eat into corporate profits and the unemployment rate stands at a postwar record. The nation's 4.9 percent unemployment rate in January was its highest since World War II.

The number of job seekers rose to 3.17 million during the month, marking the fifth consecutive monthly increase. A sepa-

【答案解析】

29. What risk is Japan's economy facing, according to the passage?

【解析】选[B]。细节题。短文一开始就指出日本的经济正面临着危机，falling prices eat into corporate profits(价格下跌造成了公司利益受损)，并且 the unemployment rate stands at a post-rate report by Japan's Health, Labor and Welfare Ministry said the ratio of job offers fell in January for the first time in 20 months to 0.65 from 0.66. This means there were 65 job offers for every 100 job seekers. Analysts warn that the ailing economy continues to spiral down in a speeding deflationary trend. [30] Falling consumer prices are dragging down corporate profit, which then forces firms to slash employment. Consumer prices in January stayed flat for the second consecutive month after dropping 0.2 percent in November. But core prices, excluding fluctuations in fresh food prices, dropped 0.5 percent after a 0.1 percent decline in December. Compared with the previous year, core prices fell for the 16th consecutive month by 0.5 percent in January, following a 0.6 percent decline in December. [31] Deflation will accelerate later in the year due to cuts in public works spending and sluggish growth in corporate capital spending, analysts predict. The first and most urgent requirement is further monetary easing by the Bank of Japan. The government may not be able to avoid introducing a supplementary budget. This is how serious conditions are getting.

war record(失业率也一直保持着战后最高水平),也就是说日本经济正面临着 the low corporate profits(公司收益锐减)和 the high unemployment rate(高失业率)的危机,故答案为[B]。

30. Which of the following can lower the corporate profit, according to the passage?

【解析】选[C]。细节题。文中提到 falling consumer prices(不断下降的消费品价格)正在 dragging down corporate profit(削减公司的收益),也就是说 the low consumer prices 能够影响到 corporate profit,故答案为[C]。

31. Why would the deflation accelerate later in the year, according to analysts?

【解析】选[B]。细节题。文中提到有些分析家预测年内 deflation(通货紧缩)还将持续下去,这都是因为 cuts in public works spending(公共建设工程支出的削减)和 sluggish growth in corporate capital spending(公司资本支出的缓慢增长),[B] 是其中的原因之一,为本题答案。

Passage Three

【听力原文】

In the 1940's and 50's, it was not likely that a young black teenager from New York's Harlem would ever have the chance to play in the world's biggest tennis tournaments. But Althea Gibson did play, and what's more, she won. [32] Althea was born in Silver, South Carolina, in 1927. When Althea was still a child, her family moved north to New York city. While Althea was in junior high school, she became interested in paddle tennis. She practiced every chance she got, and soon she was good enough to win medals.

[33] One day, a black musician named Buddy Walker saw Althea playing paddle tennis. He realized how good she was. So he bought her a real tennis racket and took her to a tennis court. Althea instantly fell in love with tennis. She started playing in the All Black American Tennis Association tournaments. When she was just fifteen, Althea played in the New York State Girl's Open tennis tournament and got as far as the finals. [34] In 1942, World War II came along, and there were no more tournaments for four years. But when the tournaments started again in 1946, Althea instantly became a star. She won every American Tennis Association tournament from 1946 to 1957.

[35] By 1958 she had won the United States Championship twice, as well as winning twice more at Wimbledon. Althea became a professional player in 1959 and won the professional championship in 1960.

【答案解析】

32. When was Althea Gibson born?

【解析】选[C]。细节题。文中提到 Althea 于 1927 年出生于 Silver, South Carolina(南卡罗莱纳州的内华达),答案为[C]。

33. Who has superior appreciation of Althea's ability in playing tennis?

【解析】选[B]。细节题。文中提到,有一天一个名叫 Buddy Walker 的 black musician(黑人音乐家)看到 Althea 正在打 paddle tennis(板球),他看出 Althea 的 paddle tennis 打得很好,所以给她买了一副真正的 tennis racket(网球拍),并且 took her to a tennis court(把她带去网球场),从此 Althea 就爱上了打网球,并且取得了举世闻名的成绩。由此可知,Buddy Walker 发现了 Althea 的才能,故答案为[B]。

34. What interrupted the tennis tournaments for four years?

【解析】选[D]。细节题。文中指出 1942 年第二次世界大战爆发,there were no more tournaments for four years(四年的时间里没有举行过锦标赛),由此可知是 World War II 打断了锦标赛,故答案为[D]。

35. How many times had Althea won at Wimbledon by 1958?

【解析】选[A]。细节题。短文结尾处提到,截至 1958 年 Althea 已经赢得了两次 the United States Championship(美国冠军杯),并在 Wimbledon(温布尔登)也获得过两次冠军,故答案为[A]。

Section C

【听力原文】

The concept of an intelligent building was born in the United States at the end of this century. The first intelligent building was built in Hartford in the United States in 1984. China's intelligent building (36) industry started in the 1990s, but its (37) momentum of fast development is (38) surprising to the world.

The intelligent building is a necessary product resulting from the information (39) era, an intelligent degree of building increasing with the development of science and technology. The major (40) indications of the development of today's world science and technology are the so-called four-Cs technologies. The four-Cs technologies are used in buildings to form a computer, an (41) integrated network in building so that the buildings are made "intelligent".

Intelligent buildings should be "investment-justified, highly (42) efficient, and quite (43) comfortable. Convenient, quick and very safe space is provided through the optimized design of four elements of buildings-structure: system, service and management, and internal relations among them. (44) Intelligent buildings can make the occupants, property managers and owners aware of the maximum beneficial returns in expenditures, comfort in life, commercial activities and personal safety."

(45) The aim of intelligent buildings is to apply four-Cs technologies to form intelligent building structures and systems, and, in combination with modern service and management methods, to provide safe and comfortable environment spaces for living, studying and working.

The house looks like an ordinary two-story building in appearance. Telephones, computers and family electric appliances are on-line to form a united communication operation platform and join its information web to the Internet. (46) Residents can use a computer or mobile phone to monitor the family electric appliances and home situation, such as the washing machine, the food in the refrigerator, someone bursting into the house and so on.

【答案解析】

36. 分析句子结构可知，China's intelligent building _____ 在句中作主语，故所填词应为名词。industry 意为"产业，工业"。

37. 空前的形容词性物主代词及空后的介词提示所填词应为名词。momentum 意为"动力，要素"。

38. 空前的系动词及空后的介词提示所填词应为形容词或动词过去分词形式，且能与介词 to 搭配使用。本分句是想表明 the world 对中国的快速发展有什么样的反应。surprising 意为"令人惊讶的"。

39. 分析句子结构可知 the information _____ 在句中作动词 form 的宾语，故所填词应为名词。era 意为"时代，纪元"。

40. 空前的形容词及空后的介词提示所填词应为名词。indications 意为"指示，迹象"。

41. 空前的不定冠词 an 及空后的名词提示所填词应为以元音字母开头的形容词。integrated 意为"综合的，完整的"。

42. 由空后的并列连词 and 可知所填词应与 investment-justified 和 quite _____ 并列，故所填词应为形容词。efficient 意为"有效率的"。

43. 根据第 42 题的分析可知，所填词也应为形容词。comfortable 意为"舒服的"。

44. 【Main Points】Intelligent buildings can make the **residents**, property managers and owners **realize** the **biggest** beneficial returns

45. 【Main Points】The **goal** of intelligent buildings is to **use** four-Cs technologies **in forming** intelligent building structures and systems

46. 【Main Points】Residents can use a computer or **handset** to monitor the family electric appliances and home **condition**

Part IV

Section A

【文章大意】

本文主要是讲海洋对人类直接的或者间接的影响。第一段讲述了海洋对人类的巨大贡献，但是海洋中仍有具大潜力尚未开发；第二段说的是海洋在提炼矿物上的商业价值；第三段说海洋的浅大陆架已经成为砂石的重要来源，并且核聚变反应堆的发展使得海洋本身也能够成为一种无限能源；第四段说的是海洋给人类带来的娱乐作用以及由此带来的负面影响。

47. 【定位】根据题干中的关键信息 chemical elements，profitable 可将搜索信息定位在第二段第二句。

　　【解析】concentrations of most chemical elements are dilute。该句指出虽然海水中含有 60 多种有价值的化学物

质,但是 most are in such dilute concentrations that commercial extraction is not profitable(由于大多数化学物质的分布非常分散,所以对它们进行提取也是无利可图的),该句的主句也是本题答案的出处。通过对其改写可知答案为 concentrations of most chemical elements are dilute。

48.【定位】根据题干中的关键信息 exploiting shallow continental shelves 可将搜索信息定位在第三段首句。

【解析】sands, gravels and petroleum。该句指出浅大陆架被开发以利用其中的 sands and gravels(沙土和砂砾)资源,但下句中的 In addition 提示浅大陆架被开发还有其他的原因,即开发海岸地区的 petroleum-bearing sands,而开发 petroleum-bearing sands 归根结底是为了其中蕴含的 petroleum,故答案为 sands, gravels and petroleum。

49.【定位】根据题干中的关键信息 Manganese nodules 可将搜索信息定位在第三段第三句。

【解析】on the deep ocean floor。该句的地点状语 on the deep ocean floor 为答案出处,即 manganese nodules 位于 the deep ocean floor(深海海底)。

50.【定位】根据题干中的关键信息 nuclear fusion reactors 可将搜索信息定位在第三段最后一句。

【解析】ocean water。该句中的 in the event that 引导条件状语从句,由此可知 ocean water itself could prove to be a limitless source of energy(海水能够成为无限的能量来源)的条件就是 nuclear fusion reactors are developed(核聚变反应堆的发展),所以如果 the nuclear fusion reactors succeeds,就可以从 ocean water(海水)中获得无限的能量。

51.【定位】根据题干中的关键信息 ocean pollution 可将搜索信息定位在最后一段最后一句。

【解析】People who dispose of wastes in the oceans。该句指出海洋污染变得更加严重是由 those who use the ocean for recreational and commercial purposes, as well as those who live nearby(利用海洋的娱乐价值和商业价值的人及住在海边的人)往海里倾倒垃圾造成的。概括地说就是 people who dispose of wastes in the oceans(往海里倾倒垃圾的人)应该为海洋的污染负责。

Section B

Passage One

【文章大意】

全球化的发展导致世界语言的数量不断减少,目前世界上语言的灭绝速度是十分惊人的,本文通过对 McWhorter 和 Dalby 的著作及观点的介绍揭示了这一现象。第一二段对 McWhorter 和 Dalby 的书进行了总体的概述;第三四段则分别阐述了 McWhorter 和 Dalby 的观点;第五六段则指出了 McWhorter 和 Dalby 之间的共识。

52. 选[C]。事实细节题。文章第一段指出 Andrew Dalby 和 John McWhorter 的两本书 map the intricate combination…that typically conspire in their demise(描述了政治、种族灭绝、地理和经济等因素之间错综复杂的联系共同导致这些语言的消失),结合下文中两位作者对语言灭绝原因的共同认识可知,这两本书主要关注的是世界语言的灭绝问题,故答案为[C]。

53. 选[D]。推理判断题。文章第三段最后一句中的 a pattern of spilled milk reveals anything specific about the bottle it came from 说明谚语"木已成舟"虽然来自于牛奶洒出瓶子,但该谚语却没有显示任何与瓶子有关的信息,将该关系带入到"说话者的世界观、说话者按照语法组织起来的表达世界观的语句、语法"这三者中来就可以知道作者的世界观与语法有关,但是语法并不能反映作者的世界观,故答案为[D]。

54. 选[C]。推理判断题。文章第四段主要阐述的是 Dalby 对语言的观点,该段第一句话中的 Rather than dissociating languages from the people who speak them 从反面表明 Dalby 对研究语言的观点:应该将语言与说该语言的人联系起来,故答案为[C]。

55. 选[C]。推理判断题。文章第五段举出单词"world"的例子,在 Yupik 语中 world 包含的事物为天气、野外、意识和感觉,而在欧洲语言中,则与"人、群体和居住者"有关,这说明同一个单词在不同的语言中所涉及的事物也是不一样的,言外之意就是说不同语言的人对事物的认识是不一样的,即每种语言都能够表现说该语言的人对事物的独特认识,故答案为[C]。

56. 选[A]。观点态度题。本文主要是介绍 McWhorter 和 Dalby 在他们的书中所表达的观点。第一二段对 McWhorter 和 Dalby 的书进行了总体的概述;第三四段则分别阐述了 McWhorter 和 Dalby 的观点;第五六段则指出了 McWhorter 和 Dalby 之间的共识。通过通读文章可以发现,作者在文章中并没有特别偏向于 McWhorter 和 Dalby 之间哪一个的观点,他始终保持客观的态度对二人的观点进行阐述,故答案为[A]。

Passage Two

【文章大意】

　　目前,中风,尤其是小中风日益成为影响人们身体健康的一大因素,中风情况不容小视,本文围绕小中风的症状及如何辨别小中风而展开。文章第一段指出世界上的中风情况;第二段主要介绍了什么是小中风;第三段重点说明小中风的严重性;第四段主要介绍了美国人患有小中风的情况;第五至七段主要说明鉴别小中风症状的方法。

57. 选[B]。推理判断题。文章第一段第二句指出 The news out of the meeting was not good(会上传来的消息不容乐观),第三句接着陈述了这样一种情况:中风人数在 1960s 和 1970s 有所下降,但现在却出乎意料地处于上升状态,该句表达的形势明显不容乐观,正好与第二句中的 not good 相对应,由此可推断 news 指的是"中风患者的数量呈上升趋势"这一信息,故答案为[B]。

58. 选[C]。事实细节题。文章第一段第一句即指出第 25 届国际中风大会的目的就是探讨 better ways of dealing with strokes,很多同学会误选[A] 正是因为看到了这一句话,但是他们没有注意题干中的形容词比较级 greater,它提示本题问的是本次大会将探讨的重点放在了哪里。根据该段最后一句话 the conference paid particular attention to the mini-strokes 可知本题答案为[C]。[B]、[D] 都只是大会探讨的一个方面,故不选。

59. 选[D]。事实细节题。文章第四段主要涉及美国人患有中风的情况。该段最后一句指出 if the public knew how to spot the symptoms of stroke…,由此可知,在患中风时,得到及时的治疗是十分重要的,故答案为[D]。排除[A] 是因为题干中的条件状语从句 if you are experiencing a mini-stroke 已经明确了患者患有中风,所以不需要再诊断。

60. 选[B]。推理判断题。文章第五段第一句指出小中风的症状十分不明显并且转瞬即逝,并且指出小中风的症状可分别表现在:脸部、手臂或腿部,尤其是身体的一侧突然出现麻木或软弱无力的症状;一只或两只眼睛视物模糊;吐字不清或说话困难,及意识模糊或意识不清;行动不便,晕眩或失去平衡;无缘无故的剧烈头疼。小中风的症状应该是暂时性的,这就可以排除[A]、[C]。[D] 与该段提出的最后一个症状相违背,故不选。而[B] 则与第四个症状中的 loss of coordination 相符,故为本题答案。

61. 选[B]。事实细节题。文章第四段倒数第二句指出美国大约有 120 万 45 岁以上的成年人很可能并不知道自己患过小中风。第三句接着提出一种假设情况 if the public knew how to spot the symptoms of stroke…,这从反面说明了大众并不知道如何辨别中风,尤其是小中风的症状,而造成这一现象的原因可以从第五段中找到:the symptoms of a mini-stroke are often subtle and passing,[B] 是原文的细节再现,故为答案。

Part V

62. and — or。连接词误用。in sedimentary rock 和 in organic matter 都是化石被保存的地点,sedimentary rock 和 organic matter 明显是两个不同的事物,所以连接词不应该使用连词 and 而应使用表示选择关系的连词 or。

63. lively — living。易混词误用。由本句后一分句中的 groups that were now extinct 所表达的意思可知,本分句是想表示"展现大多数目前仍存活的物种的化石已被发现"。lively 意为"活泼的,有生机的",明显不符合本句句意,故应将 lively 改写为 living,表示"活着的,现存的"。

64. were — are。时态错误。本分句是想表达"还有些展现现在已经灭绝的物种的化石也已经被发现了,所以应用一般现在时,故应将 were 改写为 are。

65. at — in。介词误用。range 通常和介词 in 搭配,表示某一个方面的范围,在本句中表示在年代上的范围,故应将 at 改写为 in。

66. the — /。指代错误。fossils 显然是类指,而"定冠词+名词复数"不能表示类指,只表示特指,故应将 the 删除。

67. reducing — reduced。语态错误。分析句子结构可知,or 后连接的分句也应是被动语态,故应将 reducing 改写为 reduced。

68. having — have。非谓语动词与谓语动词误用。分析句子结构可知,本句缺少谓语成分,故应将 having 改写为 have。

69. what — that/which。关系词误用。what 引导的从句应在句中充当主语从句或宾语从句,这两种从句都不符合本句的语法规范。通过句意可知,walls 后的内容应是修饰 walls 的定语从句,故应将 what 改写为定语从句的引导词 that 或 which。

70. depended — depending。非谓语动词误用。分析句子结构可知,depended on the prehistoric environment… 在句中作定语,修饰前面整句话。主语与 depend 为主动关系,所以 depend 应用其现在分词形式,故应将 depended 改写为 depending。

71. commonly ∧ there — where。连接词误用。本句与上一句话在句子结构上是相同的,上一句指出 older rocks 的发现地点,分析本句话可知,本句同样也是要表达在哪里可以发现 younger rocks,即:younger rocks 的发现地点。但本句中没有表示地点状语的副词,根据句意可知,there is active mountain building and volcanic activity 表达的是地点,故应在 there 前增加一个引导地点状语从句的连词 where。

Part VI

72. 【答案】that the new rule be adopted

【解析】本题考查对同位语从句的掌握。分析可知,所给翻译的部分是 The suggestion 的同位语。所给汉语翻译是一个无主句(没有动作的发出者),因此应翻译成英语中的被动句。

73. 【答案】when all at once the solution flashed across my mind

【解析】本题考查对时间状语从句的掌握。连词 when 可引导时间状语从句表示"就在那个时候",all at once 意为"突然"。

74. 【答案】To a certain extent

【解析】本题考查对惯用搭配 to…extent 的掌握。to…extent 中间的省略号可以添加其他词语,如 to such an extent(到这种程度),to some extent(在某种程度上),to what extent(在多大程度上)。

75. 【答案】have to shovel the snow

【解析】本题考查对主谓一致的掌握。either…or…意为"不是…就是…,或者…或者…"。当 either…or…连接两个并列主语时,谓语应与 or 后的名词一致。类似搭配还有,not only…but also…,neither…nor…,当这些惯用搭配连接主语时,谓语应与惯用搭配的后半部分(but also…,nor…)所接名词一致。

76. 【答案】their house wouldn't have been broken into

【解析】本题考查对虚拟语气的掌握。前半句中的 hadn't gone on vacation 是对过去的否定假设,故后面的句子应采用虚拟语气,谓语动词用 would have done。would have done 意为"本来可以…",但实际上并未发生。

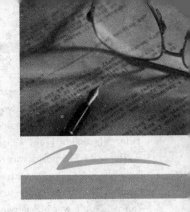

预 测 试 题 六

Part I Writing (30 minutes)

Directions: *For this part, you are allowed 30 minutes to write a composition on the topic*: ***Should Older People Live with Their Adult Children***? *You should write at least 150 words, and base your composition on the outline given in Chinese below*:

1)关于老人是否应与成年子女居住在一起,我的观点是…

2)论证说明我的观点

Should Older People Live with Their Adult Children?

_____

_____

Part II Reading Comprehension (Skimming and Scanning) (15 minutes)

The American Eagle

Family Tradition

Displaying the eagle is a traditional practice that celebrates the individual's freedom of choice guaranteed to all citizens of the United States of America. Americans through the years have displayed sculptures of eagles in prominent locations in their homes. Many families have an eagle with spread wings above their fireplace or displayed on the external surfaces of their homes above doors, entries or garages. It is often used as an ornament for flagpoles.

Background

The eagle represents freedom in the United States. The bald eagle was chosen June 20, 1782 as the emblem of the country, because of its long life, great strength and majestic looks, and also because it was then believed to exist only on this continent. It has become a tradition to display the eagle, or the seal of the United States which contains the eagle, in locations where the Federal Government has offices or conducts official business. The eagle is found on U. S. currency and coins and also forms the basis for many emblems of government agencies.

The Eagle, National Emblem of the United States

Living as it does on the tops of high mountains, amid the solitary grandeur of Nature, the eagle has unlimited freedom, whether with strong wings it sweeps into the valleys below, or upward into the boundless spaces beyond. It is said the eagle was used as a national emblem because, at one of the first battles of the Revolution (which occurred early in the morning) the noise of the struggle awoke the sleeping eagles on the heights and they flew from their nests and circled about over the heads of the fighting men, all the while giving forceful utterance to their hoarse cries. "They are shrieking for freedom," said the patriots. Thus the eagle, full of the boundless spirit of freedom, living above the valleys, strong and powerful in its might, has become the national emblem of this country and an opportunity for a full and free expansion into the boundless space of the future.

The eagle became the national emblem in 1782 when the great seal of the United States was adopted. The great seal shows wide-spread eagle, faced front, having on its breast a shield with thirteen red and white stripes, surmounted by a blue field with the acme number of stars. In its right claw the eagle holds an olive branch, in its left a bundle of thirteen arrows, and in its beak it carries a scroll inscribed with the motto: "E Pluribus Unum (合众为一)". The eagle appears in the seals of many of American states, on most of American gold and silver coinage, and is used a great deal for decorative patriotic purposes. At the Second Continental Congress, after the thirteen colonies voted to declare independence from Great Britain, the colonies determined they needed an official seal. So Dr. Franklin, Mt.

J. Adams, and Mr. Jefferson as a committee prepared a device for a seal of the United States of America. However, the only portion of the design accepted by the Congress was the statement E Pluribus Unum, attributed to Thomas Jefferson. Six years and two committees later, in May of 1782, the brother of a Philadelphia naturalist provided a drawing showing an eagle displayed as the symbol of "supreme power and authority". Congress liked the drawing, so before the end of 1782, an eagle holding a bundle of arrows in one wing and an olive branch in the other was accepted as the seal. The image was completed with a shield of red and white stripes covering the breast of the bird; a crest above the eagle's head, with a cluster of thirteen stars surrounded by bright rays going out to a ring of clouds; and a banner, held by the eagle in its beak, beating the words E Pluribus Unum. Yet it was not until 1787 that the American bald eagle was officially adopted as the emblem of the United States. This happened only after many states had already used the eagle in their coat of arms, as New York State did in 1778. Though the official seal has undergone some modifications in the last two hundred years, the basic design is the same. While the eagle has been officially recognized as America's national bird, there have been opposers who feel that the bird was the wrong choice.

Benjamin Franklin wrote: "I wish that the bald eagle had not been chosen as the representative of the United States, he is a bird of bad moral character, he does not get his living honestly, you may have seen him perched on some dead tree, where, too lazy to fish for himself, he watches the labor of the fishing-hawk, and when that diligent bird has at length taken a fish, and is bearing it to its nest for the support of his mate and young ones, the bald eagle pursues him and takes it from him. Besides he is a rank coward; the little kingbird, not bigger than a sparrow attacks him boldly and drives him out of the district. He is therefore by no means a proper emblem for the brave and honest of America. For a truth, the turkey is in comparison a much more respectable bird, and in addition, a true original native of America…a bird of courage, and would not hesitate to attack a well-equipped soldier of the British guards, who should presume to invade his farmyard with a red coat on. "

Franklin was clearly against the eagle and let everyone know it. Otherwise, the artist John James Audubon agreed with this opinion of the bald or white-headed eagle. Nevertheless, selected as the national bird, the eagle has appeared on all official seals of the United States, as well as on most coinage, paper money, and on many U. S. stamps. It is curious to note the minted eagles have been issued in a great variety of shapes and positions. Also, there is great variation in the species described. Some of the famous images have species other than the bald eagle — for example the famous ten-dollar gold pieces exhibit the "double eagle" instead. Numerous people have complained because many, if not most, of these illustrations show the wide-ranging golden eagle rather than the national bird, the bald eagle. They feel these representations mislead the general public into believing that they are looking at a bald eagle. The easiest way to distinguish between the golden and bald eagles is by the feathering on the legs. The golden is feathered down the entire leg, while the bald eagle has no feathers on the lower part of the leg until at least two or three years of age, when bald eagles also start developing the white head and tail.

1. This passage is discussing about reasons why the bald eagle was chosen the national emblem of the U. S. .

2. The eagle not only appears on American currency but also is chosen as the emblems of non-government organizations and institutions.

3. After declaring the independence from Great Britain, a committee was founded to prepare an official seal for the United States of America.

4. In 1782, the bald eagle was officially adopted as the national emblem of the U. S. .

5. The statement E Pluribus Unum is ascribed to _____ .

6. On the complete image of the seal of the U. S, the breast of the eagle is covered with _____ .

7. Experiencing some modifications, _____ of the official seal remains the same.

8. Benjamin Franklin would rather choose _____ than _____ as the emblem of the U. S. according to what he wrote.

9. Despite some opposition, the eagle was selected as national bird and has appeared on all _____ besides on most currency and many stamps of the United States.

10. The most striking difference between the golden eagles and the bald eagles is _____ .

Part III　Listening Comprehension（35 minutes）

Section A

11. [A] The man feels sick.　　[B] The man thinks the woman is being mean.
　　[C] The man has expected his suit to be ready.　　[D] The man backs up into another car.

12. [A] In the Toilet Bowl Cleaner section.　　[B] Underneath the household goods.
　　[C] On Aisle 14.　　[D] At the end of Aisle 12.

13. [A] She needs a new raincoat or umbrella.
　　[B] It will probably rain tomorrow.
　　[C] It will be clear tomorrow.
　　[D] She doesn't know where the man put his raincoat or umbrella.

14. [A] Ask someone else to compete with Mr. Smith
　　[B] Buy a new TV set.
　　[C] Ask somebody else to repair his TV.
　　[D] Mr. Smith is the best person to ask for repairing TV sets.

15. [A] No one knows how Mary gets to work.
　　[B] She doesn't think the record player works.
　　[C] She has thrown the record player away.
　　[D] It's surprising that Mary could use the record player.

16. [A] Critical.　　[B] Casual.
　　[C] Excited.　　[D] Satisfied.

17. [A] Teachers.　　[B] Lawyers.
　　[C] Students.　　[D] Editors.

18. [A] 24.　　[B] 12.
　　[C] 6.　　[D] 3.

Question 19 to 21 are based on the conversation you have just heard.

19. [A] He could read women's minds.　　[B] He could understand what women say.
　　[C] He could know what they need.　　[D] He could control women's mind.

20. [A] She is satisfied with his performance.
　　[B] She thinks his performance is out of her imagination.
　　[C] She thinks his performance still needs improving.
　　[D] She doesn't think much of it.

21. [A] Nancy Meyers is the heroine.
　　[B] The film emphasizes the necessity of learning about women.
　　[C] Gibson is a well-known serious person.
　　[D] The film doesn't have much attention paid to it.

Question 22 to 25 are based on the conversation you have just heard.

22. [A] Because it will irritate the public.　　[B] Because it will ruin his reputation.
　　[C] Because it will leave a bad influence on others.　　[D] Because he is forbidden by his golf club.

23. [A] An actor.　　[B] A model.
　　[C] A golf player.　　[D] A director.

24. [A] Being a comedy actor.　　[B] Keeping winning.
　　[C] Traveling around the world.　　[D] Keeping moving.

25. [A] When he is old enough.　　[B] When he doesn't find playing golf fun.
　　[C] When his skill retrogresses.　　[D] When he is not role model.

Section B

Passage One

26. [A] The relation between changes in the season and crime patterns.
　　[B] Different kinds of crimes.

　[C] Increasingly high crime rate in the U. S.

　[D] Seasonal changes in the natural environment.

27. [A] Monday. 　　　　　　　　　　　　[B] Thursday.

　　[C] Friday. 　　　　　　　　　　　　　[D] Saturday.

28. [A] Spring and autumn. 　　　　　　　[B] Summer and winter.

　　[C] Spring and winter. 　　　　　　　[D] Summer and autumn.

Passage Two

29. [A] Because they have a driving license.

　　[B] Because they have received a special training.

　　[C] Because the traffic conditions in London are good.

　　[D] Because the traffic system of the city is not very complex.

30. [A] It is risky. 　　　　　　　　　　　[B] It is fierce.

　　[C] It is excited. 　　　　　　　　　　[D] It is tough.

31. [A] They don't want their present bosses to know what they're doing.

　　[B] They want to earn money from both jobs.

　　[C] They cannot earn money as taxi drivers yet.

　　[D] They look forward to further promotion.

Passage Three

32. [A] An air force team. 　　　　　　　　[B] A navy team.

　　[C] A land force team. 　　　　　　　　[D] A police team.

33. [A] The dogs must be older than three. 　　[B] The dogs must be tame.

　　[C] The dogs must be tall. 　　　　　　[D] The dogs must be aggressive.

34. [A] 11-week course for control duty. 　　[B] 11-week course for patrol duty.

　　[C] 9-week course for control duty. 　　[D] 9-week course for patrol duty.

35. [A] Drug-sniffing dog is less sensitive to the danger than bomb-sniffing dog.

　　[B] Drug-sniffing dog should dig for what he finds while bomb-sniffing dog shouldn't.

　　[C] Drug-sniffing dog experiences less training time than bomb-sniffing dog.

　　[D] Drug-sniffing dog is safer than bomb-sniffing when implementing its duty.

Section C

　　The industrial revolution dramatically affected newspapers. Both the numbers of papers and their paid circulations continued to rise. In the 1850s, powerful, giant presses appeared, able to (36)_____ ten thousand complete papers per hour. At this time the first "(37)_____" weekly newspapers emerged; they featured extensive illustrations of events in the news for the first time.

　　During the Civil War, the (38)_____ demand for timely, accurate news reporting (39)_____ American journalism into a (40)_____, hard hitting force in national life. Reporters became the (41)_____ of the public and the (42)_____ of youngsters everywhere. Many accounts of battles turned in by these (43)_____ stand today as the definitive histories of their subjects.

　　Newspaper growth continued in the postwar years. (44)_____. At this period, the features of the modern newspaper appeared, bold "banner" headlines, extensive use of illustrations, "funny pages", plus expanded coverage of organized sporting events.

　　The rise of "yellow journalism" also marks this era. This is also the age of media consolidation, as (45)_____, many were reduced to vehicles for the distribution of the particular views of their owners, and so remained, without competing papers to challenge their viewpoints. By the 1910s, all the essential features of the recognizably modern newspaper had emerged. In our time, radio and television have gradually replaced newspapers as the nation's primary information sources, so (46)_____.

Part IV　Reading Comprehension（Reading in Depth）（25 minutes）
Section A

There is no readily available, comprehensive and robust source of information on the numbers of young single homeless people. Some groups of young single homeless people were only brought within the safety net of the homelessness legislation in 2002, while some are still not included. Both definitions and monitoring arrangements can vary between geographical areas and individual organizations. The adoption of different definitions means that estimates of the extent of youth homelessness vary.

The definition adopted by The Inquiry into Youth Homelessness was：

"A single person, without dependents, between the ages of 16 and 25 who is in one of the following housing situations：

- without any accommodation, e. g. sleeping rough；
- in temporary accommodation such as a hostel, bed and breakfast hotel, or squat；
- staying temporarily with friends or relatives who are unable/unwilling to accommodate in the longer term.

Research published in 2003 by the ODPM which looked at initiatives in London designed to prevent youth homelessness found that projects providing services to homeless young people, or those at risk of homelessness, reported seeing increasingly younger and more vulnerable clients. In addition, drug and alcohol misuse and mental-health problems were cited as becoming more common.

Nationally, young people from Black and Minority Ethnic groups are disproportionately vulnerable to homelessness. This is due to a number of factors, including those related directly to racial discrimination, as well as those associated with lack of provision of appropriate information, advice and support services and accommodation options. A report noted that nearly half of all the homeless young people in London are from Black African, Black Caribbean and other ethnic minority groups. The consequences of youth homelessness are serious. From its research the organization, Crisis, highlights that early experiences of homelessness can have a permanent and unforgettable effect on a young person's future. The consequences are wider than the destructive effects on the individuals concerned. The Inquiry into Youth Homelessness noted the interconnections between homelessness, alcohol and drug misuse, anti-social behavior and criminalization, making the case for investing in services both to prevent youth homelessness and to reduce its impact on individuals and communities.

47. It was until in 2002 that some groups of single homeless youth were _____ under the protection of the homelessness legislation.

_____

48. The estimates of the extent of young homeless people vary as a result of _____.

_____

49. Research published in 2003 by ODMP found that homeless youth are becoming _____.

_____

50. Homeless youth in London from Black African, Black Caribbean and other ethnic minority groups accounts for _____.

_____

51. The effect caused by the experiences of homelessness on young people's future is _____.

_____

Section B

Passage One

Parents can easily come down with an acute case of schizophrenia from reading the contradictory reports about the state of the public schools. One set of experts asserts that the schools are better than they have been for years. Others say that the schools are in terrible shape and are responsible for every national problem from urban poverty to the trade deficit.

One group of experts looks primarily at such indicators as test scores, and they cheer that they see all the indicators "reading scores, minimum competency test results, the Scholastic Aptitude Test scores" are up, some by substantial margins. Students are required to take more academic courses, more mathematics and science, along with greater stress on basic skills, including knowledge of computers. More than 40 state legislatures have mandated such changes.

But in the eyes of another set of school reformers such changes are at best superficial and at worst counterproductive. These experts say that merely toughening requirements, without either improving the quality of instruction or, even more important, changing the way schools are organized and children are taught makes the schools worse rather than better. They challenge the nature of the tests, mostly multiple choice or true or false, by which children's progress is measured; they charge that raising the test scores by drilling pupils to come up with the right answers does not improve knowledge, understanding and the capacity to think logically and independently. In addition, these critics fear that the get-tough approach to school reform will cause more of the youngsters at the bottom to give up and drop out. This, they say, may improve national scores but drain even further the nation's pool of educated people.

The way to cut through the confusion is to understand the different yardsticks used by different observers.

Compared with what schools used to be like "in the good old days", with lots of drill and uniform requirements, and the expectation that many youngsters who could not make it would drop out and find their way into unskilled jobs — by those yardsticks the schools have measurably improved in recent years.

But by the yardsticks of those experts who believe that the old schools were deficient in teaching the skills needed in the modern world, today's schools have not become better. These educators believe that rigid new mandates may actually have made the schools worse.

52. The best title for this passage would be _____.
    [A] Experts' Dissidence on Issue of Quality of Schools
    [B] Conflicting Views on Schools
    [C] Improved Quality of Schools
    [D] Poor Quality of Schools

53. What kind of condition does the word "confusion" (Line 1, Para. 4) refer to in the passage?
    [A] Schools are confused by the mandates issued by the state legislatures.
    [B] Students are confused by the doubt that whether they could get high testing scores.
    [C] Experts are confused by the question whether the testing scores should be the only standard.
    [D] Parents are confused by the two opposing views on the quality of schools.

54. The assertion of the experts who think schools are doing better is based on the _____.
    [A] test scores   [B] qualification of the teachers
    [C] reading ability of the children   [D] basic skills of the children

55. According to the experts who say the quality of the schools is worse, the high tests scores achieved by a child do not necessarily mean that _____.
    [A] he receives better education that others   [B] his scope of knowledge is wider than his peers
    [C] he is clever than his classmates   [D] his endowment is better than others

56. The author suggest that the parents should _____ in order to make themselves clearly understand the present quality of the public schools.
    [A] realize that the standard used by experts to decide the quality of schools is different
    [B] realize that the real condition of the quality of school is not like what the experts say
    [C] have their own judgement on the quality of school without being puzzled by the experts
    [D] make a comparison among different schools to find which experts are right

Passage Two

"Let's go to the mall." This comment is one of the few statements that can be heard coming from the mouths of both sexes. While typically associated with shopping, and thus automatically, and unfairly, females, going to the mall has mutual attractions to both males and females. Since the massive increase of shopping malls in this country, the popularity of "going to the mall" has increased a thousand-fold for everyone. For females the reason that "going to the mall" is so popular is very clear. Females were always taught that their rightful place is at home taking care of their families. When the car made a sudden impact on the world during the middle part of last century, even more responsibilities were added to the wife's list of "to dos". The wife no longer just took care of the family. She now was able to go out and shop for food, clothes, or anything else that her family may need. In a sense, the wife now had more freedom to take care of the family by being away from the home more.

While contemporary women are much more free-minded about their own place in society, there still lies the motherly instinct to go out and purchase for the family. This instinct may change in time, but until that change occurs this cause shall remain as the chief reason why women "go to the mall" or "go shopping".

On the other hand, males go for a completely different reason. The malls are where all the new toys are. This may sound childish, and theoretically unscientific, but it is a sound statement. Whenever a new computer product, sports equipment or "masculine" item shows up, one of the first places where these new toys are shown off are at centre concourses in malls. Nowhere else in the world can a person see flocks of guys leaving their wives at jewellery stores. When the question is really looked at, there is only one cause for both males and females going to shopping malls. Humans as a whole are a communal species. The race is very gregarious. So, after hours of being at work, sitting behind a small desk inside and even smaller cubicle, shut off from the rest of the world, men and women just long to be around others of their own species having a good time. This communal structure of human society has been around since man was in his basic primate form. This structure also seems to be continuing, despite the attempts of computer manufacturers and Internet entrepreneurs to keep the human race logged-on 24 hours a day.

Unfortunately, shopping will always be considered feminine. The only reason that can be found to explain this "fact" is the motherly instinct of most women that was mentioned earlier. According to recent history, men are not supposed to enjoy shopping or "going to the mall". However, like so many other things that history has attempted to control, the gender gap at shopping malls has been almost obliterated. Today "going to the mall" is a statement that is not uncommon to hear from males and females.

57. Women's going out to the mall _____.

[A] makes it possible to escape from taking care of the family

[B] promotes the development of the economy in their country

[C] enhances their status in both their family and society

[D] challenges the place which was imposed on them by the old society

58. Since women are not bound to the family against their will today, they still like to go out shopping for their family because of _____.

[A] their consideration　　　　　　　　　[B] their motherly instinct

[C] their carefulness　　　　　　　　　　[D] their humanity

59. In the writer's view, the only reason for human going to the malls is that _____.

[A] they want to see the new toys　　　　　[B] they want to find out some new computer products

[C] they want to meet their friends　　　　[D] they do not enjoy being alone

60. What does "masculine" item (Line 3, Para. 3) refer to, according to the passage?

[A] Something which has particular features which can attract man.

[B] Something which is related to the man.

[C] Something which can be used by man.

[D] Something which is marvellous.

61. By saying "Nowhere else in the world…leaving their wives at jewellery stores"(Lines 4−5, Para. 3), the author wants to say _____.

[A] men are so fond of the new toys that they have no time to consider the possibility of their wives' buying the expensive jewellery

[B] men leave their wives at the jewellery stores in order to have more freedom to look at the new toys

[C] men are inconsiderate enough to leave their wives alone at the jewellery stores

[D] men want to escape from their wives' prate for some time

Part V　Error Correction (15 minutes)

The initial fund of general scientific knowledge is an invaluable asset, but the young research workers should have no illusion about how little it is compared with what he or she should acquire during succeeding years. As to the precise value of this initial fund of knowledge, this depends to a great degree how it has been acquired and on who has been imparting it. Young scientists cannot realize too soon that existing scientific knowledge is not nearly so complete, certain and unalterable so many textbooks seem to imply. The original papers of great scientists describe their discoveries and expounding their theories are never as rigid and self-confident as the resumes of their discoveries and theories on textbooks by other men often suggest. Young scientists consulting these original works will find in it "it appears that", "it probably means", "it seems likely that", more than once, not as expressions of good manner or false modesty, but as expressions of elements of doubt which great men felt and honestly put them on record. Many statements which have appeared in textbooks as universal and incontrovertible truth have, in their original form, put forward as only approximately true or only in certain circumstances.

Immediately upon starting on the first serious piece of research, a young scientist must therefore do two things. The first of these should be a careful reading of original papers or books relating to the problem, written by investigators that technique and judgment he can trust. A second thing a young scientist must do, almost but not quite simultaneously with tile first, is to proceed with observations and experiments.

62. _____

63. _____
64. _____

65. _____

66. _____

67. _____
68. _____

69. _____

70. _____
71. _____

Part VI　Translation (5 minutes)

72. By the end of that year Henry _____ (已收集了一千多张外国邮票).

73. He could not plead ignorance as his excuse; _____ (他本应该知道当时发生了什么) in his department.

74. He didn't like the plan at first, _____ (但是我们终于使他回心转意了).

75. These policies _____ (使得许多老人和残疾人在困苦中挣扎).

76. The space city will rotate once per minute _____ (制造像地球重力三分之一那么大的重力).

答案与解析

Part I

【思路点拨】

　　本题属于提纲式文字命题。提纲第 1 点要求说明我对某个问题的看法,提纲第 2 点要求论证说明我的观点,由此可判断本文应属于观点论证型作文。

　　根据命题,本文的内容应该包括:关于老人是否应与成年子女居住在一起,提出我个人的观点;论证说明我的观点;总结全文。

【参考范文】
Should Older People Live with Their Adult Children?

　　One of the topics in our daily life is whether or not the older people should live with their adult children. My answer to the question is that it is better for them not to.(提出观点段)

　　To begin with, adult children, like their parents, love independence and freedom, but their parents may still take them as children. The situation will be worse when the adult children are married. If the relationship between children and parents is not harmonious, the sons or daughters will be in a difficult position. Secondly, people of different ages have different ways of life. If they live together, the old may feel that they are always disturbed and the young may feel that they are often restricted.(论证观点段)

　　In short, if parents and their adult children live seperately, both the old and the young can enjoy complete independence and freedom. Living separately does not mean separation of relations. The parents and their children can still often visit and help each other if they stay in the same neighborhood.(总结观点段)

Part II

> 【文章大意】
>
> 　　本文主要谈论美国的标志物—秃鹰。文章谈到了美国人民关于鹰的一些家庭传统、美国秃鹰的背景知识以及它如何成为美国的象征,接着讲述了以本杰明·富兰克林为代表的反对意见。

1. 【定位】题干中的 This passage is discussing about 提示本题与文章的主旨有关,故应定位于整篇文章。

　　【解析】[N]。结合文章各个小标题可知,本文谈到了关于鹰的一些家庭传统、美国秃鹰的背景知识以及它如何成为美国的象征,而秃鹰成为美国的象征的原因只是原文的一部分内容,不足以概括文章主旨。

2. 【定位】根据题干内容可将搜索范围定位在小标题 Background 下。

　　【解析】[NG]。该部分最后一句话指出 The eagle is found on U. S. currency and coins and also forms the basis for many emblems of government agencies(美国的纸币和硬币上都有鹰的图案,并且美国许多政府机构的徽章上也以鹰作为图案基础),但并没有提及其他政府外的组织机构也选定鹰作为其标志。

3. 【定位】根据题干中的关键信息 Great Britain 及 committee 可将搜索范围定位在小标题 The Eagle, National Emblem of the United States 下第二段。

　　【解析】[Y]。该段第五句指出在第二次大陆会议上,在 13 个殖民地投票要求从 Great Britain 独立出来后,这些殖民地觉得他们需要 an official seal,所以 Dr. Franklin, Mt. J. Adams 和 Mr. Jefferson 组成了 a committee(委员会)开始准备 a device for a seal of the United States of America,题干内容是原文的同义转述。

4. 【定位】根据题干中的关键信息 1782 及 officially adopted as the emblem of the United States 可将搜索范围定位在小标题 The Eagle, National Emblem of the United States 下第二段。

　　【解析】[N]。该段第一句指出 1782 年美国采用鹰为其徽章,鹰也就成为国家的标志,但并没有说明是正式采用,该段倒数第四句又提到 Yet it was not until 1787 that the American bald eagle was officially adopted as the emblem of the United States,由此可知秃鹰正式成为美国的国家标志是在 1787 年而非 1782 年。

5. 【定位】根据题干中的关键信息 E Pluribus Unum 可将搜索范围定位在小标题 The Eagle, National Emblem of the United States 下第二段。

　　【解析】Thomas Jefferson。该段出现过两次 E Pluribus Unum,第一次在第三句中,该句主要是介绍 the great seal 的设计,并没有指出是谁创作出 E Pluribus Unum 一词。第二次出现是在第七句中,由该句中的 the statement E Pluribus Unum, attributed to Thomas Jefferson 可知,E Pluribus Unum 是由 Thomas Jefferson 创作的。

6. 【定位】根据题干中的关键信息 the breast of the eagle 可将搜索范围定位在小标题 The Eagle, National Emblem of the United States 下第二段。

　　【解析】a shield of red and white stripes。本段开头和结尾部分均提到了 the seal 的设计,题干中的 On the complete image of the seal of the U. S. 提示本题不应该只局限于开头部分,应在整段中寻找答案。开头部分指出了 the seal 的设计中,鹰的胸部有 a shield with thirteen red and white 但这并不是 the complete image of the seal(印章的最终形象),倒数第五句指出 The image was completed with a shield of red and white stripes covering the breast of the bird…,该句即为本题答案出处。

7. 【定位】根据题干中的关键信息 modifications 可将搜索范围定位在小标题 The Eagle, National Emblem of the United States 下第二段。

　　【解析】the basic design。该段倒数第二句指出虽然 the official seal has undergone some modifications(公章几经修改),但是 the basic design is the same(基本设计还是一样的),题干内容是原文的同义转述。

8. 【定位】根据题干中的关键信息 Benjamin Franklin 可将搜索范围定位在小标题 The Eagle, National Emblem of the United States 下第三段。

　　【解析】the turkey, the bald eagle。该段首句 Benjamin Franklin 即指出他的观点:I wish that the bald eagle had not been chosen as the representative of the United States(我希望秃鹰不是美国的象征),在论述观点的过程中,他大力宣扬 the turkey(火鸡)的优点:火鸡值得尊敬,是美国的原始居住者,是勇敢的化身等等,从 Benjamin Franklin 对 the bald eagle 和 the turkey 的不同态度可以推测,他更倾向于将 the turkey 作为美国的象征。题干中的 would rather…than… 意为"宁可…不愿…"。

9. 【定位】根据题干中的关键信息 opposition,selected as national bird 及 stamps 可将搜索范围定位在小标题 The Eagle, National Emblem of the United States 下最后一段。

　　【解析】official seals of the United States。该段第三句指出被选为国鸟后,the eagle has appeared on all official seals of the United States, as well as on most coinage, paper money and on many U. S stamps,题干内容为该句的同义转述,由此句即可找出答案。

10. 【定位】根据题干中的关键信息 the difference between the golden eagles and the bald eagles 可将搜索范围定位在

小标题 The Eagle, National Emblem of the United States 下最后一段。

【解析】the feathering on the legs。该段倒数第二句指出 The easiest way to distinguish between the golden and bald eagles is by the feathering on the legs(辨别金雕和秃鹰的最简单方法就是看它们腿上的羽毛),金雕整条腿上的羽毛都朝下,而秃鹰的小腿上则没有羽毛。

Part III
Section A

11.

[A] The man feels sick. [B] The man thinks the woman is being mean. [C] The man has expected his suit to be ready. [D] The man backs up into another car.	M: What do you mean? My suit isn't ready yet! I dropped it off for alterations more than three weeks ago. W: Our tailor has been sick. So work is backed up about a week. Q: What do we learn from the conversation?

【解析】事实状况题。男士通过反问句 What do you mean? 及感叹句 My suit isn't ready yet! 来表达他对自己的衣服还没有改好的惊讶之情,由此可推断男士 expected his suit to be ready(本来以为他的衣服能做好)。

12.

[A] In the Toilet Bowl Cleaner section. [B] Underneath the household goods. [C] On Aisle 14. [D] At the end of Aisle 12.	M: I've been around the whole store, but I couldn't find any sixty-watt bulbs. Do you know where are they? W: Oh, they used to be on Aisle 12, but we've moved them. Now you'll find them at the end of Aisle 14, in the Household Goods section. They're underneath the toilet bowl cleanser. Q: Where can the man get the sixty-watt bulbs?

【解析】地点场景题。由女士话中的 you'll find them at the end of Aisle 14(60 瓦的灯泡在 14 号货架的尽头)可知,男士在 Aisle 14 可以找到他要的灯泡。

13.

[A] She needs a new raincoat or umbrella. [B] It will probably rain tomorrow. [C] It will be clear tomorrow. [D] She doesn't know where the man put his raincoat or umbrella.	M: It doesn't seem that it is going to rain tomorrow. It was supposed to be clear all week. W: Well, according to the forecast I heard, you should take your raincoat or umbrella with you. Q: What does the woman mean?

【解析】事实状况题。女士话中的 you should take your raincoat or umbrella with you 是在建议男士明天带上雨衣或雨伞,言外之意就是她认为明天可能会 rain(下雨)。

14.

[A] Ask someone else to compete with Mr. Smith. [B] Buy a new TV set. [C] Ask somebody else to repair his TV. [D] Mr. Smith is the best person to ask for repairing TV sets.	M: I had to have Mr. Smith come over and adjust my TV again last night. W: Maybe it's not your set. If I were you, I'd have someone else check it out. Q: What does the woman think the man should do?

【解析】行为活动题。女士通过虚拟语气说 If I were you, I'd have someone else check it out(如果换作她,她就会让别人修理电视机),由此可知,女士认为男士应该让 somebody else to repair his TV(让别人修理他的电视机)。

15.

[A] No one knows how Mary gets to work. [B] She doesn't think the record player works. [C] She has thrown the record player away. [D] It's surprising that Mary could use the record player.	M: I was surprised to see Mary using that record player you were going to throw away. W: Yes. It is very old. That she got it to work amazes me. Q: What does the woman mean?

【解析】事实状况题。女士话中的 That she got it to work amazes me 表明,玛丽居然能让女士要扔的录音机正常运转,这令女士感到很 surprising(奇怪)。

16.

[A] Critical. [B] Casual. [C] Excited. [D] Satisfied.	M: What do you think of the film? W: Well, the story is okay, but the acting is just so so, especially the leading actress who seems so inexperienced. Q: What is the woman's attitude towards the film?

【解析】观点态度题。女士话中的 but the acting is just so so…表明,女士认为尽管那部电影的情节很好,但是女主角好像没有经验,演技很一般,由此可知女士对这部电影的态度是 critical(批判性的)。

17.

[A] Teachers. [B] Lawyers. [C] Students. [D] Editors.	W: It's 4:15 now. By the time I have mailed the package and gone home, it will be time for dinner. M: Yes, we had better finish grading these papers and get going. Q: What are the speakers?

【解析】身份关系题。根据男士话中的 we had better finish grading these papers(我们最好赶紧评完卷子)可以推断出二人是 teachers(教师)。

18.

[A] 24. [B] 12. [C] 6. [D] 3.	M: This candy was cut into six squares. W: Let's cut them in half, so that each person can have one. Q: How many people would have candy?

【解析】数字信息题。男士说这块糖果被 cut into six squares(分成六块),女士说应该 cut them in half(把它们都分成两份),也就是说女士建议将糖果分成 12 块,由此可知共有 12 个人分吃糖果。

Conversation One

【听力原文】	【答案解析】
M: Welcome to "Movie on the Show", today our guest is Nancy Meyers, director of the newly released movie "What Women Want". Thank you for coming. W: Thank you. M: Meyers, How do you describe your film? Are you satisfied with it? W: Well. I am happy to see it top the US weekend box office. Have you seen the film? Ha, it tells the story of Nick Marshall, a Chicago advertising executive. [19] He acquires the power to read women's minds, not just what they say but also what he hears them think. That's amazing, isn't it? [20①] I like the way Gibson interprets his role. M: Yeah, Marshall regards himself as a gift to women. I saw the movie. Then why do you choose Mel Gibson? We know, audiences usually see him playing a man with a strong typical man side, such as in his previous action movies like "Brave Heart", while "What Women Want" is what you termed as an old fashioned romantic comedy. W: You are right. That's precisely why I choose him. Gibson has been known as a joker on the set and a fan of silly comedy, but has not done many romantic comedies. I just want him to display his "feminine" potential in "What Women	19. What special ability does Nick Marshall have in "What Women Want"? 【解析】选[A]。细节题。对话中女士在介绍她导演的新电影 What Women Want(《偷听女人心》)时说,剧中男主角 Nick Marshall 具有 the power to read women's minds(知道女性在想什么的能力),他不仅能通过女性所说的话来理解女性的想法,还能通过听女性们的思想来理解女性的想法,[B] 是对对话中 not just what they say 的误解,故答案为[A]。 20. How does Nancy Meyers feel like Gibson's performance in "What Women Want"? 【解析】选[A]。推断题。对话中,Nancy Meyers 在谈及 What Women Want 的男主角时先后说到 I like the way Gibson interprets his role 以及 And I am grateful to see that he has done a good job,由这两句话可以推断出,Nancy Meyers 对 Gibson 的表演是 satisfied(满意的),故答案为[A]。 21. What can we learn about the film "What Women Want" from the conversation? 【解析】选[B]。推断题。对话结尾处,男士问

Want". [20②] And I am grateful to see that he has done a good job.

M: What do you want audiences to learn from this film.

W: About women. [21] We should learn about women. They are individuals. What she appreciates is when you make the effort, even if you are not quite getting something she says or when the communication stops.

女士希望观众从这部影片中学到些什么,女士回答说她希望人们能够 learn about women,对女性来说只要你作出努力,即使你不能真正的理解她们的意思或者停止谈话,她们也会非常感激,由此可知,这部影片提倡的是对女性的理解,那么它的重点当然就是强调 the necessity of learning about women。

Conversation Two

【听力原文】

W: This business of having to be a role model, where you can never, relax, hang loose, can you?

M: Well, I can't exactly go to hang with my friends at some of the places we used to go to, and just basically raise hell and have a whole bunch of fun. [22①] I can't do that anymore because it's not good for the public to see that. It's not good for me.

W: Your father said you have the ability to be one of the biggest influences in history, not just golf, humanity. What do you think of that?

M: [23] I think that is more important than just my golf. I think my golf is merely a vehicle to influence people.

W: How?

M: How? Oh. So many kids look up to role models, so I can help out kids in a positive way, [22②] I can influence their lives in a positive way, and I think that's what it's about.

W: I mean you are only 21, what's the goal? Where do you go?

M: [24] Keep winning.

W: But you know, at a certain point, doesn't lose…?

M: Winning never gets old and having fun never gets old either. And you always have fun.

W: And playing these tournaments is with all the apprehension and everything, still fun?

M: Always. [25] The day it's not fun is the day I quit. And it's been fun since I was in the high chair. And it's fun today.

【答案解析】

22. Why can't the man raise hell with his friends as he used to?

【解析】选[C]。细节题。对话中男士提到,他不能再像以前一样和朋友去他们经常去的地方,也不能再大吵大闹,因为 it's not good for the public to see that,并且对自己也不好,再结合男士谈及自己作为 role model 的作用时所说的"I can influence their lives in a positive way"可知,如果男士再像以前那样大吵大闹,那么他会给别人留下不好的印象,[C]表达的正是此意。

23. What is the man's profession?

【解析】选[C]。细节题。对话中男士提到 humanity 比他的 golf 更重要,golf 只不过是 a vehicle to influence people(用来影响人们的一种工具),由此可知,男士是一名 golf player(高尔夫球手),故答案为[C]。

24. What is the man's goal in the future?

【解析】选[B]。细节题。对话结尾处女士问男士的目标是什么,男士回答说 keeping winning(保持胜利)就是他将来的目标,故答案为[B]。

25. When will the man retire from playing golf tournaments?

【解析】选[B]。细节题。对话结尾处男士说到 The day it's not fun is the day I quit(当他感到打球不快乐的那一天就是他退出的一天),由此可知,如果男士发觉打高尔夫已经不能给他带来快乐的时候就是他退出锦标赛的时候,故答案为[B]。

Section B

Passage One

【听力原文】

Crime has its own cycles, a magazine reported some years ago. [26] Police records show a surprising relation between changes in the season and crime patterns. The pattern of crime has changed very little over a long period of the years. Murder reaches its high during July and August as do other violent attacks. [27] Murder, in addition,

【答案解析】

26. What is the passage mainly about?

【解析】选[A]。主旨题。短文开头处指出警察的记录显示 a surprising relation between changes in the season and crime patterns(在季节和犯罪类型之间存在着某种令人奇特的联系),下文接着说明哪种犯罪活动通常发生在哪个季节,如 murder 在 July

is more than seasonal; it is a weekend crime. It is also a nighttime crime: 62 percent of murders are committed between 6 p. m. and 6 a. m. on a Saturday night in December, January, or February. Except for one strange statistic, May is the least criminal month of all.

Apparently our intellectual season cycles are completely different from our criminal patterns. Professor Huntington made a lot of studies to discover the seasons when people read serious books, attend scientific meetings, and make the highest scores on examinations. [28] In all examples, he found a spring peak and an autumn peak separated by a summer low. On the other hand, Professor Huntington's studies showed that June is the peak month for suicides and for admitting patients to mental hospital. June is also a peak month for marriages!

Possibly, high temperature and humidity bring on our strange and surprising summer actions, but police officers are not sure. They say that there are, of course, no proof of a relation between humidity and murder. They don't know why murders' high-time should come in the summer time.

和 August 发生得最为频繁等，这些都说明了犯罪类型和季节之间存在着某种联系，由此可知本文主要讲的是 the relation between changes in the season and crime patterns，故答案为[A]．

27. When did most murders happen, according to the passage?

【解析】选[D]。细节题。文中提到 murder 不只具有季节性，它还是 a weekend crime（一种在周末经常发生的犯罪活动），62％的谋杀都发生在 Saturday（周六）晚六点至早六点之间，故答案为[D]。

28. When do intellectual activities come to the high, according to Professor Huntington's study?

【解析】选[A]。细节题。文中提到，我们的 intellectual season cycles 与 criminal patterns 是完全不同的，Professor Huntington 为找出人们经常会在哪个季节读书、参加科学性会议或取得考试最高分数做了大量实验，结果发现在春天和秋天人们的这些活动达到顶峰，而在夏天则较低。read serious books，attend scientific meetings 及 make the highest scores on examinations 都属于 intellectual activities，故答案为[A]。

Passage Two

【听力原文】

London taxi drivers know the capital like the back of their hands. No matter how small and indistinct the street is, the driver will be able to get you there without any trouble. [29] [30] The reason London taxi drivers are so efficient is that they have all gone through a very tough training period to get a special taxi driving license. During this period which can take from two to four year, the would-be taxi driver has to learn the most direct route to every single road and to every important building in London. To achieve this, most learners go around the city on small motor bikes practicing how to move to and from different points of the city. Learner taxi drivers are tested several times during their training period by government officers. Their exams are a terrible experience. The officers ask you "How do you get from Buckingham Palace to the Tower of London?", and you have to take them there in a direct line. When you get to the tower, they won't say "Well done". They will quickly move on to the next question. After five or six questions they would just say "See you in two months' time." And then you know the exam is over. [31] Learner drivers are not allowed to work and earn money as drivers. Therefore, many of them keep their previous jobs until they obtain their licenses. The training can cost quite a lot because learners have to pay for their own expenses on the tests and the medical exam.

【答案解析】

29. Why are London taxi drivers so efficient in finding places?

【解析】选[B]。细节题。文中提到，伦敦出租车司机对伦敦大大小小的街道都了如指掌，是因为他们 have all gone trough a very tough training period to get a special taxi driving license（在考取出租车驾驶执照时经过了严格的训练），言外之意就是他们所接受的训练使他们能够很快地找到指定地点，故答案为[B]。

30. How is the training period the would-be taxi drivers experience?

【解析】选[D]。细节题。文中提到，要想取得 taxi driving license，那些 would-be taxi drivers（准出租车司机）必须得经历 a very tough training period（一段极度艰苦的培训阶段），此外，文中提到的培训时间、the would-be drivers 为通过考试所作的努力以及考试的严格性都说明了 training period 的艰苦，故答案为[D]。

31. Why do learner taxi drivers have to keep their present jobs?

【解析】选[C]。细节题。文中提到，政府不允许 learner taxi drivers 作为正式的出租车司机 work and earn money as drivers（开始工作和赚钱），所以他们中大多数人需要保留他们现在的工作，故答案为[C]。

Passage Three

【听力原文】

The dog has often been an unselfish friend to man. It is always grateful to its masters. It helps man in many ways. Certain breeds of dogs are used in criminal investigations. They are trained to sniff out drugs and bombs. They help police to catch criminals. Some dogs are trained to lead blind people.

The dogs that help in criminal investigations are trained at a school called the Military Dog Studies, branch of the US Air Force in Leak land, Texas. [32] The dogs to be trained are selected by an air force team. This team visits large cities across the country to buy the dogs. They may buy dogs from private citizens for up to $750 each. Some citizens freely give their dogs. [33] The dogs selected must be healthy, brave and aggressive. They must be able to fight back if they are attacked. The dogs chosen are between the ages of one and three. They are given a medical examination when they arrive at the school. Their physical examination includes X-rays and heart tests. [34] The trainee dogs undergo the first stage of training when they arrive in Leak land. This is an 11-week course for patrol duty. After this course, the best dogs are selected to go on another 9-week course. They learn drug-sniffing or bomb-sniffing. After this course, the dogs are ready for their jobs in the cities or on air force bases.

The training given to a drug-sniffing dog is different from that given to a bomb-sniffing dog. [35] A drug-sniffing dog is trained to scratch and dig for the drugs when he sniffs them. A bomb-sniffing dog sits down when he finds a bomb. That is the alert for hidden explosives.

【答案解析】

32. Who is responsible for the selection of dogs for criminal investigations?

【解析】选[A]。细节题。文中明确提到挑选适合于 criminal investigations(协助调查犯罪活动)的狗参加训练是由 an air force team 负责的,故答案为[A]。

33. Which of the following statements is the standard for selecting dogs to be trained for criminal investigations?

【解析】选[D]。细节题。文中提到挑选出来的狗必须是 healthy,brave 和 aggressive,它们还必须在受到攻击的时候 be able to fight back(有能力回击),由此可知 agressive 是其中的标准之一,故答案为[D]。

34. What is the first stage of training for the dogs?

【解析】选[B]。细节题。文中提到这些要接受训练的狗在到达 Leak land 之后要经过 the first stage of training(第一阶段的训练),那就是 an 11-week course for patrol duty(为期11周的巡逻),故答案为[B]。

35. What is the difference between drug-sniffing dog and bomb-sniffing dog?

【解析】选[B]。推断题。短文结尾处提到 drug-sniffing dog 所受的训练与 bomb-sniffing dog 是不同的,drug-sniffing dog 必须能够在他们嗅到毒品时将毒品挖掘出来,而 bomb-sniffing dog 在嗅到炸弹时则应该坐在那里,由此可推断 drug-sniffing dog 应该挖掘出它们发现的物品,而 bomb-sniffing 则无需挖掘出物品,故答案为[B]。

Section C

【听力原文】

The industrial revolution dramatically affected newspapers. Both the numbers of papers and their paid circulations continued to rise. In the 1850s, powerful, giant presses appeared, able to (36) print ten thousand complete papers per hour. At this time the first "(37) pictorial" weekly newspapers emerged; they featured extensive illustrations of events in the news for the first time.

During the Civil War, the (38) unprecedented demand for timely, accurate news reporting (39) transformed American journalism into a (40) dynamic, hard hitting force in national life. Reporters became the (41) darlings of the public and the (42) idols of youngsters everywhere. Many accounts of battles turned in by these (43) adventurers stand today as the definitive histories of

【答案解析】

36.空前的不定式 to 和空后的名词 papers 提示所填词应为动词原形。本句主语为 presses(新闻出版社),所填词的宾语为 ten thousand complete papers,根据常识可知,新闻出版社通常是出版发行报纸的,故所填词很可能表示"出版,发行"的含义。print 意为"出版,印刷"。

37.空前的形容词 first 和空后的名词 newspapers 提出所填词应为形容词修饰 newspapers。pictorial 意为"用图说明的"。

38.空前的定冠词 the 和空后的名词 demand 提示所填词应为形容词。unprecedented 意为"空前的,史无前例的"。

39.分析句子结构可知,所填词在句中作谓语,故所填词应为动词,且能与介词 into 搭配使用,根据上下文时态可知所填词应为动词的一般过去式。tran-

their subjects.

Newspaper growth continued in the postwar years. (44)By the 1890s, the first circulation figures of a million copies per issue were recorded. At this period, the features of the modern newspaper appeared, bold "banner" headlines, extensive use of illustrations, "funny pages", plus expanded coverage of organized sporting events.

The rise of "yellow journalism" also marks this era. This is also the age of media consolidation, as (45)many independent newspapers were swallowed up into powerful "chains", with regrettable consequences for a once fearless and incorruptible press, many were reduced to vehicles for the distribution of the particular views of their owners, and so remained, without competing papers to challenge their viewpoints. By the 1910s, all the essential features of the recognizably modern newspaper had emerged. In our time, radio and television have gradually replaced newspapers as the nation's primary information sources, so (46)it may be difficult initially to appreciate the role that newspapers have played in our history.

40. 空前的不定冠词 a 和空后的名词 force 提示所填词应为形容词,与 hard 和 hitting 并列,共同修饰 force。dynamic 意为"动力的"。

41. 空前的定冠词 the 和空后的介词 of 提示所填词应为名词。由主语 reporters 和介词宾语 the public 可推测本分句可能与 the public 对 reporters 的态度有关。darlings 意为"敬爱的人"。

42. 空前的定冠词 the 和空后的介词 of 提示所填词应为名词。根据前一分句可知,本分句可能与 youngsters 对 reporters 的态度有关。idols 意为"偶像"。

43. 空前的指示代词 these 提示所填词应为复数名词。adventurers 意为"冒险者"。

44. 【Main Points】By the 1890s, the first circulation **numbers** of a million copies **of an** issue were recorded

45. 【Main Points】many independent newspapers were swallowed up into **strong** "chains", with **regrettable results** for a once fearless and incorruptible press

46. 【Main Points】it may be **hard at first** to appreciate the role that newspapers have played in our history

Part IV
Section A

【文章大意】

本文主要讲述了单身青年无家可归这一问题。文章在前半部分对无家可归的青年人群下了一个定义,接着在后半部分讲述了这类人群给社会带来的严重后果。

47.【定位】根据题干中的关键信息 2002,some groups of single homeless youth 及 the homelessness legislation 可将搜索范围定位在第一段第二句。

　　【解析】safe。该句指出 some groups of young single homeless people 直到 2002 年才被 brought within the safety net of the homelessness legislation(纳入流浪法的安全保护之下),由此可推断 some groups of single homeless youth 直到 2002 年才 safe(安全)了。

48.【定位】根据题干中的关键信息 estimates of the extent of young homeless people 可将搜索范围定位在第一段最后一句。

　　【解析】different definitions of youth homelessness。该句指出 the adoption of different definitions(采用不同的定义)意味着 estimates of the extent of youth homelessness vary(对青年流浪者的估算就会有所变化),联系上文可知 different definitions 指的是 different definitions of youth homelessness(对青年流浪者的不同定义),故答案为 different definitions of youth homelessness。

49.【定位】根据题干中的关键信息 Research published in 2003 by ODMP 可将搜索范围定位在倒数第二段第一句。

　　【解析】increasingly younger and more vulnerable。通过分析句子结构可知,本句的主干为 Research … reported seeing increasingly younger and more vulnerable clients。本题题干是对原文的改写,所以根据语法知识可知,become 的表语应为 increasingly younger and more vulnerable。

50.【定位】根据题干中的关键信息 Black African, Black Caribbean and other ethnic minority groups 可将搜索范围定位在最后一段第三句。

　　【解析】nearly half of all the homeless young people。该句指出在伦敦 nearly half of all the homeless young people 都是 Black African, Black Caribbean and other ethnic minority。由此可知,在伦敦无家可归的 Black African, Black Caribbean and other ethnic minority 几乎占了伦敦流浪青年总数的一半。

51.【定位】根据题干中的关键信息 effect 及 the experiences of homelessness 可将搜索范围定位在最后一段第五句。

【解析】permanent and unforgettable。该句指出 Crisis 突出强调了 early experiences of homelessness can have a permanent and unforgettable effect on a young person's future(早期的流浪经历会对年轻人的将来造成永久性的、不可磨灭的影响),本题是要求填写 the effect 的性质或特点,所以原文中修饰 effect 的形容词即为本题答案。

Section B

Passage One

【文章大意】

现在公立中小学的教学质量是提高了还是下降了这一问题使广大中小学生的父母感到十分困惑,本文就两组专家的不同观点对这一问题进行分析。文章第一段首先提出了两组专家的不同意见;第二三段主要是对这两组专家的不同观点分别进行详细的阐述;第四至六段提出作者自己的观点,他建议父母们应该明白不同的观察者采用的标准是不同的,这样他们就不会对公立中小学的教学质量再感到困惑了。

52. 选[A]。主旨大意题。文章第一段第二三句分别指出两组专家的不同观点,一些认为学校现在的状况比多年以来的情况都要好,而另一些则称学校现在的情况非常糟糕,概括起来说就是两组专家对学校教学质量的不同观点,并且二三段,作为文章的主体部分,对两组专家的观点进行了详细阐述,由此可知,本文主要是与专家对学校教学质量的不同观点有关,[A]选项最能概括文章大意,故为答案。

53. 选[D]。推理判断题。文章第一段第一句中的 come down with an acute case of schizophrenia 是一种夸张手法,表明 the contradictory reports about the state of the public schools 给父母们造成的困扰极大。通过阅读全文可以发现,confusion 在文中只是指父母因两种互相矛盾的报道而对 the state of the public schools 产生疑惑,故答案为[D]。[A]、[B] 文中没有提及,故可排除;文章分别提到专家的不同观点,但是并没有提到两组专家对 testing scores 是否应作为标准而感到疑惑,故可排除[C]。

54. 选[A]。事实细节题。文章第二段是对那些认为学校教学质量有所提高的专家的观点的详细阐述,该段第一句中的 looks primarily at such indicators as test scores... 表明这些专家是因为学生们的测试分数提高了,才认为学校教学质量有所提高,故答案为[A]。该段虽然提到 reading scores,但是 reading ability 并不等同于 reading scores,故不选[C]。

55. 选[B]。事实细节题。文章第三段主要对那些认为学校质量有所下降的专家的观点的详细阐述。该段第三句中的 they charge that raising the test scores by drilling pupils to come up with... 说明的道理就是分数高并不说明学生的知识多、理解能力强、逻辑思维及独立思维的能力突出,[B] 符合原文内容,故为答案。

56. 选[A]。推理判断题。根据第53小题可知,第四段中的 confusion 指的是父母对学校质量究竟是提高了还是下降了的疑惑。由第四段可知,要想解除疑惑,就要 understand the different yardsticks used by different observes(明白不同的观察者所采用的标准不同),由第五、六段可知,第四段想要表达的意思是:因为不同的观察者采用不同的标准,所以他们最后所作出的结论就是不一样的,这就要求父母们要充分的了解观察者作出结论时所采用的标准,这样才有助于他们真正的了解公立中小学学校教学质量的情况,故答案为[A]。

Passage Two

【文章大意】

如今,"去购物中心吧"已成为男女皆喜欢的用语,本文主要对男性和女性喜欢逛商场的原因进行了分析。文章第一、二段主要分析了女性喜欢逛商场的原因;第三段对男士喜欢逛商场的原因及男性和女性喜欢逛商场的共同原因进行了分析;第四段主要讲人们历来对购物人群的性别偏见,以及当今社会中人们对此的重新认识。

57. 选[D]。推理判断题。文章第一段第六句指出了妇女旧时的地位:their rightful place is at home taking care of their families,而第八、九句指出由于汽车的出现,女性们不再只是照顾家庭,She now was able to go out...,对比前后女性的两种地位可知,女性能走出家庭外出购物说明旧社会对女性的定位渐渐被打破了,故答案为[D]。

58. 选[B]。事实细节题。题干中的 women are not bound to the family against their will today 是文章第二段第一句中 contemporary women are much more free-minded about their own place in society 的同义转述,由此可知答案为[B]。

59. 选[D]。事实细节题。题干中的 human 在文中指的即是 males and females。文中第三段后半部分主要是关于男性和女性喜欢逛商场的共同原因,由该段倒数第三、四、五句可知,男性和女性都喜欢逛商场的原因就是人类是 communal species,如果长时间与世界隔绝,他们就会 long to be around others of their own species...,也就是说人类因为不喜欢独自一人,才去逛商场,故答案为[D]。

60. 选[B]。语义理解题。文章第三段前半部分主要解释了男士爱逛商场的原因。该段第二句指出男士逛商场是为了 new toys,第四句中的 a new computer product,sports equipment 和 masculine item 很明显都属于 new toys,都是吸引男士逛商场的产品。由 item 的概括性可知,masculine 也是概括性的词语,而且该词语还应是与男性有关,故答案为[B]。

61. 选[A]。推理判断题。本文主要对男性和女性喜欢逛商场的原因进行了分析。第一、二段在提及女士逛商场的原因时只提到了女士喜欢为家庭购买所需品,但是并没有提到 jewellery,但却在以解释男性喜欢逛商场的原因为主的第三段中提到。根据常识可知,jewellery 非常昂贵,而且女士对它又非常钟爱,但男性却放心地将他们的妻子留在 jewellery stores 中而独自去浏览 new toys,这就说明商场中摆放的 new toys 对男士来说非常有吸引力,以至于他们都无暇顾及自己妻子很可能一时冲动买下 jewellery,故答案为[A]。

Part V

62. degree ∧ how — on。及物动词与不及物动词误用。depends 为不及物动词,接宾语时应借助于介词 on,故应在 degree 与 how 之间增加 on。

63. so — as。连词误用。not…so…as 为固定搭配,故应将 so 改写为 as。

64. describe — describing。非谓语动词误用。分析本句结构可知,本句的谓语为 are,如果 describe 再作谓语动词就会使句子不合乎语法规范,故应将 describe 改写为现在分词形式 describing,在句中充当主语的后置定语。

65. on—in。介词误用。通常表示"在书中"的介词用 in,而不是 on,故应将 on 改写为 in。

66. it —them。代词误用。these original works 为复数名词性短语,所以代词应该使用表复数的代词,故应将 it 改写为 them。

67. manner — manners。上下文语义矛盾。manner 指"态度",而 manners 则指"礼貌",根据本句句意可知,good manners"好的礼貌举止"才更符合句意,故应将 manner 改写为 manners。

68. them —/。赘述。put 的宾语为 which,再使用指代 elements of doubt 的代词 them 就显得重复,故应将 them 删除。

69. ∧ put — been。语态错误。本句的主语是 Many statements,谓语是 put forword,这里显然应当使用被动语态,故应在 put 前添加 been。

70. that — whose。连接词误用。technique and judgment 明显从属于 investigators,故应将 that 改写为 whose,表示所属关系。

71. A — The。冠词误用。A 应改写为 The,The second 与上一句中的 The first 对应。

Part VI

72. 【答案】had collected more than a thousand foreign stamps
  【解析】本题考查对时态的掌握。the end of that year 是过去时间,再加上 by 可知是过去某一时间以前完成的,所以应该用过去完成时。collect stamps 意为"收集邮票"。

73. 【答案】he should have known what was happening
  【解析】本题考查虚拟语气的掌握。should have done 表示对过去某事的肯定推测,意为"本应该…"。

74. 【答案】but we managed to bring him round
  【解析】本题考查对惯用搭配 manage to do 和 bring sb. round 的掌握。"manage to +动词原形"意为"设法、达成",说明终于做成了某事。bring sb. round 意为"说服某人同意某事"。

75. 【答案】resulted in many elderly and disabled people suffering hardship
  【解析】本题考查对固定短语 result in…的掌握。result in…意为"造成、导致"。

76. 【答案】to create a gravitational pull one-third as strong as Earth's
  【解析】本题考查对 as…as 同级比较和不定式的掌握。to 所引导的不定式在句中充当目的状语。as…as 意为"像…一样"。

图书在版编目(CIP)数据

大学英语六级考试巅峰训练 / 王长喜主编. —8 版. —北京:学苑出版社,2007.9
ISBN 978-7-5077-1826-3

Ⅰ.大… Ⅱ.王… Ⅲ.英语—高等学校—水平考试—习题 Ⅳ.H319.6

中国版本图书馆 CIP 数据核字(2007)第 154669 号

责任编辑:郑泽英
出版发行:学苑出版社
社　　址:北京市丰台区南方庄 2 号院 1 号楼
邮政编码:100078
网　　址:www.book001.com
电子信箱:xueyuan@ public. bta. net. cn
销售电话:010 – 67675512、67602949、67678944
经　　销:各地新华书店
印 刷 厂:保定市中画美凯印刷有限公司
开　　本:787×1092　1/16
印　　张:27.375
字　　数:448 千字
版　　次:2008 年 1 月北京第 8 版
印　　次:2008 年 1 月北京第 1 次印刷
印　　数:1 – 8 000
定　　价:26.80 元